"This is the real thing. This is what we've wanted to know. Abbey in the altogether—a chronicle of the writer we love."—Edward Hoagland

"Determined to cut through myth and rumor, Cahalan meticulously tracks the course of Abbey's often feral yet always creative and resonant life."—*Booklist* (selected as one of the year's top ten biographies of social activists)

"The story of Cactus Ed Abbey's life as told by Cahalan will engage and inspire, with as insightful a look at the times as it is of the man. Cahalan tells the whole story, and he tells it exceedingly well."—Robert Redford

"Rarely will I stay up past midnight to finish a biography, but thanks to the superior writing of James Cahalan and the tumultuous nature of Abbey's life, I did on this one."—*Education Digest*

"Ed Abbey was one of the extraordinary people of the twentieth century, trying to figure out ways for this planet to survive. This book will help you know him."—Pete Seeger

"Cahalan show[s] that the redneck image of 'Cactus Ed' he cultivated was really a fiction that he hid behind. . . . His book offers both depth and detail."—*Library Journal*

"A compelling work . . . Cahalan has achieved what all good biographers do: He brings the subject to life, and what a life it was."—*Pittsburgh Post-Gazette*

"The best trail guide for tracking the hungry life of that fabled masked man clutching a monkey wrench."—Charles Bowden

"It goes a long way toward revealing the real Edward Abbey and even further toward answering Abbey's numerous critics."—*Earth First! Journal*

"This [biography] should be definitive for many, many years. . . . I surmise that at this point [Cahalan] is the leading Abbey scholar in the country."—Ann Ronald

"This is a biography rich in well-supported facts, numerous interviews and overviews of previously unpublished writings and drafts of published works. . . . An important text for future Abbey scholars."—*Inside/Outside Southwest*

"A lucid, impressive biography . . . Those who love Abbey's books will find much to interest them here."—Larry McMurtry

"An authoritative study, this book is successful because Cahalan realized that Abbey can never be fully demystified."—*Choice*

"Cahalan fills a huge gap in our understanding of Abbey. . . . A definitive biography."—Ann H. Zwinger

"Cahalan . . . gives us the larger-than-life Abbey, the cantankerous sagebrush patriot who rolled old tires into the Grand Canyon. . . . But Cahalan also works hard to separate the threads of Abbey's life as a serious writer from those of his more politicized public persona."—*High Country News*

"A wealth of facts woven into an interesting, clear narrative, and a portrait of Abbey that is sharp, colorful, and fair. . . . An excellent companion for reading Abbey's work and understanding the spirit that animates it."—*The Hollins Critic*

Edward Abbey
a life

James M. Cahalan

The University of Arizona Press   Tucson

The University of Arizona Press

© 2001 The Arizona Board of Regents

All rights reserved

⊛ This book is printed on acid-free, archival-quality paper.

Manufactured in the United States of America

06   05   04   03   6   5   4   3   2

Permission to reprint material from the following books by Edward Abbey is gratefully acknowledged: *Abbey's Road* (© 1979 by Edward Abbey), *One Life at a Time, Please* (© 1988 by Edward Abbey), and *Confessions of a Barbarian* (© 1994 by Clarke Abbey); all reprinted by permission of Don Congdon Associates, Inc. Material from James M. Cahalan's articles "Edward Abbey, Appalachian Easterner," *Western American Literature* 31, no. 3 (Fall 1996), and "'My People': Edward Abbey's Appalachian Roots in Indiana County, Pennsylvania," *Pittsburgh History* 79, nos. 3–4 (Fall 1996/Winter 1997), is reprinted here (in different form) with kind permission of the editors.

Library of Congress Cataloging-in-Publication Data

Cahalan, James M.

Edward Abbey : a life / James M. Cahalan.

p. cm.

Includes bibliographical references and index.

ISBN 0-8165-1906-4 (acid-free paper)

ISBN 0-8165-2267-7 (pbk.: acid-free paper)

1. Abbey, Edward, 1927–   2. Novelists, American — 20th century — Biography.

3. Environmentalists — United States — Biography.   I. Title.

PS3551.B2 Z597   2001

813'.54 — dc21

2001001177

British Library Cataloguing-in-Publication Data

A catalogue record for this book is available from the British Library.

To all those who helped me
as I traced Edward Abbey and his environment,
especially those who sought to
"keep it like it was"

Contents

Illustrations

Introduction

from Home to Oracle

T his is a book in which I seek to separate fact from fiction and reality from myth. At the outset, I have to tell readers that Edward Abbey was not born in Home, Pennsylvania; he resided in several other places before his family moved close to Home. And he never lived in Oracle, Arizona. Yet he convinced almost everyone that he had been "born in Home" and "lived in Oracle." Even the author's blurb for the paperback edition of his autobiographical "fat masterpiece," *The Fool's Progress*, released the year after his death, stated (like so many of his earlier book jackets) that he was "born in Home" and had lived and "died in 1989 near Oracle."[1] Many publications about Abbey, even scholarly books, have repeated his fictionalized account of himself; his birthplace has been universally reported as Home.[2]

Abbey knew that he had not been born in Home. And he used Oracle, like "Wolf Hole" earlier, as camouflage, strategically positioning it on book jackets and even listing his Oracle post office box number in his "Preliminary Notes" to *Down the River*,[3] in order to deflect both cultists and enemies from his actual house and mailbox just west of Tucson. Periodically, he would drive up to Oracle to pick up the mail that readers sent him there. Also, he simply liked the sounds of "Home" and "Oracle." They had a nice ring on book jackets and in letters to the editor in which this sometimes prophetic trouble-maker could sign off from "Oracle."

My intention is not to perpetuate the mythology surrounding Abbey but to examine it and to understand the actual man and his work. I have tried to follow good and courageous advice that Abbey's best friend, John De Puy, gave me: to "write an honest book" about Ed Abbey.[4] Too much loose talk has already been published about this author who inspired (and continues to in-spire) wilderness activists, and who attracted (and still attracts) a cult following. Abbey helped to create this cult in his own books, developing a strong persona that was based on himself but, at the same time, was partly a fictional creation. Sometimes he enjoyed his cult image, but often he was uncomfortable with it. I intend and hope that this book is useful to readers who are already knowledge-able about Abbey and want to know more as well as to others whose impressions (whether positive or negative) may be too simple and in need of correction or complication. Cult followers of "Cactus Ed," on the one hand, will encounter in these pages another, different, more private Abbey. On the other hand, readers and teachers who have decided from some fleeting snapshot somewhere that Abbey disliked other races and women, for example, and thus do not want to read or teach his books, can read here about the Abbey who edited a bilingual English-Spanish newspaper and spoke at a Navajo rally, and the Abbey who so helpfully reviewed, advised, and befriended several women writers.

Indeed, he was neither simply a countercultural cowboy hero nor a backward villain but, rather, a very complicated person. Almost every aspect of Abbey's image is fraught with inaccuracy or contradiction. The popular and common critical version goes something like this: born in Home, Pennsylvania, and eventually settling in Oracle, Arizona, Abbey was one of our most impor-tant Western nature writers as well as an outrageous personality with some mi-sogynist attitudes toward women. The problems with this depiction, beyond its inaccuracy about his birth and his later location, include three important facts: Abbey remained very much marked by his upbringing in the Appalachian East; he insisted that he was not a "nature writer"; and he was typically very reserved in person. He certainly had massive difficulties with women and they with him, about which I tell the truth in this book. Yet his good platonic friends included women such as singer and activist Katie Lee and fellow writers Terry Tempest Williams and Ann Zwinger, who testified to his kind, even genteel qualities. Abbey also liked to give the impression to readers that he was some kind of cowboy or ranger, "Cactus Ed," who wrote on the fly, simply typing up *Desert Solitaire* straight out of his journals. In fact, he wrote and revised that book, and all of his books, very carefully—like Hemingway, another writer who created a wild public persona that belied his meticulous literary craft. It is no accident that "Cactus Ed" won Fulbright and Guggenheim fellowships and eventually became a full professor of English at the University of Arizona.

I never met Abbey myself. I moved to his native county in 1984, one year after his last appearance at Indiana University of Pennsylvania (IUP), which he had attended in 1947 when it was Indiana State Teachers College. I regret that I also never met his remarkable mother and father, who died in 1988 and 1992, respectively. I have enjoyed getting to know several other Abbeys, including his widow and his three surviving siblings, and this book depends on extensive interviews that I conducted with more than 100 people who knew Ed. These people are listed in my bibliography. The subsequent deaths of a few of them have impressed on me how quickly such knowledge is lost—a growing sense that spurred me along once I got my late start on this project.

Many individuals who helped me in various ways are thanked in my acknowledgments at the back of this book. The first was John Watta, who was Abbey's classmate in 1947, regularly brought him back later to speak at IUP, and shared stories about Abbey and his parents during the fourteen years in which John and I lived just a few feet away from each other in the town of Indiana, Pennsylvania. Now I live outside of town in woods that are reclaimed acres of a mine where Abbey's father worked seven years before his famous son was born. In addition to my interviews in this area, countless bike rides all over Abbey's home territory have helped to impress on me both how well he knew it and how much it remained a part of him.

Several trips to the Southwest, including the region stretching from Albuquerque up through southern Utah, also made me fall in love with Abbey's Four Corners country and gain an appreciation of what it all meant to him. I wandered around Arches, Canyonlands, Dead Horse Point, Natural Bridges, Escalante, both rims of the Grand Canyon, and various other places dear to him. I also revisited some places that Abbey felt had been ruined. On the way to Capitol Reef, I sped across Utah's Route 95, where he had sabotaged road-building bulldozers in April 1975. And I stood atop the dreaded Glen Canyon Dam, looking down at the drowned Glen Canyon. In particular, my sabbatical in Tucson—during which I hiked in and out of the Grand Canyon, Aravaipa Canyon, and many other places that meant a lot to Abbey, and visited his grave ten years after his death—helped me understand not just where he was coming from but where he wanted to be and what he felt he must celebrate and defend in books such as *The Monkey Wrench Gang*. I went down the San Juan and Rio Grande Rivers, waded for miles through Aravaipa Creek and the Escalante River, and even spent one long, memorable day traversing (by jeep) Abbey's ill-advised "No Road" in Big Bend National Park. I have also thought about related issues in a broader context through the course that I teach on our national parks. For more than a quarter century, Abbey worked in no fewer than sixteen different national parks and forests, ranging geographically from Montana's Glacier to Florida's Everglades.

By all accounts, meeting and knowing Abbey was a remarkable experience, as evidenced by how many of his compatriots have written about it, in essays that I quote in this book. Nevertheless, I feel that *not* meeting or knowing Abbey in person has allowed me to look at him more objectively or at least impartially. Some of the writers who understood Abbey's work best—Wendell Berry and Gary Snyder, for example—never met him either. Unlike so many others, I write neither as an acquaintance of Abbey nor as a member of any of the groups surrounding him. I have sought to stand clear of the Abbey cult and simply report what is most clearly established about the man, his life, and his writings. If I am not certain about something, I have done my best not to include it. I cannot promise that no errors have crept into this book, despite my determination to keep them out, but I have tried hard to stick to the facts. This approach has been reinforced continually by my hard-pressed editors' strict page limitation, which has provided both frustration (because there is always so much else to tell about Abbey) and discipline (making me limit myself to what is most clearly known). Also, Abbey's life needs no embellishment. The simple facts alone are more than lively enough by themselves.

In another sense, I did get to know Abbey intimately by studying everything in his large collection at the University of Arizona, including all of his unpublished journals, letters, videotapes, audiotapes, and manuscripts. I have also tried to collect and read as many of his publications as possible—no mean feat, because Abbey's essays and letters to the editor appeared everywhere from *Audubon* and *Harper's* to *Penthouse* and *The Stinking Desert Gazette*. My bibliography of his publications is the most extensive yet available. It cannot be completely definitive—perhaps no such bibliography ever will be—because Abbey sent so many letters to so many different periodicals (well-known and many little-known and short-lived ones) that doubtlessly some have not yet been found. I have done my best. It is a telling indication of the kind of author Abbey was that the greatest help I got in finding some of his most obscure publications came from a Yosemite park ranger, Dean Shenk.

My work has been informed by historically and culturally focused critical approaches. I agree with Walt Whitman biographer David Reynolds that biography is compatible with such approaches,[5] because its purpose is to provide "thick descriptions" (in anthropologist Clifford Geertz's influential phrase) of the connections of a writer's life to the particulars of history, politics, and all of the cultural issues intertwined in a lifetime and a career. My style here is not at all theoretical, however. I have sought to report the facts about Abbey and his work as clearly and simply as I can at the same time that I emphasize the complexity of the man and his writings. Within my "thick descriptions" is imbedded the even thicker, more elaborate web of Abbey's accomplishments and high points yet also his difficulties, contradictions, and paradoxes. This was a writer who could be at various times (and sometimes all at the same time) inspiring, enraging, and hilarious.

What *were* Abbey's leading accomplishments that make his life story worth knowing? He was the author of twenty-one original books of fiction and essays (in addition to a few other compilations and posthumous books), and his work had a major impact on contemporary nature writing and environmentalism. He never forgot his native Appalachian area of western Pennsylvania, and he focused on it in his first novel, *Jonathan Troy* (1954); in *The Fool's Progress* (1988), thinly disguising it there as West Virginia; and in *Appalachian Wilderness* (1970) and a number of essays. Yet his best-known books were set in his beloved, adopted Southwest. His two New Mexico novels, *The Brave Cowboy* (1956) and *Fire on the Mountain* (1962), were both turned into movies. His book of essays about southeastern Utah, *Desert Solitaire* (1968), put Arches and Canyonlands National Parks on the literary map, brought a boldly original and uniquely personal new voice to American nature writing, and remained his most celebrated book. *The Monkey Wrench Gang* (1975) was Abbey's most successful novel, a remarkable and wildly comic tale about a band of four ecological rebels and saboteurs that was the leading inspiration for the Earth First! Movement, along with that novel's sequel, *Hayduke Lives!* (1990). Yet most critics agreed that Abbey was at his best in his essays—not only *Desert Solitaire* but also such other collections as *The Journey Home* (1977), *Abbey's Road* (1979), *Down the River* (1982), *Beyond the Wall* (1984), and *One Life at a Time, Please* (1988). Abbey enjoyed a very strong "author function" (to borrow French philosopher Michel Foucault's term), creating that striking image of himself as "Cactus Ed," the defiant oracle from Home. Even though this persona was largely invented and somewhat different from the real Ed Abbey, it was so forceful that many of his readers feel that they know him personally from reading his books.

Having said all that, I turn back to my subject and his story. How in the world *did* Ed Abbey get all the way from Home to Oracle?

Edward Abbey

CHAPTER ONE

The Boy from Home
1927–1944

Demythologizing Edward Abbey starts at birth. Key to the persuasive myth that he created about himself, as reinforced in several of his essays and books, was the impression that he had been born and reared entirely on a hardscrabble Appalachian farm that had been in the family for generations, near a village with the strikingly appropriate and charming name of Home, Pennsylvania. In addition to book jackets, even Abbey's academic vita listed him as "born in Home."[1] And in his private diary as late as 1983, Abbey whimsically recalled "the night of January 29th, 1927, in that lamp-lit room in the old farmhouse near Home, Pennsylvania, when I was born" (308).[2] In fact, that night at 10:30, weighing in at nine pounds, three ounces, Abbey was born in the hospital of the good-sized town of Indiana, Pennsylvania, with doctor and nurse in attendance, as recorded on his birth certificate and noted in the baby book that his mother kept.[3] Mildred and Paul Abbey's baby, the first of five who survived, went home not to any farm but to their small rented house on North Third Street[4] in a cramped neighborhood in Indiana, the county seat of Indiana County, in the foothills of the Allegheny Mountains fifty-five miles northeast of Pittsburgh.

Nor was Abbey's origin myth only a matter of his birthplace, for his family never lived on a farm until he was fourteen years old; instead, they migrated all around the county as the Depression arrived. Before moving closer to Home (a tiny, unincorporated village about ten miles north of Indiana) when he was four and a half years old, his family stayed at several other places. These included two dwellings in Saltsburg, twenty miles southwest of Indiana,[5] and a series of campsites across Pennsylvania and New Jersey in the summer of 1931. During Abbey's early childhood, his father was not a farmer but a real estate salesman, dealing in properties for the A. E. Strout Farm Agency.[6]

The gap between Indiana and Home involves more than mileage: the larger county seat, in the valley, is the center of the county's commerce, whereas the little village, in the uplands, is merely a blip on Route 119, in a mostly rural county with one of the highest unemployment rates in Pennsylvania. But it was (and is) also beautiful countryside: rolling foothills, leisurely valleys carved by a meandering network of creeks and rivers, and everywhere — despite the ravages of coal and logging companies — trees, trees, and more trees, both pines and an endless deciduous array. Indiana County enjoys one of the most beautiful autumns in the world. After the mild green summer, everywhere trees erupt into brilliant reds and golds. The long winter can be dark, but it is also marked by some brilliant winter days with blue skies and snow-covered slopes. It is often cloudy in this area, but when it does clear up, the sky becomes shockingly crystalline, with the stars brightly radiant at night in a way never seen in any city. And when spring finally arrives, it is announced dramatically by an ongoing, late-day chorus of frogs, the "spring peepers." In short, no place could be more different than — yet in its own way sometimes just as gorgeous as — the American Southwest that Abbey would make his transplanted home and subject.

As much as he liked to conjure up "Home" as his own personal origin myth, the adult Edward Abbey was aware that he had been born in Indiana. When accuracy was important — filling out federal employment applications, for example — he listed Indiana, not Home, as his birthplace. But "Home" sounded better on book jackets — part of the self-created myth of the man. Clarke Cartwright Abbey, his last wife, recollected that "he just liked the way it sounded, the humor of being from Home."[7] He would always identify much more with the Appalachian uplands around Home than with the trade center of Indiana. People in this region seldom identify themselves as "Appalachian," but Abbey would understand that in truth Indiana County has much more in common with Morgantown, West Virginia, than with Allentown or other places in eastern Pennsylvania. He retained vivid memories of Indiana, describing it at the beginning of his significantly entitled book *Appalachian Wilderness*: "There was the town set in the cup of the green hills. In the Alleghenies. A town of trees, two-story houses, red-brick hardware stores, church steeples, the clock tower on the county courthouse, and over all the thin blue haze—partly dust, partly smoke, but mostly moisture—that veils the Appalachian world most of the time. The diaphanous veil that conceals nothing."[8] His first book, *Jonathan Troy*, is set in Indiana, Pennsylvania (thinly disguised under the Native American name Powhatan), and its immediate surroundings—the first novel with this particular setting by any author and Abbey's only book focused entirely on his home county.

Appreciating Abbey's imposing mother and father is a key part of understanding their son. He made them an important part of his story by writing about them frequently, and in their cases the reality lived up to the myth. Mildred Abbey (1905–88) was a physically tiny yet dynamic woman: a schoolteacher, a pianist, organist, and choir leader at the Washington Presbyterian Church near Home, and a tireless worker. As Abbey later told his friend Jack Loeffler, "after she put us brats to bed at night . . . our little ninety-eight-pound mother . . . would try to play us asleep with the piano. She'd be downstairs playing the piano—Chopin . . . old hymns. And we'd be upstairs slowly falling asleep under the influence of that gentle piano music. I've been a lover of music ever since."[9] He also inherited from her his preference for hills and mountains over flat country. Mildred wrote in her 1931 diary, as she wandered across Pennsylvania with her husband and three small children, "To me there isn't anything even interesting on a road on which one can see for a mile ahead what is coming. But there is something stimulating, even thrilling in a new scene that is revealed suddenly by a turn in the road or by reaching the crest of a hill."[10] (Ed echoed her opinion almost exactly in an article written for his high school newspaper, when he was seventeen: "I hate the flat plains, or as the inhabitants call them, 'the wide open spaces.' In my opinion, a land is not civilized unless the ground is tilted at an angle.")[11] She had learned her love of rolling hills, and of nature in general, growing up amidst the soft, pretty contours of Creekside, Pennsylvania, seven miles from Indiana.

Everyone knew Mildred as an outstanding, energetic person: "impressive," as her sister Betty George stressed.[12] She was always active, running her busy household, continually involved in church and other volunteer work, and then, in her little free time, regularly out walking many miles all "over the hills, through the woods, and up and down the highway," as her second son, Howard Abbey, and many others recalled.[13] People frequently remarked to Isabel Nesbitt, another sister, "Oh, we saw your sister walking up the railroad tracks up there by Home."[14] Abbey later made this a key part of the character of his autobiographical protagonist's mother in the novel *The Fool's Progress*: "Women don't stride, not small skinny frail-looking overworked overworried Appalachian farm women. . . . But our mother did."[15]

Late in her career of raising five children, Mildred returned in the early 1940s to her earlier job: teaching first grade. For a quarter century, she influenced many students in Plumville, five miles northwest of Home, until her retirement in 1967. Janice Dembosky remembered:

> She loved us. She made learning fun. The history of the American Indians came alive for us when she told us stories and showed us arrowheads. She even enlisted the help of one of her sons to come in and show each and every one of us how to transform an oatmeal box into our very own Indian tom-tom! Even through the whoops and war dances that followed, she smiled her smile. . . . Mrs. Abbey showed us how the maple trees on her farm were tapped for the sap which she then turned into shining brown syrup and wonderfully sticky maple sugar candy for us to taste.[16]

Mildred also took classes at Indiana University of Pennsylvania (IUP) until she was eighty, was active with Meals on Wheels, and did various other volunteer work. When John Watta, one of Ed's college classmates, suggested to Mildred later in life that she might want to take things a bit easier, she replied, "Well, there's so much to do, how can you?"[17] Abbey's sister, Nancy, emphasized their mother's writing ability, her love of nature, and her courage:

> When she was an elder in the church, and the Presbyterian church was considering homosexuals and their stance about homosexuality, my mother stood against all the church in her support for the rights of a gay or lesbian to be a minister. And people respected her so much that she was never ostracized for this view. They tried to understand her viewpoint because she was such a respected woman that they could really listen to her and hear her and think, "My goodness, there must be something to this if Mildred Abbey's saying this." She was revered in that way by people. Part of Ed's relish in being different also was supported so much by my mother—her not trying to hold us at home or make us fit into the mores of that little community. That takes strength of character.[18]

Iva Abbey, the wife of Ed's closest brother, Howard, called her "the best mother-in-law anyone could ever want" and "perfect," and she stressed that

Mildred was proud of Ed's accomplishments yet also always insisted that "Ned," as his family and friends called Ed as a boy, "was just one son."[19] Mildred made a point of writing to Bill, her youngest child, in his adulthood and after Ed's rise to fame, that "she was proud of all her kids."[20]

In their youth, Mildred and Paul Abbey had met on the Indiana-Ernest streetcar in Creekside, a small town midway between Indiana and Home where both of them grew up after moving there in childhood from other counties in western Pennsylvania. Paul (1901–1992) was born closer to Pittsburgh, in Donora. He liked to tell the story that he had been conceived after his mother, thinking that ten children were enough, showed some contraceptive medicine to her mother—but was told by her to "throw that devil's medicine in the fire." In 1908, when he was seven, he moved to Creekside after his father answered an ad to run an experimental alfalfa farm there. Paul remembered, "We had a team of horses and a riding horse and six head of cattle, and he rode the horse and herded the six head of cattle from down below West Newton up to this place here."[21]

As a young man, Paul pursued many different working-class jobs, as he would continue to do all of his life. He spent some time out west as a ranch hand, and he worked in various mills in Ohio, Michigan, and western Pennsylvania and in the mine at Fulton Run near Indiana. He worked in his first mill at age sixteen, but, as he later reminisced, at twenty-six he "went on strike and I'm still on strike. I never went back."[22] Paul's memories and mementos of the West were Ed's earliest boyhood incentives to go west, and his working-class defiance rubbed off on his son in a big way. He was tall, lanky, and strong—like his oldest son. His revolutionary full name, Paul Revere Abbey, was fitting.

Paul left school at an early age but carried on a lifelong, voracious self-education. He could quote Walt Whitman by heart, and he became a devoted socialist in one of the most conservative counties in Pennsylvania.[23] Whitman's advice to "resist much, obey little" became Paul's maxim—and Ed's. Howard Abbey described his father as "anti-capitalistic, anti-religion, anti-prevailing opinion, anti-booze, anti-war and anti-anyone who didn't agree with him"—but also as a hard worker and very loyal and loving to his family and friends, a good singer and whistler, an openly sentimental but fun-loving man with a ready smile.[24]

Paul also learned to overcome the racism that surrounded him while growing up in western Pennsylvania. In 1990, he recounted his youth: "Before I was a socialist, I belonged to the KKK. Back in that time, everybody was joining the KKK—pretty nice guys in there. So, I joined up too—just a kid, you know. I went to one meeting and I heard the most miserable speech, from the lousiest guy I ever knew, telling us what we should do with the Jews, and the

Catholics, and the 'niggers.' So I didn't stay in the KKK very long. Now I'm a life member of the NAACP."[25] Working in factories as a young man, Paul soaked up labor radicalism. Eugene Debs was his hero.

He remained a devout Marxist and longtime subscriber to *Soviet Life*, right up through the fall of the Soviet Union at the end of his life. His political radicalism, opposition to organized religion, and independent streak rubbed off on his oldest son at an early age. In 1939, when Ed was twelve, his Uncle Franklin George and Aunt Betty George took him to the New York World's Fair. This was his first foray to the city that would subsequently fascinate him almost as much as the Southwest. He gazed upon the Empire State Building and the Statue of Liberty with wonderment. Ed immediately asked to see the Fair's Russian Pavilion—an unusual interest for a young boy from a conservative, backwater area—because his father had told him about it.[26]

Around the same time, he stomped out of Sunday school near Home after the teacher replied to his questions by insisting that the parting of the Red Sea had really happened. Later, during high school years, when a car stopped illegally in the crosswalk in front of Ed and Howard, Ed climbed right over the car, walking across it, to the driver's amazement, while Howard walked around it.[27]

Inheriting an independent streak also meant that key differences developed between father and son. Although Paul remained a lifelong teetotaller, the adult Ed became a heavy drinker. In response to Paul's belief that socialist state control of the means of production was the answer to poverty and oppression, his son would become an anarchist, an opponent of government and bureaucracy. The socialist school dropout's son would develop into the author of a master's thesis on anarchism. Yet much as Marxism served as his father's religion, anarchism and wilderness would become Ed's. He declared in *Desert Solitaire*, "I am not an atheist but an earthiest."[28]

Abbey was also the product of class conflict resulting from the marriage of a mother from a more comfortable family and a father born and bred in humbler circumstances. Whereas Mildred was the daughter of a schoolteacher and a principal, Paul was the son of a modest farmer. Mildred's marriage to Paul on July 5, 1925, was unpopular in her family. She was the oldest of four sisters. Her father was not at all happy about her choice of a husband, convinced that he was not the type who would find a good job and give her a comfortable home.[29]

Class conflict was indeed rooted far back in Mildred and Paul's contrasting family histories. Mildred's parents, Charles Caylor Postlewaite (1872–1965) and Clara Ethel Means (1885–1925), married in Jefferson County at the turn of the century, where "C.C.," as he was known, came from a family of farmers, and Clara's father, J. B. Means, was a businessman. A housewife and seamstress, Clara died in June 1925, shortly before Mildred's marriage to Paul,[30] but C.C. remained for many years a dominant personality in his family and community. He had moved to Creekside to teach. The only male teacher at the school, he became its principal while continuing to teach; Paul Abbey was one of his students. Mildred's three younger sisters, Britta, Isabel, and Betty, married a bank teller, a housepainter, and an insurance salesman, respectively—steady jobs rooted in Indiana.

C.C. was not predisposed to approve of his eldest daughter's marriage to an uneducated young man with questionable prospects, especially when it meant that she left her own teaching position in the adjacent town of Ernest to follow Paul from town to town as he changed jobs. Mildred's family lived in a house beside a church in Creekside; Paul's family, in a farmhouse outside the town.

Paul's parents, John Abbey (1850–1931) and Eleanor Jane Ostrander (1856–1926), were of immigrant backgrounds, whereas Mildred's German and Scotch-Irish ancestors had lived in Pennsylvania since the eighteenth century. John Abbey's father, Johannes Aebi (1816–1873), had come over from Switzerland in 1869, stepping off the ship *Westphalia* in New Jersey. He was followed two years later by his wife, Magdalena Gasser (1825–1880) and children, who journeyed to New York on the German ship *Helsatia*. The family settled near Ohiopyle in Pennsylvania's Fayette County, but Johannes died of smallpox soon thereafter, leaving behind a large family facing poverty. Eleanor, Paul's mother, was of French Huguenot extraction. Married in 1877, John and Eleanor had eleven children. In 1918, Eleanor wrote a poem—the earliest known literary text by an Abbey—addressed to Paul, her youngest son: "Oh I love to hear your whistle / When you're coming home at night." [31] Both of Paul's parents died within six years of his marriage to Mildred. Among Ed Abbey's grandparents, only C.C. lived on, until 1965, sternly disapproving of Paul Abbey and his kin.

Yet it was Ed's paternal ancestors, the mysterious Swiss natives whom he barely knew, who captured his imagination, as reflected in his 1979 essay "In Defense of the Redneck": "I am a redneck myself, too, born and bred on a submarginal farm in Appalachia, descended from an endless line of lug-eared, beetle-browed, insolent barbarian peasants reaching back somewhere to the dark forests of central Europe and the Alpine caves of my Neanderthal primogenitors." [32] This pithy sentence well illustrates Abbey's selective myth-making at work: not only does he imagine himself as born on a farm, but he also omits his respectable maternal heritage in favor of a romanticized image of his paternal line in hues as "dark" as possible. In the same essay he cites his own brother, Howard, "a construction worker and truck driver," as part of this heritage; early in life Howard was tagged with the nickname "Hoots," a Swiss version (originally spelled "Hootz") of his name.

Paul and Mildred were devoted, independent souls. They lived a difficult life, yet Howard stressed that they nonetheless provided as well as they could for their children, and he remembered dressing as well as his peers and not going hungry. Nancy Abbey, however, told me that her mother "scrubbed diapers on a scrub board for years for the first three babies," getting a washing machine only in the mid-1930s. When the family moved in 1941 to the country place that Ed later dubbed "the Old Lonesome Briar Patch," they got electricity but had no running water for a couple of years and no hot water until even later. Nancy added: "She was a frail little woman. She had two miscarriages—one between myself and Bill and one after Bill. My father just never saw any reason to make money. For him, life was just fine and I think maybe I, being a girl, may have felt more deprived than my brothers because I didn't have clothes like the other girls at school and things like that."[33] Howard recalled that Mildred was "rather bitter during the Depression years, occasionally venting her frustration at us around her," but always did her best to make sure that the family survived and that the children had enough food and spoke proper English.[34]

In the literature by and about Ed Abbey, his father is characterized almost solely as a nature-loving farmer and woodsman. Paul was both of those things, but he probably earned somewhat more money over a longer period of time selling the magazine *The Pennsylvania Farmer*, beginning in the Depression, and then driving a school bus for nearly eighteen years beginning in 1942.[35] As Howard pointed out, as a schoolteacher Mildred "actually made more money than my dad did, probably."[36]

Abbey misled everyone into believing that he was "born in Home," but he was very accurate in his more general recollection, in the introduction to his significantly entitled collection of essays *The Journey Home*, that "I found myself a displaced person shortly after birth."[37] Indeed, he was "displaced" repeatedly, living in at least eight different places during the first fifteen years of his life—not counting the numerous campsites that were his family's temporary homes in 1931. Like his younger brothers Howard and Bill, who outlived him, Abbey likely could not recall the actual places where he lived during the first four and a half years of his life, as the growing family migrated around the county early during the Great Depression. It was no accident that John Steinbeck's *The Grapes of Wrath* was one of his favorite novels.[38]

By the beginning of 1929, Paul, Mildred, Ed, and baby Howard (born August 4, 1928) had moved into a larger house at 651 East Pike just outside of Indiana.[39] Until the stock market crashed in October 1929, Paul was doing fairly well. In 1990 he still proudly reminisced that, in 1929, "I sold more real estate than all the other real estate men put together in Indiana. . . . Hard times came along, and I started to sell a farm magazine, *The Pennsylvania Farmer*."[40] Ed Abbey's childhood friend Ed Mears reported that his brother-in-law delivered milk to the East Pike house during this period and that, in 1930, Paul Abbey was unable to pay his milk bill and ran up a considerable debt at the rate of ten cents per quart. Finally, after he got his job selling the magazine door to door, he was able to pay off his accumulated milk bill of thirty dollars.[41]

Unable to sell much real estate in 1930, Paul had to move his family to a cheaper rented house just outside of the smaller town of Saltsburg, and then later that year into a grim third-floor apartment in the center of Saltsburg.[42] The family thus had less and less room as it grew; the third son, John, was born on April 21, 1930. Paul worked at a Singer sewing machine shop in Saltsburg, having earlier been employed by Singer in Indiana, but, in the depths of the Depression, business was poor.[43] Mildred made all of the family's clothing herself.

For the Abbeys, as for the country, bad times grew worse. The Abbeys spent the summer of 1931 on the road, from May 25 until sometime in August. They drove from Indiana County eastward over the mountains to Harrisburg, then to New Jersey and back into Pennsylvania before returning to Indiana County, all the time living in camps as Paul picked up various jobs to try to support them while he competed in sharpshooting competitions. Mildred kept a remarkable diary of this trip. One of her most poignant entries was written somewhere in northeastern Pennsylvania: "As we drove under the big apple tree Hootsie said 'Wake up, Ned, we're home.' Poor little kids! They haven't been getting much of a show this past year. Ned gets homesick to live in a house, and frequently when we drive past an empty one he will exclaim hopefully, 'Momma, there's an empty house we could live in!'"[44]

This is a special instance, rare in the very sparse direct evidence of young Ned's attitudes, of how different his boyish mindset could be from his well-known adult points of view. The adult Abbey would generally seem defiant and independent; the four-year-old Ned, from this account, wanted what every child does: a stable, safe home. Yet the migratory nature of his early youth established the same pattern in his adulthood. In some ways Abbey was very consistent from beginning to end—he was capable of saying or writing things in youth that he would still believe in middle age—but in other ways (like everyone else) he developed and changed considerably, and we need to regard his adult statements about his youth with caution.

On that summer trip in 1931, in any event, the facts are that the Abbeys headed eastward from Indiana on the Benjamin Franklin Highway (now Route 422) right past the birthplace of the area's other leading literary light, the essayist Malcolm Cowley. Two years earlier Cowley had vividly described his visit home, in a January 1929 article in *Harper's*. He emphasized how the woods had grown back following the years of intensive timbering before his departure for college in 1916, when "it was as if my country had been occupied by an invading army which had wasted the resources of the hills, ravaged the forests with fire and steel, fouled the waters, and now was slowly retiring, without booty." Even before the stock market crashed, the lumber company had left for Kentucky and "young men, the flower of their generation, tramped off to Pittsburgh or Johnstown to look for work in the mills."[45] Returning home, Cowley climbed up into a tree and watched the Benjamin Franklin Highway rippling "with an unbroken stream of motor cars" in search of a living.

At the end of the summer of 1931, the Abbeys returned to Indiana County and moved into a house midway between Chambersville and Home — the first time they lived close to the village that their oldest son would celebrate. "Home" is indeed a real place with an appealing name — so appealing that in history it supplanted another, earlier place-name. At Kellysburg, founded in 1838, the post office came to be known as "Home" because the mail was originally sorted at the home of Hugh Cannon, about a mile away. The name "Home" stuck so well that eventually it replaced "Kellysburg" officially as the name of the village, though people often continued to refer to "Kellysburg," as did Abbey in his journal and manuscripts as late as the 1970s.[46] Because the Home post office has rural delivery, whereas several other surrounding villages (such as Chambersville) do not, a number of people living not particularly close to Home are able to claim it as their address.

The appeal of the name "Home" in the Abbey family was expressed by Bill Abbey, who retired to Indiana County in 1995 after twenty-seven years of teaching in Hawaii. He was determined to collect his mail at the Home post office even while living several miles away, closer to a different post office. "I like the name 'Home, Pa.' I wanted that all my life," Bill remarked. "When I came back here, I really needed to get a Home, Pa., address because nobody believes it back in Hawaii. I have a deal with the postmistress at Home where she stamps my letters to Hawaii 'Home.'"[47]

By the beginning of 1933, the Abbeys had moved to another house near Crooked Creek at Tanoma, an even more obscure village five miles southeast of Home. Ed later claimed in his journal that his earliest girlfriend had been Tanoma's Sarah Jane Dieffendeffer (140).[48] The Abbeys' only daughter, Nancy, was born in their Tanoma house on November 21, 1934. Her aunt Isabel Nesbitt visited them there shortly after Nancy's birth and felt very sorry for her sister Mildred, left all alone with her new baby.[49] In 1927 Ed had been born in the hospital while his father was selling real estate and renting a house in the county seat—but now the family's fortunes had declined to a new low point, with childbirth taking place at home while Paul wandered the region trying to sell magazines.

The Abbeys' unstable, obscure existence is underscored even more sharply if one contrasts it with the "beautiful life" enjoyed by a more famous, older Indiana County native: Jimmy Stewart. One also learns a good bit about Abbey's native county by means of this comparison, for Stewart persists at the forefront of the area's popular consciousness, whereas Abbey remains marginalized. It is striking that this small town managed to produce both the famous actor and the celebrated author. Yet the tendency to lionize the actor and forget the author reflects the dominance of big-screen Hollywood over the world of books and is also another marked instance of class contrast. Stewart grew up in a comfortable home literally looking down upon the commercial center of Indiana—including his father's bustling hardware store on the main drag of Philadelphia Street—from atop Vinegar Hill. Stewart would remain the town's icon, with a larger-than-life-size statue of him dedicated in 1983, fourteen years before his death, in front of the county courthouse and across the street from where the Stewart hardware store used to be. The Abbeys, in contrast, continued to attract only a peripheral reputation in the area. People's scorn for the firebrand Paul was exceeded only by their neglect of the writings of the adult Ed, who became famous in the Southwest yet remained almost unknown in his native county. The hero of *Mr. Smith Goes to Washington* and *Harvey* offered to Indiana, Pennsylvania, much more appealing public relations images than those of the rebellious monkeywrencher.

From 1936 to 1941, the Abbey family finally lived in Home itself, in another rented house right on the main highway through the village. Their youngest child, Bill, was born on September 30, 1937. As the country moved out of the Depression, life improved a bit for the Abbeys. Paul made thirty dollars a day selling *The Pennsylvania Farmer* as far afield as West Virginia, and he won an award as "high man in Pennsylvania" for his sales efforts as times improved. Ed Mears took piano lessons during this period from Mildred, who continued to do what she could to supplement Paul's earnings.[50] Mears remained loyal to the family despite an experience involving him that was recalled later by Abbey: "I haven't been in a fight since about the fourth grade when I beat up my best friend, the only guy in the class I could lick." [51]

Finally, in 1941, when Ed was fourteen, Paul and Mildred bought a home for the first time: the house and land near Chambersville (but with a Home mailing address) that their son dubbed "the Old Lonesome Briar Patch," where his parents remained for a quarter century. He had been nine years old when they moved to Home itself in 1936, thus giving him a strong, pre-teen sense of Home as "home," and now his most memorable Pennsylvania years, from adolescence to young manhood, were spent on the family farm. This countryside was then less "developed" in some ways than it is now, yet it was actually easier for children to get to the larger town of Indiana: all the Abbeys had to do was walk to the end of their road to catch the "Hoodlebug" train to town. This was the scene of everything that mattered most to Abbey about his boyhood, as recaptured in *The Fool's Progress*. Here he and his brothers wandered in and around Crooked Creek, organized baseball games, and followed the family tradition of liberating coal from passing trains on the Baltimore and Ohio line. Unlike his brothers, Ed never liked hunting much, but he relished both summer and winter sports. He would wade in Crooked Creek in the hot months, back when the water was clean enough to drink, and then skate down it in the winter and play makeshift games of hockey. He and his friends hiked and skied everywhere through the woods.[52]

Crooked Creek is aptly named; it wanders all over northern Indiana County and then into Armstrong County and (via today's dammed Crooked Creek National Recreation Area) the Allegheny River. Once the Abbeys moved to northern Indiana County in 1931, they always lived close to Crooked Creek, whether they resided near Chambersville, Tanoma, or Home. In the introduction to his collection of essays *Down the River*, Abbey would claim that his first attempt at a river trip came when he was ten years old, when he and Howard rigged up their father's cement-mixing box for boating, dragged it laboriously down to "Crooked Crick," and promptly sank to the bottom, sitting in water up to their necks.[53] His dating of this incident, if it actually happened, is probably inaccurate, since in 1937 the family was still living in Home, right next to the highway, too far from Crooked Creek to drag a heavy box to it. In any event, early in life young Ed gained a strong sense of the land as defined bioregionally rather than politically, by natural creeks, rivers, and mountains rather than by arbitrary county and state lines.

Three of the family homes, including the Old Lonesome Briar Patch, were close to an area of very tall, full-climax trees that they called the "Big Woods," on the Chambersville side of Home. The earliest extant piece of writing by Abbey is a striking, undated letter to "deer dad," presumably during one of his father's road trips selling magazines, sometime during their five years living in Home village. Complete with drawings and a map, and apparently begun at the campsite, when Abbey was about eleven years old, it describes an overnight trip in the Big Woods that he and Howard took, walking with their "blankets, potatoes, baked beans, weiners [sic], axe, etc."

Since this is the earliest sample of Abbey's writing (the only one available from before 1942), and one that sheds particular light on his lifestyle as a boy, it is worth quoting in detail:

> Hoots built a fireplace and I built a shelter. We thatched it with pine boughs. Then we roasted our weiners and cremated the potatoes. Their ashes are still unburied. We sat around the fire a good bit, watching the fire, swatting at mosquitoes. Boy thats [sic] the life. Mosquitoes were the only insects that bothered us up where we were (except daddy-long-legs which don't trouble you any unless you leave your mouth open when you go to sleep). We both went to sleep right away but then about ? o'clock I woke up to get my feet out of the ice cream freezer. We hadn't brought along heavy enough blanket [sic]. Still, it *was* the life! The last time we woke up it was morning so we dressed (put on our shoes) and got breakfast. We opened both cans sliced a couple weiners we had left over and put them in with the beans. After breakfast we took a dip and started home. We got there too! I figured up the cost of the clothes I need and its only about $11. Well, hurry home dad, we'll do some more camping like H. & I did. Ned.[54]

He added a "P.S." concluding that the campout was over: "Shelter—down!" He also added, "Get a Spanish-Am. dictionary if you can," and then scrawled across the bottom of the letter a botched attempt at a sentence in Spanish.

We can see that, even from an early age, Abbey writes with verve and imagination: he and his brother "cremated" the potatoes. This valuable specimen of his earliest writing both reinforces and complicates his later reputation. We see him writing enthusiastically and vividly about his experiences in the natural world—out of which he would make his career as an author. Yet we also witness this notorious opponent of Mexican immigration, who was called an anti-Latino racist in the 1980s, trying to write in Spanish at an early age and expressing his desire to learn more of the language—in Home, Pennsylvania, of all places, an obscure, Anglo village, a very long way away from any Latino population.

Abbey would return often to his childhood woods in his mature writing. Thinking back nostalgically in 1974, he commemorated this landscape in his superb essay "Shadows from the Big Woods":

> In childhood the wilds seemed infinite. Along Crooked Creek in the Allegheny Mountains of western Pennsylvania there was a tract of forest we called the Big Woods. . . . My brothers and I, simple-

minded farmboys, knew nothing of such mythologies, but . . . we knew that the Indians had once been here, Seneca and Shawnee.

. . . My brother Howard could talk to trees. Johnny knew how to start a fire without matches, skin a squirrel, and spot the eye of a sitting rabbit. I was an expert on listening to mourning doves. . . . We invented our boyhood as we grew along; but the forest—in which it was possible to get authentically lost—sustained our sense of awe and terror in ways that fantasy cannot.[55]

He concluded this essay by lamenting that "the Big Woods is gone—or going fast."

But in the 1930s and 1940s, northern Indiana County seemed a dreamlike place to spend a boyhood. To a young stringbean boy like Ed Abbey, these woods seemed even bigger than they were, and so did the surrounding foothills, which he described in his introduction to *The Mountains of America*: "The Alleghenies are high enough to excite the imagination of a boy. My latent acrophilia was brought out early by excursions upward through the pastures under the lightning-blasted shagbark hickories. . . . Down below—far below I would have said then—I could see the red barns, the white farmhouses, the green and yellow fields, meanders of sulfurous Crooked Creek, the winding ways of the country roads passing among the hills from farm to farm."[56]

Another important part of Abbey's boyhood was baseball, played in a country style that he would celebrate in the fourth chapter of *The Fool's Progress*, "April 1942: The Rites of Spring." There Red Ginter ends a game ambiguously by golf-swinging a pitch in the dirt into Mr. Prothrow's cornfield, a home run—but then drops his bat and heads home, refusing to run out the bases.[57] Red Ginter also appears in Abbey's first novel, *Jonathan Troy*, where he ambushes Jonathan at his school bus stop and chases him, as Jonathan narrates in a flashback.[58] Earl "Red" Ginter was the name of an actual classmate at Rayne Township Consolidated School, who was several years older than Ed but was always far behind his age group in school. Abbey apparently combined Red Ginter with Red Hankinson, a big, older boy who lived in Chambersville and, according to Howard Abbey, enjoyed "the great sport of beating up on little kids."[59] Howard also never forgot the Abbeys' pick-up baseball team of the late 1930s and early 1940s, the "Home Hellions." Ed was the "chief organizer and player manager." Paul Abbey hauled the Hellions all over the county in his small Willys automobile so they could play teams such as Decker's Point, Plumville, Canoe Ridge, and Blacklick. Howard was an adequate first baseman, Ed a pretty good southpaw pitcher, and Johnny a very talented second baseman— the best player in the family.[60]

Although the family also played tennis on a neighbor's dirt court, baseball in particular contributed to Abbey's "creative impulse," as part and parcel of his boyhood dream. He later claimed that his attempts to doctor up his batting average while serving as the scorekeeper were part of becoming a writer.[61] He described the sport in his journal as early as 1952, as part of his native, natural scene (in a passage showing that he had already read his future teacher Wallace Stegner's 1943 novel *The Big Rock Candy Mountain*), calling the "incredible heaven of boyhood" a "big rock-candy mountain of delight and mystery." He fondly recalled the woods, playing hide-and-seek and waging imaginary battles, running and rolling on the grass, with the "smell of oiled leather and the smack of the baseball in the palm, the solid smash of a good hit, the long loping runs in the outfield hauling down a high fly ball—the smell and texture of spring air" (33–34). Toward the end of Abbey's life, in *The Fool's Progress*, he nostalgically recollected these boyhood baseball games.

In that same work, Abbey fictionalized the Old Lonesome Briar Patch as "Lightcap Hollow" and, with wishful thinking, wrote of "the gray good gothic two-story clapboard farmhouse that remained, after a century, still the Lightcap family home."[62] On the very first page of *Desert Solitaire*, Abbey highlighted it as "a gray gothic farmhouse two stories high at the end of a red-dog road in the Allegheny Mountains," calling it one of the most beautiful places on earth.[63]

Paul and Mildred Abbey lived at the Old Lonesome Briar Patch from 1941 until 1967, when they moved to a little house on Route 119 just south of Home that became well known because of the rock shop next to it where Paul would sell (and more often give away) rocks from his trips west. Like his father, Howard Abbey became a woodsman and worker; he was the only one of Ed's siblings who settled for most of his life (after youthful wandering and work in many other states) near their boyhood home. Howard's many job locations included the Marines, the railroad, factories, construction, surveying, and pipe fitting, but his longest-lasting position was that of self-employed tree surgeon, trimming trees in Indiana County for over thirty years. Like their mother, Ed, John, Nancy, and Bill were all teachers at one time or another. Bill taught earth science for twenty-seven years in Hawaii, and Nancy, who settled in Santa Cruz, California, worked for a health education organization. They all got along pretty well, except for the usual kinds of boyhood sibling conflicts between Ed and Howard as two brothers close in age, the increasing distance among the far-flung siblings in their adult lives, and the friction between John and the others (particularly Ed) partly because of the increased conservatism during the Vietnam War of John, a Korea veteran.

As divergent as were their various choices of career and locale, the

Abbey children remained linked by a mutual attentiveness to nature that they inherited from Mildred and Paul. The first time I met Howard, I invited him into my house to take a look at Abbey's Web—the award-winning website run from Sweden—on my computer. He declined, instead pointing out to me a beautiful blue jay feather in my front yard that I had never noticed. Both Nancy and Bill interrupted me during our interviews to exclaim about birds they saw flying outside their windows. Nancy told me that "there's something so strong in the Abbey blood that when I read Ed's books, I find out that I like the same music, I like the same authors. We all have this writing skill, and we all have this passion for trees and birds, and we have different views about ecology and the environment, but we all have this love of the things outdoors. And that really came from my parents."[64] Bill added: "I remember Nancy's boyfriend, Bruce, mentioning one day when I was visiting her, and Nancy and I were talking about this tree and that tree over there, 'What the hell is it with these Abbeys and the trees? Every Abbey has something about trees.' It's true."[65]

The accuracy of Bill's remark is underscored in Paul's 1990 interview: "Come over here and look straight across the reflection of that light— that tallest tree over there. That is a sycamore. . . . When we were just starting to build here, twenty-two years ago, our next-door neighbor got me a little tree. That's it. Imagine that thing growing that much. That's at least a hundred feet high."[66] The Abbeys' attachment to trees and their love of nature continued throughout their lives and was passed on to the rest of the world through Ed Abbey's writings.

The Old Lonesome Briar Patch house burned down in the early 1970s. Later, when reviewing two books by Wendell Berry (who, in contrast to Abbey, returned to and restored his family farm), Abbey memorably summarized his feelings about his family's home:

> My brothers and I called our place The Old Lonesome Briar Patch. The name reveals our attitude toward it. We liked the woods, the hunting and trapping, fishing in Crooked Creek and small-town baseball, but tired quickly of pitching manure, milking cows, husking corn, fixing fence, plowing up potatoes, and the fifty other daily and seasonal chores that required, we thought, too much of our time. We had better things to do, though we had only the dimmest notion of what those better things might be. We envied our city cousins with their electric lights, indoor toilet, hot and cold running water, new car, neighbors living one hundred feet away, and the poolroom and movie-picture show only a few blocks down the street. When the war came and an opportunity to escape, we left—

in a hurry. Without regret. My father, not keen on farming himself—
he preferred the logging business—sold our farm. . . . We should
have kept the place in the family.[67]

The family's experience with the Old Lonesome Briar Patch was
not as idyllic as imagined by some writers about Abbey and perhaps sometimes
by Abbey himself. It was never a complete or very successful farm; much of
it was covered by woods (some of which Paul participated in clearing for strip
miners in the early 1950s). Yet Mildred was very upset when they moved in
1967 to a much smaller house and plot of land right next to the busy, noisy
Route 119; she wrote to Ed, "I protested as much as I could. I'd been promised,
when we moved there, that I'd never have to move again and there have been
many times when I've felt that I just couldn't survive the *fourteenth* uprooting.
I had resolved that I'd never go near the place again. To have watched its slow
dying. . . . If I can't live out my life there, then I don't want to be involved in it in
any way."[68] This quotation also reflects some of the marital difficulties between
Mildred and Paul, with Paul generally doing whatever he wanted and Mildred
understandably feeling wronged.

Abbey remained very nostalgic about the Old Lonesome Briar
Patch, writing about it repeatedly—perhaps most memorably at the beginning of *Appalachian Wilderness*, where he described "that valley" formed by
"Crooked Creek, glowing with golden acids from the mines upstream." He
vividly recounted "Coming Home," time and time again, heading "across the
creek and up a red-dog road under a railroad trestle through a tunnel in the
woods. I call it a tunnel because the road there is so narrow and winding that
the trees on either side interlace their branches overhead, forming a canopy."
Then he would come to "the house"—"at the far end of the living tunnel, beyond it and in the open, under a shimmer of summer sun or behind a cur-
tain of whirling snow or within a lavender mist of twilight condensing toward
darkness." This was "an austere and ancient clapboarded farmhouse, taller than
wide when seen from the road." Over thirty years after he had moved out of this
house and across the country, Abbey easily drew it from memory on the cover
page of his longhand draft of *The Fool's Progress*.[69] It had "filigreed porchwork,
a steep-pitched roof and on the roof lightning rods pointing straight up at the
sun or stars; half the year there would be smoke winding out of the chimney
and amber lamps burning behind the curtains of the windows. . . . Nobody even
knew if there was a key. Home again. Time to slop the hogs, Paw."[70]

However, Abbey's relatives and friends recollected that as a boy
he was not, in fact, anxious to "slop the hogs" or do other farm chores. He
seemed interested only in nature, reading, and writing. Ed did not join Paul

(who often won back his sons' meager week's wages in a Saturday night poker game), Howard, John, and Bill in hoeing corn, claiming that he had a heart problem.[71] Nancy recounted this incident: "Ed was sitting in an apple tree eating an apple and reading a book and my dad was working in a garden not too far away and my dad yelled to Ed, 'Ed, will you go down and get me a hoe?' And Ed says, 'Where are they?' And my dad says, 'You mean to tell me you live on this farm and you don't know where we keep the hoes?' And Ed says, 'Yes, and I'm proud of it'."[72] Similarly, Ed took a book along when he went out to pick blackberries with Ed Mears: "How many blackberries are you going to pick," Mears wondered, "with your hand on a book?"[73]

Clearly, Abbey was an independent, rebellious, free spirit from an early age. His Aunt Betty told me that she "couldn't hang on to Ned" while babysitting him when he was a year old.[74] The baby book that Mildred kept on him includes entries like these: "Falls out of bed at 3 months," and "Goes everywhere at thirteen months." Her June 4, 1931, diary entry captures his bold voice at age four (in the earliest known quotation from Ed Abbey): "'I'm a big man and don't cry when I get my head washed,' Ned howled, 'but I don't see why you have to do these "dumb" things to me.'"[75] At about age five, he broke his right arm while running down a "Pinchot" road, so-called for the pavement that had been installed by the former Forest Service chief, Gifford Pinchot, then governor of Pennsylvania. Howard was convinced that this was why Ed subsequently pitched and wrote left-handed.[76]

Abbey's formal education began late, at age seven, but continued for a quarter century until he finally completed his master's thesis at the end of his dissolute 1950s. Erudite learning and hillbilly grit would combine to form Abbey's distinctive voice. Though a year and a half apart in age, Ed and Howard Abbey began school together as first-graders at Rayne Township Consolidated School in 1934, when there was no kindergarten, but soon thereafter Ed was skipped ahead to second grade, and he always remained very self-assured and certain of his superiority to his peers.[77]

He was a shy, studious schoolboy, quiet and low-key.[78] In fact, the real Abbey was quite different from the image of him created by characters such as the troublemaking Henry Lightcap in *The Fool's Progress*. As he himself wrote in his journal in 1976, "The Edward Abbey of my books is largely a fictional creation: the true adventures of an imaginary person. The *real* Edward Abbey? I think I hardly know him. A shy, retiring, very timid fellow, obviously. Somewhat of a recluse, emerging rarely from his fictional den only when lured by money, vice, the prospect of applause" (246–47). Abbey clearly developed a persona in his books and as a public speaker that was not the same as his private demeanor. He remarked in a 1977 interview: "The real Edward Abbey—whoever the hell that is—is a real shy, timid fellow, but the character I create in my journalism is perhaps a person I would like to be: bold, brash, daring. . . . I guess some people mistake the creation for the author, but that's their problem."[79]

I went to Abbey's fiftieth Indiana High School reunion in September 1995, where he was posthumously honored, and I expected to hear that he was an unforgettable character and perhaps a practical joker. Instead, the word that I heard most frequently from his 1942–45 classmates was "loner." He was not popular at school, partly because he lived nearly ten miles away, out in the country, and was not involved in many after-school social activities.[80] His relatives confirm these classmates' impressions. Nancy said that, as a boy, Ed was "too shy" to be the class clown, and that he was always "a very, very complex person."[81] Aunt Betty noted that she never saw him trying to be funny.[82] Yet even from an early age, Abbey was not afraid to stand out. His classmate Eugene Bence described him as "kind of like the hippie of his day," wearing work shoes and casual clothes, with his hair askew; "he didn't care."[83] Following in his father's footsteps in conservative Indiana County, young Ed regularly wore socialist Norman Thomas buttons to school.[84]

Abbey's reputation at Marion Center High during 1941–42 had been much the same. "He was pretty much a loner," Ed Mears commented. "He didn't mingle a lot. He wasn't an enemy of anybody. But he didn't have a lot of friends."[85] Ivan McGee, who was a year ahead of Abbey at Marion Center (and later the executive director of the Historical and Genealogical Society of Indiana County), felt that Abbey was an "intellectual student" who did not fit in too well with many of his classmates.[86]

Abbey had switched in 1942 from Marion Center to Indiana High School, which was several miles farther away from home, for several reasons. He did not like walking to Marion Center, whereas he could get a ride to Indiana High.[87] Remembering that he used to take the "Hoodlebug" train into Indiana all the time, Nancy noted that her brother fancied the increased cultural stimulation of the larger town,[88] which had two theaters on the main street.[89] Late in life, Ed told Clarke Abbey that he had switched high schools in order to get more writing classes.[90]

This was the same period when he obtained his first jobs, preferring to work away from home. During the seventh and eighth grades, he delivered *The Grit*, a family magazine published across the state in Williamsport, and the *Indiana Gazette* newspaper. He earned enough money to buy himself a blue and silver bicycle, at a time when most kids in the area did not own their own bikes, and he rode it proudly on his delivery routes and wandered all over the countryside.[91] Then, when he went to Indiana High, he got a job as a stock boy at Anderson's shoe store in the center of Indiana. Also, the same Ed who disdained working on his own family's farm joined Howard and a group of twenty other boys and young men picking apples for three weeks near Mont Alto, more than 150 miles across the state. In the summer of 1943, Abbey attempted his first cross-country hitchhiking trip, but, in contrast to his celebrated trip a year later, he failed to make it past the Midwest.[92] Nonetheless, his lifelong campaign to go west and turn himself into a Westerner, becoming the author of *Desert Solitaire* and his other books, began as a deliberate effort with this botched trip.

At Indiana High, Abbey's double distance as a country boy commuting from out of town and his remarkable intellect, even at a relatively early age, increased his alienation. "I don't think anybody in our class," Eugene Bence remarked, "ever got to know Ed Abbey really well. And I think it's because, intellectually, he was on a plane above us."[93] Classmate Judy Moorhead recalled: "The one statement I remember Ed Abbey making was in a science class. We were talking about atoms; in those days no high school students heard very much about atoms. And Ed said, if anybody can ever split the atom, they'll unleash all kinds of power. He was aware of these things before the rest of his classmates."[94] As Abbey himself recalled, "I was very intellectual, especially for Appalachia."[95] In his journal, he described high school as a period of "intellectual adventure" and "social misery" (118).

Abbey's future career and interests as a writer began during his high school years. His first known publications appeared when he was fourteen and fifteen years old: an anti-Hitler editorial, "America and the Future," in the *Marion Center Independent* in December 1941, and "Another Patriot," a short story in a spring 1942 Marion Center High School compendium of student writings and news. Both are forgettable boyhood, wartime writings, though "Another Patriot" is early evidence of Abbey's flair for the dramatic, with his protagonist diving into the ocean in front of an oncoming German torpedo to sacrifice himself and save his ship.

Actually, Abbey had "published" at an even younger age, in early adolescence, developing his instinct as a professional writer by charging his siblings a penny to read his homemade comic books, "filled . . . with the further adventures of Flash Gordon and Captain Easy. 'I sold them to my relatives by subscription. But I reneged after a few issues and my father made me give back the money.'"[96] Similarly, at Rayne Township School, Abbey had created his own school newspaper, describing kids' marble tournaments and other events, again charging readers a penny. And he authored a lively comic series of "the adventures of Lucky Stevens," recounted Nancy. A cartoon hero, Lucky Stevens could crack open whiskey bottles with his teeth from earliest infancy. Another "hobo king" had a thumbnail that was like a dagger. "Lucky Stevens had to fight to the death with him."[97] Abbey's "hobo" and "hillbilly" imagination was fed not only by his father's life experiences but also by the wandering hobos who would sometimes sleep near the family's humble dwellings, tolerated and helped by them during the Depression even though the Abbeys had their own poverty to endure.

Like most boys of his generation, Abbey played cowboys and Indians and loved watching Western movies, which he took seriously and never forgot. He told *Publishers Weekly* in 1975, just after *The Monkey Wrench Gang* was published, "I'd always been strongly drawn by the Western landscape, mostly because of the movies."[98] He loved losing himself in Westerns during high school.[99] A majority of the movies listed in the *High Arrow*, Indiana High's newspaper, during Abbey's years there had such titles as *Wagon Track West*, *Frontier Badmen*, *Ride*, *Tenderfoot*, *Ride*, *Canyon City*, *Call of the Rockies*, *Light of Sante Fe*, and *Sage Brush Heroes*.[100] As Abbey wrote in *The Fool's Progress*, "What I always really wanted to be, like most American boys, was a free-lance cowboy . . . a movie-type cowboy."[101] Howard vividly recalled going to Westerns in Indiana with his brother: "They had two or three features every weekend, the Ritz. I remember Ken Maynard and Buck Jones and Tex Ritter."[102] Tom Mix, one of the cowboy screen icons whose films convinced Abbey that he had to go west, was also from western Pennsylvania.

Abbey would admit as late as 1985, in his notorious lecture at the University of Montana in which he attacked the subsidized cattle industry, that for a while after he moved west as a young man, he had remained brainwashed by the boyhood movies: "Like most new arrivals in the West, I could imagine nothing more romantic than becoming a cowboy. Nothing more glorious than owning my own little genuine working cattle outfit."[103] Joking that "Cowboys do it better—ask any cow," he added that "I know some of you resent that remark, but I don't hear anybody denying it. I can testify from my own boyhood on an Appalachian farm that country boys are a weird species."[104] He also avidly read Zane Grey, remarking as late as 1982, "I remember *Riders of the Purple Sage* like I read it yesterday, though I haven't looked at it in years."[105]

Abbey liked to claim later that he had flunked his journalism class twice in high school, explaining that he "never could get the basketball scores right";[106] actually, he dropped the course at Indiana High during his sophomore year of 1942–43 and then failed it in 1943–44.[107] It is true that all of his Indiana County transcripts—elementary through high school and his year at IUP—list high grades in English but spottier performances in other areas such as math and science, including Cs in botany and zoology at IUP. This perhaps confirms Abbey's later insistence that "I am not a naturalist,"[108] despite frequent critical pegging of his books as such. Abbey began his junior year as *High Arrow* features editor, but this lasted only two months.

Yet "I had a couple of good teachers in high school," Abbey clarified late in life to Jack Loeffler, "who introduced me to Hemingway, Thomas Wolfe, Sinclair Lewis. I read a lot. I read and read and read probably hundreds of books during my teenage years."[109] Those teachers included Raymond Munnell at Marion Center High and Mary McGregor, James Nix, and Arthur Nicholson at Indiana High. Feathersmith, the teacher who tries to guide Abbey's autobiographical protagonist in *Jonathan Troy*, was probably modeled on both Munnell and Nix.[110]

Abbey would pay public tribute to his family and teachers in a December 9, 1976, lecture at IUP, to an audience that included his parents. These telling, heartfelt remarks (which Abbey never published) are worth citing on their own merits and for what they reveal about Abbey:

> I was born and raised near Home, Pa., ten miles north of here on Highway 119. Home—population 110, not counting dogs and chickens. My parents still live there, God bless them, where they always wanted to live, in a little house by the side of the road. . . . Where is home? What is home? Thomas Wolfe said, You Can't Go There Again. Typical displaced romantic—like myself. . . . A writer down in Kentucky named Wendell Berry . . . says why can't you go home again? He has done it and found his place. Others say home is where you have your roots. . . . But I too have found my home. And I define it thus: home is where you have found your happiness. . . . There are some—many—who never make this discovery for themselves, who spend their entire lives in the search for a home. . . . Such people are not hard to identify: they are the ones who will sell their native acres for easy money; who will stripmine and clear-cut and flood with dams the place where they were born. . . . We know the type; they generally run things. . . . Though I've lived most of my life so far in the red and gold of the American Southwest, and think of myself as a desert rat and a Southwesterner, I'll never get the green of Appalachia out of my heart. Nor ever want to. These misty hills will always be a part of my life, the source of my earliest inspiration. And I want to take this opportunity—I may never get another—to pay tribute, publicly, not only to this place, but to certain people in this place, who taught me so much, to whom I shall always be in debt. I mean certain teachers—Ray Munnell of Marion Center High, Lambert Joseph and Mary McGregor and Art Nicholson of Indiana High, Rhodes Stabley of Indiana U. of Pa.—then called ISTC. Most of all I want to pay homage to my mother, Mildred Abbey, who taught

me to love music, and art, and poetry, and to my father, Paul Revere Abbey, who taught me to hate injustice, to defy the powerful, to speak for the voiceless.[111]

It is striking how frequently the adult Abbey would refer to his western Pennsylvanian background, not only when he was writing directly about it but even in writings set in the West that have been considered only in the contexts of Western and environmental literature. He could be as far away as Norway, writing in his journal in 1952 during his Fulbright year, when a scene reminded him of home, with the fertile grass and "black cows, board fences, big shiny milk cans by the road in front of every farmhouse" seemed "just like rural Pennsylvania." The sniff of manure made him "nostalgic. Must be planting time in Pennsylvania. The folks there must be busy, perhaps hopeful, emerging from dreary winter" (61). He remarked that seeing a swan fly in England seemed about as likely as an "Allegheny pig-iron barge taking off for a spin over the Triangle around three o'clock in the afternoon on Mother's Day" (88). Writing in his journal while sailing in the North Sea, he thought about his home country as his "source," a land "dark and fruitful," with green hills, where "love began and must always return." He felt that he no longer belonged in Pennsylvania yet knew that he would always be welcomed there, "no matter how evil I become; not where I choose to live, but where I must continually return." Far off in Norway, "I easily remember my home. Yes, yes, I think of home, I think of Home" (77–78).

Such an attachment reflects not merely homesick jottings in a young man's diary but a lifelong theme in many of Abbey's works. As Doc Sarvis remarks in *The Monkey Wrench Gang*, "The best men, like the best wines, come from the hills."[112] When Sandy tells Will Gatlin, the protagonist of *Black Sun*, "Gatlin sounds like a hillbilly name," he agrees: "It is, it is."[113] In *Desert Solitaire*, it takes little to shift Abbey's mind from Utah back to western Pennsylvania: "Raised in the backwoods of the Allegheny Mountains, I remember clearly how we used to chop blocks of ice out of Crooked Creek, haul them with team and wagon about a mile up the hill to the farmhouse and store them away in sawdust for use in the summer."[114] When asked about being pegged as a writer of Western books, Abbey remarked in 1977, "I'm trying to write an *Eastern*."[115]

Even those who knew Abbey only out West have recognized, as his fellow Western writer and friend Charles Bowden put it, that "he was basically a hillbilly from Appalachia who knew how to write, who wanted to restore some hollow up in the mountains."[116] Abbey's close friend Ken Sleight, the river guide who was the model for the character of Seldom Seen Smith in *The Monkey Wrench Gang*, told me that Abbey "had a fond memory of his childhood right on up" and was trying to return to his roots when he bought rural properties in Utah near Green River and Moab in the 1970s and 1980s. At Sleight's Pack Creek Ranch in the mid-1980s, he wanted to live on the land, as the Abbey family had back home at the Old Lonesome Briar Patch, and he wanted "a place for his family. He'd always think of his family. He really liked families."[117] And John De Puy noted that Abbey "really loved village society especially. He grew up in a village. He was at heart, he and his family were at heart Appalachians."[118] Clarke Abbey similarly remarked: "He never really forgot who he was and where he grew up. He said a lot of times that he was an Appalachian hillbilly who grew up in a very poor family. And I don't think that part of his life ever left him, and he never wanted it to. He never forgot it."[119]

Abbey's attachment to home and family, artistic talent, sense of humor, and creative self-presentation were all clear in a remarkable letter of December 13, 1942, to his Aunt Ida (his father's sister). His suggestions for his Christmas present were very unusual for a fifteen-year-old boy: some classical recordings such as "Going Home" from the *New World Symphony*, or a book such as Thoreau's *Walden*. "You can always depend on a book," he stressed. He updated her about the family pigs, fancifully claiming (while toying with Appalachian stereotypes), "I've become quite attached to my pig, Knight-time. He sleeps with me every night and eats all his meals at the same table." He added that he avoided hunting, as he failed to see the point of "dashing around in the rain, through swamp and swill, merely to make life miserable for the rabbits." He included a three-page account, in cartoon format, of "My Day," his typical school day. True to his relatives' recollections, he depicted himself as cursing as he reluctantly fed the pigs at 6:31 a.m., and dashing out to catch his ride to school at 8:00. Diverging from his pseudo war stories several months earlier, and foreshadowing his subsequent political radicalism, he drew his class pledging allegiance to the flag with a hand motion resembling the German salute to Hitler. His other cartoons lampooned the various classes and after-school activities of this reputedly beleaguered adolescent, right through to evening piano practice (with a sketch of the sheet music for "Little Woodpecker") and "7:45 to 10:00. I read, or study, or listen to radio or play the piano or play ping-pong or just plain loaf. At ten I turn in." Here in this amusing, factual, but also partly fictionalized letter by this Appalachian schoolboy, we see the seeds of the adult Abbey, who would write about himself so creatively and comically.

Appalachian western Pennsylvania remained an important part of Abbey. Nevertheless, he was about to take his first big trip on his own away from this region, in the summer of 1944, and after that the world would never again look quite the same to him.

CHAPTER TWO

Go West, Young Man
1944–1952

In a few short, turbulent years, Abbey grew up fast—even if he did not exactly mature. He took his first trip west in 1944, graduated from high school in 1945, put in a stint in the army during 1945–47, spent 1947 back home starting college and working, returned west to pursue his bachelor's degree during 1948–51 at the University of New Mexico, failed pathetically in his first marriage to a UNM student during 1950–52, and studied in Edinburgh on a Fulbright Scholarship and roamed Western Europe in 1951–52. Abbey also continued his career as an author during these years, publishing essays and stories, getting in trouble editing a literary magazine at UNM, and writing his first novel, *Jonathan Troy*.

From an early age, Abbey loved wandering the wilderness and writing about it. But he did not see himself as a nature writer. In the 1940s he would like to have been Thomas Wolfe or James Joyce, and in the 1950s he resembled the influential Beats, both in his lifestyle and in his writing, much more than he did Henry David Thoreau or John Muir. He was interested in adventure, women, and drinking—not necessarily in that order. Later he would be seen (and perhaps even see himself) as an early postwar pioneer in trying to save the Southwest from the ravages of American industrial society. But he first went west as a rambling teenage hobo, and he returned to the Southwest in 1948 not only because it was beautiful, as he first learned during his 1944 introductory tour via the rails, but simply because he wanted to get away from home and have a good time while living off the GI Bill. In the 1940s the word "environmentalism" was not part of the American vocabulary, and wilderness preservation was hardly visible on the national agenda. Young men like Abbey simply wanted to leave the army behind them and get on with their own lives.

Abbey's two Appalachian novels, *Jonathan Troy* (1954) and *The Fool's Progress* (1988), sit like bookends at the beginning and end of his career. With different degrees of success, both novels vividly capture his western Pennsylvania heritage and upbringing—but also his strong impulse from an early age to follow Horace Greeley's advice to "go west, young man." Like Abbey himself, young Jonathan is moved by a cowboy movie, drinking in its canyon scenes, identifying with its outlaw hero, feeling "a powerful resolution formed and clenched and knotted in his heart"[1]—the resolution to go west. In his superior, retrospective *Fool's Progress*, the "fat masterpiece" that he struggled to write for many years, Abbey highlighted young Henry Lightcap's "three-month grand tour" of the West in the summer of 1944. There it begins when his father responds to Henry's stated desire to see the country by giving him a twenty-dollar bill and the advice, "Don't let any man take you for a punk. Never eat at a place called Mom's. Don't play cards with strangers."[2]

Indeed, Abbey's 1944 hitchhiking tour, between his junior and senior years at Indiana High School, is most frequently repeated in his writings as pivotal. In a great many different places, Abbey cited it as the key formative experience of his life: "I became a Westerner at the age of 17, in the summer of 1944, while hitchhiking around the USA. For me it was love at first sight—a total passion which has never left me."[3] He was overwhelmed by the vast expanses, the great openness, the sheer freedom of the Western landscapes that he saw. Perhaps his best-known essay about this experience is "Hallelujah, on the Bum": "In the summer of 1944 . . . I hitchhiked from Pennsylvania to Seattle. . . . On the western horizon, under a hot, clear sky, sixty miles away, crowned with snow (in *July*), was a magical vision, a legend come true: the front range of the Rocky Mountains. An impossible beauty, like a boy's first sight of an undressed girl, the image of those mountains struck a fundamental chord in my imagination that has sounded ever since."[4] He saw the beautiful redrock desert and canyon country of the Southwest for the first time while riding the rails with hobos. He got arrested in Flagstaff and finally abandoned the rails in Albuquerque in favor of a bus ticket home.

Hitchhiking west was a rugged family tradition that had begun with Paul Abbey. "The thing about this heading west business," Bill explained, is that "my dad did that. Then Ed did that hitchhiking, railroading thing. Then Howard did it. I'm pretty sure my brother John did it. I did it, when I was in high school, too. Hitchhiked across the country one summer. Nancy, of course, couldn't do such a thing. But every one of us boys did that. It had to be something about how our father did it, so we have to do it—sort of a rite."[5] Nancy added: "I envied my brothers so much. To me that would have just been the most exhilarating experience. And I didn't have the nerve to do it on my own."[6] This was a solo, macho rite. After Ed's aborted 1943 trip, Howard asked his older brother if he could come along with him in 1944, but Ed curtly replied, "No way! I'll go alone." When Howard asked why, Ed's condescending reply was "because, frankly, you bore me." Howard clearly remembered a half century later that "those words resulted in a bloody nose for him and further descent of self-respect for me."[7] During the following summer, in 1945, Howard hitchhiked as far west as Oklahoma, Nebraska, and the Dakotas, working the wheat harvest from Kansas to North Dakota. But then he ran out of time and had to stay in a YMCA on the way home, in Chicago, where somebody stole his wallet containing $250—as had also happened to Ed the year before in California.[8]

Nor had this been a comfortable "grand tour" for young Ned, at age seventeen, later self-described as "wise, brown, ugly, shy, poetical; a bold, stupid, sun-dazzled kid, out to see the country before giving his life in the war against Japan."[9] His much earlier, original, November 1944 account of his departure from Indiana was no less romantic: "Within five minutes I was picked up by an official of the UMW [United Mine Workers] bound for New Castle. . . . I swore a frightful oath that I would never stop until I gazed upon the blue Pacific. . . . After about two days in the Windy City I took to the road again, hitch-hiking northwest, bound for the Mississippi, the Great Plains, the mountains and whatever was beyond."[10] Before seeing either the Rockies or the Pacific, however, Abbey had to live by his wits and raise funds along the way, by harvesting wheat with Indians in South Dakota. He arrived in Seattle after seventeen days of hitchhiking, for which he was detained by police near the Oregon line.[11] Following four days of work in Oregon and then robbery in California at the hands of a man who gave him a ride,[12] Abbey was employed from June 25 to July 19 in the fruit-canning factory of the California Packing Company in Oakdale, in the Central Valley.[13]

After indulging himself with side trips to "John Muir's range of light" in nearby Yosemite and then to William Saroyan's home in Fresno,[14] Abbey tried to hitchhike east out of Needles, California, where he spent a day learning that few people attempted to drive in daytime across Arizona in August before the existence of air conditioners. Finally, an African American hobo taught him how to ride the rails. He also made his first trip to the Grand Canyon, hitching up to the South Rim from Williams, Arizona. He asked to be dropped off a mile from the rim because he had an instinct that it would be sacrilegious to ride to the rim in a car—better to walk there on his own two feet. Then, "a little east of Mather Point, . . . the first thing I did was urinate off the rim onto a little aspen tree waiting patiently below. It was a semiconscious act, no offense meant, signifying a claim to territoriality. But I have belonged to the Grand Canyon ever since, possessing and possessed by the spirit of the place."[15]

After returning to the main rail line, Abbey hopped the train again, climbing off in Flagstaff, where he was arrested for vagrancy near the center of town and thrown into the drunk tank for the night.[16] Three decades later, Abbey allowed George Washington Hayduke in *The Monkey Wrench Gang* to take revenge for him. Hayduke hijacks the police car of the cop who had thrown him into the drunk tank years earlier, tells off the police over their own radio, and then abandons the car on the tracks, to be obliterated by a fast-moving freight train.[17] Abbey's own brush with Flagstaff law in 1944 was less dramatic: the judge reduced the bail to one dollar and "told me to get the hell out of Flagstaff and never come back," and a policeman bought him a good lunch, returned his dollar, and then drove him to the eastern edge of town and dropped him by the highway. After another futile day with his thumb out, Abbey ignored the cop's warning against rail-riding, hopping another night freighter to Albuquerque, where "homesick . . . for the warm green hills of Pennsylvania,"[18] he bought his bus ticket home.

After Abbey returned to Indiana High, his classmate Judy Moorhead stressed, he "really had a claim to fame because he hitchhiked out West and was back in class in September."[19] Abbey also attracted attention because he wrote about his trip west in a striking series of seven articles in the *High Arrow* during his senior year. These accounts of his trip show that, from an early age, he was a better writer than editorial journalist, and they are particularly exciting to compare with his boyhood World War II pieces three years earlier at Marion Center High School; these *High Arrow* articles show a writer in the process of finding his true subject and voice. We have his junior and senior English teacher, Mary McGregor, to thank for launching Abbey's career as a Western writer. After Ed arrived home two weeks late for the beginning of his senior year, McGregor punished him by assigning him the task of transcribing the diary of his trip, which he then read to her class.[20] His summer of 1944 diary itself does not survive, but we are lucky that he wrote his *High Arrow* articles so soon thereafter.

These accounts then began to appear in installments in the *High Arrow*. "Abbey Walks 8,000 Miles by Adroit Use of Thumb," announced the first headline: "Around the last of July I began to feel an itchiness in my feet that could not be diagnosed either as athlete's foot or abstinence from soap and water. It was the wanderlust, pure and simple. So I decided to act, and promptly, for in a month the gaping jaws of free education would be demanding their annual sacrifice. Two days later I packed a toothbrush and a notebook in a small grip, walked a few blocks out the western end of Philadelphia street, and began hitch-hiking in the general direction of Seattle, Washington." Abbey's other 1944–45 articles recount such episodes as swimming in the Mississippi in the middle of the night, listening to a wolf howl while hitchhiking at night near Yellowstone, and (ignoring his father's advice) playing cards while riding the rails.

They also reflect Abbey's characteristic ear for dialogue and interest in politics, as illustrated in a couple of passages worth quoting in detail for what they show us both about young Ed's experiences that summer and his youthful writing style, and because most of Abbey's readers have never before been able to sample his late-adolescent writing. One recounts a conversation that a man strikes up with him in Pierre, South Dakota:

> "Where're you from?"
> "Me? Oh, I live at Home."
> "Most people do, son, but I mean the name of the town or city you live in."
> "Home. Home, Pa. That's the name of the place."
> "Oh. . . . You're an Easterner, eh?"
> "Yes," I admitted reluctantly. Somehow you felt that that was a shameful thing to confess.
> "What's your name?"
> "Abbey. Edward Abbey. What's yours?"
> "Sharpe. I'm the governor here."
> "Oh."
> Then we had a friendly little discussion on current politics, found we differed violently as to who would win the national election. As it turned out later we were both wrong, for he had bet on Dewey and I on Norman Thomas.

The second passage recounts another conversation, this time among hobos riding the rails across northern Arizona:

"You boys wanta play a little game of poker or somethin'?"

"Sure," said "New York," pulling out a pack of cards. At the same time Bleary-Eyes pulled out his pack, the greasiest, dirtiest, most wrinkled and pock-marked set of cards I have ever seen.

Bleary-Eyes glared at "New York" and spoke in the low, ominous tone men use when they are not sure of themselves.

"Whatsamatter boy, don't yuh like mah cahds?"

"No," said "New York" and he started to deal.

Trying to change the subject, I motioned toward the Negro, now awake and looking at us. "What about him?" I said. "Maybe he would like to play."

"That's a nigger," said Bleary-Eyes, "an' I ain't playin' cards with no nigger. Besides, this is thuh white section of thuh box-car an' I don't allow no niggers here. He gotta stay where he is."

I stared in disbelief at the man and couldn't speak. The words from his pitiful little brain hung in the dusty air between us and separated me from him.[21]

Such a moral to the story was the pronouncement not of an adult Abbey but of an already discerning eighteen-year-old boy writing just a few months after his journey.

Roaming the country and then writing about it as his penance, Abbey had found his true place and best subject: the canyons and deserts of the Southwest. He would recapture his northern Arizona apotheosis as he rode the rails east from Flagstaff, like Paul on the road to Damascus: "Through the wide-open door of my sidedoor Pullman I saw for the first time in my life the high grasslands of the Navajos, the fringes of the Painted Desert, the faraway buttes and mesas of the Hopi country. . . . It all looked good to me. And then we came to New Mexico. . . . Brightest New Mexico."[22] Nothing could be more different, it seemed, from the wet green hills of his native western Pennsylvania. He was immediately attracted by the emptiness and vastness of the Southwest, a country where the sun always seemed to shine and where the predominant year-round colors were golds and browns and the unsurpassed blue of the sky. "Brightest New Mexico" (also the first three words of his 1962 novel *Fire on the Mountain*) became, from 1948 through the 1950s, the scene of his college degrees, his first two marriages, his up-and-down, multiple careers, and his permanent love affair with the Four Corners region.

First, however, Abbey had to finish high school, do his time in the army, and begin his college career at home. He continued to excel in English class, subverting grammar exercises by putting questions about literature to

Mary McGregor.[23] She later admitted that she had been unable to teach grammar to Abbey, who already had a strong command of the mechanics of writing from all of his own reading and writing.[24] He was active in the drama club, playing Herbert's father in *Moonlight for Herbert*, which McGregor directed in February 1945.[25] The caption for his senior picture in his high school yearbook was apt: "EDWARD ABBEY . . . General College . . . Dramatic and Speech Clubs. . . . Hobbies are politics, writing, and hitch-hiking. . . . Favorite course is English."[26] Abbey would quote this description almost verbatim in *Jonathan Troy*, while elevating Jonathan to the lead in *Macbeth*.[27] In his journal on his twenty-fifth birthday in 1952, he recalled that he once "played in *A Christmas Carol* to a packed house. Packed in. I was Ebenezer Scrooge and loved the part" (14).

Abbey would also identify April 1945, in January 1952, as the time when he "first fell blindly, hopelessly, completely . . . in love with a girl," remembering it as a "thick dream-syrupy golden month when time suspended itself and I walked every night through twilight and darkness for miles and miles and miles, just to see and touch a girl" (17–18). This may have been Leafy Repine, a local girl who lived between Chambersville and Ernest,[28] whose first name Abbey subsequently borrowed in *Jonathan Troy*. We cannot be certain, however. Howard Abbey recollected that, like most others at this time, Ed dated very little.[29] Like Jonathan with Leafy in his novel, Abbey's sexual experience at this time was imagined rather than real. Very uncharacteristically for an Abbey protagonist, Jonathan even leaves a waiting Leafy behind at the end, choosing solitary exile over a sexual opportunity—probably yet another reason why Abbey dismissed this novel later.

After graduating from Indiana High on May 28, 1945,[30] Abbey followed many of his classmates into the army, joining a crew of thirteen young men in Indiana who gathered at the draft board, were blessed by a Methodist minister, and then were taken into Pittsburgh for induction on June 22.[31] His physical examination found him to be just over six feet tall, 150 pounds, with blue eyes, brown hair, and a ruddy complexion. Beginning on June 30, he did his basic training at Fort McClellan, Alabama—as later riotously recaptured in the eighth chapter of *The Fool's Progress*. After a ten-day furlough back to the family's Old Lonesome Briar Patch, on November 11 Abbey shipped out via Pickett, Virginia, arriving in Naples, Italy, on December 10. He served as a clerk-typist and motorcycle policeman for just over a year, until his honorable discharge at Fort Dix, New Jersey, on February 12, 1947.[32]

According to his own account, Abbey "rose," as he ironically expressed it in his 1952 birthday journal entry, from the rank of "private to private first class; was not given a Good Conduct medal" (16). He did receive Army of Occupation and World War II victory medals.[33] He succinctly summarized his army career in his journal, while slightly exaggerating his length of service: "U.S. Army, Italy—two years of misery, frustration, exploration, physical adventure" (118). He also noted, "With the infantry in Italy I shot rats, bullied terrified chickens, ordered people around. Almost fell into Vesuvius. Got drunk in the Toledo area of Naples and made a big row. Went AWOL once, for two days, in Milan. Stole a .45 from the army. Rode a motorcycle. Once arrested a colonel" (15). The home press provided an equally flashy, if more conventional account of how "Pvt. Edward Abbey joined the famous 88th Blue Devil Division which is now on occupational duty in the disputed area of Veneziy-Giulia in the Northeastern section of Italy, in July 1946," clarifying that, after his arrival in Naples, he had been sent to the 803rd Military Police Battalion for seven months before receiving his orders to report to the "world re-known [sic] 88th Blue Devil Division." While with the "famous" 349th "Krautkiller Infantry Regiment," he served as supply clerk for Company G and was later "sent down to S-3 as a draftsman." During his term of service, he was able to visit such places as "Switzerland, Austria, and Cortina, the latter being the rest center for the famous 88th Blue Devil Division."[34]

The liveliest, fullest account of his brief motorcycle career was given by Abbey himself in his essay "My Life as a P.I.G., or the True Adventures of Smokey the Cop." He was called on first to try out for the motorcycle crew for the same reason that his superiors tabbed him for many other, less savory duties—because his last name came first in the alphabet. He claimed that he got the job despite crashing his Harley in the tryout, by the simple expedient of writing "passed" next to his name on the drunken sergeant's list.[35]

Later, in blurbs on early paperback editions of *Desert Solitaire*, Abbey included the claim that "the army made an anarchist out of me and what with one thing and another I've been living off the government ever since."[36] In "Smokey the Cop," he maintained that he wrote home to his mother, from his new position as a policeman, "'Let's stop coddling criminals. . . . Let's put father in jail where he belongs.' (My father was the village Socialist back in Home, Pennsylvania)."[37] Actually, in 1946, unbeknownst to his son, Paul Abbey was already on his way to visit him, as he narrated in 1990: "I volunteered to go with a shipload of horses that we sent over to Yugoslavia. Hitler had killed all the animals over there. We took a hundred and seventy-five brood mares." In Venice, one of his son's cohorts took Paul up to his room and asked him, "Ed, does your old man belong to the Coast Guard?" His son was suitably surprised, as he did not expect to see his father, especially "seven thousand miles from home."[38]

As antimilitaristic as Abbey would become after his tour of duty, he nonetheless clearly enjoyed his army adventures. Italy was also the site of his sexual initiation. His essay "The Sorrows of Travel" vividly describes a young woman (married, her husband off in the army) propositioning him while he rode homeward from Fort McClennan on his first furlough in the fall of 1945. He turned her down. "My rejection of her remains, in my eyes, unforgivable."[39] But among the photographs of Abbey astride his motorcycle, over in Italy in 1946, is one of him grinning widely in the company of a young woman. In "Smokey the Cop" he described "long siestas with my girl friend in her filthy villa high on Posillipo, the Harley hidden under the orange trees. Yes, I'd finally discovered sex."[40] In fact, though later Abbey would often seem dismissive of his army experience, Italy was where he first enjoyed both sex and living amidst (rather than just traveling through) warmer weather—both of which he would devote himself to for the rest of his life.

After his discharge, Abbey headed home, catching a ride the last few miles with his neighbor Joe Houser, and showing off his stolen army pistol to his younger brothers.[41] He then enrolled at his hometown Indiana State Teachers College for two semesters, the spring and fall of 1947, under the GI bill, commuting from the Old Lonesome Briar Patch. One of the first things this GI did at ISTC, in February, was to post a letter against the draft—which caused the FBI to begin the file that they would keep on him for many years: "Tomorrow, the anniversary of Abraham Lincoln's birthday, several thousand American men are going to attempt to emancipate themselves of their draft credentials, either by mailing them to the President or burning them in public bonfires. . . . Send your draft card with an explanatory letter to the President. He'll greatly appreciate it, I'm sure."[42] Abbey maintained such antimilitary attitudes throughout his life, opposing the military hierarchy (rather than soldiers themselves).[43]

A year and a half before Abbey wrote his antidraft letter, beginning his career as a troublemaker, Jimmy Stewart returned home triumphantly from the war to Indiana. We can learn much about Abbey's hometown, and particularly about the bias of the popular press in favor of Hollywood and the upper class, by contrasting Stewart's homecoming with Abbey's. Stewart was featured on the cover of the September 24, 1945, issue of *Life* magazine, on the roof of a building, looking happily across at the clock tower of the old Indiana courthouse where banners read "Welcome home, Jim" and "V" for victory; inside the magazine was an equally celebrated photo of Stewart in his father's hardware store just down Philadelphia Street, talking on the telephone, smiling, with his feet propped up on the counter. When compared to the famous, affluent, Republican movie star, the obscure, proletarian, radical Abbey emerges in sharper relief.

His classmate and friend John Watta described Abbey as a beginning college student in early 1947, immediately after his return to Indiana from the war:

> All of a sudden Ed Abbey came there in a blue workshirt, no necktie, jeans when it wasn't fashionable. And you'd swear he'd just walked in off the farm and he didn't give a damn. There would be a bunch of guys standing around talking, and Ed would sort of edge up to the back and, eventually, he'd squeeze himself into the front and before very long people were listening to Ed. There were some really hot discussions out there. I loved to be outside Leonard Hall in those days because they would almost lead to fisticuffs in many cases. A lot of them were returning GIs, like I was, and a lot older than the average college freshman. Of course, Ed was too.[44]

Sam Furgiuele, another classmate and veteran, added: "Ed was a teaser. He said a lot of things tongue in cheek. He would say things, I think, to get a reaction. And he would upset people."[45] Abbey had not yet abandoned his father's socialism, later recalling in a journal entry, "*Indiana, Pa.*: campaigning at Teachers College." He admitted that the progressive Henry Wallace "might not win" but nonetheless "confidently asserted that at least he would get more votes than Truman."[46]

At ISTC, Abbey continued his high school pattern of earning As in English and humanities but Cs in botany and zoology. While ostensibly studying secondary education, he took writing classes from English department chairman Rhodes Stabley and published his first two adult short stories, "A New Variation on an Old Theme" in *The Indiana GI Writes, 1946–1947*, and "A Fugue in Time," a rather Joycean stream of consciousness experiment, in the 1948 compendium *The Indiana Student Writes*. "A Fugue in Time" seems a strained exercise in the kind of writing that Abbey later turned his back on, and inferior to the realistic narratives of his trip west that he had already published in high school. It describes a man's thoughts and mumblings as he gets up, stumbles around, and prepares to join his wife for breakfast downstairs—except that things start to strangely repeat themselves. The protagonist sees his wife's back leaving the room more than once, and the story ends with his eating breakfast and leaving the house, but then finding himself at the top of the stairs, ready to go down to breakfast again.

The satiric "New Variation on an Old Theme," while no masterpiece either, does foreshadow the humor and politics found in his much later, mature essays. Here a young man ostentatiously reads the *Daily Worker* before a concert, where he grows increasingly irritated by two middle-aged women who come in, sit in front of him, and giggle. After he finally chastises them, he learns that they are the composer of the progressive music that he has been listening to and the wife of the conductor. "On the way home he nervously dropped his *Worker* in a cellar window. Something was terribly wrong. The next day the young man bought a life subscription to the *Saturday Evening Post*."[47]

Abbey had begun keeping a journal in Italy in 1946, at first "devoted almost wholly to highly emotional and maudlin reminiscences of one girl-passion after another," as he recalled in February 1952 (19). Its extensive volumes survive only from late 1951 forward. On New Year's Day 1954, he remembered "1947: Home—a year of baseball, pallid love, ambitious writing, desultory study, painting high-tension towers" (188). He worked that summer with his brother Howard at the tower painting job before taking a second semester of courses at ISTC in the fall.

From an early age, Abbey was drawn to writers who celebrated solitude and nature, such as B. Traven and Thoreau. Given Abbey's youthful love of the movies, his enduring attraction to the mysterious Traven may have begun with John Huston's 1948 film *Treasure of the Sierra Madre*. The image of a hero wandering anarchically into Mexican deserts and mountains remained a central one for Abbey. It was perpetuated even after his death by the cult mystique surrounding his own secret, illegal burial in the desert. Similarly, as Abbey himself later remarked, "I've been influenced very strongly by Thoreau," whom he began to read around the same time in college.[48] Traven and Thoreau would continue to be key inspirations.

Abbey's vision of the high desert of New Mexico as glimpsed from a boxcar had remained fixed in his mind, reinforced by years of reading about the West and seeing images of it on the movie screen. His stint in Italy had increased his love of sunshine and remote places. Therefore, he decided to take the GI Bill and his modest savings back to where he had concluded his 1944 train ride: Albuquerque, a small city at that time, perched astride the famous Rio Grande River, with the Sandia Mountains towering above it just to the east. In January 1948, Paul and Mildred, with young Bill also along for the ride, drove Ed down Route 66 to Albuquerque, where he enrolled at the University of New Mexico.[49] Like many other young, male GI Bill students, he took up residence in barracks at Kirtland Air Force base that the military had turned over to the university. Many of these students were from the East, too; Abbey was by no means the only GI to head to the Sunbelt. One of his cohorts in these cheap quarters reminisced that "it was just like being in the army without the discipline. Shots were fired; poker was played all night until the money ran out."[50] Transferring his two semesters of courses from ISTC, Abbey excelled in philosophy, anthropology, and music during his first semester at UNM, while earning a C in a survey of early English literature and failing Spanish and art.[51]

Abbey came to a Southwest very different from today, at only the beginning of its postwar boom, especially in its cities and towns. According to U.S. census figures, the population of Albuquerque burgeoned from 35,449 in 1940 (larger than the 10,050 of his home town of Indiana, but in the same order of magnitude) to 96,815 in 1950; it would be 201,189 by 1960 and about half a million by 2000. The city where he would spend much of the 1970s and most of the 1980s, Tucson, grew dramatically from 36,818 in 1940 and 45,454 in 1950 to over 200,000 by 1960, a quarter million by 1970, 300,000 by 1980,[52] and between half a million and a million by 2000. During the same period, the population of Indiana borough did not quite double (to its still small size of about 17,000), and the rural Indiana County of Abbey's boyhood hardly grew at all.

Abbey thought that he was escaping from the overrun East to a more pristine Southwest; instead, he relocated to what would become major sites of overdevelopment, while his native Appalachia languished far behind, with higher levels of unemployment forcing more people to leave. From his arrival in Albuquerque in 1948 until his death in Tucson in 1989, Abbey was a constant witness of this exponential postwar growth—a defining experience and nemesis for him. As he would repeatedly declare, "Growth for the sake of growth is the ideology of the cancer cell."[53]

He found the Southwest of the 1940s and 1950s, however, a place of seemingly endless beauty, wilderness, and adventure, beginning in Albuquerque, a modest, lively town bisected by that mighty Rio Grande and sitting beside those tantalizing Sandias. Even the UNM campus added to the otherworldly look of things: its architecture was pueblo in style, with wide, low buildings in earth tones, imitating the adobe houses native to the area. Older white GIs like Abbey, from other parts of the country, intermingled with Latinos and Native Americans and learned to enjoy tortillas, pinto beans, and other wholesome and cheap Mexican foods—"a student's windfall," Abbey's UNM contemporary Phyllis Flanders Dorset remembered. They found New Mexico to be a "feast," offering "stunning, sun-baked vistas of tawny earth, blue mountains, endless skies" and "energetic people, full of gratitude that the war was over and full of hope for their futures." This was "a poor man's Paris" in which "people lived art." "The spirit of the new was everywhere—new industries, new restaurants, new art galleries, new stores, new theater companies, new bookstores, new houses, new cars, new clothes and, underlying all of it, new ideas."[54]

With his new friends, he began to explore the region in an old Chevrolet that he brought back after a visit home, having picked it up from "Square Deal Andy" in Pittsburgh. On New Year's Day 1954 he recalled in his journal meeting his classmate and friend Alan Odendahl and undertaking his "first delightful explorations of the Land of Enchantment in my old Chevvy [sic]: the Sandias, Bandelier, Chaco and Aztec, El Paso and Chihuahua, the White Mountains" (118).

Abbey's manner of exploration was more like Jack Kerouac's than John Muir's—more that of the young, drugged Beat writer than the semimystical, upbeat nature prophet. He grew a Beat goatee in the 1950s. His essay "Drunk in the Afternoon" (1989) described this early period, even though it was not published until four months after his death:

> Friday was our favorite day of the operation, since none of us had classes on Saturday. . . . World War II vets, G.I. Joes loafing through school on something called the G.I. Bill. . . . We met for lunch at Okie Joe's, an all-male beer joint right off campus. We began with a pitcher of beer. Then hamburgers to help absorb the second pitcher. When the third pitcher was empty, we swaggered outside into the blaze of the New Mexico sun. . . . We climbed into Alan's car, a black Lincoln convertible about 12 years old. . . . We headed north along the Rio Grande River. . . . Passing the pint around . . . we discussed my new model for the moral universe.[55]

In the summer of 1948, Abbey took English and music courses at the UNM Taos field school, which was located on a former ranch that Freida Lawrence, the famous novelist's widow, had helped the university arrange to buy.[56] On January 1, 1954, he recalled that first wonderful summer in Taos, making new friends in Dick Volpe and Ken Lash (118). What could be more romantic than studying creative writing, contemporary poetry, and nineteenth-century music in the mountains around Taos, this budding arts center and ski resort? These higher altitudes north of Albuquerque (which baked in the summer) made it the perfect retreat.

By the fall, however, even on the GI Bill, Abbey's money had run out, so he descended from bliss in mountainous Taos to a brief stretch of drudgery in industrial Erie, Pennsylvania, joining his brother Howard on the assembly line in a General Electric refrigerator factory. The trip back east required a "sickening bus ride from Denver." Along the way home he went to a campaign rally for Henry Wallace and then spent a week in "sad and lovely Venice, Florida," before submitting himself to "six pointless months of hell" (118), as he called them in January 1954, in western Pennsylvania—worse than his own native county, from his point of view, because it was flat and plagued by factories. Or as he would put it in *The Fool's Progress*: "Home is where when you have to go there you probably shouldn't."[57] He stayed in Pennsylvania from November until late spring, when he had saved enough money to return to New Mexico.

In the summer of 1949, Abbey took more courses in English (including advanced creative writing), philosophy, and music; he lived on South High Street, in "the little community of South High Albukerk, where Volpe and I" and several others "dreamed, swore, fought, drank, suffered and rejoiced. I can almost smell," he noted in January 1954, "the smell of that small cramped dirty chaotic little wooden shoebox we lived in" (117). After his classes ended, he returned to the Grand Canyon, in his first major solo adventure in the Southwest since 1944. In the "Havasu" chapter of *Desert Solitaire*, he would claim that he had been bound for Los Angeles with his college buddies, in what was to be his first visit there, when "we stopped off briefly to roll an old tire into the Grand Canyon, . . . watching the tire bounce over tall pine trees, tear hell out of a mule train and disappear with a final grand leap into the inner gorge." His tendency to embellish his essays might make one wonder if this wilderness champion really polluted the Grand Canyon with a tire, except that a reliable friend of his vouched that, as late as the mid-1970s, Abbey did exactly the same thing, rolling another tire into the Rio Grande canyon in Big Bend National Park.[58] This maverick was no reverent John Muir walking always lightly through pristine wilderness.

A few words from a Grand Canyon park ranger made Abbey decide in 1949 "that I should see Havasu immediately, before something went wrong somewhere. My friends said they would wait. So I went down into Havasu— fourteen miles by trail—and looked things over." Here he discovered the wonderland of the inner canyon, with three astonishing waterfalls into which one could plunge to escape the summer heat. "When I returned five weeks later I discovered that the others had gone on to Los Angeles without me."[59] The rest of that chapter is a vivid account of his brief encounter with the small Havasupai tribe and his extensive solo adventures, culminating when he nearly got trapped in a side canyon but finally made it out alive. His subsequent night in the rain on the Tonto Plateau was "one of the happiest . . . of my life."[60]

During 1949–50, in addition to his ongoing work in philosophy and English, Abbey continued to take flute classes, doing quite well at what became his chosen, lifelong instrument (perhaps in imitation of his hero, Thoreau), even though his fastidious instructor always gave him Bs. That fall, in a world literature course, he met Jean Schmechel, who retained, half a century later, an image of him walking down the street "playing the flute like Pan," and who went with him to Grants, New Mexico, where he sang in a UNM chorus.[61] Abbey also met Bud Adams, another classmate, and began staying with him on his land in Tijeras Canyon, east of Albuquerque, an experience that he recalled in his essay "Desert Places":

> We lived in a cinder-block hut twenty miles from campus, commuting the distance via a hairy-scary mountain road in his black Lincoln convertible in never more than twenty minutes. Until then I had never known who it was that shot up all the road signs around Albuquerque. In return I taught him how to burn down billboards. . . . On the day before the season opened we went deer hunting with handguns; I quit when I realized he was stalking not deer but me. Of all gun-happy people I have ever known, he was the happiest. . . . In one beautiful all-night poker game, I cleaned him of $240, but lost it all at dawn when he proved on a final bet that he could break a cinder block over his head. One day he got married and I had to move out. For wedding present I gave the bride my stolen U.S. Army chrome-plated .45 automatic, loaded.[62]

Abbey would describe this character at still greater length, calling him "Mack," in his notorious 1985 lecture on "The Cowboy and His Cow" in Missoula, Montana, explaining how living with the feckless "Mack" helped him correct his own earlier mythology about cowboys as heroic emblems of the West.[63] He remembered Bud Adams as more of a picaresque vagabond than a working cowboy.

These were rough-and-tumble yet also intellectual days for Abbey, as captured in a letter of November 8, 1949, to his parents, asking them to help him buy a used Ford, now that his Chevy had died. It is worth sampling this lively document, the only available letter from this period about his own college, for what it reveals about a lifestyle that combined erudite philosophy with sophomoric adventures:

> I have not yet bought either a horse or a motorcycle and am thinking of buying a car; not any car, but a '47 Ford one of my fellow students is trying to sell. . . . I should buy something; otherwise I'll continue to fritter my money away on records and books and wild parties. It's painful to remember that a mere six months ago I had twice as much money as now—where did it all go? I can't imagine. . . . I'm doing some writing but it's all of a highly technical nature— "the planes of reality"; "Pythagorean philharmonica"; "the polarities of experience"; "Principia Aesthetica"; "the isolation of data"; "Democritian atomism"; "Attic Romanticism" and such-like pretentious frivolity. . . . Bud and I went antelope hunting last weekend

with one other fellow. Bud's friend got one. Having neither license or rifle I drove the jeep while the others did the shooting. Quite exciting—driving off the road into the sagebrush over hills and down arroyos, rounding up the antelope like cattle. My but they're fast—we clocked one bunch at 40 miles an hour. . . . Mid-term exams this week. That's why we're home so early and not in bed. Cramming. Debauchery will be resumed this coming Saturday night and will reach a high point next week for the annual Homecoming festival.[64]

In many ways this rare 1949 letter seems consistent with the rambunctious adult Abbey; later in life, however, the lack of a license probably would not have been an obstacle for him. Sometimes the twenty-two-year-old Abbey may have been more cautious than the middle-aged author would care to recall.

Abbey split his time between Bud Adams's place and other friends' apartments in Albuquerque, on South High Street and elsewhere. He would claim that he lived in twenty places in thirty-one months in Albuquerque during 1948–51 (98)—and he would live in quite a few more there during the rest of the 1950s. On weekends he traveled farther and farther out into the canyon country in his old Ford and various friends' cars. In "How It Was" in *Slickrock*, he recounted his first trips to the redrock country of southeastern Utah, making it as far as Blanding and Bluff, discovering "a landscape which I had not only never seen before but which did not resemble anything I had seen before."[65] Here he sounds like many another traveler entering that canyon country for the first time, feeling as if he had died and gone to heaven, or to another planet. It is that rare place where one does not merely tour from site to beautiful site—because *everything*, everywhere there, is resplendent. This state, with the highest percentage of national park acreage, could *all* be a national park, and its southeastern quadrant is particularly ravishing, with its massive buttes and endless orange, brown, and golden canyons. Abbey would never forget this landscape, and he would endlessly return to it.

In the spring of 1950, as Abbey himself reconstructed in his journal four years later, he wrote poems for *The Thunderbird*, the UNM student literary magazine, as well as "brilliant papers on Shakespeare" for Professor Katherine Simons, thus establishing "a kind of reputation." He bounced from one place to another, spending part of the summer in a friend's "fabulous hacienda in Carnuel," near Tijeras Canyon. He spent a "terrific hot dusty summer in Albukerk. I take three deadly English courses. . . . We visit Volpe-as-Hermit in his log cabin retreat high in Sangre de Cristo Mountains near Red River—a beautiful and unforgettable place" (118–19).

Whereas Bud Adams seemed an unromantic, postmodern cowboy,

by the fall of 1950 Abbey had met another UNM student who would become the model for *The Brave Cowboy* (1956), his second novel. A native of Rhode Island, Ralph Newcomb took a train to Wyoming right after World War II, met and married his wife in Montana, and spent a few years rambling around the inner West on horseback and jeep. Before moving to Albuquerque, he and his wife had ridden on horseback from Wyoming through Utah and Arizona, in a trip that resembled something out of the nineteenth century. Newcomb was tent-camping near Bud Adams's place when Abbey got to know him, and they shared many campfires—Newcomb singing songs and playing the guitar, Abbey the flute. They first met when Newcomb brought one of his cowboy songs to the office of *The Thunderbird*, on which Abbey was now working as an editor.[66] Abbey soon came to admire Newcomb, thinking about him while far away on the North Sea in May 1952, as "a genuine full-blooded human being, and consequently somewhat of an anachronism in modern commercial-atomic America. A kind of misfit, like I hope I am," who "doesn't own a wristwatch or alarm clock or much of anything else, and goes where he likes when he likes and is all in all a full-fledged practicing Philosophical Anarchist. Huckleberry Finn Newcomb. One of the half-dozen people I really know and really like" (77).

Abbey's friendships ranged eclectically beyond cowboys, however. His fellow editor on *The Thunderbird* was Bob Riddle, a city boy and businessman who would become a successful real estate salesman, and for whom Abbey was working part-time by the spring of 1951 (30). For part of the summers of 1950 and 1951, Abbey worked on a crew in oil fields near Farmington, New Mexico, around the same time that his own father was cooperating with strip miners back at the Old Lonesome Briar Patch in Home. In a 1982 letter he would write that "the work was a combination of high excitement and dreary monotony, as it is now, and my fellow workers the usual company of misfits, oddballs, and long-run losers. . . . There's something about the extractive industries, about all forms of mining the earth, that corrupts and destroys everything it touches. I know. I was born and raised on a sidehill farm in northern Appalachia. Part of the old place is now a strip mine."[67]

Also in 1950, from the beginning of the year, commenced Abbey's first serious romantic relationship. He had enjoyed brief flings with women in Italy and earlier in Albuquerque, but his budding romance with Jean Schmechel, who was a year ahead of him at UNM, was of a different quality. When she returned from Christmas break in the Midwest, Abbey (who had remained in Albuquerque, unable to afford a trip home) gave this tall, attractive, Presbyterian sorority member two Indian bracelets, introduced her to Bela Bartok's music, and held forth to her about the space-time continuum, his Havasu Canyon adventure the previous summer, and how on a hilltop he had invited

God to strike him dead, but God had declined to do so. He also talked to her about how outrageous the billboards around Albuquerque were and how to burn them down. Their relationship seemed promising: Ed and Jean shared interests in some of the same authors and artists, and they both enjoyed travel. Jean graduated from UNM in June 1950 and took some typing classes at a secretarial college while Abbey enrolled in summer courses at UNM. Soon they decided to get married, which they did at the home of a friend of Jean, in Albuquerque, on August 5, 1950, witnessed by Jean's family and a few of her friends but not by Abbey's family, who could not afford to come.[68]

The odds of this marriage's success, however, seemed poor, as suggested by events even before the ceremony. Both Ed and Jean would vividly recall Ed laughing out loud at the presiding minister when, in his meeting with them before the wedding, he suggested to Ed that he might want to get involved in the church. Over two years later, Abbey remained irritated with this preacher because he "accepted without offering any change in return my ten-dollar bill; $10 for a wedding! I had expected the dog to return $5, at least. No doubt he was getting even for the laugh" (103). And Abbey's mother wrote to Jean's mother, expressing the hope that the marriage would work out but also noting that she "knew what it was like to be married to a restless person."[69] (In his next three marriages, too, Abbey married above his economic station, choosing wives with more money than he had and in-laws who thought little of his prospects.)

During the 1950–51 school year, while Jean worked in Albuquerque as a secretary and Ed took his senior courses at UNM, they lived in a modest hillside house in splendid Tijeras Canyon and then a cabin in nearby Cedar Crest, camped for a week, and moved into an apartment in Albuquerque by midwinter. Jean remembered that "the trouble started right away. Ed was restless."[70] Abbey similarly recollected in his journal in January 1954, "Live in the mountains in Tijeras; fights begin almost at once" (119). Nevertheless, they tried to make a go of the relationship, escaping their stormy home life by taking several trips together to some of the most stunning places in the Southwest—to Santa Fe and Taos, to Chiricahua National Monument and Monument Valley in Arizona, and to Big Bend National Park in Texas.[71]

In the spring of 1951, however, Abbey took two rash actions that would be symptomatic of his reckless life as both artist and man: he published a deliberately provocative issue of *The Thunderbird* in March, and he began an affair with Rita Deanin, a UNM artist, in April. The magazine contained his first piece of published short fiction since "A Fugue in Time" had appeared in 1948: "Some Implications of Anarchy," the academic-sounding title of which satirically belied its racy content. In a local bar, one young Jonathan Troy—

borrowed from Abbey's first novel, which he had begun to write—concludes this story by picking up a can of kerosene. A friend asks him, "Whaddeya gonna do with it?" and follows Jonathan out of the bar after he explains, "We're going to burn down a few billboards that are marring the landscape west of town."[72]

Still more incendiary, however, was the cover of this *Thunderbird*, as designed by Abbey: it highlighted the quotation "Man will never be free until the last king is strangled with the entrails of the last priest," and attributed it to Louisa May Alcott. As Jean recollected, "I, who had loved Alcott's books when I was growing up, thought this was childish and I told him he was going to be fired if he went through with this plan. Well, he did and he was. This was an embarrassment to the University of New Mexico because the publication came out at the same time that there was a religious conference on campus. They were furious."[73] The Catholic archbishop called UNM president Thomas Popejoy, who promptly shut down *The Thunderbird*. Ralph Newcomb never forgot the big stir this caused.[74] And another classmate remained bitter, decades later, about how Abbey's thoughtless prank had gotten his friends in trouble and cost students their literary magazine.[75]

As for Abbey himself, he would remark in 1980 that the "Alcott" quotation was actually from "some Frenchman," correctly specifying "Diderot, I believe. And of course, I got the Catholics in an uproar about that. I don't blame them. It was kind of a stupid thing to do. I was just trying to attract attention."[76] He certainly succeeded at that. It seemed that UNM never forgave him. He went on to earn both his bachelor's and his master's degrees there but remained irked late in life that, though he had spoken at many universities at the height of his popularity, "I have *never* been invited back to UNM for a reading or speech. Every other college in the American West, and many in the East, have offered invites, but not me old *alma mater*. How come?"[77] His love of controversy often served him well as an independent author, but it cut short his career as an editor, like in the cases of his similarly brief stints on his high school newspaper and on the Taos paper *El Crepusculo de la Libertad* in 1959–60.

Despite his newfound notoriety in his final undergraduate semester at UNM, Abbey met with academic success. After mixed grades in all subjects during 1948–50, in the spring of 1951 he received all As in three philosophy and two English courses, and he graduated respectably at 86th in his class of 780.[78] Moreover, and doubtlessly to President Popejoy's chagrin, Abbey was awarded a Fulbright Fellowship to Edinburgh University, Scotland, for 1951–52, having been highly recommended by his philosophy and English professors, including his Shakespeare instructor, Katherine Simons.[79] He summarized his myriad endeavors, in his journal a year later, claiming that he had carried on at least seven different activities during his last semester at UNM: (1) getting As in all of his six courses except for French ("that ugly language!") and graduating with honors as a double-major in philosophy and English; (2) drafting the first part of his novel *Jonathan Troy*; (3) publishing his disastrous issue of *The Thunderbird*; "(4) working part-time in Riddle's tile factory; (5) separating from and trying to divorce my wife; (6) falling in love and carrying on an intense affair with a crazy girl sculptor and painter"; and "(7) spending the last six weeks of the semester without a roof over my head, living in a sleeping bag on top of a small hill in Tijeras Canyon" (29–30).

He also never forgot "that April in 1951 when I fell in love for the last time"—as he claimed with wishful thinking nine months later, on his twenty-fifth birthday in 1952—"those warm dark delirious nights, the complex troubled time of love and early sorrow, love against time and love against love" (18). A year behind Abbey at UNM, Rita Deanin was a dark-haired, vivacious painter and sculptor. She was the first of three Jewish women from the New York City area with whom he would have significant relationships (marrying the first two) over the next twenty years of his life. His friend John De Puy, also a painter, would note that this pattern was even more striking given that Abbey spent most of his adult life in a Southwest that was predominantly Anglo, Hispanic, and Native American.[80] Yet it was also true that Abbey was drawn to the exotic and different, singing Rita's praises in his journal in 1952 as "my Jewish princess!" (103). Two decades later, just after the death of Judy Pepper and while living with Ingrid Eisenstadter, he would poignantly ask himself, "Why do I have this fatal attraction for sweet good innocent Jewish girls?" (228).

Even before he became involved with Rita, Abbey projected into his synopsis of *Jonathan Troy*, which he had begun writing while living with Jean, a very similar premise (though not carried out in the novel itself) for Jonathan and his fiancée: "After a long and painful courtship he agrees to and does marry her, although carrying on an affair with another girl at the same time." His fiancée "becomes apprehensive, unhappy, anguished, which only adds to Jonathan's anger and disgust. He treats her cruelly."[81] In April 1951, though Jean was not yet aware of the seriousness of Ed's new relationship, they separated. By the time Ed graduated in June, however, Jean was determined to salvage their marriage, and she told him that she intended to go with him to Edinburgh.[82] Abbey would summarize the next few months of his life, two and a half years later in his journal, where he noted that he and Rita had enjoyed a "preliminary semi-experimental and poetically lovely honeymoon going to Carlsbad [Caverns] and back." After a "sad and reluctant return to Albukerk," Rita went east and "I am stuck with wife." He then went to work in the oil fields, became a "roughneck," and then, after a "hopeless meeting" with Rita, he went with Jean to Edinburgh, where despite the "delights of Scotland," Jean would finally despair of their marriage, leaving him "free again at last. Free to love and wander" (119).

After a summer of work in Albuquerque, Jean had quit her secretarial job, visited her family in Missouri, and then joined Ed at the Old Lonesome Briar Patch near Home, meeting and enjoying his family for the first (and last) time. Around Labor Day, Ed and Jean sailed from New York to Le Havre, Southampton, and London, and then traveled by train to Edinburgh. Along the way they stayed in Yorkshire, where they visited the ruins of Fountain's Abbey and Ed argued with some locals in a pub about why the monarchy should be abolished. In Edinburgh they boarded with a family at 7 Warrender Park Crescent and enjoyed several plays and concerts as well as a Thanksgiving dinner for Fulbright and other international students.[83]

But Jean soon learned that Ed was carrying on a passionate correspondence with Rita. Ed and Jean talked about divorce, Jean consulted an attorney in Edinburgh, and then she left by December 15 (11), after her family cabled her money, returning home in time for Christmas. Back in Albuquerque, she filed for divorce on grounds of irreconcilable differences.[84] On February 13, 1952, Abbey wrote in his journal, "Received today a letter from Jeannie—a letter and official documents officially decreeing us officially divorced. Fantastic. Incredible. Actually, I took it quite calmly—not a ripple of emotion, only a slight ease of relief. . . . No more matrimony for me for a good long time" (25). Jean was awarded their Ford, which she sold to their friend Dick Volpe. As the sole mementos of their year and a half of marriage, she kept the two Indian bracelets and a concho belt that he had given her. Soon thereafter, the FBI came to interview her about Abbey, and she told them that the idea that he was a traitor to his country was a ridiculous misreading of his character.[85] In August 1952 she wrote Abbey, reminding him that his box of books was still in storage in Albuquerque, and wishing him well (99).

Abbey's reference to his first wife as "Jeannie," a diminutive that neither he nor anyone else ever called her in person, was just one small indication of his dismissive attitude toward her. As early as January 1952, even before their divorce was finalized, relief outweighed the rare guilty note in his journal. Confessing to "adolescent perversity," he admitted that "no sooner was she gone than I wanted her back." He felt that she had been a "habit," a "dependable fixture," and "thinking I did not want her I had actually become quite dependent upon her." Privately to himself (rather than to Jean), he admitted to "my dear sweet loyal wife" that "how fine you are, how good, and how foolish and stupid I was . . . and am. For I am not yet convinced that marriage to you was, or could be, a good thing for either of us" (19–20). In August 1952, he reacted to her polite letter by noting that Jean had essentially "disappeared" from his life. He thought of her only "occasionally," and then with "disbelief. To think that we were once actually married is to think too much. . . . That we were central in each other's lives for almost two years seems incredible." He concluded that "I owe her so much" and that she was an "admirable girl" and he a "villain" (99).

Abbey ruminated in January 1952, "Ah, Jean, what have I done to you? And Rita, what shall I do to you? Forgive me if you can, for I know what I do. . . . Light a candle for me. Hail a few Marys. I sure need it, and them" (44). Of course, part of the appeal of Rita in early 1952 was that she was distant (back in Albuquerque, finishing her bachelor's degree at UNM) and seemed almost unobtainable. What Abbey would admit in 1980 was telling and true throughout his life: "I love to be in love."[86] He loved to be in love more than to carry on the hard work necessary to make a marriage succeed.

Especially since Abbey wrote so extensively about his own life throughout his career, it is important to introduce a note of caution about his frequent departure from autobiographical accuracy, lest readers continue to read his books as faithful records of his life. A telling instance is his essay "Disorder and Early Sorrow," which begins as follows: "The first time I investigated Big Bend National Park was a long time ago, way back in '52 during my student days at the University of New Mexico. My fiancée and I drove there from Albuquerque in her brand-new Ford convertible, a gift from her father. We were planning a sort of premature, premarital honeymoon, a week in the wilderness to cement, as it were, our permanent relationship."[87] He writes that they encountered a fork in the road with two signs, "Hartung's Road—Take the Other" and "No Road," where he drove off-road onto "No Road," destroying his fiancée's car in the process. At the end she "took the first bus out of town. . . . Nor did I ever see my fiancée again. Our permanent relationship had been wrecked, permanently. . . . Small consolation to me was the homely wisdom of the philosopher; to wit: A woman is only a woman, but a good Ford is a car."[88]

Is the object of Abbey's misogynist humor here Jean or Rita? Neither or both, one has to conclude—or rather, this is a fictional character (in this ostensibly nonfictional essay) based on but not accurate about either. Abbey was not a student at UNM in 1952, but then he was often off by a year in his writing, as when he frequently claimed that he had first arrived there in 1947. In his trip with Jean to Big Bend during the 1950–51 school year, during their marriage, Abbey was driving their Ford, and no such disaster as described in this essay occurred on that trip,[89] even though such off-road driving behavior was characteristic throughout his life. Abbey's description of a supposed 1952 "premarital honeymoon" is quite similar to his 1951 "preliminary . . . honeymoon" to Carlsbad Caverns with Rita. However, not only are the year and destination different, but their romance did not end; in fact, it resulted in Abbey's longest marriage. Abbey's earliest published version of this essay, the 1975 "Desert Driving," includes no mention of 1952 and describes these events as if they were more recent. Here and in a great many other instances throughout his career, Abbey was a practitioner of what would be called (only much later) "creative nonfiction."

One might expect that his academic studies and the failure of his first marriage would have dominated Abbey's thoughts during his 1951–52 Fulbright year in Edinburgh. But these two topics come up infrequently in his copious journal—which is dominated instead by descriptions of his rambling escapades and lengthy meditations about writing (mostly his own). He was focused primarily on *Jonathan Troy* and on touring Europe, soaking up a different world and looking for romance while also corresponding with Rita. Edinburgh University kept a record of his enrollment but not of credit for any degree or courses;[90] instead, his Fulbright was a ticket for independent writing and adventure, even more easily permitted by Edinburgh's European educational model emphasizing supposed general degree progress rather than discrete course evaluation. On his July 1952 application for federal employment, he noted, "At Edinburgh University the semester hour system not used; I took 3 courses."[91] The basic idea for the academic thesis in philosophy that occupied him, off and on, for the rest of the 1950s did occur to him in Edinburgh, on November 10, 1951: "A General Theory of Anarchism." He determined that he must read Bakunin, Geronimo, Proudhon, Kropotkin, and Tolstoy (6).

Abbey's energy as a writer during 1951–52, however, was devoted mostly to *Jonathan Troy*. His synopsis a year earlier had been broad and sweeping, including plans for later chapters in which Jonathan was supposed to follow in his author's footsteps from Pennsylvania to Naples in the army and then to the Southwest. Eventually, he was to meet his demise in "the unexplored and uninhabited area of canyon and desert in southeastern Utah, into which the young poet Everett Reuss disappeared in 1947." Later Abbey wrote derisively at this point in the margin about Jonathan, "He had it coming."[92] In the actual novel, Jonathan never makes it out of Pennsylvania, though he does begin to follow those authorial footsteps by hitchhiking out of his home town, catching a ride at novel's end with a truck driver bound for Cincinnati.

Abbey remained disgusted with this first novel throughout the rest of his life. This may have been not only because he felt that it was not well written but also because Jonathan remains mired in his home town. Abbey drew heavily from his own life, though he also changed many of its details. For example, Jonathan's mother is already dead, and he lives in town in an apartment with his father—preventing Abbey from dealing with the legacies of his own mother and rural upbringing, both of which would obsess him during the rest of his career, right through to *The Fool's Progress*. He finished most of *Jonathan Troy* while in Edinburgh but complained in February 1952 that "my terrible novel will drive me to ruin" (32).

Abbey felt that Edinburgh was "Dark" and "Grave." Enveloped in fog, the city seemed to him trapped beneath too many clouds: the "heavy foggy smoggy sky pushed damply down upon the city under its own soul-filthy fatness" (4, 5). All of his life, Abbey disliked cold climates. He also found himself homesick for America. He was surprised at a concert, while the band played the British anthem, to experience a "wave of homesickness and loneliness" and an "immense and inordinate and tearful tragic pride in my land, my country, America, *sweet land of liberty*." He felt a love of the "physical land, of the towns and farms, of the many folks I know—tragic with a sense of America as a promise yet far from complete, far from realization, and as a dream menaced by ugliness" (11).

Shortly after Jean left for the United States in mid-December, Abbey headed off to the Continent for an extended Christmas vacation (writing in his journal in Paris on December 21 and then in Spain from December 30 until mid-January). He was a bit happier in the warmer climes of Spain, but lonely, apart from both Jean and Rita. He went to bullfights but took no consolation in a whorehouse when he followed others there, spending a night solely in observation of others "In a Little Spanish Whorehouse," as he labeled this journal entry: "I had not the faintest desire to go a-whoring—I've seen too many of the mask-face bitches. . . . no harm in just lookin'" (46). He merely sat downstairs and listened "to the distant muted jangle of upstairs beds" (48). He also found that "the landscape that had seemed, from a ship, so charming and lovely," during his earlier stint in the army, "turned out on close inspection to be heavily burdened by human need. Hardly a square foot of surface was left unused; the terraced hillsides smelled of human dung, the fields were cultivated to within inches of the roads. . . . I discovered the smell of poverty, the smell of fear, the oppression of invisible but all-too-confining walls."[93]

Back in Edinburgh, Abbey remained obsessed with Rita. Asking himself on February 12 why the arrival of her letters gave him "such a thrill of magic," he confessed that it was because he associated "her head with her body and her body with the small aperture that is the whole point and purpose of all my sweating scrambling yearnings" (24). His attractions to women in Edinburgh did not progress beyond infatuation, though it seemed to him a "sin" (29) to neglect the attractive waitress he admired, and likewise the second flutist of the Scottish National Orchestra, "a tall slim woman with magic fingers and dark-brown piled-up hair and soft shadowed brilliant eyes. . . . Every time I pass a pretty girl on the street my heart gives a lurch of regret—regret that I *passed* her" (80, 81).

Encouraged by a letter from a young woman from Sweden he had met, inviting him to visit, Abbey traveled by ship and train to Austria and Scandinavia from mid-April to mid-May. In Sweden he found himself too confined by the young woman's family to consummate a romance, but, while roaming through Austria, "I fell in 'love' for a few days. I met a girl from South Africa named Penelope" (58). His journal sketch of how she went to bed with him rather than with a German with whom they were both socializing, and whom Abbey had thought she favored, was later developed more fully in "The Sorrows of Travel." The different vocabulary of this earlier time is illustrated when Abbey calls himself, in an April 25 journal entry, "a devout environmentalist": he means "environmentalist" not in the 1970s, Earth Day meaning but rather in the sense that people are shaped by their social environments and nationalities (61).

Abbey's Edinburgh and European journal is filled with many worries about and passages from *Jonathan Troy*, thoughts about early influences such as Mark Twain and James Joyce (15), and mention of a brief encounter in May with the poet Hugh McDiarmid, "a little old fat man with glasses, a huge head with leonine hair, and a querulous irritable manner."[94] It also contains a list of women's names and addresses, and a shameless running commentary on the body parts of different nationalities of women. For Abbey, there was no contradiction in thinking about novel writing and body parts at the same time. He declared in January 1953 that writing a novel felt to him "like the seduction of a woman: It begins with strategy, with a campaign, but soon—if the affair is genuine—all plans are lost in the rush of passion" (105).

By the end of May 1952, Abbey's Fulbright year was over and his money running out. Via Cornwall, Dorchester, and Cherbourg, France, he set sail across the Atlantic, returning home via New York, eager to see Rita and his parents and to resume his American journey.

CHAPTER THREE

Ranging across America

1952–1960

The 1950s marked a difficult, mixed period for Abbey as he strained toward and passed the age of thirty. Personally, he moved from his first to his second, longest, most difficult marriage. Professionally, he enjoyed his first popular success with *The Brave Cowboy* (1956)—but then spent the rest of the decade struggling as a writer. In terms of the wilderness issues that later defined his reputation, he experienced such formative experiences as his 1956 and 1957 seasons at Utah's Arches National Monument and his 1959 raft trip through the doomed Glen Canyon, the beautiful, peaceful, pristine stretch of the Colorado above the Grand Canyon. But he also did menial work on federal water projects during 1952–53 and on road crews in national forests in 1953 and 1955—the very same types of projects that he later bitterly opposed as destructive of the natural world.

In terms of environmental issues, Abbey matured only gradually, like the environmental movement itself. The Sierra Club's 1954 campaign against the proposed Echo Park dam up on the Green River transformed that organization from a fairly cautious one, during the years leading up to these events, into a strong opponent of government policy. When that dam was averted only at the price of acquiescence in the damming of Glen Canyon, Sierra Club president David Brower and many other conservationists turned even more defiantly and despairingly against what government and industry were doing to the wilderness areas of the Southwest.

Later, Abbey would become an activist and continual letter writer on these issues, but in the 1950s he spent most of his time trying to survive while juggling writing, graduate study, and a string of temporary jobs. He returned in June 1952 to the United States after his academic year abroad and was reunited with Rita, spending a week with her in Provincetown, Massachusetts; as he noted on July 26, the love that had "weakened somewhat in Europe flagged and fluttered there, was set on fire once more with the ardor of madness and passion" (96). Twenty-two years old on July 20, Rita had just finished her bachelor's degree at the University of New Mexico and was working on abstract painting on Cape Cod at the Hans Hofmann School of Fine Arts before returning to UNM to pursue her master's. In the mornings when she was at Hofmann's school, and again in the evenings while she washed dishes in a restaurant, Abbey proofread his manuscript of *Jonathan Troy*, perused other authors, and enjoyed walks along the long, cool beaches. It was too late for him to find a summer job in Provincetown, so reluctantly he accepted his old UNM classmate Alan Odendahl's offer to join him in Washington, D.C., and seek work there.

On July 16, just a week after filling out his application for federal employment, Abbey was appointed clerk-typist in the Department of the Interior at an annual salary of $2,950.[1] Given his later notoriety as an opponent of such federal river projects as the Glen Canyon Dam, it is ironic that Abbey's first civilian federal job was in the Water Resources division of the U.S. Geological Survey, presumably contributing low-level support to some of the postwar projects that he would argue against vociferously in the future. He endured his clerkship in Washington until October, while living on 21st Street N.W.

Another instance of Abbey's unscrupulous attitude and unreliability as a "nonfiction" narrator occurs in his journal when he imagines that "I steal Alan's girl, then drop her, having never really wanted her" (99). One reads this as factual at first, until noticing that he introduces it as "another tale of tortured love, betrayal, etc."—and subsequently complains by the autumn that his time in Washington had been "monastic" and "celibate," until his last week there, when he devoted himself to seducing a young woman whom he met at a party (101–3). His reference to "Alan's girl" appears to be another case in which his journal was a site of fictional creation rather than simply a diary of daily activities.

When not strapped to his desk at work, Abbey spent a good bit of time corresponding with and thinking about Rita: "When I left her and came here, I suffered horribly from loneliness and the hungry cry of unsatisfied love" (96). He detested Washington even more than he had Edinburgh. On July 26, he declared that he was "desperately homesick" for the "great Southwest" and its "wild free skies and spaces" (95). Indeed, it is clear that Abbey's time in Europe and back in the eastern United States had increased his longing for the Southwest, with his exile redoubling his sense that the Southwest must now become his true home. Three days later, he wrote that he had turned down a better job offer because it would have required remaining in Washington for another year, "something I cannot possibly do. I hate this hot smothering eastern city" (96). On her way back to Albuquerque in September, Rita visited him. He was both impressed and fretful that she seemed to love him and wanted him to father her children. "(Good Gawd! Am I ready? Am I worthy? Do I want to—yet?) But I do love her, the sweet small wild thing, I do love her" (100).

In late October, Abbey eagerly accepted a reassignment to Albuquerque, still with Water Resources at the same salary. First he enjoyed a parting visit home to the Old Lonesome Briar Patch, where he was glad to be out of the big city and back in his native Pennsylvania woods, and he observed the "proud immortal American autumn" with its "gold and death-fire of leaves" fading. Now everything seemed "black, drab lusterless brown, gray, under a bleak smoky sky. . . . But even now a few cicada are left; you can hear them at twilight, few in number but still alive" (102). By October 30 he was aboard "The Chief" to Albuquerque, eager to see Rita yet curiously prescient about their difficult future together, as he ruminated in his journal while riding the rails: heading toward reunion with Rita, he wondered, "What does it mean? What do I really want? What does she? What is the meaning of us? I don't know; we're two blind creatures in the dark, each uncertain, a little cautious, worried. We each have our literary fictions to be true to—the legend-builders. We are reluctant to abandon our personal romances for a common romance" (103).

On November 20, 1952, Ed and Rita were nonetheless married "in a small ceremony at an adobe house in Albuquerque owned by Rita's mentor, the head of the university art department."[2] Rita had wanted to be married by a rabbi but was refused because of Ed's divorced, non-Jewish status.[3] They moved into an apartment at 214 Pine N.E.[4] and, as with his first marriage, soon thereafter Abbey was writing in his journal about arguments, to the point where they now seemed to follow a pattern. His mother had advised him that, in marriage, "Crises are easier to survive than the daily routine," and his friend

Malcolm Brown had pointed out one day that "married couples who fight continually may really need each other as desperately as those apparently desperately in love—the fighting fills an important vacuum in their otherwise empty vows" (105).

Brown was an artist and former UNM classmate of Abbey who, together with his wife Rachel and their children, was becoming an important part of Ed and Rita's life in New Mexico. In July 1953, Abbey would note that Brown was the "nearest thing to an all-round human I know" (108). In January 1954, he added that he was "proud to be his friend" (122), and in September 1966, Abbey declared that "he is the only man I know who has succeeded, as Frost says, in uniting his vocation with his avocation."[5] In 1969, he would publish an article entitled "Malcolm Brown: The Artist as Architect," describing the unusual adobe homes designed and built by Brown in Taos and concluding that he was "living evidence that a different kind of life than most of us know may still be possible. Life as hazard and exploration freely chosen—an adventure in freedom and love."[6]

At the end of February 1953, Abbey's job with the Geological Survey ended while Rita continued as a graduate assistant in the UNM art department. Around this time, Howard Abbey stayed with them for a while after being laid off from a railroad job in Washington state; he worked on a surveying crew up and down the Rio Grande until late spring. He remembered Ed and Rita's little adobe place at the outskirts of the city,[7] where Howard kept his distance and was often out of town on his job. As he put it later, "Were we friends? Hell no, we weren't friends! We were brothers!"[8]

Meanwhile, Abbey was looking for work and thinking about graduate school. With the help of his teacher Hubert Alexander, chair of the UNM philosophy department, he was admitted to Yale's graduate program in philosophy for the fall. On May 12 he was hired as a laborer in Carson National Forest near Taos, the first of his many U.S. Forest Service and National Park Service jobs, at the rate of $10.40 per day. The work was menial, but he enjoyed staying in the deep forest. This job continued through July, while Rita attended a UNM art extension course, living in the Harwood Building in Taos.[9] Things were also looking up for Abbey's writing. In June he noted that he had received a $500 advance for *Jonathan Troy* from Dodd-Mead, who contracted to publish the novel in early 1954. He decided to dedicate the book "to my mother and father and to Rita" (106).

In the late summer of 1953, if we can believe Abbey the essayist in "How It Was," he took a trip to Dandy Crossing, near Hite, Utah—which today is buried under a few hundred feet of Lake Powell, having been flooded by Glen Canyon Dam since June 1964.[10] By 1954 David Brower, Wallace Stegner, and the Sierra Club would mount a successful publicity campaign against the proposed Echo Park dam up on the Green River in Dinosaur National Monument, as a result of which Brower eventually agreed (much to his subsequent chagrin) not to stand in the way of Glen Canyon Dam. In "How It Was," Abbey describes driving his pickup down hazardous, unpaved roads from Blanding to Natural Bridges and on to Hite and beyond, taking all day to make it out through North Wash after a rainfall. Even today, this region includes some of the most striking landscapes and unbelievable roads on the continent; one can still drive north from Mexican Hat toward Natural Bridges, for example, see nothing in front of oneself near the Valley of the Gods except for the massive walls of the redrock canyon, feel that one's journey is about to come to an end—yet then follow switchbacks all the way up the wall and continue atop the plateau (to one's astonishment) to Natural Bridges. This unspoiled region of the Colorado River, soon to be lost, remained an important place for Abbey. The protagonists in his early 1960s, unpublished novel "City of Dreadful Night" would sit in Hoboken and talk continually of escaping to Dandy Crossing.[11] And "How It Was" in *Slickrock* concludes as follows: "The river is gone, the ferry is gone, Dandy Crossing is gone. Most of the formerly primitive road from Blanding west has been improved beyond recognition." Politicians say that paved roads and Lake Powell have made the region much more accessible, but "that is a lie. . . . For those who go there now, smooth, comfortable, quick and easy, sliding through as slick as grease, will never be able to see what we saw. They will never feel what we felt. They will never learn what we know."[12]

At the end of the summer of 1953, Ed and Rita headed to New Haven, Connecticut, where Ed enrolled in his graduate courses and Rita got a job as a waitress at Howard Johnson's. They did not make it through September. Abbey would later succinctly summarize his career at Yale: "Two weeks. . . . I had academic ambitions then and wanted to be a professor of philosophy. . . . I got scared out by a course in symbolic logic. It was required, and I found it totally incomprehensible. . . . We both decided we were homesick for the Southwest. . . . I quit just in time to get my tuition money back."[13] He declared on September 20, while still in New Haven, that he wanted to be a "writer, not an academician. . . . My calling and my study lie elsewhere, in the sweet air and under the open sky of the broad world, among my friends and folks" (111). The combination of symbolic logic and the gray walls of Yale and even grayer streets of New Haven was enough to drive him right back to Albuquerque.

Before returning to New Mexico, however, Ed and Rita spent the rest of 1953 in Rochelle Park, New Jersey, near Rita's parents. By October 10, Abbey was working at the Dumont Television factory, "sitting at a bench winding fiberglass around transformer coils, laminating the cores, jig-boring modified specs, wedging one coil inside another, testing"—with dull co-workers and muzak continually playing (112). His escapes were partly literary: proofreading the galleys of *Jonathan Troy* and, in December, talking with Norman Mailer at a party in Greenwich Village, finding him "unnecessarily patient, tolerant; he had to listen to some dreadful crap" (115). This was the first of Abbey's several sojourns in the New York City area, where the teeming cultural life and many bars would serve as counterpoint to his beloved, still much less populated Southwest.

In January 1954, Abbey found himself laid off from his factory job, "unemployed through no fault of my own, for once" (119). He and Rita then returned to New Mexico, as he recalled on December 27, 1954, via the Smoky Mountains, New Orleans, and Big Bend. In Peralta, south of Albuquerque, he installed himself as caretaker of a "splendid old adobe mansion" owned by an "old lady named Minnebo or Menopause or something." One morning about two weeks after moving in, he "built a wood fire (scrub oak, yellow pine) in the livingroom stove. That evening the place was a heap of smoking ash. Alas! No one knows. A superb, an excellent conflagration, a blazing spectacle. Sightseers came from far and wide, and the press too" (121).

Next, Ed and Rita moved into a little "studio" adobe hut next to the house of Malcolm and Rachel Brown on North Edith Street in Albuquerque, staying there until early 1955. Soon before the Abbeys left North Edith Street, Rachel recalled, "they had this big wild party with some of the neighbors around, and the main event was burning the outhouse; guys were getting drunk and jumping over the fire."[14] In *The Fool's Progress*, Abbey eventually combined both fires—the Peralta caretaking disaster and the Albuquerque outhouse event—into a single "Housewarming Party," fictionally redated to March 1956.[15] In some respects fiction could not be any wilder than fact. For example, Abbey inserts a character named Roggoway into this "Housewarming Party."[16] The real Alfred Roggoway, as both the Browns and Abbey remembered, was notorious because "when the party gets dull," he "unbuttons his fly and lays his penis on the table. 'Mine,' he says, 'all mine'" (123).

Abbey's life in New Mexico during this period may seem the stuff of good stories, and he was glad to be back in the open spaces of his beloved Southwest, but Abbey and his wife and friends were also mired in grinding poverty that was not very inspiring or funny at the time. As Rachel Brown emphasized, "we were just struggling artists and lived in the most appalling adobe ruins that nobody would think of living in now."[17] Abbey noted that "for a goodly while we lived on pinto beans, home-baked bread, potatoes" (122). This was a decade before the days of communes, yet the Browns and Abbeys tried to help each other out in a cooperative way.

There was also some attraction, though not acted on, across the confines of the Brown and Abbey marriages. Something of Abbey's bizarre sexual fantasy life is suggested by "Sunflowers," a published chapter from his later, unpublished novel about this period. Here we meet Millie Lightcap, who calls to mind both Rachel, since Millie is the mother and homemaker of a New Mexico family resembling the Browns, and Abbey's own mother, Mildred, not only with her name but also with her "hillbilly eyes."[18] So what does Abbey's autobiographical protagonist do in this chapter? He seduces Millie Lightcap while her baby lies crying just a few steps away, thus violating taboos if viewed on a biographical and Freudian level. It did not happen in reality, but Abbey fantasized about such a seduction in the form of this story.

Another significant member of the semi-communal Brown-Abbey household was Homer, an old part-Dalmatian dog that they took turns taking care of. Abbey vividly synthesized comedy, poverty, and the dog in an unpublished, macabre narrative, "The Dog" (first outlined in January 1958 [145]) in which Homer becomes "Chief. Part Dalmatian, part damnation, all hound." After Chief takes up residence beneath his back porch, the narrator kicks him to try to get rid of him, but his wife feeds him, "so naturally he continued to hang around." "The Dog" proceeds according to a pattern of disaster yet endurance, as when the wife tries to take Chief to be vaccinated, tying him to their truck, but he jumps out, runs, and is dragged along. After a stint in an animal hospital, Chief next eats "a mixture of hamburger and strychnine" and then is caught in the inevitable house fire—yet survives both.

The narrator and his wife finally leave Chief with their friends, an only slightly exaggerated version of the Browns: "Our friends didn't want the dog. They were very poor people, with five children and no income. They made pottery for a living, which they tried to sell to tourists in the summer. They told us, quite clearly and definitely, that they could not and would not feed the dog." Returning two years later, the narrator and his wife ask for their dog back, but their friends refuse, explaining that despite the loss of an ear, Chief had somehow survived, and they had become attached to him. "However, I was able to console my wife a little later, as we drove away, by promising to get her a puppy as much as possible like Chief. I had noticed quite a number of them in the neighborhood, all looking very much like our dog. In fact, we ran over one on the road home."[19]

Again, Abbey's fiction was hardly any stranger than his reality. Later, in the fall of 1959 when the Browns moved from Arroyo Seco, near Taos, to Colorado, Homer refused to get into the truck to go with them—instead running off and turning up several miles away at the Abbeys' house, where he spent the winter. After the Abbeys left Taos, Homer lived on his own until the Browns returned to Arroyo Seco, as Malcolm reminisced: "Homer showed up one day, totally transformed, just skin and bones and scabby and almost dead. He lived out the rest of his life with us."[20]

Meanwhile, Abbey's early career as a writer was like Homer's—lively but difficult. Even before *Jonathan Troy* was published in early 1954, he had become disgusted with it, deciding while reading the galleys in December 1953 that it seemed "even worse than I had thought," too "juvenile, naive, clumsy, pretentious." He felt that he had "tried to do everything at once and succeeded in almost nothing. Too much empty rhetoric, not enough meat and bone. Not convincing. All the obvious faults of the beginner" (114). This first novel's commercial failure reinforced his dissatisfaction, as he added a year later, complaining that *Troy* had been "faintly reviewed, virtually ignored, generally unbought" (122). He had to depend on his old high school teacher Art Nicholson (by then a professor at Indiana State Teachers College) for a kind review in his hometown *Indiana Gazette* on March 3, 1954: "The fact that the setting of the story is unquestionably in Indiana, Pennsylvania, may make this well-written novel of unusual interest to the people of this area." But even Nicholson complained that "a chief weakness of this otherwise meritable and commendable novel" is that "with the exception of Jonathan, all the characters are underdeveloped. They tend to be caricatures or stereotypes."[21] Much more visibly in the *New York Times*, in an April 11 review, Herbert F. West called *Jonathan Troy* a "symphony of disgust" yet noted its "bitter, but artistically satisfying end."[22]

Abbey remained so unhappy with his first novel that he always refused to have it reprinted—though he did permit a two-page excerpt at the beginning of his 1984 collection *Slumgullion Stew* (subsequently retitled *The Best of Edward Abbey*)—and left instructions that it not be reprinted after his death. As a result, *Jonathan Troy* became a very expensive collector's item, consistently fetching four-figure prices by the end of the century. Abbey was too hard on himself; this novel is certainly flawed, yet interesting. It includes some lively writing and introduces several of the main themes that remained central in his writing—particularly the protagonist who makes a mess of his romantic life, is opposed to conventional society, and finally wanders off alone toward the western horizon. Abbey was probably dissatisfied partly because of its departures from his real life; for example, he kills off Jonathan's father, Nat, a radical strike leader, late in the novel. Nat Troy is described as "Old One Eye" (in contrast to Abbey's actual two-eyed, sharpshooting father)—a motif that subsequently appears in the mysterious one-eyed "Lone Ranger" in *The Monkey Wrench Gang*, who makes his final appearance as "one-eyed Jack" in *Hayduke Lives!* (reincarnated as Jack Burns from *The Brave Cowboy*).[23] Yet as

late as 1982, Abbey remarked that *Jonathan Troy* "was a disgusting novel, fortunately long out of print. . . . It's about the agonies of growing up in a small
town: pimples and masturbation." This writer who devoted himself to a clear
style all his own remained bothered not by his first novel's personal revelations
but by its derivative style: "There's a Faulkner chapter, an entire chapter in
one sentence. . . . There's a Thomas Wolfe wind-through-the-trees-outside-the-
farmhouse chapter, a Joyce chapter, and of course there are newspaper clips
all through the thing, like in Dos Passos's *Nineteen Nineteen*."[24] Nonetheless,
his first novel's publication did encourage him to think of himself as "Edward
Abbey—writer" (106).

More than a year before reading the galleys of *Jonathan Troy*, Abbey
had been provoked by his deadly Washington desk job to fantasize, in October 1952, about the Southwest, in the form of what became a better novel: *The
Brave Cowboy*. "(Don Quixote de Newcomb): The anachronism rides again,
this time in the modern West. A young man, perhaps, who has read too many
old books, seen too many movies; self-hallucinated, he rides the range alone
(no Sancho) among the billboards, across the highways, under the telephone
wires, seeking adventure, finding ridicule, indifference, a death without dignity" (102). Whereas his plan for *Jonathan Troy* had been amorphous, including
much material that never made it into that novel, here in his journal Abbey
outlined his entire second novel in these two succinct sentences, projecting
a focused story onto his beloved New Mexico landscape. By the end of 1954,
he had 125 pages drafted, which he felt was "tight taut compact stuff." He believed that it was better than *Troy* yet "not so much fun in the writing. . . . Why
not?" (122).

Abbey had more fun writing *Jonathan Troy* than *The Brave Cowboy* (1956) because he was happiest, and eventually most successful, in writing
about himself; as Wendell Berry has insisted, Abbey was an "autobiographer."[25]
The Brave Cowboy was a better novel and did include autobiographical details and values. But it was not essentially autobiographical like *Jonathan Troy*,
his subsequent novels *Black Sun* and *The Fool's Progress* (significantly, his two
favorites), and his later essays.

As with his third novel, *Fire on the Mountain* (1962), his inspiration
for *The Brave Cowboy* was somebody other than Abbey himself: Ralph Newcomb, who had ridden his horse from Wyoming through Utah and Arizona, like
a nineteenth-century cowboy, before moving to the postwar Albuquerque of
multiplying billboards, cars, and highways. To make sure he got his hero's story
right, Abbey handed red pencils and the manuscript of his novel to Newcomb,
asking him to make corrections and additions wherever he liked. Newcomb
complied: "When he kills the deer I had to practically rewrite that in red pencil

because he never killed or butchered a deer before. When he turns the horses loose, I suggested that he add the Mormon hobbles used at the time. I was his technical advisor."[26] Abbey remarked about Newcomb, "For two years he and his wife camped at the edge of the city limits and he rode his horse to class. I pumped him for everything he knew. I borrowed his appearance, his manner of talking, his knowledge of horses and deer-hunting."[27]

The hero of *The Brave Cowboy*, Jack Burns, was modeled primarily on Newcomb, but a few of his features also resembled those of Abbey himself. His nose was "thin, red, aquiline and asymmetrical, like the broken beak of a falcon. . . . His hands were big and long fingered like those of a flutist."[28] Most telling of all, Jack Burns had partaken of "too many westerns. Too much Zane Grey."[29] Abbey did draw from his own experiences, as well, in order to understand Burns, who gets himself locked in jail to try to rescue his friend, the draft resistor Paul Bondi, and then escapes and climbs the Sandia Mountains in defiance of the government. In 1954, Abbey "went to jail for three days: reckless driving. A grim, tedious and illuminating experience. . . . Field research, I called it then" (122). With his friend Jim Gilbert and "Homer the hound," he hiked ten or twelve miles "clear across the mesa one day from the edge of the city to the heart of the mountains," much like Jack Burns on the run. "Four hours under a fiery sun" (122). Paul Bondi combined some of the characteristics and values of Malcolm Brown as well as Abbey himself, and the character of his wife, Jerry Bondi, was based on both Rachel Brown (as homemaker with a son named Seth) and Rita (as a painter with "huge canvases splashed recklessly with color").[30]

Dodd-Mead gave Abbey another $500 advance for *The Brave Cowboy*, but one could not live long on $500, even in 1954, and Abbey was not finished with his academic ambitions or his articulation of his anarchist philosophy. Therefore, he decided to resume graduate studies in philosophy, in the fall of 1954, at UNM. In the meantime, Rita had completed her master's degree at UNM in the spring of that year and returned to Provincetown to study again with Hans Hofmann. Abbey joined her there in July. He sat on the beach watching the people ("these women with their narrow shoulders and huge bulky rumps"), thinking about *The Brave Cowboy*: "How can he hope to persuade Bondi to give up his martyrdom in prison for the ridiculous life of the outlaw?" (120). He also wrote the Browns a playful letter in which he mentioned that a swimmer was waving his arms, perhaps drowning, while Abbey enjoyed the sun.[31]

Abbey was awarded a fellowship in philosophy for the 1954–55 academic year and then a graduate assistantship for 1955–56.[32] He earned mostly As in his graduate courses in political theory, existentialism, Oriental philosophy, the early and nineteenth-century English novel, and American literature. He also registered for thesis credits from his very first semester, in the fall of 1954, but the many complications in his life kept him from completing his thesis until 1959; his master's degree was not awarded until 1960.[33] First, he had to narrow his overly ambitious topic, as he later explained: "I wanted to write a book that I was going to call the 'General Theory of Anarchism.' Fortunately, the thesis committee was not interested in that kind of tome, or I'd still be working on that first treatise."[34] His thesis became instead the more focused "Anarchism and the Morality of Violence." Even though the anarchist Abbey had moved a long way from his Marxist father, the very fact that he continued to ask the big questions and think the big thoughts about such key political issues, earning a degree in philosophy rather than literature, reflected that Paul Abbey's influence was still with him. The UNM program was very accommodating, allowing him to pursue some courses in literature and take several years to complete his degree.

As department chair, Hubert Alexander was listed on Abbey's transcript as thesis director, but he largely turned Abbey over to Cuban political philosopher Miguel Jorrín, and the committee also included Archie Bahm.[35] In *The Fool's Progress*, Abbey subsequently presented negative and comic autobiographical portraits of himself and his thesis committee. When Henry Lightcap's committee meets with him about his thesis, it becomes apparent to his readers that he has not written one (except for footnotes containing girls' phone numbers). Finally, department chair B. Morton Ashcraft demands to know if Henry really wants to be a professor of philosophy, to which Henry has to admit, "Not really."[36] Abbey did in fact eventually complete his thesis, and he felt fairly positive about his mentors: "Bahm is a good fellow," he noted in March 1955. "I've come to like him very much."[37] In the thesis itself, Abbey would "in particular . . . thank Professor Alexander, without whose patience and generous assistance this paper might never have been completed."[38] Later he dated his master's degree as 1956 on his vita—reflecting not only his typically casual approach to autobiographical chronology but perhaps also some embarrassment about how long it actually took him to complete his thesis. In contrast to his later fictional portrayal in *The Fool's Progress*, his mentors were in fact clearly very supportive and patient with the oddball Abbey, and, unlike Henry Lightcap, he was successful academically (even if slow in his degree progress).

Abbey noted in March 1955 that he and Rita had been staying in the Browns' "little mud studio" but had now moved into town, gaining gas heat, running water, and "eleektrissitie." He despised himself for enjoying it, though he did not have to work for it: "Rita does that" (124–25). In the "little mud studio," they had been much attached to the Browns, including their young son

Seth, who never forgot his boyhood days with the Abbeys. Ed and Rita would position a red bandanna on a pole either up or down according to whether or not they wanted visitors. The Browns and the Abbeys resumed this familial type of relationship in the late 1950s while living in the Taos area, where Seth Brown "used to stand near the window and wait for Ed to come driving up, and I'd run out, jump up, and grab him around the neck."[39]

Ed and Rita's arguments apparently increased, without the Browns next to them as a buffer, when they moved into an apartment at 1310 Grand Avenue N.E., Albuquerque, in early 1955.[40] The nature of their relationship became clear not only to close friends but even to Abbey's professors, as Hubert Alexander explained:

> In the middle of the night sometime Abbey got kicked out of his house because of some domestic dispute, and he got this bottle of whiskey and went over to the campus. He and his friend were in Archie Bahm's office and the campus cops came by and caught him at it. I was called in the middle of the night, as chairman of the department, and the campus police confiscated the bottle of whiskey and kicked him out of the office, and he had to go find someplace else. I was called into the dean's office the next day and asked what I should do with Abbey. I said I didn't think anything should happen—he got kicked out of his house and he had no place to go. The bottle of whiskey ended up in the vice-president's office.[41]

A still stranger (and anti-ecological) story from the same period— which Abbey liked to tell later, as he similarly liked to claim that he had rolled "an old tire into the Grand Canyon"[42]—involves his setting afire some old tires in a crater west of Albuquerque and creating quite a stir among people who thought it was a volcano erupting.[43] The most teasing postscript to this incident is that future Earth First! founder Dave Foreman remembered seeing the "volcanoes on the west mesa" as a young boy in Albuquerque in 1955, some twenty-six years before he met Abbey. When Foreman happened to tell John De Puy in 1994 about this memory, including how he had then heard that some college students had started the fire, De Puy informed him that the college student had been Abbey.[44]

More of Abbey's time in early 1955, however, was spent in the classroom and the library. As a result, by April 20 he found himself "drugged, sense and mind, by desert thoughts, canyon thoughts." He had become obsessed with the Colorado Plateau, the region surrounding the Green and Colorado and San Juan Rivers. He wanted to take a raft trip from Hite's Ferry to Rainbow Natural Bridge, exploring Glen Canyon. Thinking about those great canyons, and of the "terrible and grand and unearthly wilderness of rock that surrounds them," Abbey concluded, "Christ! I've got to go there, be there, live there; it's become an obsession with me, a passion! Those places, those names" (125–26). By April 1956 he would be working at Arches National Monument, and by June 1959 he would be taking that "journey through Glen Canyon," with the brave cowboy, Ralph Newcomb.

In 1955, Abbey had to settle for Apache National Forest in the dazzling high country southwest of Albuquerque, where he was appointed "engineering aide" from June 11 until February 16, 1956. He could manage this seasonal half-year because he had finished his master's course work, with only his thesis still to write. Salary was only half the annual rate of $2,750, but the job included free housing for himself and Rita near Reserve, New Mexico.[45] Abbey relished this as a summer of creativity, both personally and professionally. He returned to Havasu Canyon, the site of his summer 1949 sojourn, "for a second honeymoon. By the verge of Havasu Falls under the light of a desert moon, quite deliberately, we conceived our first child," Joshua, born on April 12, 1956.[46] And he finished, not his thesis, but *The Brave Cowboy*, "in the summer of 1955," as he clarified in a preface to the 1971 Ballantine edition of the novel (written at Organ Pipe Cactus National Monument in March 1970, the month before the first Earth Day). "I actually thought that me and old Ammon Hennacy of Salt Lake were the only preaching and practicing anarchists alive in the whole U.S.A. And the wilderness cult had barely begun."[47]

In February 1956, the Abbeys returned to Albuquerque, moving into an apartment on Lead Avenue S.E.[48] in time for Ed to take up a second-semester graduate assistantship and guest-teach some classes in Hubert Alexander's undergraduate humanities course. In 1970 he would notoriously (and jokingly) criticize Gary Snyder for his supposed "Hindu-Zen bullshit,"[49] but it is noteworthy that, early in the career of this reputed Anglo-chauvinist, Abbey lectured on Hindu philosophy in Alexander's class on February 29, 1956. His detailed notes included the historical background of the caste system, polytheism and the *Vedas*, "the identification of *atman* (soul) with *Brahman* (world-soul)," *Karma*, and "the four great *Yogas*." On March 7 his handout was on "East and West," including Buddhism, Hinduism, Confucianism, and Taoism.[50]

The year 1956 was an important one for Abbey: his first son was born, he spent his first summer at Arches, and *The Brave Cowboy* was published. But it was also a difficult year. He began his job at Arches just as Josh was born, and Rita went home to New Jersey "partly because of the baby," Abbey noted, closer to better medical care and to Rita's mother (129). Rita had been teaching art at Albuquerque's Highland High School but fulfilled the expectations of the 1950s by resigning her position in order to give birth to her son.[51]

Rita was unhappy with Abbey's migratory lifestyle, especially when it coincided with childbirth, pushing all the wrong buttons. "His limit seemed to be about six months," Rita complained later. "Sometimes his job was over, sometimes he was restless. He was a runner."[52] At the same time that they were starting a family, Abbey was beginning to settle into a long series of seasonal ranger jobs in the national forests and parks (extending through the 1970s). He liked the wilderness, the solitude, the chance to get some writing done—and he did not want to be tied down to one place. In the early 1970s, when he encouraged his friend Doug Peacock (the model for Hayduke in *The Monkey Wrench Gang*) to become a ranger, Abbey stressed to him that it was always great to "have quitting day to look forward to."[53]

Abbey began his first stint at Arches not simply immersed in nature, in blissful and uninterrupted solitude as *Desert Solitaire* (1968) later stressed, but also frenetically trying to juggle work and family, which were clearly in conflict with each other. On March 30, 1956, he was appointed seasonal ranger through September 22 at half the annual rate of $3,415. On March 31, Superintendent Bates Wilson assigned him to Arches[54]—close enough to the April Fool's Day starting date that he enjoyed claiming at the beginning of *Desert Solitaire*.[55] In fact, once again truth was stranger than fiction, with Abbey missing a comic opportunity in his book by failing to note that he did in fact sign a federal loyalty oath on April Fool's Day in order to begin his new job. On April 12, however, he was briefly back in Albuquerque for Josh's birth, recording his weight as 8 pounds, 12 ounces, and writing, "May he be blessed by sky and earth, Heaven and Home; may he be brave and lucky and good" (127).

Interspersed in Abbey's Arches journal were many worries about his marriage. On May 20 he wrote that his difficulties with Rita were "breaking me in two. Christ, I don't think I've ever suffered more than I suffer now." But he suffered as much from solitude as from marital difficulties, feeling like a randy animal: "Look at me, a young brown god, virile as a panther, lusty as a goat, bepricked like a veteran stud, and no women within twenty miles. . . . What a crying shame, what a parlous crying shame!" (130). He added on June 15 that Rita was "really puttin' the pressure on me," with letters arriving even from her "head-shrinker," admonishing him to be a "good dutiful obedient husband, or forever foreswear your wife—and son. . . . Do I want her or don't I? . . . God knows I'm lonesome here, I miss her . . . with an almost desperate pain, poignancy. And yet, there are other times . . . I can rejoice in myself and my powers and my world and feel no need of Rita nor of any one particular woman" (132).

Abbey's Arches residence was a trailer along the old entrance road to Balanced Rock that used to run from the main road north of Moab near the turnoff for Dead Horse Point. This location was much more remote than it is now: in the absence of today's paved roads through Arches, Abbey's drive to Moab was a largely unpaved, circuitous, twenty-five-mile journey. But Abbey did not mind too much, for this was the most fabulously beautiful, unspoiled place he had ever lived. He found himself surrounded everywhere by the red and golden arches, spires, and canyons of this otherworldly, almost Martian terrain. If he had to be alone for a while, he could have chosen no more marvelous retreat.

Chief Ranger Lloyd Pierson, who arrived at Arches later that summer, explained that, with Abbey's large cranium, "We couldn't find an official NPS Smoky hat to fit him and for a while he wore a black cowboy hat. But Bates didn't like the look of it and finally he made Ed start wearing a pith helmet with an NPS emblem. Abbey didn't think much of that pith helmet."[56] Pierson explained that "our uniform consisted of a Park Service hat and a gray shirt with the Park Service insignia on that and the badge, and usually we wore blue jeans because we did a lot of the work ourselves." Abbey reappeared for his second Arches season in April 1957 with a beard, but after Bates Wilson grumbled about it, even though there were no formal rules against it, Abbey shaved it off.[57]

Abbey later described his duties at Arches, while working Fridays through Tuesdays, as "interpretation and protection: greeted and oriented visitors; patrolled roads and trails; maintained campgrounds and picnic areas; guided small groups through trail-less areas; provided first aid and other forms of assistance to visitors in difficulty; helped with some repair and construction work; handled entrance station funds."[58] And in 1962 he memorialized "Balanced Rock at Arches, snow-covered mountains beyond and me squatting on sandstone in the clean clear chill air, coffeecup in hand, sun blazing down on snow already beginning to melt from juniper . . . brief bliss. . . . That must have been my last year of youth and confidence—ever since, nothing but struggle and terror, the horror in the heart."[59] Yet he also had some fun in his role as ranger, as he noted in July 1956, calling himself a "comedian." A tourist said to him, "That's a lousy road you got in here"—to which he replied, "If I had my way, there wouldn't be any road atall in here." When they asked him if he had a television, he growled, "If I saw a TV set in here, I'd shoot it like I would a mad dog." He was serious, but they stood there "just a-laughing at me. . . . Tourist says, 'Does it ever rain out here?' and I say, 'I don't know, I've only been here twenty-eight years'" (133).

Abbey was also writing the "Desert Journal" that became the source book for *Desert Solitaire:* He found the desert not sterile but "very much alive—exultant. . . . Great big yellow mule's ears blooming by the road; the cliffrose, gay and fragrant as a pretty girl, blossoming everywhere" (127). Here we see Abbey devoting himself in his writing to the description of nature in a newly focused way, with the sense that here was something special that needed to be recorded. Until now, he had always tried to write a novel; though he did not know it, here began his career as a nature writer. He had often described nature in his novels and earlier journal entries, but now he sought more to see it on its own terms.

Abbey never talked about his books to his fellow rangers, even though *The Brave Cowboy* was published during his first season at Arches. He would only remark enigmatically, "The world needs poets, too."[60] Lloyd Pierson recalled, "If we had known the power of his pen, we would have had him writing our usually dry governmental reports rather than picking up the garbage. Wouldn't that have set the regional office on its collective ear?"[61] Something (probably the FBI) must have attracted the regional office's attention, because not long after Abbey's two seasons at Arches, Pierson explained, "we got a memorandum from the regional office that said, 'If you intend to hire Edward Abbey as a seasonal ranger, please check with the regional office first.' These were the days when old McCarthy was burning the big light. Ed showed up, we showed him the memorandum, and he went into Santa Fe and got it squared away, because he worked for several other Park Service areas after that."[62]

Abbey recalled twenty-five years later that *The Brave Cowboy* "got a review in the Sunday *Times Book Review*; most novels did in those days, in the middle 1950s. Otherwise, it was pretty much ignored by the national press, although there were a few reviews in local and western newspapers."[63] Lewis Nordyke declared in the *New York Times* on September 9, 1956, "The idea of a romantic cowboy riding an almost locoed mare named Whisky in the speed, the noise and the civilization of the atomic age is a fascinating one and it is cleverly and engagingly handled."[64] The title *The Brave Cowboy* deliberately conjured up the tradition of the outlaw cowboy hero since at least the time of Owen Wister's *The Virginian* (1902), Zane Grey's *Riders of the Purple Sage* (1912), and, more recently for Abbey, Jack Schaefer's *Shane* (1954), with a clear formula at work: "an outsider enters a community, defends the townspeople/settlers/farmers against the Indians/wilderness/ranchers, and after restoring order, departs."[65] *The Brave Cowboy*, however, is contemporary and anarchistic: rather than restore order, Jack Burns, confronted by the billboards, highways, and lawmen of New Mexico in the 1950s, flees with his horse up into the Sandia Mountains but is eventually flushed out onto the highway, where he is mortally wounded by a truck hauling toilets. Abbey later noted that "the first edition of *The Brave Cowboy* was too closed, but I corrected that in the later editions."[66] Beginning with the November 1971 Ballantine paperback edition, he deleted the following from the novel's ending in previous editions:

"The choking had stopped. 'Sure,' the woman said, 'all right for him. He's dead now.'"[67] Burns was thus free to ride again—mysteriously in *The Monkey Wrench Gang* and more explicitly in *Good News* and *Hayduke Lives!* And *The Brave Cowboy* attracted much more attention when Kirk Douglas made it into the movie *Lonely Are the Brave* (1962).

Shortly before the end of his first term at Arches, in September 1956, Abbey got a letter from Rita telling him that they were finished. She warned him that he would find nothing back home with her except "a glimpse of what could have been." Rita's "terrible words" nonetheless made him determined to return to her "at once." He journeyed to Hoboken, New Jersey, the first of his several sojourns there, in what he described on December 6 as "an uncertain reconciliation with my family—Rita and Josh" (137). The main achievement of an otherwise unproductive winter in Hoboken was to convince Rita to return with him to Arches for his second season, which ran from April to September 1957. "Back in Abbey's country again. I walk in beauty" (139). He was elated that, this time, Rita and Josh would share it with him.

Abbey's second season was a happier one for him, and it resulted in several of the central ideas and experiences in *Desert Solitaire*, as for example when he wrote in his journal on April 8, "DICTUM: NO AUTOMOBILES IN NATIONAL PARKS. . . . God Bless America. Let's Save Some of It!" (141). He could see the changes coming, yet in 1957 Arches remained a true wilderness. Today, at the peak of the season in July, it is packed with cars and tourists, but in early July 1957, when fifteen-year-old David Sharp visited Arches with his family, they found themselves the only tourists there.[68] On August 11 and 12, Ed and his brother John (a ranger at Natural Bridges that summer) participated in the manhunt that would become "The Dead Man at Grandview Point" a decade later in his celebrated book. This incident is yet another good illustration of Abbey's techniques of "creative nonfiction." For example, he describes being called "via the shortwave radio to join a manhunt" at Grandview Point, in what later became Canyonlands National Park. In fact, Arches rangers had no radio communication within the park at the time—and the manhunt actually took place at Upheaval Dome, several miles from Grandview Point.[69] Summons by radio to Grandview must have seemed more dramatic, and Abbey never hesitated to fictionalize his ostensibly nonfictional essays. An even stronger example is "The Moon-Eyed Horse" chapter of *Desert Solitaire*, because Abbey's mysterious canyon encounter with this wild horse very likely never happened at all. As he teasingly said years later to his friend Bob Greenspan, "Did that really happen or did I make that up?"[70]

In 1957 Rita and Josh lived with Abbey in the same trailer near Balanced Rock that he had occupied alone during the previous summer. Rachel

Brown remembered visiting them that summer, with Rita trying to do her painting in and around "that hot trailer." Rita was short on supplies.[71] Ralph Newcomb also visited: "I brought some drums up there and she wanted a drum, but I didn't have one to give her."[72] As for Abbey, he wandered off on his own into town and elsewhere. Rita protested that "he would disappear for days," with only Bates Wilson checking in on Rita and Josh. "Ed was pretty defiant," Rita remembered. "I was pretty much of a rebel myself at the time."[73]

Abbey did not include Rita or Josh in *Desert Solitaire*, nor did Rita mention Abbey in her own related book, *Rivertrip* (1977).[74] His only two brief references to Rita were both vague and dismissive, when he mentioned the fact that as he and Ralph Newcomb floated through Glen Canyon, "our wives and loved ones" were "back in Albuquerque,"[75] and his reply to a tourist who asks if he was married: "Not seriously."[76] By the time that Ed and Rita published these books, they were divorced and their bitterness was too great. Abbey clearly decided, for aesthetic as well as personal reasons, to keep his book strictly "solitaire." Like Thoreau with his two years at Walden Pond, he telescoped his 1956 and 1957 Arches seasons (as well as other adventures from 1950, 1959, and 1965) into one single *Season in the Wilderness*, in the words of his book's subtitle. Later, he also deleted Bates Wilson from the introduction to his book, after highly praising him in early editions as a devotee of the land and "founder of Canyonlands National Park."[77] By the 1988 revised edition of the book, Wilson was dead, and Abbey had long ruminated on the fact that Wilson and his staff "had actually done the planning for the roads and developments he so hated and objected to. He eliminated the introduction which was so kindly towards the 'working rangers in the field' and substituted a preface in which he further decried the 'industrial tourism.'"[78]

Wilson campaigned for Canyonlands; he also oversaw the paving of Arches, which Abbey attacked so caustically in his chapter "Polemic: Industrial Tourism and the National Parks." "I remember him kidding us" in 1957, Pierson reminisced, "when we heard about the plans for the roads. He'd say, 'Well, I don't know why you don't pave the whole thing and call it Arches National Moneymint.'"[79] Abbey later wrote in "My Life as a P.I.G." that, in Arches, "I enforced the law (natural law) by pulling up survey stakes from a new road the Park Service was attempting to build into my park. That didn't do much good; I moved on."[80] However, it also appears that his jobs in 1953 at Carson National Forest and in 1955 at Apache National Forest had involved work on road crews. In *The Fool's Progress*, Abbey describes Henry Lightcap's stint on a road crew in New Mexico, immersed in asphalt, his "face and hands and neck blackened as a coal miner."[81] As much as he enjoyed driving, Abbey never liked roads, and he hated road building.

At the end of all editions of *Desert Solitaire*, Abbey is driven by ranger Bob Ferris to nearby Thompson, Utah, to catch the train to Denver. "Contrived," Pierson wrote, "because that ranger" (whose real name was Bob Morris) "wasn't at Arches at the time. I was. Besides, Ed had a car, a wife and a child to move, but it did make a good ending for a good book."[82] This ending was a version of Abbey's solo departure from Arches in September 1956. In September 1957, Ed, Rita, and Josh left Arches for El Granada, California, where they lived on Seaview Road near Half Moon Bay until the spring of 1958, while Abbey studied creative writing under Wallace Stegner at Stanford.[83]

Abbey was thus laterally mobile in his erstwhile academic career: his UNM master's thesis was still not finished, but he welcomed the opportunity to work on his writing with the assistance of a Stanford fellowship. In his 1986 "San Francisco Journal," he described his sojourn in the area three decades earlier:

> I was a member of Wallace Stegner's creative writing workshop at Stanford. Two days a week I cranked up my 1952 Chevrolet pickup —rust-red with rotted floorboards; you could see the asphalt rushing below between your feet—and commuted over the pine and eucalyptus hills to Palo Alto. I was at work on a sensational new kind of American novel that winter. The subject was sub-bohemian life and the desperate search by young Americans for spiritual enlightenment, emotional fulfillment, sexual liberation, escape from the chores of the work-place and the routines of domestic bondage. My characters spent a great part of their days and nights smoking giant joints, drinking red wine by the jugful (Gallo Is Hearty Burgundy), and racing back and forth across the continent from Green Witch Village, New York, to North Beach, California, in borrowed, stolen, unpaid-for, and boat-shaped automobiles. My title for the book was *Down the Road*. I never finished it, for reasons now historical which I have successfully blotted from my mind.[84]

Still a long way from writing *Desert Solitaire*, Abbey had begun a novel that he really called "Black Sun," just as Jack Kerouac's *On the Road* hit the bookstores and (he felt) scooped him. Except for two separate chapters in periodicals,[85] this "Black Sun" was never published, even though Abbey continued to struggle with it into the early 1960s. His 1971 novel of that title was a completely different, unrelated book, which became his own favorite, probably because (like the unpublished one) it was about his own life. The unpublished "Black Sun" depicted the picaresque New Mexico adventures of characters suspiciously resembling Abbey himself and some of his old UNM friends, such as Ralph Newcomb and the artist Al Sarvis.

Encouraging to Abbey's budding career as a writer, during his Stanford stint, were the publication of his story "Underground in Amerigo" and the paperback edition and payment for film rights for *The Brave Cowboy*. Appearing in the winter 1957 issue of the University of Illinois quarterly magazine *Accent*, "Underground in Amerigo" described UNM escapades close to his 1951 story in the infamous issue of *The Thunderbird*. It is perhaps most noteworthy because it concludes with the description of an Abbeyesque grave beneath a juniper tree: "ERNEST THOMISON FLACK, 1931–1949. Born of the earth, I give back to the earth these ashy bones, this troubled flesh; but my triumphant spirit you shall never find." [86] After *The Brave Cowboy* appeared in paperback in late 1957, Abbey received a check for $7,500, in early 1958, from Janus Films for the film rights. He still had no agent, and this amount seemed like a big windfall, which he described on January 29 as "unbelievable" (145). Three years later when the film was made, however, and he saw how much money went into its production, Abbey felt cheated.

He claimed that, in Stegner's class, a Ford Foundation representative had asked for suggestions on "what to do with their millions." Abbey said, "Why (the fuck) don't they give it all back to the people they stole it from in the first place?" (197). Stegner noted that Abbey helped evaluate new applications for the following year's Stegner Fellowships. "Among the manuscripts that he got to read was one by Ken Kesey, then still at Oregon. The manuscript was a football novel all about homosexual quarterbacks and corrupt coaches. Ed's comment . . . was one sentence: 'Football has found its James Jones.'" [87] Wendell Berry was also a Stegner Fellow the year after Abbey. Abbey continued to regard Stegner as a key elder among Western writers, and Berry became Abbey's long-distance friend and a crucial fellow writer about the land.

By way of the New York City and San Francisco Bay areas as well as Taos (an artistic center a bit like San Francisco), Abbey was now in the midst of his Beat period. The first issue of *Playboy*, with its famous nude calendar shot of Marilyn Monroe, had appeared in December 1954, with its early issues promoting male rejection of marriage and job in favor of selfish pleasure. [88] Kerouac and other Beats followed much the same code, celebrating anarchist aesthetics, reckless lives, and male bonding. John De Puy emphasized that "we were the tail end of the Beat Generation. . . . It was a formative period for all of us. It was a time of explosive energy. Kesey and Kerouac and Neal Cassady and Creeley and San Francisco and Taos and traveling on the road, hitchhiking, riding the rails. We thought we had the world by its balls at the time. . . . I think what Ed enjoyed most was that it was a manly period."[89] Similarly, Rita Abbey lamented, "Even though he had so many women, it always occurred to me that his relationships with men were more important to him. He liked to drink with them, be in the desert with them."[90]

As with Kerouac and Gary Snyder, the urban Beat experience would be tempered for Abbey by thoroughly rural stints in fire lookout towers. Stegner regretted that Abbey resigned his Stanford fellowship after two quarters—trying in vain to get paid for the third quarter—because "he yearned to be back in the sagebrush and not hanging around in classrooms."[91] He also found that $2,500 did not go far in the Bay Area: "Another fellowship like this and I'll claim bankruptcy." Rita was substitute-teaching, and he was "swindling the state of Utah," collecting unemployment compensation (145). In his "San Francisco Journal," he recalled trying to write in their leaky apartment during the rainy season, while Rita painted "on huge canvases hard to get through the front door" and Josh "toddled about among the hydrangeas in the backyard digging live snails out of their shells with his little finger and eating them."[92]

By the beginning of May 1958, Abbey was back in New Mexico, working as a Fire Control Aid through July at the Beaverhead Ranger Station in the remote, towering Gila National Forest southwest of Albuquerque; Rita and Josh retreated to Hoboken. From November 1958 until April 1959, in his first extended stay in southern Arizona, Abbey worked as a seasonal park ranger at Casa Grande National Monument, the impressive and medieval Native American site south of Phoenix, where he noted that he "greeted visitors, collected fees," and "led guided tours through archeological ruins."[93] It was during this period that he first began to imagine what would become *Desert Solitaire* as he began outlining "Canyon Country," a "book of essays and pictures on SE Utah."[94]

The Abbeys next returned to Albuquerque, from April until September 1959, with Rita settling into their apartment on Mission Avenue N.E. for the birth of their second son, Aaron, on May 28. Abbey recorded a joyful journal entry on that date, but, between jobs once again, he (and no doubt Rita) found their life grim at other times. He described "nasty grueling quarrels with Rita" on April 22, emphasizing that their economic situation was worse than ever, creating "continual insecurity," regular moves, and "all the nagging chores and perplexities that entails." He noted that, in the previous few years, they had lived in at least a dozen different places, including "Albuquerque, Moab, Hoboken, Moab, Half Moon Bay, Beavershed (Hoboken for Rita), . . . Casa Grande, now Albuquerq again." Admitting that it was "no wonder we're always snarling at each other," Abbey recorded that, as he wrote in his journal, he could hear, through the kitchen door, the tired complaints of his wife and son. "Somehow we've got to break out of this awful trap, this treadmill. Or else give up. Divorce" (147). Nonetheless, Ed and Rita would struggle on until 1965, holding on that long only because of their sons and their intermittent determination to try to stay together.

As in the case of Josh's birth and Ed's first season at Arches, Abbey once again retreated to the wilderness shortly after Aaron's arrival. Like his original trip west in 1944 and his first season at Arches in 1956, Abbey's two-week raft journey through Glen Canyon on the Colorado River in June 1959, in the company of Ralph Newcomb, was one of the most formative experiences of his life. He fell in love with the Southwest in 1944, became champion and defender of the redrock country at Arches in 1956, and now he explored the beauties of Glen Canyon for the first (and last) time, not long before its destruction by Glen Canyon Dam and Lake Powell. He would spend the rest of his life raging against this "damn" and "Lake Foul." Abbey had many flaws, but he knew how to pick his wilderness places—or maybe just got lucky sometimes. He had gone to an unspoiled Arches for his first seasonal ranger job, and now he chose for his first significant river trip what some people (ranging from the nineteenth-century pioneer John Wesley Powell to the contemporary river-runner Ken Sleight) felt was the most beautiful stretch of river in the West. So named by Major Powell because of how peaceful and quiet it was after his men's torrential voyage through Cataract Canyon in 1869, Glen Canyon before the dam offered an endless paradise of blue skies, redrock cliffs, golden and mysterious side and slot canyons, waterfalls, and other natural wonders.

Abbey provided vivid accounts of this trip—undertaken in two cheap rubber rafts bought in a drugstore and then tied together—in his journal (148–55) and in the "Down the River" chapter of *Desert Solitaire*. His descriptions were made especially poignant by his painful awareness that he was seeing everything he described for both the first and last time. It would all be flooded beginning in 1963, with preparations already visible in 1959, particularly at the enforced conclusion of Abbey and Newcomb's journey. They encountered a "white rectangular object. A sign! A billboard! Curious, I paddle closer and am able to read it: 'All boats must leave river and Kane Creek Landing one mile ahead on right. Absolutely no boats allowed in construction zone.'—U.S. Bureau of Reclamation. . . . Our voyage was over" (155).

Soon after passing the mouth of the San Juan River, Abbey accidentally started a brush fire when he burned some litter that someone else had left behind (153). Two years later, in 1961, Eliot Porter came across the remains of Abbey's little fire as he rafted down the river taking his memorable photographs for *The Place No One Knew*—a soulful commemoration of Glen Canyon introduced by David Brower, who visited the Glen repeatedly during the period just before its demise. Abbey had wanted to raft the Glen ever since first glimpsing it in 1953, and he mourned its annihilation as early as May 16, 1956, in Arches: "Glen Canyon will soon be lost. The dam-building maniacs. The hogs and pigs win again. Glen Canyon, beautiful beyond any telling of it, to be drowned forever" (130).

The second half of 1959 was a difficult, defining time for Abbey: after rafting the Glen, he finally defended his UNM anarchist thesis on August 5 and then, beginning in September, he edited the progressive Taos newspaper *El Crepusculo de la Libertad* through January 1960. Wilderness, politics, anarchism, philosophy, socialism, Spanish language and culture—Abbey was involved in all of it during this period. His eighty-page thesis sought to answer the question of how anarchists justify violence. He focused on Godwin, Proudhon, Bakunin, Kropotkin, Sorel, and (among incidents of anarchist violence) the 1887 Haymarket bombing in Chicago and the assassinations of Russian czars and German emperors, the president of France, and U.S. president William McKinley. Abbey explained that, though Tolstoy and Gandhi showed that anarchists can be pacifists, mostly anarchism has been linked to revolutionary violence, and he concluded that anarchists had failed to satisfactorily justify violence.

Here we find in the 1950s the basis of Abbey's later distinction, in the 1970s and 1980s, between terrorism (violence against people, which he consistently rejected) and sabotage (disabling violence against destructive machines, which he viewed as sometimes justifiable). Yet his thesis is dated and pre-"environmentalist," even though it incorporates lengthy passages from anarchist "how-to" manuals that are comparable to Dave Foreman's *Ecodefense: A Field Guide to Monkeywrenching* (1985).[95] But it does not yet entertain the possibility of justifiable violence against machines, nor link violence to environmental issues, even though Abbey himself had burned billboards throughout the 1950s.[96] There is no mention of environmental issues in his thesis.

After successfully defending his thesis, the anarchist Abbey was then hired by a Marxist. Craig Vincent had come to Taos in the late 1940s from Colorado, where he had served in the state legislature and run the Rocky Mountain Council for Social Action as well as Henry Wallace's presidential campaign in the state. In 1949 he and his wife, Jenny, opened the San Cristobal Valley Ranch, "a resort that catered to a multiracial, left-wing clientele from all over the United States."[97] After the Vincents sold the ranch in 1954, Craig became increasingly active in progressive Taos politics, and in July 1959, he leased *El Crepusculo de la Libertad* (a newspaper that had been founded in 1835 by Padre Martinez) for one year with an option to buy. On November 15, Abbey recounted that, two months earlier, Vincent had called him up and asked if he was interested in editing it. Reluctant, Abbey knew "instinctively" that this position would be a "big pain in the ass. I tried to talk him out of hiring me." But then he drove up to Taos, met acting editor Phil Reno, and decided to give it a try, on a two-week trial basis, at a salary of $100 per week. "So here we are." He added that Rita, he, and their two sons had moved into a "big beautiful adobe house close to the office," in the very heart of downtown Taos, while he worked "my half-ass off trying to put out a decent paper every week. It can't last long" (157).[98] But while it did, Taos offered the spectacular scenery surrounding it as well as its own teeming hub of alternative and artistic lifestyles and liberal and radical politics.

It was during this time that Abbey befriended the landscape painter John De Puy, who would become his closest friend for the rest of his life. His later essay about their friendship recounted their first meeting: "My friend Debris was staggering down Palace Avenue," in Santa Fe, "supported on the arms of an artistic woman named Rini Templeton, whom I had met a short time previously in the editorial offices of . . . *El Crepusculo*. . . . I was supposed to be the paper's editor-in-chief. . . . Debris and I have shared many adventures and some misadventures, helping each other through the anxieties of fatherhood, the joys of marriage, the despair of separation and divorce, the deep purple funk of creative inertia. And survived. And thrived. We have both been very lucky. But we deserved it."[99] In De Puy, Abbey had discovered a truly kindred soul. Each was a tall, lanky, goateed artist from the East who had fallen in love with the Southwest. Even their sonorous voices sounded much alike. Each married a series of younger women and moved house many times. Eventually Abbey would tell De Puy that he felt closer to him than to any of his own brothers.[100] De Puy's striking, bright Southwestern paintings in the tradition of Georgia O'Keeffe led Abbey to call him "the best landscape painter now at work in these United States,"[101] and he summarized his feelings in a poem:

> TO JOHN DE PUY
> Madman and seer,
> painter of the apocalyptic volcano of the world—
> *Compañero*, I am with you forever
> in the glorious fraternity of the damned.[102]

In the short term, however, Abbey was right that his editing job would not "last long": his first issue as editor of the paper appeared on October 29, 1959, and his last was January 21, 1960. He found the job so time-consuming that he could not pursue his own, independent writing; his only other publications from the fall of 1959 were two book reviews in the *New Mexico Quarterly*, of Samuel Beckett's novel *Watt* (celebrating its "grotesque suffering and comic misery"[103]) and Douglas Woolf's Arizona novel *Fade Out*.[104] *El Crepusculo* and Abbey's contributions to it are both quite fascinating. Vincent had turned this newspaper into a progressive, bilingual voice. It featured both English and Spanish on the front page, with Spanish editor Felix Valdes, and ongoing advocacy of Indian rights and a rural electricity cooperative (whose proposed sale to a private company Vincent successfully opposed).

The same Ed Abbey who would be so bitterly attacked, in the early 1980s, for his stance against Mexican immigration was, in 1959, editing this bilingual newspaper and clearly sensitive to the Spanish ambiguity of its very name, recognizing that *El Crepusculo de la Libertad* meant "The Dawn (or Twilight?) of Liberty" (157). Noting that for years Abbey wore a cap with the saying "Viva La Causa," De Puy insisted that he was sympathetic to Chicano activists in Taos and throughout northern New Mexico, many of whom still resented nineteenth-century Anglo land seizures, and who (with Reies López Tijerina in the lead) would stage a celebrated civil rights occupation of the courthouse in Tierra Amarilla, seat of Rio Arriba County, in 1966.

However, Abbey was never satisfied to subsume his own ideas to those of others. His own characteristic flourishes appeared in *El Crepusculo*. His very first issue included the editorial "In Defense of Cottonwoods": "The U.S. Reclamation Bureau is planning a campaign to kill off the cottonwood trees in hopes of providing a little more ground water for commercial farming and livestock-raising. . . . Shade and beauty are commodities difficult to sell, trade, or measure in statistics. Therefore the cottonwood, like the coyote and the mountain lion, has got to go."[105] On November 12, "The Smell of Fraud" attacked television advertising. This editorial was accompanied by Abbey's six-frame cartoon showing a beer-drinking man watching a Western on TV—and then pulling out a revolver, blowing up the TV, and leaving.[106] It preceded and foreshadowed by three decades Terry Moore's celebrated 1980s photograph of Abbey having just blown up his TV. On December 3, 1959, he lampooned the paper's rival *Taos News* in a cartoon depicting their office as an outhouse just two miles outside Santa Fe. And De Puy humorously recollected that "some fool in Las Vegas, New Mexico, the Melody Sign Company, put up about twelve immense forty-foot signs, so everybody on the paper went out in the middle of the night and sawed them down. And the next week, the owner of the company came to put an ad in the paper for the apprehension of these criminals, and Ed being the editor took the ad and burst out laughing, so Mr. Melody asked him what was so funny. He said, 'Nothing, I'm thinking of something else.'"[107]

Hints of mounting tension between the sarcastic, anarchist Abbey and the serious, socialist Vincent were evident even in the pages of the newspaper itself. In his sardonic December 24 "Christmas Greetings," Abbey promised to "abstain this year from writing a long and eloquent editorial on *The Real Meaning of Christmas* or *The Tree Beneath the Tinsel* or *What Made Christmas a Package Deal?*"[108] As if to correct him, the following week Vincent signed a December 31 counter-editorial insisting that "the true spirit of Christmas prevailed—in and out of the Churches—in spite of our community controversies."[109] The January 7, 1960, lead editorial was similarly signed by Vincent.[110]

But in a final flourish, Abbey regained the lead in his last two issues —January 14 and 21—promoting his own unmistakable voice on wilderness issues. "For Future Beauty" expressed the hope that Interior Secretary Fred A. Seaton's "Mission 66" directive (which actually paved and built visitors centers in Arches and other national parks) would protect wilderness.[111] It was accompanied by a striking, prophetic, four-frame cartoon with the words "YOU CAN'T STOP PROGRESS," with a sketch of a couple walking up a path through the woods, followed by one car driving up a single lane, then six cars on two lanes with just one tree left, and finally many cars packing four lanes with no trees. "God Bless America—Let's Save Some of It" (in which Abbey credited that much-quoted line as originating with "conservationist Weldon Heald") delivered spirited advocacy of "the Wilderness Preservation Bill about to be re-introduced into this session of Congress," as "one of the most worthy and significant pieces of legislation since the creation of the National Park system in 1916."[112]

Abbey and Vincent parted company on the newspaper shortly after that—though by 1965 Abbey jokingly described their earlier conflicts as "idiot-logical,"[113] and he took the Vincents on a summer 1967 boat trip at Lee's Ferry that Jenny Vincent still cherished, over thirty years later, as "delightful."[114] Abbey declared on February 11, 1960: "No more newspaper racket for me. Finished. Couldn't get along with the boss. Vincent was too hard on my nerves, me on his. Thank Gawd it's over" (158). Reflecting on the tension between the younger anarchist and the older Marxist, one has to wonder how much Abbey felt compelled to enact Oedipal rebellion against an authority figure who may have also seemed on some level to be a father figure, especially given that Abbey had already staked out his anarchism against the Marxism of his own actual father, Paul Abbey.

El Crepusculo did not do well financially, and within a few months Vincent had relinquished his option to Santa Fe publisher Robert McKenney. The whole project was hopelessly inefficient. Vincent had appointed an oversized cast of at least sixteen people (counting only those assembled in the staff photograph) to publish "a small weekly newspaper of only 8–14 pages," as the poet Judson Crews, one of the printers of the paper during its Vincent-Abbey run, pointed out. As for Abbey, in true anarchist fashion, "he let the staff do what they pleased," as Crews recollected, "and he did pretty damn much what he pleased. He didn't last very long."[115] This, Abbey's third stint as a periodical editor, was his final one.

Although Abbey hated this job, Rita liked the artist colony of Taos. She wanted to "make a home here," Abbey had noted on November 15. Yet he detested "this arty hate-filled town. . . . I dream of and long for the desert. But we need a home" (157). With the loss of his job, their marriage took yet another turn for the worse. Within a few months Abbey would be living in Albuquerque and Rita and the boys back in Hoboken, having been evicted from their latest Taos house. Abbey's career during the 1950s may have been desultory enough, but his most difficult years were just now beginning.

CHAPTER FOUR

Singing the Hoboken Blues
1960–1965

At first glance, the early 1960s looked like promising years for Abbey: his second novel was made into a successful movie, *Lonely Are the Brave*, which was released in the same year as his excellent third novel, *Fire on the Mountain* (1962). Beneath the surface, however, times were hard, both professionally and personally. He finished drafts of two other novels, the New Mexico "Black Sun" and the Hoboken "City of Dreadful Night," but neither was ever published — and Abbey made only modest amounts of money from *Lonely Are the Brave* and *Fire on the Mountain*. Meanwhile, he bounced back and forth between the Four Corners and New York City areas, trying to maintain his marriage to Rita while working at various public welfare, technical writing, bartending, ranger, and fire lookout jobs. During these years he increased his determination to live permanently in the Southwest, but he spent sizable chunks of time in New Jersey. Events in U.S. environmental history occurred during these years that would be important for Abbey and everyone else interested in the natural world, but he seemed quite removed from them. He was struggling obscurely in Hoboken when Rachel Carson's pivotal book *Silent Spring* appeared in 1962, when the gates of Glen Canyon Dam were closed in 1963, and when the Wilderness Act was passed in 1964.

This period was indeed punctuated for Abbey by alternating moments of good and bad luck. Soon after the end of his editing job at *El Crepusculo*, he received a check for $2,300 on February 22, 1960, as part of "the movie deal" for what became *Lonely Are the Brave*.[1] He had time to rewrite 180 pages of "Black Sun"—but also tore a ligament in early March while skiing near Taos. By early April he had to check into the Veteran's Hospital in Albuquerque for knee surgery. He left on a pre-surgery weekend pass to accompany on flute the guitar-playing Ralph Newcomb at a Beatnik club (159) and was then visited by Rita after surgery (168). This surgery cost Abbey a seasonal job at the Grand Canyon (163), and by early May Rita and the boys had flown back to Hoboken, having received an eviction notice from their Taos landlady (170).

As Abbey lamented in his journal on May 8, "As usual, no home, no job, no income, no book." McGraw-Hill had rejected his New Mexico "Black Sun" manuscript "without a word of explanation" (170). He sardonically called this rejection the "biggest publishing blunder since Simon & Schuster rejected the New Testament" (174). He had to console himself with the summer 1960 appearance of a chapter from this novel, "Amador," in *Between Worlds*, a journal edited at the Inter American University in Puerto Rico by an old UNM friend, Gilbert Neiman. Like Abbey's editing of the bilingual *El Crepusculo*, the publication in Puerto Rico of "Amador"—in which Abbey's Anglo protagonists take young Amador Martinez into a New Mexico canyon in search of the Virgin Mary, but she fails to appear—complicates and calls into question the later reputation of Abbey as anti-Latino. Such a Latino friendship was not merely the stuff of early fiction but also part of Abbey's own earlier years in New Mexico. Alberto Martinez had been among his friends at UNM.[2] At the end of his life, in his lengthy list (in *Hayduke Lives!*) of thanks to real-life friends and family, Abbey included "Amador Martinez."[3]

By the summer of 1960, Abbey was outlining "The Good Life," a novel about his Appalachian boyhood. As with his other unpublished novels during this period, it took more than a quarter-century for this material to be crystallized and published in the form of *The Fool's Progress*. In 1960 Abbey was still just thirty-three years old; many more years were required to gain enough distance on his various autobiographical adventures to be able to shape them into a meaningful form. At this time he continued to have better luck writing about the experiences of other people, as in *The Brave Cowboy* and *Fire on the Mountain*.

By September, Abbey and his family were back in Taos. On September 10 he wrote, "Here we go again. The happy family on the move again. Same tedious old story. Low on money, job-hunting." His manuscripts were "floating around New York collecting rejections." He decided to leave Rita and their sons in Taos while he went to look for work in Albuquerque, El Paso, Phoenix, and Salt Lake City. "Still no home. Still no security. A severe trial for love." On October 25 he added, "Still haven't found a job. Down to our last $40. Living in a big house in town now" (170), while by November 30 he was "working now, as a bartender at the Taos Inn. A wretched job, of course, but I endure" (171).

On January 30, 1961, Abbey began a stint as a ranger at Petrified Forest National Monument in northeastern Arizona. Usually his spirits lifted when he went to work as a ranger, but this was perhaps his least favorite assignment during his long career in national parks and forests. On February 21 he declared that it was a "detestable chickenshit sort of place" and noted that he had already applied to thirty-eight other sites (173). He hated being tied to the entrance station, as he later recalled in *Desert Images*: "My obligation was to spend eight hours a day in a little cabin at the entrance to the park and sell admission tickets to the tourists coming in off the highway. That was half of it; I also stopped and checked out each car leaving the Park. Looking the driver in the eye, I would say, 'Sir, do you have any petrified wood in your car?' The driver would look me back straight in the eye, sincere and honest as only an American can be, and reply, 'No sir, we don't.' One of the kids in the back seat would say, 'But Daddy, what about that big log we put in the trunk?'"[4] He was also miserable because Rita and the boys were once again back in Hoboken. After not hearing from Rita for ten days, he wondered if divorce proceedings were about to commence. "Give the old man another chance, Rita. I'm right for you, you know, though you don't know it yet. Our destiny—to suffer together for another forty or fifty years" (173).

On the other hand, at Petrified Forest Abbey began the novel that would be his next success: *Fire on the Mountain*, the tale of John Vogelin, a New Mexico rancher who refuses to sell his land to the government for its new White Sands missile range. Like *The Brave Cowboy*, this novel effectively combines dramatic action with strong characterizations and lyrical descriptions of the New Mexico landscape. On the one hand, it is quintessential Abbey, a taut, defiant tale just one step away thematically from *The Monkey Wrench Gang* (but without the later novel's sense of humor). On the other hand, *Fire on the Mountain* depended on popular historiography for its material and on film scriptwriting for its tight, dramatic style. Abbey's major source was C. L. Sonnichsen's 1960 book *Tularosa: Last of the Frontier West*, which included the true-life story of John Prather, who had announced at the age of eighty-four in 1957, when he was ordered off his land, "I'm going to die at home."[5] Abbey altered the ending of this story. In fact, Prather won an eviction exemption and was allowed to stay on his ranch, living on to 1965—whereas, in more dramatic fashion, Abbey's fictional Vogelin is forced off his land but then goes back there and dies.

Abbey himself provided the most succinct, telling summary of the composition and intent of *Fire on the Mountain* (originally called "Vogelin's Mountain") in a 1970 interview: "That book was written with one hand, one dusty desert March while I was working as a cop-ranger at Petrified Forest. The book was always meant quite calmly and frankly for Hollywood and someday they'll make a movie of it."[6] He was right: in November 1981, NBC aired a television movie version starring Buddy Ebsen and Ron Howard. Nevertheless, clearly motivated by the filming of *Lonely Are the Brave* in 1961, Abbey probably did not expect the movie of *Fire on the Mountain* to take two decades to appear.

The influence of scriptwriting on Abbey's novels was very direct. He read novelist and screenwriter Dalton Trumbo's script for *Lonely Are the Brave* on March 2, 1961, at the same time that he was trying to make headway on *Fire on the Mountain*. He felt that it was very good, with livelier dialogue than in his own novel, and more authentic jail and truck scenes. Trumbo's script enjoyed a "swift pace, no drag," but his own new novel proceeded slowly at first, with only seven pages, "as it was on the end of the day on which I began" (174). Yet he then finished *Fire on the Mountain* much more quickly than he had his previous novels, with a new sense of writing according to a commercially appealing design, following quite closely his detailed, ten-chapter, February 1961 outline. He wrote it with "swift pace, no drag," taking to heart the lessons learned from Trumbo's script.[7]

Abbey was beginning to develop a stronger sense of how to market his work—and of the need for an agent. Abbey had no agent when he published *The Brave Cowboy*, but it was an agent, Herb Jaffe, who sent the published novel to Edward Lewis, Kirk Douglas's producer. Lewis suggested to Douglas that he "read it as a possible starring vehicle."[8] Douglas was completely taken with the book and determined to bring it to the big screen. Universal did not want to make this movie, but a "disapproved picture" clause in Douglas's contract allowed him to make it for under three million dollars.[9] Abbey earned very little money from the movie; as his friend and fellow novelist William Eastlake later remarked, "Ed was broke when they paid a Hollywood scriptwriter a fortune and shot the film outside of Albuquerque and generously gave Ed a job as an extra."[10] Later in 1961, Eastlake gave Abbey an introduction to his own agent, Don Congdon, and Congdon took on Abbey and sold *Fire on the Moun-*

tain to Dial Press.[11] Congdon remained Abbey's agent for most of the rest of his career.

On May 4, 1961, during the production of *Lonely Are the Brave* (initially called "The Last Hero"), Kirk Douglas described Abbey to Gary Cooper, writing to "Coop" in Beverly Hills from the Western Skies Hotel in Albuquerque. Douglas noted that Abbey was "a ranger working in the Petrified Forest. They tell me before I meet him that he's written about himself. So now he comes to Albuquerque where we're shooting and I go to meet him at the airport. Fifty guys step off the plane but I spot him immediately—why? He looks like Gary Cooper."[12] Abbey had managed to convince Douglas and his producers to shoot the movie in Albuquerque and the Sandia Mountains. Its house scenes were filmed at the home of Vera and Arch Napier of the *Albuquerque Tribune*, which was much nicer than any in which Abbey and his friends had lived during the 1950s.[13] Yet Abbey could not prevail on the film's producers to change its new title, which he did not like (174), but under which the film was released. *Lonely Are the Brave* remained Douglas's favorite movie from his more than eighty roles, as he continued to assert decades later, because he was impressed by how Jack Burns proved that "you have to conform or the forces of society come down on you like a truckload of toilets."[14] He even published a letter to the editor in the *Los Angeles Times* in 1989 complaining that its Abbey obituary had failed to mention this movie.[15]

Abbey was very glad to have his Petrified Forest job end on May 12, much preferring a new appointment that began on June 3 as a fire lookout on the North Rim in Grand Canyon National Park. His knee surgery the year before had prevented him from taking this job at that time and had helped provoke his shifting from earlier stints as a patrolling ranger (as at Arches and Casa Grande) to jobs involving a lot more sitting (as at Petrified Forest, the North Rim, and his many subsequent lookout appointments). His later essay "Fire Lookout" provides only a fictionalized account of how his North Rim appointment began, but it also contains a precise, accurate description of its setting:

> The lookout tower on North Rim was sixty feet tall, surmounted by a little tin box six feet by six by seven. One entered through a trapdoor in the bottom. Inside was the fire finder—an azimuth and sighting device fixed to a cabinet bolted to the floor. There was a high swivel chair with glass insulators, like those on a telephone line, mounted on the lower tips of the chair's four legs. In case of lightning. It was known as the electric chair. . . . My home after working hours was an old cabin near the foot of the tower. The cabin was equipped with a double bed and a couple of folding steel cots, a wood-burning stove,

table, shelves, cupboard, two chairs. It made a pleasant home, there under the pines and aspen, deep in the forest, serenaded by distant coyote cries, by poor wills, and sometimes by the song of the hermit thrush, loveliest of bird calls in the American West.[16]

By June 30, however, Abbey had turned his North Rim station over to his father, who was there on one of the earliest of what soon became almost annual treks west to visit his son, occasionally to substitute for him at fire lookouts, and regularly to collect rocks for display back home at his new rock shop. At the age of sixty, Paul Abbey hiked the Grand Canyon from rim to rim with his son in 1961—a feat he would repeat in 1971, when he was seventy, and once more in 1981, at the age of eighty. Robert Creeley and Louise (Bobbie) Hawkins both remembered meeting Paul in the summer of 1961, when he visited Ed in Albuquerque, hiking at the crest of the Sandia Mountains, looking so vigorous and so like his son that at first they thought he might be an older brother.[17]

Abbey cut short his first season at the North Rim (where he later returned for three more seasons during 1969–71) in order to work on *Lonely Are the Brave*. His stint on the movie set did not last long, but he had fun, as he recalled in 1970: "I worked for them as Official Consultant, $100 a day and all expenses, best job I ever had in my life. The job lasted two days. . . . I also did a one-line bit part as a deputy sheriff which was cut out later. That completes my career as a movie actor."[18] John De Puy remembered showing up with Abbey to appear as extras in "the last scene when the Cowboy is dying on the road and there are a bunch of deputies hanging around."[19] Their appearance was indeed cut, but it was enough to get Abbey into the newspaper back home, where the *Indiana Gazette* reported that "a Home, Indiana County, man has followed the footsteps of the illustrious Jimmy Stewart onto Hollywood's sets, but he maintains he is making his 'first and last picture.'"[20] Within a few years, Abbey likewise followed Stewart as an inductee into the Cowboy Hall of Fame in Oklahoma City.[21]

Such ephemeral fame did not pay Abbey's bills, however. It is an ironic fact that, just as his name was lifted into the bright lights of Hollywood and theaters across the country, while *Lonely Are the Brave* was being filmed in 1961 and released in 1962, Abbey was in the midst of one of the darkest, poorest periods of his life. He received no more credit than money for the film, which was a modest popular and strong critical success; for example, *Time* praised it in July 1962, calling Trumbo's script "refreshingly tart and literate" while not even mentioning Abbey.[22] Abbey saw the film for the first time in June 1962, finding it an "embarrassing" experience, even though he felt that it was an "honest and lucid" film that was faithful to his book (175). On July 8 he noted that

The New Yorker had called it a "shoddy and simple-minded song of hatred for twentieth-century American society." The characteristically surprising Abbey reacted, "Exactly! Exactly what I meant the book to be. I am quite pleased by the reviewer's observation" (176).

In the fall of 1962, Abbey did receive positive credit for the book *Fire on the Mountain* in such places as the *Chicago Sunday Tribune* and the *New York Herald Tribune*. Martin Levin wrote in the *New York Times Book Review* that "if Mr. Abbey oversimplifies the twentieth century a bit by making White Sands a locus of pure evil, he states his case with a lyricism that is highly persuasive. . . . [The] striking finale [is] made all the more poignant because it is seen through the unclouded eyes of Vogelin's young [grandson]—a boy to whom the end of the ranch is a devastating tragedy."[23] Levin appreciated how Abbey had personalized New Mexico and linked it back to his own home territory by having young Billy Vogelin come from Pennsylvania to visit his grandfather.

Meanwhile, Abbey's marriage and working career were under great duress. He spent more time apart from his wife and family than with them during 1961 and early 1962, as Rita and the boys shuttled between Taos and Hoboken. During the second half of 1961, Abbey introduced yet another page to his disparate job profile, working as a caseworker for the Welfare Department in Albuquerque. In the summer of 1961, he commuted back and forth between his new job in Albuquerque and his family in Taos, spending only weekends or every other weekend with them.[24] In the fall he lived at 1012 Buena Vista in Albuquerque[25] while Rita, Josh, and Aaron once again returned to Hoboken; Abbey was separated from them until early 1962. He hated his job as a caseworker, "bleakly checking claims—an awful job," as Robert Creeley called it.[26]

Like a true Beat, as critiqued by Barbara Ehrenreich, Abbey found male bonding much easier than making a marriage work. As Abbey recollected two decades later, "One day in the summer of 1961 two ambitious young writers —Robert Creeley and myself—made a pilgrimage by Volkswagen bus from Taos, New Mexico, to Cuba, New Mexico, west of Santa Fe, to visit William Eastlake. We'd both read and admired Eastlake's first novel, *Go in Beauty*, and we wanted to meet the author."[27] According to Tucson journalist Tom Miller, who knew both Eastlake and Abbey, "they spoke little of literature and lots about the land. Eastlake saddled up his horses, Póca Mas, Pocos Menos, and Elegante, and the three rode through the high Chihuahuan Desert until they reached Eastlake's herd grazing illegally in a national forest."[28] Drinking was always a big part of such gatherings. Creeley never forgot Abbey's regular, fierce home brew that "could knock you flat for circa $5 for a lot of bottles thereof."[29]

Abbey recalled their return visit to Eastlake that fall:

One cold gloomy afternoon in November we rode out to attempt again to find his cows. We separated for tactical reasons, planning to meet at the home pasture. Snow began to fall, quickly becoming a blizzard. I could hardly see twenty feet before me and soon realized I was lost. I gave the horse free rein, letting him find the way home. The horse began to run—panicky behavior. . . . We were both lost. . . . Around midnight the wind died, the snow stopped, and I heard, not far, the sound of a gunshot, then another. It was Eastlake, hunting for me. He'd been out for hours. The horse and I, as it turned out, were only a mile from the ranchhouse.[30]

Creeley explained that "Ed charmingly spooked Bill by telling him that the simplest means of survival in such a crisis was to kill your horse, slit open his belly, and climb inside. Since Bill much loved the horse in question, Póca Mas, Ed really got to him."[31] Abbey and Eastlake remained friends, both later resettling in southern Arizona. Abbey eventually taught at the University of Arizona in the 1980s (by which time he was better known than Eastlake) after Eastlake had done so in the 1970s.

As troubled as his marriage seemed at the beginning of 1962, Abbey was determined to make a grand attempt to repair it, even returning east against all of his strongest geographical instincts. By the end of January, he was living at 528 Hudson Street in Hoboken,[32] hoping to make amends with Rita. Teaching and technical writing were two ill-fated jobs that he tried out in the New York City area.[33] He tried to teach writing at the New School for a semester—his first attempt at teaching since his guest stint in Hubert Alexander's class in the spring of 1956—but student attendance plummeted after the first meeting.[34]

Two decades later, Abbey provided a memorable if not entirely factual account of his equally brief career as a technical writer, conjuring it back up all the way from Alaska while in the middle of a river trip. It is worth citing in some detail, as it remains the only description of this obscure episode and is very revealing about his irreverent attitudes toward work and marriage. "I was employed briefly as a technical writer for the Western Electric Company in New York City," he explains. It was under contract with the Department of Defense "to prepare training manuals for the workers building the arctic radar stations and air bases of the Distant Early Warning System." Sitting among many others "at desks in one huge office ten floors above Barclay Street in lower Manhattan," Abbey sweated under fluorescent lights. "All technical writers were required to wear white shirts. With tie." Assigned to edit a manual entitled *How to Dispose of Human Sewage in Permafrost*, he suggested that he go to the Arctic so he could "conduct firsthand field studies," but his boss insisted that he stick to "spelling, grammar, and punctuation, not shit research. I returned to my desk among the other stuffed, bent white shirts—we all faced in the same direction—and stared moodily out the window for two weeks, watching the sun go down over Hoboken, New Jersey." Then, however, his boss appeared at his desk and asked, "Abbey, do you really want to work for Western Electric?" "'No sir,' I said, 'not really.' 'I thought not,' he said. 'We're letting you go as of 1700 hours today.' I could have kissed him—and knowing New York, I probably should have. 'That's all right, sir,' I said. 'I'm leaving right now, as of 1330 hours.'" He then "spent the afternoon at the White Horse Tavern on Hudson Street, then with cronies at Minsky's Burlesque in Newark. Reported to my wife, drunk and happy, at 2200 hours with what was left of my first and final Western Electric paycheck."[35]

On June 23, 1962, Abbey wrote in his journal that he had reconciled with Rita and that the future seemed a "bright gray. So much for that. Love? We need each other. One more try." He added that Rita's father was slowly dying and that her mother was an "irritable, guilty, irrational wreck. Our apartment is crawling with cockroaches, the windowsills are coated with black New York soot, everything is layered in grime." Rita herself was "sunk in dread and emptiness." He also recorded a telling dream: "Rita and I, driving a fat new car, come to a flooded stream crossing, I wade in to ascertain the depth of the water, find it over my head. I sink deeper and deeper, entangled in underwater vines, and know at once that all is lost. And do not care. Down, down, no bottom" (175).

Fourteen years later in the *New York Times Magazine*, Abbey's recollection was more fanciful:

> We were desperately in love but hopelessly incompatible . . . she aloof in her loft, me dejected in my superintendent's luxury basement apartment in Hoboken (Corsage of the Garden State), N.J. It was like Tristan and Isolde. . . . Swooning with passion, we were indifferent to the squalor of our surroundings. It was I who watered the wine and humidified the potato chips for her frequent and always successful gallery openings. But our basic conflicts could not be surmounted. We tried therapy and created only another banal triangle: I was in love with her, she fell in love with the therapist, the therapist was in love with himself.[36]

Rita had returned home to help look after her ailing father and because a doctor had told her that she had a lung infection linked to the western desert; she also felt that her marriage was over.[37] In Abbey's unpublished novel about this period, "City of Dreadful Night," Myra, the wife of the protagonist, wants to leave him because they are incompatible, he has been unfaithful, she has had a hysterectomy, and she has fallen in love with her psychiatrist.[38]

Abbey continued to love other women and have affairs, and Rita continued to keep her own separate art studio after his move to Hoboken, in addition to their small, unsavory apartment. He had fumed about her separateness in his journal as early as March 1961, off by himself in the Painted Desert. He feared that, back in Hoboken, Rita was "emotionally at ease," as she had assured him she was without him. He complained that he had sent her "mad, despairing love letters twice a week, working for her, while she has the kids, her studio," and her own life (174).

In July 1962, Abbey began work as a welfare caseworker for the Hudson County Welfare Board, continuing until March 15, 1963.[39] He was trying to persuade Rita "to return west, where he knew he belonged; meanwhile, he toiled as a welfare case worker . . . the only time in his life he's 'labored' more than five or six months a year."[40] Abbey had "quit a horrible job" (probably as technical writer) to take the welfare position, but his new job was not much fun either. Bobbie Hawkins remembered that, when she and Creeley visited Abbey in Hoboken, "he looked miserable, energy down; he hated the city, wearing a semi-ratty brown tweedish jacket, out of his element."[41] Similarly, Abbey's agent, Don Congdon, recounted that "he'd be so depressed that he'd come over and want to talk. I would give him a stiff drink of Scotch and a Cuban cigar. It took about one glass of Scotch for him to loosen up, and then he would soften up after the second drink."[42]

In "City of Dreadful Night," Abbey included a vivid version of his doomed career as a welfare worker, in a chapter entitled "A Day at the Madhouse." This chapter eventually reappeared virtually verbatim in the paperback edition of The Fool's Progress [43] —posthumously reinserted there according to his instructions after being left out of the original, hardback edition. In the welfare "madhouse," Abbey's autobiographical protagonist is bombarded by imploring phone calls from clients of various ethnic backgrounds. He tries to help each but is overwhelmed, buried in paperwork, and stymied by bureaucracy and the sheer weight of human misery. He talks to his supervisor: "Look, Mrs. Kelly, not only that but this other one, Mrs. Moore, yes, Mrs. Cynthia Moore, she says her husband stole her check and ran away and she has to go to the hospital this afternoon and there's no one to look after the kids and what's more the wheel fell off her wheelchair, I mean his wheelchair, yes, Mr. Rogelio's wheelchair, and they stole his check too, he said, and one of the children is having an epileptic fit, yes, a seizure, and the cop says he'll kill her." Mrs. Kelly tells him to "get a grip on yourself," he replies that "I've got to get out of here," but she warns him that "you're not going anywhere till you make out last week's work report and next week's field visit schedule and you're not going anywhere till you dictate your reports on the visits you made or should have made last week." [44]

Abbey's co-worker Katherine Bounds noted that "in the early 1960s, the welfare benefit laws were very restrictive. There were tight eligibility laws and residence rules. Ed was very much a free thinker and a very liberal eligibility worker. He didn't appear to be happy in that job." [45] Another colleague who regularly rode home with Abbey from the welfare office in Jersey City to their apartments in Hoboken, a seaport city packed with bars, found him always quiet, even taciturn, beneath his goatee and tweed jacket. The jacket was a concession to the relative formality of his workplace, but with his goatee and a face deeply tanned from his time in the West, Abbey stood out.

Abbey published little during this grim period, though he did make some great plans; the several books that he outlined in January 1963 included "*Solitaire in the Desert* (a journal)" and "*The Wooden Shoe Gang* (or) *The Monkey Wrench Mob*," a novel about a "Wilderness Avenger" and his gang, offering "sabotage and laughter and wild wild fun" (185). He wrote this note five years before *Desert Solitaire* appeared and twelve years before *The Monkey Wrench Gang* was published. Abbey had to be patient. "City of Dreadful Night" is a title that pretty well sums up the mood of his unpublished novel from this Hoboken period. This novel's male characters sit around Hoboken talking endlessly about getting back out west, to Dandy Crossing, Utah.

They were speaking for Abbey, who wrote ironically in his journal on October 20, 1962, about himself and Rita, that the "something seriously wrong" with him that Rita complained about was that he preferred to be living "in the bright open Southwest" instead of the "smoky iron swamps of New York. (You're sick, man.)" He wanted to do "man's work," with his hands and body, outdoors, not sit in an "overheated office all day, necktie-strangulated," with a "horde of middle-aged females, pushing papers and pressing dictaphone buttons. (Yes, man, you are in bad shape.)" He concluded that, not only did he want to live in the Southwest, and "work in the air and sunlight," but he also wanted to have his wife and children with him. "(Wow! my Gawd, you'd better see a doctor quick!)" He insisted that this was not, as it might be for other men, an "empty fantasy. . . . For me and my family, such a place, such a job, such a way of life were all within the realm of concrete actuality, all within easy reach." He was especially frustrated because he knew they could have done it, but they did not. "The boys and I had to give it all up. And why? Yes, why? (And she wonders at my bitterness)" (179). He wanted to integrate life with family and life in nature, like Wendell Berry did later, but he found himself unable to do so.

Yet Abbey, who had retreated to Hoboken from Arches as early as

1956, also developed some fond memories of the big city. In 1969 in *Natural History*, an unusual venue for the topic, he would publish "City of the Prophecies—A Hoboken Perspective," which became "Manhattan Twilight, Hoboken Night" in *The Journey Home*. It concludes with a dedication "to that city we love, that visionary city of the prophecies, humane and generous, that city of liberty and beauty and joy which will come to be, someday, on American earth, on the shore of the sea."[46] And his celebrated 1970s essay "Freedom and Wilderness, Wilderness and Freedom" would begin even more surprisingly:

> When I lived in Hoboken, just across the lacquered Hudson from Manhattan, we had all the wilderness we needed. There was the waterfront with its decaying piers and abandoned warehouses, the jungle of bars along River Street and Hudson Street, the houseboats, the old ferry slips, the mildew-green cathedral of the Erie-Lackawanna Railway terminal. . . . I loved the fens, those tawny marshes full of waterbirds, mosquitoes, muskrats, and opossums that intervened among the black basaltic rocks between Jersey City and Newark. . . . It will all be made, someday, a national park of the mind, a rigid celebration of industrialism's finest frenzy.[47]

Any full understanding of Abbey as a Western wilderness writer has to be complicated by his attachment also to his Eastern places—especially Hoboken and even more his native, Appalachian, western Pennsylvania.

In the spring of 1963, however, Abbey felt that he had to escape Hoboken and get back to the West. A lot was happening in environmental history and in the West that would be crucial to Abbey's later career, but from which he had been cut off while pushing welfare papers in New Jersey. Rachel Carson's *Silent Spring* was published in 1962. The gates of Glen Canyon Dam were closed in January 1963, at which point Lake Powell began to fill; because of this, the river-runner Ken Sleight moved to Escalante, Utah, that year, determined to rediscover an unspoiled wilderness and mount opposition to Glen Canyon Dam. Howard Zahniser and the Wilderness Society were campaigning for a major new wilderness act, which Congress would pass in 1964.

From April 15 until September 15, 1963, Abbey worked as a ranger at Sunset Crater National Monument, the colorful volcanic cinder cone and summit, nearly a thousand years old, near Flagstaff, Arizona. William Eastlake was proud that he and Abbey did their bit near there as wilderness activists: "I went on one expedition with Ed outside Flagstaff while Ed was working at Sunset Crater, and we carved down a huge Las Vegas girlie sign that was hiding the West. I can't say this is true, because that is illegal, but someone did it while we were in that area."[48]

In his journal on May 29, Abbey fully exposed his tortured inner world as well as the beautiful outer world around him, noting that back in the West at his ranger post, he found himself "lost and bewildered again" as before, lonely, but finding the air and light "exhilarating" and the desert landscape "marvelous." He anticipated that Rita and the boys would be there soon "if I can rely on Rita's latest letter." She had put him "through the wringer" again, keeping him "guessing for two months and ain't through yet, neither, I guess, since she plans to visit her eunuch-saint in Taos" en route. "More anguish, heartache and uncertainty" seemed to lie in store. He was convinced that "drama" was what Rita liked. Abbey confessed that he was "bitter," even though he knew that this "weary game" was partly his own fault, as he had not been a "good husband when she needed me." He felt that now she was getting her revenge, "grinding it in," and that he could only "endure it and hope for eventual good luck" (186).

Ed and Rita saw little of each other during the rest of the year. Instead, Abbey had an affair with a ranger who was working at the South Rim of the Grand Canyon. He alluded to this when writing of being on the South Rim with Rita and their sons, in June 1963, "minutes after a fateful secret farewell," with his heart "black with despair" and "almost ready to vault the rail and leap into the chasm, so bleak and empty seemed my life" (191). Only two decades later could he joke about it, in his essay "Forty Years as a Canyoneer": "In 1963 I fell recklessly in love with a girl who lived in Grand Canyon village. (After a summer of passion she left me for another man—her husband)."[49] This lover was one of the inspirations for *Black Sun*, the 1971 novel in which Abbey's protagonist falls in love with a woman who finally disappears in the Grand Canyon.

In the fall of 1963, with both his summer lover and his family once again gone and his latest job ended, Abbey reached a new nadir. He began a period so grim that the article in which he described it, "Hard Times in Santa Fe," was not published until after his death, in April 1989. Although the exact dates of this Santa Fe episode cannot be established, and Abbey (who was often unreliable about dates) set it in wintertime in his much later essay, the forwarding address that he left at Sunset Crater on September 25, 1963, was 511 East Palace Avenue in Santa Fe.[50] As Abbey recounted, when he happened to return to "the narrow street called Palace Avenue" and see the "high adobe walls" of the house that John De Puy's in-laws had owned, male bonding had reached new depths among the house-sitters from hell:

> He left me and another friend, a Yogi fakir from New Jersey named Frank Wohlfarth, in charge of his fifteen-room *palacio*.

A serious mistake. John knew better. But love had deranged his mind.

Frank and I cleaned out the pantry and emptied the freezer the first week. Ate everything available, the canned goods, the frozen meats, the dried pastas, the last jar of peanut butter, the final box of cornflakes, the ultimate tin of smoked baby clams. We consulted our finances and each discovered that the other was broke, penniless, bankrupt. Neither of us had a job or any intention of finding a job. I was a writer, not a bloody *employee*.[51]

He added that their gas, electricity, and water were all shut off, after which "I pawned the household furnishings piece by piece." Soon joined by a third deadbeat artist, this motley crew burned chairs and other household items in the fireplace. Given Abbey's propensity for "creative nonfiction," one cannot know how many of his lurid details are actually true, but it is clear that things were bad. He also spent some time wandering, as elsewhere he remembered visiting Las Vegas on November 22, 1963, thinking about Kennedy's assassination while aimlessly watching the flashing marquees along the Vegas strip.[52]

When a telegram came from De Puy stating that he was now divorced and his ex-relatives were coming to reclaim their house, Abbey and his housemates left quickly. Abbey and De Puy remained good friends, despite what Abbey had done to the house that De Puy had entrusted to him. De Puy confirmed that "he stole all my furniture. We had a good laugh about that afterwards. It didn't matter because Rita had just left him and Claudine had just left me, so we were both pretty depressed. One night we ended up at a bar on Canyon Road and came out at two in the morning singing Schiller's 'Ode to Joy.'"[53]

Desperate, Abbey returned one last time, at the beginning of January 1964, to Hoboken, Rita and their sons, and his job as a caseworker. As he lamented in his journal, "What a life. From Hoboken to Sunset Crater to Santa Fe to Death Valley to Santa Fe to Hoboken" (183). He added on May 26, 1964, that he had arrived in Hoboken on January 1 and returned to work at the Welfare Department, once more ostensibly reconciled with Rita (187). His life in the West had been going nowhere, and his writing seemed equally doomed. His two unpublished novels, Abbey noted later that year, had been rejected everywhere, and even his agent, Don Congdon, did not like either book (187). For the ten years beginning with the publication of *Jonathan Troy*, followed by two better novels and the Kirk Douglas movie, Abbey calculated that he had earned from his writing a total of $12,605 "minus taxes." He began an outline for the "*Monkey Wrench Band*," to include "three men and a girl,"[54] but was unable to write any of it yet.

By the end of October 1964, Abbey claimed that his relationship with Rita was "very good at present" and began making plans to move to San Diego as a compromise between his desire to return to the West and Rita's attachment to the big city (188). His own parental model for a long-lasting marriage, however, appeared none too appealing to him at Halloween, when he drove the "long long drag through the raggedy woody hills of Pennsylvania," returning home "to ye olde lonesome briar patch." He was depressed by "my poor sad rejected mother and father, their sad and lonesome lives," with his mother "terribly thin, pale, tense, constricted, a soul in a straightjacket, worn-out by overwork and over-worry," and his father "moaning over his minor physical afflictions as if he were Job reincarnate." Abbey declared, "Gawd how I dislike these domestic martyrdoms! Why don't they *do something*?" (190).

In September, a new, young, attractive caseworker, fresh out of Jersey City State College, had come to work at the Welfare Department: Judy Pepper. A child of the 1960s, a fan of Joan Baez, Judy was quite taken with Abbey, who was fifteen years older. They soon began an affair. Judy's gentle, trusting, impressionable personality was very different from that of the older, more assertive Rita. Yet their backgrounds were actually very similar: both came from Jewish families, on the New Jersey side of the Hudson River, who were more prosperous than Abbey's Appalachian family. Both Rita and Judy wanted to be rebels, yet both also wanted comfortable lives that he was not much good at providing. As he admitted toward the end of his life, "My wives got sick and tired of the constant moving around and the poverty level income. It was enough to survive on, but no surplus."[55]

Judy's old friend and co-worker at the Welfare Department, Katherine Bounds, explained that Judy "was very impressed" by Abbey, his three novels, and his defiant view of the world. He was "a father figure, someone strong, and someone probably very flattering to her. He saw in her someone who was unspoiled, and fresh, as nature is." Judy was shapely, with pale red hair and a fair complexion, an idealistic Kennedy Democrat whose "mother would smother-love her; Lord and Taylor's and Bloomingdale's were the stores of choice. Judy had been protected, but was ripe for adventure." As for Abbey, "he had a deep tan and creviced face, with a real outdoors man kind of look about him, tall and lean, and she was head over heels, just like that."[56]

On March 14, 1965, Abbey described "more terrible, bitter, lacerating" arguments with Rita because he wanted to take a river trip in May, which she felt spoiled their plans (193). He was determined to do what he wanted to do anyway. On the same day, he recorded significant career changes: his firing from the Welfare Department in February after a "nasty argument with Stapleton the witch." He had a job offer from the Welfare Department in Las Vegas but did not want to take it. "May go with the Park Service this summer" (192). He agreed to a new contract with McGraw-Hill for two books, with a $2,500 advance and another $2,500 on delivery of an acceptable manuscript. The first book would change his life, whereas the second fizzled out in the short run: "(1) *A Desert Journal*, and (2) *Lives, or, American Lives*—a study of welfare clientele and their actual way of life" (192–93).

Abbey did accept the Las Vegas job offer as a short-term ticket back to the Southwest. As in the case of his loyalty oath nine years earlier, when he had started his first term at Arches, his new job as a caseworker for the Nevada State Welfare Department began on April Fool's Day, appropriately enough.[57] Hopelessly, he tried to juggle his relationships with both Rita and Judy. "After her father died," according to Susan Zakin, "Abbey asked Rita to take the boys and meet him in Las Vegas. He lived with her for several weeks," and then left. Even while planning marriage to Judy, "he tried to keep his relationship with Rita going by telephone."[58]

On June 17, 1965, Abbey "bolted," as he confessed in his journal, heading to Moab to begin a summer season as ranger at Canyonlands National Park. What more appropriate landscape to escape to? Here he could leave behind the responsibilities of family life and city work, and instead gaze upon some of the biggest, most remote vistas in North America, with nothing but endless expanses of redrock canyons towering above the Green and Colorado Rivers. He asked Rita to go with him, but she refused. He admitted that he had left them in favor of "exile in the desert. Am I mad? . . . My only hope now is Judy—good sweet delightful Judy." He knew that Rita was now divorcing him, and he claimed that he could not "blame her one bit" (194). That same night he called Judy in Pearce, Arizona, where she was enrolled in a residential geology program run by the University of Arizona, while on leave from her Welfare Department job back in New Jersey. Judy felt completely disoriented in the strange terrain of southeastern Arizona and in this male-dominated program; she missed Abbey, and she wanted to know when she would see him and when they would get married. By the beginning of July she was back east, attending the Newport Jazz Festival in Connecticut.[59]

As with Rita, when they had traded love letters during his year in Edinburgh, Abbey once again loved being in love, carrying on a new correspondence between Canyonlands and the East with Judy. "I've become a convert to Judyism," he declared in his journal on July 24 (195). Judy visited him in Moab in early August, then returned home to her welfare job and began looking for an apartment for the two of them while awaiting Abbey and the finalization of his divorce. She was willing to return west to live with Abbey, but she feared the isolation of a season in a ranger trailer (as earlier endured by Rita). When Abbey's Canyonlands season ended in September, the very first thing he did, rather than speed to Judy, was to disappear into the Maze district of Canyonlands with a male friend, Bob Waterman, for a few days. He described this male-bonding, wilderness experience in a chapter in *Desert Solitaire*, "Terra Incognita: Into the Maze," which concluded with their entries in the visitor's book: "I write, 'For God's sake leave this country alone — Abbey.' To which Waterman added 'For Abbey's sake leave this country alone — God.'" [60]

Finally, on September 20, he boarded a plane in Denver, flying to New York City and "my sweetheart, my love, my one and only honey-pot, Judy Pepper. My God how I've missed her — it's been a long and lonesome five weeks" (195). As the plane took off, he added: "Judy, my sweet, my darling, I'm coming, coming, coming, in a great crescendo of an orgasm, at six-hundred mph" (196). His divorce was now final, and he and Judy had set a wedding date. A month before his third wedding, Abbey made the telling notation, "Divorced August 25, 1965 — Married October 16, 1965. (Idiot!)" (197).

Neither the fates nor even Abbey himself seemed to smile upon his impending third marriage. He also remained haunted for the rest of his life by leaving behind the mother of his two sons from what remained his longest marriage. His divorce from Rita was also complicated by the fact that it came just a few years before his rise to fame and relative success. Their divorce decree stipulated that a percentage of his royalties would henceforth go toward the support of Josh and Aaron, but probably neither Rita nor Ed thought that this clause would mean much, in 1965 when very little money was coming in.

In the 1970s and 1980s, however, with *Desert Solitaire, The Monkey Wrench Gang*, and numerous other Abbey books flourishing in the mass market, that divorce decree would mean a great deal and continue to be a major bone of contention. Rita remained bitter that he had abandoned his family, seldom visited his sons, and often ignored his responsibilities. "I've never been a good family man," he later admitted.[61] Abbey came to resent that their 1965 divorce decree, with no age limitation, later diverted large royalties to his sons even in their adulthood, by which time they continued to remain very close to their mother while seldom seeing him. In 1975, just as *The Monkey Wrench Gang* was about to be published, he would complain about Rita's $13,000 court judgment against him in Arizona that year (240). When he refused to pay a further judgment against him, some of his royalties were garnished. In May 1979, Abbey made note of "another embittered letter" from Rita asking for money (264).

Rita had followed Abbey to Las Vegas, but it was he who left and she who stayed. Subsequently, she became a successful art professor at the University of Nevada at Las Vegas, continued her career as an exhibiting painter and sculptor, and remarried (to a doctor). But she had to witness the rise to fame of her ex-husband, who had struggled as a writer late in their marriage, only to become a much more famous writer after the appearance of *Desert Solitaire*. The popular press would help to remind her of this fact, as in 1979 when the *Las Vegas Sun*, in a review of a play that Josh was in, identified him as son of the "noted author Edward Abbey" and "UNLV art professor" Rita Deanin Abbey.[62]

In 1965, of course, none of this could yet be imagined. Prosperity was several years in the future for Abbey. As this thirty-eight-year-old rushed from one marriage to the next—marrying young Judy, back in New Jersey, when she was about the same age that Rita had been at the time of their 1952 wedding—he wondered how he would earn a living. Once again, Abbey would make his way back to his beloved Southwest only via a very roundabout route, involving yet another eastern setting as different from the desert as one could conceive: the Everglades, where he accepted another seasonal ranger job in December 1965.

CHAPTER FIVE

Writing the Wild
1965–1970

In the mid to late 1960s, as in U.S. politics in general, environmental controversies were heating up, though higher-profile struggles such as the Vietnam War and the Civil Rights Movement tended to keep conservation issues in the shadows. Only with the first and hugely popular Earth Day of April 1970 did new talk of "environmentalism" move to the forefront of the national agenda. Meanwhile, the one book that, more than any other, defined Abbey's reputation appeared at the beginning of 1968: *Desert Solitaire*. This book would prove vital to his career—not only because it was acclaimed as his best but also because, as his first nonfiction book, it firmly established his persona as a spunky, independent outdoorsman and thinker, later called "Cactus Ed" (though this character, too, was as much invented as based on reality). However, even this very successful book would only slowly gain a wide following. It was released in a year dominated nationally by the assassinations of Martin Luther King and Robert Kennedy and by the Chicago Democratic convention riots, which overshadowed other significant 1968 events such as the passage of the National Wild and Scenic Rivers Act and the publication of Paul Ehrlich's book *The Population Bomb*, a stern warning about the problems created by the exponential growth of the human race.

Abbey's masterpiece of that same year had to wait until after Earth Day, two years later, to attract a substantial readership. It would have a big impact. As James Hepworth writes, "Is it merely coincidence that Rachel Carson published *Silent Spring* in 1962, Edward Abbey published *Desert Solitaire* in 1968, and . . . one year later Congress passed the National Environmental Policy Act?"[1] Yet it was also not the case that Abbey himself was interested only or even primarily in environmental issues, waiting impatiently for Vietnam to fade eventually from the top of the national news. Like many others, he was involved in speaking out against the war, though Abbey's activities on that subject have been obscured by a narrow pigeonholing of him as strictly a nature writer. When he appeared in Denver in April 1968 to promote *Desert Solitaire*, he offended many by focusing on the war instead. Characteristically, his consciousness was overwhelmed even more by the complexities of his personal life. In 1965 his second marriage had ended in a bitter divorce. During the second half of this decade, his third marriage would proceed from happiness to tragedy.

Although his subsequent popular image might picture Abbey as always defiantly positioned at such Southwestern wilderness sites as Arches and the Grand Canyon, he actually began this period lost in the swamps of Florida. He was stationed twelve miles southwest of Homestead as a ranger in Everglades National Park from December 6, 1965, to April 9, 1966[2]—his first visit to Florida since 1948, and apparently his last. Later he declared, "One winter in that low-rent bog was enough."[3] Nevertheless, he remembered this as one of the happiest times in his marriage to Judy Pepper (228), and he had some entertaining times while working there, as he recalled in his essay "My Life as a P.I.G." He enjoyed zooming up and down the Everglades entrance highway in the Park Service's "souped-up Plymouth Interceptor with siren concealed behind the grill," writing "a few warning tickets, out of meanness," stopping traffic to help diamondback snakes across the road, and "chasing skunks and drunks and alligators out of the rest rooms, which were left unlocked at night" at the visitor center.

> But the best part of the job was lying in wait for 'Gator Roberts, the most famous alligator poacher in the state of Florida, maybe in the whole Southeast; a legendary figure, phantom outlaw, folk hero, and a bone in the throat of Everglades park rangers. We hated him.
>
> We had an informant, a waitress who worked at the Redneck

Café near Pine Island; she had connections with the alligator underworld and would tell us from time to time (for a price) exactly where old 'Gator Roberts was planning to strike next. We'd stake out the place—some stinking, stagnant slough deep in the dismal swamp—and wait there through the night, sweating, cursing, scratching chigger bites, slapping mosquitoes, fondling our guns. He never appeared. Next morning we'd learn that sixteen skinned alligator carcasses had been found at the other end of the park, forty miles away, with a note attached: "You Smokies aint got the brains Gawd give a spoonbill duck, regards, Gator."[4]

Abbey was anxious to escape south Florida's humidity and mosquitoes and get back to the West, where, once again, environmental events that mattered to him were happening. On the negative side, from his point of view, "Mission 66," a full-scale campaign of new roads and visitor centers in the national parks (including his beloved Arches), was being rushed to completion to mark the fiftieth anniversary of the founding of the National Park Service in 1916. But the good news was that David Brower and the Sierra Club successfully countered Bureau of Reclamation head Floyd Dominy's attempt to build more dams on the Colorado River, within the Grand Canyon itself. They placed full-page ads in the *New York Times* and other newspapers that cemented public opinion against these dams and forced their cancellation, overcoming Dominy's argument in his publicly financed book *Lake Powell: Jewel of the Colorado* that such dams as Glen Canyon made it easier for visitors to come in by boat and see the marvels of nature, with the "lake" thus bringing people "a little closer to God." In contrast, the most inspired Sierra Club ad asked, "Should we also flood the Sistine Chapel so tourists can get nearer the ceiling?" When articles in such mainstream magazines as *Reader's Digest* and *Life* joined the opposition to the dams in the spring of 1966, it was obvious that the Grand Canyon dams were doomed.[5]

Abbey accepted a job as fire lookout in Lassen Volcanic National Park in California to begin in June 1966. Before going there, he and Judy traveled northeast from Florida, visiting relatives and old friends. They dropped by Appomattox Court House National Historical Park in Virginia to say hello to its superintendent, Lloyd Pierson, Abbey's former co-worker at Arches. In Washington they attended a rally against the Vietnam War, joining the small contingent from New Mexico.[6] Abbey gets typecast as a single-issue environmentalist, but it is clear that his limited activism during these years included opposition to the war, much as he would take an interest in the antinuclear cause in the late 1970s.

From June 20 to September 17, 1966, Abbey stayed atop his north-central California fire tower in Lassen Volcanic National Park.[7] This was the first time he had lived in California since early 1958, and he was glad to be there, in a fire lookout tower "8,045 feet above sea level, . . . all alone with my new and lovely and delightful wife Judy" (197). He much preferred his new mountain-top room with a view to Florida's flat swamps: here he was surrounded by the "drab-green coniferous forests" of northern California. West of him stood the "plug-dome volcano" of Lassen Peak, northwest the "shining Fuji-like form of Shasta, fourteen-thousand feet high and eighty miles away" (201). He enjoyed a visit there from his old friend Ralph Newcomb for a couple of days in the middle of the summer.[8] He was lonely in September when Judy was away for a while (206), but he got a lot of writing and thinking done. On September 5, he noted that the "big issues" in his life included his desire to arrive at an "ac-commodation of some sort" with Rita, so that he could visit his sons; his need to earn a living so he could make his support payments and not be "entirely de-pendent upon Judy (bless her sweet, generous heart!)"; and helping Judy earn her master's degree, "since her heart is set on it" (201).

Abbey liked the remote parts of California well enough that he stayed there until the spring of 1967, moving south to the Death Valley area after the end of his season at Lassen in October 1966. He was fascinated with Death Valley as "of all deathly places the most deadly—and the most beau-tiful."[9] If Arches had seemed like Mars to him, Death Valley appeared to be something like Mercury, hot and devoid of conventional life forms, and so spec-tacular. In an essay published in *Sage* magazine in the spring of 1967, he wrote of "*Telescope Peak, October 22.* To escape the heat for a while, we spend the weekend up in the Panamints. . . . Surely this is the most sterile of North Ameri-can deserts."[10] To prolong his stay in the area, he took a job on a school bus route, deriding himself in his journal on February 12 as "paralyzed." Now he was a school bus driver, "just like the old man" (210), Paul Abbey, who had done that job earlier for nearly two decades.

Like many others, Abbey had demonstrated against the Vietnam War, and similarly he took LSD for the first (and apparently last) time, on Octo-ber 19, 1966. He chose Death Valley as his acid test site, as Michel Foucault also did a few years later, after Michelangelo Antonioni called attention to the mind-bending possibilities of the area in his 1970 film *Zabriskie Point*.[11] With Judy nearby but not partaking, Abbey was initiated by an experienced friend— but his mind was not productively bent. His sole LSD experiment was an "un-comfortable and inconclusive failure: the stars quivered in a cloudy cobweb but the big spider-God failed to appear" (209). Soon thereafter he drafted an account of this experience in the form of an unpublished short story that he called "The Web of the Stars"[12] and subsequently published a nonfictional version of it a decade later. As he revised his 1976 "Death Valley Acid" article in the *Mountain Gazette* as "Death Valley Junk" in *Abbey's Road* (1979), he tried to make his acid trip a bit more exciting, but both versions concluded by noting that "for weeks following my abortive flight, I suffered from a shade of disappointment and loss. Some ancient way remembered but not found. The trail not taken. For myself at least, it now seemed clear—there was not going to be any magic shortcut into wisdom, understanding, peace. There would be no easy way."[13] He returned to his tried and true mind-altering drug, to which he would stick for the rest of his life: alcohol.

Abbey was now happy, not only in his marriage to Judy but also because he was involved in some of the best writing of his career, as he shifted from novels to essays. Later, Abbey explained that *Desert Solitaire*

> was written in 1966–67 during a year of wandering. . . . The final chapters were composed in the corner of a bar serving a legal house of prostitution at Ash Meadows, Nevada, where I waited each day with my little yellow schoolbus (I was the driver) to pick up the children from Shoshone High School for transfer to the village of Furnace Creek in Death Valley. While waiting, I scribbled. . . . We mailed the thing to New York (book rate), and in January 1968, on a dark night in a back alley in the dead of winter, *Solitaire* was released from its cage and turned loose upon an unsuspecting public. Nothing happened. . . . Later, however, *Desert Solitaire* was exhumed and resurrected in paperback, in which form it has enjoyed a modest but persistent life, burrowing along from year to year about two feet underground like a blind and seditious mole.[14]

By the mid-1960s he had begun to despair of further success as a novelist, after failing to find any publisher for "Black Sun" and "City of Dreadful Night." Abbey was a member of a generation of writers for whom the novel was the most revered genre, and even though (with the notable exception of *The Monkey Wrench Gang*) he would enjoy more success as a nonfiction writer, he always regarded essays as "light casual work."[15] In the 1980s he recounted to Clarke Cartwright Abbey that, under the weight of his rejected novels in the 1960s, he had been at a loss for what to write about, and his agent, Don Congdon, told him, "Just write about your camping trips." Abbey replied, "That's easy. Can I really do that? Will that make a book?" For him that kind of writing flowed easily, helping him to find his niche.[16]

Abbey later gave the impression that, for *Desert Solitaire*, he had simply typed up his old Arches journals and sent them in: "I rummaged through my trunk, dug out my old notebooks and journals, and transcribed by type-writer the entries I had made during those two seamless perfect seasons."[17] His agent's encouragement to write about his own experiences further reinforces an impression that this was not a carefully crafted or self-motivated book. But to the contrary, Abbey had been planning it since 1958, before he had any agent, already thinking then of "Solitaire" as part of its title. He did draw from his 1956 and 1957 Arches journals, but he thoroughly transformed his source material, and most of the book was written elsewhere, several years afterward and many miles away from Arches. Both the original and the revised manu-scripts of *Desert Solitaire* (the second marked by the publisher as received on July 24, 1967) were thoroughly carved up and characteristically much rewrit-ten by Abbey.[18] His most celebrated book was the result of very deliberate de-sign and careful revision. Although in truth the autobiographical experiences described in it were drawn from several years and diverse places, the book seemed to unify them as a single *Season in the Wilderness*, as its subtitle put it, following Ranger Ed Abbey from April Fool's Day to September.

Although ostensibly "set" mostly around Arches, this book contains many ideas that he developed in other places. This was reflected in a January 12, 1967, journal entry when he decided, in "Gravel Gulch, Dead Valley," to write "another fifty pages for *Desert Solitaire*, plus a straight magazine-type article on 'Industrial Tourism and the Parks.'" In this perhaps most influential chap-ter of the book, which would have an impact thirty years later on changes at the Grand Canyon's South Rim and Yosemite, Abbey's attack on road building appears to be focused on Arches. Actually, however, his ideas were finalized in Death Valley, as he also indicated on January 12. He felt that Death Val-ley's main flaw was "simply far too many roads. . . . One does not feel here the sense of wilderness, of remoteness, still available in other parks. You cannot *see* wilderness from a road" (210).

Abbey's time in Death Valley was a key source not only for *Desert Solitaire* and other subsequent nonfiction but also for *The Monkey Wrench Gang*. Charles "Seldom Seen Slim" Ferge of nearby Ballarat, California, in the Panamint Valley, was a celebrated Death Valley character, a spunky, indepen-dent soul who attracted enough attention that his August 1968 funeral was broadcast on television, and the nearby "Slim's Peak" was named after him.[19] In early 1968, Abbey wrote in his journal, "Seldom Seen Slim. (short story?)"[20] Instead, he saved the name for *The Monkey Wrench Gang*, slightly altering it to Seldom Seen Smith. In *Cactus Country* (1973), on the subject of why one loves the desert, Abbey wrote, "I have often wondered what the answer would have been from one of the most famous of Death Valley old-timers, a prospec-tor named Seldom Seen Slim. But he never answered his telephone. He didn't have a telephone. And he was never home. Didn't have a home."[21] He noted in "The Great American Desert" that he "searched for and never did find Seldom Seen Slim."[22]

Another telling example of the growth of *Desert Solitaire* is Abbey's celebration of naturalistic "surfaces," which he first generated at Lassen on July 23, 1966: "Do I seem to write only of the surfaces of things? Yet, it seems to me that only surfaces are of ultimate importance—the touch of a child's hand in yours, the taste of an apple, the embrace of friend or lover, sunlight on rock and leaf, music, the feel of a girl's skin on the inside of her thigh, the bark of a tree, the plunge of clear water, the face of the wind" (199). This striking journal entry was made even more distinctive and lyrical in his original introduction to *Desert Solitaire*, in a much-quoted passage worth comparing with his journal entry: "I know nothing whatever about true underlying reality, having never met any. . . . I am pleased enough with surfaces—in fact they alone seem to me to be of much importance. Such things for example as the grasp of a child's hand in your own, the flavor of an apple, the embrace of friend or lover, the silk of a girl's thigh, the sunlight on rock and leaves, the feel of music, the bark of a tree, the abrasion of granite and sand, the plunge of clear water into a pool, the face of the wind—what else is there? What else do we need?"[23] Note how he increased his defiant pose, shifting from the tentative question that begins the journal entry ("Do I seem to write . . . ?") to the declarative statement in the book ("I know nothing whatever . . ."). And he sharpened his style and imagery, revising for example "the feel of a girl's skin on the inside of her thigh" into "the silk of a girl's thigh."

By turning to nonfiction, to essays, Abbey had now hit upon a method by which he could draw very directly from his copious journals and also become more successful as a writer. Understandably, he might have thought that more money was to be made by writing the great American novel, not essays. But now (as he would tell students at the University of Arizona in April 1980) he had "discovered I could sell each thing I wrote twice—first as a magazine article, then as a chapter in a book. Or even three times—first as a reading at some university, then as a magazine article, then as a part of a book. That seemed like a good deal; and I was hooked. Corrupted."[24] The readings came later, beginning in the 1970s, after *Desert Solitaire* and *The Monkey Wrench Gang* had cemented his popularity. Yet he put his new strategy of "magazine article, then book" into practice even before *Desert Solitaire* appeared. And this process was no mere double- or triple-dipping of his work; it encouraged him to be forever revising and sharpening his essays, as he would do not only with the chapters of *Desert Solitaire* but also with all of his subsequent essay collections.

Abbey's regular editor in later years, Jack Macrae, wrote that "Bob Gutwillig, then a hotshot editor, had signed Abbey to a two-book contract in 1966; as with many such hotshots in book publishing, Gutwillig had departed his job before the first book, *Desert Solitaire*, was published. The manuscript languished in a pile of contracted but unread manuscripts in a small office at McGraw taken over by Walter Clemons."[25] At Lassen on July 1, 1966, Abbey noted that he was on page 191 of *Desert Solitaire*—"two-thirds completed thank Gawd" (197). In December, part of his "Water" chapter appeared as "The West's Land of Surprises, Some Terrible" in *Harper's*, where it provoked interest even beyond those pages. Keith Green wrote in the *Taos News* soon thereafter, "A fellow named Edward Abbey, evidently a Utah resident, expounded this month on the trials and (to give him credit) beauties of the desert. . . . Abbey perhaps seeks with his article to keep the Southwest empty—his own preserve. . . . One can admire Abbey's writing, but one also must object to his sweeping generalities."[26]

The condensed "West's Land of Surprises" then appeared in the February 1967 *Reader's Digest*. On February 28 in Death Valley, Abbey comically lamented that this was a "literary disgrace." *Harper's* had been "bad enough," but now "Gawd help me! . . . Aaah . . . the lures of mammon." He added that he had received about twenty fan letters because of his *Harper's* and *Reader's Digest* appearances, more than he had yet received from any of his books, as well as a request to speak at the University of Nevada and a critical review in *Western Review*. "Could the ice finally be breaking? E. Abbey, the famous unknown author" (211). The *Western Review* piece was William T. Pilkington's "Edward Abbey: Southwestern Anarchist," a critique of *The Brave Cowboy* and *Fire on the Mountain*. In the fall of 1966, Levi Peterson very positively discussed *The Brave Cowboy* right after Walter Van Tilburg Clark's classic novel *The Ox-Bow Incident* in the inaugural issue of *Western American Literature*, the journal destined to become the most common site for scholarly studies of Abbey.[27] Abbey did indeed have reason to believe that the critical ice was breaking.

In late 1966, *Sage* magazine included "Snake Dance," which became "The Serpents of Paradise" chapter in *Desert Solitaire*. This was the first of Abbey's nine contributions during 1966–69 to *Sage* (a Las Vegas quarterly nature magazine), most of which eventually made their way, in one revised form or another, into subsequent books through the rest of his career: *Desert Solitaire*, *Slickrock* (1971), *The Journey Home* (1977), *Abbey's Road* (1979), and *One Life at a Time, Please* (1988). A synopsis of his *Sage* periodical history underscores Abbey's new method of recycling his essays, his *modus oper-*

andi for the rest of his career. "Death Valley Notebook" (1967) was source material for a shorter discussion of the area in the 1973 National Geographic book *Wilderness USA*[28] and then fully reprinted in *The Journey Home*. "A River to Explore" (1967) was transformed into "Down the River with Major Powell" in *The Journey Home*. His interview with Joseph Wood Krutch (1968) was rewritten as his preface to Krutch's *The Great Chain of Life* (1978) and then recycled as "Mr Krutch" in *One Life at a Time, Please*. "Glen Canyon Dam" (1968) became "The Damnation of a Canyon" in both *Slickrock* and *Beyond the Wall*.

Even the three *Sage* pieces that did not reappear in Abbey's books helped set him up for other writings. "Running the Wild River" (1968), about the Colorado in the Grand Canyon, was never reprinted; instead, Abbey developed his writing on that same subject in several other essays. His most obscure contribution to *Sage* was an interview with William Eastlake (1969), because he published it under the pseudonym Peter M. Kenyon, identified as "a free lance writer" who "has written extensively about people and places of the Southwest."[29] Abbey may have published it under another name simply because he already had another, signed contribution in the same issue: "The Artist as Architect" (1969), his article about Malcolm Brown. Like Brown, Eastlake remained a good friend as well as an important influence, and several of Eastlake's attitudes expressed here—his admiration for Mark Twain and Thomas Wolfe, his boredom with Henry James, his disgust with being ignored as a Western writer—were clearly shared by Abbey.

As with the "Water" chapter in *Harper's* and *Reader's Digest*, the pieces of *Desert Solitaire* in *Sage* are telling reflections of how carefully he revised, despite his self-cultivated, Hemingwayesque image as a rough-and-ready type who lived his adventures and then simply typed them up. "A Day in the Life of a Park Ranger" (1967), for example, includes the striking first page of the book and then a version of much of the "Cliffrose and Bayonets" chapter. Yet it is missing perhaps the most striking flourish in the book chapter: his gratuitous killing of a rabbit, which he hits with a rock and then declares, "The wicked rabbit is dead."[30] How could he possibly have failed to include such a memorable detail in his first version of this chapter? Is it perhaps because, as he suggested to his friend Bob Greenspan about "The Moon-Eyed Horse," it never really happened[31]—and was instead later invented and added to make a strong effect on readers (which it certainly always does)? Abbey's readers have tended to read this book as factual, and much of it is, but the insertion of fictional stories about rabbits and horses should probably come as no surprise. After all, the chapter on "Rocks" slides from factual descriptions into a lengthy shaggy-dog story about the Husks and Mr. Graham, a triangle of ill-starred prospectors, that Abbey admits is "a story based on events which may or may not have happened but which," following the patterns of folklore, "all who tell it will swear is true." [32]

Also of biographical interest are Abbey's later changes to his list of friends and alter-egos at the end of this original article. "Where are you now, J. Soderlund? Alva T. Sarvis? Bob Riddle? Henry Lightcap? Malcom [*sic*] Brown?" becomes, in the 1968 book, "Where are you now, J. Soderlund? Alva T. Sarvis? John De Puy? Wilton Hoy? Malcolm Brown?" and finally, in its 1988 revision, "Where are you now, J. Soderlund? Alva T. Sarvis? Bob Riddle? Jack Loeffler?" [33] Riddle and Brown, his old New Mexico friends, come and go, just as his later close compatriots Loeffler (whom he did not yet know when writing *Desert Solitaire*) and De Puy crop up.

By the late 1960s, Abbey had settled into a productive pattern of using his seasons as park ranger and fire lookout not only as his means of support but also as the sites and subjects of his writing. After his 1966–67 stint in California, he accepted an appointment as park ranger at Lee's Ferry, Arizona, on the Colorado River, to begin in May 1967. On his roundabout way there, he took a two-week raft trip down the Green River with Malcolm Brown and Harvey Mudd (Brown's friend, architectural client, and wealthy namesake of the California college). They left from the town of Green River, Utah, and descended to the confluence of the Green and Colorado Rivers, in Canyonlands National Park below Moab. This was Abbey's first big river trip since his float through Glen Canyon with Ralph Newcomb in 1959, and he remained hooked, taking many more such expeditions throughout the rest of his life.

All was not calm and bliss, however, as Brown memorably recounted:

> We had three little banana boats—little individual one-person inflatables, with just enough space in them for one person and their gear and their food. But the great question that arose was what to do about liquor, which was very important to Harvey and Ed. They wanted to have a large stash of it for fourteen days on the river. The question was how to carry the stuff. They looked around Green River and found a garage with a huge tractor tire innertube. They bought this innertube—about five or six feet in diameter—blew it up and wrapped a piece of canvas around the bottom of it and up over the top and tied it with strings, and filled up the space with bottles of whiskey. Then they tied it behind either one of their boats and took turns pulling this thing down the river. It didn't make it hardly any of the way; the canvas got a tear in it, and all the liquor

fell out. They didn't know it and they lost it all, barely into the trip. A great dismay![34]

Brown also explained that "Ed popped a branch through his ill-fated banana boat. He tried to patch it with duct tape, but there were many sad instances. Ed's boat would just slowly begin to collapse and Ed would start to sink into the river. An inflated boat is such a joyous thing when it's inflated, and it's such a sorry thing when it begins to crumple up."

Nonetheless, they made it to the Confluence, spending "four blissful days of camping," Brown fondly recalled, "on a beautiful rolling sand dune right at the top of Cataract Canyon," where at night they heard "tremendous deep rumbles, and the whole earth would shake. It was boulders at the top of Cataract Canyon that would get dislodged at the bottom of the river by the roiling water and just roll down under water." Some marijuana sufficed to appease the liquor-lovers. "Ed was very scornful about consciousness-enhancing drugs, but since there was no liquor, he smoked some, and I remember him waxing eloquent, reciting long lines of Shakespeare and various authors." Four days later the jet-boats that they had hired arrived and sped the threesome up the Colorado to Moab—the only easy way out of the Confluence.[35]

In his summer 1967 *Sage* article about this trip, "A River to Explore," Abbey established his credentials as a literary and philosophical river-runner. Here he mostly avoided riotous real-life details about sunken whiskey bottles and sinking banana boats in favor of lofty quotations from Major John Wesley Powell's journal about his maiden journey down the Colorado River in 1869, carrying on a running commentary with Powell that he subsequently emphasized by retitling this essay "Down the River with Major Powell" (in *The Journey Home*, where he inexplicably misdated his own Green River trip as "May 1971"). Even before *Desert Solitaire*, which transformed the previously obscure Arches area into a popular destination for his many readers, Abbey decided to be careful about communicating the location of beautiful wilderness places to his readers. He names a side canyon on the Green River, but then notes, "This is our discovery and our name, and because of the lovely things it contains I prefer not to specify its location."[36] This became his common practice, taken a step further in many subsequent writings that deliberately mislead readers about various wilderness locations. In this essay, he gives the last word to Powell, who speaks for him: "The great river shrinks into insignificance as it dashes its angry waves against the walls and cliffs that rise to the world above. . . . We have an unknown distance yet to run, an unknown river to explore."[37]

Abbey's season at Lee's Ferry ran from May 19 to October 20, 1967.[38] As he clarified a year later in the essay that he eventually called "The Damnation of Glen Canyon," "During my five-month tour of duty I worked at the main marina and headquarters area called Wahweap, at Bullfrog Basin toward the upper end of the reservoir, and finally at Lee's Ferry downriver from Glen Canyon Dam. In a number of powerboat tours I was privileged to see almost all of our nation's newest, biggest and most impressive 'recreational facility.'"[39] His appointment was as a ranger within the new Glen Canyon National Recreation Area, soon to be the most visited such site in the country, crowded with house-boats and speedboats. In his journal at Lee's Ferry in August, he called himself "the motorboat ranger," with twenty-three miles of river as his domain (211).

In 1959 he had floated blissfully through Glen Canyon; in 1967, this patrol took him to Page and the base of the towering Glen Canyon Dam, which by now had drowned Glen Canyon with the huge reservoir ironically called Lake Powell. Staring up at the dam, Abbey had ample opportunity to think about what had been done to beautiful Glen Canyon—and soon he began to think about how it could be undone. By October he asked himself, "If dam removed, could Glen Canyon recover its former beauty? . . . Already the 'desert varnish' has come down over the bathtub rings." In June 1969, gazing down into Grand Canyon from his lookout tower on the North Rim, Abbey wrote, "Glen C.? Gone—but could be recovered. The dam is obsolete, should be removed."[40]

Even in 1967, this area attracted a lot of visitors, including old friends from his New Mexico days such as Al Sarvis (211) and Craig and Jenny Vincent.[41] He also made an important new friend, one who would influence his thinking about Glen Canyon Dam more than anyone else: the veteran river-runner Ken Sleight, who had grown up in Idaho, graduated from the University of Utah, and then (before going off to Korea for two years in the army) rafted through Glen Canyon for the first time in 1951, from Hite (near Dandy Crossing) to Lee's Ferry. In 1953 he began Ken Sleight Expeditions and soon co-founded the Western River Guides Association. However, not long after he had commenced rafting Glen Canyon regularly, he was astonished to watch David Brower and the Sierra Club agree to its doom when they cut the deal that saved Dinosaur Canyon upstream. Brower and Eliot Porter would call Glen Canyon "the place no one knew," but Sleight knew it well. After moving to Escalante in 1963, he directed both the Escalante Chamber of Commerce and the Friends of Glen Canyon. As Russell Martin writes, "Short, mischievous, gregarious, and sweet-tempered until you crossed him—an epic beer drinker in the great jack-Mormon tradition—Sleight was suited to his chosen field."[42]

In his May 1989 eulogy at Arches, Sleight described his first meeting with Abbey, when he arrived at Lee's Ferry in the summer of 1967 to lead an expedition through the Grand Canyon: "As I pulled down to the river, you as a National Park Service Ranger came strolling down to announce your presence and to inspect my outfit. After the rigging chores, we sat for hours on those ugly rubber rafts, swapping tales, some lies. As you know we spoke with derision about the Glen Canyon Dam. That God awful dam was destined to become the object of many discussions. We commiserated together. . . . We were determined that something had to be done about that dam." [43] Sleight later added that, after he first left Abbey at the river and had been heading downstream for a couple of hours, Abbey pulled alongside in his ranger powerboat to watch him run Badger Creek Rapid and called out to him, "Ken, we'll take that god-damned dam down yet!" [44]

Abbey subsequently followed Sleight's course down the river, with Ron Smith's Grand Canyon Expeditions. Observing him looking wistfully at their boats while inspecting them, as Abbey recounted in his essay "Up the Creek with the Downriver Rowdies," Smith invited him to join his crew for the trip. "'I'll get fired.' 'Who cares?' Smith said, opening a can of beer with his boatman's pliers. . . . I gave my boss due notice—30 seconds—and went along." [45] Abbey characteristically gives readers the impression that he walked off the job in midseason, but this trip came at the end of his Lee's Ferry season, in October (212). For him this was "the first of several voyages down the Colorado, through the heart of the Canyon (The Canyon as its lovers call it) to its terminal necrosis in Lake Mead." [46]

After his time on the Colorado River ended, Abbey visited San Francisco at the end of October before moving to 342 North Park Avenue in Tucson in November, joining Judy, who was studying at the University of Arizona. [47] This was his first time living in the city that became his almost permanent home in the 1970s and 1980s. That winter he met Joseph Wood Krutch, the English professor turned author of such books as *The Voice of the Desert*, and Abbey interviewed him for *Sage*. His January 1968 encounter with this veteran desert essayist toward the end of his life represented a passing of the guard of sorts. Abbey found him a "calm, cool, clear-minded old man" but also fairly "old-fashioned, still living largely in the '20s. Good ole gray fuddy-duddy, J. W. Krutch" (214).

Abbey learned that he shared with this Tennessee native a preference for the open desert over the comparatively crowded hills of Appalachia, and an opposition to building roads through the desert. By the end of February 1968, Abbey would be living and working in the desert himself, beginning the first of his three seasons at Organ Pipe Cactus National Monument, in the rugged, stunning terrain near the Mexican border, so named for its large number of cacti resembling the pipes of a church organ. Yet he also found Krutch more conservative on Vietnam than he was: "I was unable to get him to take a stand against what seemed to me then and seems to me now the most shameful episode in our nation's history since the time of legalized human slavery."[48]

Abbey's opposition to the Vietnam War was shared by other members of his family (except for his brother John), and Judy was also a strong opponent of the war. During this period he renewed correspondence with his by now far-flung relatives. On December 30, 1967, his youngest brother, Bill, wrote Ed from Micronesia, where he was living with his Filipina wife and teaching high school. On the subject of Vietnam, Bill remarked, "I often think about changing my citizenship, but then what the hell good would that do?"[49]

On May 29, 1967, back home in Pennsylvania after another rock-collecting expedition during which he visited Ed at Lee's Ferry, Paul Abbey wrote to Judy that "Mildred has another week of teaching and then she is going to join me in doing what she wants to do when she wants to do it." Retiring from a quarter century of teaching first grade, Mildred reluctantly moved into their tiny new house, which Paul had built along busy Route 119 in Home. They sold the Old Lonesome Briar Patch to another family rather than accept an offer from John to buy it, because the broken-hearted Mildred (as Paul lamented on August 28) "for some ununderstandable reason says she doesn't ever want to see it again, hence she does not want to sell it to Johnny."[50]

John felt alienated from the other Abbeys because of his support of the war, their disagreements over land, and his generally cantankerous personality. He obtained another, smaller property near the Old Lonesome Briar Patch from Paul, and then refused to sell it back to him; he kept it and eventually willed it to Bill, though other family members lived on it.[51] Paul sought to reassure Ed on August 27, "Don't feel too badly about Johnny," who had recently "spent only an hour with Nancy at the airport" in San Francisco. "He has nothing against you. He admires you, but of course would never say anything like that except when he was drunk. He is so proud of the fact that he is *almost* as smart as you. He is lonesome and confused, feels that all is futility."[52] Yet John remained true to his own convictions, his own adopted life in southern California, and his own friends.

In his October visit to San Francisco, Ed was surprised that, as a "hater of cities," he nonetheless found it "a sweet town" and enjoyed a better visit with his sister than John had, finding Nancy "bright and gay" in the company of her "three golden children," Bill, Abigail, and Kelly. Nancy was very much the "independent woman, now, since her divorce. *Her* divorce. Says she's happy enough. Moderately happy, like any other Abbey. Still looks good—not pretty, no, but beautiful" (212).

Abbey corresponded not only with his relatives but also with Judy, because they were often apart during Abbey's ranger seasons. While he was at

Lee's Ferry in the summer of 1967, she returned to the University of Arizona's geology camp at Pearce,[53] where she had been so unhappy two years earlier. They traded romantic letters and looked forward to the occasional visit, such as when Judy took a bus to Flagstaff and was met by Ed. Their marriage has been represented as Abbey's first happy one, but Judy had to contend with her husband's pronounced model for a one-sided open marriage. At Lassen in September 1966 — a couple of weeks after Judy's departure, and less than a year after their marriage — he composed in his journal "A Modest Proposal" in favor of legalized prostitution, which he saw as a positive step toward the "ideal utopian society of free love" (207). He also wrote at length about the animal desirability of the right kind of woman, who should be between fifteen and thirty in age, with "bright eyes, glossy hair, clear skin, sweet breath, full and normal bodily development, strength, agility, sexual appetite, good disposition, and attractive figure — meaning a normal and healthy body (neither too thin nor too fleshy)" (204). This entry was eventually published as "How to Pick a Woman" in *Esquire*, appropriately enough.[54]

His motto was Don Juan's, which he had quoted in November 1964 (while married to Rita but having an affair with Judy): "How can I be true to one without being false to all the others?" (191). In June 1965 in Las Vegas, a couple of weeks before leaving Rita, he remained "obsessed with sex. An overpowering lust is driving me mad — everywhere I look I see only ripe young female flesh — cunt, ass, thigh, knee, swelling breast and soft lips parted to receive my torpedo of love — ah! As the Scotch say, the standing cock hath no conscience" (194). A month later in Moab, he wrote of "all the pretty girls — Abbey's downfall, his destruction. And his only regret — the ones he missed. (Judy, come! Quickly!) I wish my arms were around you now and your legs around me and my tongue down your throat and your fingernails in my back and my hands on your bottom and your hair in my eyes and your nipples on my chest and my et cetera in yours, et cetera. And my feet against the wall" (195).

In March 1968 at Organ Pipe, he similarly complained of a "furious eroticism" that was "driving me mad," with "hard-ons all day long." He confessed that he was a "satyr-maniac" (216). Three months later, he admitted that he "loved them all, that was the trouble. Could never willingly give up any of them, could never forget. He wanted them all around him, all his life. Never did he *want* to lose one for another. But they, of course . . . they never understood. And so, one goddamned tragedy after another" (220).

A decade later, in *The Hidden Canyon*, Abbey celebrated his 1967 summer season at Lee's Ferry, where "I took my girl friends for rides. . . . I used to lie on the sand and watch my favorite birds — turkey vultures, shrikes, ruby-throated hummingbirds, rosy-bottomed skinnydippers."[55] Even if one were willing to credit such descriptions to Abbey's typically lively imagination, it is clear that his version of open marriage, during his three seasons at Organ Pipe, was exciting for him but difficult for his wife. Abbey loved the warm winters at Organ Pipe, which he delighted in calling "Organfeeler National Orgasm" (216) in his journal. In early 1968, Judy learned that she was pregnant, and she remained mostly in Tucson while Abbey worked at Organ Pipe, three hours southwest of Tucson next to the Mexican border, from February 27 to April 18. Judy and their daughter Susannah, born on August 28, lived with Abbey in a Quonset hut at Organ Pipe during much of his second and third seasons there between December and April of 1968–69 and 1969–70. His fellow rangers got along well with Abbey, gave him plenty of room when he received female visitors beginning in his first season, and tried not to listen when they heard boisterous arguments between Ed and Judy emanating from the Quonset hut.[56] Abbey himself recorded on March 17, 1968, that he had had a fight with Judy over old love letters of his. "She left me here *sans* typewriter, *sans* clock, *sans* towel, *sans* stew pot and *sans* wife" (215).

Organ Pipe was one of Abbey's favorite national park assignments, rivaled in that regard only by Arches and the Grand Canyon, partly because of its pristine desert setting and partly because of the camaraderie he enjoyed among the rangers there. This was a male world. Significantly, when Abbey first arrived at Organ Pipe, he did so in the company not of his wife but of his best friend, John De Puy. His first season there was a short one; he replaced a ranger who left in midseason to take a job elsewhere. Living in a trailer mostly by himself that year, Abbey enjoyed being "just one of the guys," and that is how chief ranger Jim Carrico and head naturalist Bill Hoy remember him at Organ Pipe. He knew the rules, both written and unwritten; for example, he showed up with a full beard at first but then shaved it off in time for his first day on the job.[57] Just as he had gone through the entire 1956 Arches season without ever mentioning *The Brave Cowboy*, in 1968 his many topics of conversation with fellow rangers did not include *Desert Solitaire*, which was beginning to earn a national reputation.

This book did not take off in the mass market until well after the first Earth Day, in April 1970, when Simon and Schuster released its 1970 paperback edition and Ballantine its 1971 mass-market paperback. But the positive reviews that the original edition received did bode well from the beginning. These commenced even before publication (with a November 15, 1967, entry in the *Kirkus Reviews*), continued on New Year's Day in the *Library Journal*, and peaked in prominence with Edwin Way Teale's review in the January 28 *New York Times Book Review*: "His is a passionately felt, deeply poetic book. It has philosophy. It has humor. It has sincerity and conviction. It has its share of nerve-tingling adventures in what he describes as a land of surprises, some of them terrible surprises." Teale added that, to "the builders and developers" among park administrators, "his book may well seem like a wild ride on a bucking bronco. It is rough, tough and combative. The author is a rebel, an eloquent loner." He also cited "Mencken's definition of nature as 'a place to throw beer cans on Sunday.'"[58] Abbey subsequently made notorious his own preference for throwing beer cans onto highways.

At first Abbey thought that *Desert Solitaire* was "another book dropped down the bottomless well," as he complained on February 6, 1968. "Into oblivion. The silent treatment. . . . Abbey: He wanted the same thing all writers want—fame, money, beautiful girls. An *audience!*" (215). But he was encouraged by the good reviews and by some glowing notes from family and friends. Paul Abbey wrote on New Year's Day 1968, "You should get the Nobel Prize in literature. . . . *I have not lived in vain,*" adding to Judy, "I give you credit for this in large part. You gave Ed the peace of mind that he needed to put together this fine, thoughtful and much needed book."[59] Al Sarvis wrote four days earlier, "YOU HAVE DONE IT! SOLITAIRE is a magnificent book—by far the best thing you have written, and by far the most moving thing I have read in recent years. . . . The whole thing is a heroic feat, my old friend. I am proud to know you. You had me close to tears more than once."[60]

Paul Abbey correctly observed that his son had found new happiness with Judy. Ed Abbey had also found a new genre for himself, carving out a niche as a nature writer. And he had rewritten himself by writing *Desert Solitaire*, creating a new persona, seemingly nonfictional (if also often fictional). This was the turning point in his career; after *Desert Solitaire*, Abbey's life and his writings would never again be the same.

Abbey also enjoyed hearing from two other old friends who were actually in his book: Ralph Newcomb and Lloyd Pierson. He teased Newcomb on January 22, 1968, that "any resemblance between Ralph Newcomb and an utterly fictitious creation named 'Ralph Newcomb' in SOLITAIRE is absolutely coincidental," and he replied to Pierson on April 10, "Hope you enjoyed your own part in it—Floyd Bence?" and telling him to give his best to Bates Wilson: "If he actually builds a paved road into Chesler Park we'll condemn him to two years in Orange County, California. Without parole."[61]

Moreover, *Desert Solitaire* soon drew new friends and followers in ways that Abbey had not anticipated. In the fall of 1968, Wendell Berry pulled a copy of the book—with the McGraw-Hill jacket, which included glowing blurbs by Krutch, Walter Van Tilburg Clark, and A. B. Guthrie—from Wallace Stegner's bookshelf at Stanford, where both Stegner and Berry were teaching, and he then bought *Fire on the Mountain* and became a regular reader of

Abbey.[62] Soon many other readers would tell similar stories of "the first time I read *Desert Solitaire*." Annie Dillard remembered analyzing Abbey's book while outlining *Pilgrim at Tinker Creek*.[63] And Abbey's readership included more wilderness fans and activists than fellow literary types. Dave Foreman remarked that *Desert Solitaire* was "the first book I'd ever read that I totally agreed with."[64] Within a few years Abbey's book became "word-of-mouth required reading," as Russell Martin put it, "a kind of *Catcher in the Rye* for the coming-of-age of the environmental movement."[65]

Yet when Abbey left Organ Pipe on April 21, 1968, and went to Denver for a few days on a promotional trip for *Desert Solitaire*, it was not environmentalism that he talked about. Around the same time that Gary Snyder read his "Smokey the Bear Sutra" at an environmentalist teach-in at Berkeley,[66] Abbey abandoned his prepared text on wilderness, in his April 23 talk at the Rocky Mountain Book Festival, and instead spoke out against the Vietnam War and overpopulation. The normally quiet Abbey, in what he himself later called his "maiden public speech,"[67] thus became from the outset a deliberate troublemaker as a speaker, with a public demeanor quite different from his private manner. Pierson, who was living in Denver at the time, recollected that "he made one little old lady madder than hell and she got up and left."[68] As the *Rocky Mountain News* reported the next day, "he was mildly booed, while a handful of his audience showed their indignation by staging a walkout in the middle of his presentation." To their reporter, Abbey commented, "I guess in a way I don't blame them for walking out. I expected some ruffled feelings, but the booing surprised me. I am glad to see people can react, however. And to express your feelings openly is better than secretly."[69]

In that momentous year of 1968, Abbey did not see himself as the wilderness prophet into which *Desert Solitaire* readers would transform him, even though he spent the next couple of months, from May 18 to July 23, at a remote fire lookout tower on Atascosa Mountain in Arizona's Coronado National Forest near Nogales.[70] Indeed, after the appearance of *Desert Solitaire*, similarly isolated federal assignments far from the public eye and the more developed national parks became standard for Abbey. Yet in 1968, like everybody else, he paid attention to big events that had the nation's attention—such as the assassinations of Martin Luther King in April and of Robert Kennedy in June, and the riots at the Chicago Democratic convention in August—juxtaposing them with events in his complex personal life. On April 14, Paul Abbey wrote from Home about Vietnam debates at Indiana University of Pennsylvania, his own involvement in the Eugene McCarthy campaign, and his African American friend Charley Sadler's trip to King's funeral;[71] in May, Paul joined his son in the Atascosa lookout tower for a week, with their close quarters getting on Ed's nerves (220). A decade later, Abbey still remembered a woman visiting him for a liaison in his lookout tower on the night of Kennedy's assassination,[72] and he recalled that his daughter was "born the night of the police riot at the Democratic convention in Chicago."[73]

After Susannah's birth, during which the progressive-minded Judy used the new Lamaze technique,[74] Abbey felt a need to find a job with a salary and a setting more conducive to family life. He accepted an invitation from Al Sarvis to join him at Western Carolina University in the mountains west of Asheville in Cullowhee, North Carolina, where Sarvis had been teaching art and helped get Abbey a teaching position in the English department. Ed, Judy, and baby Susie lived in the nearby town of Sylva, in the basement of the rambling home of Marcellus Buchanan, a colorful local politician.[75] This was the first time that he had lived in Appalachia in over twenty years, after leaving his native county for the University of New Mexico at the beginning of 1948.

Abbey hated this area and his job. He noted on October 8, 1968, that, "like a bloody idiot," he had accepted a teaching job "here at Redneck U. All for monetary greed. . . . $7,800, or almost $1,000 per working month, good wages for me." He dreaded the "horror the tedium the *drudgery* of academic life. How I despise it. How I loathe it. All those pink faces in the classroom three fucking hours, five fucking days per week. . . . Always there's tomorrow's shit to prepare, to read, to grade" (221). He would return to teaching more successfully in later years, but his first term as full-time instructor of record was not an auspicious one. Having been hired by WCU English department chair Mabel Crum strictly on Sarvis's recommendation and his growing reputation as a writer, Abbey had no training or experience in teaching freshman composition, and he did not do well in class. His English department colleague D. Newton Smith explained that Abbey was "very shy about that process. He didn't know what to do, pretty much." Smith added that Abbey's training in philosophy, "a very contemplative kind of thing," was certainly "not the same thing as teaching English."[76]

Outside of class, rather than establish a quiet life with his wife and new baby, Abbey carried on rambunctiously. He tried to overcome not only the "drudgery and tedium and horror" of the classroom, as he lambasted it also in a letter to Ralph Newcomb, but also "the continual sexual frustration of having all those goddamned little coeds, essentially untouchable, flipping their tails in my face all day."[77] At one point, without mentioning that he was married, Abbey asked out a young freshman student who was so startled when he escorted her to an illegal tavern that she made him take her home.[78] In dry Jackson

County, he and Sarvis drank a lot of home brew at a great many parties, with Sarvis carrying on about creativity, anarchy, and the absence of God. On wild, drunken, reckless drives through the countryside, Abbey threw his homebrew bottles out the window and raged against the ugly billboards defacing the landscape, telling Newt Smith that the most glorious sight he had ever seen was "the sight of a billboard burning against the sky." He particularly resented a billboard with a squirrel pictured on it along one of the area's main highways, and one day Smith noticed that it was no longer there.[79]

When Abbey got word that he could return to Organ Pipe for a second full season, he was so eager to flee the classroom and the coming Appalachian winter for the Arizona desert that he quit his teaching job before the end of the quarter, as he recorded on November 22: "Done it. Gave 'Model T.' Crum my resignation letter." He planned to leave on December 10 and head back to "Organ Pipe National Orgasm" (221). Newt Smith clarified that "he simply gave everybody in his class a B and left. It was not well received!"[80] This also marked a falling out with his old friend Sarvis, who remained angry that Abbey had walked out on him and felt that his own reputation had been tarnished; Sarvis's contract was not renewed at WCU for the following year.

Abbey was indeed delighted to return to sunny Arizona, working at opposite ends of the state—in cactus country from winter until spring, and then in canyon country in the summer. He loved his assignments as an Organ Pipe ranger, from December 13, 1968, to April 9, 1969, and as a fire lookout at the Grand Canyon's North Rim, from May 16 to September 17.[81] He returned to both jobs in 1970, and these settings provided material for some of his best writing. In *Cactus Country*, his book about Organ Pipe and the surrounding desert regions of southern Arizona and northern Mexico, he wrote: "A man or woman could hardly ask for a better way to make a living than as a seasonal ranger or naturalist for the National Park Service. . . . There's something about the Park Service that attracts good men and women." At Organ Pipe in 1969 and 1970,

> I lived in the south half of an old military Quonset hut, vintage World War II, that had been relocated there in the early development days of this park. The north half of the hut was occupied by Bill Hoy, ranger-naturalist and desert rat first class. I spent one or two working days each week tending the public campground, and that was the least interesting part of my job. . . . I was the only full-time patrol ranger. The job fell to my lot because I was relatively inexperienced, not very bright, wore my sideburns long and was only a seasonal, not a career, man. . . . One patrol might cover what is called the Puerto

Blanco Drive. This is a 51-mile loop road that begins near park head-quarters, close to the highway, and winds over the hills and across the flats of the western side of the park.[82]

Such patrols functioned like an experiential writer's library; *Cactus Country* and other keenly observant nature writing grew directly out of his ranger duties and logbooks.

Abbey enjoyed many adventures in the company of Organ Pipe's career rangers, especially Jim Carrico and Bill Hoy. One night in the winter of 1969, the three of them and their friend Hal Coss (like Hoy, a gifted naturalist) got good and drunk and decided to climb Montezuma's Head, the most imposing, monolithic mountain in Organ Pipe, right then and there, at midnight. This was Abbey's first time, whereas the others had scaled it before. Carrico and Abbey worked their way up the cliff in the dark, while Hoy and Coss slept on a shelf down below, following them up at dawn.[83] When they had all reached the summit, an innocent remark was made that Abbey enjoyed preserving in *Cactus Country*: "'What's to do up here?' said Hal Coss, looking bored."[84]

Abbey's friends also took him on his introductory tours of two striking and remote desert regions to which he often returned: the black, volcanic Pinacate region of Mexico, and the beautiful series of rolling desert valleys and mountains in southwestern Arizona known as the Cabeza Prieta (Black Head, after one of its mountains)—one of the largest wilderness areas in the lower forty-eight states. His first visit to the Pinacate had come in March 1968, when "Bill Hoy rappelled down into the well-like opening of a sixty-foot fumarole in the heart of a lava flow and nearly never emerged," as Abbey recalled in *Cactus Country*, but managed to pull himself "upward and out with the aid of a pair of jumars—clamplike metal devices that grip a rope with many times the leverage of human hands."[85] John De Puy was along on this trip, as he was also the following year when Ann Woodin—a writer and at that time the wife of Bill Woodin, the director of Tucson's Desert Museum—took Abbey camping in a seldom visited area of the Pinacate. There Ed confessed to Ann, "I've discovered that I'm not a desert rat; I'm a desert mouse." He found the black, barren Pinacate very harsh and foreboding—a feeling that he repeated in 1972 to another friend, Sandy Newmark—and may not have minded too much when, in 1969, he had to leave early to take De Puy, who had developed a fearsome toothache, to a dentist.[86]

However, Abbey fell in love with the Cabeza Prieta on his earliest visits there with Carrico and other rangers, such as a great jeep caravan trip in 1969.[87] "It was in February," Abbey noted in *Wilderness USA*, "that three friends and I ventured into one of the largest areas of mostly primitive Sonoran

Desert this side of Mexico: the Cabeza Prieta Game Range, 860,000 acres big." They followed the old Mexico-to-California trade route of El Camino del Diablo (the Devil's Highway) and camped "in the middle of a broad and lovely wash where great mesquite and ironwood trees towered above clean, bright, untrampled sand. . . . Nobody could sleep; we sat through most of the long winter's night telling stories and singing songs, giddy on moonshine, starshine, and the penultimate case of beer. We rose the next day at the crack of noon."[88]

Beginning his journey up toward the North Rim lookout tower in early May 1969, Abbey climbed into his old Volkswagen van after drinking wine with friends and picked up some hitchhikers who shared some marijuana with him. He pulled off the road, passed out, was abandoned by the hitchhikers, and was apprehended by the police. Ann Woodin got a call from him at a police station in the middle of the night, took him to a Tucson hospital, and then brought him to her home to recuperate for a few days.[89]

Abbey was keen to make it back to the North Rim, noting on June 6 that he was glad to be back at "the old stand" again. "The cabin in the woods. The steel tower. The sea of treetops, spruce and fir and aspen. The violet-green swallows and the hermit thrush. The crooked forest" (222). "The Crooked Wood" was the title of the article that he would publish about his North Rim seasons in the November 1975 *Audubon*. In November 1969, his "Escalante Canyon" essay appeared in *Natural History*, based on his three-day hike into the "semi-subterranean" world of the last discovered and mapped river in the forty-eight states. This essay is another good example of Abbey's careful revision process: it ended with a long addendum attacking road-building plans in the area, but when the essay reappeared as "Fun and Games on the Escalante," the fourth chapter of *Slickrock* (1971), this material was much better integrated.

By now Abbey had resumed much the same pattern as in his marriage to Rita: Judy retired to the city with Susie part of the time, while he maintained his distant post. In late June 1969, he admitted that "I can't bear monogamy. . . . I crave sexual excitement. Which means, for me, a new girl now and then in bed." By June 30 he was relishing his "summer with a girl ranger. Big sweet friendly good-lookin' blonde Californian. Screwing in the sunshine, on the pine needles. In the cabin while it rains. Up in the lookout tower, on the floor. In my VW here and there and everywhere. In her hot and musical Springdale apartment (Near Zion). In the Towne House, seventeenth floor, Phoenix. In Taos. Many sweet and delightful weekends" (223). He would similarly commemorate this summer in another essay about the North Rim, "Fire Lookout," in *Abbey's Road* (1979).

By the end of September 1969, however, Abbey was rejoined by

Judy and Susie and went back east in order to work on writing about his native Appalachian region. In March 1968 he had received a $2,500 advance from McGraw-Hill for "The Good Life" (216).[90] This was the novel about his family and upbringing that he had been planning since at least 1960—but did not succeed in finishing for another twenty years, in the form of *The Fool's Progress*, even though he received a second $2,500 payment in early 1970.[91]

He had better short-term success with *Appalachian Wilderness: The Great Smoky Mountains* (1970), a "coffee table" book that Jack Macrae at Dutton persuaded him to write on the strength of *Desert Solitaire*. The first of Abbey's half-dozen such endeavors, this book was filled with handsome photographs by Eliot Porter. At Dutton and later Holt, Macrae would extract from Abbey most of his several collections of essays as well as edit *The Fool's Progress*. Whereas *Desert Solitaire* championed the canyon country to which Abbey had journeyed, *Appalachian Wilderness* returned him to his home region of the country. On June 23, 1969, Abbey wrote Macrae concerning the latter project, "That I like very much and would like to do. I was born and raised in the northern fringe of the Appalachian country—western Pennsylvania—and know the life of the marginal farmer and out-of-work coal miner in my bones and blood. I am now laboring over a long novel for McGraw-Hill which deals partly with this material. . . . If you prefer not to take a chance on such last-minute work I would like to suggest Mr Wendell Berry as a good man for the job."[92]

By the early fall of 1969, Abbey, accompanied by Judy and Susie, was visiting his native county, corresponding from 203 Water Street in Indiana[93]—his longest stay in the town of his birth for many years. As nostalgic as he was later when writing about Appalachia, he was not happy to be there in October 1969: "Back home, where you can't go, said Wolfe. Why not? says Wendell Berry. I'm with Wolfe." He now felt that, to him, his hometown and native area meant "nothing. I feel nothing, no emotion whatever. Might as well be visiting Fargo ND for all it means to me. . . . A dismal scene, man." He did not appreciate that "the town is now three times bigger," with "schools and children everywhere" and "devastated farmland—hills disemboweled to make room for highway interchanges," "new factories and coal-burning power plants," and "all the old-style general farms . . . gone" (223–24).

It seemed to Abbey's childhood friend Ed Mears that Abbey expected Indiana to be "the same as it was when he left." Mears told him in 1969, "Ned, everybody and everything changes. When you're away from here eight to ten years, the people here change. We've all changed. You've changed." But the transformation of his native place clearly upset Abbey. Concerning the various forms of "development" that he saw, he told Mears, "It's all right to do it back here, but we don't want anything west of the Mississippi. They should have put a barricade up when we got to the Mississippi. Nobody should have gone west of that." [94]

On December 5, 1969, Abbey was presented with an "Ambassador Award" by the Indiana County Tourist Promotion Bureau at a banquet at the Rustic Lodge. His old college classmate Sam Furgiuele was there and retained this vivid memory:

> When they gave him the plaque, he stood up, a kind of imposing guy, and looked at the plaque and grinned, as if to make it very clear that this didn't mean a thing to him. Then, literally, he simply tossed it the way you would do a magazine or a card onto the table. His first words were, "You must know I don't believe in professional tourism." He said that there should be no need for a professional tourist bureau or tourism if you did the things in a community that you ought to do. He said, "Make Indiana beautiful and people will come to it." He said, "Get that goddamned traffic off main street and put in a parkway, benches, and trees." Some were extremely upset with his abrasive attack on the community leaders and on the chamber of commerce. Yet what he was saying was true. [95]

Afterward, Abbey left the plaque with his brother Howard, not bothering to take it back to the West with him.

His visit to the home of IUP English professor Raymona Hull, to speak to her class in December 1969, was also not a popular success. Her students were overawed, Abbey seemed ill at ease, and afterward when she asked if he would like some refreshment, he requested a beer; she had none to offer since it was a freshman class, and finally an older student took Abbey out to a bar. "I think the whole interview was a disaster," Hull summarized. "I felt as if there was a universal sigh of relief when he left." [96]

Abbey's family life was equally a catastrophe. On October 10 he noted that he was "alone again." Judy had left, swearing that she would not return and that he would never see her again. "So be it. I'll survive. (Somehow)." Two weeks later he wrote, "Last night I made love to a bonnie lass. Ah! The sweetness and the beauty and the madness of that hour. And her name: Bonnie! An unusual, almost Asiatic beauty. A Hollywood Indian princess. 'I want to be dominated,' she said. How true!" (224–25).

But with his writing he was positively "busy," as he indicated on the same date. "More book reviews for *Times*, *Post*, and *American West*, article for *Natural History* and *Life*, picture story in *Look*, interviews with press, Vietnam Moratorium." [97] My chronological bibliography of Abbey's writings reflects a sharp contrast between his difficult earlier years, with far fewer publications, and the late 1960s, when he became "busy" indeed, as he remained for the rest of his life. The pattern was now in place: he struggled to finish big novels, especially the one that eventually became *The Fool's Progress*, but he prolifically zipped off one article and book review after another.

After the pivotal appearance of *Desert Solitaire*, Abbey's writing was more and more often invited rather than unsolicited, and he developed a heightened sense of picking and choosing what he wanted to write. For example, he brushed aside Macrae's suggestion that he build a collection of essays along the lines of the "Industrial Tourism" chapter of *Desert Solitaire*,[98] which had been revised as "How to Save Our National Parks" in the March 1969 *Field and Stream*. He felt that he had already said his piece there and was more interested in new topics, as reflected in his strikingly diverse articles and book reviews during this period.

Two of these book reviews are worth mentioning because they contradict later attacks on Abbey as misogynist and racist as well as his own perception that he had no voice in New York. In his March 1969 review of Josephine Johnson's *The Inland Island* in the *New York Times Book Review*, Abbey praised this "green book of marvels" and helped bolster Johnson's reputation as a nature writer. Abbey's November 1969 review of the Native American writer Vine Deloria's *Custer Died for Your Sins: An Indian Manifesto*, again in the *New York Times Book Review*, is the earliest of his several sympathetic reviews and articles on Native American subjects. He emphasized that Deloria's book included important history that was not being taught in schools, and he noted that "the many parallels between the war in Vietnam and the war against the American Indian has not escaped the American Indian."

In Abbey's June 1969 *Times* review of Wallace Stegner's *The Sound of Mountain Water*, he argued that, in light of "politico-industrial vandalism" such as Glen Canyon Dam, "there is no West anymore." In the city where Abbey soon became a leading controversialist, the Tucson *Arizona Daily Star* promptly attacked this remark in a June 29 editorial headlined "Baloney!" From his North Rim lookout tower, Abbey sent a reply, printed by the *Star* on August 18, calmly clarifying that "I meant the West as a distinct *cultural* region."

Similarly, as much as Abbey disparaged his own native area in his journal and his public remarks, he assiduously researched Appalachian history for *Appalachian Wilderness*, which includes citations of numerous sources on the subject and an epilogue by the noted Appalachian author and activist Harry Caudill. Abbey's lyrical writing affirms the identity of Appalachia as a bioregion that transcends state lines, and he refers to Native American names in preference to the imposed name of Abbey's birthplace, Indiana: "Tennessee seems today something like Punxsutawney, Pennsylvania, thirty years ago. Like

Seneca and Powhatan, like Home, Pa., where many of us were once brung up. All of it Appalachian, winter or summer, then and now. Land of the breathing trees, the big woods, the rainy forests." [99] Abbey outlined and criticized the devastation of the Native Americans who once lived in Appalachia. [100] He also included a fourteen-page social history of the "Scotch-Irish" settlement, movement deeper into the mountains, increasing isolation and self-sufficiency, home remedies and other material culture, typical cabin structure, crops, and animals. He analyzed their distinctive subculture as broken down by modern capitalism in general and strip mining in particular as well as logging, the "damning" of the rivers, and eventually mass tourism and its transformation of Appalachian people into "curiosities." [101] He identified "western Pennsylvania" first in his list of areas strip mined, and first by quite a margin in the number of acres "disturbed." [102]

Later, Abbey tried to rediscover his Appalachian roots by buying land at Pack Creek, Utah, and elsewhere in the West. [103] He established a cabin behind his Tucson home in which he did all of the most important writing of his later years, and where he chose to die. In *The Poetics of Appalachian Space*, Parks Lanier emphasizes the traditional cabin as a key to Appalachian identity. [104] Similarly, Abbey stressed that "each householder built his own home. . . . Such cabins, when properly built, would last for a century." [105] He disdained the "immobilized 'mobile homes'" that he saw people inhabiting in Indiana County. When he left his native county in December 1969 (rejoined by Judy and Susie) to return to Arizona, he drove there via the Smoky Mountains, describing what he saw in *Appalachian Wilderness*. This book received nothing like the attention that *Desert Solitaire* drew, but the *New Republic* did praise Abbey for writing "tenderly and lyrically about Appalachia's wilderness, its plentiful water, its imposing hills, its valleys of refuge, its mighty trees and fragile wild flowers." [106]

Once again, Abbey was very eager to return west, fleeing Appalachia for the second December in a row for Organ Pipe, where he resumed his ranger job between December 23, 1969, and April 1, 1970. [107] During this season he made three new friends who remained important to him for the rest of his life, both personally and as environmentalist allies: Katie Lee, Doug Peacock, and Ingrid Eisenstadter. The latter two soon joined Ken Sleight as Abbey's inspirations for three-quarters of the central quartet in *The Monkey Wrench Gang*. Like Sleight, the folksinger, author, and activist Katie Lee had been rafting Grand and Glen Canyons since the early 1950s and remained a defiant opponent of Glen Canyon Dam. After reading *Desert Solitaire*, she had mailed her album *Folk Songs of the Colorado River* and some survey stakes to Abbey in the late summer of 1969; he replied from Indiana in September, "Muchas gracias for the surveyor's stakes. Keep up the Lord's work." At the end of December she met Abbey, Judy, Susie, and Abbey's visiting parents at Organ Pipe, where Abbey showed her an isolated place to camp.[108]

Like many others, the Vietnam veteran and wildlife advocate Doug Peacock read Abbey's March 1970 *Life* magazine article "Let Us Now Praise Mountain Lions," a sharp attack on hunting them in Arizona. This article prompted several positive letters in *Life* and a new national visibility for Abbey well beyond its pages. Paul Abbey reported to him that this issue had quickly sold out in his home town of Indiana.[109] It also showed Abbey that he could make as much money for such an article as for a whole book. Concerning this article's commissioning, Abbey wrote in his journal on August 26, 1969, "$1,500 plus expenses—for about 2,000 words! 75¢ a word! . . . You're getting too commercial, Abbey. Gonna end up as a mere hack if you're not careful."[110]

Just after this article was published, Peacock met Abbey at William Eastlake's house in Tucson, where they talked about mountain lions. At Abbey's invitation the burly, bear-like Peacock then visited him at Organ Pipe, toting a bottle of whiskey and talking about the Cabeza Prieta. Abbey told him that Organ Pipe was "relatively tame compared with the wild and empty valleys and ranges of the Cabeza Prieta," as Peacock wrote in 1998. "His last request," nearly twenty years later, "was that he be buried in such a place. . . . Ed Abbey considered the Cabeza Prieta our greatest intact desert wilderness—largely unknown, unvisited."[111] Abbey and Peacock subsequently shared several trips there.

Environmental issues were now coming to the forefront of people's minds. On January 1, 1970, the National Environmental Policy Act was signed into law by President Nixon, requiring federal agencies to take into account the environmental effects of their actions. April 22, 1970, was a day that had a crucial impact on events for Abbey and millions of other people. Proposed by Wisconsin senator Gaylord Nelson and organized by Harvard student Denis Hayes, the first Earth Day drew twenty million people at numerous locations around the United States.

One of those locations was Logan, Utah, where Utah State University English professor Thomas J. Lyon and former USU student Ingrid Eisenstadter were involved in organizing the local event for the Logan "Earth People." Eisenstadter journeyed all the way to Organ Pipe, before the event, to invite the author of *Desert Solitaire* to appear at Earth Day in Logan. Abbey did so, speaking carefully from prepared notes against corporations and in favor of environmental action. He found a receptive audience—in Logan and far beyond, with sales of *Desert Solitaire* steadily picking up after Earth Day, and a ready market available for more such writings. Abbey struck Lyon as quite shy when they first met in Logan, but he loosened up afterward in a nearby bar.[112]

In other ways, Abbey was not shy at all. He became involved with Ingrid, a feisty, dark-haired young woman who, like Rita and Judy, was Jewish and from the New York City area. At the beginning of May, while the attention of the rest of the nation was riveted on the Kent State shootings, Ed and Ingrid rafted through the Colorado River's Cataract Canyon with Ken Sleight. Sleight recalled Abbey's oar cracking as their boat plunged into "Satan's Gut": "Pulling the splintered oar to the surface, you looked at it with a silly grin, and then at the frothing hole ahead. Then turning to me, still with a silly grin, you said, 'Ken, do we have another oar? This one seems to have an imperfection,' as we suddenly dropped into the hole." [113]

Meanwhile, Judy had grown ill in 1969, felt worse during Abbey's 1969–70 season at Organ Pipe, and soon returned home and sought medical attention while her mother took care of Susie. Abbey visited her in New Jersey in May 1970, in between his Cataract Canyon trip and his flight back west later that month to join a group of people who were working on the Sierra Club's *Slickrock* book. On June 6, 1970, Abbey returned to his North Rim fire tower on an appointment good until August 31. He wrote on June 15 that, at the age of twenty-seven, Judy was back east in Mt. Sinai Hospital, "slowly dying of acute leukemia" (225). Less than three weeks later, on July 4, she was dead.

CHAPTER SIX

In the Canyons
1970–1974

Ed Abbey in particular and the environmental movement in general both rose to prominence in the early 1970s. It was no accident that, only a few months after the April 1970 Earth Day, the Ballantine paperback edition of *Desert Solitaire* began to attract a much larger readership and a growing critical reputation. During 1970–74, Abbey also wrote *The Monkey Wrench Gang*, his most popular novel and the book that would cement his reputation as an icon of the radical environmentalist movement. In the early 1970s, however, most environmentalists stuck to lobbying for such legislation as the Endangered Species Act of 1973, working through comparatively mainstream (and rapidly growing) organizations like the Sierra Club, the Audubon Society, and the Wilderness Society.

Rather than join them, Abbey characteristically continued to live and write way out on the fringe, though he did publish in *Audubon* and write *Slickrock* (1971) for the Sierra Club. From spring 1972 until June 1974, he spent most of his time commuting between his new house in Esperero Canyon, outside of Tucson, and the only year-round ranger job he ever held, in Aravaipa Canyon, an hour northeast of Tucson. His personal life took up much of his energy, as he struggled to overcome the death of his third wife, devoted himself to short-term relationships with other women, and then became involved with and married his fourth and youngest wife.

In late June 1970, Abbey took leave from his North Rim lookout tower, drove to the Tucson airport—where he "looked like hell," when his friend Katie Lee happened to encounter him there—and flew to New York.[1] During his two-week deathwatch with Judy, his demeanor was even worse. He walked daily from Mt. Sinai Hospital "on Ninety-second Street—where I watched my young wife dying—to my brother-in-law's apartment building on Thirty-fifth Street," as he recalled in the early 1980s. "Fifty-seven blocks, about three miles. I was seeking sleep through physical exhaustion, hoping a mugger would accost me so that I could kill him. (I carried a piece, a .45 automatic, under my coat.) . . . Maybe the look on my face scared them off."[2] In his journal a week after Judy's death, he noted that he had spent her last two weeks with her, sleeping in her hospital room with her during the last few nights, "except the very last two, when I could no longer bear to watch and listen to her suffering. . . . I wish I could forget. Oh, more than anything, I wish I could forget Judy's pain and fear, and all the hurt I gave her during our 4-1/2 years of marriage" (225).

Judy was the victim of "a rare, virulent, fast-acting myoblastic leukemia which kills real quick," as her friend Katherine Bounds remembered, adding that Judy knew instinctually she was dying and that she had religious visions toward the end.[3] No one wanted to tell her the truth about her condition, beginning with the Tucson hospital that suggested she return home to New York, and continuing with Mt. Sinai and even Abbey—in violation of his longstanding belief in looking death squarely in the eye. He told his old friend Malcolm Brown, who was living in New York City at the time, that he was "too much of a coward" to bring himself to admit to Judy that he knew she was dying.[4] A few years earlier he had watched as Rita's father died a slow, miserable death, and now, after watching Judy deteriorate quickly, he would redouble his determination to die with dignity one day himself. He felt that hospitals stripped patients of their humanity. For example, he had to bring Susie to the Mt. Sinai parking lot so that Judy could see her standing below, because the hospital did not permit children to come inside during visiting hours.[5]

Abbey wrote in his journal on July 11 that he should have told Judy the truth, "while she was still whole and rational, and given her the *choice* of the hideous hospital ordeal or of taking her own life. . . . She had a right to an honorable death—and we denied it to her! . . . I cannot escape the conviction that we betrayed her: the doctors because they knew best what was in store for Judy if the drug treatment failed, as it did; and myself because I knew best what a brave girl Judy really was" (227). Given how many times Abbey had been unfaithful during their marriage, his guilty conscience had other kinds of betrayal to mull over. "I killed her," he declared that summer.[6] Later he projected his guilt into *The Fool's Progress*, where Henry Lightcap crashes his truck while trying to drive his young wife Claire (a version of Judy), when she goes into labor, from the wilderness to a hospital; she dies and Henry wakes up in the hospital to learn that Claire is dead, with his mother-in-law standing beside him clutching their newborn daughter in her hands, telling him, "I knew you'd find a way to kill her sooner or later."[7]

The Peppers gave Judy "a nice quick Jewish funeral" the day after her death, and, as Abbey also recorded, she was "buried at Mt. Moriah, near Fairview," New Jersey (226). He asked Malcolm Brown to build a monument that he could take back with him to Arizona, so Brown fashioned a wooden Gothic arch with Judy's name and dates on it, which Abbey subsequently positioned behind his Esperero Canyon house while living there during 1971–74. After a visit to his parents in Home, Abbey flew back to Arizona and resumed his North Rim post—along with his daughter, "to her grandparents' sorrow," as he admitted (227). With Susie still less than two years old, her short-term surrogate mother was Ingrid Eisenstadter (228). Ingrid did not stay full-time at the North Rim, however, and by late July Bess Pepper, Judy's mother, visited Abbey and told him that she wanted Susie to come live with her. On August 13, Abbey's own mother suggested in a letter to him that Susie might be better off with Bess.[8]

A lookout tower with half of the actual Monkey Wrench Gang as parents was not an ideal place for a two-year-old. By September 16, Abbey resigned himself to his inability to maintain full-time care of his daughter, lamenting that he had now flown her back to her grandmother in New Jersey with Ingrid. "Sweet utterly lovable little Suzi—I feel I've betrayed her, forsaken her. But there was nothing else I could do. Nobody would help me" (229). Mildred Abbey reassured him on October 26, after a visit to Bess and Susie in Jersey City, that Susie was in very good hands.[9] Throughout her youth, Susie would be shuttled between her grandmother and her father—and later boarding school and summer camps.

Abbey's relationship with Ingrid remained touch and go: "What does she hope or expect from me? I don't know—but I'd like her to be my mistress and buddy for about twenty-five years, then I'll drop dead" (228). They shared some lively, wild times together. During Abbey's last season at Organ

Pipe, in the spring of 1970, they had found themselves marooned when Abbey's old Volkswagen van broke down. A car lover who knew little about engines, he thought at first that his van's acceleration was a bit weak, but then had to admit, when it died entirely, that something more serious was wrong. Stuck in the middle of the desert with no other liquid anywhere in sight, Ed and Ingrid popped open a warm bottle of wine and drank it all, giddily laughing through what they imagined might be their last few hours, until a truck happened along and towed them with a six-foot rope to an Ajo service station.

In the late summer of 1970, with Ingrid gone, Abbey was visited by his friend Ann Woodin, who had rescued him from jail the year before. As he remembered in his essay "Fire Lookout," "She came to my part of the forest bearing apples, a flagon, black caviar and a magnum of Mumm's. We sat on a log under the trees at evening, by a fire, and listened to the birds, and talked, and ate the caviar and drank the champagne and talked some more. She helped me very much. A lady with class, that Ann."[10] Ann herself recalled that "he was in the pits. It was guilt, because of his philandering and lack of being faithful to Judy. He just had a lust for young women." But Ann, who was a year older than Abbey, was surprised to find a whimsical side of him that she had not seen before, "just like a little boy, at night when he started to talk about his childhood and his relationship to the outdoors."[11]

Abbey was also visited by his old friend John De Puy, who remembered that "we hiked down to Thunder River and spent a whole night in a cave crying because Judy had died and my father had died."[12] Abbey likewise recalled descending from "North Rim down to Thunder River" and lying "in the shade of limestone ledges while the sun roared like a lion three feet away," discussing "the mystery of the death of a father, of a wife—that inexplicable *disappearance*."[13] De Puy claimed that Abbey blamed the military for Judy's death because of nuclear fallout in the Southwest.[14] On November 8, 1970, Abbey wrote to Utah senator Frank Moss in opposition to nuclear missiles.[15] Similarly, the Utah author Terry Tempest Williams would later write about the prevalence of breast cancer in her family as a result of radiation from nuclear testing in the region.

As usual, Abbey's personal life during this period was inextricably intertwined with his career as a writer. During his two weeks in New York City, he had visited not only Judy but also Ingrid and "a smart, attractive New York editor" who "persuaded him to publish the novel *Black Sun* . . . with Simon & Schuster without benefit of Don Congdon, Ed's longtime agent" for a $5,000 advance plus $7,500 for the paperback. The publishing relationship with Simon & Schuster was to last only one book, yet Jack Macrae believed "that the attentions of Ed's friend within the house helped to position *Desert Solitaire*, which was then considered a title of limited appeal, in the paperback market." [16] Abbey wrote to her on July 13, "You've been very kind, and a great help," outlined various projects to her, and remarked concerning Congdon, "It's the first time in my life I ever had a chance to fire somebody and you can easily imagine how delighted I am." [17]

The day before, he had written Congdon that he wanted to terminate their relationship because he felt that he could place his work with publishers just as well on his own, without paying 10 percent of his royalties to an agent.[18] He then proceeded to publish, in 1971, both *Black Sun* and *Slickrock* without an agent, though he did hire another agent for a while, as he noted in May of that year.[19] *Slickrock* and *Cactus Country* (1973) were photographic coffee-table books for which he was paid flat sums rather than royalties. Around the time that *Cactus Country* came out, however, Abbey had William Eastlake ask Congdon if he would be willing to be his agent again, Congdon resumed the relationship, and they stuck together for the rest of Abbey's life.[20] In fact, during the 1980s, friends would tell Abbey that he ought to switch to a different agent, but he insisted on remaining loyal to Congdon.[21]

Abbey had composed his letter of termination just eight days after Judy's death, and Congdon understood that he wrote it in a bad frame of mind and under a lot of stress. Abbey did his best to continue with his writing and his activism. This shows either that he was numbed to what had happened in his life and was simply trying to carry on, or that he was well able to function despite the impression that *Black Sun* would leave in many readers' minds—or both. On July 11, the day before he wrote to Congdon, he had moved quickly from his personal life to Utah politics in a note to Katie Lee: "Judy did not make it. She died early in the morning, July 4th. Acute leukemia—the poor kid never had a chance. Sent a copy of your protest letter to the Escalante Wilderness Committee. They want to make sure all such letters are included in the record." [22] And two days later, on July 13, he wrote not only his letter to his female friend at Simon and Schuster but also a review of three books for the *New York Times Book Review* [23]—all this while manning his lookout tower and living with Ingrid and Susie. After Will Gatlin's young lover disappears in the Grand Canyon at the end of *Black Sun*, Will spends all of his time hopelessly searching the trails for her, but in reality Abbey, as grief-stricken as he was, moved on expeditiously with his life, relationships, and work.

Because *Black Sun* is an obviously autobiographical novel about a North Rim fire ranger and was published with a dedication "For Judy, 1943–1970—*wherever*," many of Abbey's readers have assumed that it is a version of his relationship with Judy (in the form of young Sandy MacKenzie). *Black Sun* remained a favorite of his (253). Its third main character, Will's friend Art Ballantine—who is filled with racy talk and invites Will to sleep with his wife and to join him at the college where he teaches—was inspired by Abbey's old friend Al Sarvis. Such close autobiographical connections might further encourage the impression that this novel was an account of Abbey's third marriage. Yet Sandy was based not on Judy but on another woman with whom Abbey had had an affair in 1963. He finished his first draft of *Black Sun* in April 1968 (219), over two years before Judy's death, and it was a bone of contention in their marriage. He reported on March 17, 1968, that Judy hated it, "thinking it the story of one of my old love affairs, which in a way it is, but only in a greatly altered and much exaggerated way. If only she understood that there's nothing deader than a dead romance" (215).

Abbey remained attached to this sexy novel because it was a very personal account of his love life—with Sandy's disappearance at the end becoming even more meaningful to him because of Judy's death. But it has to be said that, as a work of art, *Black Sun* is perhaps too personal or too self-centered. Sandy is Adam's rib—a sex object who is more a means to Will Gatlin's gratification than an independent character of her own: "He kissed her mouth, unbuttoned her blouse and stroked the small soft breasts, feeling the nipples rise and harden under his touch. 'Yes. There. Kiss me there.' "[24] Will Gatlin is free of Jonathan Troy's adolescent inhibitions, but as a romantic object in the woods, Sandy is scarcely advanced beyond Leafy of *Jonathan Troy*. *Black Sun* is Abbey's *Lady Chatterley's Lover*, but the opposites that attract are not class differences, as in Lawrence's novel, but rather age: Sandy is very young, and Will middle-aged. Age difference was increasingly central in Abbey's relationships. Growing older, he continued to marry young women. All of his wives were in their twenties (or younger) at the time of marriage, whereas on his five wedding days Abbey was in turn twenty-three, twenty-five, thirty-eight, forty-seven, and finally fifty-five years old.

Black Sun enjoyed neither the popular nor the critical success that Abbey had hoped for. Its later Avon paperback edition sold over 100,000 copies[25]—but this was in contrast to *Desert Solitaire* and *The Monkey Wrench Gang*, each of which exceeded the half-million mark. And the reviews were not kind. The *New Yorker* called *Black Sun* "an embarrassingly bad novel."[26] Even Abbey's new friend Edward Hoagland—who had first written to him on March 19, 1970, praising *Desert Solitaire*—lamented in the *New York Times Book Review* that *Black Sun* was "not a masterpiece" like *Desert Solitaire*, complaining that "he does not always finish his books but publishes next-to-last drafts."[27]

It seemed that everyone wanted another environmental tract like *Desert Solitaire*, not a love story like *Black Sun*. By 1971, the 95-cent Ballantine mass-market edition of *Solitaire* was taking off in the bookstores and attracting a new round of positive reviews.[28] The new perception of Abbey as a nature essayist (rather than novelist) was reinforced by many of the kinds of books that he was asked to review, as in his critique of eleven conservation books, headlined "How to Live on This Planet Called Earth," in the April 19, 1970, *New York Times Book Review*. The author that he reviewed least favorably there, Edward Higbee, bitterly complained on May 24 that having the environmentalist Abbey review him, a proponent of the technological theories of Buckminster Fuller, "was like sending the Little Old Lady from Dubuque to cover 'Hair.'"[29]

Desert Solitaire was beginning to win Abbey, formerly a comparatively obscure Southwestern author, a national reputation. Soon it was also attracting further speaking invitations—even at the Navajo Community College at remote Many Farms, Arizona, where the mostly Native American audience listened to him, in the fall of 1971, with only passing interest.[30] On April 24, 1972, Abbey lectured at the rather different venue of Princeton University, where he assured the assembled colloquium on environmental studies, in a talk on wilderness, that Hoboken was America's Calcutta.[31] During the same period he began the essay that eventually became the celebrated "Freedom and Wilderness, Wilderness and Freedom" in *The Journey Home*, the beginning of which appeared in the August 28, 1972, *New York Times* as "On the Need for a Wilderness to Get Lost In." Abbey informed his startled readership that he had enjoyed "all the wilderness we needed" when living in Hoboken.[32]

Desert Solitaire also won Abbey a new chance at teaching, in a more palatable position than he had endured two years previously as a freshman English instructor in North Carolina. He had been in touch with Les Standiford at the University of Utah, who published an interview with Abbey in the autumn 1970 *Western Humanities Review* that Standiford noted was actually "assembled from correspondence with the author in 1969." It included Abbey's subsequently much-quoted complaint that capitalists could not understand that "growth for the sake of growth is the ideology of the cancer cell," an idea he had introduced in *Solitaire*.[33] He then accepted an appointment as the first Writer in Residence at the University of Utah, during the fall 1970 semester. He taught just one graduate course in creative writing, which required him to be in Salt Lake City only one or two days a week. He took up residence with Ingrid at 641 North 6th East in Logan,[34] an hour and a half north of Salt Lake City in the mountain and canyon country.

This time, teaching creative writing in a prestigious position created for him by people who were helping to further his reputation, Abbey was determined to try to do a good job as a teacher. When he went backpacking along the Utah-Arizona border that fall with Utah State University professor of English

Tom Lyon, he talked a lot about how to teach creative writing. He repeatedly asked Lyon, "What do you say about writing? How can you possibly teach writing?" He seemed nervous about teaching at the University of Utah and being the Writer in Residence.[35] Abbey joked about teaching a "writing sweatshop," but his introductory remarks for his first class on September 29 came from a seven-page, single-spaced document that he composed, in advance, in complete sentences: "I'm not sure whether a course or workshop like this has any value for the writer, or would-be writer, except as offering a certain stimulus to actually produce something, to actually sit down, grab paper and a pen, and actually begin." He filled a notebook with detailed notes for each class—while also brainstorming ideas, on its facing pages, for *The Monkey Wrench Gang*.[36]

On October 13, 1970, Abbey wrote on the blackboard the mottoes that became his mantra as a teacher, recycled in the 1980s at the University of Arizona: "Write right. Write good. Right Wrong. Write on!"[37] He meant that a successful author's prose must be well composed, interesting and moral, opposed to power and evil, and that one "must write, be rejected, and rewrite until someone listened," as William Marling clarified. "At the time, he was the paragon of his own program. His gritty *Desert Solitaire* . . . was becoming a brush fire in the popular market."[38]

By now Abbey had developed a style all his own, with a strong preference for clarity and directness. Early in his career his influences had included erudite modernist techniques—such as James Joyce's stream of consciousness and John Dos Passos' inclusion of newspaper headlines—and he had filled his Edinburgh journal with lengthy responses to Joyce and Samuel Beckett. In the essays that he had been writing since at least the late 1960s, however, he developed a blunt, pithy style. In an August 30, 1970, review in the *New York Times Book Review*, he expressed his disdain for "the traditional Jamesian art of saying as little as possible, in the greatest possible number of words."[39] Similarly, he encouraged his students to develop their own voices and styles.

In a later interview, Abbey characteristically derided his own teaching: "One poor guy, I'm sure, I discouraged from writing forever. He wrote a Mormon love story. I read it aloud to the class . . . and I couldn't help laughing at all the wrong places. For half the story the hero agonized over whether or not to kiss the girl."[40] But one student in that Utah class, Ernie Bulow, himself subsequently a teacher and book dealer, vouched that it was a good course. Bulow already knew Ingrid from undergraduate days at Utah State, and he had signed up for the class because he wanted to meet Abbey, whose books he had read. The two of them became lasting friends.

Abbey enjoyed living that fall in Logan's beautiful surroundings. Tom Lyon had to work hard, as they explored the area, to keep up with the long-legged Abbey, the son of two great walkers: "He could move; he could step out." After he received a check for "Appalachian Pictures," an excerpt from *Appalachian Wilderness* that appeared in *Audubon* that September, Abbey immediately took his Logan friends out to dinner. "He had that kind of expansive generosity," Lyon stressed, "despite being a pretty shy person socially." [41]

The success of *Desert Solitaire* was teaching Abbey the salutary lesson that he could make good money and reach a growing readership by writing about his own wilderness adventures. He had been invited by the Sierra Club to write the text for *Slickrock*, a coffee-table book with photographs by Philip Hyde, that was aimed at celebrating and protecting the redrock canyon country of southeastern Utah. John G. Mitchell, a Sierra Club editor, had met Abbey at the Newark airport in May 1970 (where a fading Judy saw him off) to fly to Moab via Chicago and Salt Lake City. [42] "From the Moab airport," Mitchell recounted in the book's introduction, "we drove south toward the canyons in a Sunkist-colored four-wheel-drive wagon." "Six-foot-three Abbey" was "fish-hooked between his new straw sombrero (ninety-eight cents at the Moab drugstore)" and the "aisle seat (an overturned washbucket)." Mitchell recaptured their mood: "Crowded? Who cared? We were heading for canyon country. To get *uncrowded*." [43]

They wanted to "share in conceiving the book even before the first photograph was selected or the first word written." [44] This was Abbey's first meeting with Philip Hyde. Often he did not even meet the photographers of his coffee-table books. Later he expressed disdain for such publications, convinced that readers ignored his text and looked only at the photos. On this trip, Abbey joked to Hyde that "one good word is worth a thousand photographs"; [45] he repeated the line (attributing it to Confucius) in his preface to *Beyond the Wall* (1984), his collection of essays (without any photos) from four of his coffee-table books. [46] The positive but sparse reviews of books such as *Slickrock* and *Cactus Country*, in contrast to the much more numerous notices of *Desert Solitaire*, *The Monkey Wrench Gang*, and Abbey's collections of essays, certainly bear out his sense that readers were not paying enough attention to his writing in the photography books. [47] Yet, like *Desert Solitaire*, both *Slickrock* and *Cactus Country* very effectively combined striking descriptions of the natural world with entertaining and interesting narratives of their author's experiences, for readers who took the trouble to read past the photographs. These two books also nicely complement each other, with *Slickrock* following up *Desert Solitaire* as a celebration of the beautiful redrock canyon country of southeastern Utah and northern Arizona, and *Cactus Country* extending Abbey's geographical range southward into the desert regions to which he would devote so much of his subsequent life and writings.

"I remember Abbey," Mitchell noted in his introduction to *Slickrock*, "in a sandstone window overlooking a maze of canyons that wind off toward the deep gorge of the Colorado River. He was chewing on a blade of grass and the sombrero was low again in observance of sundown. *Just like Abbey*." He added that "darkness was coming on fast. Time to return to camp. Abbey removed the hat and, holding it level, slowly extended his arm toward the big river. Though it struck me as an unusual gesture, it was at once natural and moving. Abbey, saluting the slickrock with that silly sombrero, reaching out to bless the stark chiseled bounties of that wild beyond."[48]

When he wrote his chapters for *Slickrock* during 1970–71, Abbey drew directly, as was his style, from his own experiences. "Days and Nights in Old Pariah," for example, described his August 1970 hike, with John De Puy and his wife Judith Colella, into the splendid Paria River Canyon near Bryce Canyon National Park, and his return trip there that fall with Tom Lyon. Judith persuaded Abbey to free a cow they found stuck in the canyon, after which he complained vociferously about these "hooved locusts" grazing everywhere on public lands—until she pointed out to the bemused Abbey his hypocrisy in ordering a steak the same night.[49] Abbey and Lyon "walked for three and a half days," as Abbey described their trek through many redrock wonders, "and came out at Lee's Ferry. We celebrated with a swim in the icy green Colorado River."[50]

Nevertheless, Abbey was interested in doing different kinds of writing. In 1969 he had brushed aside Jack Macrae's suggestion that he write a collection of essays like "Industrial Tourism" in *Desert Solitaire*, but in late August 1970 he drafted a strident, heavily documented attack on Glen Canyon Dam for *American Heritage*, which never published it, probably finding it too hot a potato for its pages. However, Abbey knew how to "write on," in the words of his advice to his students, persisting even with rejected work. And he was learning the value of an effective title. Mitchell noted that he had joked to his *Slickrock* collaborators in May 1970, "For the title, . . . how about *Help Stamp Out Rape*?"[51] On the manuscript of his unpublished article attacking Glen Canyon Dam, Abbey crossed out the subtitle "The Assault on the Canyonlands" and substituted "The Rape of the Canyon Country."[52] Five years later, he recycled this basic idea and title, dropping the footnotes, widening his critique into a livelier account, and matching the "rape" title to a periodical rather different from *American Heritage*: *Playboy*, in his December 1975 article "The Second Rape of the West," which was subsequently reprinted in *The Journey Home*. Thus, an offhand remark in the canyon country in 1970 gradually worked its way into the title of a highly remunerative article for a large male readership. One of those readers was his own father, Paul Abbey. He asked for a copy of the magazine in a bookstore back home in Indiana, Pennsylvania, telling the clerk that he wanted it not for the pictures but for his son's article. When she joked that he therefore wouldn't mind if she cut out the photographs, Paul replied, "Don't you dare."[53]

Ed Abbey had begun to develop ideas about gender issues that would get him into trouble later with feminists. In the fall of 1970, he drafted, for the University of Utah magazine the *Wasatch Front*, an essay that he called "Some Second Thoughts on Women's Lib." Too racy—like his *American Heritage* submission—it was not published, but again Abbey held onto its basic ideas, which appeared more than a decade later when he reviewed books by Gloria Steinem and Susan Brownmiller for the *Bloomsbury Review* in 1984, in an essay that reappeared as "The Future of Sex" in his last collection, *One Life at a Time, Please*, in 1988. Abbey's thesis remained essentially the same: he supported equal rights for women, but he felt that feminists did not take into account the fundamental biological distinctions between men and women, and he believed that *la différence* between the two genders was what made possible a liberated sexuality.

On December 15, 1973, from his trailer in Aravaipa Canyon in the outback of southern Arizona, Abbey dashed off a letter to "Mizz Magazine," mischievously addressed to "Dear Sirs," which he quoted in the introduction to *Abbey's Road* (1979), changing only the name of his actual rancher friend, Cliff Wood, in his mailed typescript, to the printed "Marvin Bundy":

> Some us menfolks here in Winkelman aint too happy with this here new magazine of yourn. Are old wimmin is trouble enuf to manage as is without you goldam New Yorkers sneaking a lot of downright subversive ideas into their hard heads. Out here a womin's place is in the kitchen, the barnyard and the bedroom in that exackt order and we dont need no changes. We got a place for men and we got a place for wimmin and there aint no call to get them mixed up. Like my neighbor Marvin Bundy says, he says "I seen men, I seen wimmin, I haint never seen one of them there persons. Least not in Pinal County." Thems my sentiments too. You ladies best stick to tatting doilies. Much obliged for your kind consideration, I am Yrs truly, Cactus Ed.[54]

In print he attributed the reply he got to Gloria Steinem, but it was actually written by Valerie Monroe on December 17, 1973: "Dear Cactus, Many thanks for your amusing and thorough expression of sentiments concerning *Ms.* and the Women's Movement. I'm pleased to learn that some Winkelman women are reading the magazine and becoming hard to manage as a result. Seems like it must be kind of boring out there with everybody in his or her place, especially if it's in your kitchens, barnyards or bedrooms. . . . P.S. I ain't never tatted a doily in my life."[55] Abbey gives the last word to *Ms.* here in *Abbey's Road*. He clearly enjoyed adopting the backward pose of "Cactus Ed"—and also being "crushed," as he put it, by their reply.[56] It appears that Valerie Monroe was also entertained by their exchange. Neither appears to have taken the other too seriously. The joke's the thing.

In the 1980s, Abbey would play to the hilt this role of the offensive curmudgeon. His readers might be surprised to learn how seriously he had approached these issues in 1970, in his unpublished "Some Second Thoughts on Women's Lib." For example, three years before Roe v. Wade, he declared that "a woman's womb is not the property of the State. . . . She must be mistress of all that's enclosed within her skin." He added that "full employment opportunity" for women was "long overdue." This father of two-year-old Susie, and companion of Ingrid, asserted that "girls should be encouraged from infancy on to see the whole world as a playground of potentiality," lamenting women's under-representation in most fields of endeavor, and that "no man who is really a man will feel his manhood demeaned or threatened by the act of washing dishes." He then parted company with several feminist tenets as he perceived them.[57] The progressive, pro-feminist sentiments in this essay would not fit conveniently into the backward, outrageous persona of Cactus Ed.

The essay that the *Wasatch Front* did publish was more somber: "Science with a Human Face." Here Abbey argued that neither science nor religion was really capable of understanding the mysteries of nature. He faulted the feel-good fads of "Zen, om, I Ching, and tarot," criticizing "the life weariness of Buddhism, the world negation of Hinduism, the doper's heaven of institutional Christianity."[58] This essay was drafted around the same time that he dashed off what would become an infamous note to Gary Snyder. On September 27, 1970, signing off from the North Rim but really writing from Logan, this former lecturer on Buddhism and Hinduism (in 1956 at the University of New Mexico) thanked Snyder for sending him his environmentalist manifesto "Four Changes," adding that "it's good sound doctrine (except for the Hindu-Zen bullshit)."[59] He subsequently made this line public by inserting a slightly exaggerated version of it in *Abbey's Road*, right before his letter to *Ms.*: "Long ago, returning a friendly greeting from the poet Gary Snyder, I wrote: 'Dear Gary, I admire your work too, except for all that Zen and Hindu bullshit.' One potentially lengthy correspondence craftily nipped in the bud."[60]

As with the "Dear Sirs" letter to "Mizz," Abbey meant to offend and entertain with his ostensible insult of Snyder—which was ironic not only because he himself had lectured on Hinduism fourteen years earlier but also because a decade later, during the 1980s, he remained fascinated with Zen Buddhism, according to John De Puy.[61] On July 26, 1972, he noted in his journal at Aravapai, "Gary Snyder don't write to me no more since I noted the 'Hindu-Zen bullshit' in his poetry."[62] After sending Annie Dillard a long letter in January 1984 that he described as "five pages of single-spaced sulfurous fulminations," he similarly concluded that it "should be sufficient to stifle *that* correspondence in its cradle."[63]

Actually, neither Snyder nor Dillard—both of whom remained, like Wendell Berry, long-distance friends whom Abbey never actually met in person—were offended. Snyder knew that Abbey was kidding and that there was no substance in his wisecrack, and when he wrote his own "Letter to Ed Abbey" for the 1985 collection honoring him, *Resist Much, Obey Little*, he began by noting that "the reason that we never had further correspondence (I guess) was not—as you suggest in the book—because of any comments about Buddhism, but just because it didn't happen." He disagreed with Abbey's view of Eastern religions but concluded, "I hope you consider me in your boat as I consider you in my boat, and hope we can walk some ridge or canyon together somewhere sometime."[64] Later he added that "arguing with Ed was fun, and of course we both knew we were really brothers at heart."[65] As for Abbey's letter to Dillard, one of several cordial exchanges, it concluded with best wishes for her forthcoming baby and an invitation to take her out to dinner if she ever came to Tucson.[66]

In mid-December 1970, Abbey successfully completed his semester as Writer in Residence at the University of Utah. His career as an author had picked up considerably by then, but his personal life remained as scattered as ever. *Life* magazine commissioned him to go to Israel to write about the effects of warfare on the desert there, and he made it as far as New York City, with Ingrid, in January 1971, but then returned to the Southwest rather than take the overseas trip. He visited Susie at her grandmother's in New Jersey and vowed to bring her back to rejoin him and Ingrid at the North Rim that summer.

By the end of February, Abbey was writing in his journal at Kanab, Utah, north of the North Rim, declaring on February 28 that it was "time to be thinkin' of work, man. Time for the Wild bunch to ride again, the wooden shoe mob, THE MONKEY WRENCH GANG! Strikes! Again!" (229). On March 9 he added that he wanted to "be good to my good Ingrid" (230), clarifying that he had called off the Israel trip and postponed another, to Australia, for *Audubon*, instead agreeing to travel to Yosemite at Easter to write a different article for *Life*. He also worked on *Slickrock*.

In the remote North Rim country, Abbey made a new friend, one who would join John De Puy as one of his closest comrades during the rest of his life: Jack Loeffler. De Puy had suggested to Loeffler that he should meet Abbey because they shared common interests. Loeffler visited him near the North Rim, in the winter of 1971, while traveling in the area with some friends.[67] The two came from similar backgrounds: Loeffler had grown up in West Virginia, not far from Abbey's Appalachian end of western Pennsylvania. He was a gregarious man with a booming laugh, and his upbeat personality provided a helpful antidote to Abbey's inward, brooding nature. As with Ken Sleight and his opposition to the Glen Canyon Dam, Abbey was drawn to Loeffler because of his politics. In 1970 Loeffler had founded the Black Mesa Defense Fund in Santa Fe, where he lived, in opposition to the Peabody Coal Company's strip-mining project in the Navajo region of Black Mesa, in northern Arizona. He reminisced that "Ed and I spent a lot of time out there just poking around and thinking dire thoughts with regard to it all. We both found this destruction (of Black Mesa) disgusting and it was largely over this issue that Ed and I became friends."[68]

Soon Dave Foreman, the future founder of Earth First!, was stuffing envelopes in the Black Mesa Defense Fund office in Santa Fe—and Abbey was gathering more ideas for *The Monkey Wrench Gang*. Loeffler described an occasion during this period "when we got to the bridge that crosses above Lee's Ferry and Marble Canyon," near the Glen Canyon Dam, "and we got out of our truck and went over and knelt and prayed for an earthquake, hoping that the dam would collapse. I think maybe that was the last vestige of that particular form of religiosity that either one of us ever experienced, because nothing happened!"[69] More pragmatically, with the encouragement of Loeffler and his Black Mesa Defense Fund, on May 28, 1971, Abbey read a statement at a Senate Interior Affairs Committee hearing at Page, Arizona, about power plants in that region. Endorsing the opposition to the plants by the Hopi and Navajo tribes and several conservation organizations, he sternly remarked that "strip mining, in particular, is a plague which blights everything it touches, as I well know, for I was born and raised in Appalachia." Noting that the threatened lands were tribal and public, he concluded that "we cannot have both wilderness and industrial development; the two are absolutely incompatible."[70] Reading the testimony of Hopi elders into the microphone, Loeffler was so drained by the hearing that, when he was finished, he collapsed—and had to be picked up by Abbey. By 1972 the Black Mesa Defense Fund had "quietly expired"[71]—only to be revived three years later, in fictional form, in *The Monkey Wrench Gang*.

Meanwhile, Abbey's spring 1971 visit to Yosemite for *Life* led to "The Park That Caught Urban Blight" in its September 3 issue, an article that *Life* cut quite a bit; Abbey returned to his fuller, April 14, 1971, typescript[72] when this essay reappeared in *The Journey Home* as "Return to Yosemite: Tree

Fuzz vs. Freaks." He recounted the July 1969 "battle of Stoneman Meadow," when park rangers and hippies fought over an Independence Day weekend encampment in the valley. Ever since Chief Tenaya and his tribe had been driven out in 1851, Yosemite Valley had become entirely too crowded, in Abbey's view, especially because of its jam-packed road, with rangers therefore required to focus on law enforcement. Ahead of his time, he noted that "sometime in the future the Park Service hopes to ban all private automobiles from Yosemite Valley, substitute a clean quiet nonpolluting mass transit system. They'll need it." He concluded that, in the case of this once "holy place," the best thing to do was to *"keep it like it was."* [73]

On May 10, 1971, Abbey returned to his North Rim fire tower, joined once again by Ingrid and Susie. He was also visited later that month by his father. On May 26, Ed noted that Paul had spent a week with him, hiking the Grand Canyon together, rim to rim. He looked "awful in the face, ravaged and gaunt, sunken eyes, yellowish complexion." Yet he seemed to be still in good shape, hiking the epic trails "happy and whistling and never faltered, in fact walked almost as fast as I would have walked, though he stopped much more often" (230). His son added, "I love him—but I can't bear to live with him day by day. . . . Sunday morning, his last day here, he walked up the trail-road to say good-by: 'I don't approve of everything you say and do, Ned,' he said (he did not approve of *Black Sun*, naturally), 'But I love you anyway.' We embraced. 'I love you too, Dad.'" Paul walked away, looking "quite handsome then, in his big coat and silver-gray Stetson and his white hair" (231).

Also that month, Katie Lee visited Abbey, leaving behind with him the manuscript of a novel that she had written about Glen Canyon, which he volunteered to read. Later that summer, he wrote her with advice that she did not want to hear then but would eventually follow, much later, in the form of her nonfictional book *All My Rivers Are Gone* (1998): "I agree with your agent. Rewrite the book as a straightforward autobiography. Why? Because the truth in this case is more interesting than your fictional version." [74] Abbey had become a generous reader and astute critic.

At the North Rim, Abbey was delighted to be reunited with Susie, whom he found to be "a sheer delight," and with Ingrid, "the best so far." His happiness did not last long, however. On May 19 he lamented "sad and bitter quarrels with Ingrid. She's been brooding over all the wrongs I've done her over the past year. But—she hasn't left me (completely) yet. . . . Of course I have a couple of other lady-friends waiting in the wings (Boston, Berkeley). But none so beautiful and young and wise and witty as my Ingrid. . . . What to do? The old dilemma" (230).

The assertive Ingrid determined what to do: she left him. His offer to marry her had only made matters worse, because it forced her to make a decision about their relationship. She felt that Abbey had always neglected Josh and Aaron, his two sons from his marriage to Rita, which still complicated his life. And she was convinced that he had no realistic sense of how to take care of Susie, with no permanent job, no health insurance, and no way to carry on a romantic relationship while he attempted to provide childcare from a lookout tower. As for Susie's time at the North Rim, she would remember only an unpleasant diet of wheat germ for breakfast every morning[75] and her father retrieving her in the forest after she had wandered off.

On June 9, Abbey was despondent, returning to his cabin to find Ingrid gone, with only a note left behind, as he bemoaned the next day, quoting what she had written: "Where was my Ingrid last night? Sick with longing and anxiety, I searched for her for an hour. Oh where? 'I loved you so much. . . . I will miss you for a long time.'" At the same time, his self-confessed lust was turning to even younger females; he admitted right after recording Ingrid's departure that, on June 4, he had given a graduation speech in Aspen, Colorado, and was overwhelmed by "lovely girls in minimal skirts. Maddening lust! . . . No wonder dear sweet Ingrid has given up on me" (231). His prepared remarks to these Aspen students were not the usual graduation pieties: "So you're finally getting out of high school? . . . *Free At Last!* . . . Public education is basically a penal institution. . . . Console yourselves with this thought, however: much as you have suffered, your teachers have suffered even more."[76]

During a Sierra Club speech the following year in Phoenix, the forty-five-year-old Abbey would gaze into the audience to find himself riveted by a beautiful, tall, willowy, sixteen-year-old student, Renée Downing. He introduced himself afterward, got her phone number, and began sending her love poems.[77] Thus would begin his next major relationship—with a woman three decades younger than him. In June 1971, however, he was crushed by Ingrid's departure. After adding (perhaps later) some bitter, dismissive remarks about her, he wrote nothing in his journal for exactly one year, until June 10, 1972, when his new job at Aravaipa Canyon, amid solitary beauty, provoked him to write again (231). Over time he and Ingrid, who eventually settled in her native New York City, enjoyed a strong friendship, one always tinged by both their previous happiness together and the bitterness of their breakup.

Abbey's fire-tower appointment at the North Rim was good until September 1, but he resigned in mid-summer, on July 24.[78] Though she had split up with him, Ingrid remained nearby (but estranged) that summer, working as a park ranger at the North Rim. Feeling unable to take care of Susie by himself, Abbey had sent his daughter back to her grandmother. Now he wanted to get away from even his beloved North Rim. Appropriately enough, this was not only his last season there but the last year for the fire tower itself, which was closed in 1972. In "Fire Lookout," Abbey claimed that "one day somebody in Park headquarters, down on the South Rim of the Canyon, the bad rim, said to somebody else, 'Do we really need a fire lookout on North Rim?' And the other man said, 'I didn't know we had one.' The lookout was closed at the end of my fourth season and has never been used since."[79]

Abbey was now ready for new adventures and, more than ever before, felt that he could begin to make a living from his writing. In the case of *Cactus Country* for Time-Life Books, as he had asked himself on May 18, "$20,000 for 40,000 words? How could I say no?"[80] He therefore "again postponed the FAT MASTERPIECE," as he had now begun to call the novel that would eventually become *The Fool's Progress*, "for another year" in order to work on *Cactus Country* and various invited articles. At the same time, he was bemused to receive a letter from a librarian at Boston University indicating that they wanted to start an Abbey collection in the Mugar Memorial Library;[81] although it did not materialize, with Abbey agreeing in 1974 to donate his papers to the University of Arizona instead, this invitation certainly intimated to the forty-four-year-old author that his work was deemed to be of lasting significance.

In July 1971, Abbey got as far away from his breakup with Ingrid as he possibly could: he took a trip to Australia commissioned by *Audubon*. As long before as 1952, he had fantasized about going there (25–26). Quickly enamored of this huge country with lots of wilderness and comparatively few people, he would return there again in 1976 and express interest in writing a book about it as late as March 1987.[82] Flying via San Francisco and Honolulu to Brisbane, and then walking around that city, Abbey nevertheless felt that he might as well be back in the United States. And when he learned about how the Great Barrier Reef and some of Australia's other wonders were threatened by industrial pollution, he advised the readers of the January 1972 *Audubon* (and, later, *Abbey's Road*) that "the forces that are fouling up America are hard at work in Australia too." But he loved what he saw of this continent's unspoiled interior and the folksy personalities and speech of the rural people he met: "Australia seemed to me not so much another country as my own country in another time."[83]

Back in the Southwest, Abbey made a trip to Las Vegas, in August, to visit his sons—and a showgirl named Rose whom he had met a few months earlier at the Grand Canyon. In the early fall he visited Ingrid in Germany, where she lived for a while in Berlin, and where Abbey stayed just long enough to get mugged. Then he looked up an old girlfriend in England, in his first (and only) return trip there since his Fulbright term twenty years earlier. By mid-

October he was in Tucson, the city to which he had been wanting to return. He was making enough money from *Desert Solitaire* and from magazine articles that he felt able, for the first time in his life, to buy a house, in Esperero Canyon, northeast of the city (addressed at that time as 274 Sabino Canyon Road, though it was on a side dirt lane off that main road).[84]

This was the most striking house Abbey ever lived in. It was built from stone, with jagged, unusual angles in unity with the stone bluff atop which it stood rather than in keeping with conventional architecture. The stone house was a bargain in 1971, before the development of this area (which eventually became a gated community). Abbey planted Malcolm Brown's memorial to Judy behind this house, which served as his home base until June 1974.[85] His friend Linda Newmark happened to visit him there on one occasion just after three-year-old Susie had left with her grandmother. Having not known that he had a daughter, Linda asked him about her, and Abbey ended up in tears as he told of how he had loved Judy and felt unable to take proper care of Susie.

Abbey enjoyed the beautiful vistas of the Santa Catalina Mountains, just above him to the north, and the city of Tucson in the distance to the southwest. However, he had a sure instinct for what was coming. One evening in early 1972, as Linda and Sandy Newmark sat with him at the house after dinner, he told them that he would have to move soon, since the beautiful valley into which they were gazing would be filled with houses, stretching from Tucson to Esperero Canyon.[86] The Newmarks did not believe him, but Abbey insisted that he was right—and he was, as a drive up today's congested Sabino Canyon Road quickly illustrates.

In the early 1970s, however, the stone house was isolated enough that Abbey could stand outside and urinate in peace—as his friend Dick Felger once observed him doing from the roof of the house, after Abbey called out to him when he was driving by.[87] This was Abbey's privacy test; when outdoors urination was no longer feasible, it was time to move on. He told Sandy Newmark that "if you can't pee in your own front yard, you live too close to the city."[88] Like hiking and wandering the country, this was a paternal family tradition. Abbey had urinated off the South Rim of the Grand Canyon upon first arriving there in 1944, and on May 1, 1982, his father, on one of his many treks westward, would be fined in Oklahoma for public urination after failing to locate a restroom in a small town and getting arrested in a back alley. Paul Abbey then continued to Gallup, New Mexico, where he borrowed money from Ernie Bulow—and rather than go on to Tucson to visit his son, he turned around and drove all the way home to Pennsylvania,[89] where in his inimitable fashion he dashed off an angry, four-page letter to the governor of Oklahoma.[90]

During the first few months of 1972, Sandy Newmark stayed in the little guest apartment attached to the stone house—until Abbey encouraged him to leave, describing himself as a misanthrope and loner who could not bear to spend too much time even with his closest friends. Yet Abbey also hosted some wild parties at the stone house. On one occasion, he came home and, like Goldilocks, found Sandy and Linda Newmark sleeping in his bed.[91] At another gathering early that year, Ed, Sandy, and John De Puy (who was living in nearby Vail) ended up dancing drunkenly all over the house to the accompaniment of Indian drum music on the stereo—and to the horror of some staid visiting Sierra Club officials. Abbey perpetuated his irreverent attitude to the Sierra Club, delivering "insolent remarks" to their meeting in Phoenix on March 11.[92]

As much as Abbey felt that he was a loner, he enjoyed the friendships that both Esperero Canyon and Tucson offered. The canyon was a place for alternative lifestyles. The Newmarks built a geodesic dome—to the consternation of Abbey, who viewed Buckminster Fuller as a misguided technocrat. Dick Felger was an ethnobotanist who accompanied Abbey "Down to the Sea of Cortez," as he described the trip in *Cactus Country*. Andrew Weil, who eventually became the most famous resident of the area as a proponent of New Age medicine, lived at that time in another "of the old rock houses at the mouth of Esperero Canyon," and he remembered Abbey as "a seldom seen but valued member of our informal community."[93] "Loner" though he might often have been, Abbey fit in well enough. His review of Stewart Brand's countercultural *Last Whole Earth Catalog* in the November 1971 issue of *Natural History* seemed an appropriate contribution for a member of the Esperero community.

He also enjoyed spending time in the liberal, progressive city of Tucson with such friends as William Eastlake, who had moved to southern Arizona from New Mexico, and with other personal and publishing friends who now found Abbey living near a relatively major airport for the first time in years. Jack Macrae and his wife would see Abbey in 1974 at Eastlake's. The four of them played a wild game of doubles on an old tennis court that culminated in Eastlake's collapse when he lunged for a shot and his toupee fell off, while Abbey laughed hysterically.[94] At the end of April 1973, Ingrid, then working for Sierra Club Books, visited him at the stone house. Reading his journals, which Abbey had once promised to her, Ingrid was irritated to find herself included in a list of women that he had compiled.

Indeed, he continued to enjoy the company not only of friends but also of a series of women who visited him at the stone house.[95] During 1971–72 he was involved with an infatuated Tucson English teacher, until she realized that Abbey was simply exploiting her infatuation.[96] On June 10, 1973, exactly two years after he had stopped writing in his journal when Ingrid left him, Abbey bragged in those pages that he enjoyed "amazing success" with women.

"I could pick up a new one every week if I wished. But I don't; too much bother." He told himself that, after a year, he was still "largely pleased with my darling Janet," a woman who stayed off and on with him at the stone house. "And Renée—my 'Natasha,' my 'Sandy,' my forbidden delight" (233). As usual, his relationship with Janet did not prevent him from beginning others and from mailing a plane ticket to Ingrid with a note saying "Don't tell Janet." In July 1973 he wrote of "Susan G." and the "violence of her passion! She came so hard and so fast and so often, I could hardly come myself. . . . Women *are* better than men. I ought to know" (234). And he had begun his practice of picking up women on the lecture circuit, at Colorado State University that same month, for example.

Abbey was also happy because he was getting a lot of writing done. Remarking to Sandy Newmark that he was well paid for his articles, he worked hard during the daytime, relaxing with drinks only later. He finished *Cactus Country* and wrote some of *The Monkey Wrench Gang* at the stone house. *Cactus Country* begins "on the terrace of this old stone house above Tucson in the foothills of Arizona's Santa Catalina Mountains," as he thinks "about the deserts I have known" while "the city glitters softly, 10 miles down and away, under its tender veil of smog. Airplanes like fireflies circle slowly through the twilight."[97] As early as September 20, 1972, Abbey complained testily to the *Arizona Daily Star* about police helicopters buzzing Esperero Canyon.[98] But in *Cactus Country* he expressed appreciation of the view of "moonrise over the Rincon Mountains, beyond a shore of clouds. Great gory sunset in the west, behind the jagged pinnacles of the Tucson Mountains."[99] He also described his hike up Baboquivari—the Native American "Sacred Peak," as he entitled his chapter describing it, southwest of Tucson—that he enjoyed exploring with John De Puy, and which remained a beloved place for him.

Moreover, life was also looking up because, in the spring of 1972, Abbey was hired by the Defenders of Wildlife as caretaker of their new Whittell Nature Preserve at Aravaipa Canyon. This appeared to be his dream job, because like his federal ranger and lookout positions, it offered plenty of time to write in a beautiful wilderness setting, yet it was also an ongoing, year-round appointment that allowed him a great deal of freedom. On June 10 he noted that he was the "manager" or "coordinating custodian" of the new Aravaipa preserve, "forty-thousand acres of rugged canyon and mountain country. I should be happy as a pig in shit. And I am" (213). He also had plenty of time to read. Early the next year he was bitten by an Aravaipa scorpion while reading *Gravity's Rainbow*, but the same writer who had echoed Robinson Jeffers by declaring in *Desert Solitaire* that he would "rather kill a *man* than a snake" calmly killed the scorpion and continued with Pynchon's book.[100] He finished

it in the summer of 1973 while helping Jack Loeffler build his house in Santa
Fe, where he "snapped the book shut, and said, 'There. I finished it. Someone
had to do it. Now you do it.' He handed me the book, rolled over in his sleeping
bag and went to sleep."[101]

Within southern Arizona, Aravaipa Creek is unusual: it runs all year
in a deep, beautiful canyon through which javelina, deer, and even mountain
lions roam. For years this canyon had been a favorite site for hunters, but, beginning in the late 1960s, the Defenders of Wildlife, headed by the wealthy animal rights activist Ted Steele and represented by Tucson attorney Lou Barassi,
began to buy ranchlands at both the western and eastern ends of the canyon,
thus sealing off and protecting the canyon itself. They offered ranchers such as
Cliff Wood, who became Abbey's good friend, the opportunity to live out the
rest of their lives on their ranches if they would sell to the Defenders.[102]

Abbey was hired largely to patrol the canyon and make sure that
hunters stayed out. He soon decided to share the job and its $10,000 salary with
his friend Doug Peacock[103] so that he would not be tied down to his post, remaining free to spend time in Tucson and elsewhere. When Loeffler showed
up at Abbey's Aravaipa trailer one day, he found him feverishly working on *The
Monkey Wrench Gang*. Abbey snatched off his reading glasses, which seemed
to embarrass him, drank two beers with his friend, announced that he was
leaving, asked him to look after things, abruptly departed, and was gone for a
week.[104] During 1973, Abbey managed a two-week vacation in August to Telluride, Colorado, and an October trip back east, to New York City, where he
visited friends and publishing contacts, and then home to Pennsylvania, where
he was depressed by the inertia and aging of his relatives.[105]

During 1972–74, Peacock often stayed with Abbey both at his Tucson stone house and in the ranger trailer that the Defenders soon installed at the
west end of Aravaipa Canyon. Abbey commuted back and forth between the
two places, also often hosting his daughter and women such as Janet and Renée.
Peacock is best known as the model for Hayduke in *The Monkey Wrench Gang*,
but a version of him also appears in *The Fool's Progress*, where a Vietnam veteran named Lacey transplants the engine of a hunter's high-powered truck into
Henry Lightcap's old pickup after hunters have forced their way, at gunpoint,
past Lacey and Lightcap to gain entry into the canyon.[106]

Peacock and Abbey remained close friends, wilderness explorers,
and eco-warriors, but their friendship was often a tense one. Concerning their
escapades with women, Peacock claimed that "he was right at the door when I'd
break up with a girlfriend; and once he moved in a little too soon, so I threw him
around the backyard. It cost him 60 bucks in chiropractic readjustments."[107] As
late as January 1988, while hiking through their beloved Cabeza Prieta wilder-

ness, Abbey summarized the nature of their friendship: "Doug is like a brother. And maybe that's why, most of the time, I can't stand him. He's too much like me to love" (338).

Abbey also wrote some vivid essays about Aravaipa Canyon. A straightforward source for the hunting episode in *The Fool's Progress*, "Trouble on the Old Preserve" was written in December 1973 for the newsletter of the Defenders of Wildlife. This essay was not reprinted in any of his books, but it outlines confrontations between hunters and patrolmen very similar to that episode in *The Fool's Progress*.[108] Abbey also noted that he had once been a hunter himself, until the early 1960s. It is clear that working in close quarters against "sport" hunters at Aravaipa solidified his change of heart and mind.

In both *Cactus Country*—completed while he was patrolling the canyon—and his later essay "Blood Sport," Abbey made a strong distinction between hunting out of necessity and hunting for sport.[109] First written as a foreword to Vance Bourjaily's book about hunting, *The Unnatural Enemy* (1984), "Blood Sport" focused on Paul Abbey, who was "a hunter—not a sportsman," during the Depression. "He hunted for a purpose: to put meat on the table." A crack shot, he killed his deer just before "opening day" because "he believed, as most country men did, that fear tainted the meat and therefore it was better to get your deer before the chase." Actually, Paul seldom ever hunted deer, preferring smaller game such as rabbits and pheasants.[110] When times got better, he gave up hunting altogether, explaining that "we don't need the meat any more." His son remembered his example, many years later, when thinking about how he too had stopped hunting, though in truth Ed Abbey had hardly ever hunted to begin with. He ends this striking essay with a description of his father asking him to hold a light to help "still hunt" deer at night. "'Yes, sir,' I whisper back. 'Sure will, paw.'"[111]

"Aravaipa Canyon" in *Down the River* describes this twelve-mile-long canyon whose name comes from an apt Native American word meaning "laughing waters."[112] It also focuses on Abbey's only encounter with a mountain lion, which is described still more memorably at the end of "Freedom and Wilderness, Wilderness and Freedom." In that essay, he characteristically moves from polemic to narrative in order to illustrate how people need wilderness in order to be free: "Let me tell you a story"—the story of how he followed the big cat at Aravaipa, feeling a healthy fear but also an affection and a "crazy desire to communicate, to make some kind of emotional, even physical contact with the animal." He concludes that "I want my children to have the opportunity for that kind of experience."[113] As he had already highlighted in his March 1970 *Life* article, "Let Us Now Praise Mountain Lions" (before he had ever seen one), why would anyone ever want to kill such a rare, beautiful animal?

Abbey attacked Arizona hunters more satirically in his two essays "The Great Globe Arizona Wild Pig and Varmint Hunt" and "Sportsmen." Originally solicited by *Sports Illustrated* but never published there, appearing instead in *The Journey Home*, his Globe essay exposed the annual "Javelina Derby" in which the town's chamber of commerce gave out prizes for dead javelinas. "Sportsmen" was written in the form of advice for sports hunters about how to kill endangered species—"How to Use Your SIRENIA Wildlife Caller"—which he asserted were "verbatim excerpts from an anonymous printed leaflet found on a dirt road in central Arizona." [114]

As different as the profound, impressive "Freedom and Wilderness" is from the light, unimpressive "Sportsmen," both essays well illustrate Abbey's resilience in revising and recycling his work. The two-part title "Freedom and Wilderness, Wilderness and Freedom" in *The Journey Home* (1977) reflects the origins of this essay in two separate pieces written four years apart: his 1972 *New York Times* article "On the Need for a Wilderness to Get Lost In," to which he then added the 1976 "Wilderness and Freedom" from *Not Man Apart*, wherein he told his Aravaipa mountain lion story, noting that it was "drawn from a speech he gave at the 'Wilderness and Freedom' conference in Oregon last March." [115] "Sportsmen" was drafted in 1975 but not published until it appeared as the last item in Abbey's final collection of essays, *One Life at a Time, Please* (1988). [116] Although some essays moved fairly expeditiously from magazines into his books, these two illustrate how drawn-out that process sometimes became, with Abbey determined nonetheless to "write on."

A further excellent instance of such a process is Abbey's essay "The Great American Desert" in *The Journey Home*. *Desert Solitaire* had established Abbey as a "desert expert." His work was now solicited, as in the case of two of his 1973 publications: *Cactus Country* and "The Southwest: A Thirst for the Desert." The latter was an essay that appeared in the National Geographic Society's *Wilderness USA* and is very similar to "The Great American Desert," which was solicited by Ingrid Eisenstadter in the same year for a Sierra Club hiking "totebook." That book, Peggy Larson's *Sierra Club Naturalist's Guide to the Deserts of the Southwest*, was finally published in 1977, with a version of "The Great American Desert" as its foreword—at about the same time that this essay also appeared in *The Journey Home*. As with several of the chapters in *Desert Solitaire*, "The Great American Desert" was then reprinted *after* its book appearance, at least three times, in *Reader's Digest, Mariah*, and *Sierra*. Such republication not only brought in more money but also attracted more attention—and controversy, such as when a geologist published a letter in *Mariah* protesting Abbey's recommendation that hikers remove all mining claim stakes. [117]

Another essay set at Aravaipa nicely synthesizes Abbey's light-hearted and serious moods: "Merry Christmas, Pigs!" Originally published three days before Christmas 1973 in the *Tucson Daily Citizen*, this article tells of being surrounded that month at Aravaipa by a herd of javelina that made their typical snuffling noises while they chomped on prickly pear cacti. Abbey stood nearby, fascinated if nervous, as he had been with the mountain lion. "Some of those little fifty-pound beasts carry tusks and have been known to charge a full-grown man right up the hairy trunk of a saguaro cactus." They finally parted company on good terms: the javelinas "had the whole east slope of Brandenburg Mountain to ramble over," and Abbey returned to his trailer, "where I keep my bearskin and this neurotic typewriter with a mind of its own." The essay closes by wishing them well: "Happy Christmas, brother and sister. Long live the weeds and the wilderness. Merry New Year, pigs!" [118]

Abbey loved living at Aravaipa, where he had two horses and a straw-berry garden and enjoyed the company of Susie as well as Janet and then Renée. When University of Arizona librarian Lawrence Clark Powell visited him there for an interview, Abbey explained that *Cactus Country* was a less angry book than *Desert Solitaire* "because there is less to be angry about in southwestern Arizona." Powell felt that "he looks more the lover of *Black Sun* than the an-archist of *Desert Solitaire*." [119] Abbey wrote that this was the longest he "held a steady job" since he had left the U.S. Army in 1947 (233).

In *The Fool's Progress*, Henry Lightcap quits his canyon caretaker position after refusing to cooperate in restocking part of the preserve with cattle. On May 30, 1974, Abbey made note of his termination from his job at the Aravaipa preserve after having fallen "out of favor with Steele" (237). According to Lou Barassi, Ted Steele had hired Abbey because he admired his writings and, as a gay man, was possibly even attracted to him. But now he had heard about a photo of Steele that Abbey had tacked up on his trailer wall, with the caption "Bah, humbug!" It was Merry Christmas, pigs, but not Merry Christmas, Ted Steele. Barassi was given the job of firing Abbey. When Abbey asked him why, Barassi told him about the photo.[120]

Abbey had already gotten himself in trouble after people in the area complained about him skinny-dipping in Aravaipa Creek [121] and because of his controversial letters to the editor. On June 13, 1973, he published a letter in the *Arizona Daily Star* in Tucson arguing that the return of American prisoners of war was nothing to celebrate in view of how disgraceful the Vietnam War had been.[122] This letter also appeared in the San Manuel *Miner*, close to Aravaipa, in the heart of conservative mining and hunting country. Barassi's phone "rang for two days" with a series of angry calls from people in the area whose cooperation the Defenders of Wildlife needed, provoking Steele to view Abbey as a liability.[123]

Meanwhile, Abbey's romantic life had taken a pronounced turn. On November 17, 1973, he wrote of a "nasty scene with Janet. I'm afraid it's all over with us," noting at the same time that Renée had "grown up at last—eighteen a week ago!" (235). Chuck and Carol Downing, Renée's parents, were actually slightly younger than Abbey. Shortly after she turned eighteen, Renée announced to her parents that she was getting married to Abbey. On December 30, 1973, the forty-seven-year-old Abbey "married once again and—I swear—for the final time." He added that Renée had been "sixteen when I met and fell in love with her" (237). With the Downings standing uncomfortably nearby, the event was held in a picnic area at the foot of the Rincon Mountains just outside Tucson, in the eastern branch of Saguaro National Monument, with the help of Abbey's old friend Hal Coss, a ranger there. It was followed by a raucous party at the nearby Webb Steak House.[124]

Having lost his Aravaipa job, Abbey decided that it was time for a change of scenery, so in late June 1974, he and Renée moved to Moab, which would remain their home base for the next four years. Such migration back and forth between cactus country and canyon country remained his pattern for the rest of his life. Neither marriage nor a new home, however, meant that Abbey would settle down—far from it.

CHAPTER SEVEN

The Bard of Moab

1974–1978

During the mid to late 1970s, Ed Abbey attracted new fame and notoriety as author of *The Monkey Wrench Gang* (1975), the book in which he successfully synthesized his serious politics, his comic fiction-writing abilities, and his friendships. The notion that politics is personal had grown out of such movements as feminism and Black Power—thus developed in contexts quite different from Abbey's point of view—but he made politics personal in his own inimitable way. *The Monkey Wrench Gang* was a very timely book. In the years following its appearance, it was read by a great many people, some of whom were wilderness activists becoming increasingly disenchanted with mainstream politics and looking for new kinds of environmental activism. Dave Foreman, who had not yet met Abbey but whose activism had been spurred, beginning in 1971, by his work in Santa Fe for the Black Mesa Defense Fund[1] (begun by Jack Loeffler), would go to Washington in the late 1970s as a lobbyist for the Wilderness Society. But there he would find himself frustrated by how comparatively few acres of western wilderness were designated for protection by such conventional legislative measures as RARE II, the U.S. Forest Service's Roadless Area Review and Evaluation project. Having read *Desert Solitaire* and *The Monkey Wrench Gang* with escalating admiration for Abbey and anger against business as usual, by 1980 Foreman would resign his Wilderness Society job and begin Earth First!, a radical action group inspired by Abbey's books.

For Abbey himself, *The Monkey Wrench Gang* not only articulated his politics and brought him heightened attention as a writer but also turned him into a cult figure in ways that had significant effects on his personal life. Having lost his Aravaipa ranger job, he retreated to the scenic and congenial Utah town of Moab. He attempted domestic home life with his new, very young wife, Renée, but was soon easily distracted by other women who had read his books and were eager to know their author. Once again, Abbey's writings built a politicized public persona for him, while behind this persona was a man much more interested in his own private life of friendships and sexual relationships, which proceeded from happiness to difficulty and disaster.

At first, though, life in Moab was great. Abbey felt comfortable there because he loved the canyon country and because he already had a number of friends in the area, dating from his 1956, 1957, and 1965 ranger seasons in the region and many other visits. Ken Sleight had moved to nearby Green River in 1969. In March 1974, Ed and Renée took a trip down the Rio Grande in Big Bend National Park with Sleight and a few friends. This trip culminated when Abbey traversed the last ten miles downriver by himself in an old, bashed-up canoe that they found, as Abbey recounted in "On the River Again" in *Abbey's Road*.[2] Afterward they took the canoe back to Green River and saved it as a memento—perhaps leaving some Mexicans stranded without their ferry.[3]

In the summer of 1974, he and Renée bought twenty acres near Green River for $3,000 (238)—a "watermelon and gopher ranch"—and he and Sleight acquired some additional ranchland nearby at Willow Bend. They socialized and played poker with Sleight's fellow river-runners in Green River, the Quist brothers, Bob and Clair. Abbey and Sleight liked the idea of getting back to the land, returning to farm settings like where they had grown up, but by November 1974 Abbey had decided that he had actually been "swindled" (244) for the land that he had earlier thought a bargain, and eventually he and Sleight had to sell their land because they both traveled too much to be able to take adequate care of it.

Abbey also joined a circle of newer friends in Moab during this period, including Bill Benge, whom he had met at the Needles area of Canyonlands National Park in the fall of 1971 and who became his attorney in Moab; Tom Arnold, whose "Volkswagen museum" he had first visited for repairs in

1972; Bob Greenspan, a musician who had journeyed to Aravaipa in April 1973 to meet him; and Roger Grette, a fellow wilderness wanderer who first encountered him in the company of John De Puy while hiking around Navajo Mountain, on the Utah-Arizona border, in May 1973. After settling in Moab, Ed and Renée also befriended Marilyn and Karilyn McElheney, twin sisters living nearby who dated (respectively) Greenspan and Grette, and whose phone Abbey regularly used because he did not want to have one himself; Jim Stiles, a park ranger, writer, and illustrator from Kentucky; Owen Severance, a crusty park worker and wilderness activist; Gil Preston, a doctor and part-time writer from the East who had fallen in love with the West; and (after her move there in March 1977) Laura Lee Houck, their next-door neighbor, who often baby-sat Susie.

Many of Abbey's friends in Moab, and later in Tucson, were the proud possessors of books that he gave them, both his own and others'; he read continually and delighted in sharing what he read. He remained attached enough to his Moab friends that he made a point of putting most of them into his books, even years after he had moved away from that town. For example, in *Desert Images* (1979) he described how Tom Arnold, who regularly flew him around the Southwest during the 1970s, let him steer his plane all the way to Las Vegas in 1978 while Arnold read *Playboy*.[4] In April 1979, Bob Greenspan was surprised to hear that he and his song "Big Tits, Braces, and Zits," which Abbey described as "a song of adolescent passion,"[5] were highlighted in that month's issue of *Penthouse*, and he rushed out to discover "In Defense of the Redneck." Abbey claimed that Greenspan had drunkenly insulted the police in "Glob" (Globe), Arizona, thereby shutting down the bar, but in fact Greenspan had never played in Globe; Abbey had heard him in Moab (where he did once swear at some rangers, in 1975, but the bar was not closed).

Greenspan—who reappears as "Singing Bob" in *Good News* (1980) —did not at all mind Abbey's poetic license, however, because the *Penthouse* article attracted a lot of gigs for him.[6] As for Abbey, he argued in his journal right after "In Defense of the Redneck" appeared that *Penthouse* and *Playboy* are sexist magazines because "they exploit men," and that the appearance of his article left him "nothing to do now but sit back and wait for the libel suits from the Ruins Bar, Antonio, Glob Chamber of Commerce—and goons layin' for me up on Aztec" (262).

Not all of Abbey's Moab contacts remained enamored of him. His poker compatriot Gil Preston, for example, reacted much less favorably to "In Defense of the Redneck" and to Abbey in general, viewing him as an overrated writer with significant psychological problems. He did not appreciate Abbey's characterization of the "Instant Redneck," who "migrates west, buys himself a hobby ranch, a pair of tight jeans, a snap-button shirt, one of those funny hats with the rolled brim like those the male models wear in cigarette ads, and a ninety-dollar pair of tooled leather boots. . . . Now in full cowboy costume, he buys his first pickup truck. . . . He buys a gun for the gun rack, pops the top from his first can of Coors, and roars off in all directions to tear up the back country and blast away at the wildlife. A real man at last. The Instant Redneck."[7] As Abbey himself suggested in the rest of this essay, in his background and lifestyle he himself had more in common with the "real" rednecks who often bitterly opposed his radical politics than with many of the nouveau environmentalists who agreed with him.[8]

Abbey did have some good platonic women friends in Moab: Laura Lee Houck and the McElheney sisters. An interesting example of how he transformed his friends into fictional characters is "Loralee Croissant" in *The Fool's Progress*, a San Francisco hippie with whom Henry Lightcap has an affair after she greets him with a banner hanging outside her apartment: "WELCOME, HENRY LIGHTCAP."[9] Abbey and Laura Lee never had any affair, though he expressed his interest and asked her about her old San Francisco days. In Moab she once hung out a butcher-paper banner saying "WELCOME HOME, KARILYN" for her friend after she had been away. During 1977–78, when Renée returned to Tucson to study at the University of Arizona, Laura Lee regularly took care of nine-year-old Susie when Ed was away, delighting in how clever she was with words and becoming almost her temporary surrogate mother.[10]

Abbey shared many good times with his new friends, such as a giddy outing in his van through the desert near Moab at breakneck speed in the company of Susie and Karilyn and Marilyn McElheney while they sang happily about "clear cool water."[11] Karilyn was immortalized in his essay "A Walk in the Park," in which he remembered Utah senator Frank Moss telling her, "Miss McElhenny [*sic*], you're much too pretty to be an environmentalist."[12] As for Marilyn, who had come to Utah in 1973 to work as the first female seasonal ranger at Natural Bridges, in his "Preliminary Notes" to *Down the River* Abbey fulfilled his promise to "put her and her dog in a book. Here they are."[13]

Abbey was regularly visited in Moab by his best out-of-town friends, such as John De Puy, Doug Peacock, and Jack Loeffler. Loeffler described coming through Moab with his mother and father, whom he was showing around the Four Corners region, and asking Abbey on the phone, "'Are you really older than your father-in-law?' 'It is true, you miserable bastard. I'll meet you at the La Vida Bar in fifteen minutes.'" "Brother Ed" and "Brother Jack" gave Loeffler's mother a beer-driven tour of the La Sal Mountains. Abbey then invited Loeffler on a camping trip to the Piceance Basin in northwestern Colorado, where he investigated an oil company development project. On that trip the two of them swore an oath to each other that neither would let the other die in a hospital.[14]

By this time Abbey and his beer-drinking friends had established the tradition of measuring mileage in six-packs, at the rate of one per hour per passenger: "It was considered a one six-pack trip from Santa Fe to Albuquerque," Loeffler explained, and "a two six-pack trip from Tucson to Phoenix."[15] The same practice was followed by Hayduke in *The Monkey Wrench Gang*: "He and his friends measured highway distances in per-capita six-packs of beer. L.A. to Phoenix, four six-packs; Tucson to Flagstaff, three six-packs."[16] And Abbey confounded environmentalist proprieties about "littering" by tossing his beer cans out the window onto roads he hated, such as the new paved road to the Bullfrog Marina at the Glen Canyon National Recreational Area.[17] As he explained in "The Second Rape of the West," "Of course I litter the public highway. Every chance I get. After all, it's not the beer cans that are ugly; it's the highway that is ugly."[18]

Upon first moving to Moab, Ed and Renée lived in an apartment on Main Street, where Abbey bumped into Roger Grette on June 28, 1974, and told him that they were settling in the area.[19] In September Abbey noted that they had "bought a crumbly old house" that summer, at 2240 Spanish Valley Road, "for $26,000" (238). In contrast to his previous, unusual stone house outside Tucson, this one was a much more conventional frame house with a picket fence and a metal barn behind it. But it afforded views just as dazzling as the ones in Esperero Canyon, off into the redrock vistas surrounding Moab.

Abbey expressed "vain useless regrets" about selling his "beautiful old stone house at Sabino—the only real-value property I ever owned" (238). He considered buying it back a year later, but with the Tucson area growing rapidly, its price had already doubled by then. Thus had begun the tug of war between the Utah canyon country and the Arizona cactus country that dominated the rest of Abbey's life. It was reflected in his writing—as in a satiric essay in which an angel descends from heaven and carries a redneck rancher on a wild flight above the countryside, revealing development projects that God wants him to stop. The voice of this narrator, called "Big Ed" in the first version, is similar to that of his December 1973 "Cactus Ed" letter to *Ms.* magazine. This essay first appeared in *Arizona* magazine in March 1974 (when Abbey was still working at Aravaipa) as "A State Plan from Upstairs: It May Have Come From God, Or a Sharp Blow on the Head." It opens with its narrator on horseback near Aravaipa Canyon, as if Abbey imagined what would happen if his rancher friend Cliff Wood were visited by God.

Subsequently, however, Abbey revised this piece as "God's Plan for the State of Utah: A Revelation," for a May 1975 reading in Salt Lake City, and subsequently published it in the *Mountain Gazette* in March 1977 and in *The Journey Home*. Here he substituted a Utah setting for Aravaipa in order to hit home to his new audience: "We're riding along the rimrock above Pucker Pass Canyon, me and this red dun horse, minding our own business and generally at peace with the world, such as it is."[20] Similarly, in "Dust: A Movie," a short impressionistic "script" describing the end of the world, he changed the setting from Wolf Hole, Arizona, in its original September 1975 *Not Man Apart* version to "Pariah," just across the line in Utah, in *The Journey Home*.[21] Both "God's Plan" and "Dust" show Abbey experimenting more with fantastic rather than realistic storylines, as he would do more extensively in his 1980 novel *Good News*, a futuristic Western that he began outlining in late 1975 and writing during 1976.

As Abbey declared in his essay "Come On In": "The canyon country of southern Utah and northern Arizona is something special. Something else. Something strange, marvelous, full of wonders. So far as I know there is no other region on earth much like it, or even remotely like it. Nowhere else have we this lucky combination of vast sedimentary rock formations exposed to a desert climate, of a great plateau carved by major rivers—the Green, the San Juan, the Colorado—into such a wonderland of form and color."[22] He loved both the canyons and the desert but preferred Utah in summer and Arizona in winter, as he never liked cold weather. By the mid-1980s he would summer in Moab and spend the rest of the year in Tucson, but in the mid-1970s he was not yet able to do that. By the fall of 1974 he wished he had stayed in Tucson, and on September 11 he wrote to William Eastlake in Tucson, "I need a tennis partner. Come back to Moab!"[23]

Abbey did find plenty of tennis partners in Moab, however: Roger Grette, who recorded in his diary their many tennis dates between 1975 and 1977; Ken Sleight, who remembered that Abbey regularly "took him to the cleaners" when they played; and Bill Benge, who recalled Abbey deliberately trying to hit cracks in the court with a shot he called the "crevasser," and Peacock once playing with them while taking frequent drinks from a canteen of bourbon strapped to his side.[24] Abbey also enjoyed regular poker sessions, often on Wednesday nights and frequently at "Tom Tom" Arnold's, involving Arnold's friend Rex Scharf and friends such as Grette, Severance, Greenspan, and Preston. Abbey would linger at the poker table, drinking and laconically exclaiming, "Baby needs new shoes!"[25]

For Susie Abbey, six years old in August 1974, this was the most stable phase of her otherwise scattered childhood with (and often without) her father. She went to school in Moab and settled in with Ed and Renée in the early, domestic phase of their marriage. Renée was trying some gourmet cooking and did her best to entertain their friends with fancy meals at their Spanish Valley house, though Ed preferred more basic fare, delighting in making hot dogs for Susie and his friends when Renée was out of town. Abbey would satirize this situation in *The Fool's Progress*: Henry's wife Elaine proudly shows him her latest concoction, "poached egg in aspic," and Henry thinks that it looks "like something out of a horse's hoof" and ends up flinging it into the chinaberry tree behind their house.[26]

Abbey's diet regularly included lots of grease and alcohol. On October 5, 1974, he admitted to himself that he was "drinking too much again: insulting cell tissues, all them brain cells rotting away, cirrhosis of the liver, kidney stones, the shakes — Jesus Christ! Gimme a drink!" (239). His Moab friends from this period maintained different opinions on the question of whether or not Abbey was an alcoholic. Those who felt that he was an alcoholic pointed to the regularity of his drinking and the fact that the physical problems he developed a few years later are typically linked to alcoholism. Those on the other side of the question noted that he limited his big drinking to occasional outings with friends; Renée said to one of them that, most of the time, Abbey didn't drink that much.[27] Of course, the fact that Abbey seldom gave the appearance of being drunk is itself typical of alcoholism, and we see here that he seemed aware of his problem but also unable to do much about it.

Ed and Renée did for a time settle into "domestic bliss." After a while Renée went to work at the Rim Rock flower shop, in the central part of town, spending a lot of time with her co-workers Marilyn and Karilyn McElheney and later Laura Lee Houck. Though at this point she was only a high school graduate, Renée was very bright and shared Abbey's passion for environmental issues. Often he wrote statements for public hearings and — convinced that listeners would pay more attention to an attractive young woman than to him — he had Renée read them.[28] Abbey soon became one of the most regular and certainly the best known and most notorious letter-writer to Sam Taylor's *Moab Times-Independent*, from 1974 until 1987. In a letter printed on September 19, 1974, for example, he attacked motorboats on the Colorado, assuring Taylor and his readers that John Wesley Powell and many others had made it down the river without the aid of motors. Paul Abbey could have been speaking for his son when he wrote him on December 3 of that year from Home, "I just finished a 'letter to the editor'. . . . It's a masterpiece of Iknowbetterness."[29]

From the position of his new home in Moab, Abbey set himself up in opposition to the East Coast. He disdained urbanized Eastern novelists such as Tom Wolfe and John Updike. In the September 1976 *Harper's*, he attacked Wolfe — whom he always distinguished from "the real Thomas Wolfe," author of the Appalachian novels he so admired — as "a sycophant to the wealthy and powerful." A month earlier, in an article called "Nothing to Do," he explained to readers of the *New York Times Magazine* that "we live in a place called Spanish Valley, not too far from the ghost town of Wolf Hole, Ariz." He described the earlier "squalor of our surroundings" when he had lived in Hoboken to be near to Manhattan and Rita (identified here only as a "painter" of "Esso gas stations"). Responding to a visitor who asks him what there is to do, by contrast, in Spanish Valley, Abbey looks out at his breathtaking surroundings, including mountain peaks clearly visible ten miles away, sighs, and replies, "I can't tell you."

With Susie in school and under his care in Moab, Abbey traveled less than usual at first. On November 18, 1974, he wrote to his friend Alan Harrington, the Tucson writer, "I haven't been in Tucson since last August, when I moved our furniture out of the old stone house."[30] He chopped a lot of firewood in preparation for the Utah winter and disappeared regularly into the room that he established as his study in the Spanish Valley house, working hard on his writing. It was there that he revised *The Monkey Wrench Gang* for publication, having completed a 740-page draft of the novel on June 10, 1974,[31] just before moving to Moab. *Desert Solitaire* had attracted a devoted band of readers, and Abbey had made it into the 1974 edition of *Contemporary Authors*, later revising his entry so as to mischievously list his religion as "Piute."[32] Yet as he comically complained in his journal, he was still "tired of obscurity! I want to be famous! Like everybody else! At least for fifteen minutes. (Like Andy Warhol promised)." He made this declaration on November 30, as he was "nearing the final end of agony in revising *MWG*." On October 5 he had signed a book contract with a $37,500 advance from Lippincott, which made him feel "embarrassed by this sudden wealth" but also convinced that it was really all just "fantasy. A bunch of paper. One-third to the IRS, one-third to Rita" (239).

Abbey had little contact with his sons, Josh and Aaron, who were now teenagers. He managed to visit his sons in late 1975 and in April 1977 (when he took Susie, who met them for the first time), but such meetings were difficult and infrequent. On March 21, 1975, he noted that Rita had won a court judgment against him in Arizona for $13,000, and that he had paid $4,500 "but received absolutely no concessions in return. Hiding. Secret addresses. Oh, the humiliation and indignity of it all. . . . And alimony is not even tax deductible" (240).

Meanwhile, Abbey consoled himself with his friendships and his writing. In *The Monkey Wrench Gang*, he immortalized himself and several of his friends as the novel's main characters, giving them different but familiar names. Doc Sarvis, whose name was lifted straight from his erstwhile pal Al Sarvis—much to Sarvis's irritation[33]—was a fictionalized combination of

Abbey himself and John De Puy (who had been a medic in Korea). Ingrid Eisenstadter became Bonnie Abbzug, whose spunky New York Jewish personality was reinforced by her novelistic name—borrowed from Congresswoman Bella Abzug, whom Abbey subsequently suggested should be Secretary of State.[34] Ken Sleight starred as Seldom Seen Smith, a polygamous, Jack Mormon outfitter, handy with boats, ropes, and machinery, calm in speech but dramatic in action.

Doug Peacock was the chief inspiration for George Washington Hayduke, the Vietnam veteran, eco-warrior, and wild man of this novel. Abbey, who often recycled material, had already used "George Hayduke" for completely different characters, a decade before he first met Peacock, in his two unpublished novels of the early 1960s, the New Mexico "Black Sun" and the Hoboken "City of Dreadful Night."[35] Now, in *The Monkey Wrench Gang*, the third time was the charm for "Hayduke," a name that can still be found in western Pennsylvania; in Ed's youth, the Abbeys had lived near the Duke family of Home.[36] As he noted only when the novel was going to press, Abbey had been delighted to learn that "Hayduke," coincidentally and appropriately for its monkeywrenching reincarnation, "is a *hajduk, heiduk*: a Magyar, Serbian, Turkish word meaning 'brigand' or 'robber' or Balkan bandit-resister (*Oxford English Dictionary*)," or "thanks to Katie Lee" (who had sent him a postcard about its etymology), "in Hungarian, 'foot soldier'" (244). As for Peacock, Hayduke brought him much attention, yet he later remarked that "to the extent that I was seduced by the hype, it placed enormous strain on my friendship with Ed, which from the start carried the imbalance of paternalism" between the older Abbey and the younger Peacock.[37]

Each of these real-life friends found dialogue in the novel that they felt had been lifted straight from their actual conversations. Even some of the interpersonal relationships of the novel's characters echoed those of their factual models. Doc often finds the cantankerous Hayduke difficult to deal with at the same time that he admires his defiance and courage (much as was the case with Abbey and Peacock). Calling to mind Ed and Ingrid's relationship during 1970–71, Bonnie Abbzug becomes Doc's "part-time mistress" after his wife's death; he proposes a year later but she turns him down.[38] Abbey's ragtag foursome falls together into a band of saboteurs, eventually deciding to blow up the Glen Canyon Dam, and failing, but surviving to try again another day.

Yet Abbey insisted later that, though Seldom Seen, Hayduke, Bonnie, and Doc were inspired by real people, they were "not portraits. I just borrowed what was useful to create the fictional characters."[39] He also projected some of his own thoughts and experiences onto all of his characters, not just Doc. For example, Hayduke's revenge on a Flagstaff policeman who had locked him up several years earlier was most likely provoked by Abbey's own night in a Flagstaff jail way back in 1944, on his first hitchhiking trip through the West. A character called the "Lone Ranger" first appeared in a chapter entitled "Strangers in the Night," which was published before the novel, in December 1974, as "Where's Tonto?" in the *Mountain Gazette*. For readers of Abbey's second novel, *The Brave Cowboy*, this solitary, rebellious old cowboy resembled Jack Burns, a character who would reappear more explicitly in both *Good News* and *Hayduke Lives!* He noted on November 6, 1975, that "the one-eyed stranger in *MWG* is really the reincarnation of Jack Burns, the 'Brave Cowboy'—some fan pointed this out to me; I'd never thought of it; incarnated a third time as The Old Man in *Sundown Legend*" (244), which became *Good News*.

Abbey immortalized not only his friends but also some of their adversaries, especially the pro-development Utah Mormon Cal Black, who stars as Bishop Love in both *The Monkey Wrench Gang* and its sequel, *Hayduke Lives!* Ken Sleight later recalled that Abbey would regularly call him up during these years and ask, "What damn thing is Cal Black up to now?"[40] Abbey regularly published attacks on development projects supported by Black in the *Moab Times-Independent*, and now Black could recognize himself as caricatured in Abbey's novels.

Abbey must have enjoyed lending the completed manuscript of his new novel to Sleight. Certainly Sleight relished reading it, carrying it down beside the Dolores River, in 1974, and absorbing it all in a single day.[41] Here he found the fulfillment of what he and Abbey had been talking about since the summer of 1967: the need to get rid of Glen Canyon Dam. He also recognized many scenes described by Abbey, including some of the rivers and canyons that they had explored together. In early 1975, Abbey had his galleys sent to Ingrid Eisenstadter in New York City, because he had learned that she was worried about the appearance of a version of herself and their relationship in the book. By now an experienced editor herself, she did not ask for any changes. Also, in Moab, Abbey had Bill Benge and Gil Preston review his manuscript to make sure that the novel was legally and medically accurate.[42]

At the beginning of 1975, Doug Peacock and Abbey met for a week-long camping trip in the Cabeza Prieta wilderness in southwestern Arizona, ringing in the New Year there during Abbey's three-week return trip to southern Arizona. Peacock then came to Moab for an extended visit during the period soon before *The Monkey Wrench Gang* was published.[43] After he had worn out his welcome during a couple of weeks at the Abbeys' house, where Renée did not appreciate his drinking and his dogs, he stayed for quite a while at the McElheney sisters' house nearby. One day, after reading a pre-publication copy of the novel, as most of Abbey's Moab friends had already done, Peacock burst out of the McElheneys' house, complaining loudly that Abbey had stolen his personality.[44] Yet the two of them continued to hike the canyons and especially the Cabeza Prieta together, many more times, and Abbey later helped launch Peacock's own writing career by putting him in touch with his New York publishing contacts. Peacock would be at Abbey's side when he died.

Abbey once told John De Puy that, in *The Monkey Wrench Gang*, he changed the names of his friends "to protect the guilty."[45] We know that he had destroyed billboards in New Mexico in the 1950s (and in North Carolina in 1968), but did Abbey actually do "field research," as he would slyly and euphemistically call it,[46] concerning the sabotage of bulldozers as described in *The Monkey Wrench Gang* and *Hayduke Lives!*? Another friend of Abbey remembered accompanying him on such an expedition, in April 1975, just a few months before the publication of *The Monkey Wrench Gang*. One moonlit night the two of them drove into White Canyon, west of Blanding, where Utah state route 95 was being paved. This was the same area that Abbey had enjoyed slowly traversing, back in 1953, via unpaved roads and the Hite ferry, as recounted in "How It Was."[47] The 1970s road project transformed a backcountry dirt road into a highway facilitating tourists' high-speed trips into the heart of the canyon country (with three new bridges replacing the one old ferry at Hite, now long since submerged beneath Lake Powell). As Seldom Seen Smith explains in *The Monkey Wrench Gang*, Route 95 was "to help out the poor fellas that own the uranium mines and the truck fleets and the marinas on Lake Powell, that's what it's for. They gotta eat too."[48] Abbey declared in his novel that "almost all the country within their view was roadless, uninhabited, a wilderness. They meant to keep it that way. They sure meant to try. *Keep it like it was.*"[49]

While his friend stood guard, Abbey poured damaging substances into the gas tanks of a fleet of bulldozers, doing more than $20,000 worth of damage. He wanted to destroy a bulldozer—to "get this fucker started," as he has Hayduke explain in *The Monkey Wrench Gang*, "take it up to the top of the ridge and run it over the rim."[50] But Abbey was unable to start the engine. Instead, he had Hayduke fulfill his fantasy by driving a bulldozer over a cliff in *The Monkey Wrench Gang* and doing the same to a massive GOLIATH earthmover in *Hayduke Lives!*[51] Following his April 1975 sabotage, the authorities searched for the perpetrators, investigating Ken Sleight—but Sleight, De Puy, and Peacock were not part of this incident. Abbey decided that it would be wise for his friend and him to bury their boots and tires so they could not be tracked. They did exactly that, and then Abbey spent a few days in Arizona during the Utah investigation. The leading principles of monkey-wrenching, as he later explained in *Hayduke Lives!*, dictated that one should work in small groups of trusted friends, sabotage machinery rather than hurt people, and not get caught.[52] He and his friend had thus faithfully followed these principles—but they did little to stop Route 95, which was completely paved by 1976 as a "bicentennial highway." Abbey admitted "with a grin" in a 1984 interview about *The Monkey Wrench Gang*, "I did quite a bit of field research for that book. . . . I spent whole nights on construction sites in Utah, putting sand in transmissions, shooting holes in truck tires and radiators. I was full of rage and it made me feel good temporarily."[53]

Following an additional $16,500 advance in February 1975 from Lippincott and $25,000 from Palladium Productions for a movie option,[54] *The Monkey Wrench Gang* was published in the late summer of 1975. The Palladium payoff was the first of many options on a movie that never quite seemed to get made (even though it would be scripted and planned many times). Gary Snyder would put his finger on the perversity of Hollywood film culture, in a 1982 letter to Earth First! founder Dave Foreman, explaining why he thought a *Monkey Wrench* movie would never be released: one can spray as much human blood across the big screen as one likes, but one should never dare depict the sabotage of machinery. This is because that violates the most sacred American value: industrial private property. As Abbey noted in agreeing with Snyder, "in our culture, property is sacred, valued far above human life" (280). Abbey remained clear about distinguishing unacceptable violence against people—terrorism—from sabotage, "an act of force or violence against property, or machinery, in which life is not endangered, or should not be."[55] Financial sponsors would get cold feet about producing a movie of this book in which nobody gets killed. According to the terms of the distinction, terrorism is everywhere in Hollywood films, but environmental sabotage remained censored and invisible.

The reviews of *The Monkey Wrench Gang* in 1975, however, were numerous and mostly positive, and sales were strong—and stronger still after the book went into paperback the following year. For example, Elizabeth Ashton called it "a scriptwriter's dream" in the *Houston Chronicle*. Vincent McCaffrey in *Fiction* and Kenneth Caldwell in *Landscape Architecture* both predicted that it would soon become a successful movie.[56] By November 1979, Abbey noted sales of 270,000 (270). Through 1998, the Avon paperback edition had sold nearly 700,000 copies,[57] and of course this figure did not include Lippincott's hardback sales or those of the 1985 revised edition from Dream Garden Press. Not surprisingly, Abbey would identify this as the turning point in his career: as he remarked in 1987, "I've made my living by writing since

1975, when *The Monkey Wrench Gang* was published."[58] By the end of the century only *Desert Solitaire*, Abbey's most popular book in college courses, had surpassed *The Monkey Wrench Gang* in total sales.

Abbey was, naturally, pleased with the success of his novel, though he regretted that he had agreed to leave out chapter 21, "Seldom Seen at Home," which he published separately in the August 1975 *Mountain Gazette* and then restored in the 1985 edition of the novel—much as his Hoboken welfare episode would later be left out of *The Fool's Progress* but then reinserted in its paperback edition. Moreover, by July 1977 he would conclude that the reviewers had consistently *"misrepresented* the character" of *The Monkey Wrench Gang* (250). Typical was his reaction to Jim Harrison's October 1976 review in the *New York Times Book Review*. He felt that it was "one year late." It was "favorable" but characterized the novel as a "'revolutionary' tract for the old 'New Left.' Jeez! No mention of the comedy, the word-play, the wit, humor and *brilliance*!" (245). He stressed that "I intended it to be mock-heroic, or perhaps a little more than that. But above all I wanted it to be entertaining."[59] Abbey may have wanted his novel to inspire a new brand of environmentalist activism, but he even more clearly designed it to set up his jokes. It is partly a shaggy-dog story in which, for example, Hayduke (nicknamed "Rudolph the Red") settles an argument with Bonnie by insisting that he was sure it had been raining in the night, because "Rudolph the Red knows rain, dear."[60] *The Monkey Wrench Gang* and *The Fool's Progress* would remain his two best novels because both of them were not only thought-provoking works with memorable characters and important themes but also hilariously funny books.

Abbey always felt that *Desert Solitaire* had typecast him as an ecological essayist, and now that he had published a rollicking novel, he believed that it was misread as merely another environmentalist tract. To be fair, *Newsweek* called it a "comedy played out in a vast open space Abbey loves and knows well," Peter Wild pronounced it a "picaresque novel of continuous thrills" in *High Country News*, the *Pittsburgh Post-Gazette* said that it was "a great lot of entertainment," the *Memphis Commercial Appeal* declared that "the chase sequences represent some of Abbey's best writing and some of the funniest in American prose," and the *Chicago News* concluded that it "does for ecology what M°A°S°H did for the Korean War."[61]

Abbey's books have for years carried the blurb "the Thoreau of the American West," crediting this phrase to his fellow Western writer Larry McMurtry. How these words—the signature tag most frequently quoted in writings about Abbey—came to be positioned at the center of his reputation is a curious instance of how a slogan gets produced in the publishing business. True, McMurtry compared Abbey to Thoreau in his September 1975 review of *The Monkey Wrench Gang* in the *Washington Post*—a linkage made over seven years earlier by Clifton Fadiman, who called Abbey a "road-company Thoreau" in his April 1968 review of *Desert Solitaire* in the *Book-of-the-Month Club News*,[62] and later encouraged by Abbey's own 1981 essay "Down the River with Henry Thoreau." Thoreau had been Abbey's hero for many years, and it was natural to compare *Desert Solitaire* to *Walden*. However, "the Thoreau of the American West" were neither McMurtry's actual words nor quite true to their context. He reviewed *The Monkey Wrench Gang* together with William Eastlake's now mostly forgotten novel *Dancers in the Scalp House*, which also dealt with a group that wanted to do away with a dam. Eastlake had bet Abbey that *The Monkey Wrench Gang* would sell more copies than his own novel— and he won the bet easily.[63] McMurtry praised Eastlake's novel, if anything preferring it to Abbey's, which he said was "good to read, but *Desert Solitaire* is still his masterpiece." Buried toward the end of his review was the claim that "Eastlake is the Kafka of the American desert; Abbey is its Thoreau." McMurtry's correspondence with Abbey began, a few months after this review, when he acquiesced in March 1976 to Abbey's complaint that he seemed fixated on *Desert Solitaire* to the detriment of his subsequent work.[64]

Nonetheless, the Thoreau comparison got picked up, as in a 1977 review of *The Journey Home* which noted that "Abbey has been called the Thoreau of the American Desert."[65] In 1984 Abbey himself encouraged the use of "the Thoreau of the American West" as a blurb on the hardback jacket of *Beyond the Wall* but then changed his mind about it. On July 5, 1984, he had written to his publisher Jack Macrae that he liked the blurb. But then he reported that he had just had dinner with McMurtry, who felt sorry that he had "branded me as one more goddamned Son of Thoreau." On March 2, 1985, Abbey wrote Macrae again, asking him to remove the phrase from future printings of *Beyond the Wall*: "I know it was my idea in the first place (to quote his remark) but now I find it an embarrassment. I am not the Thoreau of the American West (there was only one Thoreau) and wish to break out of that limiting categorization."[66] However, the phrase stuck, and Abbey had already contributed to its solidification perhaps even more than had its supposed author, McMurtry.

The year 1975 marked a turning point in Abbey's fortunes, not only with the appearance of *The Monkey Wrench Gang* but also with the awarding of a Guggenheim Fellowship, in March, with the help of recommendations by two Tucson friends, Alan Harrington[67] and University of Arizona librarian Lawrence Clark Powell (240). This $12,000 award, good for one year beginning in July,[68] was to help Abbey complete "The Good Life," the big Pennsylvania novel that he had been trying to write for years and that Eastlake and others had encouraged him to finish. He declared on March 21 that he needed to "start thinking" about that project—"the farm, the old man, the glory and tragedy of hard work" (240). However, during this period he never got past page 149 of his manuscript, once again setting aside this novel, which he transformed into *The Fool's Progress* over a decade later.

Instead, Abbey did a lot of other writing, particularly nonfiction articles and reviews. Later he would complain, as he put it in his preface to the 1988 edition of *Desert Solitaire*, that this book "trapped me . . . in the box labeled 'nature writer,'"[69] seducing him into dissipating his talents by spending too much time dashing off nonfictional pieces, solicited and well paid, instead of working on his novels. Certainly some of his articles and reviews are anything but masterpieces. Yet it often seems that Abbey did not recognize his own strongest talents. Sometimes he was at his best in essays that he viewed merely as diversions.

A good example is "Shadows from the Big Woods," one of his very best essays—which he wrote for a calendar. This four-page work, which is stylistically and structurally tight as a drum, begins with the much quoted lines, "The idea of wilderness needs no defense. It only needs more defenders," and then proceeds from a lyrical description of playing with his brothers in the lost "Big Woods" of their childhood—populated by wildlife and Indian spirits—to a biting attack on the destruction of wilderness and the need to face the industrial "machine."[70] "Shadows from the Big Woods" first appeared on a single long page in the *Sierra Club Wilderness Calendar 1974* and was republished three years later in *The Journey Home* with hardly a word changed. Abbey was glad to contribute to a Sierra Club calendar, but it seems unlikely that he felt it would bring him any literary prestige. How could he know that he was at his best in this short, nonfictional form, writing unselfconsciously, with the illusion of one person talking to another? Another such example is "Walking," which leaps off the pages of *The Journey Home* as Abbey's spunky response to Thoreau. "Whenever possible I avoid the practice myself," he begins by telling us, before going on to develop the idea that "walking makes the world much bigger and therefore more interesting."[71] This essay was written for the 1976 *Sierra Club Trail Calendar*, as was "A Walk in the Woods" for its 1980 *Wilderness Calendar*.

During the rest of the 1970s, Abbey regularly migrated away from Moab, particularly during the warm months. Time-Life paid him to travel to Mexico in the spring of 1975, and *National Geographic* sent him to Australia in May and June 1976. He put in four more seasons as a fire lookout—on Numa Ridge in Montana's Glacier National Park from June 25 through August 1975, and at Aztec Peak in Arizona's Tonto National Forest, in his final three lookout seasons, from May through September in 1977, 1978 (the year he moved back to Tucson), and 1979. He enjoyed these paid sabbaticals in the wilderness, and he wrote successfully about them. As he told an interviewer at Numa Ridge, "It's ideal for reading and writing. . . . All you have to do is get up and have a good look around every 15 minutes or so."[72]

Abbey kept a journal of his summer 1975 Glacier sojourn that became "Notes from a Lookout Logbook" in the May 1976 *Audubon* and "Fire Lookout: Numa Ridge" in *The Journey Home*: "Renée and I walked up here on July 2nd, packs on our backs, two hours ahead of the packer with his string of mules. The mules carried the heavier gear, such as our bedrolls, enough food and water for the first two weeks, seven volumes of Marcel Proust, and Robert Burton's *Anatomy of Melancholy*. Light summer reading."[73] Doug Peacock was living a couple of hours away that summer, because he regularly migrated to the grizzly bear country of Montana during the warm season. But even though Abbey would revisit this region in the company of his friend Peacock, "himself half-grizzly," and later travel to Alaska, he never did manage to see a grizzly bear. By 1984 he would decide that "the grizzly bear is a myth." Yet he agreed with Peacock that "it ain't wilderness . . . unless there's a critter out there that can kill and eat you."[74] However, he always preferred the hotter, brighter desert and canyon country of Arizona and Utah to "the dark cold wet Northwest," dreaming in Montana on August 25, 1975, of "Vermillion Cliffs, of White Rim, of Grand and Slickhorn gulches, of Waterpocket Fold and San Rafael Reef and Book Cliffs and my little hay farm and gopher ranch on the banks of the golden Green" (244).

Abbey frequently accepted paid travel assignments by big-budget publishers but then wrote articles too racy for their pages, publishing them in Denver's alternative *Mountain Gazette* instead. For example, in the spring of 1975, he and Renée met his old friend Bill Hoy and his wife for a trip, financed by Time-Life,[75] into Mexico's Barranca del Cobre or Copper Canyon, described in "A Tale of the Sierra Madre" in the July 1975 *Mountain Gazette* (and later *Abbey's Road*). He and Hoy carried on a friendly debate about the relative merits of the Barranca del Cobre versus the Grand Canyon: Hoy felt that the Copper Canyon was the greatest unspoiled canyon on the continent, whereas the nativist Abbey preferred the Grand Canyon. They had a fabulous trip, feeding Abbey's Mexican fantasies about his hero B. Traven, but he was repelled by Mexico's poverty and glad to go back to the United States.[76] Yet he would return to Mexico often. In February 1977, in the company of his river-running friend Clair Quist, he journeyed to Angel de la Guardia Island off the Baja peninsula, describing the trip at the end of the year in both *Outside* and *Backpacker* magazines, where he disguised the island as "Isla de la Sombra."[77]

Similarly, Abbey enjoyed his 1976 trip to Australia, but *National Geographic* surely regretted funding it, because the magazine found his bawdy accounts of outback ranching and aboriginal life inappropriate for its pages. Instead, after submitting three articles with a similar lack of success to the *New York Times Magazine*, Abbey published them during 1977 and 1978 in the *Mountain Gazette* (which recorded its thanks to *National Geographic* for rejecting them) and then in *Abbey's Road*: "Anna Creek," "The Outback," and "Back of Beyond." On the one hand, Abbey felt at home in the Australian outback because, with its arid climate and wide-open spaces, it reminded him of his beloved Southwest. He could attribute to an Australian rancher the same joke that Abbey had first used at Arches in the late 1950s: "When did he expect the next rain? 'Couldn't say,' he answered. 'Only been here twenty-three years.'"[78]

On the other hand, he loved what was different about Australia: its much lower population and its fascinating dialects. Abbey called up his old Arizona friend Hal Coss after his Australian trip to borrow his lexicon of Australian English, so that he could get the dialogue right.[79] In "Back of Beyond," Abbey began to sound like an Australian himself: "Say what you like about my bloody government, . . . but don't insult me bleedin' country."[80] He uttered this line when he picked up a rental car—and then proceeded to destroy it, in a series of mishaps recalling his account of an early 1950s jaunt to Big Bend, "Disorder and Early Sorrow." Automotive misadventures are nearly as recurrent in Abbey as environmentalism.

With *The Monkey Wrench Gang* and *Desert Solitaire* selling very well, Abbey had now attracted a cult following. By November 1976, as he remembered telling Grace Lichtenstein of the *New York Times*, he had mixed feelings about becoming a "cult hero," having insisted to Lichtenstein that he wrote not for "hippies or college sophomores" but rather for "literate, educated people like yourself, who enjoy a good story told with style, passion and wit" (246). She had interviewed him in January 1976 after hearings in Page, Arizona, over the proposed Kaiparowits Power Plant on the southern Utah border, and her article "Edward Abbey, Voice of Southwest Wilds" had brought him increased national attention.[81] Abbey recognized that "Cactus Ed" was a persona that he had created, quite different from his private self. He seemed simultaneously bothered and pleased by all the attention he was receiving, with people pursuing him even to remote Aztec Peak, as part of the "Hack's Progress." Interview requests had come in from *Voice*, "*Pipple* magazine, *Mudduh Jones*," *New Times, Mariah*, and others. "What to do? My instinct is to crawl into my cave, refuse to see any of 'em. On the other hand, who's going to buy my books if nobody's ever heard of me? Edward Albee—who? I owe it, you might say, to my books" (255). He was amazed to receive a four-figure royalty check in July 1977 from so modest a publisher as the University of New Mexico Press,[82] which had reprinted *The Brave Cowboy* in 1977, in the wake of the success of *The Monkey Wrench Gang*, and which had similarly reissued *Fire on the Mountain* in 1978.

One way in which Abbey compromised and toyed with all of the attention was by concealing his geographical locations. He granted interviews at Aztec Peak only on the condition that magazines not mention its name or location high in the mountains northeast of Phoenix.[83] Abbey coyly described his tower, in "Meeting the Bear," as situated "somewhere between Sombrero Butte on the east, Noisy Mountain to the south, Malicious Gap on the west, and several small rivers . . . to the north and northwest."[84] He began to sign off many of his publications and letters from Wolf Hole and then Oracle. Wolf Hole was a ghost town, a "fabled" blip on the map near the Grand Canyon, which he had driven out of his way to see back in June 1965, finding exactly "nothing" (193). Soon after *The Monkey Wrench Gang* appeared with a book jacket claiming that Abbey lived there, Jim Stiles climbed into his Volkswagen in Kentucky and drove all the way to Wolf Hole to meet him—and found nobody and nothing there. Instead Stiles met him at their mutual friend Doug Treadway's Moab house in December 1975, where Abbey had come to play poker. When he heard that Stiles had searched for him in Wolf Hole, Abbey grinned and asked him, "What's it like down there?"[85]

It was partly because of such goose chases—and because the regional post office in St. George, Utah, got tired of forwarding his "Wolf Hole" mail[86]—that Abbey began to sign off instead, for the rest of his life, from Oracle. Oracle is of course a real town, near Tucson. Unlike Wolf Hole, it had a post office where Abbey fans could appear—and learn that they would not actually find him there. During his 1972–74 career at Aravaipa, Abbey had gotten a postal box in Oracle, where he stopped on his regular commutes to and from Tucson. After he moved to Tucson in 1978, he continued to use this as his address for all but his most important and private correspondence. He would come up to Oracle every few weeks to sort through his mail—which flooded in particularly after he announced, in the 1982 "Preliminary Notes" to *Down the River*, that "I welcome more letters. I want to hear from my readers, whoever you are. I want to know what's going on out there in the great American boiling pot. My mailing address is P.O. Box 628, Oracle, Arizona"—his actual box number at that time.[87]

As for Jim Stiles, Abbey rewarded him for looking for and finally finding him. At their first meeting, Stiles showed him his drawing that *The Monkey Wrench Gang* had inspired and that he had hauled to Wolf Hole: the cracking of Glen Canyon Dam. Six months later, Stiles opened a letter from Jack Macrae at Dutton publishers, asking if he would be willing to illustrate Abbey's forthcoming collection of essays, *The Journey Home*. Abbey had not forgotten his cartoon of the cracked dam—and it showed up on the cover of early paperback editions of the book, which Abbey would delight in displaying (both the drawing and the significant title, *The Journey Home*) to his audience in his native country, at Indiana University of Pennsylvania in May 1983. Abbey and Stiles became fast friends. By the summer of 1976, Stiles had followed in Abbey's footsteps, working as a ranger at Arches, where he encountered so many misguided Abbey fans that he hung a sign on his trailer: "NO, this was NOT Edward Abbey's trailer!"[88]

One of the Abbey fans who found that sign on Stiles's trailer, in July 1976, was IUP student Tom Lynch, who like Stiles had journeyed west from Appalachia in search of the author. He found him only five months later, back at IUP, when Abbey was brought in by his old classmate and friend, English professor John Watta, for a reading and lecture on December 9 and 10. Along with "God's Plan for the State of Arizona," Abbey read his two great essays about his Pennsylvania youth, "Shadows from the Big Woods" and "Hallelujah on the Bum."[89] Then he paid tribute to his parents (who were in the audience), his early teachers, and his native area in general. Next, Tom Lynch and his fellow editor Nick Suzich interviewed Abbey for IUP's *New Growth Arts Review*.[90] Abbey told them that he had not "given up on this area (western Pennsylvania) environmentally, but because I no longer live here, I'm not primarily concerned with it. Most people who do live here don't care about it enough to fight for it. . . . There are probably more trees in this state than in any other. And yet what you see from the highways is so depressing."[91] Yet he liked traveling back east, often combining visits to Home with trips to New York City to confer with his publishing contacts and see friends. In October 1974, Renée had enjoyed a trip to New York with Abbey. He stayed up all night at a gathering at Jack Macrae's, talking with William Gaddis, whom he appreciated meeting because he was an admirer of Gaddis's work.[92]

Abbey's celebrity and combativeness often masked a different private self. John Watta visited many bars with Abbey between the Pittsburgh Airport and Indiana, after picking him up for this visit in December 1976. When Watta dropped him off at his mother and father's little house in Home, he glimpsed another side that contrasted with the argumentative drinker in the bar—as Abbey tenderly embraced his mother.[93] Yet when Tom Lynch, Abbey, and a young woman unknown to either of them ended up in a restaurant for dinner, Lynch left early when he saw that Abbey (typically) and the young woman had hit it off.[94] Abbey felt that the best aspect of his newfound celebrity was that it sold books and helped him meet pretty young women. As he remarked a decade later, "Mainly I go for the girls. . . . To that extent I enjoy being a cult figure."[95]

Celebrity also attracted more celebrity, as in the case of Robert Redford, who had met Abbey while working on his own book *The Outlaw Trail* (1976), which contains one photograph of just the two of them rafting down a river together, and another of Ed and Renée among several other friends. Abbey subsequently sent Redford notes about his actor son Joshua; as a result Josh would get a bit part in *The Natural* in 1984 as the photographer who flashes a picture of Redford sliding into home plate (315).[96] In *The Fool's Progress*, Henry Lightcap makes collect phone calls under the name of "Robert Redford,"[97] and in his definitive, final list of acknowledgments at the beginning of *Hayduke Lives!*, Abbey doubtlessly enjoyed identifying him, in his long list of mostly unidentified, more obscure friends, as "Bob Redford (an actor)." There was once hope that Redford would film *The Monkey Wrench Gang*, but it failed to happen.

By 1976 Abbey was becoming an accomplished, entertaining public speaker, with invitations increasing dramatically. As Peter Carlson wrote perceptively several years later, "the glib, gruff jokester he plays in public is . . . a fiction, the product of his profound shyness about meeting strangers—and of the firewater with which he fortifies himself for such events."[98] In March, at a conference at Mt. Hood in Oregon, Abbey read a version of what would become his essay "Freedom and Wilderness, Wilderness and Freedom" (the second half of which appeared in *Not Man Apart* in July). He also read Sierra Club "archdruid" David Brower's statement after Brower had gotten sick with Montezuma's revenge: "If you wanted someone else to read your speech for you, whom above all would you ask for? I asked, and got him, and what I wrote was read for me by Edward Abbey," Brower later reminisced. "Montezuma lost after all."[99] In August, Abbey led a workshop called "On the Rocks" in Arches that was organized by University of Utah professor Florence Krall,[100] and he also spoke at a symposium in Vail, Colorado: "I am pleased to be invited to Vail to speak (once again) about overpopulation, overcrowding, war, pollution, urban squalor, mental anguish, social injustice, vanishing wildlife, the breakdown of the family, starvation, civil war, ski resorts, and women. World misery is my favorite subject, and I am always happy to talk about it."[101]

On the one hand, Abbey continued carefully to write out his talks in advance, as in the case of a dozen-page longhand text for his IUP speech,[102] where one might think he would have just spoken casually and extemporaneously, at this college he had first attended back in 1947. On the other hand, he recycled some of the same lines, especially jokes, from one place to the next. At IUP he used the line that he had invoked in Denver seven months earlier, on May 3, 1976, when he spoke on "Fiction and the Land" at the University of Denver, before a sizeable audience including his hosts, professors Donn Rawlings and Ed Twining: "The last time I spoke here, I gave a very moving speech — about half the audience moved right out of the hall." [103] In Denver he was re- ferring to his April 1968 remarks about Vietnam; in his home town of Indiana, he meant his December 1969 attack on development in the area. As with many of his best lines, he would use this one again, and remain proud of the numer- ous occasions on which his talks would send sizeable portions of his audiences "right out of the hall."

Abbey also took time out to speak his mind on national politics by publishing a set of suggestions for President Carter, just as he was about to take office in January 1977, in Friends of the Earth's *Not Man Apart*. These in- cluded "Appointment of Joan Baez or Bella Abzug as Secretary of State" and "Remodeling of the Pentagon by Allen Ginsburg and Gary Snyder." [104] In April 1978, he followed up with a report card in the form of a letter to "Dear Jimmy": "Well, old buddy, here it is one year later and I see you ain't accomplished any more than me and my brother-in-law Henry Pepper" (his third wife Judy's brother) "managed to accomplish in the same amount, when we took over the Winkelman, Arizona, Transcendental Meditation franchise." He remonstrated in his letter to Carter, "Goddamnit, we didn't expect too much anyhow." [105]

Complete with Jim Stiles's artful illustrations, *The Journey Home* was published by Dutton in February 1977. This was the first of five collections of essays encouraged and edited by Jack Macrae, who recognized Abbey's tal- ent as an essayist, the need to bring together his pieces from many diverse (and sometimes obscure) sources, and the considerable sales potential because of his newfound popularity. *The Journey Home* included twenty-three of Abbey's essays, most of which had been published during the first half of the 1970s in magazines ranging from nationally known ones, such as *Audubon* and *Life*, to regional ones that had attracted his loyalty, such as *American West* and the *Mountain Gazette*. Some of the essays appeared virtually unchanged from their magazine versions. Others, however, were carefully rewritten. For example, "Come On In" had included, in *Plateau: The Magazine of the Museum of North- ern Arizona*, ponderous asides about Keats and other references that he short- ened in the book version, giving more weight to his most memorable lines about the desert: "Enter at your own risk. Carry water. Avoid the noonday sun. Try to ignore the vultures. Pray frequently." [106]

All of these essays dealt with wilderness, yet the first words of *The Journey Home*, in Abbey's cantankerous introduction, were "I am not a natu- ralist." He added, "If a label is required say that I am one who loves unfenced country," and he insisted that this was not nature writing but "a book of per- sonal history." [107] He had a point, for even his most didactic attacks on devel- opment of wilderness areas combined the fictitious with the factual, and the comic with the serious. A good example is "The BLOB Comes to Arizona," published earlier in the *New York Times*. Here he accurately recounted, for example, a conversation with University of Arizona English professor Peter Wild about how Arizona was living beyond its means—but only after spinning an apocryphal tale about visiting the governor of the state, who had been sitting at his desk "with nothing much to do, feeling bored and maybe a little lonely." His strident conclusion that Arizonans must "finally begin to make some sort of accommodation to the nature of this splendid and beautiful and not very friendly desert we are living in" appeared in the same pages in which he assured his readers that "I've never met a pretty girl I didn't like," after he claimed that one such beauty told him in a Phoenix street that, ideally, "the optimum population of Arizona" should be "40,000 savages . . . and me." [108]

The Journey Home received many positive reviews, boosting Abbey's reputation as an essayist. In the *Los Angeles Times*, Wallace Stegner, Abbey's old teacher and dean of Western letters, insisted that, despite his protestations, Abbey was in fact a naturalist and called him "a voice crying in the wilderness." In contrast, Larry McMurtry assured *Washington Post* readers that Abbey was not a naturalist, because after McMurtry's *Monkey Wrench Gang* review, he had been "brought up short by a letter from the non-naturalist himself, pointing out that he should have been plunked down with Rabelais, Villon, Knut Hamsun and B. Traven." Ted Morgan declared in the *New York Times Book Review* that he liked Abbey "best when he is most ornery." Another reviewer felt that *The Journey Home* was even better than *Desert Solitaire* because, in the former, Abbey "seems more urgently aware that he is a shrill voice crying to be heard." [109] Indeed, one could make a strong case that *The Journey Home* remains his single best collection of essays.

Abbey published a second book during 1977, *The Hidden Canyon: A River Journey*, a photographic coffee-table book from Penguin that incorporated his journal of his August 1976 run through the Grand Canyon with Renée, boatman Martin Litton, and photographer John Blaustein. He later republished most of his text in *Beyond the Wall* because, as with his other coffee-table writing, he was convinced that readers had mostly skimmed past it while focusing on the pictures. The paucity of reviews of *The Hidden Canyon* supports his impression. Abbey felt that he was generally ignored in the East, like most other Western writers, yet the most positive review of this book appeared in William F. Buckley's *National Review*, where Priscilla Buckley wrote that he "makes you feel what it is like to confront the . . . racing, dangerous waters of the Colorado and its thundering rapids in a light dory." [110]

Both of these books demonstrated that Abbey was anything but a conventional nature writer. In *The Hidden Canyon* he quoted from Major

Powell and hoped for the demise of Glen Canyon Dam, but he also described "the approach of two of my twenty or so fellow passengers. Some fellows. One is a brown exotic wench in a tiger-skin bikini; she has the eyes and hair of Salome. The other is a tall slim trim sloop of a girl with flaxen hair and perfect sateen thighs emerging from the skimpiest pair of Levi cutoffs I have ever seen." This passage is actually a toned-down version of "White Water Ramblers," an article that appeared in the August 1977 issue of *Playboy*—which continues with a still racier description of the taller female "lying on top of her sleeping bag, naked as a nymph." Continuing in the soft-pornographic style of the country's most popular magazine in the genre, Abbey wrote, "She says nothing as I unroll my bag beside hers, undress and lie down next to her. . . . I reach out and touch the girl, softly on her warm, rounded hip. 'Took you long enough to get here,' she says. 'Sorry, honey.'"[111] He reveals her to be "Renée—my wife."[112]

Abbey had trouble distinguishing his wife from other attractive women not only in his writing but also in his life. His marriage to Renée was perhaps doomed from the very beginning. Just before their wedding, in February 1974, he had written to Ingrid Eisenstadter asking her if he should go through with it and suggesting that she might want to talk him out of it; as late as 1979, he invited Ingrid to join him on a trip to Alaska, but when she ascertained that he was still legally married to Renée, she declined. Many of Ed's friends felt that he regarded the beautiful, young, quiet Renée as merely his ornament.[113] He insisted to her that they would not have any children—but then fathered two more after he remarried in 1982.[114] Abbey believed that he was in love with Renée, but, as in his previous marriages, for him loving his wife and making love to other women were not mutually exclusive propositions. As he put it in a poem (recycling old journal entries), "The standing cock / hath no conscience. . . . / How can I be true to one, / without being false to all the others?"[115]

Abbey's settled domestic life with Renée in Moab did not last long. His companions on his hikes at places in southeastern Utah and northern Arizona such as Navajo Mountain were not limited to his male compatriots but occasionally also included women. One of his male camping friends once complained that Abbey monopolized tent space when he made these other arrangements. Mostly, however, his meetings occurred at locations that remained private. Soon Abbey was regularly telling Renée that he was driving up to their Green River property—but then actually going in other directions, to see other women.[116] When heading off to see another woman, he confessed to a friend, "You know, I don't know what's wrong with me. I've got a perfectly beautiful wife and I love her. I don't know why I'm doing this." Nor was his unfaithfulness limited to just one or two other women; he was known to pick up a total stranger in a Moab bar, and to tell a friend working in California to let him know if he met any attractive starlets, for he would be happy to come on out and meet them.[117] As he admitted to an interviewer a decade later, he had "several marriages destroyed by his womanizing — 'I could never get enough sexual variety, or so I thought.'"[118] Some of Abbey's friends were aware of his promiscuity and skeptical that his marriage to Renée would last;[119] one of them with medical training noted that, if Abbey had been born just slightly later — with his peak 1970s promiscuity occurring instead a decade or two later, at the height of the AIDS epidemic — he would not have lived as long as he did.[120]

Abbey's unfaithfulness and the demise of his marriage were encouraged by his cult status after the appearance of *The Monkey Wrench Gang* in 1975, which attracted more women to him, and by Renée's own restlessness and dissatisfaction. On February 6, 1975, Abbey noted that she was "bored" with him and Moab and wanted to go to college (239); nine months later, on November 6, he made note of her "losing interest" in him (244). He sought to restore their relationship in the Montana wilderness that summer, rejoicing on Numa Ridge in Glacier Park on July 10 that Renée was a "delightful" companion. She was "cheerful, clever, sharp and unafraid, and growing prettier every hour — I have never loved her so much as I do now. How fortunate I am, ugly hairy smelly morose old man, to have so good and strong and beautiful a wife" (242).

When he traveled by himself to Australia in May and June 1976, he left an unhappy Renée (still only twenty years old) at home to take care of seven-year-old Susie by herself.[121] She met him in San Francisco upon his return and spent a week with him in northern California, in late June, traveling and visiting his sister Nancy and her children. Abbey enjoyed a fiftieth birthday party and poker game in the company of Renée and several friends, at their Moab house, on January 27, 1977 (247). By March 22, 1977, however, his thoughts about the prospects of his marriage were mixed. He resolved that he must be good to Renée and that he would never find a better woman. Yet he realized that he continued to make "careless, thoughtless, mindless gestures toward break-up and disaster. Out of sheer sloth! stupidity! Some atavistic blind urge to self-destruction. . . . Why? Is happiness a bore?" (248–49).

Abbey had given an outrageous reading at the University of Arizona on February 2, 1977. It served both as an entrée to his subsequent teaching job there — which began four years later, despite this unlikely introduction — and as public evidence of his sexual adventures. He was invited by Lois Shelton, director of the university's Poetry Center on Cherry Street. Speaking in the Modern Languages Auditorium to a packed house, Abbey began by explaining, "I'm not really a professional poet . . . but I am living in your poet's cottage this week, so I am your official poet. God knows I've written a lot of poetry, but I've never published any of it anywhere. I think I'll read some of it to you so you'll understand why." He then read a series of bawdy "love poems," introducing each with an inquiry about a different woman: "This one's for Ingrid. Is Ingrid here tonight?" [122] "You say / you love me now. / Okay. / But will you love me / when I'm old / and bald and fat / and impotent / as an empty sock / and cold?" [123] Part of the audience was entertained; another segment of it "moved right out of the hall," and even in the liberal *Mountain Newsreal*, Margaret Hernandez wrote that "Abbey should have stayed home . . . to preserve his image as a cactus jumping Henry David Thoreau. . . . Instead he came to Tucson to treat his audience to low-class erotic poetry." [124] Yet in private conversation, Abbey seemed shy and unassuming. He had developed a public persona much at odds with his normal personality.

When Abbey headed to his Aztec Peak lookout tower in May 1977, hoping that another wilderness sojourn would restore Renée and him to the happiness that they had experienced on Numa Ridge, it worked at first—but not for long. Now back in her native Arizona, Renée left Aztec Peak regularly to visit family and friends in Tucson and Phoenix. Abbey's father visited him at the tower in May 1977 but stayed for only one day (250). Abbey enjoyed reading, writing, and playing his flute in the tower. When his friend Katie Lee visited him there in August 1977, she walked up to see him one morning and was greeted by enchanting flute music wafting through the air from atop the tower.[125] Jack Loeffler recalled playing a Vivaldi trio in the tower—he and his wife on recorders, Abbey on flute—and watching a falcon hover in the air near them, eating a mouse and apparently listening to them.[126]

In Renée's absence, Abbey was visited by another woman with whom he had begun a relationship, calling her long-distance after having met her at a January 1977 party where he autographed her parka with "Hayduke lives!" (the earliest instance of what would become a catchphrase of Earth First! in the 1980s and then the title of his last novel).[127] With his self-confessed skirt fetish, Abbey liked her to arrive at Aztec Peak wearing one—at which point he would carefully follow her all the way up the stepladder to the lookout tower. He would send her scenic postcards, letting her know when it was a good time to visit. They got along well also because neither was looking for a permanent relationship at the time. One weekend Susie was with him when she visited, but usually he was by himself while Susie stayed with her grandmother, who had moved to Tucson.

It was as if Abbey had separate compartments in his brain for different kinds of relationships, one for "home" and another for "the road," believing that he could love his wife and other women at the same time. As he had already noted in June 1968 at another Arizona fire tower, Atascosa, he loved them "all" and could not bear to give up any of them, but they did not understand (220). His new Aztec Peak visitor, however, understood: "Ed loved women. In order to be around Ed, you had to accept that this was the way he was. He just wasn't monogamous. He was handsome in a craggy way. He liked legs. All I had to do was put a skirt on, and he was blind to anything else in the universe." Abbey would admit in *The Fool's Progress* that he (in the form of Henry Lightcap) had "a fetish for skirts. The word itself—*skirt!*—excites him instantly."[128] His skirted Aztec Peak visitor further recollected: "I liked his voice, and he was witty, funny, and intelligent. I just loved him for what he was: I liked his music, I liked his conversations, and I enjoyed his friends. We took long walks; he could outwalk any young people I know twenty times over, in the desert. He was a robe and slippers and pipe and a real big book in your lap kind of guy. He was a wonderful, civilized human being with the most remarkable memory of anyone I've ever met. He was a gentleman and a scholar."

Another woman, Norah Booth, who photographed Abbey at Aztec Peak for a magazine article, explained his appeal in an article of tributes published after his death: "Sign me up as another woman who fell madly for Ed Abbey the moment she saw him. My portrait for the magazine showed a man who had to smile at the overwhelming approval of yet another young woman. Somehow, I knew I was going to love this man."[129] As noted above, this photographer was only a distant admirer.

In the fall of 1977, Abbey again sought to salvage his marriage, returning to Moab and his ostensibly settled life with Renée. But by the end of the year, Renée announced that she was returning to the University of Arizona in January as a full-time student. During the first few months of 1978, separated from Renée, he remained in Moab with Susie. Then in May he returned to Aztec Peak and his on-again, off-again relationship with Renée while Susie went to summer camp in Prescott. In a last-ditch attempt to repair matters, he agreed to move back to Tucson, buying a "cute little desert house" (255) that spring on four and a half acres of land a few miles to the west of the city, on a side road off Sweetwater Drive, just beneath the Tucson Mountains, where he would rejoin Renée in the fall of 1978 after his Aztec Peak season.

Abbey regretted leaving behind his friends in Moab, where his swan song was the unpublished, satiric little play "Best of the West: A Morality in One Short Act," staged in Star Hall on January 4, 1978. It comically depicted conflicts between developers and "Sahara Clubbers," with God appearing as a burning bush. The program stipulated "No Calls for Author, Please. . . (He Has Left Town)."[130] In May, Abbey did leave town. Jim Stiles stopped by his house to say goodbye, expecting to find a crew of friends loading up his truck, but instead encountered Abbey packing up his whole house by himself. After Stiles spent the afternoon helping him, Abbey took him out for dinner.[131] He gave away many of his books, and his John De Puy paintings went to Owen Severance.[132]

That summer Renée once again came and went to and from the lookout tower. On August 5, 1978, Abbey noted that Renée had been gone for eighteen days, "off on her third dory trip down the Grand," leaving him feeling "very lonesome, much forsaken, deeply unnecessary. I miss her!" (257). He consoled himself that summer with a solo trip of his own—his first journey to Alaska, where he would return a year later and once more in 1983, subsequently writing about those later two river adventures. He lamented on September 8 that even though he had a "good sweet loving wife, . . . like a fool, I'm always exposing the worst aspects of my character: my melancholia, my volatile irritability, my jealousy and suspicion, the most narrow of my prejudices." He decided that he needed to be careful and try harder, or he would "lose this one too. And I don't, I really don't, I really *must not* lose again" (259). Yet he was about to do exactly that.

Young "Ned" Abbey suited up for cowboys and Indians in the mid-1930s, in this undated photo presumably taken in or around Home, Pennsylvania. He grasps a toy revolver in his right hand and wears a cowboy handkerchief around his neck, similar to the next, adult photograph taken near Tucson about a half-century later.

Here the notorious postmodern cowboy appears to have shot his television set in his own backyard near Tucson, in this celebrated magazine-cover photograph from November 1986 by Terrence Moore. Note how he assumes much the same pose in both photographs: gun on his right, handkerchief around his neck, left hand in repose, but ready to playfully fight, enjoying the role of cowboy, never quite growing up.

In this earliest available photograph of Edward Abbey, originally from his Pennsylvania family that owned no camera and saved very few photographs, he is pushing his toy wheelbarrow—already actively busy on the land. This photo was taken in 1928, when he was about a year and a half old, in Indiana, Pennsylvania, probably behind the Abbeys' rented house on North Third Street.

An animated, early-adolescent Ed Abbey, undated.

In this undated teenage photograph, the
budding young writer seems bemused in
his most stylish adolescent phase.

Serving as an army motorcycle cop in Italy in 1946, the nineteen-year-old Abbey had found
his true element, happily grinning beside an unidentified woman and various Italians.

With Jean Schmechel, Abbey's first wife, circa 1950, in Albuquerque, with the Sandia Mountains in the background.

Abbey and Homer, the celebrated dog that he shared with Malcolm and Rachel Brown, undated but likely ca. 1953.

The thirty-year-old Abbey rock-climbing in the Fiery Furnace at Arches, May 1957.

The Abbey family in late 1956, gathered next to the holiday table, at the "Old Lonesome Briar Patch" midway between Chambersville and Home, Pennsylvania: seated (from left to right) are Rita Deanin (Ed's second wife), Iva (Howard's wife), and Ed's sister Nancy; his mother Mildred stands in the middle holding Joshua (Ed and Rita's first son); and standing behind Mildred are (left to right) his father Paul, Ed, and brothers Bill, John, and Howard.

Towering above the rest and sporting a Beat goatee, Abbey joins the entire staff (nearly half Latino and half female) of the Taos *El Crepusculo de la Libertad* newspaper as they appeared in the November 5, 1959, issue. From left to right: Douglas H. Vincent, business manager; Don Hanan, mechanical superintendent; Ferdie Cortes, floorman; Felix Valdes, Spanish-section editor; Fred Aguilar, floorman; Manuelita Mondragon, bookkeeper; Rini Templeton, art editor; Ruth Fish, county reporter; Craig Vincent, publisher; Dolores Montoya, circulation manager; Ed Abbey, editor; Preciliana Garcia, receptionist; Judson Crews, printer; Mildred Crews, staff photographer; Otto Pitcher, society reporter; and Sister Jesusita Perrault, columnist. As Judson Crew noted, there were more staff members here than pages in the newspaper—part of the reason that it had to be sold the next year.

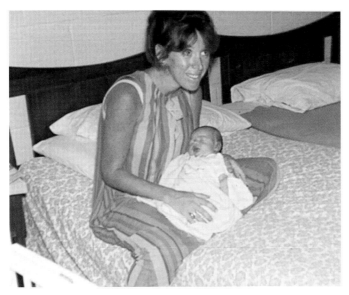

Ed's third wife, Judy Pepper, and baby Susannah Abbey, Ed's third child and first daughter, in the fall of 1968.

The author of *Desert Solitaire* somewhere in the Utah canyon country in the late 1960s, at about age forty.

Abbey's best friend, John De Puy, in his studio in 1973, flanked by two of his Southwestern landscape paintings, with some influence perhaps from Georgia O'Keefe but projecting De Puy's own bold view of the Southwest that he shared with Abbey.

Abbey in his element, among his male ranger (and ranger-type) friends, somewhere along El Camino del Diablo (the Devil's Highway), during their February 1969 jeep caravan trip from Organ Pipe Cactus National Monument into the Cabeza Prieta Wildlife Refuge. From left to right, we see Abbey, Fred Goodsell, Roger Weber, Jim Carrico, Hal Coss, an unidentified friend of Matt Ryan, Scotty Steenbergh, and Organ Pipe superintendent Matt Ryan.

Admiring the Mexican desert, El Gran Desierto, in extreme northwestern Sonora, on the edge of the Pinacate region, May 1982.

Abbey the professor squinting over student papers in his office at the University of Arizona during his first semester teaching there, spring 1981. The studious, scholarly, fifty-four-year-old Abbey that we see here is at odds with the much wilder image of "Cactus Ed" that he projected elsewhere.

With Earth First! leader Bart Koehler (known as "Johnny Sagebrush" when he sang Earth First! songs) cheering him on in the background, Abbey delivered a feisty, comic speech at the July 4, 1982, Earth First! Rendezvous in the Gros Ventre Mountains of northwestern Wyoming. His audience was laughing too.

Paul, Mildred, and Ed Abbey during his April 1983 visit to Indiana University of Pennsylvania (IUP).

Showing off an appropriately entitled book during his April 1983 visit to IUP: *The Journey Home*. Visible is Jim Stiles's cover illustration imagining a cracked Glen Canyon Dam.

With his good friend, fellow writer, and key influence, William Eastlake, in Bisbee, Arizona, in August 1984.

Ed's fifth and last wife, Clarke Cartwright Abbey, baby Rebecca, and Ed at their home near Tucson in 1984.

Abbey in his cabin study (where he later died) behind his house in 1984. He is flanked by his manual Royal typewriter and Honoré Daumier's painting *Don Quixote,* on the right, and by a picture of Beethoven and an old Industrial Workers of the World poster, on the left.

Near Tule Well along El Camino del Diablo in the Cabeza Prieta (the wilderness area where he was later buried) in 1987. Abbey proudly sports his R. Crumb "Hayduke" T-shirt.

With the countercultural illustrator R. Crumb at the Arches book launching for the tenth-anniversary edition of *The Monkey Wrench Gang*, March 24, 1985.

The last known photograph ever taken of Ed Abbey, sixty-two years old, at his final public appearance—appropriately enough, a Tucson Earth First! rally against the University of Arizona's development of an astronomy station on Mount Graham. This was March 4, 1989, just ten days before his death.

Doffing his hat, getting ready to say goodbye, in the Grand Gulch, Utah, May 1988.

"The Journey Home": the big sunrise wake for Abbey on Rough and Rocky Mesa, adjacent to Arches National Park, on Saturday, May 20, 1989. Emcee Ken Sleight, the inspiration for Seldom Seen Smith in *The Monkey Wrench Gang*, is at the podium to the left, next to the American flag.

Doug Peacock, the model for George Washington Hayduke in *The Monkey Wrench Gang,* commemorating his old friend at the May 1989 Moab wake.

Abbey's gravestone at his illegal burial site in Arizona's Cabeza Prieta wilderness.

CHAPTER EIGHT

The Bard of Tucson
1978–1982

Abbey's return to Tucson in the fall of 1978 initiated what eventually became a very successful, influential, and happy period for him, personally as well as professionally and politically. Yet surely he must not have guessed how positively events would develop, given how unhappy he was at first, back in the city that remained his home base for the rest of his life. He was not at all pleased initially to be living in the Tucson area again, and then his fourth marriage disintegrated entirely, plunging him into one of the deepest depressions of his life. However, at the same time, in early 1979, he met the woman who would become his final wife, in his fifth and by far most successful marriage: Clarke Cartwright. But it would be more than a year before they reconnected and began living together, and more than three years until their 1982 wedding. Soon thereafter, he would have his first big brush with his own mortality.

Meanwhile, Abbey's writings and political influence continued to burgeon, with a concerted environmental movement growing in particularly gratifying response to *The Monkey Wrench Gang*. The success of that racy novel and, more modestly, the essay collection *The Journey Home* made publishers eager to publish his subsequent books of this period: the photo/essay book *Desert Images* (1979), the futuristic Western novel *Good News* (1980), and his second and third collections of essays, *Abbey's Road* (1979) and *Down the River* (1982). *Monkey Wrench* fans enthusiastically snapped up these books, and Abbey's legend continued to grow.

His popularity would peak after the creation of Earth First! in 1980. Earth First! founder Dave Foreman and his cohorts conceived this band of anarchist, direct-interventionist eco-warriors out of frustration due to the failure of conventional political activism, and they were directly inspired by *The Monkey Wrench Gang*. Ronald Reagan's ascension to the presidency in 1981 and his appointment of the most reactionary secretary of the interior in U.S. history, James Watt, redoubled the determination of Earth First! to counter the conservative onslaught on wilderness, ensuring the growth of this spunky new group. In a strange combination, Abbey would simultaneously enjoy both countercultural notoriety and newfound academic respectability. In the spring of 1981, he would begin a new position teaching creative writing at the University of Arizona and, during that same semester, appear as featured speaker at the "Cracking of Glen Canyon Dam" demonstration organized by Earth First! It seemed that *The Monkey Wrench Gang* was not merely a fiction but becoming a reality, and its author was not merely a cult figure but an influential force in American letters and environmental activism.

All this must have been hard for Abbey to imagine in the fall of 1978. At the end of September, he finished his second season atop the Aztec Peak fire tower and shipped off the revised manuscript of *Abbey's Road* to his editor, Jack Macrae, in New York. Then he went to Tucson and picked up ten-year-old Susie, who had spent the summer at camp in Prescott and was living again with her grandmother, now that Ed and Renée's once stable Moab household was in loose transit to Tucson. He took Susie on a camping trip to California, driving through Nevada, Death Valley, and the Owens Valley (Mary Austin's "land of little rain") to the ghost town of Bodie.

On October 19, Abbey described in his journal his early-morning walk from their campsite "above Owens Valley," when he heard "a thin high desperate cry." After "returning hurriedly to camp," he found his daughter heading toward the highway, "crying with relief" at the sight of her father. "Poor little kid. She said she thought I'd gotten lost or killed—was dead. (Waking there alone.)" The terrified Susie had dressed and, finding her father's briefcase too heavy for her to carry, extracted and took along his knife ("for snakes"), money, address book, and journal (260). Abbey described this trip in more up-beat terms in an article that he sent to the new nature-travel magazine *GEO*, which surprised him by promptly accepting it for their May 1979 issue. He felt that this article, later reprinted as "Fool's Treasure" in *Down the River*, was "dull, tedious, uninspired" (261), but he used his visit to this ghost town as the occasion for a thoughtful meditation on the old West.

Abbey did not care much for the new West that he found in Tucson upon his return there, assailing it in his journal on November 7 as "Shithead-ville" and "Greater Smogsville." He remembered that, in 1965 in Las Vegas, he had "left a wife and two children because I refused to live in the midst of the Consumption Society. And here I am again, full circle, back in the city, living in a place I detest, betraying everything I believe in." [1]

A week later, Abbey temporarily escaped Tucson again in favor of Colorado, to speak on behalf of antinuclear activists there and to attend and write about their trial. On November 16, after a warmup by his friend Bob Greenspan on the guitar, he delivered to a capacity crowd at the University of Colorado in Boulder a talk that he called "Nuclear Weapons and the Attack on the Human Condition," in which he criticized nuclear power as a form of tyranny [2] and complained that nuclear weapons "take all the fun out of war." [3] The next morning he was in the courtroom in nearby Golden for the trial of the April 1978 Rocky Flats antinuclear protestors, where he met Daniel Ellsberg. It ended after Thanksgiving with trespassing convictions. A couple of years later, on September 7, 1980, he would join Pete Seeger in speaking against nuclear power at a rally in Santa Fe. [4]

Abbey had become a writer with a wide range. In December 1978, Ed Twining and Donn Rawlings, his hosts two years earlier in Denver, visited Abbey at his new Tucson home, talking about many issues in Western let-ters and politics. They were struck by the breadth of his interests. [5] His obser-vations about the Rocky Flats trial appeared in the March 1979 *Harper's* as "One Man's Nuclear War" — reaching a wide readership just in time for the in-famous March 28 accident at the Three Mile Island nuclear power plant in his native Pennsylvania. Contributing very visibly to the nuclear power debate at its height, Abbey thus confounded those who viewed him as interested only in wilderness issues. He concluded that "I felt a guilty envy of the protestors, of those who actually act, and a little faint glow of hope—perhaps something fundamental might yet be changed in the nature of our lives." Drawing inspi-ration from a source similarly not in line with those who would narrowly see him as an anti-Chicano racist, Abbey added, "If we could not celebrate exactly a victory, then—as César Chavez has said—we would celebrate our defeat." [6] His father wrote to him on March 10, after reading the *Harper's* article, that though he had suggested earlier that his son should "write something for the Indians or for Cesar Chavez," this article convinced him that "you *are* writing for the Indians, for Chavez, and for us all."[7]

Paul Abbey's words cheered up his son at a time when his private life in Tucson was in disarray. In the same letter, Paul reported that he had been handing out socialist leaflets at the student union at Indiana University of Pennsylvania. Ed Abbey's ornery nature as well as his admiration for his father and mother were both well illustrated after he received a request from Clarence Stephenson, who was writing a history of Indiana County, for information about himself as a notable native. On April 18, 1979, Abbey replied to Stephenson that he would rather not be included in his book unless it also featured his parents, assuring him that Paul and Mildred's "sum contributions (so far) to the economic, social, cultural, intellectual and educational life of Indiana County" far exceeded his own.[8] His parents' different styles were also well illustrated by their reactions. Writing jointly to him on May 9, Paul delighted in his son's riposte to Stephenson as "the funniest thing I ever read" and joked to him that he was a "crazy galoot" and "traitor to our illustrious county." In contrast, Mildred was "downright *crushed* by your response," since she felt that Stephenson was "a good man who has spent uncounted hours, years, effort in researching and writing that volume."[9]

Father and son enjoyed more banter later the same year when Ed published a letter in his hometown *Indiana Gazette*, headlined "Yes, There Is a Home, Pa.": "I have read with pleasure two recent letters in your 'Readers Write' column from a certain Paul Abbey of 'Home' (is there really such a place? or is the writer putting us on?), Pa. In any case, Mr. Abbey demonstrates a rare talent for polemical satire—or satirical polemic—and I do not hesitate to predict that this young man, if he persists, will go far in his chosen field. Whatever it might be."[10] Paul reported to his son on September 7, 1979, that he had read with interest this "hatchet job you done did on that poor old aspiring writer from a place called Home."[11] Ed enjoyed his father's correspondence more, however, than his parents' actual lifestyle and their cramped little house along the busy highway through Home. On November 19, after a three-week lecture tour that took him back east, Abbey described a couple of days and nights in "cold brown drizzly" Home, Pennsylvania (269). He enjoyed walking in the woods and splitting logs with Paul, but he had mixed feelings about his "silent embraces" with his mother, who was convinced that she would die soon, and about his paternal Aunt Ida's remark that "I'll be dead pretty soon, . . . and frankly I don't give a damn" (270). Afterward he was glad to escape back to sunny Arizona from gray Pennsylvania.

Abbey liked to insist that he was no naturalist, claiming in his introduction to *The Journey Home* that "the only birds I can recognize without hesitation are the turkey vulture, the fried chicken, and the rosy-bottomed skinny-dipper."[12] Yet in "Watching the Birds: The Windhover" (originally published in 1978 as "Flights of Reincarnation"), he showed that, even though he had once gotten Cs in zoology, he had now certainly learned his birds, after many seasons in the wilderness. Here he provided a vivid account of a gray-backed peregrine falcon attacking and soaring through the sky above Aztec Peak, and announced that he would like to be reincarnated as a "humble turkey buzzard" so that he could "contemplate this world we love from a silent and considerable height."[13]

This essay and several Aztec Peak magazine interviews that Abbey did during this period mentioned Renée and included idyllic descriptions that gave readers the impression that all was well in their relationship.[14] Back in Tucson, however, things were not going well at all. Abbey had moved there after Renée went back to school at the University of Arizona, but their marriage was now only a sometime, weekend affair. Renée would remember an occasion when she sent Ed to the store for groceries in Tucson and he returned home two days later.[15]

Around the same time, Abbey invited a young woman to his house for a party, the "party" consisting of "Ed with a bottle of whiskey" waiting alone for her. But she came accompanied by her boyfriend and a group of anti-nuclear activists from the University of Arizona. Her boyfriend remembered that Abbey literally "drank me under the table," where he came to just long enough to see him "kissing my girlfriend." When he awoke the next morning in his own bed, he learned that Abbey had invited his girlfriend to join him that summer in his lookout tower at Aztec Peak, but she declined.[16]

And this was at home in Tucson; on the road, Abbey was even less inhibited. He wrote very openly about his behavior in the "Coda" to *Abbey's Road*, published in the spring of 1979, where he explained that he enjoyed the lecture circuit not just for the money and "ego massage" but "to meet those lovely girls. 'My name's Sharon,' she says. Or Susan. Or Kathy. Or Pamela. Or Tammy. And, 'Oh Mister Abbey, I've been wanting to meet you for years!' 'That's funny,' I reply, 'I've been wanting to meet you too; how about a drink as soon as we can sneak away from this mob?' 'Oh, I'd *love* to,' she says," and in a description reflecting Abbey's disdain for the young men he met while on tour, "she tugs at the arm of a shy, pimply, long-haired, very tall and thin young lady standing a bit to her rear — 'and this is my boy friend George.' Jack. Henry. Willy. 'He wants to meet you too.'"[17]

At the end of 1979, when Abbey traded letters in *Mariah/Outside* magazine with his fellow Western writer Tom McGuane, complaining that McGuane ought to try to help save the West, McGuane replied that "I don't belong to organizations of any kind," stingingly adding that "I have never breathed 'Mountains, rivers, forests . . .' at coeds from the lectern."[18] It should have come as no surprise to Abbey that, shortly after he returned to Aztec Peak at the beginning of May 1979 for his final season of federal employment, Renée visited him and told him, "We're through," asking for a divorce, as he noted in his journal on May 29. "She's bored with our marriage ('lacks intensity') and fed up with me—says I'm away too much, that I don't talk to her when I *am* with her, that I'm indifferent, that I don't love her, etc. She suspects me of fooling around with other women; doesn't trust me." But Abbey, who wanted to remain married and still have his affairs, "said I would not give her a divorce." Susie was about to head off from her grandmother's house to another summer of camp in Prescott: "Poor Suzi—no mother and not much of a father. Renée is torturing herself with guilt over Suzi; I tried but failed to console her." Abbey also promised himself on May 30 "one thing for sure: no more hasty or impulsive marriages for me," after having a letter from Rita requesting money that he owed her (264).

Abbey's failed marriages did indeed continue to come back to haunt him. He had been glad to see his first marriage with Jean end; his second marriage concluded when he abandoned Rita and his sons; and his third marriage ended with Judy's abrupt death. The difference this time was that Renée, who remained very angry, left him against his will. He was therefore especially morose that summer, spending a lot of time wandering back and forth between John De Puy and Jack Loeffler, bemoaning the loss of Renée.[19] In 1971 he had taken solace in his first trip to Australia just after Ingrid Eisenstadter had broken up with him, and now in July 1979 he journeyed to the Canadian Yukon and Alaska for the second summer in a row, joining river-runner Mark Jensen in a two-week trip down the Tatshenshini River that he described in an article for *Mariah/Outside*.[20] He also visited a psychiatrist in Tucson for quite a while after Renée left him. On January 30, 1980, he noted that "the last words I heard directly from Renée" were " 'Stop loving me.' " He declared that he would "never—never!—fully recover from the pain of that separation"—yet clarified later in the margin of that journal entry, "Took about six months" (273).

Meanwhile, among the several other women Abbey saw during 1979 was one who would change his life: Clarke Cartwright. He could not at first know that, even though he was quite smitten with her. A striking woman with a very direct way of expressing herself, Clarke was a native of College Station, Texas (where her father was a scientist at Texas A&M University); her own youthful first marriage had ended in 1976 when she was twenty-three years old. (Abbey's previous wives had each married him when they were very young and without the experience of a previous marriage.) One day in late 1978 she had been playing frisbee with a neighbor in Salt Lake City, Richard Firmage, an employee of Abbey's sometime-publisher Gibbs Smith, and told him that, if she won, he would have to get Abbey's address for her. She did, and he did. After tearing up a long first draft, Clarke mailed to Abbey's post office box in Oracle a short note thanking him for writing his books, indicating that she had never written a fan letter before, and inviting him to dinner if he was ever in Salt Lake City.[21]

Conveniently enough, Abbey was invited to Salt Lake in February 1979 to address a gathering of the Western River Guides Association. He phoned Clarke from Tucson and asked if she would pick him up at the airport. "Ed delivered his standard inflammatory words of eco-rebellion to the river runners," their friend Jim Stiles reported, "and later, he and Clarke ate dinner and danced at a local Greek restaurant."[22] Back in Tucson on February 27, Abbey announced in his journal that he had met Clarke Cartwright, a "darling!" (262). As for Clarke, she was "surprised when I met him by how quiet and gentle he was. I always expected him to be more of a Hayduke type, just from reading his books. . . . But he was really quite gentlemanly and soft spoken."[23]

Abbey told all about this trip in his May 1979 article in the new Denver *Rocky Mountain Magazine*, "Up the Creek with the Downriver Rowdies"— all except for Clarke, since he had just met her and was still married to Renée. "One cold evening in February," he wrote, "I checked into the Tri-Arc Travelodge in Salt Lake City, a respectable hotel in a decent, law-abiding town. I was dismayed to find the place swarming with hairy ruffians in cowboy hats, greasy down vests, wool shirts, boots. . . . The clerk smiled a reassuring smile. 'Don't be alarmed,' he said, 'it's only another boatmen's jamboree. They'll all be in jail by midnight.'" These "hairy ruffians" included Abbey's close friends Ken Sleight and the Quist brothers. Actually only one river rat was arrested, after urinating in the parking lot late at night. When Abbey was leaving the gathering at its conclusion, Bob Quist told him that he looked like a politician because he was wearing a tie and shaking everybody's hand—at which point Abbey gave him the finger, only to be upstaged, as he walked away, by Quist, who dropped his pants and mooned him. "Never turn your back on a boatman." Abbey also described Sleight inviting his compatriots to join hands in a circle, visualize Glen Canyon Dam, concentrate hard, and thus cause its destruction.[24]

Ed and Clarke arranged to meet again a few weeks later for a trip across southern Utah, but "the rendezvous was an underwhelming success," Stiles explained, because Clarke now found him a bit grumpy and began to think about their age difference: "It was not love at first sight," she said. Then she spent six months in Mexico learning Spanish and traveling, and she worked for four months tutoring some doctors in English in Guatemala, where she fell in love with Leonel, a physician and opponent of the government. Back in her hometown of College Station, she corresponded with him, but then soon received a letter from Leonel's mother informing him that he had "disappeared." Leonel was never found.[25]

Not long thereafter Abbey called Clarke, and they resumed their correspondence. He visited her in College Station in June 1980, and they spent much of that summer traveling together—in New Mexico and Utah, and up to Montana to see Doug and Lisa Peacock at Peacock's "Grizzly Hilton" residence. At the end of that summer they picked Susie up from summer camp and Clarke moved in with Ed in Tucson,[26] where she would become certified in special education and teach for two years in the Tucson public school system.[27] On October 16, 1980, Abbey wrote in his journal that Clarke had been living with him for nearly three months, since July 20. He loved her "very much, but she remains a bit cautious." He felt that he had now recovered from the "malaise of loneliness and rejection." He was convinced that Clarke was a "fine woman; I want and plan and hope to marry her, even make a child with her. With the blessings, I hope, of her parents" (274). He added the following summer, on August 16, that he could even accept the "prospect of another baby without panic or terror. Hell, Clarke really is a good woman" (276).

In a simple ceremony in front of a Tucson justice of the peace, witnessed only by Susie and her grandmother, Bess Pepper,[28] fifty-five-year-old Ed and twenty-nine-year-old Clarke were married on May 21, 1982. His journal entry on that date was simply "Clarke and I are married! Yay! Hooray!" (279). This one included none of the troublesome quality of his wedding to Jean, when things had turned sour after he laughed at the minister, or the merely matter-of-fact quality of his notation about marrying Rita ("Today I married Rita" [104]), or the self-flagellating pessimism of his entry after marrying Judy ("Idiot!" [197]), or his similar attitude when he married Renée only after asking Ingrid to talk him out of it. Not long after his marriage to Clarke, he explained to an interviewer who asked him why he had broken his oath not to marry again, "I was premature." [29]

Abbey was convinced that Clarke was "the best I've ever known and loved," as he declared in August 1981 (276). It seems that, in his mid-fifties, he had finally begun to grow up—and had finally met his match. All stories of Abbey's philandering cease with his marriage to Clarke. His last indication of a different encounter was noted in Jackson Hole, Wyoming, on January 30, 1980, when Clarke was still in Central America and before they had begun their steady relationship: "Just spent a week here with L., a beautiful, generous, brave, talented and clever woman" (272). There is no evidence that Abbey was ever unfaithful to Clarke, and he continued to write lovingly about her in his journal throughout the rest of his life.

As his good friend and fellow writer Alan Harrington wrote, in the 1970s Abbey had been "inclined not to take women seriously," but his marriage to Clarke "seemed to change him over, drive out the sardonic side, the jocular regrets. . . . He would invariably speak of her and his new family with joyous admiration. She evidently helped release his affections. . . . With Clarke he walked the line."[30] Other friends confirmed this sense that he "settled down" with Clarke in a way that he had not with any of his previous wives.[31] On November 24, 1981, for example, at an Earth First! event at the University of Arizona, a young woman handed Abbey her phone number. He passed it along to Dave Foreman and joked, "Here, you can use this more than I can."[32]

Like everyone else who knew her, Ed found Clarke to be a very generous, smart, dynamic, determined, strong person. Well aware of his personal history, she let him know in no uncertain terms that she expected him to be faithful to her. When Ed and Clarke visited his friend Katie Lee in Jerome, Arizona, soon before their marriage, it was clear to her that Clarke would tolerate no fooling around from Ed.[33] Similarly, when Ed's old friend Malcolm Brown visited them in Tucson after they were married, Clarke spoke darkly and impressively about the fearful consequences that would befall Ed if he ever left her,[34] and this made an impression on Ed that he cited to friends elsewhere.[35] His closest friend, John De Puy, stressed that Clarke was the woman who understood Ed best and stood up to him.[36] She had difficulties with how he wrote about women and how he "lived inside his head a lot."[37] But Clarke loved Ed and admired his intellect, his views about the environment, and how he finally became a doting father during the 1980s.

In 1980 Abbey bought some acreage overlooking the Vermillion Cliffs near the Grand Canyon and subsequently often fantasized about building a home there.[38] But instead he and Clarke settled into his house just west of Tucson, which remained his home base for the rest of his life. He often hankered to move back to the redrock canyon country, settling for summer sojourns in Utah. He told the *Bloomsbury Review* in 1980 that his Tucson house "suits me fine," though he accurately predicted (as he had about Esperero Canyon in 1972) that "very likely, this will all be built up in a few years." He admitted that "I've got myself trapped in the same sort of mortgage situation as most other people."[39]

During this same period, when he finally achieved personal happiness, Abbey became more in demand than ever as a public speaker. On November 19, 1979, he made note in his journal of a lecture tour from which he had just returned to Tucson; it included Phoenix ("a thousand or so at the Heard Museum"), Salt Lake City ("about 2,500 at the U. of U.!"), Tempe ("five hundred"), Boulder ("1,500!"), and the University of New Hampshire ("five hundred") (269). His return visit to Salt Lake was especially significant, not only because that audience was his largest but also because he met there for the first time three nature writers who would provide vivid accounts that, taken together, illustrate yet again the many different faces of Edward Abbey: Barry Lopez, John Tallmadge, and Terry Tempest Williams.

Invited by Professor Florence Krall (who had organized Abbey's workshop at Arches three years earlier), Abbey joined Lopez at the University of Utah on October 29 for a benefit reading for the Utah Wilderness Association. Beforehand he visited Krall's environmental education class, where he answered questions put to him by her friend John Tallmadge, and then went out for dinner and drinks at the Green Parrot with Krall, Tallmadge, Lopez, Williams, and several local wilderness activists. In the packed auditorium, Abbey then read a book review and "Notes from a Cold River," his account of that summer's river trip in the Yukon and Alaska, where he had been impressed by the wilderness but, as in Montana in the summer of 1975, he failed to see any grizzly bears and did not like the cold. Afterward he retired to a party at Krall's house.

A comparatively young, lesser known author at the time, Lopez was struck by Abbey's generosity in merging their speaking dates after each had been invited separately, so that he got to address the huge crowd that had assembled mostly to hear Abbey. At dinner he mentioned to Abbey his feeling that the author should respect the reader's vulnerability, and after Abbey "paused with his fork in the air," he registered his agreement, "from somewhere far away in himself. . . . It was a moment of trust." Lopez concluded that "as I listened to him read, I thought, well, here is a good man, a fine and decent neighbor," who wrote out of "a hunger for greater clarity." [40]

What struck Lopez as Abbey's hidden thoughtfulness seemed instead a crusty reserve, in the different arena of the classroom, to Tallmadge (who was unknown then but subsequently became a noted author and president in the 1990s of the Association for the Study of Literature and the Environment). Abbey met his questions with short, noncommittal replies—indicating that people should simply read his books—with Tallmadge "sweating hard" after a few minutes of such perfunctory answers. Drinking and "trading war stories" in a smaller group at the Green Parrot, Abbey relaxed considerably and then drove to the reading "with exuberance, heading up Fourth South in the wrong lane before screams from the others made him realize his error. He grinned, gunned the engine, and hauled the truck over the median, crunching the transaxle." For Tallmadge, Abbey's "fictional self" remained "more real to me than the man"—whether the cause was the head cold Abbey had at the time, his natural reserve, or his discomfort about being a cult figure. "As Keats once observed, 'a poet is the most unpoetical of any thing in existence.'"[41]

At Flo Krall's party after the reading, Terry Tempest Williams's spunky Mormon grandmother spoke up: "Mr. Abbey, I will not read all of your books. I don't have time. But I will read one of them. Which one is your favorite?" The room fell silent in anticipation of Abbey's reply, but instead he said, "Mrs. Tempest, follow me into the bedroom"—where they went and conversed privately, so that his answer was not revealed to the partygoers. Afterward her granddaughter asked her, "So Mimi, which book?" but she replied, "'I vowed to secrecy and I will keep my word to Mr. Abbey.' I noticed the next time I was at my grandmother's house that on her nightstand was a copy of *Desert Solitaire*."[42] Soon thereafter Williams received a postcard reading, "Nice meeting you in Salt Lake City, Tempest. Come to Tucson. I would like to show you around the desert. Love, Ed."[43] Like Lopez and Tallmadge, Williams went on to become an accomplished author herself, eventually speaking at Abbey's May 1989 Arches wake (where she remembered that first postcard) and responding to *Desert Solitaire* with *Refuge*, her own Utah nature-essay book.

Abbey's audiences were larger than ever now. He was publishing prolifically and attracting a great deal of attention. In the spring of 1979, Dutton released his collection of essays *Abbey's Road*—a title that played up his increasing cult of personality by alluding to the Beatles' almost identically entitled album of ten years earlier. This book collected some twenty pieces: his introductory accounts of his exchanges with Gary Snyder and *Ms.*, his essays about such trips as his 1971 and 1976 expeditions to Australia and his 1975 and 1977 jaunts to Mexico, and other notable ones such as "In Defense of the Redneck," "Fire Lookout," and "Merry Christmas, Pigs!" Picking up on this collection's title, many of its numerous and mostly positive reviews focused on his personality. *Kirkus Reviews* declared, "There's more of him here than in earlier books," and Ray Murphy wrote in the *Boston Globe*, "Supposing, God forbid, that Thoreau drank, smoked and ran after women. If he had, he'd probably have written a lot like Edward Abbey."[44] Whereas the narrator of *Desert Solitaire* had been merely an independent loner, hiding out in the wilderness, the persona of *Abbey's Road* was that of a more deliberate troublemaker, always looking for a fight. This book contains some of Abbey's most entertaining essays, and it also extended his range, with essays not only about the American Southwest but also those new pieces about Australia and Mexico.

Abbey often complained about his New York reviews, yet *Abbey's Road* attracted not one but two notices in the *New York Times* and its *Book*

Review. On June 19, 1979, John Leonard called him "one of the good guys. . . . Reading him is often better than being there was." On August 5, Lucinda Franks wrote, "He is a macho man and proud of it. . . . We do not really take his sexism seriously."[45] Ironically, Abbey chose to reply to this review via deliberate provocation, as in his 1973 letter to *Ms.* (but in a very different style). He concluded that "I suspect that she objects to the book because the author is a man (by choice) and writes like a man—not like a Garp, a Cowgirl with the Blues, or some other species of androgyne. In short, *I accuse* Mizz Franks of *raw sexism!*" The *New York Times Book Review* published Abbey's letter on October 7 along with Franks's reply: "His reaction to my positive review (I daresay one of the most positive his new literary effort has yet received) would be amusing were its tone less hysterical."[46]

Glad to stir up trouble and attract attention with *Abbey's Road*, Abbey was much less happy about the publication price and reception of his other 1979 book, *Desert Images*. On November 19 he was "embarrassed" that this "dinner table" book cost $100—too expensive for his friends, to whom he joked that soon there would be a "cheap paperback edition" for only $49.95 (279). He was also not pleased that reviewers mostly ignored the book, and he had to wait for a second chance until he could reprint four of its chapters in *Beyond the Wall* (1984). His distaste for the New York literary establishment was increased by John Russell's brief dismissal of the book in the *New York Times Book Review* as "oversize, overpriced, overproduced and overwritten." Six months before Russell's review, Abbey had already concluded, in May 1979 at Aztec Peak, that he still could not overcome his bitterness at the "condescension or total indifference" with which his books were treated by the New York literary establishment. "But why should I be surprised by it? I've always been a loner, an outsider, a misfit in all respects; why should I not also be the same in the literary world?" (263).

Scornful of David Muench's photographs and unaccountably calling Abbey's writing "all but impossible to read," Russell revealed his New York snobbery and ignorance by concluding, "give me the filthy air of Fifth Avenue any day."[47] He made no specific mention of any of the actual contents of *Desert Images*, such as Abbey's thoughtful meditations on the ancient Native American petroglyphs and pictographs found everywhere on Southwestern canyon walls: "The art served as a record. As practical magic. And as communication between wanderers. Water around the next bend, a certain zigzag sign might mean. We killed eleven bighorn here, only two hundred years ago, says a second. *We were here, say the hunters. We were here, say the artists.*"[48] This passage echoes (and the italicized lines repeat almost verbatim) a similar discussion of petroglyphs and pictographs in *Desert Solitaire*, where Abbey had announced his interest in the subject a decade earlier.[49] Indeed, thinking in April 1979 about his oft-repeated comic line "when I die, if I live that long," he asked himself, "Where'd I use this old gag? I am plagiarizing myself quite a bit these days. In my decline. Failing powers, fading vision, diminishing energy. Only my self-pity seems as powerful as ever. Fortunately" (262).

Abbey continued his Native American interests in the 1980s, going so far as to publish a scholarly study of Navajo sand paintings in *Architecture Digest*.[50] In *Desert Images* he showed that his interest was more than casual: "These are speculations. Only a few anthropologists, like New Mexico's Dr. Polly Schaafsma, have given the Indian rock art serious attention."[51] In such passages, Abbey confounded those who dismiss him simply as a racist and cite passages in *Desert Solitaire* or *The Fool's Progress* in support of the notion that he disdained Native Americans.

Abbey's interest was more than merely academic or aesthetic, and his attitudes toward Native Americans were reflected not only in his books but also in his actions, complicating the picture of this complex, sometimes contradictory writer. His September 7, 1980, antinuclear appearance in Santa Fe with Pete Seeger was at a Navajo miners' benefit event. The same writer who had claimed in *Desert Solitaire* that he had crawled into his sleeping bag one night "drunk as a Navajo" also spoke sympathetically on behalf of native peoples.[52] He traveled to the Navajo benefit shortly after he and Susie ran in a Labor Day race at New Oraibi, Arizona, in the middle of the Hopi reservation. His article about this experience two months later in *Running* magazine did not focus much on the running itself: "I hate running, and most other forms of physical effort." Instead he meditated upon Hopi prophecies and history, telling the story of the Hopi after whom the race was named, a classmate of Jim Thorpe at Carlisle Academy in Pennsylvania.[53] He also became interested in the Navajo-Hopi land dispute in Arizona, subsequently publishing a review on this topic which concluded that these Native peoples' difficulties with overpopulation and industrialization were shared by all Americans.[54] It provoked the accusation that he was too critical of Navajo overpopulation and not sympathetic enough to the threat of their removal by capitalists.[55]

In the same November 19, 1979, journal entry in which he complained about the price of *Desert Images*, Abbey was more encouraged to note that the experimental novel on which he had been working since late 1975, *Good News*, was "now on page 242" (270). By mid-December he had mailed off the completed novel (271), which Dutton published in the fall of 1980, following the appearance of excerpts earlier in the year in the *Tucson Weekly News* and *TriQuarterly*. Continuing in the satiric and futuristic mode of such 1970s essays as "God's Plan for the State of Utah" and "Dust," in which he similarly imagined the destruction of the environment and the end of the world, *Good News* was set in Phoenix under the rule of a fully authoritarian, industrialized state. However, when he tried to reach beyond the tall-tale tradition on which "God's Plan" depended, into the fuller fantasies of "Dust" and *Good News*, Abbey was on shakier ground. "Dust" was a thin, overly abstract piece, an unhappy conclusion to the otherwise generally very strong *Journey Home* collection, and it has to be said that *Good News* is his weakest later novel.

If *Black Sun* (1971) was Abbey's erotic *Lady Chatterley's Lover*, then *Good News* was an attempt at his didactic *1984*. It was built upon two of his favorite, oft-repeated ideas. First, he always responded to the charge that he was a pessimist by insisting, as he told his audience in Boulder on November 3, 1979, "I'm an optimist; I think the 'ever-growing' military industrial state will eventually collapse."[56] Second, *Good News* illustrated Abbey's premise that, if wilderness is outlawed, then only outlaws can save wilderness. This modest novel focused on the adventures of a small band of anarchist dissidents hiding out in the mountains near the hated city that had become the "BLOB" that ate Arizona, as Abbey had suggested in his 1976 article "The BLOB Comes to Arizona." These were promising premises, but the actual novel does not satisfactorily enact them. *Good News* is a fragmentary rather than a unified work, and instead of combining drama and humor like *The Monkey Wrench Gang*, it descends into melodrama.

Abbey's outlaws were led by Jack Burns, reincarnated from the pages of *The Brave Cowboy*, and Native American chief and shaman Sam Banyaca. Abbey always wished he could return the Southwest to the hunter-gatherer society that had once dominated the region. In 1977 he had praised Scott Momaday's *The Names: A Memoir*, using his review as an occasion to lament that "the great horse and hunting culture of the Kiowas (and all other plainsmen) is gone. It may have been the best, most adventurous, most beautiful way of life ever known on this or any other of the earth's five continents. But it could not withstand the violent advance of European-American industrialism, the rapacity of overwhelming numbers. The overt violence is now part of the past; the seductive violence of our greed-and-consumption."[57]

Abbey filled *Good News* with chase scenes like those that had made *The Monkey Wrench Gang* so popular, and his most loyal environmentalist readers enjoyed the novel, but his characters were not nearly so strong. Abbey himself admitted in February 1981 that, in this book, he had "tried to do too many things at once and got too complicated. The characters never did get developed."[58] His new version of Jack Burns included several promising (but underdeveloped) strands, such as Burns's search for his son, who has been turned against him by his ex-wife—into which it is difficult not to read Abbey's feelings about his own sons Josh and Aaron and his ex-wife Rita. His thin characterizations were also unfortunate, since he had never tried before (or afterward) to develop, for example, a significant Native American character. He had wanted to incorporate a Native American perspective on wilderness, which he felt was quite different from mainstream ideas. In his essay "Floating: The River of the Mind" (first published in April 1980), he wrote that "the American Indians had no word for what we call 'wilderness.' For them the wilderness was home."[59]

Reviewers inevitably compared *Good News* to *The Monkey Wrench Gang*, to the detriment of the new novel. Some were reluctant to dismiss this flawed book because of the perceived importance of its subject matter. Alan Cheuse noted in the *Los Angeles Times* that *Good News* "leaves much to be desired" but concluded that, at the outset of the 1980s, it was "the only doomsday book we've got thus far." John Berry wrote in the *Washington Post* that "if Phoenix after the collapse seems two-dimensional, part of Abbey's point is that Phoenix . . . is an unnatural growth that cannot survive." Yet even Abbey's old benefactor a decade earlier at the University of Utah, Les Standiford, concluded in the *El Paso Times* that this novel "fails as 'eco-satire' partly because of the gloomy seriousness that has come to replace the fine leavening humor of Abbey's earlier comic novel, *The Monkey Wrench Gang*."[60]

By January 1981, Abbey was convinced that his new novel was "another bomb, down the well," with the "usual mediocre reviews." He felt that everyone had missed his point that *Good News* "really is an *optimistic* book, in that it forecasts the imminent collapse of the military-industrial State. The title is not ironical, but the plain truth." But the reviewers were "baffled" by his title. Abbey echoed the resisters in his novel and indicated his anger about the reviews by writing in his journal, "Traded my .22 for a .357; ready for the wars" (274–75). He told an interviewer in February that this novel was about Phoenix in 1999, just barely still alive. "The mere thought of the demise of Phoenix puts him in a better mood."[61]

At the same time that Abbey was fantasizing in *Good News* about an anarchist band of outlaws defying an authoritarian state, a handful of real-life wilderness activists and admirers of *The Monkey Wrench Gang* were planning to make his fantasy come true. In April 1980, Dave Foreman, a thirty-five-year-old Albuquerque native, was heading home to New Mexico after a trip to the Pinacate region of Mexico, which Abbey's book *Cactus Country* had inspired him to visit. A big, bearded man very much at home in the wilderness, he was preparing to resign from his job in Washington, D.C., as a lobbyist for the Wilderness Society. Frustrated by the failure of politics as usual, he was looking for a new kind of activism. According to Rik Scarce in *Eco-Warriors*,

Foreman was particularly angry about "RARE II, the Forest Service's Roadless Area Review and Evaluation project that had seen the old-line environmental groups compromise so much internally that less than one-fourth of the eighty million acres under study was designated as wilderness." [62]

On April 3, Foreman and his traveling companions and fellow activists—Bart Koehler, Mike Roselle, Ron Kezar, and Howie Wolke—pulled off at a rest stop north of Tucson on their way to Albuquerque. This core group perceived the need for a "radical wing," in Foreman's words, "that would make the Sierra Club look moderate." In a moment of inspiration, Foreman suggested that they form a group called "Earth First!" and Roselle immediately came up with a logo—a clenched fist within a circle, like the one on Foreman's motorcycle helmet. Their motto would be "No Compromise in Defense of Mother Earth." [63] As Foreman later recalled, "the way I defined Earth First! in the beginning stages was that Earth First! was made up of Ed Abbey style conservationists." [64] "Back in those days," he explained, "we were 'rednecks for wilderness'; we were all Ed Abbey fans." [65] The fact that Abbey was very much in the popular consciousness had already been underscored in Boulder, Colorado, two weeks earlier, on March 19, when "'The Monkey Wrench Gang,' a group of 'concerned citizens,' . . . admitted the weekend theft of light bulbs from the star on Flagstaff Mountain and left the bulbs at the *Daily Camera*." [66]

On July 4, 1980, Foreman and his friends gathered near Moab for their first "Round River Rendezvous," which became an annual Independence Day rite. "The 200 people at that first Rendezvous, many from mainstream groups, drank lots of beer, sang to Johnny Sagebrush (Koehler's stage name) songs, and complained about RARE II," Scarce notes.[67] On the same day, the conservative local county commission counter-demonstrated by sending "a flag-flying bulldozer," Foreman later recalled, "into an area the Bureau of Land Management had identified as a possible study area for Wilderness designation. The bulldozer incursion was an opening salvo for the so-called Sagebrush Rebellion, a move by chambers of commerce, ranchers, and right-wing fanatics in the West claiming federal public land for the states and eventual transfer to private hands." [68] The next day Earth First! held their own "'Sagebrush Patriots' Rally' to make it clear to the newly emerged Sagebrush Rebellion just who the real Americans were." [69] A new war over Southwestern wilderness was on.

On November 1, 1980, Foreman began to publish the *Earth First! Newsletter* (which soon became a fuller *Earth First! Journal*). It numbered 1,500 subscribers by early 1981 and eventually 10,000 by the late 1980s.[70] That same month, shortly after his election, Ronald Reagan sent a telegram to the second conference of the League for the Advancement of States' Equal Rights: "I renew my pledge to work toward a sagebrush solution." It was clear whose side he would be on. The coming to power of Reagan and Watt galvanized not only Earth First! but also the environmental movement in general, with Sierra Club membership rising from 181,000 in 1980 to 346,000 by 1983 and similarly dramatic growth in Wilderness Society and Audubon Society rolls.[71]

Foreman and Abbey had both known Jack Loeffler since the early 1970s, but Foreman did not actually meet Abbey until March 21, 1981.[72] On that date, Earth First! staged a demonstration that remained its single most dramatic action: heading out from Page, Arizona, onto the top of the dreaded Glen Canyon Dam, they unrolled a huge black plastic strip (which Abbey had helped fund) down the side of the dam, simulating a crack—as preserved in a video of the event disseminated afterward by Earth Image Films under the title "The Cracking of Glen Canyon Damn."

Abbey stood in the back of a pickup truck and offered some trenchant remarks: "Surely no man-made structure in modern American history has been hated so much, by so many, for so long, with such good reason."[73] "I see this as an invasion. . . . I would advocate sabotage, subversion, as a last resort when political means fail."[74] He concluded in stirring fashion (with a line borrowed, in truth, not from his grandmother but from John De Puy): "We'll outlive our enemies and, as my good old grandmother used to say, 'We'll live to piss on their graves.'"[75] Deputy Sheriff Ed White had been taking down information about the demonstrators, but then he got distracted, asking "Is that Ed Abbey?" An admirer of Abbey's books, he got his autograph, and no arrests were made that day.[76] Afterward, however, another investigator dusted the entire top of the dam for fingerprints.[77]

Abbey continued to support Earth First!, often contributing to the *Earth First! Journal* and speaking at the group's events. His last public appearance in March 1989, ten days before his death, would be another Earth First! demonstration, in Tucson. Having inspired the group with *The Monkey Wrench Gang*, he would return the favor with his last novel, *Hayduke Lives!*, whose subject was Earth First! Yet rather than get involved in the nitty-gritty organizational work, he always preferred to remain on the periphery, sending in generous checks and zipping off incendiary speeches and letters.

Abbey would rather be wandering the wilderness and writing. On election day in November 1980, for example, while the whole nation buzzed about Reagan's victory, Abbey was floating down Utah's Green River. He kept a journal that became an introduction to *Walden* and (after a couple of published permutations and combinations) his celebrated essay "Down the River with Henry Thoreau." On November 8 he wrote: "Who won the election? What election? . . . I rebuild the fire on the embers of last night's fire."[78] He would continue this tradition by floating down the Colorado River from Moab for ten days surrounding Reagan's reelection in 1984 and writing about the experience in his essay "River Solitaire" (1987). Like his hero Thoreau, with whom he carried on a running conversation, Abbey preferred to live on his own and go against the grain. Nevertheless, immediately after climbing out of Lake Powell at the conclusion of his November 1980 river trip, he went straight to Salt Lake City and spoke at another benefit, on November 14, for the Utah Wilderness Association,[79] as he had also done a year earlier.

At the height of such political notoriety, Abbey also enjoyed more and more scholarly attention and critical acclaim. In 1977, two years after *The Monkey Wrench Gang*, Garth McCann had published a short volume on Abbey in the Boise State Western Writers Series. Journals such as *Western American Literature* included articles on Abbey with increasing regularity. Ann Ronald's *The New West of Edward Abbey* appeared in 1982, and Abbey himself found it a "good sympathetic scrutiny" of his books, though he felt that she "takes 'em all much too seriously" (286). He then sent Ronald a postcard in which he stressed how much he had revised his essays between their periodical and book publications.[80] Abbey was not egotistical about his own reputation; when he met John Gardner at the University of Arizona in the spring of 1982, he sat quietly, impressed because he had read *On Moral Fiction*, while Gardner did all the talking, asking Robert Houston afterward "who that 'Lincoln looking guy' was."[81] Yet McCann's monograph and Ronald's book served to expand Abbey's reputation and broaden his academic legitimacy. This unconventional troublemaker was now also an English professor as well as increasingly the subject of research and writing by professors, especially members of the rapidly growing Western Literature Association, who had already presented him (in absentia) with a lifetime achievement award at their 1978 meeting in Park City, Utah.[82] During this period, WLA members sought to carve out a new academic niche for themselves, much as those devoted to nature writing would do in the 1990s. Abbey's rise in popularity and his shifting identities as both Western and nature writer were partly the result of such academic politics.

In the late 1970s, Abbey began depositing his papers in Special Collections at the University of Arizona, as he had agreed to do in 1974. He donated them for free; only after his death did his agent, Don Congdon, extract from the library a fee of $10,000 that was paid to Clarke Abbey, his widow.[83] For a while—until UA librarians convinced him that they could send him photocopies of whatever he wanted—Abbey used his collection not as evidence of his own immortality but as his own organizational resource for work in progress, especially as he assembled the three collections of his essays published during the 1980s. He often came in to pull out something he needed, leaving notes for librarian Lou Hieb: "Borrowed some crap. —Ed Abbey."[84] Or he would call up and say something like, "Somewhere in one of those boxes is a piece I published in *Outside* in 1980. Could you please send me a copy of that?"

In January 1981, the University of Arizona also became Abbey's employer. He surprised many by surpassing his friends William Eastlake and Alan Harrington, both of whom also taught at the UA; Eastlake had been fired in 1973 after he regularly failed to show up for class,[85] and Harrington remained only a part-time instructor. Poet, nonfiction writer, and director of the UA creative writing program Richard Shelton went out on a limb in 1980 by recommending the appointment of Abbey as full-time lecturer beginning with the spring 1981 semester. Because of Abbey's iconoclastic persona, many in the English department were not at all happy with this appointment.[86]

Abbey remained good friends with colleagues such as Shelton and Robert Houston, each of whom served as director of the UA creative writing program. Soon after Abbey began teaching, another recently appointed UA faculty member, Leslie Marmon Silko, dropped him a note, visited him in his office, and struck up a friendship. Those who call Abbey racist and sexist—who typically teach or otherwise promote Silko's books, not Abbey's—may be surprised to learn that the Anglo male and the Native American woman were good friends, and that Silko's novel *The Almanac of the Dead* (which she was writing when they met) shows the influence of *The Monkey Wrench Gang*. Knowing that his appointment had been opposed by many, Silko identified with Abbey as an outsider and wanted him to know that she welcomed him as her colleague. One day about a year later, Ed and thirteen-year-old Susie came out to Silko's beautiful place looking into Saguaro National Park to ride Fred, a horse owned by English professor Larry Evers. Abbey subverted his image as a wilderness cowboy that day: he could not get Fred to go through Silko's gate, and he could not name some of the common desert vegetation outside of her house.[87]

Abbey surprised many people by becoming a very successful teacher. By choice he taught only in the spring semester, continuing through 1988 (except for 1983 and 1986, when he took leave to devote himself more fully to his writing). His fire lookout job at Aztec Peak ended after the 1980 season, and now teaching became his seasonal job instead, as he ambivalently noted on May 10, 1981: "Would much rather be a fire lookout than a college professor. I think. Wouldn't I?"[88]

By now, however, Abbey had warmed up considerably to the prospect of teaching since the days of his brief initiation as a graduate assistant at the University of New Mexico in 1956 and his disastrous term at Western Carolina University in 1968, with his 1970 stint as Writer in Residence at the University of Utah as a turning point. From the latter experience he remembered, as he remarked in 1980, that writing classes could be useful because "they give you pressure to write. That's the hardest thing about writing—to get started, to put the first things down on a page." [89] As his entrée to teaching nonfiction at the UA, he gave a guest-lecture there in a course on this subject in April 1980, coming with a ten-page prepared text on "The Art of Nonfiction" and telling students that regular work habits were important, even though he did not stick to them himself: "To avoid steady work for half a century, as I have done, requires talent." [90] He was equally jocular on April 20 when he spoke at the UA's Alternative Energy Festival: "My solution to the energy crisis is conservation. Conservation of energy. I got up at 6 o'clock this morning to write this important speech, sat down at my desk for five minutes, thought about it, and then went back to bed." [91]

As with Les Standiford a decade earlier at the University of Utah, at the UA Abbey did not want to let down Richard Shelton, whose poetry he admired enough that he had quoted from it as an epigraph in *The Monkey Wrench Gang*. He was hired to teach his specialty, creative nonfiction, a new academic field at that time, in an established undergraduate writing program at the UA as well as in a relatively new master's of fine arts program that was just then beginning to burgeon. This was by no means a cushy appointment, however: in the spring of 1981, Abbey taught three courses for $10,000. Only seven years later, at the end of his teaching career in the spring of 1988, did he enjoy a higher status, as a newly appointed full professor with a lighter teaching load and a $30,000 one-semester salary. [92] His first UA graduate course (as representative of his whole teaching career there) deserves close attention, both because enough information is available that it can be reconstructed in detail and because yet another side of Abbey emerges from it.

On January 19, 1981, Abbey walked into English 597ax, his graduate nonfiction writing workshop, to find a very large class sitting before him. The dozen or so pale-faced English graduate students were outnumbered by a large group of tanned Abbey fans, wearing hiking boots and shorts, who had managed to sign up just to take his course, eagerly waiting to sit at the feet of their guru. Abbey was wearing a red bandanna beneath a plaid shirt, with blue jeans and a jean jacket, smoking a pipe and squinting past his reading glasses—looking nothing like the image of Hayduke that his fans expected. Previously he had enjoyed the fringe benefits of being a cult figure on the lecture circuit, but returning to the classroom after a decade away from it, he had neither time nor patience for such nonsense.

Abbey immediately announced that the chief requirement of this course would be three to six publishable pages of writing every week, to be graded and regularly read aloud to the class. He also assigned an impressive list of magazines to be searched for models of writing and possible places to submit work—the *New Yorker, Harper's, Mother Jones*, and several others—and a longer list of essayists to read, beginning with classics by Montaigne, Thoreau, and Orwell and continuing with contemporary writers such as Didion, Berry, Hoagland, Harrington, Dillard, and others.[93] He expected his students to address him as "Mr. Abbey," and he addressed them by last name as "Mr." or "Ms." There was no mention of environmentalist causes, Earth First!, or his own books. As his friend, fellow writer, and UA nonfiction instructor Alan Harrington later remembered, Abbey was "kind and courteous to his students at the University of Arizona" except for those who "fell in love with 'the environmentalist' too quickly."[94] In his literary tastes, "he was a classicist," Robert Houston recalled.[95]

A week later, most of the tanned cultists had dropped the course. So much for sitting at the feet of their master! Abbey walked back into the classroom on January 26, grinned at the sight of a much smaller class of mostly pale-faced graduate students, and exclaimed, "Now, this is more like it!"[96] Soon enough, even the survivors were terrified, especially when they got their first submissions back with letter grades on them, including Bs and Cs. Accustomed to no grades or only As, several were upset, and some of them registered complaints with the English department.[97] But the best students in the class appreciated Abbey's rigor, directness, and encouragement. Several of the students who completed this course went on to become successful teachers, writers, and editors themselves: Jim Hepworth, Nancy Mairs, Rod Kessler, Kathy Miller, and Gale Walden, for example. Like Barry Lopez, Terry Tempest Williams, and John Tallmadge after Abbey's visit to the University of Utah in October 1979, four of Abbey's spring 1981 students—Hepworth, Mairs, Steven Schwartz, and Robert Baird—were impressed enough that each later published their reminiscences about the experience.

This was all the more remarkable in the cases of Schwartz and Baird, because both of them dropped the course early in the semester. "We were all looking forward to having Ed Abbey as our teacher," recalled Schwartz five years later in his editor's column at the *Colorado Review*, but he was surprised when Abbey came back very late after the class break, explaining that he had gotten lost.[98] He could get quite distracted; a colleague once encountered Abbey ogling sunbathing coeds outside the Modern Language building,[99] and his subsequent office mate Peter Wild felt that Abbey would visit him at his home as well as the office in order to keep an eye on Wild's attractive young wife.[100] Schwartz was even more surprised when Abbey "pulverized" his first piece in class and gave him a B, at which point he dropped the course. Abbey signed his drop form only after telling him, "You're one of the best writers in the class," and when he spoke at Colorado State University over four years later, he immediately greeted his former, short-lived student as "Mr. Schwartz," was pleased to see him, and wished him well.[101]

His ability to remember Robert Baird was no less remarkable. Baird's mother, Joan, had been a couple years ahead of Abbey at Indiana High School in the early 1940s, but after Baird mentioned this at the beginning of the course, he felt rebuffed when Abbey seemed to register no reaction whatsoever, and he dropped the course. Over seven years later, they happened to see each other again: "'Keep at the writing. I'll be looking for you,' he said, with one of those wry smiles that never gave too much away. And say hello to your mother.'"[102] Baird later became music editor of Santa Fe's *Stereophile Magazine*. Even those who dropped Abbey's course could become successful editors.

He made an even more lasting impression on those who survived English 597ax. Standing at the blackboard with "green pants, boots, battered briefcase, big hands," Abbey wrote advice:

1. Write right—correct.
2. Write good—with style and wit, so it's entertaining.
3. Right wrong: be a crusader.
4. Write on! (It does pay to be persistent.) Specialize! Seek controversy. Honesty is the best policy in art and journalism.

Soon, class member Rod Kessler got in the spirit of things by giving Abbey a grading sheet containing the statement, "Mr. Abbey thanks you for submitting your work" and a drawing of him handing back a paper with the comment, "You write good."[103]

Week after week, Abbey asked students to read their work aloud to each other, with everyone responding, critiquing, and making suggestions. This procedure was unnerving to those who were used to being able to read assigned writing in advance, but it did force everyone to attend to the importance of the spoken voice in what they wrote and listened to. Like everyone else, Abbey sat at a classroom desk—which looked like an elementary school desk with him squeezing into it. He told his students to write every day, but admitted that he did not do that himself and that he never spent more than twenty-four hours writing an article, though he always regretted that afterward. "We wrote this down too," Steven Schwartz recounted. "There didn't seem any contradiction between what he said and did. Sometimes one's persona can embrace contradictions that in others would be screamingly hypocritical."[104]

Abbey also brought some memorable guests into English 597ax, such as Alan Harrington and John G. Mitchell. Author of *The Immortalist*, Harrington (who died in 1997) befuddled students by explaining seriously and in detail why they should never have to die. Mitchell, Abbey's old friend from Sierra Club Books, came to town while he was working on an article about Abbey for *Rocky Mountain Magazine* and stayed with him at his house. After Abbey played his flute early in the mornings, they took long walks through the desert, where he complained to his visitor about new development already evident in the area, which made him want to move to Australia or back to Utah. Mitchell observed drafts of magazine articles and student papers strewn everywhere on Abbey's desk, with his book manuscript pushed off to one side. Abbey told him that he had been wasting his time "on magazine articles . . . when what I should have been doing was writing a really good book. . . . I write in a hurry. . . . Three thousand words a day. You make careless mistakes at that speed."[105] In class, Mitchell talked just as frankly as his host typically did, getting into a lively debate about hunting with a vegetarian student who brought her dog to class.[106]

After a few weeks confined to the classroom, Abbey took English 597ax to the Big A, his beloved beer-and-hamburger joint along the main drag of Speedway near campus. Someone ratted on them, however, and they were forced to return to the classroom since meeting off-campus violated university policy. But everyone seemed to relax after that, including Abbey, "his shyness now natural and close-fitting, not a piece of armor." For the last meeting of the class, he once again flouted UA policy by inviting the class to his house, where he and Clarke served them hot dogs in tortillas and everyone drank beer and watched the sunset.[107]

When Jim Hepworth (later coeditor of the first collection of essays about Abbey, *Resist Much, Obey Little* [1985]) mentioned early in the course that he feared failure as a writer, Abbey said that perhaps he should go see a shrink.[108] But Hepworth survived to earn an A in the course—which felt so undeserved coming from Abbey that he protested, but was met by the retort, "Who's the teacher for this here course?" Hepworth notes that Abbey was a tough grader of his own work, too, as in April 1983 in his journal, where the average "grade" that he assigned to his own books was a C+, including a B for *Desert Solitaire* (286).[109] It was this hard-headed self-scrutiny that most impressed Hepworth, who appreciated being told that "only a blockhead would write for anything but money."[110] Similarly, Nancy Mairs (who was also a student in his spring 1985 seminar on the essay) found that Abbey treated her "not as a potential, even a promising writer, but a writer in fact." "You write good, Ms. Mairs," he wrote at the end of one of her essays, "on a professional standard. Which is why I judge you so hard. . . . Don't get mad. Don't give up."[111]

Mairs eventually published not one but three separate essays about Abbey as a teacher. These pieces chart a fascinating series of responses, both good and bad, constituting just about the most thorough student evaluation ever composed. In the 1985 *Resist Much, Obey Little* and the April 1989 *Tucson Weekly*, as fitting for two collections of tributes to Abbey both before and just after his death, she sang his praises for "the debt I owe you for staking me to a writer's life." In "597ax," she quoted his pragmatic advice at the end of one of her long essays: "I can understand that your reminiscences seem precious to you, as mine do to me, but somehow you've got to find a way, a device, a meaning, to make these memoirs readable to an ordinary bored, busy, hard-nosed, cynical, weary, cigar-smoking, whisky-drinking, fornicating old fart like—not me!—but your typical magazine or book editor."[112] Abbey was also willing to comment on politics, as when he wrote on Rod Kessler's essay about El Salvador, "You should also have mentioned Archbishop Romero, who pleaded with Carter to send no more arms to the junta. The Archbishop was shot in his church, while performing the Mass."[113]

In Mairs's 1994 feminist book *Voice Lessons: On Becoming a Woman Writer*, however, Abbey is not named (though nonetheless unmistakably identified) in a much more distanced critique of how he inevitably had approached her writing in a patriarchal fashion: "I deferred to the values of the Fornicating Old Fart . . . because he'd published a lot of books and I hadn't published any. . . . I began to recognize that in fact nine-tenths of the literature I was familiar with had been written for FOFs, of which, by virtue of my gender, I could not be one." She noted that "I took a long time to free myself of FOF's notion that one merits one's memoirs through acquiring fame, and to develop the divergent sense of purpose I'm describing."[114] She wanted to "write a female body" rather than phallocentrically call attention like Abbey always did. Even while deliberately staking out a different territory for herself, Mairs returned to Abbey as a key, influential reference point.

Abbey had become a very effective, memorable teacher, but he always remained frustrated with teaching both because he was so self-disparaging about his own abilities in the classroom and because he worked so hard at it that even one semester of teaching significantly interfered with his own writing. For this latter reason he would take leave in 1983 and 1986, especially to work on the book that became *The Fool's Progress*. "The better teacher Ed becomes," Mairs noted in "597ax," "the more tempted I am to burst into his office, shouting and shooing: 'Off with you! Now! Go breach a dam. Lock the door behind you. And lose the key.'"[115]

As we have already seen, Abbey *did* "go breach a dam," at the March 21, 1981, Cracking of Glen Canyon Dam, right in the middle of this course. And two days before this event, *Rolling Stone* published his attack on the MX missile and nuclear testing in Southwestern deserts, in its March 19 issue.[116] But he kept his work as a teacher and his career as a polemicist quite separate from each other. He never mentioned the Cracking of Glen Canyon Dam in English 597ax.[117] In the UA English department where his appointment had been less than universally popular, Abbey kept his reputation as a writer who was likely to say just about anything in the popular press, regularly creating controversy in Tucson and beyond. Yet at meetings of the creative writing faculty, he tended to sit quietly as if "on a stump back in Home or Moab," as Robert Houston put it, participate conscientiously in deliberations, and generally (once again) contradict his public image as a firebrand. However, in the different setting of a public reading, even someone else's reading, his personality changed. When Houston read from his novel *Bisbee 17* at the UA on March 24, 1982, his friend and colleague Abbey comically heckled him from the audience.[118]

After a relatively quiet summer, two events in the fall of 1981 brought more attention to Abbey both in Tucson and beyond: James Watt's visit to the city on September 15, and NBC's airing of the television movie *Fire on the Mountain* in November. When Watt appeared to speak to a Republican gathering, 2,500 protestors jammed the parking lot of his motel. Abbey told them that he had "predicted several years ago," in *Desert Solitaire*,[119] "that National Park Service officials were going to turn the national parks 'into Disneylands.' I was only kidding at the time," but now it seemed as if Watt were actually trying to enact the idea.[120] Watt assured the Republican faithful that "there is one particular species he would like to see endangered and eliminated—liberals."[121] Abbey wrote fondly of these events in a December 1981 article in *Rolling Stone*, "Waiting for the Fifth Card."

By May 19, 1983, Earth First! would up the ante to the point that, when Watt appeared at Glen Canyon Dam to celebrate its twentieth anniversary, they returned to the scene of its "cracking" and mounted a full-fledged assault by land, by air, and by sea: demonstrators chanted from the roadway beside an effigy of Watt, a plane sailed over pulling a banner reading "Earth First! Free the Colorado!," and a houseboat harassed the boat on which Watt was ceremoniously perched. Watt told the press there that "he had 'never heard' of Edward Abbey or his Monkey Wrench Gang."[122] Earth First! would follow him relentlessly the rest of that summer—to Wyoming, Alaska, and Arches National Park—and Watt eventually resigned after one of his more egregious verbal gaffes. On February 2, 1984, Abbey would publish a letter in the *Earth First! Journal*: "I've been thinking: Hey! Why not—recruit *James Watt* for Earth First!? Now, right now, might be the ideal time. Think how pissed, disconsolate, shaken and embittered he must be these days. (He's a great fund-raiser—and a wit!)."[123]

On November 23, 1981, Abbey's brand of defiant defense of the land came to national television, albeit in TV's inevitably watered-down version, in Charmaine Balian's NBC production of *Fire on the Mountain*, starring Buddy Ebsen as John Vogelin and Ron Howard as his friend Lee Mackie. Abbey had written his novel "frankly for Hollywood" over twenty years earlier, and not only had he waited two decades to finally see it on the screen, but he had to go to a neighbor's house to watch it, since he no longer owned a TV set.[124] Ebsen felt that it was "one of the most important pieces of film I've ever done,"[125] and he was fairly impressive as the crusty Vogelin, as was Michael Conrad in the role of his adversary, Colonel DeSalius.

However, overall this movie (which was rebroadcast by WTBS in 1991) was something like "The Waltons"—but armed.[126] Ron Howard and Julie Carmen were scripted to play a Lee Mackie and Cruza Peralta who bore only slight resemblances to Abbey's characters. Here Mackie is a land speculator who has returned to New Mexico after a long time away, and Cruza is Vogelin's housekeeper but has no husband. None of this was the case in Abbey's novel. These changes set up Mackie and Cruza for their inevitable TV romance, likewise completely fabricated. As in *Lonely Are the Brave*, only a brief credit indicating that this movie was "based on the work by Edward Abbey" flashed by, though this time he was paid much better, and the NBC movie did bring something of his views to many who had never read his works. His fame was also increased a month later when Russell Martin featured him in a *New York Times Magazine* cover story on "Writers of the Purple Sage."[127]

Abbey was determined to get back out into the wilderness on his own terms. In early December 1981, he took a two-week solo hike, over 110 miles, through the pristine mountain and desert country from Wellton to Lukeville, Arizona, crossing the U.S. Air Force Gunnery Range, the Cabeza Prieta wilderness, and Organ Pipe Cactus National Monument. He fantasized about taking "Abbey's Last Walk," disappearing like B. Traven (292). Afterward, as he recorded on December 11, Clarke met him in Ajo, in a "sweet, sexy, passionate reunion." But then she found in his journal "something silly I'd written about what a great lover of 'many women' I have been." He resolved that "I must learn to control my pen" (278). He followed this with a two-week camping trip—over Christmas and beyond New Year's, with Clarke, Susie, and John De Puy and his wife—to Sierra Desemboque on the Sonoran coast in Mexico.[128] This was just a month before he published "My Friend Debris" in the *Bisbee Times*, but he did not show his tribute to his old friend, preferring to surprise him.

Abbey spoke about his December 1981 desert solo trek on April 22, 1982, as the fourth annual Belkin Lecturer at the University of California at San Diego (289), and then published "This Antique and Empty Land" in the April 1984 *GEO*—an abridged version of what became "A Walk in the Desert

Hills" in *Beyond the Wall*. Here he characteristically concealed the route of his walk through beloved wilderness places, disguising Lukeville—where he arrived near the Mexican border, after following the old Camino del Diablo that he had driven with his ranger pals in February 1969—as "Bagdad," [129] a town located impossibly across the state, west of Prescott.[130]

In mid-January 1982, Abbey commenced his second year of teaching at the University of Arizona, confessing to himself on January 28 that "vanity and greed" kept him on the job, along with his "economic fears" (268). He also made public appearances in Los Angeles, Flagstaff, Missoula, and several other places, largely to help sell his third collection of essays, *Down the River*, which was published by Dutton early that year. This was his first book to feature, at his insistence, his own illustrations. It also included some essays that he had managed to write while teaching full-time a year earlier at the UA, such as "Aravaipa Canyon," which he had read aloud to his English 597ax students [131] and then published in the *New York Times*. This book received good reviews, most visibly in the *New York Times Book Review*, where Tim Cahill wrote that "running like a river through all these essays is the sound of rippling water." [132]

Abbey himself felt that it was "a damn good book, my *best* nonfiction so far," and he was pleased by its Western sales though dissatisfied with its Eastern reviews (279–80). He replied to a review in *The Nation* by sardonically agreeing ("from personal acquaintance"), in a letter to the editor, that "Edward Abbey is indeed an 'arrogant,' 'xenophobic,' 'puerile,' 'smug' and 'dopey' sort of fellow. So far, fair enough. But what about the book? Drabelle never does get around to saying what the book is about. Rivers, maybe?" [133]

True to its title, *Down the River* incorporated several of Abbey's articles about earlier river adventures, such as his summer 1979 Yukon/Alaska journey in "Notes from a Cold River" and his November 1980 Green/Colorado trip in "Down the River with Henry Thoreau," as well as his 1979 article about that year's lively Western River Guides Association gathering in Salt Lake City, "Up the Creek with the Downriver Rowdies," now retitled simply "River Rats." His "Preliminary Notes"—in which he invited readers to write to him at his P.O. box in Oracle—returned to his roots to relate an anecdote about sinking to the bottom of Crooked Creek in his boyhood and to quote a letter from his father in which Paul Abbey had advised him that "every man has to go down a river sometime." [134] This book's "river" title and theme seemed to offer more unity than any of his essay collections since *Desert Solitaire*, but other sections of the book slid easily away from that topic, and overall it is a good but more uneven collection than his others.

"Running the San Juan" recounted one of his outings with his daughter Susie; they ran the San Juan twice and the Green River once during 1979–

81. For one of those trips he left his two dogs, Ellie and Bones, in Oracle with his friend Tom Thompson, who had made his acquaintance in 1976 in his capacity as the mailman tending Abbey's post office box. In an incident recalling the troubled career of Abbey's 1950s dog Homer, Thompson inadvertently drove his truck right over Bones's head—but Abbey shrugged it off when Thompson sheepishly told him what had happened, and Bones lived on for a couple of years afterward, his head carrying a distinctive road rash.[135]

Especially after his May 1982 wedding to Clarke, life finally looked good for Ed Abbey. He had also shared some good times with Susie and was glad to have her living with him in his first secure household in years. This made him regret that he had so little contact with his two sons, Josh (who was trying to make it as actor in New York City) and Aaron (who, "too busy to write" [278], was working on a master's degree in writing at the University of Southern California in Los Angeles).

Abbey had landed a promising new teaching job, another new book was doing well, and he enjoyed a larger readership than ever before. Earth Day had launched *Desert Solitaire* a decade before, and now Earth First! offered a more radical brand of environmentalism in an Abbey mutual admiration society. *The Monkey Wrench Gang* was Earth First!'s inspiration, and these eco-warriors returned the favor throughout the 1980s by providing its author with an expanding audience, a lively notoriety, and a growing legend.

It came as no surprise to Abbey that the FBI had been keeping a file on him for thirty-five years, when he obtained it under the Freedom of Information Act. On May 25, 1982, he noted that he had received his FBI dossier and found it "disappointing—130 pages of tedious dithering" mostly a result of his 1947 "anti-draft letter at Indiana" (279). But he did not assume that they were done with him; six months later, on December 1, he recorded his suspicion that the FBI was probably tapping his phone "right now" (285).

At Earth First!'s July 4, 1982, Round River Rendezvous in the Gros Ventre mountains of northwestern Wyoming, the assembled faithful applauded Abbey's feisty speech, even when he told them, "I'm here today in support of the E.R.A. . . . I mean Equal Rocks Amendment, or equal rights for rocks, and for trees and grass and clouds and flowing streams and bull elk and grizzly and women—yes, ladies, I also support the E.R.A. for women." He grinned and his listeners, both male and female, laughed.[136] Earth First! itself was now becoming more than symbolic. They had chosen Little Granite Creek in Gros Ventre as their meeting place because Getty Oil planned to drill there for oil, but Earth First! blockaded the site, Bart Koehler filed an appeal, and eventually Congress declared the area a protected wilderness.[137] It seemed that the tide was turning for environmentalists. Abbey had also taken great delight from a February 6, 1982, report of a giant saguaro cactus near Phoenix falling on a man and killing him after he shot it: "Hey! there is a God! there is justice in this world."[138]

Fresh from the successful Earth First! Rendezvous in July, Ed and Clarke retreated to southern Colorado, near Great Sand Dunes National Monument, for an extended vacation in a cabin owned by Jim and Ginny Carrico, his old friends from Organ Pipe, who were spending the summer in West Virginia.[139] When his Denver friends Donn and Carol Rawlings visited them there for an afternoon, Abbey explained that (in the style of "The Serpents of Paradise" in *Desert Solitaire*) he had brought a bull snake into the cabin to try to clear out the mice.[140] Life seemed grand—and this was Abbey's kind of life. He and Clarke planned to spend the rest of the summer at the cabin.

In early August, however, Abbey became ill, with pains in his midsection, so he and Clarke drove to Santa Fe to visit Jack Loeffler and ask if Ed could see Jack's doctor. After an attack in Loeffler's living room, Abbey was rushed to the hospital. Doctors did a CAT scan and told Abbey that it looked like he had pancreatic cancer and would have only a few months to live. He immediately turned to Loeffler and quipped, "At least I don't have to floss anymore."[141] Just three months married, he and Clarke lay in his hospital bed, listened to the music of Bach, and wept (283).

Abbey had thought about death for many years, and now it knocked at his door. He had written out detailed "funeral instructions" for Clarke in October 1981, seven months before their wedding, and now, on August 12, 1982, he determined to review his will, make Clarke its executor, write letters to his friends and family, arrange for publication of "two more books" salvaged from his previous writings, and "say good-bye and go for a walk 'in the spirit of adventure, never to return'" (280–81).

CHAPTER NINE

"If there's anyone here I've failed to insult . . ."
1982–1985

The next few years of Ed Abbey's life involved a curious mix of poor health and the threat of death, personal happiness with his new wife and the beginning of another family, and political controversies provoked by his own defiant writings. A month after being told in August 1982 that he had only a few months left to live, Abbey noted that, while he was greatly saddened at the idea of being "forced so suddenly, abruptly, prematurely, to leave my beloved Clarke and Susie, and the desert hills and sunsets, and music and books and my friends and my work," he nevertheless "felt no fear" (281). It occurred to him that he had been preparing "for this very hour for the last thirty-five or forty years of my life" (283). Indeed, as early as December 15, 1951, at the age of twenty-four in Edinburgh, just after his first wife's departure, he had written a journal entry on "HOW TO DIE" ("*Alone*, elegantly, a wolf on a rock") and "how not to" ("*Not* in snowy whiteness under arc lights and klieg lights . . . under clinical smells and sterilized medical eyes") (12). Now he felt "no anger, fear or dismay or any of the alleged five stages of the terminal patient (fuck Kubler-Ross)." He resolved that he "would hold out as long as possible, settle my affairs, do what literary work I could, and then, as the pain and debilitation became too much, I would take a walk" (283).

Then, however, exploratory surgery at the end of August revealed that it was not cancer after all. As he wrote to his old friend Ralph Newcomb: "When they opened me up they found a few little gallstones and a somewhat inflamed pancreas gland. Nothing more. No trace of cancer. For lack of anything better to do, they chopped out my gall bladder and my appendix and stitched me back together. . . . For three weeks—from diagnosis to the day after the surgery—I was staring Old Mother Death right in the face. . . . And discovered that I was ready."[1] Abbey explained later to an interviewer: "The dark blob on the X-ray screens and CAT-scans turned out to be some kind of portal vein thrombosis, which means that I may die at any moment of a massive internal hemorrhage. But in the meantime I feel fine and carry on as usual. . . . Like everyone else, I've lived close to death all of my life."[2] Getting the right diagnosis took some time. Robert Beliveux, a physician and the second husband of Rita Deanin Abbey, told him in September that he had "acute and chronic pancreatitis," Abbey noted, requiring a "strict dietary regimen" for the rest of his life, "if any." He was supposed to eliminate alcohol and caffeine and sharply reduce animal fats, dairy products, pork, and beef. "Shit" (282).

But the most accurate diagnosis was esophageal varices, which caused periodic and severe hemorrhaging.[3] This condition, which is often linked to drinking, plagued Abbey for the rest of his life, eventually killing him. He confessed that it was "an old wino's disease."[4] He actually lived longer than could be expected; another physician reported that, typically with esophageal varices, Abbey could be expected to survive less than two years.[5] "For the most part he was able to carry on with what he did on a regular basis," Clarke Abbey recalled. "There would just be occasions where he would have a bleed and it would really bring him down for a month or two, just until his blood level came back up."[6] He cut back on his drinking but did not entirely stop. For the rest of his life, Abbey often concealed his condition from all but his most intimate friends and family. He never wanted people to treat him like a dying man, neither soon after his 1982 attack nor when he was more closely approaching death six years later.

Privately, however, Abbey had written his own epitaph in his journal in October 1981, stipulating that the words "NO COMMENT" were to be inscribed on his gravestone (277). Seven and a half years before his death, his funeral instructions were specific and most unconventional. He wanted his corpse to be slipped into "an old sleeping bag or tarp" and hauled "in the bed of a pickup truck and buried as soon as possible after death." If the burial site proved to be "too rocky for burial," then he asked that sand and stones be piled over him "sufficient to keep coyotes from dismembering and scattering my bones." He explained that he wanted his body to "help fertilize the growth of a cactus, or cliffrose, or sagebrush, or tree." His order was to "disregard all state laws regarding burials" (276). He concluded that it was not death or dying that was tragic but rather to have "existed without fully participating in life—that is the deepest personal tragedy" (277).

Having received a reprieve less than a year after writing these words, Abbey lived up to them, throwing himself back into life, letters, and controversy with a vengeance. He returned to Tucson and his new life with Clarke. At the beginning of September 1982, Susie went to Verde Valley School near Sedona, four hours away, but she was unhappy there and asked to come home. Ed decided that he missed her "as much as she misses me" and that he should never have sent her to "that detention camp for unwanted teen-agers of wealthy families" (282). Susie then stayed in Tucson through her four high-school years.

Sitting above the Goosenecks of the San Juan River at Muley Point, Utah, on October 25 (284), Abbey wrote a poem "For Clarke," concluding (though "we love one day and we battle the next") that "I'm cleaving to Clarke till I croak."[7] He had "sown his wild oats," as his old friend Ann Woodin was convinced.[8] At the end of 1982, Clarke learned that she was pregnant. On October 10, 1983, she gave birth to Rebecca Claire Abbey, and Ed noted that they were both "delighted by our Becky" (309). Happily married, with two daughters and a position at the university (though he did not teach again until the spring 1984 semester), Abbey settled back into his Tucson house, the most stable home he had known since adolescence. He told Eric Temple in December 1982 that he wanted to "write a few more good books and die. . . . I've got a teenaged daughter, got to get her through the agonies of adolescence before I can shunt her off to college. I'd like to grow wise and venerable, but I haven't figured out how to do it yet."[9]

As a citizen of Tucson, Abbey was no more settled in accepting the status quo than he had ever been. For the rest of his life, he appointed himself the city's and the region's leading radical curmudgeon, zipping off a series of letters to newspapers and magazines and delivering incendiary speeches. As his friend Charles Bowden—fellow Tucson writer and eventually inheritor of Abbey's mantle as a champion of the Arizona desert—wrote later, Abbey "seemed hardly able to get through a day without firing off a broadside to some newspaper or magazine."[10] And as Abbey himself would write in *The Fool's Progress* (also using the line in his "Preliminary Remarks" in *One Life at a Time, Please*): "Brahms said in farewell to the assembled lords and ladies, 'If there's anyone here I've failed to insult—I apologize.' Good man." [11] Soon he would be embroiled in the two controversies in which he stirred up more trouble than at any other time in his life: his opposition to Mexican immigration, which peaked in 1983, and his 1985 attack on the cattle industry.

Abbey declared in his journal on October 4, 1982, that he wrote to "amuse my friends, and to aggravate—exasperate—ulcerate—our enemies" (284). He added to Temple: "I'm trying to write good books, make people laugh, make them cry, provoke them, make them angry, make them think if possible. To get a reaction, give pleasure." [12] His October 29 letter in the *Arizona Republic* assured voters that it was time for "another make-believe election" with "Tweedledum, tweedledee and tweedledoo—the bad, the worse, and the ridiculous." On December 12 he argued in the *Arizona Daily Star* that people should learn to live within their means and keep Tucson from growing right up into Phoenix. That same month in *American West* (in a letter appropriately headlined "Ed Abbey Takes a Shot"), he renewed his central thesis: "The American West as a whole is under a massive attack by industrial greed."

Abbey increased his letter-writing barrage during 1983, increasingly going against the grain on such issues as gender and immigration. As he admitted to himself in September 1983, he had "indulged in a frenzy of irascible letter-writing this summer. Letters against illegal immigration, against Tucson's growth, against androgyny," appearing in such places as *New Times* and the Tucson papers (307). He called himself "Abbey the crank," admitting that he had become "just one more cranky, cantankerous, dyspeptic, choleric, poker-playing, whiskey-drinking, cigar-smoking evil old man. The curmudgeon. Good" (308).

The most heated issue that Abbey ever took on was immigration. He had been convinced for a long time that overpopulation was a big part of the reason why the environment and economy of the United States were under such stress—a belief that had been reinforced earlier by Paul Ehrlich's 1968 book *The Population Bomb* and that would later be taken up (partly because of Abbey's influence) by Earth First! throughout the 1980s and by elements of the Sierra Club in the 1990s. In southern Arizona, exponential population growth was exacerbated both by U.S. migration to the sunbelt from such areas as the Northeast and by immigration from Mexico. Nothing could easily be done about migration within the United States, but Abbey felt that illegal immigration from Mexico had to be stopped.

He had been irked by a review in the October 1981 *New York Review of Books* in which the reviewer had repeated what struck Abbey as a "facetious 'calculation'" by Tucsonan Tom Miller, in his book *On the Border*, that it would take "two and a half million men, standing shoulder to shoulder, to close the Mexican border to illegal aliens." In contrast, Abbey argued in his December 18, 1981, letter to the *Review* that 20,000 men "properly armed and equipped" could stem illegal immigration. He added that illegal immigrants "take jobs away from American citizens and that the estimated ten billion dollars remitted annually from Mexican aliens to their relatives still in Mexico is money that should be going into the pockets of American workers." He also noted that this immigration really benefited American employers and border merchants as well as Mexican employers and politicians (who needed a "safety valve" for their grossly underpaid workers). While admitting that closing the border was a "harsh, even cruel" proposition, Abbey concluded that, because "the American boat is full if not already overloaded, the U.S. cannot afford further mass immigration," and "the most compassionate thing we can do for nations like Mexico is to encourage them, somehow, to commence the policies of deep internal reform and population stabilization that are clearly necessary."[13]

Abbey's initial argument here was focused on economics, not ethnicity, and it was aimed not specifically at readers in the Southwest but rather at a national readership via the *New York Review of Books* (albeit in its seemingly marginal letters column). He had known Hispanos in New Mexico throughout the 1950s, including Amador Martinez, whose name figured both in his fiction and in his definitive list of real-life friends.[14] In 1959, Abbey had edited the bilingual Taos newspaper *El Crepusculo de la Libertad*; in a 1979 article he had quoted César Chavez.[15] Throughout his life, one of his favorite (and most frequently quoted) assertions—right up there with Whitman's "resist much, obey little"—was one he borrowed from the Mexican revolutionary Emiliano Zapata: "The earth, like the sun, like the air, belongs to everyone—and to no one."[16] Abbey had visited Mexico several times and would continue to do so. His old friend John De Puy insisted that Abbey believed the Mexican government was an abominable betrayal of the Zappatista revolution and should be forced to confront its own problems rather than continue to "dump people on us because they couldn't deal with their own people."[17]

Abbey's economic argument for a national readership, however, was swiftly turned into an ethnic controversy in Arizona, where he was pressed into a defensive corner. Having thrown down the gauntlet, this defiant controversialist would not let it go—even if it meant that the shift to an ethnic focus would only make him look worse to many readers. On December 30, 1981, Tucson's *Arizona Daily Star* published a snide attack ironically entitled "A Nice Fellow": "A hero to some," Abbey was believed to be "a passionate defender of humanity as well as the environment"—until the appearance of his *New York Review of Books* letter. "It is a smugly elitist proposition to argue that any cultural influence—other than the good old U. S. of A.—cheapens and degrades American life."[18]

Rather than reply only with a simple clarification—that he had focused on the economics of overpopulation, not on ethnicity or culture—Abbey was provoked by this editorial attack, as well as invited by the *New York Times*, to turn his letter into a full-fledged essay. As "Immigration and Liberal Taboos," this essay would eventually reach its widest audience in *One Life at a Time, Please* (1988). He made it clear, in his inimitable style, that it was not about culture but rather about the problems inherent in large-scale immigration, and that he was certainly not opposed to a better economic situation for Mexicans: "Stop every campesino at our southern border, give him a handgun, a good rifle, and a case of ammunition, and send him home. He will know what to do with our gifts and good wishes. The people know who their enemies are."[19]

Before being included several years later as his "favorite" essay in *One Life at a Time, Please*, however, Abbey's most controversial essay underwent the most torturous periodical history of any in his career. He explained in his "Preliminary Remarks" in that book that he had written it "on assignment from the editors of *The New York Times* Op-Ed page," but after several months of revision and delay, they rejected it, and he endured several other rejections before it appeared in *New Times* as "The Closing Door Policy" at the end of June 1983.

> I sent the editors a bill for my time, trouble, and expenses, and asked for the return of my essay. This letter was not answered and my original copy never returned. Four years later *The New York Times* still owes me five hundred dollars plus eighty-eight cents in postage expenses.
>
> Rejected by the *Times*, I mailed my immigration piece to other periodicals. In quick succession it was turned down by *Harper's, The Atlantic, The New Republic, Rolling Stone, Newsweek's* "My Turn" and—automatically—by *Mother Jones*. I should have known. Giving up on the national press, I persuaded Mike Lacey, editor of *New Times*, a Phoenix weekly, to publish my loathsome little essay in his magazine. Bravely, he agreed to do it, though covering himself by giving equal space for reply to a local Chicano politico. I did my part for interracial goodwill by donating my two-hundred-dollar fee to a Mexican American arts center in Phoenix. The politico did his by calling me a racist.[20]

Abbey upped the ante by responding to Alfredo Gutierrez in *New Times* in August 1983: "Exactly as I stated, anyone who dares to oppose immigration will be attacked as a racist by our Hispanic politicos. Nevertheless, race is not the issue. Like most other people, I am opposed to mass immigration *from any source*. On this point, if we can believe opinion polls, some 80 to 90 percent of American citizens agree with me." He then dug himself an even deeper hole with readers by adding, "I will confess to cultural bias. Though an *aficionado* of tacos, Herradura tequila, and ranchero music (in moderate doses), I have no wish to emigrate to Mexico. Nor does Alfredo Gutierrez. . . . At some point soon our Anglo-liberal-guilt neurosis must yield to common sense and enlightened self-interest." [21]

When Abbey asked himself if he was racist in his journal on September 9, 1983, he admitted that he was, if that meant that he did not want to live in a society controlled by Africans, Mexicans, or Asians (307). The very next day, he had a fierce argument with his old friend William Eastlake about Mexican immigration.[22] However, in a 1987 letter to the editor of the *Earth First! Journal*, Abbey would make a distinction between chauvinism and racism: "I am guilty of cultural chauvinism—I much prefer life in the USA to that in any Latin American country; and so do most Latin Americans—but chauvinism is not racism. Racism is the belief that all members of one race are innately superior to all members of some other race. I do not subscribe to any such belief." [23] He would further develop these ideas in a January 3, 1988, journal entry, adding the thought that, if measured in terms of who has done the least harm to the earth, the only "superior" races would be the Australian Aborigines, the "Bushmen of Africa," and perhaps the Hopi tribe of Arizona (337).

In the *Arizona Daily Star*, which had first brought Abbey's controversy to Tucson readers, he had already escalated it with a May 22, 1982, letter: "Since the editors of the *Daily Star* are so devoted to promoting mass immigration from Mexico, it seems to me you might as well change the name of your paper to the *Daily Estrellita*. Better yet, set up your editorial offices in South Nogales, where you can enjoy today the poverty, misery, squalor and gross injustice which will be the fate of America tomorrow, if we allow the Latino invasion of our country to continue." The predictable wave of negative responses that this letter provoked was then followed a year later by the *Arizona Republic*'s story "Author Wants Illegal Aliens Returned to 'Garbage Dumps.'" This inflammatory headline belied the more balanced content of the interview, including Abbey's remarks that "I don't like being called a racist and a bigot and a fascist" and that he opposed "all immigration legal or illegal, from any source, not simply Latin America, Haiti, Asia but from England, France, anywhere." [24]

Although he had begun with the economics of immigration, this clearly became a free-speech issue for Abbey. He felt that liberal taboos against any criticism of "minority" ethnic groups represented a form of censorship. In a March 1985 letter to the *New York Times Book Review*, he criticized a review that had called a travel writer prejudiced for describing loud amplified noise frequently heard on a trip through Turkey, asking if that meant "that a writer must not report what he actually sees in third world nations if that observation conflicts with New York liberal sentiments about third world culture? . . . It is an author's duty as well as right to speak the truth, offensive though it may be to this or that group." [25]

This controversy continued to haunt Abbey in Tucson. He told the *Arizona Republic* that "I'd much rather keep quiet on this issue" and that he felt "squeamish about talking about such things as deportation." [26] When "Immigration and Liberal Taboos" appeared in *One Life at a Time, Please* in 1988, Charles Bowden quoted from it in his Tucson *City Magazine* — and received a string of angry phone calls. He asked Abbey to call one angry Latino reader, at which point Abbey sheepishly told Bowden that "he wished he'd never written that piece, that it had hurt too many people and raised too much bad feeling for whatever value the ideas in it might have." [27] In that same collection of essays, Abbey sought to explain himself further in a passage in "A San Francisco Journal": "I acknowledge that we are all the descendants of illegal aliens — including the American Indians, who apparently crossed the Bering Strait or land bridge only twenty-thousand years ago. But sooner or later we must draw the line. . . . Mexico needs not more loans — money that will end up in the Swiss bank accounts of *los ricos* — but a revolution." [28]

Rather than remain master of the controversy, as he usually did, in this case the controversy mastered him. Yet, as in the case of his proposal in *Desert Solitaire* to keep cars out of national parks, his argument was not popular at the time but was taken up by others later. U.S. border patrols became much more vigilant of the Mexican border, anti-immigration initiatives were mounted in states such as California, and, by the late 1990s, the Sierra Club would conduct a referendum on immigration and its impact on the U.S. environment.

This dispute would continue to follow Abbey even after his death. In April 1990, a Latino politician in Tucson, Pima County supervisor Raul Grijalva, refused to accept an environmental award named after Abbey, explaining that he was "uneasy because of Abbey's views on immigration, Mexicans, and population growth." [29] In 1984, while still in the midst of the controversy, Abbey wrote a generous endorsement for the Latino writer Luis Urrea, which helped him win a Western States Book Award. [30] Yet in 1996, Urrea's essay "Down the Highway with Edward Abbey" — in which he carried on an imaginary conversation with Abbey while driving his Cadillac, which had been bought by Abbey's friend Ernie Bulow — was less than complimentary. Urrea concluded that Abbey had been guilty of "Pete Wilsonesque scapegoating" (as in the anti-immigration campaign led by the California governor) but that if "Ed Abbey had feet of clay," that made him "just like me."[31] In short, the "racist" tag remained attached to Abbey—one much more simplistic than the picture that emerges from a full reading of his life and writings.

His literary sparring partner and fellow Western writer Tom McGuane eventually delivered a warning that Abbey should beware of becoming "a professional curmudgeon instead of a productive writer. That's a much smaller role than Ed can comfortably occupy. I would like him to be what he can be, an energetic, original comic novelist, a fresh American voice, and stop being such a fucking sourpuss."[32] In early 1983, several years before this admonishment, Abbey was determined to return to his big book projects. He therefore chose not to teach that year. On January 15 he wrote his old friend Ralph Newcomb that he was working on "a long semi-autobiographical novel" in which he planned to "include a few episodes from our Beatnik days in Albuquerque," such as the "great house-warming party" in which he had "burned down the adobe hacienda in Peralta."[33] But it would take him a few more years to finish his "fat masterpiece," *The Fool's Progress* (1988).

In the meantime, Abbey negotiated to complete the collection of essays that he had long wanted to extract from his coffee-table books—without the photographs. By the end of March 1983, his editor Jack Macrae had left Dutton for Holt, where he would oversee his own line of books, and his agent Don Congdon had similarly formed his own independent agency. Abbey followed them both and shaped *Beyond the Wall* from pieces of *Slickrock, Cactus Country, The Hidden Canyon*, and *Desert Images*. His University of Arizona colleague Peter Wild noted in his review that "some of these volumes bore such a high price tag, the writer quips, that only his enemies could afford them. Now, we give thanks, this edition makes them available to Abbey's friends." Abbey's instinct that reviewers and readers would pay more attention to these writings once they had been separated from the photographs was accurate, and the essays in this book are some of his best. Following its release in early 1984, *Beyond the Wall* attracted many positive reviews. Bruce Brown declared him "one of the nation's great writers on the arid wildernesses of the West" in the *Washington Post*; in the *New York Times Book Review*, Alice Hoffman called him "the voice of all that is ornery and honorable."[34] In June, Abbey was featured in *People* magazine.[35]

The year 1984 was a big one in the canonization of Ed Abbey, especially after Dutton released *Slumgullion Stew: An Edward Abbey Reader*. Here "the Author's Preface to His Own Book" and his own illustrations accompanied extracts from all of his previous books except for *Beyond the Wall* and the coffee-table books excerpted in that collection. His instinct did not serve him so well as with *Beyond the Wall*: against editorial advice, he insisted on the title *Slumgullion Stew*,[36] and this book did not sell very well or receive many reviews until Sierra Club Books, in its 1988 paperback edition, retitled it simply *The Best of Edward Abbey*. Only then did the *New York Times* sit up and take notice that Abbey had insisted "on editing his own anthology."[37] Like *Abbey's Road*, these books show the extent to which Abbey now enjoyed a strong "author function," with a readership on the lookout for his name regardless of what his current subject might be.

The more original "fat masterpiece" would be slow in coming—not only because Abbey was now embroiled in editing these other books, and in his new family and his teaching position (resumed in 1984), but also because he began to travel a lot again. He continued to receive many speaking invitations, but prestige was not always enough to attract him. In early 1983, he spoke at Notre Dame along with Susan Sontag, Barry Lopez, and Richard Brautigan (286)—but then he turned down an invitation that spring from Yale.

Instead, Abbey returned to Indiana University of Pennsylvania, where he gave a reading and a talk on April 28, 1983, and was honored as an "IUP Ambassador." He had sent his mother a plane ticket so she could come see him in Tucson for a few days at the beginning of February, and now he was interested in getting back home and in seeing the country along the way, which he had not done for quite a while. He wanted to research *The Fool's Progress*, in which Henry Lightcap would make the long drive home. Abbey had hoped to take that same trip (for which he would have to wait for another three years) in April, but, after flying to Pittsburgh and being delivered to his mother and father's house by his old friend, IUP English professor John Watta, he took the train back to Tucson. His visit to his hometown happened to come shortly before the town's gala "75th birthday party" in May for Jimmy Stewart, during which the actor was greeted by a big new statue of him that was unveiled in front of the county courthouse. Any attention to Abbey in his native county was buried far beneath the barrage of media hype surrounding the Hollywood icon's return home.[38]

In early June, Ed and Clarke traveled through the canyon country of southeastern Utah. He left a note on his friend Jim Stiles's cabin door near Monticello on June 16, shortly after finding out about attempts to develop an area of the La Sal National Forest near Mount Tukuhnikivats (which he had described climbing in *Desert Solitaire*): "We stopped by to say 'Hell-O!' But you ain't here. . . . P.S.: Evil doings a-foot up in Gold Basin. Better send some of the Gang up there quick." That same summer, Abbey spoke at an Earth First! rally at Jackson Hole, Wyoming, where activists had gathered to protest Getty

Oil's plans to carve more roads into the wilderness.[39] He also followed up by sending Stiles a card on August 28, adopting his common practice of seeing to it that Utah politicians received his statements from a Utah address: "Please mail the enclosed cards for me, with fake addresses. I see the phucking Forest Service is allowing phucking Exxon to phuck up Gold Basin. Disgraceful! Can you do anything about that?"[40]

He would stick with this issue like a bulldog, publishing a letter in the *Moab Times-Independent* on July 24, 1986, during his summer living in a cabin at Ken Sleight's nearby Pack Creek Ranch: "The family and I took a little drive up into Gold Basin the other day to inspect the oil company's vandalism in that area. . . . Citizens, wake up. The public lands belong to all of us." This one short letter would provoke a stream of responses for a month, mostly negative, from reactionary business interests.

Abbey had considered going back to work for the Forest Service that summer but noted in his journal on April 13, 1983, that he had declined an offer to return to his 1975 lookout post on Numa Ridge in Montana because of an offer from *Outside* magazine to run the Kongagut River in Alaska's Brooks Range with Mark Jensen and his Alaska River Expeditions.[41] He had wanted Clarke to join him, but her doctor advised against it because she was beginning her third trimester of pregnancy when Abbey, Jensen, and his crew began their river journey in late June.[42] As late as January 1987, Abbey wrote a letter expressing interest in returning to ranger work—at Bates Well in Organ Pipe Cactus National Monument, but the superintendent decided to close that area to visitors.[43]

An interesting contrast emerges between Abbey's March 1984 *Outside* article concerning his 1983 Alaskan trip and his private journal entries about it. In the magazine that had paid for the trip, he maintained a comparatively cheerful, spunky, entertaining tone. He described not only the river journey but also his dream of robins back in Home and his brief career as a technical writer in Manhattan. Even though he once again failed to see a grizzly bear, he sang the praises of Alaska as "after the Australian outback, . . . the most remote spot on which I've managed to install myself, on this particular planet, so far." He called this article "The Last Pork Chop" in light of an anecdote about a friend of his who took two pork chops when everyone else ate just one and then, when only one remained and everyone else hesitated to take it, he ate that too. "Alaska is not . . . the Last Frontier," Abbey concluded, but "the last pork chop. . . . Alaska is the final big bite on the American table, where there is never quite enough to go around."[44]

In his journal, however, he wondered, even before he set out on what turned out to be his final trip to Alaska, why he felt "no pleasure, no excitement?" (305). He grumbled about the trip in his private journal entries, in contrast to his public *Outside* article. He had to overcome a stomach virus at the beginning of the trip, and, as in 1979, he found that he did not enjoy cold weather, especially in the summer. When the river voyage ended on July 4, Abbey was glad to leave Alaska behind for the final time.

He was happy to return to Tucson, where he spent the rest of the summer. Unable to attend an Earth First! rally in Salt Lake City in September, he sent them a memorable letter instead:

> The undersigned deeply regrets that he cannot be here in the flesh — or what there is left of it. . . . Although my feet, head, belly, etc., are out yonder, my heart is here with all of you posie-sniffers, toadstool worshippers, eco-freaks, earth-lovers, anti-nuke hardheads, environmental blowflies, FBI agents, innocent onlookers, Mothers for Peace and Winos for Ecology. You are the new salt of the Earth. . . . We need more heroes and more heroines — about a million of them. One brave deed, performed in an honorable manner and for a life-defending cause, is worth a thousand books. . . . Philosophy without action is the ruin of the soul. . . .
>
> Climb those mountains, run those rivers, explore those forests, investigate those deserts, love the sun and the moon and the stars and we will outlive our enemies, we will piss on their graves, and we will love and nurture and who knows — even marry their children. . . .
>
> Who's in charge here? We're all in charge: every man his own guru, every woman her own gurette. . . . Down with Empire! Up with Spring! We stand for what we stand on! I thank you, partners.

He then traveled with Clarke to New Mexico and Colorado during the second half of September, in search of the source of the Rio Grande River, in an expedition paid for by *National Geographic*. Unlike his 1976 trip to Australia — as a result of which he wrote articles that *Geographic* deemed unsuitable for its pages — this time the magazine recouped its investment. Abbey's essay about this experience appeared as "The Rio Grande: All Vigor Spent" in the National Geographic Society's 1984 book *Great Rivers of the World*; it was subsequently reprinted (and casually misdated by a year) as "Round River Rendezvous: The Rio Grande, October 1984" in *One Life at a Time, Please*. After making a second funded trip in September 1984, Abbey also published "Big Bend: Desert Rough and Tumble," which described the southern stretch of the Rio Grande, in the autumn 1985 *National Geographic Traveler* (also reprinted in *One Life at a Time, Please*). He thus fulfilled his obligations this time, but he was not overly happy about it. As he memorably explained on September 23, 1984, writing for *National Geographic* was, in his experience, "like trying to jerk off while wearing ski mitts" (316).

Once again, Abbey's published travel writings were happier and more efficient than some of his actual travels. In September 1983, Ed and Clarke enjoyed reunions with Malcolm Brown and Jack Loeffler in New Mexico as they made their way through Gallup, Santa Fe, and Taos on the way to Creede, Colorado. Then, however, as they drove farther and farther into the mountains in search of the sacred source, it started to rain. Nine months pregnant by now, Clarke said, "Ed, maybe we should go back." Determined to reach his elusive destination, Ed drove on through buckets of rain and "we kept climbing," Clarke recounted, "ever upward and onward. Finally the hillside in front of us slid across the road, blocking our forward progress. Ed tried to back up and another mudslide blocked our retreat. I thought, this is not my favorite place to have a baby." Finally Clarke climbed out of the truck, and Ed plowed, in reverse, over the mudslide to safety. "I still remember that truck swerving toward the edge and thinking of Ed going with it."[45] Three weeks later, back in Tucson, Clarke gave birth by cesarean section to Becky. She had survived her Colorado wilderness adventure with Ed—and also the tasty water that he brought home that summer from Tom Thompson's well in Oracle. Ed filled jugs with this water because it tasted so pure and natural to him—until Thompson informed him that the water had tested positive for coliform and was not safe for a pregnant woman to drink.[46]

At the beginning of November 1983, Abbey traveled to Hall's Crossing, Utah, joining a group of geologists from Dartmouth who had invited him to accompany them as "philosopher in residence" on their houseboat on Lake Powell. They had all read *The Monkey Wrench Gang*, and now they made use of "Lake Foul" for their floating field trip to inspect the geology of the Colorado Plateau. Having been advised to lay off the alcohol a year earlier when he had been told he was terminally ill, Abbey was delighted when one of the geologists, Hendrik von Oss, pressed a bottle of Molson's Ale into his palm upon meeting him. He thanked von Oss in the article that he published about this outing in the *New York Times Magazine*, "Houseboat in the Desert"—and again when he reprinted it as "Lake Powell by Houseboat" in *One Life at a Time, Please*, and yet again in his list of acknowledged friends at the beginning of *Hayduke Lives!*[47] A friend in need of a drink was a friend for life.

"Willem van Hoss" also became the name of Henry Lightcap's wild, fictional Santa Fe friend in *The Fool's Progress*. Abbey was not making much progress yet on his big novel, but he was soaking up experience for what he would soon write. When he visited Malcolm Brown that summer, he noticed how thin his old friend had become—and later turned him into that novel's caricaturized aesthete with the same initials, Morton Bildad.

Abbey was writing some articles and making better money than ever before, but since his long-awaited novel still languished, he felt unproductive. He quizzically noted on October 27 that he was doing "nothing," yet "the money continues to flow in." He received regular and healthy royalty checks from publishers such as Dutton and Holt, sizeable sums from the movie option on *The Monkey Wrench Gang*, and payments from magazines such as *Outside* and *National Geographic*. He found it almost "embarrassing." He would return to teaching in January at the University of Arizona—"more easy, unearned increment. Shame, shame." He accused himself of living "falsely. I do not practice what I preach. I wanted a life of freedom, passion, simplicity; I lead instead a life of complicated deals, petty routines, rancorous internal grievances, moral compromise, sloth, acedia and vanity. The only generous thing I ever do is write checks" (309). A couple of weeks later, he told the *Tucson Weekly*, "I don't intend to write any more about environmental issues," though he would "continue to write checks, if not books, for the cause."[48]

Abbey did not stick to his plan to stop writing about the environment. He railed against development in his January 29, 1984, *Arizona Daily Star* editorial, "Arizona's Future: How Big Is Big Enough?" In February he outlined Earth First!'s wilderness proposal in the *Tucson Citizen*, inviting readers to write to his P.O. box in Oracle to get more details, and the *Earth First! Journal* reprinted this article in May. Yet he felt constrained by his reputation, and he wanted very much to return to his big novel. It was during this period that he began instructing his agent, Don Congdon, to refuse requests to reprint selections from *Desert Solitaire*, telling him to ask them to choose other essays. Abbey stuck to this position for the rest of his life, insisting even to his old friend Tom Lyon that he not use anything from *Desert Solitaire* in his 1989 anthology of nature writing;[49] instead, Lyon reprinted "The Great American Desert" from *The Journey Home*.[50]

Abbey not only wrote generous checks to Earth First! and other causes but also often turned down offers of money from his friends. On December 3, 1983, he drove up to Jerome, Arizona, at the invitation of his friend Katie Lee, to speak at a showing of *Lonely Are the Brave* to the Jerome Historical Society. When she called him beforehand to ask what his fee was, encouraging him to quote one since the society had a budget for it, he replied, "Hell, Katie, I don't want a fee. . . . I'd like to see old Jerome again. . . . Just buy me a drink."

He sent her a blurb listing some of his books and adding, "I live near Oracle, Az., have a wife, children, house, bills to pay, the whole catastrophe, and am looking forward to becoming a mean, nasty, ugly, wise old man. Love, Ed."[51]

Abbey was loyal to his old friends, and for a "mean, nasty, ugly, wise old man," he was also surprisingly willing to make new ones. Harvard writer Richard Marius had traveled to Tucson at the beginning of March 1983 to give a reading and talk at the University of Arizona and attend a conference there. He asked his host to call Abbey, who agreed to meet him on March 5, following Marius's last luncheon at the conference. When Marius arrived at Abbey's house, no one was home, and he was filled with beverages from lunch, so he relieved himself near the house—just as Ed and Clarke drove up. While Clarke went inside, Ed—proud outdoor urinator for many years in such scenic spots as Grand and Esperero canyons—gave Marius a friendly greeting. They took a walk in the desert, and then Abbey offered to drive him back into town, but Marius declined, expressing a desire to walk. After he hiked about a mile in his tweed jacket and bow tie, he found Abbey waiting for him at the next intersecting road. "I just wanted to see if you could walk in a straight line," Abbey said, and gave his guest signed copies of several of his books.[52]

He preferred friendship one-on-one. In the late summer of 1983, Ed and Clarke stopped by to visit his old friend Bill Hoy in Bowie, Arizona. Abbey was delighted to see Hoy, and they enjoyed a hike together, after which Hoy invited Ed and Clarke to a party he was hosting. However, uncomfortable meeting so many new people, several of whom were admirers of his work, Abbey excused himself and left with Clarke after they had been at this gathering for only a few minutes.[53] Abbey admitted to himself on May 27, 1984, that he had "come to dislike parties" (314) as his hearing had now become poor.

Abbey had acknowledged to himself many years earlier that he wanted "fame" and "an audience" as a writer (215). He recognized that appearances at bookstores to sign books were necessary for selling his work and extending his reputation. Yet he never enjoyed these appearances, since meeting a series of strangers—even (or perhaps even especially) admiring ones—was never his idea of a good time. In 1984, when *Beyond the Wall* and *Slumgullion Stew* came out, there were plenty of books to sign in a series of bookstores. At Tucson's Book Mark that April, Abbey complained to the *Arizona Daily Star*: "Every time I do one of these things, I swear it'll be the last time. . . . Sure, I like to have my books read and admired, but I don't like to see anyone infatuated with me or my writing. That's obscene."[54] Mike Ives tellingly described Abbey's demeanor at another such appearance in Phoenix in May 1984: "One cheery matron pauses after receiving her autograph and asks brightly, 'Do you enjoy this sort of thing? Signing autographs, I mean?'" Abbey thought about it for a quick moment. "'No.' That is all. No reasons, no elaborations. . . . The woman nods nervously, then departs in disarray."[55]

Nor was this startlingly frank response unusual for Abbey. In Tempe, one reader told him that he had read *The Monkey Wrench Gang* four times and "passed it on to a bunch of friends." Abbey responded, "That's more times than I have read it," and complained, "Do you realize that every time you lend that book to someone I lose 10 cents?"[56] At yet another such appearance, a man told Abbey that he had been on one of his Alaskan river trips with him, apparently expecting Abbey to greet him like a long lost friend. Instead, Abbey replied, "So?" This incident was often repeated as evidence of his coldness, but Ernie Bulow—Abbey's old friend, who happened to be there to witness this exchange—felt that it was simply part of his natural shyness and uncomfortable feeling about people who approached him in large groups.[57]

In contrast, Abbey was always glad to meet another author whose work he admired—and it need not necessarily be a big name (as with John Gardner in 1982). In January 1984, Charles Bowden went to Abbey's house to interview Dave Foreman—who was visiting Abbey and preparing to move to Tucson, where his partner Nancy Morton would study nursing at the UA and where Earth First! would be headquartered until 1989.[58] Bowden was writing an article about Earth First! for the *Tucson Citizen*, and this was his first meeting with Abbey. He later recalled tapping timidly on Abbey's door, at which point Abbey "opened it up, introduced himself and instantly thrust a copy of my first book into my hands"—*Killing the Hidden Waters*, a book about abusive water policies in Arizona, "a text that had fallen dead from the press and taken almost ten years to sell two thousand copies. He asked if I would autograph it, and went on and on about its wonders. So he may have had pretty bad literary taste, but he was one of the kindest men I have ever known."[59] In his *Tucson Citizen* article, Bowden described his host's demeanor during the interview with Foreman: "Abbey teeters on the edge of the talk but mainly puffs his pipe and listens. He is trying to retire from the wars for the West and looks upon Foreman and Morton and their kind as new troops."[60]

Abbey and Bowden shared an interest in environmental issues and opposition to the development of southern Arizona. Yet during the friendship that they quickly formed, "I don't think I ever spent ten minutes," Bowden recollected, "kicking around environmental issues with him," as many of Abbey's friends also remembered. "I guess they were simply a given."[61] Instead, they talked about books. Abbey regularly attacked John Updike—whom he described in *The Nation* as "the Engelbert Humperdinck of contemporary American Lit"—and Saul Bellow ("friend of power, hierarchy, techno-industrialism").[62] He regularly gave Bowden "armloads of books" that he admired and wanted to share.[63]

Bowden also edited Abbey. Once Abbey forgot to write a piece that he had promised him, so when Bowden stopped by to pick it up just before the deadline, Abbey wrote it in his car as Bowden sped across town. "When I got there it was finished, the pages were full of pen marks moving sentences, scratching out words, adding new thoughts. The damn thing looked like a snake pit packed with writhing serpents and he was still at it with his pen as I pried it out of his hands."[64] On another occasion in 1984, Abbey "suggested that a suitable memorial should be created for a leading local developer," Roy Drachman. "He wanted to name the Ina Road sewage treatment plant after him. Neither newspaper would publish the letter."[65]

Abbey also wondered, understandably enough, if the *Bloomsbury Review* would print his long review of Susan Brownmiller's *Femininity* and Gloria Steinem's *Outrageous Acts and Everyday Rebellions*, but they did publish it in September 1984. As he later noted in his "Preliminary Remarks" to *One Life at a Time, Please*, where this review was reprinted, "'The Future of Sex' began as a routine book review for the *Bloomsbury Review* but escaped its ball and chain and took off for the territory ahead."[66] Ironically, Abbey had taught "The Art of Reviewing" (along with "The Art of the Essay") as one of his two spring 1984 courses at the UA,[67] but he did not follow whatever advice he gave students about tactfully matching the review to the occasion. As with his outrageous letter to *Ms.* magazine in 1973, Abbey once again got himself in trouble with feminists. He had been provoked by Steinem's April 1984 appearance at the UA, where he felt that her positions were those of a Milquetoast liberal rather than a real radical.[68]

This time Abbey was not joking, as he had done with his letter to *Ms.* He wanted to address seriously (though not somberly) the issue of feminism. As William Plummer had reported in 1982, "in person, he is solidly behind the ERA and even goes so far as to argue that women are 'morally superior' to men. He says things like, 'I think they are a different race and sometimes wonder that we men can even interbreed with them.' It's not women after all, but androgyny that turns his stomach."[69] Abbey would write in his journal on August 2, 1986, "Most women really are better than most men. No doubt about that" (329). He supported the equality of the sexes but remained fascinated with the differences between them and insisted that these differences not be lost in the campaign for equality.

In "The Future of Sex," Abbey was characteristically forthright about his own responses to people's sexuality, laying his cards on the table more honestly than most others are willing to do: "Like most men, I suppose, the first thing I sense in approaching another member of the human race is the sex of that person. Another male? Or a *female*? (Emphasis *added*.) If another male, my reaction is one of indifference, unless the circumstances are such as to suggest an element of danger in the situation. But, if it's a female, a little flag goes up, automatically, somewhere."[70] This *Bloomsbury Review* essay reached a geographically diverse audience.

More local embarrassment was provoked by *Tucson Citizen* reporter Judy Carlock at the end of June 1984, when she noted that Abbey had applied for the rezoning of his four-and-a-half-acre property. Having been the author of controversy, Abbey now became its target. This reporter seemed delighted to reveal that the seemingly uncompromising Cactus Ed had now supposedly compromised himself. That same month he had angrily told the *Arizona Daily Star* concerning "controlled growth," "That's bull. . . . Growth isn't inevitable, it's the result of deliberate policies. . . . They just give the developers and slum builders everything they want. . . . The more density, the more conflict between people."[71]

Carlock's story about the rezoning application dripped with holier-than-thou tones: "Edward Abbey, . . . vociferous defender of wild things and eloquent foe of urban sprawl, has applied to rezone the rolling desert land he lives on near Tucson to one day build two more houses on it." "All the surrounding property has already been rezoned," Abbey explained. "We're just taking a defensive measure." He expected that development would force him to move — maybe farther out from Tucson or perhaps to Moab or even Australia — and that the rezoning would make his property more marketable when that time came. "I don't want to live on a four-and-a-half acre island in the middle of a suburb, and unless we live here forever, there's no way we can keep even these four acres together."[72]

Abbey's rezoning application, which had actually been filed by a realtor friend, was approved in mid-September 1984,[73] but he never developed his property, nor did he sell it. As with his forecast of a developed Esperero Canyon while he was living in his old stone house there in 1972, his fear that his property beneath the Tucson Mountains would one day be trapped "in the middle of a suburb" was also accurate. At the end of the century, ten years after Abbey's death, another rapid-fire Tucson subdivision was built immediately behind his old four and a half acres.

In the summer of 1984, Abbey felt forlorn not just because he had been victimized by the local press but even more so because Clarke and baby Becky left for Salt Lake City to stay with her relatives for several weeks. Having decided to spend much of the summer at home, he found that "I am one lonesome hounddog. Susie is still here, and she is good sweet company, but she too will be gone in a week," back to camp in Prescott (315). Abbey had grown very attached to his new family, and it almost surprised him how much he finally enjoyed being a father. He told a reporter that spring, "Rebecca is the most wonderful thing to ever happen to me. I have finally grown old enough to enjoy being a father. I used to resent it. I considered it an infringement of my liberty. But now, at 57, I really enjoy the little nipper. She is a delight, makes me feel loved. Wonderful!"[74] He asked his old Moab neighbor Laura Lee Houck, "Why is this joy wasted on the young?"[75] As he noted to another interviewer, "I'll be in my 70s when she's a teenager."[76] Clarke Abbey emphasized later that "he was a terrific father" who had finally become "wonderfully patient," having "settled down into fatherhood by then," spending a lot of time "reading and drawing" with Becky.[77]

Abbey no longer relished solitude quite so much. In March 1984, he had taken another solo hike in the Cabeza Prieta wilderness, but after four days he had to cut it short when he became ill after drinking some bad water and developing blisters.[78] He loved being with his new family, and he also felt a renewed need to reconnect with extended family. "How tragic that we are so scattered about," he would lament on June 6, 1984 (315). He continued to wish that he could see his sons—now busy young men—more often.

At the end of March 1984, Ed flew to Pittsburgh with Clarke and Becky, rented a car, and headed to Home, where they stayed for three nights in the big, drafty, old house of his brother Howard and his wife Iva. He enjoyed visiting his parents at their little place along Route 119, but he wished that he "had the money to buy them a better house than that little shanty beside the highway, where the coal trucks thunder past every 30 seconds."[79] Yet his father was reasonably happy—and even happier that summer when he flew to Cuba, which he convinced himself was nearly a utopian socialist society.

Then the Abbeys drove through the Appalachian mountains and valleys of West Virginia and Virginia down to South Carolina, where they saw Clarke's grandparents. Ed gave a reading on April 4 at the University of North Carolina. Having stopped at his old hero Thomas Wolfe's house in Asheville on the way down, he made a point of telling his Chapel Hill audience that he was pleased to be there partly because he had long been a fan of Wolfe.[80]

Back in Tucson, Abbey resumed his life of controversy. In 1977 he had defended "The Right to Arms" to the large male readership of *Playboy*: "I am a member of the National Rifle Association, but certainly no John Bircher. I'm a liberal—and proud of it. Nevertheless, I am opposed, absolutely, to every move the state makes to restrict my right to buy, own, possess, and carry a firearm." He approved of the Swiss tradition (inherited on his father's side of the family) of soldiers taking their guns home to keep when they left the service—as he himself had done with his .45 revolver when he left the army at the beginning of 1947. And the author of *The Monkey Wrench Gang* and *Good News* was convinced that "if guns are outlawed, only the government will have guns. Only the police, the secret police, the military. The hired servants of our rulers. Only the government—and a few outlaws. I intend to be among the outlaws." But he also qualified his argument by agreeing to limits—no gun sales to children and criminals—and underscored his earlier decision to stop hunting: "I gave up deer hunting fifteen years ago, when the hunters began to outnumber the deer."[81]

He was no longer interested in hunting animals, and, since he opposed violence against people (as distinct from anti-industrial sabotage), by the 1980s the gun had become a purely symbolic artifact for Abbey, part of his mystique as a postmodern, anarchist cowboy. His most revealing boyhood photo showed him dressed up for cowboys and Indians, with a toy revolver in his hand, and perhaps the single most famous photograph would be Terry Moore's shot of him leaning on a shotgun, looking like he had just blown up his television set. And he acquired a Winchester from Ernie Bulow, who appears in *The Fool's Progress* as Don Williams, the Gallup, New Mexico, gun dealer whom Henry Lightcap visits.[82]

In 1984, Abbey resumed his advocacy of the right to bear arms as a retrograde cause to go along with his stands on immigration and feminism. He had already argued in "The Closing Door Policy" that the best way to help a struggling Mexican was to "give him a handgun" and send him back across the border. His July 14, 1984, letter to the *Arizona Daily Star* was headlined "Right to Own Guns": "The real issue is democratic freedom."[83] And at a December 5, 1984, ACLU forum on censorship that also included a stellar Tucson cast of Leslie Marmon Silko, Byrd Baylor, Andrew Rush, and Ann Woodin, Abbey got into a disagreement over guns with his colleague and friend Robert Houston, who supported limited gun control. The *Daily Star* reported that on this occasion Abbey, "the most outspoken" speaker, "supported the right to bear arms," advancing his usual line that citizens needed guns to protect themselves from the government.[84] Houston, on the other hand, pointed out that an individually owned gun would be of little use against B52 bombers and other big-time governmental firepower.[85]

Abbey had ended his immigration essay with a bang, and likewise—on April Fool's Day 1985—he would deliver his equally notorious attack on "The Cowboy and His Cow" in Missoula, Montana, deep in the heart of cattle country, "while waving a pistol," as the local press confirmed.[86] Abbey noted in his journal: "Missoula—waving a huge (unloaded) .44 hogleg about. The audience—standing room only—seemed to love my jokes" (320). He later claimed that he had truly shot from the hip even in his composition of this speech: "'Free Speech: The Cowboy and His Cow' began as notes for a speech written on an airplane flight, . . . delivered next day under alcoholic conditions at the University of Montana before a rowdy crowd of five to six hundred students, ranchers, and instant rednecks (transplanted Easterners)."[87] His version of this oration in *One Life at a Time, Please* projected the bombardment onto his audience, giving them the final word: "*Sitting ovation. Gunfire in parking lot.*"[88]

"The Cowboy and His Cow" debunked the romantic myth of the American cowboy—to which Abbey himself had been prey, he admitted, until 1949 when he began staying outside Albuquerque with the very unromantic Bud Adams (called "Mack" in his essay). Following his comic anecdotes about "Mack," Abbey proceeded to attack cattle grazing on public lands as a form of publicly subsidized welfare for ranchers. As different as this topic was from immigration, the history of "The Cowboy and His Cow" was strikingly similar to his anti-immigration campaign: once again, Abbey unstintingly delivered his stinging critique in several places (both as a speech and then as an article), and it was greeted everywhere with endless strife and a debate that persisted for years.

Before making his bigger splash in Missoula, Abbey had led off at Idaho State University in Pocatello on March 28, 1985, and the following night at Lewis-Clark State College in Lewiston, at the other end of the state. His old UA graduate student Jim Hepworth brought him to Lewis-Clark (where Hepworth was teaching) as the Wallace Stegner Lecturer. If the Lewis-Clark audience expected a sedate lecture under this endowed sponsorship, they were in for a surprise. As in Pocatello and Missoula, Abbey carried on riotously under the title "Dead Horses and Sacred Cows." Bill Francis succinctly reported the scene in Pocatello: "'Cattle are devastating our public lands,' he told a large audience. . . . 'Overgrazing is much too weak a term. American lands are cowburnt.' The crowd laughed at Abbey's dry, witty, often rambling and mostly irreverent lecture."[89]

Angry letters to the editor of the *Lewiston Morning Tribune* followed Abbey's talk there. "When Edward Abbey and his kind go out in the dark of night and commit sabotage," Bill Hall opined on April 4, "they mount an elitist throne of their own righteousness, declare public opinion irrelevant and close down a corner of democracy." "I agree with Bill Hall," Guy Trotter responded. "The only problem is that he didn't go far enough. . . . Do sponsors have an obligation to ensure that the content of a guest speaker's lecture is something less than sedition?" Bing Young added on April 5: "Mr. Abbey failed to mention one of the greatest of the American 'parasitic rats': himself. After all, I imagine this charater [*sic*] gets paid real American dollars from the public coffers to carry his non-message to faculty and students nationwide." Only Roy DeYoung registered dissent with these bitter attacks: "Abbey has brought many people and politicians to their senses over protecting and preserving our only environment."[90]

Carlos Pedraza reported in Missoula that Abbey "spoke . . . from an electronic podium he likened to a 'console of an ICBM launcher' and, while waving a pistol, told potential detractors that he would gladly be available after the lecture for questions and answers. . . . His pistol-brandishing must have worked, because by the end of the lecture, nary a hand was seen raised for a question."[91] Abbey was indeed paid "real American dollars" for each of these appearances, including $3,000 by the University of Montana;[92] even before going on to Harvard to lecture on May 10, Abbey was pleased to note in late April that he had made $7,000 thus far from his "sacred cows" tour.[93] After speaking at Harvard, he was able to stop off in New York and Home on the way back to Tucson.

Next, Abbey moved his campaign against public "welfare" grazing into print, reaching even larger audiences. He later summarized this process in his "Preliminary Remarks" in *One Life at a Time, Please* (into which "Free Speech: The Cowboy and His Cow" found its way):

> It was reprinted verbatim, bawdy stories and all, in the Montana magazine *Northern Lights*. From there, much abridged but only slightly revised, this "speech" or "lecture" found its next home six months later in the pages of *Harper's* magazine. . . . It was rewarded by the usual blizzard of abuse, some seventy-five letters from outraged cattlepersons, including one Gretel Ehrlich of Shell, Wyoming (another instant redneck), who called me "arrogant, incoherent, flippant, nonsensical, nasty, and unconstructive. . . ." A typical reaction: our cowgirls and beef ranchers are such sensitive people. . . . ("Nasty and unconstructive"—I love that.)[94]

Ehrlich was only the best known of the several opponents to Abbey's essay after it appeared as "The Ungulate Jungle" in the July/August 1985 issue of *Northern Lights*.[95]

Ralph Beer of Helena asked Abbey to pay him $90,000 since he had argued that his publicly grazing cattle ought to be viewed as publicly owned "game animals."[96] Abbey gladly took the bait, replying in *Northern Lights*, "Tell Mr. Beer I'll pay his $90,000 bill if he can get the cattlemen's association to pony up the $25 billion or so which they owe the American public for damages done to *our* property. EAT LESS BEEF." A lover of fat, juicy hamburgers at such eating establishments as Tucson's Big A, Abbey himself always had trouble trying to eat less beef. He began his *Northern Lights* letter self-derisively: "The long, tedious and rambling 'speech' by Edward Abbey reads as if it were based on notes scribbled on a memo pad by a drunken author during a bumpy airplane ride from Pocatello to Lewiston, Idaho (so it was), and then further mangled, garbled, expurgated and redacted by a baffled stenographer trying to make sense of that same interminable lecture (she did the best she could)." Signing off from Oracle, he noted that he wanted to "humbly apologize for the generally meek, mild, temporizing tone of my address to the citizens of Montana," because public grazing was even worse in Arizona, as he learned after returning home after his speech in Missoula.[97]

Indeed, a month after his essay appeared in the January 1986 *Harper's* as "Even the Bad Guys Wear White Hats: Cowboys, Ranchers, and the Ruin of the West," Abbey saw to it that it was also reprinted in the *Arizona Daily Star* as "Taking Stock of the Cowboy Myth." *Harper's* printed six letters about the piece in its May issue, whereas no fewer than sixteen letters (one of them a full guest column) appeared in Tucson's *Daily Star* between February 14 and March 11, 1985—eight alone on February 14 under the headline "Abbey Causes Letter Stampede."

In *Harper's*, Wyoming governor Ed Herschler asked, "Without us cattlemen you would be starving. Where do you think all the hamburgers and steaks in the supermarkets come from?"[98] Abbey replied that "Herschler is partly right: as a place to live, Wyoming is still more pleasant than Texas, Florida, New Jersey, or California. But he and his fellow promoters, developers, and empire builders—throughout the West—are doing their best to change all that." He added that "about a hundred" other letters "were sent to my home address, many of a highly personal nature and most too enthusiastic to be printed in a decent family magazine like *Harper's*." Responding to each *Harper's* correspondent in turn, Abbey wrote "to Robert A. Jaynes—always talk back. Don't let an old desert rat like me buffalo a young cattleperson like you."[99]

Indeed, Abbey clearly enjoyed all the attention of this entire debate, particularly relishing the letters that most vociferously told him off. After *Redneck Review* editor and rancher Penelope Reedy registered her disagreement with Abbey in *Northern Lights*, he sent her a postcard: "Loved your letter. Give that bastard hell." Because they both believed in productive debate, they tried to continue it in *Northern Lights*, but its editors told them that they had had enough. Abbey and Reedy became good friends, and a few years later, he gave her "blanket reprint rights" to use anything of his she wanted whenever she liked, without fee, in her *Redneck Review*.[100]

In the *Arizona Daily Star*, Peter Vokac claimed that "Abbey has been eating too much quiche" and did not understand ranchers' realities. Sierra Vista cattleman James H. Gregovich called him "one-sided and inflammatory." Garth Flint added that "perhaps a few days on a working cattle ranch would be a good education for Edward Abbey."[101] A handful of readers actually agreed with Abbey, but then the big cattle guns fired. The executive vice president of the Arizona Cattle Growers' Association, Len Mattice, complained that "to have some self-styled expert come from who knows where and tell everyone just how to operate is sheer lunacy. Please let's get the facts straight the next time and not just go for some 'Johnny-come-lately' that has nothing to sell but ink."[102]

Even at the end of the millennium, ranchers in southern Arizona still remembered Abbey's essay. In late 1999, one rancher who otherwise admired Abbey told me—speaking outside on his cell phone while he kept an eye on his cattle—that he felt Abbey had gone wrong in "The Cowboy and His Cow."[103] Abbey had written him in 1986, "I'm glad to know we are still friends despite those mean things I wrote about the public-lands beef growers, and the harsh things I've written about Latino culture. I'd like to be a good liberal . . . but the temptation to defy old American taboos often gets the best of me."[104]

Once again Ed Abbey had achieved notoriety and academic success at the same time. Who else would lecture at universities in such a defiant vein? He taught at the UA in the spring of 1985, earning a little over $24,000.[105] Nancy Mairs was his student again, this time in his seminar on the essay.[106] Abbey was characteristically weary of teaching but proud of his students' accomplishments: "My . . . student Mike Crockett," he noted on April 24, "sells a story to *American West*. Delightful."[107] Yet having declined an invitation to lecture at Yale two years earlier, in January 1985 he made note of his reply to a Professor Link at "I.S.U., after receiving his 'you will' do this, 'you will' do that letter: 'Dear Professor Link: I don't like the tone of your letter. I don't take orders from anybody, not for a measly $2,000 or for any imaginable sum.' . . . Let's see what he makes of that" (318).

The year 1985 saw the appearance of *Resist Much, Obey Little: Some Notes on Edward Abbey*, edited by James Hepworth and Gregory McNamee and including essays by Wendell Berry, William Eastlake, Nancy Mairs, Barry Lopez, Richard Shelton, Robert Houston, Gary Snyder, and others. Here Abbey received the kind of sympathetic critical attention that he had long craved. For example, Berry's lead essay, "A Few Words in Favor of Edward Abbey," reprinted from the *Whole Earth Review*, insisted that, as a writer, Abbey was not really an environmentalist but predominantly "an autobiographer."[108] On March 2, 1985, Abbey had advised his editor Jack Macrae, "For the first good serious literary criticisms of my work see Wendell Berry's article in the March issue of 'Whole Earth Review.' Berry is the first and so far only good writer who understands what I am up to."[109] On May 27, 1984, in the midst of a journal entry complaining about how his books were always assigned for review to nature writers and naturalists, "who have only a dim comprehension of what I'm about," Abbey added, "Just *once* I'd like to see a book of mine reviewed—favorably or unfavorably—by one of my *peers*!" But he did realize that Robert Houston had written a "truly good essay about *Down the River* for the Hepworth anthology" (314). Houston's "Down the River with Edward Abbey" was written in the form of a letter to him, which he gave his UA colleague in May 1984, before it appeared in *Resist Much, Obey Little*.[110] Gary Snyder's contribution was likewise "A Letter to Ed Abbey."

Here, at last, Abbey was truly being reviewed by his peers, and they spoke directly to him. In contrast, he had been stung by his other UA colleague Peter Wild's 1983 critique of him as a "middle-class maverick."[111] And not all of the contributions to *Resist Much, Obey Little* were met with universal acclaim. Gregory McNamee's essay on Abbey as "The Bard of Oracle" appeared in *The Tucson Weekly* in March 1985 as well as in *Resist Much, Obey Little*.[112] In Oracle, readers were upset because they felt that McNamee had portrayed their town negatively, particularly since Abbey had never lived there;[113] having invoked Oracle only metaphorically, McNamee switched to "Tucson" in the book's later editions.

The other gratifying 1985 publication was Dream Garden Press's tenth-anniversary edition of *The Monkey Wrench Gang*, which was the first to restore the "Seldom Seen at Home" chapter and included pop-comic-book-styled illustrations by the celebrated countercultural cartoonist R. Crumb. Abbey and Crumb met for the first (and only) time at a book-launching party in Arches National Park on March 24, 1985.[114] Abbey noted the following day, "Met Crumb, a very dry droll delightful fellow—'a true gentleman and a great artist,' as I wrote in his copy of MWG."[115] Movie options for *The Monkey Wrench Gang* were also renewed annually—never yet leading to the making of a film, but regularly offering generous supplemental incomes to Abbey, his new family, and his sons Josh and Aaron.

As with his March 29 Stegner Lecture in Idaho, Abbey was capable of combining academic success and comic outrageousness in a single stroke. His UA colleague Richard Shelton invited him to San Diego to give the keynote address to the April 1985 meeting of the Associated Writing Programs, of which Shelton was then president. Abbey gave a serious and respectable enough talk, based on his essay "A Writer's Credo," in which he argued that the writer's chief responsibility is to be a critic of society.[116] But he did so only after characteristically entertaining the audience, following a lofty introduction by Barry Lopez, who sang his praises. Abbey strolled to the podium, scratched his chin, and led off with an impromptu recollection about *Desert Solitaire*. He explained that his classic book had been slow to take off even though all the early reviews were good—except for one, which said that the book was no good at all. And who wrote that? Barry Lopez, Abbey claimed. Everyone laughed except for his friend Lopez, who turned bright red.[117]

All of these achievements and typically rabble-rousing activities are all the more remarkable because Abbey was suffering from painful, poor health during the early months of 1985. For a while after he had recovered from his August 1982 scare, everything seemed to be all right. He went so far as to offer a "Recipe for a Long and Healthy Life" in the November/December 1984 issue of *Environmental Action*: "Since my father (age 83) and my mother (age 78) are both still thriving and active, emotionally, physically, mentally, I assume I'll do about the same, if I don't fall off a rock somewhere. The secret, therefore, is good genes: Choose your parents with care. . . . And finally, never *worry* about your health—those who worry too much may be already dead." But privately, Abbey worried frequently about his health. On January 2, 1985, he reported in his journal, a "lousy flu" had turned out to be "something called bleeding 'esophageal varices.'" A couple of weeks earlier, "feeling sick as a dawg," he had fallen down "in a faint," and had to go to the hospital and get "eight units of AB+ blood (now—AIDS?) to bring me back to life. Damn near blew the whole ball game" (317).

On February 8, motivated by "intimations of mortality," he wrote out a new set of "LAST WISHES" for Clarke, to augment his October 1981 "funeral instructions." He indicated that, in the event of his death, she should obtain a certificate of death to "avoid legal problems" and then, "as quickly as convenient" and without changing his clothes, put his body in his favorite sleeping bag and "load me into the back of a pickup. . . . Take me either to our property at Cliff Dwellers or Green River (either would be fine) and bury me at once. Cover me with plenty of rocks so old Cousin Coyote cannot dig up my body. . . . Then, hold a wake, as described elsewhere in these journals" (318–19).

On February 27, Abbey complained to himself that the "old bod is breaking down, falling apart, like an old car: one part goes, something else begins to malfunction—gallstones, portal vein obstruction, pancreatitis, burned-out stomach, esophageal varices, high blood pressure, abdominal fluid, anemia, enlarged spleen—and now another kidney stone" (319). Indeed, this kidney stone was Abbey's particular torture in the spring of 1985, just as he was charging all over the West attacking cowboys and cows and re-launching *The Monkey Wrench Gang*. On the outside he came across as a countercultural hero; on the inside, he could barely function.

At the Arches launching party, Abbey urged Ernie Bulow to take R. Crumb for a walk in the Fiery Furnace, while he stayed back and sat in the car writing his cowboy and cow essay, which he later claimed was penned (and was likely revised) on a bumpy plane ride. He really needed to stay behind because of his pain from the kidney stone.[118] When he came to Lewiston on March 29 to deliver his Stegner Lecture, he talked with Jim Hepworth about deep family matters, as if he might never get another chance. After he admitted to Hepworth that his kidney stone was giving him a lot of pain, Hepworth took him to a doctor, who gave him some major pain medication. Then he flew to Missoula, where he was relieved to finally pass the stone. A few days later Hepworth received a small parcel, postmarked April 1. It was the kidney stone, in a plastic bag, accompanied by a simple note: "Thought you'd like to have the result of all my labors."[119]

Abbey felt much the same about the prospect of death as he had in 1982 — except that now he was the father of his beloved young Becky. He experienced "no fear" of death, only a "great sadness, an irremediable sorrow, at the possibility that I may not live long enough to help our Rebecca become a girl, a teen-ager (another insolent teen-ager!), a woman. That thought hurts" (319–20). On November 5, 1985, he memorably wrote: "Life is a bitch. And then you die? No: Life is a joyous adventure. And *then* you die" (325).

Several significant events in Abbey's life each happened on April Fool's Day: his signing of a loyalty oath to begin his first season at Arches in 1956; his first day at his short-lived Nevada State Welfare Department job in Las Vegas just before he left Rita in 1965; and his delivery of the "Cowboy and His Cow" speech at the University of Montana — the same day that he mailed his kidney stone to Hepworth. "My job began on the first day of April," he had claimed at the beginning of *Desert Solitaire*. Concerning his Missoula speech, he confirmed to Lewis Lapham at *Harper's* on September 23, 1985, that "I really did deliver the talk on April first."[120] In the spring of 1987, he gladly donned a clown's outfit at a party: "Ed Abbey was a perfect fool."[121] He was also capable of unintentionally playing the fool; that same year he insisted to Charles Bowden that he planned to run for mayor of Tucson, just to stir things up — until Bowden pointed out that Abbey did not live within the city limits and was thus not eligible.[122] With the specter of death looming closer, Abbey finally focused on the writing of his significantly entitled "fat masterpiece": *The Fool's Progress*.

CHAPTER TEN

One Life at a Time, Please
1985–1989

Ed Abbey's tragedy was that he would die so soon after finally discovering mature happiness and the achievement of some key long-time goals. Yet, by the same token, his final years—unlike those of many people—were his most fulfilling ones. He remained happily married to Clarke, who gave birth in 1987 to their second child, Ben. He continued to support Earth First! during its glory years, as the movement lived and died with him. Abbey was made a full professor ("fool professor," he liked to say),[1] with tenure, at the University of Arizona in the spring of 1988, earning $30,000 for that semester. And he completed the big autobiographical novel that he had been trying to write for thirty years, *The Fool's Progress* (1988). Also published was his final collection of essays, the aptly entitled *One Life at a Time, Please* (1988). The final year of his life was marked by a frenetic burst of creativity, because he knew that he would die soon, as he finished two other books that were published soon after his death: a book of aphorisms culled from his journals, *Vox Clamantis* *in Deserto* (1989), subsequently reprinted as *A Voice Crying in the Wilderness* (1990); and the long-awaited sequel to *The Monkey Wrench Gang*, *Hayduke Lives!* (1990).

In order to focus on *The Fool's Progress*, and with the help of an advance for it, Abbey did not teach in 1986 but returned to his nonfiction courses at the UA again in the spring 1987 and 1988 semesters. Ed and Clarke followed a pattern of spending the school years in Tucson and the summers in such beautiful and milder climes as southeastern Utah and the mountains of Colorado. Their three pleasant summers of 1985, 1986, and 1987 can be described together in order to illustrate how good life could be in between Abbey's difficult bouts with his failing body and his complicated books. After he passed a kidney stone and terrorized the masses in Missoula on April Fool's Day 1985, Ed, Clarke, and little Becky spent that summer visiting their friends and Clarke's relatives and camping. On June 4, Ed anticipated with relish heading "off to the hills" with Clarke and Becky, to Santa Fe, Taos, Telluride, Durango, Moab, Salt Lake City, and Idaho—a "summer of camping" (320). He was only occasionally interrupted by such obligations as a book-signing appearance in Berkeley, California, on July 12.[2]

Things would not proceed without a hitch, as he noted on June 20 in Salt Lake City: "Done the camping bit. Drove my truck into a steel post set in concrete in Santa Fe and wrecked the bumper, grill and radiator. $550." He had helped Jack Loeffler with his "famous *cabrito* roast" and spent a "glorious week in the mountains near Telluride" (320). Part of that week was not quite so "glorious," however: even more seriously than when he had gotten temporarily stuck in September 1983, searching for the source of the Rio Grande when Clarke was nine months pregnant, Abbey's Ford pickup became mired up to the axles on a jeep road near Telluride. He insisted on trying to dig himself out, but Clarke went for help after two days and came back with the county sheriff, a friend of Ed's, and was met by a scowl from Ed.[3] On August 3, back in Colorado, Abbey explained that "after a tedious month of house-camping in SLC, we finally left. Then down here to Durango for two weeks (?) maybe a month (I hope) in the beautiful mountain cabin of Dusty Dick"—who was Dusty Teal, an old river-running friend (320). Ed, Clarke, and Becky returned to Tucson in late August 1985.

Near mountainous Monticello, Utah, that summer, they spent a couple of weeks in Abbey's old friend Jim Stiles's cabin. When Stiles returned there after their departure, he found a note from Ed: "Thank you very much for the hospitality. We enjoyed our stay in your lovely rustic Shangri-La very much. We *did* do some damage: burnt out the mantle in your Aladdin lamp and tore a hole in your Sun Shower bag. I enclose a $20 to cover the destruction, as well as two more trashy Abbey books to complete your collection. See you again in August or September."[4] Ed and Clarke did indeed identify the Moab area as the place to which they most wanted to return. Ed enjoyed seeing his old friends there. At one point he pulled into the entrance station at Arches, on his way to visit Stiles at the campground, and found his old next-door neighbor from Spanish Valley Road, Laura Lee Houck, working the booth. She pretended that she did not know him: "That will be one dollar." After Abbey hemmed and hawed, she waved him through with a smile.[5]

This notorious opponent of television made a more auspicious return to Arches in late October 1985 with a TV script in hand for a subsequent eight-minute segment on *NBC Almanac*: the entertaining and wise "TV Show: Out There in the Rocks" (which appeared in *One Life at a Time, Please*). The old *Desert Solitaire* pioneer lampooned the "industrial tourism" that now made Arches anything but solitary: as he sped along a paved road in a red Buick, he intoned, "That's the road to Delicate Arch. Don't have time to go there right now. Maybe later. That's the road to Fiery Furnace. I think. Was. Maybe next time." He also slyly reminisced: "Part of my job was to sit here in the shade, on a folding chair like this, and answer questions, in case a tourist might show up. (*The narrator assumes a rangerlike pose on a chair.*) Sometimes one did." Pointing to the site of his old trailer near Balanced Rock, now occupied by a gravel dump, he quipped: "When I die, if I live that long, I hope to be buried under that pile of gravel." Yet the technological medium belied the Luddite Abbey's opposition to it, for even better than reading Abbey's script is watching the video—with its breathtaking footage in which the camera peeks through a little rock window at the spectacular Delicate Arch while viewers listen to Abbey's closing meditation: "What will it be like out here when I'm gone and you are gone and our great-grandchildren are gone. . . . ? What then?"[6]

On November 5, 1985, Abbey noted that shooting this video was "mostly fun, me and a red convertible" (324). The red Buick was only a loaner from Moab, but Abbey enjoyed driving around in it so much that, on his sixty-first birthday in January 1988, he would go out and, unbeknownst to Clarke, buy a Cadillac Eldorado convertible that he drove everywhere for the rest of his life. "It was one of those things that I thought was pretty stupid," Clarke remembered. "But he had a great time."[7] Soon thereafter, Abbey noted in his journal that he had "finally bought my Pimpmobile," a "'75 Caddie convertible," a "maroon beauty, vulgar and gorgeous, with an eighteen-inch front overhang and white sidewalls and push-button gadgets, half of which don't work" (342). There was never a dull moment with Abbey and his vehicles. In June 1987 he had appeared late for lunch with Charles Bowden, apologized, and then admitted only afterward, when they walked outside and found Abbey's pickup truck with its front end crumpled up, that he had been involved in a head-on collision on the way to lunch. Later, Jack Dykinga photographed Abbey and his truck with a funereal plastic flower on its hood.[8]

As late as February 1989, Abbey was showing off his Cadillac to Bowden, who remarked, "Christ, Ed, you've got no shame"—at which point Abbey grinned widely and gave his friend "a look like I'd made his day."[9] At another point Abbey pulled into Oracle in his Cadillac and found himself sitting beside his old mailman Tom Thompson, who was driving an electric-powered grounds cart that he used within the town's small confines. Abbey offered on the spot to trade vehicles, but Thompson assured him that his cart could not make it back to Tucson on its electric charge.[10] In the fall of 1988, Abbey told Jim Fergus of *Outside*, "I just wanted to show you my birthday present," explaining that, with its special radio antenna, "You turn the radio off and it retracts like a tired penis. . . . When I first started driving around in this, I assumed the girls would sort of come climbing aboard. It hasn't worked out that way . . . though they do look. Anyway, I'm a happily married man, don't forget that . . . but I'm not dead. . . . 'He old, but he ain't dead!'"[11]

As for his marriage, Abbey admitted in his journal on November 5, 1985, that it was undergoing some strain. Clarke felt that he was too often antisocial. But he was determined to avoid yet another marital breakup. "I'd sure die. Without my Rebecca, how could I live? For what? Nothing imaginable could possibly console me for the loss of my angel-child Becky. Or for Clarke either." This time, his marriage did not fail, and Abbey clung not only to Clarke but to Becky. After his trip to Moab to shoot the TV show, he was glad to get back to Tucson just in time for "Rebecca's first real Halloween. Dressed as a black kitty-cat, she went trick-or-treating (with us) to the Peacocks'" (324). He was still haunted by his earlier, failed marriages and was determined to make this one last. In the same entry in which he delighted over Becky's first Halloween, he complained about having to pay percentages of his royalties to his adult sons, now in their late twenties, and noted that Josh was getting married to a Swiss woman, Yve, in Las Vegas, but that he had been discouraged from attending (325).

Instead, Abbey enjoyed spending time with old friends. On January 22, 1986, he noted that he and Clarke had just returned from a week in Mexico with Jack and Kathy Loeffler, camping on the beach at Tepoca Bay, north of Kino, on the Sea of Cortez (325). And after he worked on his writing in Tucson during the next few months, Ed, Clarke, and Becky spent the summer of 1986 near Moab at Pack Creek Ranch, which Ken Sleight and his new wife Jane had bought and were running as a kind of dude ranch and resort. The Abbeys stayed that summer in "the leaky old 'Road House,'" as Sleight called it, which had a small cabin beside it in which Abbey wrote.[12] By now Ed and Clarke had settled into their ideal geographical migration pattern—winters in the warm cactus country around Tucson, tucked beneath the resplendent mountains just west of the city, and then retreat from the blazing Tucson summers to the canyon country near milder Moab.

Abbey and Sleight saw more of each other that summer than at any other time except for their earlier river trips. Yet the separate cabin also gave Abbey space; when Sleight approached it and heard his old friend's typewriter clicking away, he would walk away and leave him alone. Clarke took little breaks that summer from full-time motherhood by working at the Sleights' Country Inn restaurant. Her parents, Tom and Carolyn Cartwright, were in the process of buying property at Pack Creek in order to build a house there, and Ed and Clarke soon bought a lot as well. Ed had characteristically wanted to build at a remote site beneath a cliff, but Clarke prevailed in choosing a more practical location with access to water.[13]

On July 25, 1986, Ed exclaimed in his journal that Clarke had announced she was "preggers again. Oh my Gawd!" (328). On March 19, 1987, back in Tucson, he recorded, "Benjamin Cartwright Abbey is born today, at 5:00 a.m., by cesarean section, at the Tucson Medical Center. Seven pounds, twelve ounces. Mother and child both are doing well. Hallelujah!" (331). Ben would be five days short of his second birthday on the date of his father's death. During the relatively short time that he could enjoy them, Ed Abbey relished his two young children and was delighted with their every move. On April 18, 1987, he wrote that he had just come back from two days "up in the hills" with Becky. They camped the first night in Molino Basin "beside a trickling stream. Becky caught a frog and floated it on a pond in a tiny plastic boat." He exclaimed, "God I love that kid. She is so beautiful and can be so sweet and loving. Every night she cuddled in my arms as I told her stories of Bill the Bug, Kokomo Joe the Giant Lizard, Joe the Jackrabbit, Felix the Kat and a dozen others improvised and invented. . . . Rebecca my sweetheart my treasure I love you I love you—'right up to the sky!'" (331–32).

At the same time, Josh and Aaron—by then thirty-one and twenty-eight years old, respectively—were long gone. Abbey did spend a rare day with Aaron in the spring of 1987 at Petrified Forest, where he was surprised to learn that, following in his footsteps, his son had sold a story to *Playboy*, a strange fantasy about sex in ancient Egypt.[14] Aaron, "poor devil" (334), hoped to become a writer, but, as with Josh, he was not to match his father's creative success; this story was both the beginning and the apparent end of his writing career.

Even Abbey's beloved Susie was on her way out into the world and away from him. She attended the University of Arizona during 1986–87 and subsequently went on to Sarah Lawrence College to complete her undergraduate degree. Adolescent angst had already come between them, as Abbey lamented on New Year's Day 1986: "Despondency." He had suffered through a "quarrel over nothing" with "my dear Susie" the night before, and he felt "lower than whale shit" (325). On August 2, 1986, while looking across his Pack Creek cabin and watching Becky sleeping, making him feel "such a *rush* of unlimited love," he noted that "Susie calls, says she's feeling 'depressed.' Why? She doesn't know. I'm feeling depressed too." Yet he added that "We are at our best when we live for others. No doubt about that. It's that quality of caring so much for others, always for others, that makes my Clarke such a fine distinguished woman. Like my mother" (329).

The Abbeys spent the summer of 1987 in Moab, renting a house on Moenkopi Road on the northwest edge of town, while they tried to decide what to do about their options at Pack Creek, where they put down a deposit that fall.[15] Ed expressed high hopes on June 11, 1987, about heading to Moab soon thereafter, to "find a real home at last, I hope" (334). He wrote frequently in his journal during these years about achieving a simpler life, leaving Tucson in favor of a cabin at Pack Creek or near the Grand Canyon's Vermillion Cliffs. He felt like a failure for not making such a permanent move, instead remaining in his home beside Tucson, which now felt more like a suburban residence than a desert retreat. But the Abbeys did stay in Moab through October 1987, before returning to Tucson.

On October 12, he expressed pleasure that he had spent several days the week before with John De Puy and Jack Loeffler on Muley Point, above the spectacular Goosenecks section of the San Juan River, gazing at the serpentine twists and turns carved out by the river below them (336). And, in September, he had taken a hike in Millcreek Canyon with Terry Tempest Williams, who had eighty stitches down her forehead from a recent hiking fall. "So I hear you're trying to etch the Colorado Plateau on your face, Tempest," Abbey told her. "Better make sure your words are as tough as your skin." She wrote later that "the rest of the day was spent sitting in pools, climbing in and out of alcoves, simply walking across desert meadows of prickly pears, globe mallows and cow pies. The same cow pies that fueled the *Moab Times Independent* with letters to the editors after his call for 'no more cows, period!'"[16]

As usual, Abbey was almost always writing—or trying to. Earth First! continued to offer him a strong, ready-made audience for essays about the environment. Yet that was not what he wanted to deliver. On February 6, 1986, he appeared at an Earth First! rally at the El Rio Community Center in Tucson along with Earth First! leader Dave Foreman and long-time singer and activist Katie Lee. Although Abbey did throw in a few slogans for the environmental-

ist faithful—"Earth first, Gila monsters second, and human beings third!"[17]—
for the most part he read his rambling story about the adventures of "Mack"
from the "Cowboy and His Cow" essay, which had appeared a month earlier
in *Harper's* and was about to appear in Tucson's *Arizona Daily Star*. His friend
Charles Bowden remembered the scene:

> The evening chugged along with the expected dose of environmen-
> tal pep talks, sensitive poetry readings, and we-ain't-going-to-take-
> this-anymore war cries. The audience was wall-to-wall waffle stomp-
> ers and plaid flannel shirts, the women had long hair and no makeup.
> Then Abbey's turn came and he pulled some pages out of his pocket
> and started reading a long, shaggy-dog story about his earlier days in
> Albuquerque, about roaring down the road with a pal, tossing beer
> cans out the window and firing a pistol wildly into the countryside.
> I could feel the crowd get edgy. Abbey droned on seemingly oblivi-
> ous, and his text somehow segued into the charms and joys of vari-
> ous sorority girls encountered in those college adventures. I sensed
> a sullen steam begin to rise up off the audience. Suddenly he was
> finished and the evening returned to environmental proprieties. I
> thought: well, why pander?[18]

Afterward, Bowden told Abbey, a bit ironically, "That was really great, Ed." "I
know," Abbey replied, fully satisfied.[19]

Nor was he interested in cashing in on Earth First! to sell his books.
On May 1, 1985, he made that clear in a letter to the editor of the *Earth First!
Journal*: "I would not want your readers to think that I am using the EF! journal to peddle my books and line my pockets. Therefore I would like to explain
that the Abbey books sold through Earth First! are donated by the publisher.
The author receives no royalty. All proceeds go to Earth First!" He was glad
to write for the cause, for free. That same year, his "Forward!" (in which he
invented a fictionalized aunt) appeared in Dave Foreman's subversive manual
Ecodefense: A Field Guide to Monkeywrenching:

> If the wilderness is our true home, and if it is threatened with in-
> vasion, pillage, and destruction—as it certainly is—then we have
> the right to defend that home, as we would our private quarters,
> by whatever means are necessary. . . . Eco-defense means fighting
> back. . . . Spike those trees; you won't hurt them; they'll be grate-
> ful for the protection; and you may save the forest. Loggers hate
> nails. My Aunt Emma back in West Virginia has been enjoying this
> pleasant exercise for years. She swears by it. It's good for the trees,

it's good for the woods, and it's good for the human soul. Spread the word.[20]

For the most part, however, Abbey was interested in moving on to other kinds of writing; he wanted to finish his big autobiographical novel. And as Earth First! moved into the late 1980s, Abbey's views began to fall out of fashion with some of the movement's newer, younger followers. Foreman had begun Earth First! in 1980 as "rednecks for wilderness" and "Abbey fans," but by 1987 more and more hippie anarchists had become involved. Looking back in 1998, Foreman reflected that "if somebody really analyzed early Earth First!, they would see that it was actually much closer originally to a militia, right-wing kind of group than the kind of left-wing, anarchist thing it is now."[21]

In July 1987, Abbey appeared at the Earth First! Round River Rendezvous at Parissawampitts Point, at the Nankoweap Trailhead on the North Rim of the Grand Canyon.[22] At the only other Rendezvous he attended, in 1982 in Wyoming, the Earth First! faithful had laughed at all his jokes, even those about the "ERA." But now things had changed: Abbey was drawn into an argument with urban anarchists who did not care for his views on immigration and feminism. By then there was a "women's circle" at the Rendezvous, and Abbey was perceived as a "chauvinist pig" and a member of the old guard. As always, Abbey did not mind an argument, but Foreman and some of the other original Earth First!ers were upset by how he was treated and felt increasingly alienated from the movement that they had begun. At a competing "Green Conference" that same month in Amherst, Massachusetts, the Eastern socialist environmentalist Murray Bookchin painted Abbey and Foreman as "eco-brutalists" with ties to fascism through a "crude biologism." Bookchin was soon joined by "a chorus of East coast leftists displeased with the perceived antihumanism of Edward Abbey and Foreman, variously labeled as sexist, racist, and fascist."[23]

Author of a thesis on anarchism three decades earlier, Abbey had articulated his own "Theory of Anarchy" in the *Earth First! Journal* in August 1986, distinguishing himself from the new wave of younger anarchist faddists.[24] At the end of 1987, in response to the disagreements evident at the Rendezvous, Abbey declared his allegiance in spunky, comic fashion in the *Journal*: "Words can be dangerous. . . . If Foreman is an 'Eco-fascist,' then so am I. EAT TOFU, ECO-MUTUALIST POOH-BEAR ANARCHISTS! VIVA ZAPATA!"[25] Foreman and other old-guard Earth First!ers did not appreciate how the new wave treated Abbey, but Abbey relished the controversy. In 1988, advertisements for *One Life at a Time, Please* ran in the *Earth First! Journal* with a photo of Abbey grinning mischievously in the middle, under the headline, "Why Do Left-Wingers Hate This Writer? Why Do Right-Wingers Hate This Writer?

(And Why Do They Hate Him So Much?)." Down the left-hand column appeared a string of representative leftist attacks, such as "'A racist and an eco-fascist . . .' Murray Bookchin, *Utne Reader*"; to the right, similar lines from more conservative writers, such as "'Arrogant, incoherent, flippant, nasty and unconstructive . . .' Gretel Ehrlich's 'sensitive' dismissal in *Northern Lights*." [26]

Such controversy subsequently provided the rhetoric of the most riotous chapter in *Hayduke Lives!*, "Earth First! Rendezvous," a hilarious parody of the whole movement. At the 1987 Rendezvous, Foreman was so alienated that he spent most of his time fly-fishing down at the river, far away from the speeches.[27] But Abbey has him speak in his memorable fashion, with a can of Coors in hand—as a result of which Foreman (who normally never drank that brand) would eulogize Abbey at Arches in May 1989 while grasping a Coors. In Abbey's novel, Foreman is met with vitriolic opposition:

> "Terrorist, sexist, racist, rightwing libertarian eco-brutalist!" screamed all . . . in chorus, snakes writhing in their hair. . . .
> "Eat shit, Nazi Foreman!" screamed a slightly deeper, somewhat normal maler voice.
> "Tofu to you, Doctor Mushkin," Foreman replied.[28]

Abbey then has an all too thinly disguised Bookchin—who was in fact nowhere near the Grand Canyon in 1987—appear: "Bernie Mushkin, old-time Marxist, sectarian revolutionary, tenured professor, academic writer, pedagogue, demagogue, ideologue, was drawn to political controversy as a moth to the flame—or a blowfly to a rotting hog." "Mushkin" holds forth for three pages, during which he claims, among other things, that "your enthusiastic support of immigration control, as preached by your official ideologists Hardin and Abbey, has revealed you as nationalists and xenophobes, quite the opposite of the fun-loving anarchists you pretend to be." Afterward, Mushkin's followers "drove him to his hotel in nearby Las Vegas only three hundred miles away, in their eyes and in his the nearest outpost of proper civilization in the entire northern Arizona-Utah-Nevada region." [29] *Hayduke Lives!* may be a more uneven novel than *The Monkey Wrench Gang*, but parts of it are even funnier.

Abbey also engaged in serious debate in the *Earth First! Journal*. In February 1988, the *Journal* published his review of Wendell Berry's *Home Economics* in which Abbey called Berry "the best serious essayist now at work in the United States." Abbey disagreed with Berry's notion of "stewardship," however, as "not good enough. The US Forest Service practices stewardship." What was needed, Abbey felt, was not stewardship but change. Berry replied that he felt Abbey had misunderstood what he meant by "stewardship." Berry was convinced that people could not be kept out of wilderness, felt that Abbey's view tended toward "misanthropy," and noted that "I think he suspects me of being a Catholic." He concluded that Abbey's books were "an indispensable source of delight, instruction, and comfort to me. In spite of the differences that are the subjects of this exchange, I will continue to think of myself as his ally and friend."[30] Afterward, Abbey wrote privately to Berry, suggesting that they simply forget all about it, since their friendship was too important to sacrifice to an ideal or a disagreement. Berry readily agreed, and the two of them remained solid, long-distance friends—who never met, but whose camaraderie was so strong that Berry would journey all the way to Arches for Abbey's May 1989 wake.[31]

Abbey's May 1988 "reading list for nature lovers" in the *Earth First! Journal* began in a surprisingly straightforward and accommodating manner, recognizing *Our Synthetic Environment*, by the same Murray Bookchin with whom he otherwise so scurrilously disagreed, as having "anticipated Rachel Carson by several years."[32] Simultaneously, the University of Arizona Press released a handsome new twentieth-anniversary edition of *Desert Solitaire*— with a preface by Abbey in which he claimed that, while he agreed he was "a nature *lover*. . . . I did not mean to be mistaken for a nature *writer*. I never wanted to be anything but a writer, period." He mischievously and disingenuously added that "I have never looked inside a book by Muir or Burroughs and don't intend to."[33] Yet in the *Earth First! Journal* he included as essential authors Thoreau ("of course"), Muir ("dull but important"), Faulkner, Dillard, Zwinger, Austin, and Carson. Thus, ironically, we see Abbey carrying on more wildly under the distinguished covers of a university press book yet telling the truth in the more informal and typically rowdier pages of the *Earth First! Journal*. In both places, however, he stressed, as he put in the *Journal*, that "those I most admire in the conservation movement are those who act: such men as David Brower, Paul Watson, and the legendary Bulgarian brigand Georges Heiduk. Sentiment without action is the ruin of the soul. One brave deed is worth a hundred books, a thousand theories, a million words." He then reverted to comic fiction as he concluded his *Journal* piece: "As my Aunt Minnie used to say, back in Stump Crick West Virginny, '*too much* readin' rots the mind.'"

Hayduke Lives! would come last in Abbey's life, in a final, eight-month run toward the novel's contracted February 1989 deadline. He had chosen not to teach in the spring of 1986 in order to work on *The Fool's Progress* —but ended up spending most of that semester struggling with a script for *The Monkey Wrench Gang* instead. Thus, his earlier, greatest novelistic success continued to haunt him—because everyone was waiting for both a movie and a sequel—as encouraged in 1985 by the new edition of *The Monkey Wrench Gang* and by his scriptwriting success with "Out There in the Rocks" for *NBC*

Almanac. On May 15, 1986, Abbey complained in his journal that he had not written "a word on novel since January. Have wasted a good three months fooling around with Ballard, Kaplan, Paramount and that exasperating MWG screenplay. . . . But Lord, I would *love* to see my beloved book (*I* love it!) made into a decent movie!"[34] Carroll Ballard of Fantasy Films in Berkeley, California, spent two years working with Abbey and trying to convince Paramount Pictures to make the movie. In 1987 they replaced Abbey's script with a new one by a professional scriptwriter (who was paid much more), but again the movie was not made, and Ballard gave up late that year. Thus continued the seemingly endless saga of the *Monkey Wrench* movie: regularly and remuneratively optioned, but never yet actually made, after sponsors ran scared, fearing lawsuits for provoking "ecotage."

During the late 1980s, Abbey wrote somewhat fewer essays than he had from the late 1960s through the early 1980s, because he was determined to devote himself to *The Fool's Progress*. Most of the essays in his final collection, *One Life at a Time, Please*, had been written in the early 1980s. Even "River Solitaire: A Daybook," though it was first published in *American Country* in July 1987, described his November 1984 trip down the Green and Colorado Rivers. His lecturing and teaching produced two of the later essays in his book: "A Writer's Credo," delivered in San Diego in April 1985, at Harvard in May 1985, and at the Western Literature Association conference in Durango, Colorado, in October 1986; and "Emerson," developed for his course on the essay at the UA.

Like "The Remington Studio" (originally published in *Architectural Digest Travels* in the fall of 1986), these were unusually serious, scholarly essays. And, like his piece that same year on Navajo sand paintings in *Architecture Digest*, they might not even be recognized as Abbey essays, so somber and straightforward were they, if his name did not appear on them. As he remarked about these essays in his "Preliminary Notes" to *One Life at a Time, Please*, "I was trying hard . . . to appear sober, rational, respectable. I failed. But I tried."[35] Jack Macrae or some other sage editor must have advised Abbey to set the record straight in that book's introduction. In his introductions to all of his other collections of essays, he had carried on polemically, and only vague acknowledgment pages left us mostly in the dark about the prior publications of the essays. In *One Life*, however, to the great relief of bibliographers, Abbey devoted his introduction to (mostly) clarifying where this book's essays had previously appeared or for what occasions each had been written. As in *Hayduke Lives!*, which opens with a long list of thanks to seemingly every friend he ever had, perhaps Abbey could hear the footsteps of mortality and history beating down upon him.

Now and then, Abbey received an invitation for a new essay that was simply too good to turn down. Such was the case when he was flown (along with Clarke and Becky) to San Francisco by the *San Francisco Examiner*, for two weeks in late November and early December 1986, as a writer in residence. "Edward Abbey's Bay Area Journal" then appeared in four successive issues of the *Examiner* in mid-December and subsequently in *One Life at a Time, Please* as "A San Francisco Journal." His thoughts were far-ranging. Among many other descriptions, he delighted in how young Becky looked upon everything with glee and wanted to ride the airport escalator over and over. He reminisced about his 1957–58 sojourn at nearby Half Moon Bay as a Stanford student and about passing through the area en route to Australia in 1976. He explained that he planned to flee Tucson ("never meant to be more than a temporary expedient") for "my adopted home of Moab"—because "the developers have got us surrounded" in Tucson, and "in the nine years we've lived there the population has nearly doubled. . . . Not a wholesome way to live. The Hopi Indians have a word for it: *koyaanisqatsi*, meaning 'life out of balance' or 'weird craziness, man.'" He also advanced his standard explanation in response to his own contribution to overpopulation: "How many children have you begat, Abbey? I've fathered four. But I've been married five times. That comes to only 0.8 child per marriage. If every American couple would exercise similar restraint, we'd make a better, roomier, healthier America within two generations." [36] He wrote this three months before the birth of Ben, his fifth child, in March 1987—but this passage remained unchanged in the essay's 1988 book appearance, failing to keep a correct count of all his children and amend his statistics to the final figure of 1.0 child per marriage. He did make that correction in an interview, which also shows his ability to quote in conversation such one-liners out of his essays: "Yes, I've fathered five children. But I've been married five times. That comes to an average of, let's see . . . one child per marriage. I urge all couples to exercise similar restraint." [37]

Abbey also mentioned, in his San Francisco essay, his sidetrip in late November 1986 "to share a Thanksgiving dinner with my sister and her family," followed by a solo drive to "Tor House and Hawk Tower, the former home of Robinson Jeffers. This is a literary pilgrimage to the shrine of one of America's best, most reclusive, least known and most unpopular poets." Abbey also made clear that he was not closely following doctors' advice to stay away from alcohol: in response to an old friend's suggestion that they remember Pearl Harbor on December 7 and "get bombed," they met "at a bar on Lombard Street called Shea's." [38]

Back home in Tucson, Abbey worked with renewed determination on *The Fool's Progress*. A full account of the writing of this novel has to dip briefly back into earlier periods of his life, for its gestation process was very long and complex indeed. *The Fool's Progress* also deserves special and detailed attention, because it was the only book in which he attempted to describe his entire life, summing it all up before he died. It was also his only novel set partly in his native Appalachia, except for his very first novel, *Jonathan Troy*. If *Troy* had been his failed *Iliad*, then he was determined to make *The Fool's Progress* his successful *Odyssey*. There is no doubt that Abbey conceived both novels partly in terms of the Homeric framework: it is no accident that his first protagonist was named "Troy" and that Henry Lightcap thinks to himself in *The Fool's Progress*, "Yes, I am Ithaca-bound." [39] Jonathan watches his father fight the good fight, and, after he loses it, Jonathan leaves to conquer other kingdoms. *The Fool's Progress* is all about Henry Lightcap's odyssey to Home, after the wars (both worldly and personal). Abbey had written in his journal as early as November 1951 that he hoped "to write a book called "*Ithaca* — an improvement on the *Odyssey*. Man seeking Home — a man trying to get home, after years of sorrow and danger, reaches home, to find it." [40] This remained the basic premise of *The Fool's Progress*, published thirty-seven years later. In August 1956, he planned a book to be called *Confessions of a Barbarian*, to include sections "at home on the farm (absurd desperation)" and about "the factory in Hoboken," "love in Hoboken," and "the infantry in Alabama" [41] — all of which made it into *The Fool's Progress* three decades later.

The Abbey had spent several years in the 1960s working on "The Good Life," the unfinished typescript that contains much of the raw material of *The Fool's Progress*. Its nine-page outline and 149-page typescript include many of the same ideas and characters — the same two parents and four siblings, as modeled on the Abbeys. Interestingly, "The Good Life" focused more on the parents' marital conflicts, based on those of Mildred and Paul Abbey, than *The Fool's Progress* does. The father likes to go off to work by himself in the woods "out of selfishness" and gets into financial difficulties, the result of which is that he leases the family's field to strip-miners and ruins it. The typescript includes the mother's thoughts about how she dreads her marriage but maintains "a hard mask of stoicism." [42]

The Fool's Progress still contains plenty of such attention to Henry Lightcap's parents, but it is more distanced and positive, and the point of view is more consistently Henry's rather than theirs. In "The Good Life," Abbey's autobiographical perspective is less settled. As in *The Fool's Progress*, there are two brothers who resemble his own brother Howard (the harder-working, earthier one) and himself (the more artistic, adventurous one), but there is more overlap between the two. Some of the experiences that are Henry's in *The Fool's Progress*, such as being scooped up in the field by his father when a small child, are assigned to the "Howard" character in "The Good Life," Will Gatlin (the name later given to the protagonist of *Black Sun*), who becomes Will Lightcap in *The Fool's Progress*. Abbey transformed Will into a much more interesting character in *The Fool's Progress* by modeling him not only on his own brother but also on Wendell Berry, who had reclaimed his Kentucky family homestead and returned to living on the land.[43] "The Good Life" was a very promising attempt, but it stopped in midstream after 149 pages—as if Abbey had lost perspective, was not sure where to take it, and perhaps did not yet have enough distance on the events of his youth and know how to integrate them with his new life in the West.

In his journal, Abbey had written extensively about gathering ideas and information for "The Good Life" that remained central in *The Fool's Progress*. In August 1962, he noted that he wanted to focus on "the primal scene: the home place, the farm: the Old Lonesome Briar Patch," and added ample notes about traditional Appalachian materials and the experiences of his boyhood, such as "original genu-wine authentic square dances in the Old Grange Hall at Kellysburg." In July 1966, he made further notes about "the Ginter boys in their stinking long underwear, put on in Fall and not removed till Spring," and "the Home Hellions baseball team" with "my father as ump advising me where to pitch."[44] In October 1967, he was hypothesizing about the possible Native American, Senecan strain in his family and writing about his sister, Nancy, as "an Indian maid if I ever saw one,"[45] though Nancy emphasized later that "it didn't show up in our family tree."[46] In *The Fool's Progress*, Abbey invented a Native American great-grandfather and grandmother, "Doctor Jim" and "Grandmaw Cornflower."

Abbey had long been actively researching his novel, as he indicated in his journal in 1968: "Father here for a week, pumped him considerable [*sic*] for information on farmlife in 20's and 30's."[47] In a July 1976 letter, he wrote, "Mother, could you find for me a collection of some of the classic old-time hymns? . . . I need the text of them for this novel I have in mind."[48] He tried to develop "The Good Life," like *Jonathan Troy*, as "a documentary novel, full of documents," as he wrote in his journal, making a note to "check back files of *Indiana Evening Gazette* for ads, news, styles, cars" and sitting through a session in the "Indiana County Courthouse 11-5-69."[49] "The Good Life" was so "documentary" that one of its interchapters consisted of the father's budget figures. This may be another reason why Abbey had abandoned "The Good Life": such interchapters were pretty deadly stuff.

Abbey never gave up on his struggle to write his big novel. The 1975 Guggenheim Fellowship had been intended to help him write it—but he had turned then to travel and nature essays instead. Similarly, his early 1960s Hoboken novel "City of Dreadful Night" remained unfinished and unpublished—later serving as source material for the Hoboken sections of *The Fool's Progress*. The earlier manuscript's "A Day at the Madhouse" chapter, concerning his days as a New Jersey welfare worker, reappeared almost verbatim in the 1990 paperback edition of the novel,[50] according to his wishes, after it had been deleted from the hardback (much as the "Seldom Seen at Home" chapter had been reinstated to *The Monkey Wrench Gang* in its 1985 edition). *The Fool's Progress* developed positively as Abbey realized that his "fat masterpiece" had to move beyond his western Pennsylvanian boyhood in order to link it to his adult experiences elsewhere, particularly in Hoboken (where he tried to salvage his second marriage during the early 1960s while working in a welfare office) and in the West, which had long since become his new home. By November 1977, he had planned a big novel to be entitled "*Confessions of a Barbarian, An Honest Novel.*" He wanted to reach back into not only "The Good Life" and "City of Dreadful Night" but also "the original *Black Sun* or *Firedogs* novel (movie script) of sub-bohemian life at UNM"; it would begin "*in media res*" and move "back and forward through time, a series of retrospections: UNM in the 50's, the U.S. Army in the 40's, Naples, at home on the farm, the Depression (days of hope!), infancy and infantilism as the Barb regresses."[51] Here he conceived the basic structure of *The Fool's Progress*—an imaginative, double-edged, alternating East-West chronology that is one of this novel's chief strengths. As he expressed it in a 1980 outline to his editors, it would be "a picaresque novel, told largely but not entirely in the first person, which details the adventures of one Henry Lightcap, an Appalachian hillbilly, from his birth around 1927 to his displaced status in contemporary 1980's America."[52]

Every other chapter was a version of Abbey's earlier life: his birth, boyhood, and family (chapter 2); baseball and other adolescent adventures (chapter 4); departure for the tail-end of World War II (chapters 6 and 8); 1950s misadventures in New Mexico (10); his double life at Arches and in Hoboken (12); his returns home to Appalachia to see his family (14 and 22); the dissolution of one marriage and the beginning of another (16); his many other affairs with women (18); his intense, abbreviated marriage to "Claire Mellon," a version of Judy Pepper (20); and the failure of his marriage to "Elaine" (a version of Renée Downing) and his diagnosis of a terminal illness (24). Meanwhile, all of the odd-numbered chapters narrated the older Henry Lightcap's departure from Tucson and cross-country drive home, visiting some old friends along the way such as "Don Williams" (Ernie Bulow) and "Morton Bildad" (an exaggerated version of Malcolm Brown).[53] These two alternating narrative "halves" of the novel ultimately converge in chapters 25 and 26, where a ghostlike Henry arrives at the scenes of his childhood, and in "A Postlude," in which, apparently in the next life, he escorts "Ellie" (a version of Susie) back to his beloved Southwest.

The Fool's Progress is autobiographical in such a detailed way that the natural tendency for many readers is to accept it as a straightforward account of Abbey's life and to view Henry Lightcap as simply another name for Edward Abbey. Yet this novel's fictionalized departures from reality are at least as numerous as its bases in fact, and there are so many such non-facts in the novel that listing them all would require another chapter. They begin with the invention of Native American ancestors and continue by changing Will (Howard) into Henry's older brother who goes to war, by making "Claire" (Judy) a native of Denver who dies in an auto accident caused by Henry— and with many, many other fictional inventions. Reader, beware. Despite its full title, The Fool's Progress: An Honest Novel, it is, after all, a novel, *not* an autobiography. Abbey noted in his journal, probably alluding to Henry's terminal illness: "Honest? Well, that's a teaser, a come-on, a secret between me and the reader" (333). And Henry Lightcap is an exaggerated, much less successful character than Abbey was. Henry is not a writer; he is not an influential environmentalist; he never finishes his master's thesis; he directly causes the death of his most beloved wife. In short, Henry Lightcap is just the opposite of a heroic version of his author; he is a fictional, picaresque, often offensive, always lively character—meant to entertain, not inspire.

Significantly, Abbey made no attempt to include any version (fictional or otherwise) of Clarke Cartwright, his last two children, or his happy family life in the 1980s; Henry's life stops before 1980. Abbey had decided in 1983 that "fifty years is enuf for our hero" (311). Nonetheless, Clarke was offended by Henry's attitudes to women at the beginning of the novel. Abbey noted on December 12, 1988, that Clarke hated the novel's first chapter (351). She remarked later that her husband treated women "as sexual objects in his books. He didn't treat me that way. He didn't treat the women he knew that way. But he would write about women in that way. It just seemed to be a real narrow view."[54] His father was similarly offended by the novel's first chapter; Paul Abbey refused to read any further.[55]

Although Abbey ranged far beyond Appalachia in The Fool's Progress, just as he had in his life, this novel is richer than ever in Appalachian and Abbey family materials. "Viva la Appalachia," Henry thinks to himself.[56] Not all of this material made it into the published novel. For example, Abbey's handwritten draft includes intermittent, tall-tale chapters about two Appalachian horses called "Ned and Fred." The death of Henry Lightcap's father is much more drawn out in the early draft, with the whole family driving him home from the hospital while Henry caustically observes the decayed environment of his youth. In the published novel, the father's death is much more dramatic: he is crushed by a falling tree and Will finds him only just in time to forgive him for strip-mining the farm and then bring his body home. Abbey may have based this part of his plot on a close call with a tree in which his father was nearly killed.[57] In real life, Paul Abbey outlived his son by three-and-a-half years. The fictional father's death allows Henry to deliver a eulogy, which Abbey probably wanted his father to read (though he apparently did not read it). He calls the father "a true independent" and a "mountaineer" who believed that "mountain men will always be free."[58]

By the beginning of 1985, Abbey had returned to the completion of his novel in a focused way. He express-mailed its first three chapters, 151 pages, to his agent Don Congdon on January 17 of that year—on the basis of which he received, on June 4, an advance contract from Jack Macrae at Holt.[59] An unusual clause—a reflection on the projected length of this book and the earlier editorial struggles between Macrae and Abbey—was included in the contract: "A bonus of Fifteen-thousand Dollars ($15,000.00) against earnings will be paid if the final manuscript conforms to Publisher's editorial request." By the time that bonus was paid, Abbey had forgotten all about it. But during 1985–87 he engaged in an editorial tug-of-war with Macrae over his "fat masterpiece." On August 23, 1985, for example, he wrote Macrae: "Sacco and Vanzetti executed on this date in 1927, the year of my birth. Jack Macrae is next."[60]

At the end of January 1986, Abbey sent Macrae another 225 pages of his novel, but it was still a long way from finished, and then he got distracted with writing and revising his script for *The Monkey Wrench Gang*.[61] In April of that year, in an attempt to pump new life into his novel, he journeyed all the way to Pennsylvania from Bluff, Utah, to visit his family and research Henry's trip in *The Fool's Progress*, riding with his friend Dick Kirkpatrick, who later remarked, "The homing instinct was obvious in that." Abbey filled a notebook and three audiotapes with copious impressions. When they got to Kentucky, Abbey took special notice, pronouncing into his tape-recorder: "We enter hillbilly country: . . . junked automobiles everywhere, trashy little houses, barns, stores, Shell gasoline, Sunoco, graveyards, little muddy cricks. More up ahead on the horizon. Northeast and south are the little pointy hills of Appalachia. The foothills of Appalachia. . . . One little cabin on the road. One old man sitting on the front porch and the laundry about a half-mile long hanging there by him. Crick full of old tires, stick, cans, . . . beer cans. Classic hillbilly decor."[62] Abbey's sharp, spoken, impromptu observations became part of his novel: "The first hillbilly town—a rough and wary look on every face. . . . Fuzzy little conical hills begin to appear through the haze of afternoon. . . . The foothills of Appalachia at last. Now we're getting somewhere." Henry notices "a lounging sullen homicidal primitive in every doorway" and declares, "My people."[63]

Abbey set *The Fool's Progress* ostensibly in West Virginia—the only state in the Union that is entirely in Appalachia—and he took notes on Sutton, West Virginia, as a source for his fictional town of Shawnee. However, in the novel's typescript, he crossed out some names that he had copied from a war memorial in Sutton, substituting names specific to Home, Pennsylvania, such as Fetterman and Ginter.[64] These seem acts of homage, whereas the name "Kovalchick," the name of the refuse magnate whose junkheaps still defiled the landscape of the town of Indiana at the end of the 1990s, may be something else. Henry's baseball nemesis is Tony Kovalchick, and he loses his virginity in the back seat of Will's 1935 Hudson Terraplane with Mary Kovalchick.[65]

In the spring of 1986, Capra Press published a version of the novel's first chapter under the title *Confessions of a Barbarian* (later used for the posthumous edition of Abbey's journals). It included a remarkable, highly entertaining preface in which Edward Abbey, academic editor, is approached by Henry Lightcap, redneck author, and handed the manuscript of the novel—the oldest novelistic ruse in the game, of course, dating back to at least the eighteenth century. "Abbey" set himself up as Swiftian satirist, noting that Lightcap was

> an American type now totally anachronistic. . . . They persist, alas, these atavists, throwbacks and living relics, in various dark grimy pockets around the nation, wallowing like pigs in the boué of their animal-like refuges, gathering from time to time—amidst the whining schmaltz of "country music" in their "family bars" and "honky-tonk" saloons . . . then appearing regularly at state Department of Employment Security agencies to apply for unemployment checks. . . . Nostalgia for the frontier mode of life is understandable but no longer intellectually respectable. . . . The Henry Lightcaps of America, like the redskinned buffalo-hunting horseman of the West, had their day—a century ago! They are the final incarnations of the Vanishing Americans. Let us let them vanish.[66]

Reluctantly agreeing to take a look at Lightcap's manuscript, "Abbey" then cuts a contract with him according to which he will collect the royalties if Lightcap fails to claim them himself. He subsequently gleefully notes, "Granted, the entire Appalachian region, from northern Georgia up through Western Pennsylvania, is inhabited by numerous descendants of the family Lightcap, but none has come forward to present himself as the author of a book—any book."[67] An

"Editor's Afterword" was later drafted (but not published) in which Lightcap emerges, "armed with two attorneys."[68] The preface and afterword are not only entertaining comic romps but also interesting exercises in the delineation of a fictional author and Appalachian alter ego.

Abbey ran the risk of looking to many readers like a "kitchen-sink" novelist in *The Fool's Progress*, as he himself joked in a 1985 interview: "you toss in everything that's been dangling in your mind for years: all the jokes you always wanted to use somewhere; everything except the kitchen sink — and before I'm done with it, I might even throw in the sink, too." He did.[69] However, Abbey was really much more like Hemingway, another novelist with a rough-and-ready image who revised and cut his work as scrupulously and as mercilessly as he could. One need not even examine the earlier handwritten and typed drafts of *The Fool's Progress* in the Abbey archive (though it helps to do so) in order to get a good sense of how significantly Abbey revised and cut. One can simply study earlier *published* extracts — such as the 1986 version of the novel's first chapter published as *Confessions of a Barbarian* and, more easily obtainable, the version in *The Best of Edward Abbey* of chapter 4, "The Rites of Spring." From the 1984 version, for example, Abbey deleted — in the process of getting down from more than 1,000 manuscript pages to 485 printed ones in the hardback (513 in the 1990 paperback) — an entire page-and-a-half conversation early in the chapter between Henry and his leading baseball adversary, Tony Kovalchick. Gone is such dialogue from Kovalchick as "Naw, we don't play farmers; you ain't in our league."[70] His cuts and tightening are continual, aimed at shortening and also avoiding any stodgy diction: early in this same chapter, for example, "sharp absolute loathing" becomes simply "hatred,"[71] "a wealth of talent" becomes "much talent,"[72] and so on. *The Fool's Progress* may read like a wild romp, but in fact no page of typescript or galley escaped the pen of Abbey the editor.

Just before leaving on his San Francisco trip, Abbey proudly declared in his journal on November 19, 1986, that *The Fool's Progress* was a novel with "greatness in it, the best thing I've written yet, and I'm proud of it. Yes. Lightcap is an arrogant, swaggering, macho, obnoxious and eccentric character — but he learns some humility in the end. Good for him" (330). However, he still had to survive extended editorial struggles throughout 1987 in order to see the book into print. On January 23 he noted that he had begun "the painful and difficult task of cutting and revising *The Fool's Progress*." By April Fool's Day he thought he was done, as he indicated on April 4: "final revisions of novel sent to typist 5 days ago!"[73] But he had to cut and revise some more, and it was not until August 3 that he mailed Macrae what he similarly described to him as "the final revised version."

In November 1987, however, he was still at work on the novel, still trying to hang onto various details that Macrae wanted to cut. On November 10, he wrote his old friend Donn Rawlings, who was teaching in Prescott, to read the manuscript. Abbey asked him, "Do you agree that the novel could be improved by cuts here and there? . . . How about the old jokes and Archie Bunkerisms?"[74] They met for dinner in Phoenix, took a long walk afterward, and talked about the book.[75] During the same period, his Tucson friend and University of Arizona Press editor Greg McNamee also read the manuscript and suggested that he eliminate many of the "Archie Bunkerisms"—Henry Lightcap's various racy observations about, for example, women and Native Americans.[76] Rawlings also suggested deleting some of those, but he was more in favor of preserving the novel mostly as it was. He had already received a lively introduction to *The Fool's Progress* when Abbey read from its opening chapter about Henry and Elaine, in Prescott, as part of the Western Writers Series organized by Rawlings, on April 27, 1987. A number of female members of Abbey's audience walked out while he was reading.[77]

Abbey naturally preferred Rawlings's advice, and, as he continued to review his manuscript, he sent McNamee a series of postcards explaining why he wanted to keep the various details that McNamee had suggested cutting.[78] When he mailed yet another "final revised version" to Macrae on Christmas Eve, he enclosed Rawlings's supportive letter, in which Rawlings advised him, "Don't let those eastern editors get their scissors on this one—they may not understand where the frontiers of American fiction really are."[79] Macrae later wrote that "despite Dr. Rawlings's advice the published book came in at under five hundred pages; Ed wrote me a gracious note in appreciation of the editing, which I hasten to add was in large measure his, not mine." Macrae added, "Even though Rawlings made my job more difficult I knew he was right when he wrote Ed, 'The complacent critical cranks will go on cranking without ever allowing themselves to see what is there.'"[80]

Concerning the proposed deletion of his "Archie Bunkerisms," Abbey wrote to Macrae: "I'm not going to toady to chickenshit liberalism anymore; fuck it. I've already been called fascist, racist, élitist as well as communist, terrorist, misanthrope, bleeding-heart, etc. so often it doesn't bother me anymore. To hell with all those petty, taboo-ridden dogmatic minds."[81] As he explained in his journal in 1988, "my publisher and I have a perfect agreement: he tells me how to write my books, I tell him how to publish them."[82] Abbey admitted in a nationally visible interview of August 1988, "There are a lot of things" in *The Fool's Progress* "that will annoy a lot of people. . . . Joking about sex, religious groups and ethnic groups. It's a habit of mine. I can't seem to help it."[83]

When *The Fool's Progress* appeared in October 1988, most of the reviews were surprisingly positive. Sales were strong, yet not as outstanding as either Abbey or Macrae might have wished. E. A. Mares pronounced it one of the four greatest picaresque novels; John Murray noticed that it was "a modern version of the story of Ulysses"; and the reviewer for *Chronicles* understood that Abbey was a humorist in the tradition of Mark Twain. But Abbey was dismayed by two more negative and visible critiques. Howard Coale in the *New York Times Book Review* recognized some wonderful scenes in the novel but complained that "they are drowned out to almost a murmur by the harpings of a slightly malevolent and self-indulgent voice." In the *National Review*, Ed Marston called it "part pun," "part wisecrack," "part ethnic slur," "part a voyage across America," "uneven," and lacking "the magical descriptions of air and land and the joy of destruction" of *The Monkey Wrench Gang*, though "Abbey finally achieves his goal" and Henry "is redeemed by love." [84]

On New Year's Day 1989, Abbey described Coale's review in his journal as "a slight silly superficial review (buried on page twenty-two) by some 'free-lance writer' I never heard of. As usual, the reviewer devotes so much space to attacking the author that he barely gets around to mentioning the book." He felt betrayed by Marston's review, which Marston reprinted in his own *High Country News*, because he was a Western editor whom Abbey had regarded as an ally. He found Marston's review filled with "cant and sham and hypocrisy, intellectual dishonesty and moral cowardice" (351); it failed to mention the book's actual content until the final paragraph. Abbey's friends Tom Lyon, Terry Tempest Williams, and others sent letters to *High Country News* protesting Marston's review.[85]

On February 2, 1989, Abbey wrote New York's *Village Voice* lampooning their review, which faulted his treatment of women. Just twelve days before his death, he reverted to the style of his satiric 1973 letter to *Ms.* magazine about men's interest in "wimmen": "Out here in the backlands (rest of the world) near everybody still takes that kinda interest as a incurable natural disease of the grownup male animal. . . . I could of wrote that review one hell of a lot better myself if you'd only asked me." [86] In his journal on the same date, on the question of why reviewers "hate my books," Abbey wondered: "Because the books are really no good? Perhaps. But I think I've got a better explanation. Almost all reviewers, these days, are members of and adherents to some anxious particular sect or faction. . . . As such, any member of any one of those majority minorities is going to find *for certain* a few remarks in any of *my* books that will offend/enrage 's/he' to the marrow" (352–53).

The year 1988 was Abbey's biggest publishing period since 1984; in fact, it was arguably the biggest year in his career. In addition to *The Fool's Progress*, Macrae had released *One Life at a Time, Please* at the beginning of the year, and the Sierra Club's paperback reprint of *Slumgullion Stew* as *The Best of Edward Abbey* and the University of Arizona Press's new hardback edition of *Desert Solitaire* both appeared in the late spring. The two new books naturally received more attention than the two reprinted ones, but *The Best of Edward Abbey* did sell better than *Slumgullion Stew* had, and the new hardback of *Desert Solitaire* was reviewed more widely than the original 1968 edition of the book.[87]

Despite (or sometimes because of) such controversial essays as "Free Speech: The Cowboy and His Cow," "Theory of Anarchy," "Eco-Defense," and "Immigration and Liberal Taboos," *One Life at a Time, Please* was reviewed positively more consistently than *The Fool's Progress*. It also contained several nature essays, the more preferred genre: "River Solitaire: A Daybook," "River of No Return," "Big Bend," and others. Randy Dykhuis in the *Library Journal*, for example, emphasized that the "marvelous portraits of the Rio Grande and the Salmon rivers showcase Abbey's ability to evoke a feeling for the majesty of these places." Yet even such positive reviews irritated Abbey, because once again he felt that he was too narrowly pigeonholed as a "naturalist." When Bill McKibben praised such essays in the *New York Review of Books*, Abbey wrote complaining that "by seizing on one narrow strain in my writing and ignoring the other 90 percent," McKibben "misrepresents the whole and mythologizes my life."[88] It does have to be said that the most memorable essays in this strong collection are Abbey's manifestos in the "Politics" section that opens the book ("Free Speech," "Theory of Anarchy," "Eco-Defense," and four others) and indeed the book's "Preliminary Remarks."

Past the age of sixty, Abbey distrusted the East Coast literati—even in the form of a "nice young man" such as McKibben—even more than he had when he was younger. The most unforgettable proof came in 1987 when Irving Howe invited him to a banquet inducting Abbey into the American Academy of Arts and Letters. Abbey replied to Howe on March 20, 1987: "I appreciate the intended honor but will not be able to attend the awards ceremony on May 20th: I'm figuring on going down a river in Idaho that week. Besides, to tell the truth, I think that prizes are for little boys. You can give my $5,000 to somebody else. I don't need it or really want it."[89] His old friend Edward Hoagland had lobbied for him to receive this award and was disappointed when Abbey refused it, though as a fellow nature writer, Hoagland understood that Abbey had felt marginalized and that the offer came too late.[90] As for Howe, he remarked, "Was I offended? No. It's a free country."[91]

The "river in Idaho" was the Owyhee. In his essay "River of No Return," he celebrated running the Salmon River in Idaho—but he did that in July, not in May as he claimed to Howe.[92] Despite the specter of illness and impending death, Abbey was determined to enjoy as many more wilderness adventures as he could, and his final talks and essays show him more determined than ever to be a spunky Westerner. On January 15, 1988, he delivered the "third annual Archdruid lecture" to the Sierra Club in Salt Lake City, remembering Glen Canyon and fulminating against Glen Canyon Dam.[93] On April 15, he gave a benefit reading for the Prescott National Forest Friends—again outraging many by reading racy parts of *The Fool's Progress*.[94]

In "The Secret of the Green Mask," which would appear in the *Condé Nast Traveler* in the month of his death, Abbey described his May 1988 horseback expedition, commissioned by the magazine, into Utah's Grand Gulch with Ken Sleight, the wrangler Grant Johnson, and the photographer Mark Klett.[95] Abbey chose the place; he had not been there in many years, and he felt that he could celebrate it in print since it was already well known and he was thus not giving away any wilderness secrets. He enjoyed the trip, both wandering the canyons by day and starting arguments about politics beside the campfire by night.[96]

Abbey had hoped to make some further international wilderness trips as well, entertaining late in life the notion of writing books about both Mexico and Australia.[97] In early 1987, he had pursued with photographer Jay Dusard a proposal for a book on Australia, writing Martha Lawrence at Harcourt, Brace on March 3, 1987, "I'd be willing to spend a year in Australia if necessary—or if possible." But on September 26, he wrote Dusard postponing the project until the summer or fall of 1989 because of the pressures of his spring 1988 teaching and his February 1989 deadline for *Hayduke Lives!*[98]

After teaching what turned out to be his final semester at the University of Arizona in the spring of 1988, Abbey did not return to Moab that summer. In late June, he spent a few days near Eagle Tank in southwestern Arizona's Cabeza Prieta wilderness, working on an annual governmental count of bighorn sheep in the area. Along the way he got his pickup stuck offroad near Ajo for nearly two days, walking many miles with little water and in sheer terror before he could get himself and his truck out safely (344–45).

With the completion of *The Fool's Progress*, Abbey had a sense that his work was coming to an end. He joked meaningfully in the *Whole Earth Review*, "One more novel and then, as Chief Joseph said, I shall type no more forever."[99] But he was not quite done. Feeling the pressure of mortality and his February 1989 deadline for *Hayduke Lives!*, he holed up for several weeks in a room at the Amerind Foundation (to which Charles Bowden gave him an introduction) near Benson, Arizona, where he could work intensively on the novel, isolated from family, friends, and phone calls. He commuted back and forth to Tucson—and on one occasion the opposite direction to Bowie to visit his old friend Bill Hoy—in his old Cadillac: "Sheet! Drove me Caddie all the way from Benson to here in fuckin' low gear. Didn't notice until the red lights went on. Damn near burned up the engine" (349). He emphasized his new discipline on July 9, with a self-imposed rule that he could not go home "until I do forty pages." That kept him in Benson for "four or five days at a time. If I can keep up the pace, then I should complete a first draft and fulfill my contract within ten weeks." Yet he missed his "sweet little Becky and Benno so much, so very much! And my sweet lovely sexy young wife also. I'm sixty miles, or about ninety minutes from home" (348). As Clarke Abbey recalled, "There was always the real complex issue of wanting to be married and have a family and wanting to be totally on his own and doing what he wanted." [100]

At least in terms of his writing, Abbey's regimen worked: he would send the conclusion of his final, 300-page novel to Little, Brown on February 13, 1989, almost precisely one month before his death. Several of his journal entries while writing the novel make clear that he wanted to finish the novel, which he knew would sell well, in order to provide for Clarke, Becky, and Ben, leaving future royalties behind for them after his death. For much the same reason, on February 15 he signed a contract for *Vox Clamantis in Deserto*,[101] a book of maxims selected from his journals.

In September 1988, Abbey did take a break from *Hayduke Lives!* long enough to enjoy his latest controversy in Moab, even in his absence. Because of his participation in a Moab newspaper that Jim Stiles and others had started, called *The Stinking Desert Gazette* (the forerunner of Stiles's subsequent *Canyon Country Zephyr*), Abbey had been faulted by feminists, in their rival paper *The Slinking Dessert Glace*, for his hypocrisy as an opponent of overpopulation who had fathered five children. In reply, "An Open Letter from Edward Abbey" appeared in the September *Stinking Desert Gazette*:

> To the Wild Wanton Women of Moab, Utah.
> Dear Sirs:
> Your "Open Letter" to me was noted and much appreciated. Believe me, I've been trying for years to get a vasectomy but my public simply will not permit it. Last time I even reached my physician's operating table but as she examined me, wondering why I'd never been circumcized and then going further to make sure everything was in good functioning order, at that climactic moment another mob of tearful young women burst into the room and carried me off, begging me to "have my baby," as you ladies say. So . . . what could I do? I haven't even been allowed to make a deposit in a sperm bank;

flinging their skirts in the air, the tellers hurl their bodies in my path, causing me to stumble and fall over and over again.

One might well consider that subject closed!

Abbey also took time out to dash off several other letters, reviews, and introductions. He often belittled New York writer Tom Wolfe in contrast to his boyhood hero, "the real Tom Wolfe"[102] and author of *You Can't Go Home Again*, but he did defend *The Bonfire of the Vanities*.[103] Penguin reprinted Mary Austin's 1903 desert classic *The Land of Little Rain* in 1988 with an introduction by Abbey in which he (in a completely different tone than his Moab "Open Letter") recognized that Austin had been "an active feminist at a time when that particular cause entailed risk and trouble." Unfortunately, he also offended feminists by describing the style of the book as "too fussy, even prissy at first," though "you are soon absorbed by the accuracy of her observational powers."[104] Earlier, Abbey had helped several contemporary women writers such as Josephine Johnson, Katie Lee, Terry Tempest Williams, and Ann Zwinger, but his introduction to Austin met enough resistance that Penguin soon replaced it in future printings with a different introduction by another writer.

Abbey's attitudes to women writers remained complicated and inconsistent. At the beginning of January 1989, just a couple of months before his death, Abbey and Barbara Kingsolver—a fellow Appalachian emigré to Tucson—met for the first and only time, as fellow judges in a writing contest. Kingsolver had dreaded meeting him because of his reputation but was surprised to find him "gracious, respectful to the point of deference, and wonderfully guileless. . . . It dawned on me that the revolution of his youth was not the same one as mine. While Abbey was inspiring the ire of cowboys with his black turtleneck and beret, Gloria Steinem and Malcolm X were still awaiting conversion and I hadn't yet learned to walk. His language came out of a time I never knew. I decided to lighten up a little on Ed." Kingsolver soon regretted that she had no further opportunity "to cultivate his acquaintance."[105] What she could not know was that, though Abbey found her witty and charming, he did not approve—shortly after he had returned from his own extended publicity trip for *The Fool's Progress*, ironically enough—of her leaving her young child behind while she traveled on her own book-signing tour.[106] In contrast, he praised his own wife, Clarke, not only as "my love, comrade and wife for the last ten years" but also pointedly as "full-time mother to our children."[107]

Abbey remained somber when thinking about his private life. Behind his late, often gleeful writing lurked a man who was dying during the same period when some of his relatives passed away; the rare reunions of the Pennsylvania Abbeys were now confined to funerals. Earlier, despite his own August 1982 terminal diagnosis and subsequent illnesses, Abbey felt that ancestral longevity, inherited from his mother and father, surely meant that he himself would nonetheless live for a long time. Yet events in 1987 and 1988 changed his mind. First, his younger brother Johnny got cancer, just a couple of years after Johnny's wife, Dolores, had died from the disease. Ed visited him at his apartment in Los Angeles in the late summer of 1987, after he had a tumor removed from his stomach and shortly before he began chemotherapy. The two brothers had long, private conversations about John's will and repairing family ties.[108]

On November 17, Johnny died, and Ed flew back to Los Angeles for his funeral, met there by his mother, his sister Nancy, his brother Bill, and his brother Howard's wife Iva. Afterward, Johnny's ashes were to be buried beside those of his wife in Nanticoke, Pennsylvania—but first Howard deposited half of them at the family gravesite above Washington Presbyterian Church near Home, and Paul saw to it that John's name and dates were inscribed on the gravestone that would also be Mildred's and Paul's.[109] Johnny left nothing to Ed in his will because he felt that he did not need anything—and Ed agreed with this decision. At the end of the year, Bill wrote to Ed from Honolulu wondering what to do about the land that John had willed him, and Ed advised him to keep it.[110] Ed wrote in his journal on November 19 about John, "What do I feel? A dull sorrow, a poignant regret that I never knew him. Most of his life he considered me some kind of enemy, 'just another bleeding-heart liberal.' He quarreled with all of us, sooner or later, but forgave all in his holographic will. Mother says, defiantly, 'His life was not wasted. He made some people very happy'" (336).

A year later, on November 15, 1988, eighty-three-year-old Mildred Abbey was struck by a truck as she was pulling out onto busy Route 286 midway between Indiana and Clymer, Pennsylvania, and "died instantly," as Ed wrote in his journal. "We buried her, a week before Thanksgiving, in the family plot at Washington Church. A simple ceremony. The preacher read from Isaiah and Ecclesiastes and the 23rd Psalm—exactly my own preferences. About a hundred people standing about. A chill and windy day, scattered clouds, cold sunshine. We cried" (350). Ed shivered through the ceremony, covered only by a light Western jacket. For once he had stuck true to his own real feelings when he had Henry Lightcap think about his mother in *The Fool's Progress*: "That woman is meant to live forever. She will too. He felt a surge of blood-pride rise from his heart."[111]

His big autobiographical novel had been published just a month before his mother's death, and he attended her funeral at the beginning of a grueling, month-long book-signing tour for his novel which (ironically or perhaps appropriately) just about killed him off. "Never again. *Never!*" he promised himself on December 12 (350). Many of his old friends saw him for the last time on this tour (including some who had not laid eyes on him for many years), such as Ralph Newcomb, Karilyn McElheney Brodell, Bob Greenspan, Jim Stiles, and Ken Sanders.[112] To none of them, however, did Abbey admit that he felt ill; true to form, he remained stoic, not wishing to be treated as the dying man that he was. He struck much the same note as late as February 1989 in a postcard to David Quammen: "There's nothing to get alarmed about. Got this little medical problem that kicks up every 4–5 years. Our friend Peacock tends to exaggerate a bit. Am finishing a book now, then going exploring around the Sea of Cortez in March. All's well."[113]

As bad as he felt, Abbey remained very generous to his friends. Earlier that fall he paid a final visit to Bill Hoy in Bowie—and typed out on the spot a preface to a book by his old friend that was published two years later: "This young fellow Hoy, I first met him back at the so-called University of New Mexico early in the 1950s—those antique and Neolithic times. But didn't get to know him well or rightly until 1968, when we shared a Quonset hut at Organ Pipe Cactus National Monument. . . . There is a big fat volume of history and lore in the head of this man and someday, somehow, we're going to set him down and prop him up and force him, at gunpoint if necessary, to put it all down on paper and into a book. Meanwhile, we'll have to settle for Bill's glossary of Sonoran Desert terms."[114]

To himself, Abbey was honest about his condition, admitting on March 2, 1989, "Here I sit, bleeding to death (look, Maw!)" (352). A couple of weeks before that, he had indulged in similar gallows humor with Charles Bowden, mentioning to him at lunch that earlier he had written "that nobody in his family ever died. And then, suddenly, his brother had died from cancer, his mother had been run over and killed by a truck. He looked up at me with a mad twinkle in his eyes." Bowden told him, "Maybe you ought to print a retraction."[115]

Abbey had been writing about his failing health with black humor since 1985, when he recorded that he had been "off my cough syrup (codeine) habit" for a week, but still experienced pain, withdrawal symptoms, and "that run-down miserable flulike ache-all-over feeling." He still suffered from "general debility," yet could ride a bicycle. After he had taken a fall beside a Utah creek, he noticed "how the pale gray cow-flies did swoon and swarm around my shanks!" (320).

He suffered from another kidney stone in early 1986, having it surgically removed on April Fool's Day (326). In June 1987, he believed that he was dying from another attack of bleeding esophageal varices. Internal bleeding is especially nefarious, because it remains hidden. Often Abbey would know he was in trouble only from how he felt and from the darkened color of his feces. On July 26, 1987, after exhausting himself by swimming in the Colorado River and into White Canyon's Black Hole with his friend Glen Lathrop, Abbey found a trace of blood in his stool and suffered from iron deficiency. "Will I live another year? Who knows. Who cares" (335). He asked himself the same questions on July 20, 1988, as he cranked himself up for the final stretch of writing *Hayduke Lives!*, and then added, "Anyhow, you've got to do it. Promises to keep" (348).

After his fall 1988 book-signing tour, Abbey faded steadily. A year after being promoted to full professor—with letters of support by Wallace Stegner and Wendell Berry—he took leave from teaching at the University of Arizona, just as he became eligible for social security on his sixty-second birthday on January 27, 1989. He had been planning his retirement for quite a while.[116] By February 2, 1989, he decided that he had better end *Hayduke Lives!* more abruptly than he had intended, allowing "Doc, Bonnie and Seldom [to] escape free and clear from the hijacking of the GEM, get off undetected, unidentified, and therefore never arrested or indicted. This way, we'd still have a complete novel, satisfy the contract, and I can croak, if necessary, in peace." He added, "(Doc MacGregor sez I lost at least half my blood that awful Friday and Saturday, only ten or eleven days ago. It seems and feels to me that I may not really recover this time.) 'I've gone for a little walk. Into the West. I'll be home by sunset'" (352).

On March 4, 1989, Ed Abbey made his final public appearance, at (appropriately enough) an Earth First! rally. Along with Dave Foreman and the singer Bill Oliver, he spoke against the proposed positioning of a telescope on Mount Graham by his own employer, the University of Arizona. He looked very gaunt but was as spunky as ever. After being introduced by a woman who later turned out to be an FBI plant, he fittingly read a section from *Hayduke Lives!* that included a description of FBI agent J. Oral Hatch.[117] On the same day, Abbey wrote his last known letter—yet another statement of protest, this time to an ambulance service that he felt had been slow and inefficient a few days earlier in getting him to the hospital.[118]

One week later, Abbey suffered yet another bad onset of esophageal hemorrhaging and was rushed to the hospital by Dave Foreman and Nancy Morton. At first, temporarily revived by blood transfusions, he seemed better there, so Foreman left on a scheduled trip the next day to Belize, figuring that Abbey would recover, as he had done so many times before.[119] Doug Peacock took over for him at bedside, joined by Clarke and by Jack Loeffler. Next doctors enacted a portal shunt in an attempt to bring Abbey around. When it became apparent that it was not working, on March 12, Loeffler fulfilled a pledge that he had made to Abbey in 1974 by helping detach him from the apparatus and escorting him out of the hospital.[120]

Outside in the desert, Clarke lay with Ed in a sleeping bag for hours, both of them thinking that he was about to die there. Instead, he felt a bit better, so he asked to be taken home, where he lay down in his writing cabin behind his house and lasted for another day and a half. Peacock, a former Vietnam medic, stayed with him through the night, later calling it the bravest dying that he had ever seen, and remembering that Abbey's last smile passed over his face when Peacock told him the illegal site in the desert where he planned to bury him.[121] Clarke was nearby, in the company of Susie (who had flown home from college), Becky, and Ben. Ed Abbey died on March 14, 1989, just as the sun was rising.

CHAPTER ELEVEN

Conclusion

Waking a Legacy

Many writers and public figures loom larger in death simply because the event of their death attracts attention and often more readers. This pattern certainly applied to Abbey, but it was further magnified by three other factors: the mystique of his illegal burial at an unspecified site in the desert; the two similarly unconventional public wakes held in his memory in Saguaro National Monument near Tucson in March 1989 and next to Arches National Park near Moab in May 1989; and the subsequent appearance of no fewer than five posthumously published books (six if one counts the revised paperback edition of *The Fool's Progress*). Each of these factors was augmented by the others. Abbey's private burial created a psychological need on the part of many of his friends and readers for the separate, public, large-scale memorials, with the mystery of his gravesite increasing the aura surrounding these wakes as well as the appeal of his books.

The sales of Abbey's books—the eighteen books still in print at the time of his death, and the five posthumous ones—peaked in the 1990s, with his books and the cult surrounding Abbey feeding off each other. During that period, sales of his earlier books were more than double what they had been during his lifetime.[1] *Desert Solitaire* and *The Monkey Wrench Gang* continued to lead the way, each selling more than a half-million copies and heading toward the million mark. *Desert Solitaire* enjoyed a popular readership while it remained his book most commonly assigned in college courses; these two different types of readers make it Abbey's single best-selling title. In 1999, it garnered third place on the *San Francisco Chronicle*'s list of the best 100 Western nonfiction books, right after Mary Austin's *The Land of Little Rain* (the desert classic introduced by Abbey in its 1988 reprint) and *Beyond the Hundredth Meridian* by Wallace Stegner (Abbey's old teacher during 1957–58).[2]

Several books published after Abbey's death extended his appeal. *Vox Clamantis in Deserto* (1989), subsequently reprinted as *A Voice Crying in the Wilderness* (1990), was a collection of wise sayings from his journals, including some of his funniest one-liners. *Hayduke Lives!*, *The Monkey Wrench Gang*'s sequel, created quite a splash when it appeared in 1990. David Petersen's two editions of previously unpublished writings, *Confessions of a Barbarian: Selections from the Journals of Edward Abbey, 1951–1989* and *Earth Apples (Pommes des Terre): The Poetry of Edward Abbey*, were released in 1994, as was the journalist James Bishop Jr.'s book *Epitaph for a Desert Anarchist: The Life and Legacy of Edward Abbey*. Growing interest in Abbey's life was reinforced in 1995 by *The Serpents of Paradise: A Reader*, with selections from Abbey's books arranged chronologically and a series of biographical introductions by Abbey's veteran editor Jack Macrae.

Abbey's afterlife commenced on March 15, 1989, when obituaries began to appear in many newspapers around the country. Tucson's *Arizona Daily Star* memorably declared on March 16: "He was Tucson's own by-God S.O.B., and now he's gone and we are all diminished by his death."[3] The most conclusive evidence of his celebrity in Tucson, in contrast to the large-scale neglect back home, was reflected in the fact that the *Tucson Weekly* devoted an entire dozen-page magazine supplement to "A Celebration of Edward Abbey," whereas his hometown *Indiana Gazette* simply ran a fairly unobtrusive, standard obituary: "Author Dies in Tucson."[4]

How did Abbey's mysterious burial come about? As early as 1971, Jack Loeffler had promised that he would give him a "proper burial" illegally in the desert.[5] Abbey had specified in his journal in 1981 that he wanted to be placed in his favorite sleeping bag and buried beneath a pile of rocks to keep the coyotes off, with "No Comment" engraved on his gravestone (276, 277). His wishes were granted. On March 16, 1989, in southwestern Arizona's Cabeza

Prieta wilderness, Abbey was buried by Loeffler, Doug Peacock, Tom Cartwright (Clarke Abbey's father), and Steve Prescott (her brother-in-law). His gravesite offered a striking view of some of the area's most beautiful mountains and rolling desert terrain. After his compatriots had dug the grave, Peacock lay down in it to make sure that it was acceptable. Remembering "how Ed once said he wanted to be reincarnated as a turkey vulture," Peacock took it as a sign that buzzards quickly gathered in the sky above him, looking down upon his inviting body and then "banking over the volcanic rubble and riding the thermal up the flank of the mountain, gliding out and over the distant valley."[6] After Abbey's body was buried, a basalt boulder was placed on top, reading "Edward Paul Abbey. 1927–1989. No Comment." Only these four men were present at this rite, but later the gravesite would be visited by Clarke, Becky, and Ben, who surrounded the boulder with seashells, crystals, and heart-shaped rocks.

The story of Abbey's illegal burial fascinated many readers, not only because it was illegal—on federal land without any permission—but also because the specific location of the grave remained a secret guarded by family and a few close friends. More than any other single article, Edward Hoagland's May 7, 1989, tribute in the *New York Times Book Review*, "Edward Abbey: Standing Tough in the Desert," immortalized the burial and its aftermath for a national audience. Hoagland claimed that "afterward in a kind of reprise of the antic spirit that animates *The Monkey Wrench Gang*, and that should make anybody but a developer laugh out loud," one of Abbey's outlaw undertakers "went around heaping up false rockpiles at ideal gravesites throughout the Southwest, because this last peaceful act of outlawry of Abbey's was the gesture of legend and there will be seekers for years to come."[7] As late as March 1998, many became angered when Peacock published an article about the Cabeza Prieta in *Audubon*, "Desert Solitary," which appeared to reveal the location of the grave[8]—though afterward Peacock correctly insisted that his narrative was not specific enough to allow anyone to find the grave.[9] Nonetheless, one overzealous friend, afraid that *Audubon* readers would beat a path to the gravesite, drove out to it that spring and moved the gravestone in order to conceal the site. In March 1999, Clarke Abbey had to restore the gravestone (and its accompanying shells and heart-shaped rocks) to the previous location.

Abbey had also included his own funeral specifications in his October 1981 journal entry: "Ceremony? GUNFIRE! And—a little music, please: Jack Loeffler and his trumpet. Maybe a few readings . . . Then—*a Wake!* . . . I want dancing! And a flood of beer and booze! A bonfire! And lots of food! . . . Lots of singing, dancing, talking, hollering, laughing and love-making instead" (277). These wishes were likewise honored at Abbey's first wake, on March 22, in Saguaro National Monument. At the most distant picnic area west of the

Tucson Mountains, beneath the mountains and the towering saguaros that Abbey loved so much, over a hundred people gathered. They consumed champagne while a bagpiper opened with such Scottish tunes as "Amazing Grace" and "The Bonnie Lassie." Then Abbey's colleague at the University of Arizona, Robert Houston, read his essay "Down the River with Edward Abbey." At a party, Abbey had asked Houston who the best reader he had ever heard was, and Houston had jokingly replied, "I think *I* am, Ed." When Clarke called him and said Ed had wanted him to read at his wake, Houston wondered if his old friend, from the grave, was returning the joke.[10]

Houston was followed by Leslie Marmon Silko, who read movingly from *Desert Solitaire*, crying as she ended. Susie Abbey then read her father's essay entitled "Theory of Anarchy." Jack Loeffler played taps, and Doug Peacock served a "slow elk" stew, made from a cow that had been grazing on public lands. University of Arizona librarian David Laird had everyone sign a copy of the twentieth-anniversary edition of *Desert Solitaire*. Dave Foreman—who was especially grief stricken because he had been in Belize when Abbey died— took up a collection, and Earth First!ers returned in the late afternoon with beer, tequila, scotch, and vodka. *Earth First! Journal* editor John Davis played a tape of Abbey's last reading, his hilarious March 4 rendition of the "Earth First Rendezvous" chapter of *Hayduke Lives!* Abbey's eldest son, Josh, mingled with the crowd and said a few words, but his shy second son, Aaron, removed himself to a nearby promontory from which he watched only from a distance.[11] This wake ended after Abbey's old pal Bob Greenspan played Abbey's favorite Greenspan song, "Big Tits, Braces and Zits," Peacock fired a pistol into the air, and, as Greg McNamee recalled, "a child announced that he had seen two people making love in a dry wash nearby."[12] Afterward, on the plane back to Las Vegas, Aaron asked Karilyn McElheney, "Can you tell me about my father?" and she did her best to fill in the life story of a father whom Aaron felt that he had largely never known.

Abbey had thoroughly concealed the terminal nature of his illness from all but the very inner circle of his friends and family. Even his father, brothers, and sister had not known that he was dying until the very end, and only Nancy and Howard Abbey and his son Mike were able to make it to the Tucson wake.[13] Many felt a need for a second memorial service, even some of those who were present at the first one—including Clarke (who was still in shock at the Saguaro wake). Many of Abbey's friends had been stunned by the news of his death. Charles Bowden remembered that "the day he died was the first time in years I raised my hand in anger at another person,"[14] and he left the Tucson wake after only a few minutes.[15] Donn Rawlings explained that "I was probably more upset about Abbey's death than I was upset about my father's death, probably because I knew my dad was going to die."[16] Laura Lee Houck's reaction was typical. Picking up the morning newspaper in Las Vegas, where she was living at the time, she encountered the news of Abbey's death, and "just totally freaked out." She called all of her old Moab neighbors "and just said, 'Hey, what happened?' We all knew he was sick, but he really guarded his privacy. He didn't want the pity and to feel like he was an old wreck."[17]

Soon, Ken Sleight, Ken Sanders, Terry Tempest Williams, and Jim Stiles began to organize a larger wake for Abbey. Sanders explained that "the Saguaro wake wasn't enough. We needed some public commemoration. People just weren't through letting go of Ed."[18] Stiles found the ideal location: atop spectacular Rough and Rocky Mesa (which Abbey had enjoyed three decades earlier), not far from the old dirt entrance road into Arches, but just outside the national park boundary on Bureau of Land Management land, so participants could do whatever they wanted without having to worry about National Park Service regulations.[19] Soon invitations were mailed out for "A JOURNEY HOME, a sunrise memorial service for Edward Abbey" on Saturday, May 20, at 7 A.M.; "Just north of Arches about a half mile, look for an old crumbling washed-out road with weeds growing through it that runs parallel to Highway 191 for a few hundred yards and then turns east and climbs to the top of Moab Canyon, overlooking Arches. It is about a mile walk."[20] In *Desert Solitaire*, Abbey had urged everyone to stop driving through national parks and to walk instead, explaining that visitors might see something worth seeing "when traces of blood begin to mark your trail."[21] Now, two decades later, with paved roads running everywhere through the park, friends and followers would walk up onto Rough and Rocky Mesa to honor him, while gazing off into the breathtaking redrock expanses that he had immortalized.

About 600 people attended the Moab wake.[22] These included Clarke, Susie, Becky, Ben, Howard, and Nancy Abbey. Standing nearby, but aloof, during the entire ceremony was a mysterious woman all in black—hat, veil, cocktail dress, hose, and spiked heels—whom John De Puy dubbed "the black widow":[23] Abbey's old lover, friend, and the model for Bonnie Abbzug in *The Monkey Wrench Gang*, Ingrid Eisenstadter.[24] Participants in this event encountered some old acquaintances as well as many strangers who had also been Abbey's comrades—for he had lived virtually multiple lives in many places, making many friends who had never met other people who had known him in other locations.[25]

News of the Moab wake reached far beyond its 600 attenders. The *Los Angeles Times* published an account, reporting that "a string quartet played Mozart" and "someone had set an American flag beside the small podium, from which speakers addressed the several hundred people spread out across a gentle slope of lichen-mottled sandstone."[26] A transcript of the whole event was published a year later in the University of Utah's *Journal of Energy, Natural Resources, and Environmental Law*. Ken Sleight read "A Letter to Ed Abbey" in which he reminisced about his old sidekick and thanked him "for the monkey wrench."[27] After Katie Lee and two others sang a Kate Wolf song and C. L. Rawlins read his elegy for Abbey, Abbey's friend of thirty years, John De Puy, explained that not long before "Ed told me all painters should sew their mouths shut. So all I'm going to say is 'Earth First!'"[28]

Following the singing of "Amazing Grace," Wendell Berry—who had journeyed from Kentucky in homage to this kindred spirit whom he had never met in person—paid tribute to Abbey by first reading a letter by Wallace Stegner, who was unable to attend. Stegner wrote that Abbey's "books were burrs under the saddle blanket of complacency. . . . He had the zeal of a true believer and a stinger like a scorpion when defending the natural, free, unmanaged, unmanhandled wilderness of his chosen country." Berry noted that "a sort of law at our house has been that I should not read an Abbey book after bedtime, for if I did I would be apt to laugh loud enough to wake people up," and that "I never laid down a book by Edward Abbey when I did not feel more encouraged than when I picked it up." Praising Abbey as a patriot, Berry read two poems in his honor.[29]

Dave Foreman called Abbey "a great American," but, following Berry, he changed the tempo, hoisting a can of Coors—a brand he never drank except on this occasion and in *Hayduke Lives!*—and giving a rousing "one-beer speech." He emphasized that Abbey "knew where he came from. He knew that he was born out of the hillbilly bones of this country," and he called his old mentor "the Mudhead Kachina," in the Zuni Indian tradition, "of the whole social change movement in this country. . . . Ed was a trickster farting in polite company. Pissing on overblown egos, making a caricature of himself and laughing at himself. . . . Ed was the wise prophet from the desert that tried to keep us on track and to not take ourselves too seriously." He concluded that, though Abbey had disparaged himself by claiming that "one brave deed is worth a thousand books," truly "every book of Ed Abbey's, every essay, every story has launched a thousand brave deeds."[30]

Barry Lopez then stressed that "Ed Abbey had a capacity for outrage. He espoused Jeffersonian ideals. He liked calling a spade a spade. . . . To read *Desert Solitaire* was to hear a clarion call, like *Silent Spring*." After the singing of "Will the Circle be Unbroken," Terry Tempest Williams delivered an eloquent "Eulogy for Edward Abbey." She called Abbey "Coyote, a dance upon the desert" and held up an old postcard from him, inviting her listeners to "think about the thousands of postcards with Abbey's words, his scribblings that have crossed these lands, these sacred lands like a blizzard, like migrating birds, like shooting stars, U.S. Mail, Abbey's courier, keeping in touch."[31]

Doug Peacock ("a/k/a George Washington Hayduke") lamented that "we always had Abbey to walk point"—and right then the American flag posted beside him in a pile of rocks fell over in the breeze. After an Earth First! chant and another song, Ann Zwinger remarked that Abbey had done her "the greatest honor by writing a review of one of my books for the *New York Times*." His 1975 review was the type "that any author would kill for. Ed, I owe you one, and that's why I'm here."[32] Abbey had deliberately raised the ire of many feminists during his lifetime, but the gender-balanced makeup of the Moab wake was striking, including two notable women writers—Williams and Zwinger—both of whom underscored his influence and help.

Following Stephanie Demus's drum solo while the crowd dispersed,[33] Abbey's satiric play "Best of the West," originally staged in 1978, was performed that afternoon at the City Park in Moab.[34] That night a party was held at the Sleights' Pack Creek Ranch. The *Los Angeles Times* reported that "It probably was not as raucous as Abbey had wanted, but someone did let the horses out of the corral, and at least one young woman, wearing only a blouse, staggered across a lawn littered with cars and trucks. . . . About midnight, while young Abbeyites hooted and spun yarns and sashayed to twanging goat-roper music, Peacock and Sleight embraced, grappled, laughed."[35] Also, what would become two mainstays of Moab cultural life by the end of the century sprang into life just as Abbey passed. The first issue of Jim Stiles's countercultural newspaper *The Canyon Country Zephyr* was printed on the day Abbey died, featuring his essay "Hard Times in Santa Fe."[36] In addition, Back of Beyond Bookstore was founded by several of Abbey's old friends, including Karilyn McElheney, around the time of the wake.[37]

A week later, on May 28, yet another wake was held, in Aspen, Colorado, with about 100 in attendance, including several who had heard Abbey speak at the 1971 Aspen High School graduation."[38] They commemorated him "with a keg of beer chilled in snow scooped from a snowbank somewhere on Red Mountain."[39]

Not everyone, however, was sad that Ed Abbey was gone. In Prescott, shortly after his death, "Ronald Kermit Frazier noted the event in the diary he had been keeping for the FBI. 'Abbey dead,' he wrote. 'Hooray!'"[40] Indeed, at least in the form in which Abbey had inspired it and Foreman and others had led it in the early 1980s, Earth First! died (or mutated) along with Abbey.

More than Abbey's death, however, two other key factors combined to force Foreman and other "rednecks for wilderness" out of Earth First!: the increasing alienation of his old guard from the new wave of Earth First!, which had come to the fore at the 1987 Round River Rendezvous at the Grand Canyon's North Rim, and a new FBI crackdown. Two days after he returned home to Tucson from the Arches wake, on May 31 (his wedding anniversary), Foreman was arrested by the FBI.[41]

On June 25, the *Arizona Daily Star* revealed that the FBI had been tracking Abbey for many years, and it quoted Foreman: "'I think my case is more serious, but it's the same type of thing,' Foreman said of the FBI records on Abbey. 'You have an agency that's very good at compiling data on its citizens, but is really poor in analyzing that data.'"[42] He told Susan Zakin that "Abbey's death changed things for me. Ed could say outrageous things. He could be a gadfly. . . . Right now, I only want to speak for Dave Foreman." By the time of his arrest he had severed his formal relationship with Earth First! When he agreed to go along with the plea bargain that ended the 1991 Earth First! trial in Prescott, he "said that while he was making his decision he'd thought about something Ed Abbey had written. 'Never sacrifice a friend to a cause,' he paraphrased."[43]

However, Abbey's writings continued to inspire many wilderness activists. For a while, judging from his publications, it appeared that Abbey was not yet dead. Three new essays appeared in 1989: "The Secret of the Green Mask" in the March *Condé Nast Traveler*; "Hard Times in Santa Fe" in the April *Canyon Country Zephyr*; and "Drunk in the Afternoon" in the July *Northwest: The Sunday Oregonian Magazine*. Also published that year were his "Forward!" to a new *Backcountry Handbook* and an excerpt from the beginning of *Hayduke Lives!* in *Mother Earth News*. His spirit lived on in his introductions and prefaces to books by his ranger pal Bill Hoy (1990) and Earth First! leader Howie Wolke (1991).

Abbey's posthumous books provoked still more notice. *Booklist*, for example, praised his collection of epigrams and aphorisms, *A Voice Crying in the Wilderness*, as "a handy concentration of his beliefs" and "a fitting finale to a potent life." Of course, *Hayduke Lives!* generated more reviews and sales than any of these books from the grave. The idea of Abbey living on was the prevalent theme of its reviews. One reviewer exclaimed, "Thank God for Edward Abbey—an artist with purpose, humor, and true grit. Abbey lives!"[44] Charles Bowden similarly declared in his *Los Angeles Times* review, "The damn thing is alive."[45] However, Grace Lichtenstein, who had interviewed Abbey for the *New York Times* fourteen years earlier, spoke for some dissenting reviewers when she opined in the *Washington Post* that it was in nonfiction books such as *Desert Solitaire*, "more so than in this farewell novel, that Abbey lives, forever."[46] In late 2001 airport police detained a man for reading this novel.[47]

A mixed trio of books in 1994 brought further attention to Abbey.

Confessions of a Barbarian brought to print about a quarter of his journal entries from 1951, when he was a student in Edinburgh, until just a few days before his death in 1989. At least as early as June 28, 1985, Abbey had contemplated seeing his journals into publication himself,[48] and *A Voice Crying in the Wilderness* had been the partial fulfillment of that aim. In 1981, he had written that "I keep a journal, a record book, and most everything begins in the form of notes scribbled down on the pages of that journal."[49] A reading of his unpublished as well as published journal entries continually bears out the truth of that observation. As my own frequent citations of *Confessions of a Barbarian* indicate, that book is an invaluable source for understanding Abbey's life and writings. Tim Sandlin noted in his review in the *New York Times Book Review* that it is striking in the journals, beginning in 1951, "how quickly Abbey focused on the themes that would obsess him for the next 38 years: anarchy, sex, defense of the natural world and how best to die."[50] Nevertheless, the problem with posthumous publications edited by someone other than Abbey is that occasionally the editor intrudes, inserting sometimes inaccurate identifications.[51]

Similarly, *Earth Apples (Pommes des Terre): The Poetry of Edward Abbey* is useful in making available texts that would not otherwise be accessible to most readers—yet one has to wonder if Abbey would have wanted some of these poems published. This is the writer who refused to have *Jonathan Troy* reprinted because he felt that it was a failure as a novel, and who told his Tucson audience in February 1977, when he read some of these poems, that they would understand why he had never published them.[52] If these poems deserve publication, then why not also print Abbey's unpublished novels of the early 1960s? Furthermore, there appear to have been editorial changes in some of the poems, as former University of Arizona librarian Louis Hieb noticed when he compared *Earth Apples* with his manuscript copy of Abbey's poems.[53] This time the reviews were not so favorable; even the normally positive *Library Journal* remarked that "Abbey has a tiny but legitimate poetic ability. . . . Not recommended."[54]

James Bishop's *Epitaph for a Desert Anarchist: The Life and Legacy of Edward Abbey* contributed to the growing cult surrounding Abbey and his life and death. This book sold well and was enthusiastically positive about Abbey and his writings—yet struck those who knew him as an inadequate and often inaccurate book. For example, it was advertised as a biography but was really only a general tribute, leaving entire parts of Abbey's life unexamined.[55] Bishop was wrong about where Abbey was born and when his mother died.[56] Among his errors about Abbey's life in the West was his description of the setting of his job at Arches—"high above the desert, in a tower with sixty steps."[57]

A more accurate and more aesthetically appealing introduction to

Abbey's life and works had appeared a year earlier, in the form of Eric Temple's excellent video documentary *Edward Abbey: A Voice in the Wilderness* (1993), which featured striking footage of Abbey and his Southwest and fascinating clips from interviews with Abbey and several of his relatives and confidants. A collection of essays edited by Peter Quigley, *Coyote in the Maze: Tracking Edward Abbey in a World of Words* (1998), brought his writings under the gaze of contemporary critical theory. And in late 2000, Ann Ronald's *The New West of Edward Abbey* was republished, with a new afterword by Scott Slovic. This book remains a valuable, thoughtful study of its subject (especially up until about 1980), with special attention to the broader contexts of Western literature and how Abbey both borrowed from and transformed this tradition. One long-awaited other book, as yet unpublished at this writing, is Ken Sanders's annotated bibliography of his writings.

Much unfinished business remains in regard to Abbey's own writings. A collection of his letters is very much needed, and it will have to range far beyond those in the archive at the University of Arizona, which contains a number of his letters but covers only 1969–89 and is limited mostly to carbons of his business (and some family) correspondence; there are no love letters, and no letters at all written before he was 42 years old. Abbey's letter to his father from the late 1930s, his December 1942 letter to his aunt Ida, his February 1947 anti-draft letter, and his November 1949 letter home from UNM are the only letters from those two decades that were available, and they were not in the archive. The archive's letters represent a much paler, thinner account of his personal life than his much fuller, livelier journals. Also, another collection of previously published writings could be made available. My bibliography lists more than fifty uncollected essays, about forty letters to the editor, and nearly forty book reviews. Most of these publications are now very difficult to find. Like his master's thesis, they would be of interest to many readers.

Abbey and his ideas continue to live on in the public consciousness, often in surprising contexts. In 1995, a set of elaborate web pages and an increasingly active e-mail discussion list, called respectively "Abbey's Web" and "Abbeyweb," sprang up—hosted in Stockholm, Sweden.[58] This development might have horrified Abbey, who quipped (with a pen) that "my computer tells me that in twenty-five years there will be no computers."[59] Yet some participants were convinced that Abbey actually would have approved of the anarchistic, democratic nature of the Internet. In any event, Abbeyweb prospered as a very busy forum for discussions about Abbey, wilderness, and politics. Unusually enough for a predominately nonacademic discussion list, "Abbeywebbers" also began annual gatherings, the first held in Bluff, Utah, in October 1997, the second in Death Valley in November 1998, the third in the Moab area in

October 1999, and the fourth at Lee's Ferry in October 2000. One participant arrived at the Death Valley gathering in Abbey's old, battered 1973 Ford pickup truck, which she bought for $26,500 at a May 1998 fundraising auction for the Southern Utah Wilderness Alliance.[60]

In September 1996, a Pennsylvania state historical marker about Abbey was dedicated at Home, across the road on Route 119 from Paul Abbey's old rock shop and Paul and Mildred's little house. Paul Abbey had died on May 7, 1992, but Bill, Nancy, Howard, and Iva Abbey and nearly 100 others attended this 1996 dedication. After a local news report mentioned that Robert Redford had written a letter in support of the marker, the Associated Press wire picked up the story, which ran as far away as Honolulu, under the headline "Redford Honors Activist."[61] Yet *The Monkey Wrench Gang* continued to be kept from the big screen (or even the little screen). In the spring of 1998, a wire story circulated about Dennis Hopper's forthcoming film of Abbey's novel, but at the novel's twenty-fifth anniversary at the turn of the century (though the book was reprinted then), once again no such movie had been made.

In March 1999, a "Remembering Ed Abbey" week was held in Phoenix and Tempe, organized by Dick Kirkpatrick, and culminating on March 14 with remembrances by two of the best writers in Abbey's tradition, Charles Bowden and Terry Tempest Williams. As Williams had stressed in *Outside* in October 1997, Abbey "loved to be in our faces. Still does, no doubt."[62] Various commemorative articles appeared in March 1999 in the Tucson and Phoenix newspapers, and a week-long radio series ran on Tucson's KUAT/KUAZ radio station.[63] When Grace Lichtenstein of the *New York Times* had accused Abbey of being "thirty years behind the times" in 1976, Abbey had boasted to her, "I'm a *hundred* years behind the times!" (254). Yet at the end of the millennium, a decade after his death, he was still very much in the air.

This was true even of some of Abbey's least popular positions. His argument that cars should be kept out of national parks fell on deaf ears when he made it the centerpiece of *Desert Solitaire*, but, three decades later, Grand Canyon National Park was preparing to implement a modified version of his proposal. Light rail will now transport most visitors to the South Rim from parking lots several miles away. Yosemite is moving ahead with a similar plan. When one writer ruminated in the *New York Times* in May 1997 about possible compromises for Yosemite, she described how Abbey's ghost had come back to haunt her, telling her to "go the whole hog" and ban cars entirely in Yosemite Valley.[64] President Clinton outraged many Utahns when he designated the huge Grand Staircase–Escalante National Monument in September 1996 to protect it from threatened development—but he gratified a great many wilderness activists who think more like Abbey. Even Abbey's by far least popular proposition—that immigration from Mexico be stopped—could be seen reflected in the April 1998 Sierra Club referendum proposing stricter limits on immigration. This proposal was defeated, but the very notion that the Sierra Club membership was seriously considering such an idea would have been unimaginable in earlier times. In the year 2000, proposals about limiting cattle grazing on public lands—such an outrageous idea when Abbey advanced it in 1985—were now mainstream.[65]

It has not been my intention to deliver sweeping judgments about Edward Abbey and his writings, but rather to provide as much information as I can so that readers can make their own informed decisions. It does seem appropriate, however, to end this book by examining some of the questions that people will most likely continue to ask about Abbey and his work.

How could a man with so difficult a personal life emerge as such a popular hero? Abbey himself admitted, as late as 1984, that "I've not been a very good family man or father."[66] He forgot his first wife as quickly as he could. He abandoned his second wife and their two sons after nearly thirteen years of marriage. He sadly remembered his third wife after her early death, but he was often unfaithful to her while she was alive—fueled by separation, lust, and alcohol—as he also was with his fourth, youngest wife. Abbey had a big drinking problem, and he paid for it with his life. Only in the 1980s, with Clarke Cartwright, did he find lasting happiness and relative stability. By then, his reputation as a wilderness hero—a kind of eco-cowboy—was already firmly established in the public mind.

That raises another question: how could Ed Abbey be thought of as some sort of postmodern cowboy at the same time that he attacked (in the words of his notorious essay on the subject) "The Cowboy and His Cow"? Here Abbey managed to mount his spurs atop the tradition of Western novels and films since at least the time of Owen Wister's *The Virginian* (1902) and John Ford's *The Searchers* (1956). The Western hero was always partly an antihero, an outsider, a troublemaker. This was part of what drew Abbey to the West—his imagined West—to begin with, as he readily admitted at the beginning of that infamous essay: "Just out of the army, I thought, like most simple-minded Easterners, that a cowboy was a kind of mythic hero."[67] By attacking cowboys, Abbey angered some actual ranchers, and yet, with all of his rabble-rousing and his desire to walk off into the sunset, Abbey fit right into that tradition of the mythic cowboy.

How could such a naturally reserved person become such a troublemaker? Abbey clearly developed a persona in his books and as a public speaker that was not the same as his private demeanor. Working through the Abbey archives in Tucson, I watched videotapes of the wisecracking Abbey speaking at colleges, and then I found manuscripts in which he had carefully written out every line in advance, just as he had scripted his own television performance in "TV Show: Out There in the Rocks," meticulously playing a role. He became like the polished stand-up comic, telling an interviewer that he was "an entertainer,"[68] yet insisting in "A Writer's Credo" that "the writer worthy of his calling must be more than an entertainer."[69] Abbey was publicly racy and sardonic but privately shy, somber, and self-conscious.

That double-edged nature is key to his writing, too, which is all the richer because of how funny and public, yet how serious and private, it can be. Abbey complained, "I've never read a review of one of my own books that I couldn't have written much better myself"[70]—and many of us understand and appreciate the sentiment. When he thinks about Western wilderness, pronouncing, "*Keep it like it was*,"[71] we pick up the ironic side of that line—at the same time that we get the serious point. Abbey never saw any contradiction between humor and seriousness, explaining, "I write to entertain my friends and to exasperate our enemies."[72]

Why did Abbey insist, while writing so persistently about the natural world, that he was not a nature writer? It is true that Abbey was not a naturalist in the scientific way that Rachel Carson or even Annie Dillard was qualified to be; he got mediocre grades in subjects such as zoology. Wendell Berry was right (and Nancy Abbey agreed) that Abbey's real subject was himself—that as an author he was primarily an "autobiographer" more than an "environmentalist."[73] Yet *Desert Solitaire* and *The Monkey Wrench Gang* activated more than a generation's worth of activists toward a radical new brand of direct action in defense of wilderness. While telling the story of himself and his friends, Abbey managed to change the world.

Abbey's devotion to the wilderness was not like John Muir's. This maverick did not—in the typical sense—just meditate or pray in the desert or the forest; he also often drove cars and trucks to their demise in places where they never should have been. He tossed beer cans onto highways because he was convinced it was the highways that were ugly, not the beer cans, but he offered no environmentalist rationale for rolling old tires into canyons at Arizona's South Rim and Texas's Big Bend. He was perhaps himself one among the wild animals that he felt should be protected. And, like Walt Whitman, Abbey felt not only that he should "resist much, obey little" but also that he surely did "contain multitudes." He could speak at a Navajo rally and write appreciatively about Navajo art, on the one hand, after making a wisecrack in *Desert Solitaire* about how he was "drunk as a Navajo," on the other.[74] He recorded "Piute" as his religion and wished that he had been born a Native American warrior, and he edited the bilingual *El Crepusculo de la Libertad* and made several trips to Mexico, yet Abbey could also flirt with racism. He defiantly wrote "in defense of the redneck."

Was Abbey a misogynist? Sometimes he was, even though he insisted that he loved women and found them altogether superior to men. The more useful question to ask—as with so many aspects of this deceptively complex figure—is how much misogyny was a real ideology for Abbey and how much it became a role he played to the hilt. Barbara Kingsolver's story about meeting Abbey at the end of his life, when she was surprised to find him cordial and even genteel, reminds me of one the critic Mary Colum told about James Joyce. In a visit with Joyce, she propounded some psychoanalytic readings of his fiction, at which point Joyce interrupted by growling, "I hate women who know anything!" But Colum called his bluff by replying, "No, you don't, Joyce; you like us." She recalled that he looked irritated for a moment, as if his secret had been discovered, but then a big smile passed over his face, and "the rest of the afternoon was spent pleasantly." [75]

How did Abbey convince virtually everyone that he had been born in Home and lived in Oracle, though neither was the case? This life story is finally, in a sense, a book ghost-written by Abbey himself. The great American novel that he always wanted to write was really the story of his own life. All of the questions I have been asking, in fact, have one central answer: because he wrote it that way, powerfully establishing his own version of his life. Abbey never published a full-length memoir, but, in his books, he created his own autobiography. His "fat masterpiece" was not just *The Fool's Progress* but his whole life story and its mythology throughout his books. All the way from the elegiac *Brave Cowboy* to the satiric "Cowboy and His Cow," this naturally shy Easterner and quite unheroic man created a persuasive portrait of himself as a brash, Western hero. When he was not writing his two dozen books (and sometimes even when he was writing them), Abbey spent his life out in the natural world, and so the life story of this self-confessed "nature lover" was also that of a nature writer, despite his protestations to the contrary.

It has to be said—and I hope it has become clear in this book—that there was very often a gap and a contradiction between the rhetoric of his writing and the realities of his life. Yet another example is his series of attempts to idealize a place for himself in the wilderness. He repeatedly tried to recreate the "Old Lonesome Briar Patch" of his Appalachian youth in the Southwest, as for example in the land at Willow Bend, Utah, that he bought in 1974 with Ken Sleight. But Abbey never managed to return to his imagined farm; in that case he and Sleight had to sell their land because neither was ever around long enough to take proper care of it. Abbey finally settled down in the wilderness only when he was buried in the Cabeza Prieta—which therefore became a powerful part of his legend.

In his personal life, Ed Abbey was very seriously flawed, as he himself admitted (in his books as well as in his journals). Many of his essays are quite confessional, and he made the autobiographical protagonist of *The Fool's Progress* commit sins even worse than his own. Abbey mixed fact and fiction, drawing in his novels from his own experiences and those of his friends, and often departing from fact in his nonfiction to cover his tracks and achieve desired aesthetic and rhetorical effects.

At the same time, the very high quality of Abbey's strongest prose has frequently been overshadowed by his influential politics and cantankerous persona. It has also often been overlooked because of his very natural, seemingly easy style at its best. Many of his best essays draw readers in because they sound as if "Cactus Ed" is simply talking to his audience from the next barstool—yet that effect was achieved only through a lot of very careful writing over many years. Abbey agreed with the Irish short-story master Frank O'Connor that complex stylists like Joyce had moved twentieth-century prose too far away from the desirable "tone of a man's voice speaking."[76] The natural, "speaking" style of a Hemingway or an Abbey is perhaps even more difficult to perfect, in some ways, than is the experimental prose of a Joyce or a Pynchon, because if that seemingly simple style is even the least bit off, it can be very bad in painfully obvious ways, degenerating into parody (as in the annual Bad Hemingway Contest, in which writers ludicrously imitate it). In essays such as "Shadows from the Big Woods," "Blood Sport," "Merry Christmas, Pigs!" and "My Friend Debris," Abbey mastered such a style, achieving prose as sharp as a canyon wall. At his best—in *Desert Solitaire, The Monkey Wrench Gang, The Fool's Progress*, in many individual essays, and very nearly in *The Brave Cowboy* and *Fire on the Mountain*—Abbey was a writer of the first rank, one of the most underrated writers in American literature. When all the shouting is over about the man himself and his various causes, readers will return more quietly to Abbey's writings, discovering artistry and delight.

Notes

Complete references for the works cited in short form are given in the Bibliography.

INTRODUCTION

1. Abbey, *The Fool's Progress* (1990 [1988]). Here I cite the 1990 paperback edition, but, as with all of Abbey's published writings, publication information (including subsequent reprintings and revisions) is listed under the original year of publication (1988 in this case).

2. Just a few examples of the many sources that have misreported Abbey's birthplace as Home are James Bishop, Jr., *Epitaph for a Desert Anarchist: The Life and Legacy of Edward Abbey* (New York: Atheneum, 1994), xi; Bruce Hamilton, "Edward Abbey, Druid of the Arches," *High Country News*, March 27, 1989, 12; Michael Moore, "Out There Somewhere Lies Edward Abbey," *SMART*, no. 5 (Sept./Oct. 1989), 82; Carl L. Davis, "Thoughts on a Vulture: Edward Abbey, 1927–1989," *RE Arts and Letters* 15, no. 2 (1989): 16; and "Abbey, Edward," *Contemporary Authors: New Revision Series 41*.

3. Abbey, *Down the River* (1982), 7.

4. Interview with John De Puy. All cited interviews are my own, as detailed in my bibliography, unless otherwise specified.

5. Reynolds, "Biography Can Give the Humanities a Firm Scholarly Backbone," *Chronicle of Higher Education*, April 25, 1997, B4.

CHAPTER 1. THE BOY FROM HOME

1. "Academic Vita," Abbey Papers, box 1, folder 1.

2. Abbey, *Confessions of a Barbarian* (1994), 308. All parenthetical page citations throughout my main text refer to this book—the only one that I cite parenthetically.

3. I am thankful to Howard Abbey for helping me obtain Ed's birth certificate, and to both Howard and Iva Abbey for lending me Mildred Abbey's baby book about Ed.

4. Interview with Betty George (Abbey's aunt). More details (and photographs and maps) about Abbey's Indiana County experience can be found in my article "'My People'" (1996–97). Abbey's first home was most likely the present 254 North Third Street in Indiana.

5. Interview with Betty George.

6. Interview with Paul Abbey by Jim Dougherty.

7. Interview with Clarke Cartwright Abbey, Feb. 6, 1996.

8. Abbey, *Appalachian Wilderness* (1970), 13.

9. Abbey, interview with Loeffler, Jan. 1, 1983, Abbey Papers, box 27, folder 4.

10. Mildred Abbey, unpublished "Memoirs 1931." I am indebted to Iva Abbey for lending me her typed copy of this otherwise unavailable manuscript.

11. Abbey, "Vagabond Lover Has Drink with Governor" (1944).

12. Interview with Betty George.

13. Interview with Howard Abbey, Oct. 18, 1995.

14. Interview with Isabel Nesbitt.

15. Abbey, *The Fool's Progress* (1990 [1988]), 51.

16. Janice Dembosky, "Mildred Abbey Touched Many Lives," *Indiana Gazette*, Dec. 22, 1988, 10.

17. Interview with John Watta.

18. Interview with Nancy Abbey.

19. Interview with Iva Abbey, Oct. 18, 1995.

20. Interview with William T. Abbey, Oct. 18, 1995.

21. Interview with Paul Abbey by Jim Dougherty.

22. Ibid.

23. He recorded himself as a socialist on his voter registration card in Home in 1931. I am grateful to Howard and Iva for lending me a copy of this card.

24. Howard Abbey, written remembrance of Aug. 4, 1992, which I am grateful to him for lending to me.

25. Interview with Paul Abbey by Jim Dougherty.

26. Interview with Betty George.

27. Howard Abbey, written remembrance, Aug. 4, 1992.

28. Abbey, *Desert Solitaire* (1988 [1968]), 163. Later Abbey explained that "earthe-ism" is "a basic loyalty to our planet, a reverence for our lives and lives of our families and friends, and a respect for the lives of the animals and plants that exist around us. Those are the only things that we can know well enough to revere, I think. . . . I wouldn't call myself an atheist because . . . they *could* be wrong. . . . Most of those who call themselves atheists are a silly, semi-fanatical bunch, not unlike the worst of fundamental Christians" (David Petersen, "The Plowboy Interview—Edward Abbey: Slowing the Industrialization of Planet Earth," *Mother Earth News* 87 [May/June 1984]: 19).

29. Interview with Betty George.

30. Interview with Betty George, and "Abbey Family Tree" compiled by Ida Abbey (Paul's sister), Abbey Papers, box 1, folder 1.

31. "Abbey's Web" genealogy page, accessed in September 2000 at http://www.abbeyweb.net/bio/genealogy.html.

32. Abbey, "In Defense of the Redneck" (1979), 82.

33. Interview with Nancy Abbey.

34. Howard Abbey, written remembrance, Aug. 4, 1992.

35. Interview with Paul Abbey by Jim Dougherty.

36. Interview with Howard Abbey, Oct. 18, 1995.

37. Abbey, *The Journey Home* (1977), xiv.

38. I am grateful to Robert Houston of the University of Arizona for sending me a copy of Abbey's list of favorite books (including *The Grapes of Wrath*), which he wrote for Houston on April 27, 1988.

39. Interview with Betty George.

40. Interview with Paul Abbey by Jim Dougherty.

41. Interview with Ed Mears.

42. Interview with Betty George.

43. Interview with Paul Abbey by Jim Dougherty.

44. Mildred Abbey, "Memoirs 1931."

45. Malcolm Cowley, "My Countryside, Then and Now: A Study in American Evo-lution," *Harper's*, Jan. 1929; reprinted, *Harper's*, Aug. 1999, 73.

46. Abbey referred to Kellysburg in the draft manuscript of his unpublished novel *The Good Life* (Abbey Papers, box 4, folder 8) and in the handwritten draft of *The Fool's Progress* (box 13, folder 2), and he changed "Kellysburg" to "Home" in the original *printed* version of his

essay "Hallelujah, on the Bum" in *American West Magazine* (1970), for its anthologization (box 24, folder 5, p. 13) in *The Journey Home* (1977).

47. Interview with William T. Abbey, Oct. 27, 1995.

48. Interview with Howard Abbey, Oct. 18, 1995.

49. Interview with Betty George.

50. Interview with Ed Mears.

51. David Solheim and Rob Levin, "The *Bloomsbury Review* Interview," in Hepworth and McNamee, eds., *Resist Much, Obey Little* (1996), 148.

52. Interview with Bernard Stadtmiller.

53. Abbey, *Down the River* (1982), 1–2.

54. I am grateful to Lynn Hankinson for locating this letter and to Howard Abbey for lending it to me. Since Abbey's letters in box 3 of the Abbey Papers at the University of Arizona begin only at 1969, this boyhood letter is especially valuable.

55. Abbey, "Shadows from the Big Woods" (1974) in *The Journey Home* (1977), 224.

56. Abbey, "Mountain Music" (originally published as "The Lure of the Mountains" [1975]), in *The Journey Home* (1977), 210.

57. See Abbey, *Slumgullion Stew* (1984), for the publication history of this chapter of *The Fool's Progress* (1988).

58. Abbey, *Jonathan Troy* (1954), 199.

59. Interview with Howard Abbey, Oct. 18, 1995.

60. Howard Abbey, written remembrance, Aug. 4, 1992.

61. William Plummer, "Edward Abbey's Desert Solecisms," *TWA Ambassador*, Nov. 1982, 34.

62. Abbey, *The Fool's Progress* (1990 [1988]), 85.

63. Abbey, *Desert Solitaire* (1988 [1968]), 1. "Red dog" roads were paved with red slag from coal mines. Metaphorically, the mines also followed this curiously canine pattern by massing their ugly back refuse in what are still called "bony piles." Although many of these piles continue to deface the countryside today, the red-dog roads are virtually all gone, replaced by gravel and pavement.

64. Interview with Nancy Abbey.

65. Interview with William T. Abbey, Oct. 27, 1995.

66. Interview with Paul Abbey by Jim Dougherty.

67. Abbey, "On Going Home Again" (1982).

68. Mildred Abbey, letter of May 29, 1967, to Edward Abbey, Abbey Papers, box 2, folder 1.

69. Abbey Papers, box 13, folder 1.

70. Abbey, *Appalachian Wilderness* (1970), 14.

71. Interview with Howard and Bill Abbey, Oct. 18, 1995.

72. Interview with Nancy Abbey.

73. Interview with Ed Mears.

74. Interview with Betty George.

75. Mildred Abbey, "1931 Memoir."

76. Howard Abbey, written remembrance, Aug. 4, 1992.

77. Interview with Howard Abbey, Oct. 18, 1995.

78. Interview with Bernard Stadtmiller.

79. James R. Hepworth, "The Poetry Center Interview," in Hepworth and McNamee, eds., *Resist Much, Obey Little* (1996), 60.

80. Interviews with Judy Moorhead and Eugene Bence.

81. Interview with Nancy Abbey.

82. Interview with Betty George.

83. Interview with Eugene Bence.

84. Interview with Leonard Abrams.

85. Interview with Ed Mears.

86. Interview with Ivan McGee.

87. Interview with Ed Mears.

88. Interview with Nancy Abbey.

89. In the fall of 1931, for example, while Ed's family was struggling to make ends meet near Home, Ireland's Abbey Players had performed at Indiana's Ritz Theatre. See Patricia Kane and James M. Cahalan, "The Abbey at the Ritz," *Oak Leaves* (Indiana University of Pennsylvania) (Winter 1995): 8–11.

90. Interview with Clarke Cartwright Abbey, Feb. 6, 1996.

91. Interview with Bernard Stadtmiller.

92. Interview with Howard Abbey, Oct. 18, 1995.

93. Interview with Eugene Bence.

94. Interview with Judy Moorhead.

95. Plummer, "Abbey's Desert Solecisms," 34.

96. Ibid.

97. Interview with Nancy Abbey.

98. John F. Baker, "Edward Abbey," *Publishers Weekly*, Sept. 8, 1975, 6.

99. Interview with Ed Mears.

100. *Wagon Track West* was advertised in the Sept. 29, 1943, issue of the *High Arrow*, p. 4; *Frontier Badmen*, Nov. 10, 1943, 6; *Ride, Tenderfoot, Ride*, Nov. 17, 1943, 4; *Canyon City*, Jan. 12, 1944, 4; *Call of the Rockies*, Nov. 22, 1944, 4; *Light of Sante Fe*, Dec. 20, 1944, 3; and *Sage Brush Heroes*, March 28, 1945, 4. I am grateful to Darlene Marco, Indiana Senior High School librarian, for making back issues of the *High Arrow* available to me.

101. Abbey, *The Fool's Progress* (1990 [1988]), 69.

102. Interview with Howard Abbey, Oct. 18, 1995.

103. Abbey, "Free Speech: The Cowboy and His Cow," in *One Life at a Time, Please* (1988), 9. Originally published as "The Ungulate Jungle" (1985).

104. Abbey, lecture, Univ. of Montana, May 1, 1985, Abbey Papers, box 27, tape 6.

105. Plummer, "Abbey's Desert Solecisms," 34.

106. Abbey, "A San Francisco Journal," in *One Life at a Time, Please* (1988), 57. Originally published as "Edward Abbey's Bay Area Journal" (1986).

107. Indiana High School transcript, courtesy of Indiana Area Senior High School.

108. Abbey, *The Journey Home* (1977), xi.

109. Abbey, interview with Loeffler, Jan. 1, 1983, Abbey Papers, box 27, folder 4.

110. Interview with Howard Abbey, Oct. 18, 1995.

111. Abbey Papers, box 8, folder 2.

112. Abbey, *The Monkey Wrench Gang* (1985 [1975]), 161.

113. Abbey, *Black Sun* (1982 [1971]), 60.

114. Abbey, *Desert Solitaire* (1988 [1968]), 87.

115. Pamela Bothwell, "Novelist, Environmentalist Edward Abbey Says 'I'm a Wild Preservative,'" *Greensburg Tribune Review*, Jan. 2, 1977, n.p.

116. Interview with Charles Bowden by Eric Temple, Apr. 1992.

117. Interview with Ken Sleight, Jan. 17, 1996.

118. Interview with John De Puy by Eric Temple, Apr. 1992.

119. Interview with Clarke Cartwright Abbey, Feb. 6, 1996.

120. Courtesy of Dean Shenk, from his private collection.

CHAPTER 2. GO WEST, YOUNG MAN

1. Abbey, *Jonathan Troy* (1954), 109.

2. Abbey, *The Fool's Progress* (1990 [1988]), 145.

3. "Ed Abbey: Tearing . . . Down with Words," *Econews*, Jan. 1981, 6. Abbey made very similar statements in "How It Was" (1971) in *Beyond the Wall* (1984), 51; his 1981 preface to *Black Sun* (1971); David Petersen, "A Conversation with Edward Abbey," *Basin and Range*, Aug. 1985, 10; "Forty Years as a Canyoneer," in *One Life at a Time, Please* (1988), 123; James Hepworth, et al., "Literature of the Southwest Interview," in Hepworth and McNamee, eds., *Resist Much, Obey Little* (1985), 126; and "Mountain Music" (originally "The Lure of the Mountains" [1975]), in *The Journey Home* (1977), 211.

4. Abbey, "Hallelujah, on the Bum" (1970), 11.

5. Interview with William T. Abbey, Oct. 27, 1995.

6. Interview with Nancy Abbey.

7. Howard Abbey, written remembrance, Aug. 4, 1992.

8. Interview with Howard Abbey, Aug. 28, 1998.

9. Abbey, "Hallelujah, on the Bum" (1970), 11.

10. Abbey, "Abbey Walks 8,000 Miles by Adroit Use of Thumb" (1944).

11. Abbey, "Abbey Hitch-Hikes to Jail After Viewing Blue Pacific" (1945).

12. Abbey, "Hallelujah" (1970), 12.

13. Federal Bureau of Investigation file, "Subject: Edward Abbey," obtained by author under the Freedom of Information Act, henceforth cited as "FBI file."

14. Abbey, "Hallelujah" (1970), 12.

15. Abbey, "My 40 Years as a Grand Canyoneer" (1984), 124.

16. "Hallelujah, on the Bum" (1970) makes no mention of this Grand Canyon trip, making it seem that Abbey stayed on the train straight from Needles to Flagstaff, in apparent contradiction of his subsequent essay about his first visit to the canyon. This is another example of Abbey's "creativity" and unreliability as autobiographical narrator.

17. Abbey, *The Monkey Wrench Gang* (1985 [1975]), 25–30.

18. Abbey, "Hallelujah" (1970), 14.

19. Interview with Judy Moorhead.

20. Written correspondence by William P. Kinter, Nov. 1, 1996.

21. The South Dakota conversation is in Abbey, "Vagabond Lover Has Drink with Governor" (1944); the hobo poker conversation is in Abbey, "Abbey Finally Arrives Home" (1945).

22. Abbey, "Hallelujah" (1970), 14.

23. Written correspondence by William P. Kinter, Nov. 1, 1996.

24. Interview with Nancy Abbey.

25. See *High Arrow*, Feb. 13, 1945, 1.

26. *L'Indien* yearbook, 1945, in the library of the Indiana Area Senior High School.

27. Abbey, *Jonathan Troy* (1954), 262.

28. Interview with William T. Abbey, Aug. 27, 1998.

29. Interview with Howard Abbey, Aug. 27, 1998.

30. Graduation program of Indiana Senior High School, 1945, kindly supplied to me by 1945 alumna Lois Parks Antram.

31. "Pvt. Edward Abbey," *Indiana Gazette*, n.d., n.p., supplied to me by Howard and Iva Abbey.

32. U.S. Army, "Enlisted Record and Report of Separation," obtained with the assistance of William T. Abbey.

33. Ibid.

34. "Pvt. Edward Abbey," *Indiana Gazette*, n.d., n.p.

35. Abbey, "My Life as a P.I.G., or the True Adventures of Smokey the Cop," in *Abbey's Road* (1979), 152. Originally published as "Edward Abbey as Smokey the Cop" (1978).

36. Quoted in Lawrence Clark Powell, "A Singular Ranger," *Westways* 66 (March 1974): 34.

37. Abbey, "My Life as a P.I.G.," in *Abbey's Road* (1979), 150.

38. Interview with Paul Abbey by Jim Dougherty.

39. Abbey, "The Sorrows of Travel" (1978) in *Abbey's Road* (1979), 183.

40. Abbey, "My Life as a P.I.G.," in *Abbey's Road* (1979), 152.

41. Interview with William T. Abbey, Oct. 18, 1995.

42. Abbey, letter reproduced in FBI file.

43. For example, as late as 1987, two years before his death, Abbey wrote a jacket blurb praising Brendan Phibbs's *The Other Side of Time: A Combat Surgeon in World War II* (Boston: Little, Brown), a scathing account of how American officers sent their soldiers into lethal traps. My thanks are due to Dean Shenk for sending me a copy of this blurb.

44. Interview with John Watta.

45. Interview with Samuel Furgiuele.

46. Journal entry, Abbey Papers in Special Collections, University of Arizona, box 4, folder 6.

47. Abbey, "A New Variation on an Old Theme" (1947), 6.

48. Lyman Hafen, "An Evening with Edward Abbey," *Desert Southwest Supplement* 1, in *St. George Magazine* 4, no. 4 (Winter 1986–87): 12.

49. Interview with William T. Abbey, Aug. 27, 1998.

50. Interview with a source who prefers to remain anonymous.

51. University of New Mexico transcript, obtained with the assistance of William T. Abbey.

52. C. L. Sonnichsen, *Tucson: The Life and Times of an American City* (Norman: University of Oklahoma Press, 1987), 280.

53. Abbey, "Arizona: How Big Is Big Enough?" (1988), 21. This essay originally appeared as "Arizona's Future: How Big Is Big Enough?" (1984), and Abbey introduced the idea of "growth" as cancer in *Desert Solitaire* (1988 [1968]), 114.

54. Phyllis (Flanders) Dorset, "Phyllis Dorset's Story," *Albuquerque Journal*, Nov. 5, 2000, E10 (also containing the companion "Mel Firestone's Story," E10, E12, under the linking headline "A Vast Horizon: UNM Alumni Remember Heady Years of Shared Adventure"). See also "Strangers in a Strange Land: Three UNM Alumni Look Back on the Unforgettable Post-War Years," and Ben Duncan, "Ben Duncan's Story," *Albuquerque Journal*, Oct. 29, 2000, E1, E10. I am grateful to Jean Schmechel for sending me these three wonderful accounts of student life at UNM and in Albuquerque during the late 1940s and early 1950s.

55. Abbey, "Drunk in the Afternoon" (1989), 24.

56. Interview with Hubert Griggs Alexander.

57. Abbey, *The Fool's Progress* (1990 [1988]), 10.

58. Interview with Roger Grette.

59. Abbey, *Desert Solitaire* (1988 [1968]), 173.

60. Ibid., 180.

61. Interview with Jean Schmechel.

62. Abbey, "Desert Places" (1977), 65. Abbey originally drafted this essay in 1975 under the title "Death Valley and Other Desert Places."

63. Abbey, "The Ungulate Jungle" (1985).

64. I am thankful to Howard and Iva Abbey for allowing me to copy and quote this letter and to Dean Shenk for Ed's 1949 paper on 19th-century economics (awarded an A).

65. Abbey, "How It Was," in *Slickrock* (1971), 20.

66. Interview with Ralph Newcomb. Abbey edited *The Thunderbird* during 1950–51. His own previous individual contributions to this magazine during 1948–50 (the poems and musical reviews listed in my bibliography) are fairly forgettable, especially in relation to his later mature writings, but they do reflect his early attempts at poetry and his strong interest in classical music during this period.

67. Abbey, letter to "Mr. Williamson" of Sept. 19, 1982, Abbey papers, box 3, folder 14.

68. Interview with Jean Schmechel.

69. Ibid.

70. Ibid.

71. Ibid.

72. Abbey, "Some Implications of Anarchy" (1951), 9.

73. Interview with Jean Schmechel.

74. Interview with Ralph Newcomb.

75. This interview source prefers to remain anonymous.

76. Quoted in David Solheim and Rob Levin, "The *Bloomsbury Review* Interview," in Hepworth and McNamee, eds., *Resist Much, Obey Little* (1996), 148.

77. Journal entry, Abbey papers, box 5.

78. University of New Mexico transcript.

79. Interview with Jean Schmechel.

80. Interview with John De Puy.

81. Abbey, Dec. 1950 "Synopsis of the Projected Novel, *Jonathan Troy*," University Manuscript S274, Center for Southwestern Research, University of New Mexico.

82. Interview with Jean Schmechel.

83. Ibid.

84. Ibid.

85. Ibid.

86. Quoted in Solheim and Levin, "The *Bloomsbury Review* Interview," 154.

87. Abbey, "Disorder and Early Sorrow" (1977), 23. Originally published as "Desert Driving" (1975).

88. Abbey, "Disorder and Early Sorrow" (1977), 29.

89. Interview with Jean Schmechel.

90. University of Edinburgh record of attendance by Edward Abbey, issued Jan. 26, 1998, obtained with the assistance of William T. Abbey.

91. July 9, 1952, application for federal employment in Abbey's federal employment records, obtained from the U.S. Office of Personnel Management on Apr. 20, 1998, with the assistance of William T. Abbey.

92. Abbey, Dec. 1950 "Synopsis of the Projected Novel, *Jonathan Troy*."

93. Abbey, "Thus I Reply to René Dubos" in *Down the River* (1982), 115.

94. Abbey Papers, box 4.

CHAPTER 3. RANGING ACROSS AMERICA

1. Notification of Personnel Action, federal employment file, 1952.

2. Zakin, *Coyotes and Town Dogs*, 173.

3. E-mail interview correspondence with Anne Howard.

4. *Hudspeth's Albuquerque City Directory 1953*. I am grateful to Jean Schmechel for sending me this information.

5. Abbey Papers, box 5.

6. Abbey, "Malcolm Brown: The Artist as Architect" (1969), 7.

7. Interview with Howard Abbey, Aug. 27, 1998.

8. Howard Abbey, written remembrance, Aug. 4, 1992.

9. U.S. Department of Agriculture, Forest Service, Notice of Employment, federal employment file, 1953.

10. Abbey, "How It Was," in *Slickrock* (1971), 28. It is interesting to note that, when Abbey revised this essay for its appearance in *Beyond the Wall* (1984), he changed a reference to "my wife" (22) in the earlier version to "my girl friend" (56), perhaps as part of his process of writing Rita out of his nonfiction.

11. Abbey Papers, box 10, folders 5–6.

12. Abbey, "How It Was," in *Slickrock* (1971), 31.

13. Quoted in James Hepworth et al., "Literature of the Southwest Interview," in Hepworth and McNamee, eds., *Resist Much, Obey Little* (1985), 125.

14. Interview with Rachel Brown.

15. Abbey, *The Fool's Progress* (1990 [1988]), 176.

16. Ibid., 208.

17. Interview with Rachel Brown.

18. Abbey, "Sunflowers" (1967), 20.

19. My thanks are due to Howard and Iva Abbey for lending me their copy of Abbey's unpublished manuscript "The Dog."

20. Interview with Malcolm Brown.

21. Arthur Nicholson, "Indiana High Grad, Ed Abbey, Turns Novelist; Authors 'Jonathan Troy,'" *Indiana Gazette*, March 3, 1954: 25.

22. Herbert F. West, "A Bitter Young Man," *New York Times*, April 11, 1954, n.p.

23. Abbey, *Jonathan Troy* (1954), 5; *The Monkey Wrench Gang* (1985 [1975]), 210; *Hayduke Lives!* (1990), 274.

24. Quoted in William Plummer, "Edward Abbey's Desert Solecisms," *TWA Ambassador*, Nov. 1982, 34.

25. Wendell Berry, "A Few Words in Favor of Edward Abbey" (1984) in Hepworth and McNamee, eds., *Resist Much, Obey Little* (1996), 5.

26. Interview with Ralph Newcomb.

27. Quoted in Plummer, "Abbey's Desert Solecisms," 34.

28. Abbey, *The Brave Cowboy* (1992 [1956]), 6.

29. Ibid., 98.

30. Ibid., 31.

31. Interview with Rachel Brown.

32. Interview with Hubert Griggs Alexander.

33. University of New Mexico transcript.

34. David Solheim and Rob Levin, "The *Bloomsbury Review* Interview," in Hepworth and McNamee, eds., *Resist Much, Obey Little* (1996), 147.

35. Interview with Hubert Griggs Alexander.

36. Abbey, *The Fool's Progress* (1990 [1988]), 196.

37. Abbey Papers, box 4.

38. Abbey, "Anarchism and the Morality of Violence," University of New Mexico master's thesis (University of New Mexico library), 1959, iii.

39. Interview with Seth Brown.

40. *Hudspeth's Albuquerque City Directory 1955*. Thanks to Jean Schmechel for sending this information to me.

41. Interview with Hubert Griggs Alexander.

42. Abbey, *Desert Solitaire* (1988 [1968]), 173.

43. Interview with Roger Grette.

44. Interview with Dave Foreman.

45. U.S. Department of Agriculture, Forest Service, Notice of Employment, federal employment file, 1955.

46. Abbey, "My 40 Years as a Grand Canyoneer" (1984) in *One Life at a Time, Please* (1988), 124–25.

47. Abbey, *The Brave Cowboy* (1971 [1956]), n.p.

48. *Hudspeth's Albuquerque City Directory 1956*, kindly sent to me by Jean Schmechel.

49. Letter of September 27, 1970, by Abbey to Gary Snyder, with the kind courtesy of Gary Snyder and the Snyder Papers at the University of California at Davis.

50. I am thankful to the late Professor Hubert Griggs Alexander for giving me Abbey's syllabi.

51. E-mail interview correspondence with Anne Howard.

52. Zakin, *Coyotes and Town Dogs*, 173.

53. Interview with Douglas Peacock.

54. National Park Service, Notification of Personnel Action, federal employment file, 1956.

55. Abbey, *Desert Solitaire* (1988 [1968]), 8.

56. Quoted in Jim Stiles, "The Good Old Days: Lyle Jamison and Lloyd Pierson Remember the Quiet Times at Arches National Monument in the 1950s," *Canyon Country Zephyr*, Aug./Sept. 1997, 18. Originally published as "Quiet Times at Arches N.M. with Lloyd Pierson and Lyle Jamison," *Canyon Country Zephyr*, May 1989, 22–23.

57. Interview with Lloyd Pierson.

58. Abbey, Application for Federal Employment, federal employment file, 1965.

59. Abbey Papers, box 4.

60. Interview with Lloyd Pierson.

61. Pierson, "Edward Abbey (1927–1989)," 9.

62. Interview with Lloyd Pierson.

63. Quoted in Hepworth et al., "Literature of the Southwest Interview," in Hepworth and McNamee, eds., *Resist Much, Obey Little* (1985), 128.

64. Nordyke, "Lonesome Jack Burns," *New York Times Book Review*, Sept. 9, 1956, n.p.

65. Susan J. Rosowski, "The Western Hero as Logos, or, Unmaking Meaning," *Western American Literature* 32, no. 3 (Nov. 1997): 270.

66. Quoted in Solheim and Levin, "The *Bloomsbury Review* Interview," 139.

67. I am thankful to Dean Shenk for pointing out this change to me.

68. Interview with Fr. David Sharp.

69. Pierson, "Edward Abbey (1927–1989)," 7.

70. Interview with Bob Greenspan.

71. Interview with Rachel Brown.

72. Interview with Ralph Newcomb.

73. Quoted in Zakin, *Coyotes and Town Dogs*, 174.

74. Rita Deanin Abbey, *Rivertrip* (Flagstaff, Ariz.: Northland Press, 1977).

75. Abbey, *Desert Solitaire* (1988 [1968]), 140.

76. Ibid., 204.

77. Abbey, *Desert Solitaire* (1971 [1968]), xi.

78. Pierson, "Edward Abbey (1927–1989)," 8.

79. Interview with Lloyd Pierson.

80. Abbey, "My Life as a P.I.G., or the True Adventures of Smokey the Cop" in *Abbey's Road* (1979), 153.

81. Abbey, *The Fool's Progress* (1990 [1988]), 198.

82. Pierson, "Edward Abbey (1927–1989)," 7.

83. Abbey, Security Investigation Data form, federal employment file, Apr. 15, 1963.

84. Abbey, "A San Francisco Journal" in *One Life at a Time, Please* (1988), 61. Originally published as "Edward Abbey's Bay Area Journal" (1986).

85. See Abbey, "Amador" (1960) and "Sunflowers" (1967).

86. Abbey, "Underground in Amerigo" (1957), 28.

87. Letter by Stegner to Eric Temple, Feb. 23, 1992, courtesy of Eric Temple.

88. See Barbara Ehrenreich, *The Hearts of Men: American Dreams and the Flight from Commitment* (New York: Anchor/Doubleday, 1983), 42–54. Thanks to Tom Lynch for recommending this book.

89. Interview with John De Puy by Eric Temple. Abbey never forgot Kerouac's *On the Road* and his own picaresque manuscript. In his afterword to the second edition of Ann Ronald's *The New West of Edward Abbey* (Reno: Univ. of Nevada Press, 2000), Scott Slovic argues concerning Abbey's *The Fool's Progress* that "Kerouac's imprint on this work is inescapable," situating it within the tradition of "Beat novel" with its "frenzied search for truth on American highways" (260) and its "search for a celebration of friendship" (261).

90. Quoted in Zakin, *Coyotes and Town Dogs*, 174.

91. Letter from Stegner to Eric Temple, Feb. 23, 1992.

92. Abbey, "A San Francisco Journal," in *One Life at a Time, Please* (1988), 61–62.

93. Abbey, Application for Federal Employment, federal employment file, 1965.

94. Abbey Papers, box 4.

95. Dave Foreman, *Ecodefense: A Field Guide to Monkeywrenching* (Tucson: Earth First!/Ned Ludd, 1985).

96. The poet Robert Creeley long remembered Abbey, for example (as Creeley e-mailed me on March 17, 1998), "trying to demolish a large billboard on the road coming into Ranchos de Taos (before Taos to the east) by putting copious stuff around the timbers supporting it, then dousing these with gasoline, then lighting same to produce a great glare from the burning junk."

97. Ellen Schrecker, *Many Are the Crimes: McCarthyism in America* (Boston: Little, Brown, 1998), 310. Schrecker adds: "Here, in a former boarding school deep in the Sangre de Cristo mountains, not far from Taos, union officials, blacklisted screenwriters, and other denizens of the left could vacation in a congenial political atmosphere. . . . Vincent, like so many other leftists forced out of public life in the late 1940s and 1950s, found a niche within the world of American Communism. But it was a shaky haven, indeed. Because the Vincents and their patrons were often under surveillance, it was clear that a sojourn at the San Cristobal Valley Ranch might well be politically lethal" (310).

98. Canyon Road is listed as Abbey's 1959 address on his 1963 Security Investigation form, but Rachel Brown recalls a more central house before that.

99. Abbey, "My Friend Debris," in *Down the River* (1982), 216.

100. Interview with John De Puy.

101. Abbey, "My Friend Debris," 223.

102. Abbey, *Earth Apples* (1994), 72.

103. Abbey, review of *Watt* (1959), 383.

104. Abbey, review of *Fade Out* (1959).

105. Abbey, "In Defense of Cottonwoods" (1959).

106. Abbey, "The Smell of Fraud" (1959).

107. Interview with John De Puy by Eric Temple.

108. Abbey, "Christmas Greetings" (1959).

109. Craig Vincent, "Ave Atque Vale!" *El Crepusculo de la Libertad*, Dec. 31, 1959, 2.

110. Craig Vincent, "1960—Looking Forward," *El Crepusculo de la Libertad*, Jan. 7, 1960, 2.

111. Abbey, "For Future Beauty" (1960).

112. Abbey, "God Bless America—Let's Save Some of It" (1960).

113. Abbey Papers, box 4.

114. Interview with Jenny Vincent.

115. Interview with Judson Crews.

CHAPTER 4. SINGING THE HOBOKEN BLUES

1. Abbey Papers, box 4.

2. Abbey listed Alberto Martinez among his old UNM friends in a spring 1984 journal entry (Abbey Papers, box 5).

3. Abbey, *Hayduke Lives!* (1990), opening dedication.

4. Abbey, *Desert Images* (1979), 157. Abbey also included an almost identical recollection in his essay "My Life as a P.I.G." in *Abbey's Road* (1979), 154.

5. C. L. Sonnichsen, *Tularosa: Last of the Frontier West* (New York: Devin-Adair, 1960), 286.

6. Quoted in Les Standiford, "Desert Places: An Exchange with Edward Abbey," *Western Humanities Review* 24 (Autumn 1970): 397.

7. In 1969 Abbey would work on a film script for "Black Sun" with a $2,000 grant from the American Film Institute, and during 1985–86 he would spend a lot of time writing and rewriting a film script for *The Monkey Wrench Gang* that has been preserved in the Abbey Papers, box 5.

8. Kirk Douglas, quoted in "County Hand Tries Hand in Movie Role," *Indiana Gazette*, June 9, 1961, n.p., kindly supplied to me by Howard and Iva Abbey.

9. Kirk Douglas, *The Ragman's Son* (New York: Simon and Schuster, 1988), 337. Thanks to Dave Cotey for sending me this information.

10. William Eastlake, "A Note on Ed Abbey" in Hepworth and McNamee, eds., *Resist Much, Obey Little* (1996), 16.

11. Interview with Don Congdon.

12. *Kirk Douglas Writes to Gary Cooper: A Letter—May 4, 1961* (Santa Barbara: Santa Teresa Press, 1992), n.p.

13. E-mail interview correspondence with Anne Howard.

14. Douglas, *The Ragman's Son*, 493.

15. Douglas, "Death of Writer Edward Abbey," *Los Angeles Times*, Mar. 23, 1989, metro part 2, p. 6.

16. Abbey, "Fire Lookout" (1979), 176–77.

17. E-mail interview correspondence with Robert Creeley and Louise (Bobbie) Hawkins.

18. Quoted in Standiford, "Desert Places: An Exchange with Edward Abbey," 397.

19. Interview with John De Puy.

20. "County Native Tries Hand in Movie Role."

21. "Cowboy Hall of Fame Honors County Native," *Indiana Gazette*, n.d., n.p., supplied by Howard and Iva Abbey.

22. "The New Westerns," *Time*, July 13, 1962, 66.

23. Martin Levin, *New York Times Book Review*, Sept. 30, 1962, 44. See also V. P. Hass, *Chicago Sunday Tribune*, Sept. 23, 1962, 3, and *New York Herald Tribune Books*, Oct. 14, 1962, 11.

24. Interview with Judson Crews. Rita and sons lived near Taos in Arroyo Seco.

25. Security Investigation Data form, federal employment file, Apr. 15, 1973.

26. E-mail interview correspondence with Robert Creeley, Mar. 17, 1998.

27. Abbey, "William Eastlake: *Para Mi Amigo*" (1983), 18.

28. Tom Miller, "Fighting the Good Fight: Tucson's Literary Troika—Bill Eastlake, Ed Abbey, and Alan Harrington—Remembered," *Tucson Monthly*, Jan. 1998, 56, 58.

29. E-mail interview correspondence with Robert Creeley, Mar. 17, 1998.

30. Abbey, "William Eastlake: *Para Mi Amigo*" (1983), 19.

31. E-mail interview correspondence with Robert Creeley, Mar. 17, 1998.

32. Security Investigation Data form, 1963.

33. It remains unproven exactly when he held these jobs, though both were most likely during this time.

34. E-mail interview correspondence with Robert Creeley, Mar. 17, 1998.

35. Abbey, "The Last Pork Chop" (1984), 55.

36. Abbey, "Nothing to Do" (1976).

37. E-mail interview correspondence with Louise (Bobbie) Hawkins, May 3, 1998.

38. Abbey Papers, box 10.

39. Brian Lonergan, personnel officer, Hudson County Division of Social Services, phone conversation of Jan. 14, 1998.

40. Morton Kamins, "Son of the Desert," *Gallery* 12, no. 4 (Apr. 1984): 102.

41. E-mail interview correspondence with Bobbie Hawkins, May 3, 1998.

42. Interview with Don Congdon.

43. Abbey, *The Fool's Progress* (1990 [1988]), 263–90.

44. Ibid., 278.

45. Interview with Katherine Bounds.

46. Abbey, "Manhattan Twilight, Hoboken Night" in *The Journey Home* (1977), 100–101. Originally published as "City of the Prophecies—A Hoboken Perspective" (1969).

47. Abbey, "Freedom and Wilderness, Wilderness and Freedom" in *The Journey Home* (1977), 227–28.

48. Eastlake, "A Note on Ed Abbey," 15.

49. Abbey, "Forty Years as a Canyoneer," in *One Life at a Time, Please* (1988), 125. Originally published as "My 40 Years as a Grand Canyoneer" (1984).

50. Notification of Personnel Action form, federal employment file.

51. Abbey, "Hard Times in Santa Fe" (1989), 8.

52. Abbey, "Desert Places" in *The Journey Home* (1977), 67–68. I'm very grateful to Jacek Macias for information concerning this and several other publications by Abbey.

53. Interview with John De Puy.

54. Abbey Papers, box 4.

55. Quoted in Lyman Hafen, "An Evening with Edward Abbey," *Desert Southwest Supplement* 1, in *St. George Magazine* 4, no. 4 (Winter 1986–87): 11.

56. Interview with Katherine Bounds.

57. Phone conversation with the Nevada State Records Office, Jan. 14, 1998.

58. Zakin, *Coyotes and Town Dogs*, 174.

59. Abbey Papers, box 2, folder 3.

60. Abbey, *Desert Solitaire* (1988 [1968]), 231.

61. Plummer, "Abbey's Desert Solecisms," 36.

62. "Plays Should Instruct, Too: 'Living' Art Show at UNLV," *Las Vegas Sun*, Nov. 11, 1979, n.p.

CHAPTER 5. WRITING THE WILD

1. Hepworth, *"Canus Lupus Amorus Lunaticum"* in Hepworth and McNamee, eds., *Resist Much, Obey Little* (1996), 127.

2. Federal employment file, 1965–66.

3. Abbey, "My Life as a P.I.G." in *Abbey's Road* (1979), 155.

4. Ibid.

5. Marc Reisner, *Cadillac Desert: The American West and Its Disappearing Water* (1986; rev. ed. New York: Penguin, 1993), 286.

6. Interview with Gail Baker.

7. Notification of Personnel Action, federal employment file, 1966.

8. Interview with Ralph Newcomb.

9. Abbey, "Death Valley," in *The Journey Home* (1977), 80. Originally published as "Death Valley Notebook" (1967).

10. Abbey, "Death Valley," 74.

11. SueEllen Campbell, "Foreword II: Magpie," in Quigley, ed., *Coyote in the Maze* (1998), 39.

12. Abbey Papers, box 24, folder 3.

13. Abbey, "Death Valley Junk," in *Abbey's Road* (1979), 175. Originally published as "Abbey's Road, Take the Other (or Death Valley Acid)" (1976).

14. Abbey, preface to *Beyond the Wall* (1984), xii—xiii.

15. Interview with Charles Bowden by Eric Temple, quoted in *Edward Abbey: A Voice Crying in the Wilderness* (Bethesda, Maryland: Canyon Productions video documentary, 1993).

16. Interview with Clarke Cartwright Abbey by Eric Temple, quoted in *Edward Abbey: A Voice Crying in the Wilderness*.

17. Abbey, *Desert Solitaire* (1988 [1968]), viii.

18. Abbey Papers, box 11, folders 5–6 and 7–8.

19. Keith A. Fieler, "The official web site of Ballarat, California," http://www.fieler .com/ballarat/ballarat_residents_seldom_seen_slim.htm, accessed in Sept. 1998 with the kind assistance of Kent Duryee. See also "Death Valley's Ballarat Ghost Town," *Desert USA*, Apr. 1999, accessed in Sept. 2000 at http://www.desert.usa/com/mag99/apr/stories/ballarat.html.

20. Abbey Papers, box 5.

21. Abbey, "The Ancient Dust" (1973), in *Beyond the Wall* (1984), 156.

22. Abbey, "The Great American Desert" (1977), 16.

23. Abbey, *Desert Solitaire* (1971 [1968]), xi.

24. Abbey, "The Art of Nonfiction," Abbey Papers, box 8, folder 6.

25. Macrae in Abbey, *The Serpents of Paradise* (1995), 164.

26. Keith Green, "The Image Battle," *Taos News*, n.d., n.p., supplied by Howard and Iva Abbey.

27. See William T. Pilkington, "Edward Abbey: Southwestern Anarchist," *Western Review* 3 (Winter 1966): 58–62, and Levi Peterson, "The Primitive and the Civilized in Western Fiction," *Western American Literature* 1 (Fall 1966): 197–207.

28. Abbey, "The Southwest: A Thirst for the Desert" (1973), 114–16.

29. Abbey, "Of Cowboys, Indians and the Modern West" (1969), signed by "Peter Kenyon." My thanks are due to the Tucson writer Tom Miller, who kindly sent me this interview with Eastlake and identified "Kenyon" as Abbey.

30. Abbey, *Desert Solitaire* (1988 [1968]), 33.

31. Interview with Bob Greenspan.

32. Abbey, *Desert Solitaire* (1988 [1968]), 62.

33. Abbey, "A Day in the Life of a Park Ranger" (1967), 17, and *Desert Solitaire* (1971), 43, and (1988), 38.

34. Interview with Malcolm Brown.

35. Ibid.

36. Abbey, "A River to Explore" (1967), 18.

37. Quoted in Abbey, "A River to Explore" (1967), 19.

38. Notification of Personnel Action, federal employment file, 1967.

39. Abbey, "The Damnation of a Canyon," in *Beyond the Wall* (1984), 96. Originally published as "Glen Canyon Dam" (1968).

40. Abbey Papers, box 5.

41. Interview with Jennie Vincent.

42. Russell Martin, *A Story That Stands Like a Dam: Glen Canyon and the Struggle for the Soul of the West* (New York: Henry Holt, 1989), 170.

43. Ken Sleight, "A Letter to Ed Abbey," *Canyon Country Zephyr*, July 1989, 26, reprinted in "Eulogy to Edward Abbey," 5.

44. Ken Sleight, "Abbey and Me," *Canyon Country Zephyr*, Apr./May 1999, 8.

45. Abbey, "Up the Creek with the Downriver Rowdies" (1979), 44.

46. Abbey, "Forty Years as a Canyoneer," in *One Life at a Time, Please* (1988), 125. Originally published as "My 40 Years as a Grand Canyoneer" (1984).

47. Abbey, letter of Jan. 22, 1968, to Ralph Newcomb from 342 North Park Avenue, in which he clarified that he was spending the winter there while Judy worked on her master's degree. I am grateful to Mr. Newcomb for sending me this letter.

48. Abbey, "Mr Krutch" (based on "An Interview with Joseph Wood Krutch" [1968]), in *One Life at a Time, Please* (1988), 192.

49. Abbey Papers, box 1, folder 8.

50. Abbey Papers, box 2, folder 1.

51. Interview with William T. Abbey, Aug. 27, 1998.

52. Abbey Papers, box 2, folder 1.

53. Abbey Papers, box 2, folder 3.

54. Abbey, "How to Pick a Woman" (1994).

55. Abbey, "A Colorado River Journey," in *Beyond the Wall* (1984), 108. Originally published as *The Hidden Canyon* (1977).

56. Interview with James Carrico.

57. Ibid.

58. Edwin Way Teale, review of *Desert Solitaire, New York Times Book Review*, Jan. 28, 1968, 7.

59. Abbey Papers, box 2, folder 1.

60. Abbey Papers, box 2, folder 10.

61. I am thankful to Ralph Newcomb and Lloyd Pierson for sending me these letters.

62. Interview with Wendell Berry.

63. See Jim Fergus, "The Anarchist's Progress," *Outside*, Nov. 1988, 125, where Dillard is quoted regarding *Desert Solitaire*.

64. Quoted in Zakin, *Coyotes and Town Dogs*, 26.

65. Martin, *A Story That Stands Like a Dam*, 287.

66. Todd Gitlin, *The Sixties: Years of Hope, Days of Rage* (New York: Bantam, 1987), 360.

67. Abbey Papers, box 7, folder 7.

68. Interview with Lloyd Pierson.

69. Michael Howard, "Desert Man Raises Thorny Issue at Book Festival," *Rocky Mountain News*, Apr. 24, 1968, 12.

70. Federal employment file, 1968.

71. Abbey Papers, box 2, folder 1.

72. Abbey Papers, box 5.

73. This date is incorrectly printed as "August 28, 1969" in Abbey, *Confessions of a Barbarian* (1994), 260; Abbey actually and correctly wrote 1968 in his journal (Abbey Papers, box 5).

74. Interview with D. Newton Smith by Randall Holcombe.

75. Ibid. See also Nathaniel H. Axtell, "Abbey in Appalachia," *Appalachian Voice* (Boone, North Carolina) (Winter 1998): 8. Thanks to Susan Congelosi for sending me this article.

76. Interview with D. Newton Smith by Randall Holcombe.

77. Abbey, April 25, 1969, letter to Ralph Newcomb, kindly sent to me by Mr. Newcomb.

78. Written interview correspondence with Cindy Gray about the freshman student.

79. Interview with D. Newton Smith by Randall Holcombe.

80. Ibid.

81. Federal employment file, 1969.

82. Abbey, *Cactus Country* (1973), 62, 63–64.

83. Interview with Harold Coss.

84. Abbey, *Cactus Country* (1973), 75.

85. Ibid., 157–58.

86. Interviews with Ann Woodin and Sandy Newmark.

87. Interview with James Carrico.

88. Abbey, "The Southwest: A Thirst for the Desert" (1973), 106, 108.

89. Interview with Ann Woodin.

90. Abbey Papers, box 5.

91. Abbey Papers, box 3, folder 2.

92. Abbey Papers, box 3, folder 5.

93. Ibid.

94. Interview with Ed Mears.

95. Interview with Sam Furgiuele.

96. Interview with Raymona Hull.

97. Abbey Papers, box 5.

98. Ibid.

99. Abbey, *Appalachian Wilderness* (1970), 16.

100. Ibid., 67–68.

101. Ibid., 74–87.

102. Ibid., 82, 84–85.

103. In his interview with me of Jan. 17, 1996, Ken Sleight stressed that Abbey "was returning to his roots when he bought some property here in Pack Creek."

104. Parks Lanier, *The Poetics of Appalachian Space* (Knoxville: University of Tennessee Press, 1991), 1–9.

105. Abbey, *Appalachian Wilderness* (1970), 75.

106. Review of *Appalachian Wilderness, New Republic*, Feb. 20, 1971, 29–30.

107. Federal employment file, 1969–70.

108. Interview with Katie Lee. See Katie Lee, "His Heart to the Hawks," 9, 14. I am grateful to Katie Lee for sharing this and other material from her private collection.

109. Letter from Paul Abbey to Edward Abbey, Apr. 1, 1970, Abbey Papers, box 2, folder 1.

110. Abbey Papers, box 5.

111. Doug Peacock, "Desert Solitary," *Audubon* 100, no. 2 (Mar./Apr. 1998): 93.

112. Interview with Thomas Lyon.

113. Sleight, "Eulogy to Edward Abbey," 5.

CHAPTER 6. IN THE CANYONS

1. Interview with Katie Lee.

2. Abbey, "A Walk in the Desert Hills," in *Beyond the Wall* (1984), 12. Originally published as "This Antique and Empty Land" (1984).

3. Interview with Katherine Bounds.

4. Interview with Malcolm Brown.

5. Interview with Katherine Bounds.

6. Interview with Judith Saum.

7. Abbey, *The Fool's Progress* (1990 [1988]), 431.

8. Abbey Papers, box 2, folder 1.

9. Ibid.

10. Abbey, "Fire Lookout" (1979), 180.

11. Interview with Ann Woodin.

12. Interview with John De Puy.

13. Abbey, "My Friend Debris," in *Down the River* (1982), 217.

14. Interview with John De Puy.

15. Abbey Papers, box 3, folder 6.

16. Macrae in Abbey, *The Serpents of Paradise* (1995), 164.

17. Abbey Papers, box 3, folder 6.

18. Ibid.

19. Abbey Papers, box 5.

20. Interview with Don Congdon.

21. Interview with Gregory McNamee.

22. Katie Lee, "His Heart to the Hawks," 9.

23. Abbey, "Short Stories: Auchincloss, Deck, Madden, and Others" (1970).

24. Abbey, *Black Sun* (1982 [1971]), 33–34.

25. Avon Publishers reported to me in a fax of Jan. 15, 1999, that their edition of *Black Sun* had sold 115,570 copies as of Dec. 1998.

26. Review of *Black Sun*, *New Yorker*, July 17, 1971, 87.

27. Edward Hoagland, Abbey Papers, box 2, folder 6, and his review of *Black Sun*, *New York Times Book Review*, June 13, 1971, 6, 12.

28. See, for example, the review of *Desert Solitaire* in the *Saturday Review of Literature*, Apr. 24, 1971, 33, and Roger Jellinek, "The Last Word: Wild Men," *New York Times Book Review*, Sept. 12, 1971, 71.

29. Edward Higbee, letter to the editor, *New York Times Book Review*, May 24, 1970, n.p.

30. Interview with Jerry Tecklin.

31. Abbey Papers, box 7, folder 6.

32. Abbey, "Freedom and Wilderness, Wilderness and Freedom," in *The Journey Home* (1977), 227.

33. Quoted in Les Standiford, "Desert Places: An Exchange with Edward Abbey," *Western Humanities Review* 24 (Autumn 1970): 396. See Abbey, *Desert Solitaire* (1988 [1968]), 114.

34. In the letter of Nov. 8, 1970, to Senator Moss cited in the text above, Abbey listed his address as 641 North 6th East, Logan.

35. Interview with Thomas Lyon.

36. Abbey Papers, box 7, folder 9.

37. Ibid.

38. William Marling, review of *Abbey's Road, Southwest Review* (Winter 1980): 103.

39. Abbey, review of *The Best American Short Stories 1970* (1970).

40. Quoted in Hepworth, "The Poetry Center Interview" (1985), in Hepworth and McNamee, eds., *Resist Much, Obey Little* (1996), 60.

41. Interview with Thomas Lyon.

42. Interview with John G. Mitchell.

43. Mitchell's introduction to Abbey, *Slickrock* (1971), 7. Mitchell clarified that "we were six," including also "Kent Frost of Monticello, driver and guide, river-runner, cowboy, prospector, campfire raconteur; beside him, Hyde and August Frugé of Berkeley, chairman of the Sierra Club's publications committee; in back, our art director from New York, Charles Curtis" (7).

44. Ibid., 8.

45. Interview with John G. Mitchell.

46. Abbey, *Beyond the Wall* (1984), xii.

47. Positive reviews of *Slickrock* in *Natural History*, Jan. 1972, 86, and by Thomas J. Lyon in *Western American Literature* 12 (Aug. 1977): 67–68, were just about *Slickrock*'s only reviews.

48. Mitchell's introduction to Abbey, *Slickrock* (1971), 11.

49. Interview with Judith Saum.

50. Abbey, "Days and Nights in Old Pariah," in *Beyond the Wall* (1984), 75. Originally published in *Slickrock* (1971), 45–51.

51. Mitchell's introduction to Abbey, *Slickrock* (1971), 8.

52. Abbey Papers, box 24.

53. E-mail interview correspondence with Tom Lynch, Dec. 15, 1999.

54. Abbey, *Abbey's Road* (1979), xvi.

55. Ibid., xvii, and Abbey Papers, box 3, folder 7.

56. Abbey, *Abbey's Road* (1979), xvii.

57. Abbey Papers, box 24.

58. Abbey, "Science with a Human Face" (1971), in *Abbey's Road* (1979), 127.

59. Gary Snyder Papers, University of California at Davis, quoted with Snyder's kind permission.

60. Abbey, *Abbey's Road* (1979), xvi.

61. Interview with John De Puy.

62. Abbey Papers, box 5.

63. Abbey Papers, box 3, folder 15.

64. Gary Snyder, "A Letter to Ed Abbey" (1985), in Hepworth and McNamee, eds., *Resist Much, Obey Little* (1996), 182, 188.

65. Gary Snyder, "Tributes," *Tucson Weekly*, Apr. 5–11, 1989, 5.

66. Abbey Papers, box 3, folder 15.

67. Jack Loeffler, "Strolling Along the Edge of Mortality," 27.

68. Gershon Siegel, "Deep Friendship and Radical Environmentalism: Jack Loeffler, Edward Abbey, and 'Night Work,'" *The Sun* (Santa Fe) 5, no. 11 (Sept. 1993): 9.

69. Interview with Jack Loeffler by Eric Temple, in *Edward Abbey: A Voice in the Wilderness* (1993 video).

70. Abbey Papers, box 7, folder 6.

71. Zakin, *Coyotes and Town Dogs*, 54, 57.

72. Abbey Papers, box 24, folder 5.

73. Abbey, "Return to Yosemite: Tree Fuzz vs. Freaks," in *The Journey Home* (1977), 142, 145.

74. Katie Lee, "His Heart to the Hawks," 9. Abbey's letter to her was dated Aug. 26, 1971.

75. Interview with Ernie Bulow.

76. Abbey Papers, box 7, folder 6.

77. Interview with Karilyn (McElheney) Brodell.

78. Notification of Personnel Action, federal employment file, 1971.

79. Abbey, "Fire Lookout" (1979), 180. The tower (not cabin) has since been used.

80. Abbey Papers, box 5.

81. Ibid.

82. Abbey, letter of Mar. 18, 1987, to Martha Lawrence at Harcourt, Brace; Abbey Papers, box 3, folder 18.

83. Abbey, "The Reef," in *Abbey's Road* (1979), 6. Originally published as "Man and the Great Reef" (1972).

84. Abbey's letters during this period carry this address (Abbey Papers, box 24).

85. Interview with Malcolm Brown.

86. Interview with Linda Newmark.

87. E-mail interview correspondence with Richard Felger, Nov. 4, 1998.

88. Interview with Sandy Newmark.

89. Interview with Ernie Bulow.

90. Abbey Papers, box 2.

91. Interview with Sandy Newmark.

92. Abbey Papers, box 8, folder 1.

93. Andrew Weil, "Tributes," *Tucson Weekly*, Apr. 5–11, 1989, 8.

94. Interview with Jack Macrae.

95. Interview with Linda Newmark.

96. Interview with Judith Saum.

97. Abbey, *Cactus Country* (1973), 20.

98. Abbey Papers, box 3, folder 7.

99. Abbey, *Cactus Country* (1973), 20.

100. Abbey, *Desert Solitaire* (1988 [1968]), 18; Hepworth, "The Poetry Center Interview," 52.

101. Loeffler, "Edward Abbey, Anarchism, and the Environment," in Hepworth and McNamee, eds., *Resist Much, Obey Little* (1996), 34. Originally published in *Western American Literature* 28, no. 1 (May 1993): 43–49.

102. Interview with Lou Barassi.

103. Interview with Douglas Peacock.

104. Interview with Jack Loeffler by Eric Temple, in *Edward Abbey: A Voice in the Wilderness* (1993 video).

105. Abbey Papers, box 5, folder 2.

106. Abbey, *The Fool's Progress* (1990 [1988]), 410–12.

107. Interview with Douglas Peacock.

108. Abbey Papers, box 24, folder 6. It is not clear that "Trouble on the Old Preserve" was ever published.

109. See Abbey, *Cactus Country* (1973), 113–17.

110. Howard Abbey, written communication, Aug. 2000.

111. Abbey, "Blood Sport," in *One Life at a Time, Please* (1988), 35, 37, 40. Original version published as "Foreword" to *The Unnatural Enemy* (1984).

112. Abbey, "Aravaipa Canyon," in *Down the River* (1982), 155. Originally published as "In the Land of 'Laughing Waters'" (1982).

113. Abbey, "Freedom and Wilderness, Wilderness and Freedom," in *The Journey*

Home (1977), 236, 237, 238. This section of the essay was originally published as "Wilderness and Freedom" (1976).

114. Abbey, "Sportsmen," in *One Life at a Time, Please* (1988), 221, 225.

115. Abbey, "Wilderness and Freedom" (1976), 1.

116. For the draft of "Sportsmen," see Abbey Papers, box 24, folder 7.

117. Joe V. Meigs, "Geologist Jumps on Abbey," letter to the editor, *Mariah*, Aug./ Sept. 1978, 6.

118. Abbey, "Merry Christmas, Pigs!" (1973), in *Abbey's Road* (1979), 139, 141.

119. Lawrence Clark Powell, "The Angry Lover," in Hepworth and McNamee, eds., *Resist Much, Obey Little* (1996), 71, 76. Originally published as "A Singular Ranger," *Westways* 66 (Mar. 1974), 32–35, 64–65, and then reprinted as "The Angry Lover" in Powell's collection *From the Heartland: Profiles of People and Places of the Southwest and Beyond* (Flagstaff: Northland Press, 1976), 108–18.

120. Interview with Lou Barassi.

121. Interview with Douglas Peacock.

122. Abbey, "Great Overdone" (1973).

123. Interview with Lou Barassi.

124. Interview with Harold Coss.

CHAPTER 7. THE BARD OF MOAB

1. Interview with Dave Foreman.

2. Abbey, "On the River Again," in *Abbey's Road* (1979), 106.

3. Ken Sleight, "A Letter to Ed Abbey," *Canyon Country Zephyr* (July 1989), reprinted as "Eulogy to Edward Abbey" (1990), 5.

4. Abbey, *Desert Images* (1979), 14.

5. Abbey, "In Defense of the Redneck" (1979), in *Abbey's Road* (1979), 159.

6. Interview with Bob Greenspan.

7. Abbey, "In Defense of the Redneck" (1979), 133.

8. Preston was sickened by the sight of a headless, naked doll tied to the fencepost of Abbey's Moab house, and by his continual drinking and womanizing (e-mail interview correspondence with Dr. Gilbert Preston).

9. Abbey, *The Fool's Progress* (1990 [1988]), 348, 349.

10. Interview with Laura Lee Houck.

11. Interview with Karilyn (McElheney) Brodell.

12. Abbey, "A Walk in the Park," in *Abbey's Road* (1979), 111. Originally published as "Ed Abbey Would Prefer to Walk" (1978).

13. In *Down the River* (1982) Abbey wrote, "I have a friend named Marilyn McElhenny [*sic*]. . . . She is a wildlife biologist by profession but makes her living these days as a florist. She is a sweet, rosy, generous, thoroughly delightful young woman, pretty as a marigold. She owns a dog, a shaggy yellow mutt named Toley, ingenuous and friendly, though he lost a leg a few years back while rock climbing near Moab, Utah." It was here that Abbey concluded that he had thus fulfilled his promise to Marilyn to "put her and her dog in a book" (8).

14. Loeffler, "Strolling Along the Edge of Mortality" (1994), 24, 31.

15. Ibid., 26.

16. Abbey, *The Monkey Wrench Gang* (1985 [1975]), 25.

17. Interview with Ken Sleight, Dec. 10, 1998.

18. Abbey, "The Second Rape of the West" (1975), in *The Journey Home* (1977), 158–59.

19. Interview with Roger Grette.

20. Abbey, "God's Plan for the State of Utah: A Revelation," in *Mountain Gazette* (1977), 11. Originally published as "A State Plan from Upstairs" (1974).

21. Abbey, "Dust: A Movie" (1975), in *The Journey Home* (1977), 239.

22. Abbey, "Come On In" (1976), 3. Originally published as "Welcome to Canyonlands" (1975).

23. Abbey Papers, box 3, folder 8.

24. Interviews with Roger Grette, Ken Sleight (Dec. 10, 1998), and Bill Benge.

25. Interview with Karilyn (McElheney) Brodell.

26. Abbey, *The Fool's Progress* (1990 [1988]), 26, 27. Henry then tries to explain to Elaine that "I was born and bred on a sidehill farm in Appalachia. . . . Ain't we got no pokewood greens? turnips? smoked ham? red-eye gravy? sweet corn? sowbelly? venison sausage? even beans? And I mean beans, not bean sprouts" (30). Henry and Elaine's dietary conflicts come "near the end of the honeymoon, the typical ninety days of passion before the grim reality of domestic bliss begins to sink into the mutual consciousness of man and wife" (27).

27. Interview with Karilyn (McElheney) Brodell.

28. Ibid.

29. Abbey Papers, box 2, folder 1.

30. Abbey Papers, box 3, folder 8.

31. Abbey Papers, box 5.

32. "Abbey, Edward," *Contemporary Authors* (Detroit: Gale, 1974), vol. 45. "Piute" was listed in *Contemporary Authors: New Revision Series* (Detroit: Gale, 1994), vol. 41.

33. Zakin, *Coyotes and Town Dogs*, 178.

34. Abbey, untitled list of suggestions for Jimmy Carter (1977).

35. See, for example, Abbey, "Amador" (1960), a chapter from the first novel.

36. Interview with William T. Abbey, Oct. 27, 1995.

37. Peacock, "Chasing Abbey," *Outside*, Aug. 1997, 80.

38. Abbey, *The Monkey Wrench Gang* (1985 [1975]), 44–45.

39. Quoted in Hepworth, "The Poetry Center Interview" (1985), in Hepworth and McNamee, eds., *Resist Much, Obey Little* (1996), 54.

40. Sleight, "Around the Bend Again . . . Reporting from San Juan County," *Canyon Country Zephyr*, Oct./Nov. 1997, 24.

41. Interview with Ken Sleight, Dec. 10, 1998.

42. Interview with Bill Benge.

43. Interview with Douglas Peacock.

44. Interview with Karilyn (McElheney) Brodell.

45. Quoted in Temple, *Edward Abbey: A Voice in the Wilderness* (1993 video).

46. Quoted in Winfred Blevins, "Edward Abbey: 'The Thoreau of the American Desert,'" *Mariah*, Oct./Nov. 1978, 90.

47. Abbey, "How It Was," in *Slickrock* (1971).

48. Abbey, *The Monkey Wrench Gang* (1985 [1975]), 74.

49. Ibid., 78.

50. Ibid., 83.

51. Ibid., 115, and *Hayduke Lives!* (1990), 269.

52. Abbey, *Hayduke Lives!* (1990), 110.

53. Quoted in Peter Carlson, "Edward Abbey," *People Weekly*, June 25, 1984, 63. Thanks to Dean Shenk for sending me this article.

54. Abbey Papers, box 5.

55. Quoted in Temple, *Edward Abbey: A Voice in the Wilderness* (1993 video). See also Abbey, "Property vs. People?" (1983): "I read the article 'Eco-Terrorism' with interest and pleasure. However, I must object to Ron Arnold's terminology." Making the same distinction be-

tween *terrorism* and *sabotage*, Abbey concluded, "Myself, I am absolutely opposed to terrorism, whether by government or by 'unlicensed' individuals."

56. Elizabeth Ashton, *Houston Chronicle*, Sept. 28, 1975, 8; Vincent McCaffrey, *Fiction* annual (Boston), 1976, n.p.; and Kenneth C. Caldwell, *Landscape Architecture* (Louisville), Oct. 1975, n.p.

57. Avon Publishers, fax of Jan. 15, 1999.

58. Quoted in Paul Bousquet, "Western Winds Feature Interview: Edward Abbey," *Western Winds*, Winter 1987–88, 15.

59. Quoted in John F. Baker, "PW Interviews: Edward Abbey," *Publishers Weekly*, Sept. 8, 1975, 6.

60. Abbey, *The Monkey Wrench Gang* (1985 [1975]), 264.

61. *Newsweek*, Jan. 5, 1976; Peter Wild, *High Country News*, Oct. 10, 1975, 12; James E. Alexander, *Pittsburgh Post-Gazette*, Aug. 30, 1975; Marvin Bailey, *Memphis Commercial Appeal*, Sept. 14, 1975; and David E. Jones, *Chicago News*, Sept. 27, 1975.

62. Larry McMurtry, "Fertile Fiction of the American Desert," review of *Dancers in the Scalp House*, by William Eastlake, and *The Monkey Wrench Gang, Washington Post*, Sept. 8, 1975, c8; and Clifton Fadiman, review of *Desert Solitaire, Book-of-the-Month Club News*, Apr. 1968, 10.

63. Tom Miller, "Fighting the Good Fight: Tucson's Literary Troika—Bill Eastlake, Ed Abbey, and Alan Harrington—Remembered," *Tucson Monthly*, Jan. 1998, 61.

64. Abbey Papers, box 2, folder 8.

65. George Vukelich, *Capital Times* (Madison, Wisc.), May 9, 1977.

66. Abbey Papers, box 3, folder 16.

67. Abbey Papers, box 2, folder 6.

68. "United States and Canadian Appointments 1975," courtesy of the Guggenheim Foundation.

69. Abbey, *Desert Solitaire* (1988 [1968]), x.

70. Abbey, "Shadows from the Big Woods" (1974), in *The Journey Home* (1977), 223, 226.

71. Abbey, "Walking" (1976), in *The Journey Home* (1977), 203, 205.

72. Quoted in Baker, "PW Interviews," 6.

73. Abbey, "Notes from a Lookout Logbook" (1976), 82.

74. Abbey, "The Last Pork Chop" (1984), 52.

75. Interviews with Bill Hoy and Karilyn (McElheney) Brodell.

76. Abbey, "Sierra Madre," in *Abbey's Road* (1979), 96–97. Originally published as "A Tale of the Sierra Madre" (1975).

77. Interview with Tom Thompson.

78. Abbey, "Anna Creek," in *Abbey's Road* (1979), 18. Originally published as "The World of Anna Creek" (1977).

79. Interview with Harold Coss.

80. Abbey, "Back of Beyond" (1978), in *Abbey's Road* (1979), 52.

81. Grace Lichtenstein, "Edward Abbey, Voice of Southwest Wilds," *New York Times*, Jan. 20, 1976, 24.

82. Abbey Papers, box 5.

83. See Tom Miller, "Abbey's Road," *New West*, Oct. 23, 1978, 48–51; Buddy Mays, "The Environment of a Writer," *New Mexico Magazine*, Nov. 1978, 38–39; Buddy Mays, "Novelist in a Fire Tower," *Empire* (Sunday magazine of the *Denver Post*), Mar. 25, 1979, 10–13; and Doug Biggers, "From Abbey's Tower," *Tucson's Mountain Newsreal*, Sept. 1979, 6–7.

84. Abbey, "Meeting the Bear," in *Down the River* (1982), 57. Originally published as "A Walk in the Woods" (1980).

85. Interview with Jim Stiles.

86. K. Western, "'Big Bad' Abbey's Wild, Wild West," *Colorado Springs Sun*, May 16, 1984, 23.

87. Abbey, *Down the River* (1982), 7; interview with Tom Thompson.

88. Interview with Jim Stiles.

89. Lisa Garfield, "Abbey Talks about His Craft," *Indiana Gazette*, n.d. [Dec. 1976], n.p., courtesy of Howard and Iva Abbey.

90. E-mail interview correspondence with Tom Lynch, Feb. 12, 1999.

91. "Edward Abbey at Indiana," *New Growth Arts Review*, 1, no. 2 (Winter 1977): n.p.

92. Interview with Jack Macrae.

93. Interview with John Watta.

94. E-mail interview correspondence with Tom Lynch, Feb. 9, 1999.

95. Quoted in Jim Fergus, "The Anarchist's Progress," *Outside*, Nov. 1988, 125.

96. Also in Abbey Papers, box 2, folder 9.

97. Abbey, *The Fool's Progress* (1990 [1988]), 377, 460.

98. Carlson, "Edward Abbey," 60.

99. David Brower, *For Earth's Sake: The Life and Times of David Brower* (Salt Lake City: Peregrine Smith, 1990), 296.

100. "Abbey on the Rocks," *High Country News*, July 16, 1976, 14.

101. Abbey, "Joy, Shipmates, Joy!" (1976), 1.

102. Abbey Papers, box 8, folder 2.

103. Abbey Papers, box 7, folder 7.

104. Abbey, untitled list of suggestions for Jimmy Carter (1977).

105. Abbey, "Dear Jimmy" (1978).

106. Abbey, "Come On In" (1976), 6. Originally published as "Welcome to Canyonlands" (1975), but that earlier version does not include this memorable passage.

107. Abbey, *The Journey Home* (1977), xiii.

108. Abbey, "The BLOB Comes to Arizona" (1976), in *The Journey Home* (1977), 156, 150, 157, 153.

109. Wallace Stegner, *Los Angeles Times*, Apr. 17, 1977, 1; Larry McMurtry, *Washington Post*, Apr. 25, 1977; Ted Morgan, *New York Times Book Review*, July 31, 1977; and Larry Robinson, *Mountain Kisco, New York Patent Trader*, Apr. 30, 1977.

110. Priscilla L. Buckley, *National Review*, Feb. 17, 1978, 230.

111. Abbey, "White Water Ramblers" (1977), 90.

112. Abbey, "A Colorado River Journey," in *Beyond the Wall* (1984), 107. Originally published as *The Hidden Canyon* (1977).

113. Interview with Judith Saum.

114. Interviews with Karilyn (McElheney) Brodell and Laura Lee Houck.

115. Abbey, *Earth Apples* (1994), 85. See journal entries above, p. 111.

116. Interviews with Bob Greenspan and Karilyn (McElheney) Brodell.

117. Interview with Bob Greenspan.

118. Quoted in Carlson, "Edward Abbey," 64.

119. Interview with James Carrico, for example.

120. This medical source, who knew Abbey well, asked to remain anonymous.

121. Interview with Laura Lee Houck.

122. Hepworth, "The Poetry Center Interview," 49.

123. Abbey, *Earth Apples* (1994), 81.

124. Hepworth, "The Poetry Center Interview," 49.

125. Katie Lee, "His Heart to the Hawks," 14, courtesy of Katie Lee.

126. Loeffler, "Tributes," *Tucson Weekly*, Apr. 5–11, 1989, 2.

127. This source wishes to remain anonymous.

128. Abbey, *The Fool's Progress* (1990 [1988]), 184.

129. Norah Booth, "Tributes," *Tucson Weekly*, Apr. 5–11, 1989, 7.

130. Abbey Papers, box 25, folder 6.

131. Interview with Jim Stiles.

132. Interview with Laura Lee Houck.

CHAPTER 8. THE BARD OF TUCSON

1. Abbey Papers, box 5.

2. Abbey Papers, box 8, folder 4.

3. Kathleen Wieck, "Edward Abbey: Nuclear Weapons Take 'All the Fun Out of War,'" *Colorado Daily*, n.d., n.p., courtesy of Howard and Iva Abbey.

4. Peter Kobel, "Edward Abbey: 'War Horse, Wild Horse,'" *Albuquerque Journal*, Sept. 5, 1980, B1.

5. Interviews with Edward S. Twining and Donn Rawlings.

6. Abbey, "One Man's Nuclear War" (1979), 18.

7. Abbey Papers, box 2, folder 2.

8. Abbey, letter to Clarence D. Stephenson, Apr. 18, 1979, courtesy of Mr. Stephenson. Stephenson did list Paul and Mildred as well as their parents and all five of their children, in his *Biographical Sketches of Noted Citizens, Past and Present*, vol. 4 of *Indiana County, 175th Anniversary History* (Indiana, Pa., 1983).

9. Abbey Papers, box 2, folder 2.

10. Abbey, "Yes, There Is a Home, Pa." (1979).

11. Abbey Papers, box 2, folder 2.

12. Abbey, *The Journey Home* (1977), xiii.

13. Abbey, "Watching the Birds: The Windhover," in *Down the River* (1982), 54–55. Originally published as "Flights of Reincarnation" (1978).

14. Buddy Mays, "The Environment of a Writer," *New Mexico Magazine*, Nov. 1978, 39; Buddy Mays, "Happy Drifters in an Arizona Fire Tower," *Grit*, Dec. 10, 1978, 40; Buddy Mays, "Novelist in a Fire Tower" *Empire* (Sunday magazine of the *Denver Post*), Mar. 25, 1979, 12; and Doug Biggers, "From Abbey's Tower," *Tucson's Mountain Newsreal*, Sept. 1979, 6.

15. Interview with Laura Lee Houck.

16. Kevin Dahl, "Tributes," *Tucson Weekly*, Apr. 5–11, 1989, 4–5.

17. Abbey, "Coda," in *Abbey's Road* (1979), 191.

18. Abbey, "Abbey on McGuane" (1979); "Thomas McGuane replies," *Mariah/Outside*, Dec. 1979/Jan. 1980, 4.

19. Interview with John De Puy by author, and interview with Jack Loeffler by Eric Temple, Apr. 1992, in *Edward Abbey: A Voice in the Wilderness* (1993 video).

20. Abbey, "Down the Tatshenshini: Notes from a Cold River" (1979).

21. Jim Stiles, "Clarke Abbey: Gentle Voice of Defiance," *Canyon Country Zephyr*, June–July 1998, 16–17.

22. Stiles, "Clarke Abbey," 17.

23. Interview with Clarke Cartwright Abbey by Eric Temple, Apr. 1992, in *Edward Abbey: A Voice in the Wilderness* (1993 video).

24. Abbey, "Up the Creek with the Downriver Rowdies" (1979), 41, 46.

25. Stiles, "Clarke Abbey," 17.

26. Interview with Clarke Cartwright Abbey, Feb. 11, 1999.

27. Stiles, "Clarke Abbey," 17.

28. Interview with Clarke Cartwright Abbey, Feb. 11, 1999.

29. William Plummer, "Abbey's Desert Solecisms," *TWA Ambassador*, Nov. 1982, 33.

30. Alan Harrington, "Tributes," *Tucson Weekly*, Apr. 5–11, 1989, 8.

31. Interview with Donn Rawlings and James Hepworth.

32. Interview with Dave Foreman.

33. Interview with Katie Lee.

34. Interview with Malcolm Brown.

35. Interview with Bob Greenspan.

36. Interview with John De Puy.

37. Stiles, "Clarke Abbey," 17.

38. Abbey, "My 40 Years as a Grand Canyoneer" (1984), in *One Life at a Time, Please* (1988), 125; interview with Clarke Cartwright Abbey, Feb. 11, 1999.

39. Quoted in David Solheim and Rob Levin, "The *Bloomsbury Review* Interview," in Hepworth and McNamee, eds., *Resist Much, Obey Little* (1996), 141, 153–54.

40. Barry Lopez, "Meeting Ed Abbey" (1985), in Hepworth and McNamee, eds., *Resist Much, Obey Little* (1996), 99.

41. John Tallmadge, *Meeting the Tree of Life: A Teacher's Path* (Salt Lake City: University of Utah Press, 1997), 105, 107.

42. Interview with Terry Tempest Williams by Eric Temple, Apr. 1992, in *Edward Abbey: A Voice in the Wilderness* (1993 video).

43. Terry Tempest Williams, "A Eulogy for Edward Abbey. Arches National Park. May 20, 1989" (1990), reprinted in Williams, *An Unspoken Hunger: Stories from the Field* (New York: Vintage/Random House, 1994), 73–78.

44. *Kirkus Reviews*, May 1, 1979, 2; Ray Murphy, *Boston Globe*, June 28, 1979, 44.

45. John Leonard, *New York Times*, June 19, 1979; Lucinda Franks, *New York Times Book Review*, Aug. 5, 1979, 9, 21.

46. Abbey, "Abbey's Road" (1979); reply by Franks, *New York Times Book Review*, Oct. 7, 1979, 45.

47. John Russell, *New York Times Book Review*, Nov. 25, 1979, 92.

48. Abbey, *Desert Images* (1979), in *Beyond the Wall* (1984), 92.

49. Abbey, *Desert Solitaire* (1988 [1968]), 89–92.

50. Abbey, "Art: Ceremonies in the Sand. Painting the Myths and Legends of the Navajo" (1986).

51. Abbey, *Desert Images* (1979), in *Beyond the Wall* (1984), 93.

52. Abbey, *Desert Solitaire* (1988 [1968]), 194. However, SueEllen Campbell has a point when she notes that Abbey made no mention in *Desert Solitaire* of the Ute tribe still living near Arches, in her "Foreword II" to Peter Quigley, ed., *Coyote in the Maze: Tracking Edward Abbey in a World of Words* (Salt Lake City: University of Utah Press, 1998), 42.

53. Abbey, "Footrace in the Desert," in *Down the River* (1982), 189, 193. Originally published as "Casting Shadows in the Desert" (1980).

54. Abbey, review of Krammer, *The Second Long Walk* (1981).

55. Sue Legrand, letter to the editor, *New York Times Book Review*, Apr. 19, 1981, 29.

56. Abbey Papers, box 7, folder 7.

57. Abbey, "Memories of an Indian Childhood" (1977), 95.

58. Quoted in James Hepworth, et al., "Literature of the Southwest Interview" (1985), in Hepworth and McNamee, eds., *Resist Much, Obey Little* (1996), 128.

59. Abbey, "Floating," in *Down the River* (1982), 237. Originally published as "Floating: The River of the Mind" (1980).

60. Alan Cheuse, *Los Angeles Times*, Oct. 22, 1980, V10; John D. Berry, *Washington Post*, Nov. 11, 1980, B9; and Les Standiford, *El Paso Times*, Mar. 22, 1981, n.p.

61. Quoted in Mike Ives, "Southwest's Literary Subversive has Natural Dislike of Progress," *Arizona Republic*, Feb. 16, 1980, B20.

62. Rik Scarce, *Eco-Warriors: Understanding the Radical Environmental Movement* (Chicago: Noble Press, 1990), 58.

63. Zakin, *Coyotes and Town Dogs*, 70, 133.

64. Interview with Dave Foreman by Eric Temple, Apr. 1992, in *Edward Abbey: A Voice in the Wilderness* (1993 video).

65. Interview with Dave Foreman by author.

66. Sarah Hoover, "'Monkey Wrench Gang' Behind Burgled Bulbs," *Daily Camera* (Boulder, Colo.), Mar. 19, 1980, 1.

67. Scarce, *Eco-Warriors*, 62.

68. Dave Foreman, *Confessions of an Eco-Warrior* (New York: Harmony, 1991), 16.

69. Scarce, *Eco-Warriors*, 62.

70. Manes, *Green Rage*, 76.

71. Hal K. Rothman, *The Greening of a Nation? Environmentalism in the United States since 1945* (New York: Harcourt Brace, 1998), 178, 180.

72. Interview with Dave Foreman by author.

73. Quoted in Manes, *Green Rage*, 6.

74. Quoted in Scarce, *Eco-Warriors*, 58.

75. *The Cracking of Glen Canyon Dam* (Earth Image Films, 1981).

76. Zakin, *Coyotes and Town Dogs*, 151.

77. Interview with Jim Stiles; Foreman, *Confessions of an Eco-Warrior*, 22.

78. Abbey, "Down the River with Henry Thoreau" (1981), in *Down the River* (1982), 33.

79. Abbey Papers, box 7, folder 7.

80. Professor Ann Ronald kindly summarized Abbey's postcard in a written communication to me of June 2000.

81. Robert Houston, "Tributes," *Tucson Weekly*, Apr. 5–11, 1989, 4.

82. Ann Ronald, e-mail to me of Sept. 6, 2000.

83. Interview with Don Congdon.

84. E-mail interview correspondence with Louis Hieb.

85. Tom Miller, "Fighting the Good Fight: Tucson's Literary Troika—Bill Eastlake, Ed Abbey, and Alan Harrington—Remembered," *Tucson Monthly*, Jan. 1998, 59.

86. Interview with Richard Shelton.

87. Interview with Leslie Marmon Silko.

88. Abbey Papers, box 5.

89. Quoted in Solheim and Levin, "The *Bloomsbury Review* Interview," 146.

90. Abbey Papers, box 8, folder 6.

91. Quoted in H. G. Laetz, "Abbey Speaks in Gallagher," *Wildcat* (University of Arizona), Apr. 1980, n.p.

92. Abbey's record of appointments, kindly supplied to me by the University of Arizona's Office of Human Resources.

93. Nancy Mairs, "597ax" (1985), in Hepworth and McNamee, eds., *Resist Much, Obey Little* (1996), 62.

94. Alan Harrington, "Tributes," *Tucson Weekly*, Apr. 5–11, 1989, 8.

95. Interview with Robert Houston.

96. Interview with Katherine Miller.

97. Interview with James Hepworth.

98. Steven Schwartz, "Editor's Circle," *Colorado Review* 13, no. 2 (Spring/Summer 1986): 5.

99. Interview with Karilyn (McElheney) Brodell.

100. Written interview correspondence with Peter Wild, Nov. 8, 1998.

101. Schwartz, "Editor's Circle," 7–8.

102. Robert C. Baird, "Tributes," *Tucson Weekly*, Apr. 5–11, 1989, 9.

103. E-mail interview correspondence with Rod Kessler.

104. Schwartz, "Editor's Circle," 5.

105. John G. Mitchell, "The Howling Last Stand," *Rocky Mountain Magazine*, May/June 1981, 48–49, 52.

106. Interview with James Hepworth.

107. Mairs, "597ax," 65, 68.

108. Schwartz, "Editor's Circle," 6.

109. James R. Hepworth, "*Canis Lupus Amorus Lunaticum*," in Hepworth and McNamee, eds., *Resist Much, Obey Little* (1996), 124–25.

110. Interview with James Hepworth.

111. Nancy Mairs, "Tributes," *Tucson Weekly*, Apr. 5–11, 1989, 8.

112. Mairs, "597ax," 66.

113. Quoted in e-mail interview correspondence with Rod Kessler, Apr. 9, 1998.

114. Mairs, *Voice Lessons: On Becoming a Woman Writer* (Boston: Beacon Press, 1994), 106, 109.

115. Mairs, "597ax," 67–68.

116. Abbey, "Before the Boom: A Last Look at the Towns and Trails in the Shadow of MX" (1981).

117. Interview with James Hepworth.

118. Interview with Robert Houston.

119. Abbey, *Desert Solitaire* (1988 [1968]), 216.

120. Quoted in Steve Meissner, "Tucson Protestors Voice Disapproval," *Arizona Daily Star*, Sept. 16, 1981, 6A.

121. Tom Beal, "Interior Chief Takes Aim at Liberals," *Arizona Daily Star*, Sept. 16, 1981, 6A.

122. Paul Brinkley-Rogers, "Protest Fails to Wrench Visit," *Arizona Daily Star*, May 20, 1983, 2A.

123. Abbey, letter to the editor about James Watt (1984).

124. David Hatfield, "Oregonian Could Stoke Fires in TV News Ratings," *Arizona Daily Star*, Nov. 23, 1981, 4D.

125. Jerry Buck, "Ebsen is Crusty Rancher in 'Fire on the Mountain,'" *Arizona Daily Star*, Nov. 23, 1981, 5D.

126. I am thankful to Josh Randall for making it possible for me to see this television movie and for sharing his thoughts about it.

127. Russell Martin, "Writers of the Purple Sage," *New York Times Magazine*, Dec. 27, 1981, 18–22, 40–43.

128. Interview with Clarke Cartwright Abbey, Feb. 11, 1999.

129. Abbey, "A Walk in the Desert Hills," in *Beyond the Wall* (1984), 3.

130. Interview with Bill Hoy.

131. Mairs, "597ax," 65.

132. Tim Cahill, *New York Times Book Review*, May 30, 1982, 6.

133. Abbey, "Abbey Reviews Drabelle" (1982).

134. Abbey, *Down the River* (1982), 4.

135. Interview with Tom Thompson.

136. Zakin, *Coyotes and Town Dogs*, 216–17.

137. Manes, *Green Rage*, 82.

138. Abbey Papers, box 5.

139. Interview with James Carrico.

140. Interview with Donn Rawlings.

141. Jack Loeffler, "Edward Abbey, Anarchism, and the Environment," *Western American Literature* 28, no. 1 (May 1993): 44.

CHAPTER 9. "IF THERE'S ANYONE HERE I'VE FAILED TO INSULT . . ."

1. Abbey, letter of Jan. 15, 1983, courtesy of Ralph Newcomb.

2. Quoted in Paul Bousquet, "Western Winds Feature Interview: Edward Abbey," *Western Winds*, Winter 1987–88, 15.

3. Jim Stiles, "Clarke Abbey: Gentle Voice of Defiance," *Canyon Country Zephyr*, June–July 1998, 17.

4. Abbey, letter of Feb. 27, 1989, to John Nichols, Abbey Papers, box 3, folder 20.

5. Interview with Karilyn (McElheney) Brodell.

6. Interview with Clarke Cartwright Abbey by Eric Temple, in *Edward Abbey: A Voice in the Wilderness* (1993 video).

7. Abbey, *Earth Apples* (1994), 108.

8. Interview with Ann Woodin.

9. Quoted in Eric Temple, "An Interview with Ed Abbey," *Canyon Country Zephyr*, Apr./May 1999, 12.

10. Bowden, "The Voice Laughing in the Wilderness," *New Times*, Mar. 22–28, 1989, 4.

11. Abbey, *The Fool's Progress* (1990 [1988]), 25; see also *One Life at a Time, Please* (1988), 5.

12. Quoted in Temple, "An Interview with Ed Abbey," 12.

13. Abbey, "Holes in the Fence" (1981).

14. Abbey, "Amador" (1960) and *Hayduke Lives!* (1990).

15. Abbey, "Of Protest," in *Down the River* (1982), 109. Originally published as "One Man's Nuclear War" (1979).

16. Abbey, "Come On In," in *The Journey Home* (1977), 88. Originally published as "Welcome to Canyonlands" (1975), but Abbey added the lines from Zapata only in *The Journey Home*.

17. Interview with John De Puy.

18. "A Nice Fellow," *Arizona Daily Star*, Dec. 30, 1981, A6.

19. Abbey, "Immigration and Liberal Taboos," in *One Life at a Time, Please* (1988), 44. Originally published as "The Closing Door Policy" (1983).

20. Abbey, "Preliminary Remarks," *One Life at a Time, Please* (1988), 1, 2.

21. Abbey, "Abbey Strikes Back" (1983).

22. Tom Miller, "Fighting the Good Fight: Tucson's Literary Troika—Bill Eastlake, Ed Abbey, and Alan Harrington—Remembered," 61.

23. Abbey, letter to the editor about chauvinism and racism (1987).

24. "Author Wants Illegal Aliens Returned to 'Garbage Dumps,'" *Arizona Republic*, May 31, 1983, B2.

25. Abbey, "Another Taboo" (1985).

26. "Author Wants Illegal Aliens Returned to 'Garbage Dumps,'" B2.

27. Bowden, "Epilogue" to James Bishop, Jr., *Epitaph for a Desert Anarchist* (1994), 242.

28. Abbey, "A San Francisco Journal," in *One Life at a Time, Please* (1988), 70. Originally published as "Edward Abbey's Bay Area Journal" (1986).

29. Chris Limberis, "Grijalva Refuses to Accept Activism Award Named for Abbey," *Arizona Daily Star*, Apr. 21, 1990, 5B.

30. Interview with James Hepworth.

31. Luis Alberto Urrea, "Down the Highway with Edward Abbey," in Hepworth and McNamee, eds., *Resist Much, Obey Little* (1996), 44, 46.

32. Quoted in Jim Fergus, "The Anarchist's Progress," *Outside*, Nov. 1988, 126.

33. Thanks to Ralph Newcomb for sending me this letter.

34. Bruce Brown, *Washington Post Book World*, Apr. 1, 1984; Alice Hoffman, *New York Times Book Review*, Apr. 15, 1984.

35. Peter Carlson, "Edward Abbey," *People Weekly*, June 25, 1984, 58–65.

36. Interview with Jack Macrae.

37. *New York Times*, May 1, 1988.

38. Abbey was one of four IUP alumni ambassadors honored in April 1983. The *Indiana Gazette* did run a front-page photo on April 29 with the caption "IUP Ambassador—Writer Edward Abbey, back at IUP to be designated an IUP Alumni Association Ambassador this weekend is shown reading some of his materials and talking to a group of students last evening in Pratt Hall ("IUP Ambassador," *Indiana Gazette*, Apr. 29, 1983, 1). But then he got lost in front-page coverage of "Stewart/Indiana Delegation at Statue Unveiling," *Indiana Gazette*, May 2, 1983, 1; one has to turn to p. 15 of that issue to find passing mention of Abbey's honor, and even there Abbey is merely listed among fourteen other alumni, as a "distinguished author" ("Outstanding Alumni, Two Seniors Honored at IUP Alumni Weekend," *Indiana Gazette*, May 2, 1983, 15, 26). Abbey got one phrase about his visit; Stewart got most of the front page, before his visit had even occurred. The *Gazette* then featured almost daily coverage of Stewart from May 12 through his visit on May 20–21, including a full-page spread on a Stewart film festival ("Relive Jimmy's Classic Movie Career at Film Festival, *Indiana Gazette*, May 16, 1983, 13) and a 40-page insert on May 19 dedicated to his whole life ("It's a Wonderful Life," *Indiana Gazette*, May 19, 1983, insert 1–40). After all the fuss over Stewart finally began to quiet down, the *Gazette* did finally run three belated articles in the following month: "Faculty Names Abbey Alumni Ambassador" (p. 10) on June 14, and, on June 18, "Edward Abbey Returns Home" and "Paul and Mildred Keep Up the Pace" (n.p.).

39. Dave Petersen, "The Plowboy Interview—Edward Abbey: Slowing the Industrialization of Planet Earth," *Mother Earth News*, May/June 1984, 18.

40. Thanks to Jim Stiles for sending me these letters.

41. Abbey Papers, box 5.

42. Interview with Clarke Abbey, Feb. 11, 1999.

43. Zakin, *Coyotes and Town Dogs*, 185.

44. Abbey, "The Last Pork Chop" (1984), 54, 55, 52, 58.

45. Stiles, "Clarke Abbey," 16–17.

46. Interview with Tom Thompson.

47. Abbey, "Houseboat in the Desert" (1984), 89; "Lake Powell by Houseboat," in *One Life at a Time, Please* (1988), 86; and *Hayduke Lives!* (1990).

48. Carla McClain, "Relax, Dam. Ed Abbey's Pen Has Run Dry," *Tucson Citizen*, Nov. 17, 1983, magazine section, p. 6.

49. Interview with Thomas Lyon.

50. See Abbey, "The Great American Desert" (1977).

51. Katie Lee, "His Heart to the Hawks."

52. E-mail interview correspondence with Richard Marius.

53. Interview with Bill Hoy.

54. Quoted in Cindy Hubert, "Abbey Seeks to Be Read, Not Adored," *Arizona Daily Star*, Apr. 19, 1984, 10B.

55. Mike Ives, "Ed Abbey and the Way It Used to Be," *New Times* (Phoenix), May 30–June 5, 1984, 6.

56. E. J. Montini, "Desert Defender," *Arizona Republic*, May 1984 (n.d.), G4, courtesy of Howard and Iva Abbey.

57. Interview with Ernie Bulow.

58. Zakin, *Coyotes and Town Dogs*, 282; interview with Rod Mondt.

59. Bowden, "Epilogue" to Bishop, *Epitaph for a Desert Anarchist* (1994), 244.

60. Bowden, "Earth First! Wants More Wild People, Not Just Wilderness Areas," *Tucson Citizen*, Jan. 31, 1984, 2C.

61. Bowden, "Epilogue," 244.

62. Abbey, "Reading Updike" (1987), 410, and "The Folly Wise Men Commit" (1988), 9.

63. Interview with Charles Bowden.

64. Bowden, "Epilogue," 242.

65. Bowden, "Voice Laughing in the Wilderness," 4.

66. Abbey, *One Life at a Time, Please* (1988), 4.

67. Abbey Papers, box 2, folder 1.

68. Abbey Papers, box 5.

69. Plummer, "Abbey's Desert Solecisms," 33.

70. Abbey, "The Future of Sex," in *One Life at a Time, Please* (1988), 199. Originally published as "Sexual Evolution" (1984).

71. Quoted in Iver Peterson, "Laments for Loss of Beauty and Heritage Are Becoming a Familiar Sound in Tucson," *Arizona Daily Star*, June 10, 1984, 13I.

72. Judy Carlock, "Foe of Sprawl Asks to Rezone Desert Home," *Tucson Citizen*, June 28, 1984, 1A, 2A.

73. Vicki Kemper, "Desert Solitaire vs. Planning Ahead," *Arizona Daily Star*, June 30, 1984, 1B, and Kemper, "Supervisors Unlikely to Resolve Kino," *Arizona Daily Star*, Sept. 16, 1984, 3B.

74. Montini, "Desert Defender," G1.

75. Interview with Laura Lee Houck.

76. Quoted in Lyman Hafen, "An Evening with Edward Abbey," *Desert Southwest Supplement* 1, in *St. George Magazine* 4, no. 4 (Winter 1986–87): 15.

77. Interview with Clarke Abbey by Eric Temple, in *Edward Abbey: A Voice in the Wilderness* (1993 video).

78. Interview with Clarke Abbey, Feb. 11, 1999.

79. Abbey Papers, box 5, folder 6.

80. Abbey Papers, box 5, folder 6, and box 7, folder 7.

81. Abbey, "The Right to Arms" (1977), in *Abbey's Road* (1979), 132.

82. Interview with Ernie Bulow. See Abbey, *The Fool's Progress* (1990 [1988]), 136–43.

83. I thank Tom Thompson for copying this letter for me.

84. Pam Izakowitz, "Censorship Well-Camouflaged, Local Artists, Authors Tell ACLU Forum," *Arizona Daily Star*, Dec. 6, 1984, 3D.

85. Interview with Robert Houston.

86. Carlos A. Pedraza, "Edward Abbey Punctuates Lecture with Pistols," *Montana Kaimin*, Apr. 2, 1985, 1.

87. Abbey, "Preliminary Remarks," *One Life at a Time, Please* (1988), 3.

88. Abbey, "Free Speech: The Cowboy and His Cow," in *One Life at a Time, Please* (1988), 19. Originally published as "The Ungulate Jungle" (1985).

89. Bill Francis, "Noted Author Urges Taking Cattle Off Public Lands," *Idaho State Journal* (Pocatello), Mar. 28, 1985, B2.

90. Bill Hall, "Edward Abbey's Special Kind of 'Truth,'" *Lewiston Morning Tribune*, Apr. 4, 1985, 1D; Guy Trotter, "Edward Abbey Is Wrong—and Dangerous, Too," *Lewiston Morning Tribune*, n.d., n.p.; Bing Young, "Abbey, the 'Parasite,'" *Lewiston Morning Tribune*, Apr. 5, 1985, n.p.; Roy DeYoung, "In Defense of Abbey," *Lewiston Morning Tribune*, n.d., n.p., courtesy of Jim Hepworth.

91. Pedraza, "Edward Abbey Punctuates Lecture with Pistols," 1.

92. Larry Howell, "'Monkey-wrenching' Mentor," *Missoulian*, Apr. 2, 1985, n.p., Abbey Papers, box 25.

93. Abbey Papers, box 5.

94. Abbey, "Preliminary Remarks," *One Life at a Time, Please* (1988), 3.

95. In the next (Sept/Oct. 1985) issue of *Northern Lights*, C. R. McElligott noticed that Abbey's "statistics appear to be taken directly from Denzel Ferguson's book *Sacred Cows at the Public Trough*" (19).

96. Ralph Beer, letter to the editor, *Northern Lights*, Sept./Oct. 1985, 19.

97. Abbey, letter to the editor, *Northern Lights*, Sept./Oct. 1985, 22.

98. Ed Herschler, letter to the editor, *Harper's*, May 1986, 7.

99. Abbey, "Edward Abbey Replies" (1986), 71, 72.

100. E-mail interview correspondence with Penelope Reedy, Mar. 27, 1998.

101. Peter Vokac, James H. Gregovich, and Garth Flint, letters to the editor, *Arizona Daily Star*, Feb. 14, 1986, 12A.

102. Len Mattice, letter to the editor, *Arizona Daily Star*, Feb. 22, 1986, 16A. Arizona Beef Council Manager Barbara Gast added that "Abbey has grossly distorted the data," 16A. Phyllis Cortina, who had obviously never read Abbey's writings that opposed hunting, claimed that he "and his ilk" wanted to "go out and butcher that wildlife with high-powered guns and off-road vehicles. I find it very ironic and insidious how hunters pass themselves off as lovers of nature and the wildlife" (Feb. 23, 1986, 6A). In a full-length guest column, Alan Day plaintively wrote about his three-generation ranch as a good way of life, concluding that "we can make the West a better place for all forms of life if we don't get caught up in hysterical negativism" (Feb. 26, 1986, 11A).

103. Interview with Jay Dusard.

104. Abbey, letter of Jan. 6, 1986, to Jay Dusard, courtesy of Mr. Dusard.

105. University of Arizona Office of Human Relations.

106. Mairs, "Tributes," *Tucson Weekly*, Apr. 5–11, 1989, 8.

107. Abbey Papers, box 5.

108. Berry, "A Few Words in Favor of Edward Abbey," in Hepworth and McNamee, eds., *Resist Much, Obey Little* (1996), 5.

109. Abbey Papers, box 3, folder 16.

110. Interview with Robert Houston.

111. Peter Wild, "Edward Abbey: The Middle-Class Maverick," *New Mexico Humanities Review* 6 (Summer 1983): 15–23.

112. Gregory McNamee, "Edward Abbey, The Bard of Oracle—Scarlet 'A' on a Field of Black," *The Tucson Weekly*, Mar. 20–26, 1985, 4–5, reprinted in Hepworth and McNamee, eds., *Resist Much, Obey Little: Some Notes on Ed Abbey* (1985), and then as "Scarlet 'A' on a Field of Black" in Hepworth and McNamee, eds., *Resist Much, Obey Little: Remembering Ed Abbey* (1996), 18–30.

113. Interviews with Tom Thompson and Ann Woodin.

114. Abbey, *The Monkey Wrench Gang* (1991 [1975]), frontispiece photograph.

115. Abbey Papers, box 5.

116. Abbey, "A Writer's Credo," in *One Life at a Time, Please* (1988), 161–78.

117. Interview with Richard Shelton.

118. Interview with Ernie Bulow.

119. Interview with James Hepworth.

120. Abbey Papers, box 3, folder 16.

121. Norah Booth, "Tributes," *Tucson Weekly*, Apr. 5–11, 1989, 7.

122. Interview with Charles Bowden.

CHAPTER 10. ONE LIFE AT A TIME, PLEASE

1. Abbey, letter of Feb. 1988 to Susannah Abbey, Abbey Papers, box 3, folder 19.

2. Abbey Papers, box 5.

3. Jim Stiles, "Clarke Abbey: Gentle Voice of Defiance," *Canyon Country Zephyr*, June—July 1998, 16.

4. Thanks to Jim Stiles for sending me this undated note.

5. Interview with Laura Lee Houck.

6. Abbey, "TV Show: Out There in the Rocks," in *One Life at a Time, Please* (1988), 145, 143, 149.

7. Interview with Clarke Cartwright Abbey by Eric Temple, Apr. 1992, in *Edward Abbey: A Voice in the Wilderness* (1993 video).

8. Charles Bowden (text) and Jack W. Dykinga (photographs), *The Sonoran Desert* (New York: Harry N. Abrams, 1992), 159.

9. Bowden, "Tributes," *Tucson Weekly*, Apr. 5–11, 1989, 2.

10. Interview with Tom Thompson.

11. Quoted in Jim Fergus, "The Anarchist's Progress," *Outside*, Nov. 1988, 129.

12. Ken Sleight, "Abbey and Me," 9.

13. Interview with Ken Sleight, Dec. 10, 1998.

14. Aaron Abbey, "An Ancient Affair," *Playboy*, Feb. 1988, 64–66, 145.

15. Interview with Clarke Abbey, Feb. 11, 1999.

16. Terry Tempest Williams, "A Eulogy for Edward Abbey. Arches National Park. May 20, 1989" (1990), in Williams, *An Unspoken Hunger: Stories from the Field* (New York: Vintage/Random House, 1994), 76.

17. Carmen Ramos Chandler, "Environmental Group Urges 'Negative Growth,'" *Arizona Daily Star*, Feb. 7, 1986, 5B.

18. Bowden, "Tributes."

19. Interview with Charles Bowden.

20. Abbey, "Eco-Defense," in *One Life at a Time, Please* (1988), 31–32. Originally published as "Forward!" (1984).

21. Interview with Dave Foreman.

22. Interview with Rod Mondt.

23. Manes, *Green Rage*, 20–21.

24. Abbey, "A Reply to Schmookler on Anarchy" (1986).

25. Abbey, letter to the editor about chauvinism and racism (1987).

26. Advertisement for *One Life at a Time, Please*, in the *Earth First! Journal*, Aug. 1, 1988, 33.

27. Interview with Dave Foreman.

28. Abbey, *Hayduke Lives!* (1990), 188.

29. Ibid., 202, 205.

30. Abbey, "Stewardship Versus Wilderness" (1988); Berry, "My Answer to Edward Abbey," *Earth First Journal*, Feb. 1988, 33.

31. Interview with Wendell Berry.

32. Abbey, "Abbey on Books—and Gurus" (1988).

33. Abbey, *Desert Solitaire* (1988 [1968]), x, xi.

34. Abbey Papers, box 5.

35. Abbey, *One Life at a Time, Please* (1988), 3.

36. Abbey, "A San Francisco Journal," in *One Life at a Time, Please* (1988), 59, 71. Originally published as "Edward Abbey's Bay Area Journal" (1986).

37. Quoted in Paul Bousquet, "Western Winds Feature Interview: Edward Abbey," *Western Winds*, Winter 1987–88, 15.

38. Abbey, "A San Francisco Journal," in *One Life at a Time, Please* (1988), 63, 71, 80.

39. Abbey, *The Fool's Progress* (1990 [1988]), 221.

40. Abbey Papers, box 4, folder 1.

41. Abbey Papers, box 4, folder 6.

42. Abbey Papers, box 17, folder 2, p. 23, and box 17, folder 3, p. 71.

43. In his journal entries about *The Fool's Progress*, Abbey wrote of "brother Will who, like Wendell Berry, keeps alive and functioning the old farm back in Home" and "Will Lightcap as Wendell Berry" (Abbey Papers, box 5, folder 5).

44. Abbey Papers, box 4, folders 8 and 9.

45. Abbey Papers, box 5, folder 1.

46. Interview with Nancy Abbey.

47. Abbey Papers, box 5, folder 2.

48. Abbey Papers, box 3, folder 10.

49. Abbey Papers, box 7, folder 2.

50. Abbey, *The Fool's Progress* (1990 [1988]), 263–90.

51. Abbey Papers, box 5, folder 4.

52. Abbey Papers, box 13, folder 1, p. 1.

53. Unlike the Jewish New Yorker with whom he shared the initials of his name, Morton Bildad, Malcolm Brown was a Presbyterian from New England and, though he was a devotee of Eastern religions and had become emaciated during his stay in India, he certainly never took it as far as the fictional Bildad.

54. Interview with Clarke Cartwright Abbey by Eric Temple, Apr. 1992, in *Edward Abbey: A Voice in the Wilderness* (1993 video).

55. Howard Abbey, written communication to me of Aug. 2000.

56. Abbey, *The Fool's Progress* (1990 [1988]), 188.

57. Jim Dougherty recorded Paul Abbey remembering, as late as 1990, "Had a few close calls. I was cutting the head of a strip job, a couple of miles up here. And I cut a big red oak one day, and the tree went down. . . . Knocked me on my ass. The blood gushing out of there. I tried to stop the blood and then I got to thinking, I better get to the truck. Lay here and bleed to death, they'd have a hard time finding me. So I got to the truck, and I had an undershirt and I stopped the bleeding."

58. Abbey, *The Fool's Progress* (1990 [1988]), 321–22.

59. Abbey Papers, box 5.

60. Macrae in Abbey, *The Serpents of Paradise* (1995), 270–71.

61. Abbey Papers, box 3, folder 17.

62. Abbey Papers, box 27, audiotape 8.

63. Abbey, *The Fool's Progress* (1990 [1988]), 459, 460.

64. Abbey Papers, box 15, folder 1, p. 880; Abbey, *The Fool's Progress* (1990 [1988]), 498.

65. Abbey, *The Fool's Progress* (1990 [1988]), 101.

66. Abbey, *Confessions of a Barbarian* (1986), 16, 17.

67. Ibid., 17.

68. Abbey Papers, box 14, folder 1.

69. Quoted in David Petersen, "A Conversation with Edward Abbey," *Basin and Range*, Aug. 1985, 11. Abbey does refer to the "kitchen sink" in *The Fool's Progress* (1990 [1988]), 12.

70. Abbey, "From *The Rites of Spring*," in *Slumgullion Stew* (1984), 359.

71. Ibid., 356, and *The Fool's Progress* (1990 [1988]), 84.

72. Abbey, "From *The Rites of Spring*," in *Slumgullion Stew* (1984), 359, and *The Fool's Progress* (1990 [1988]), 86.

73. Abbey Papers, box 5.

74. Abbey Papers, box 3, folder 18.

75. Interview with Donn Rawlings.

76. Gregory McNamee, "A Desert Anarchist's Legacy," *Tucson Weekly*, Mar. 25, 1999, accessed in Sept. 2000 at http://www.tucsonweekly.com/tw/03-25-99/feat.htm.

77. Interview with Donn Rawlings.

78. Gregory McNamee, "A Desert Anarchist's Legacy."

79. Quoted in Abbey, *The Serpents of Paradise* (1995), 270.

80. Ibid., 270, 271.

81. Ibid., 271.

82. Abbey Papers, box 5.

83. Quoted in Mary Ellin Barrett, "Edward Abbey, Novelist Whose Time Is Now," *USA Weekend* magazine, Aug. 26–28, 1988, 4.

84. E. A. Mares, *Santa Fe Reporter*, Nov. 23–29, 1988, 27; John Murray, *Bloomsbury Review*, Mar./Apr. 1989, 10, 12; *Chronicles: A Magazine of American Culture*, Feb. 1989, 36; Howard Coale, *New York Times Book Review*, Dec. 18, 1988; Ed Marston, *National Review*, Feb. 10, 1989, 60.

85. Interview with Thomas Lyon.

86. Abbey Papers, box 3, folder 20.

87. See, for example, the notices of *Desert Solitaire* (1988 [1968]) in the *New York Times*, May 8, 1988; *Bloomsbury Review*, July/Aug. 1988; and Paul W. Rea, "Abbey's Country," *Journal of the Southwest* 31 (Summer 1989), where he declared that it "remains his best book" (265).

88. Randy Dykhuis, *Library Journal*, Feb. 1, 1988, 66; Bill McKibben, *New York Review of Books*, Aug. 18, 1988, 42; Abbey, letter to the editor responding to Bill McKibben's review (1988).

89. Abbey Papers, box 3, folder 18.

90. Interview with Edward Hoagland.

91. Quoted in David Streitfeld, "Book Report: Gone Fishin' Instead," *Washington Post Book World*, Nov. 15, 1987, 15.

92. Abbey, "River of No Return," in *One Life at a Time, Please* (1988), 107.

93. Russell Martin, *A Story That Stands Like a Dam: Glen Canyon and the Struggle for the Soul of the West* (New York: Henry Holt, 1989), 330.

94. Interviews with Donn Rawlings and Rod Mondt.

95. Abbey, "The Secret of the Green Mask" (1989).

96. E-mail interview correspondence with Mark Klett.

97. Sharon Santus, "Edward Abbey Returns Home," *Indiana Gazette*, June 18, 1983, 20, and Lyman Hafen, "An Evening with Edward Abbey," *Desert Southwest Supplement* 1, in *St. George Magazine* 4, no. 4 (Winter 1986–87): 14.

98. Thanks to Jay Dusard for sending me these letters.

99. Abbey, "Abbey Interrogates Abbey: An Exercise in Existential Angst" (1988).

100. Quoted in Zakin, *Coyotes and Town Dogs*, 184.

101. Abbey Papers, box 22, folder 3.

102. Abbey Papers, box 3, folder 12.

103. Abbey, "Wolfe and Tolstoy" (1988).

104. Abbey, introduction to *The Land of Little Rain* (1988), x, xi—xii.

105. Barbara Kingsolver, "Tributes," *Tucson Weekly*, Apr. 5–11, 1989, 6.

106. Abbey Papers, box 5.

107. Abbey, *Hayduke Lives!* (1990), opening list of thanks.

108. Interview with William T. Abbey, Aug. 27, 1998.

109. Interview with Howard Abbey and William T. Abbey, Oct. 18, 1995.

110. Letter from Bill Abbey to Ed Abbey, Dec. 27, 1987, Abbey Papers, box 1, folder 8; interview with Bill Abbey, Aug. 27, 1998.

111. Abbey, *The Fool's Progress* (1990 [1988]), 507.

112. Interviews with Ralph Newcomb, Karilyn McElheney Brodell, Bob Greenspan, Jim Stiles, and Ken Sanders.

113. Quoted in David Quammen, "Bagpipes for Ed," *Outside*, June 1989, 29.

114. Abbey, "Introduction to Bill Hoy" (1990), iii.

115. Bowden, "The Voice Laughing in the Wilderness," *New Times*, Mar. 22–28, 1989, 14.

116. Interview with Robert Houston.

117. Interview with Rod Mondt.

118. Abbey Papers, box 3, folder 20.

119. Interview with Dave Foreman.

120. Loeffler, "Strolling Along the Edge of Mortality," 31.

121. Jonathan Waterman, "Ed Abbey's Journey Home," *Backpacker*, Oct. 1989, 12.

CHAPTER 11. CONCLUSION

1. Interview with Don Congdon.

2. David Kipen, "West-Side Stories: Readers Rank the 20th Century's Best Nonfiction This Side of the Rockies," *San Francisco Chronicle*, May 27, 1999, n.p. Thanks to Nancy Abbey and Bill Abbey for sharing this article.

3. "Edward Abbey: Uncompromising 'Troublemaker' Pulled No Punches," *Arizona Daily Star*, Mar. 16, 1989, 14A.

4. "A Celebration of Edward Abbey," *Tucson Weekly*, Apr. 5–11, 1989; "Author Dies in Tucson," *Indiana Gazette*, Mar. 15, 1989, 1, 4.

5. Zakin, *Coyotes and Town Dogs*, 54.

6. Peacock, "Counting Sheep," in *Counting Sheep: Twenty Ways of Seeing Desert Bighorn*, edited by Gary Paul Nabhan (Tucson: University of Arizona Press, 1993), 98.

7. Edward Hoagland, "Edward Abbey: Standing Tough in the Desert," *New York Times Book Review*, May 7, 1989, 45.

8. Doug Peacock, "Desert Solitary," *Audubon* 100, no. 2 (Mar./Apr. 1998): 92–98.

9. Interview with Douglas Peacock.

10. Interview with Robert Houston.

11. Interview with Laura Lee Houck.

12. Gregory McNamee, "Saying Adios to Ed," in Hepworth and McNamee, eds., *Resist Much, Obey Little* (1996), 224.

13. Howard Abbey, written communication to me of Aug. 2000.

14. Bowden, "Epilogue" to Bishop, *Epitaph for a Desert Anarchist*, 240.

15. Interview with Charles Bowden.

16. Interview with Donn Rawlings.

17. Interview with Laura Lee Houck.

18. Interview with Ken Sanders by Eric Temple, in *Edward Abbey: A Voice in the Wilderness* (1993 video).

19. Interview with Jim Stiles.

20. Printed invitation to "A JOURNEY HOME: A sunrise memorial service for Edward Abbey." Thanks to Jay Dusard for sending me his copy.

21. Abbey, *Desert Solitaire* (1971 [1968]), xii.

22. McNamee, "Saying Adios to Ed," 224.

23. Interviews with Jim Stiles and John De Puy.

24. Stephen Trimble, "Abbey Felt a Passion for the Desert," *Milwaukee Journal*, Aug. 6, 1989, 3H.

25. Interviews with Gregory McNamee and Ernie Bulow.

26. Bob Sipchen, "In Desert Solitude, Faithful Pay Tribute to the Abbey Myth," *Los Angeles Times*, May 22, 1989, 2, 1.

27. Ken Sleight, "A Letter to Ed Abbey," *Canyon Country Zephyr* (July 1989), reprinted in "Eulogy to Edward Abbey," 7.

28. *Journal of Energy, Natural Resources, and Environmental Law* 11, no. 1 (1990): 7–9; C. L. Rawlins, "Elegy for Edward Abbey," in Hepworth and McNamee, eds., *Resist Much, Obey Little* (1996), 251–52.

29. *Journal of Energy, Natural Resources, and Environmental Law* 11, no. 1 (1990): 9–13.

30. Ibid., 14–15.

31. Ibid., 18–20.

32. Ibid., 24, 26.

33. Ibid., 28.

34. Abbey, "Best of the West: A Morality in One Short Act," Abbey Papers, box 25, folder 6.

35. Sipchen, "In Desert Solitude," 2.

36. Interview with Jim Stiles.

37. Interview with Karilyn (McElheney) Brodell.

38. Brighid Kelly, "Celebrating Abbey's Inspiration," *Aspen Times*, May 25, 1989, 7A.

39. Paul Andersen, "Aspen's Tribute to Abbey," *Aspen Times*, June 1, 1989, 27B.

40. Zakin, *Coyotes and Town Dogs*, 315.

41. Interview with Dave Foreman.

42. Quoted in Eric Volante, "FBI Tracked Abbey for 20-year Span," *Arizona Daily Star*, June 25, 1989, 2A.

43. Zakin, *Coyotes and Town Dogs*, 439.

44. Donna Seaman, *ALA Booklist*, Apr. 15, 1990; Nov. 15, 1989.

45. Charles Bowden, *Los Angeles Times Book Review*, Jan. 7, 1990, 13.

46. Grace Lichtenstein, *Washington Post*, Jan. 28, 1990, n.p.

47. Gwen Shaffer, "Novel Security Measures," *Philadelphia City Paper*, Oct. 18–25, 2001, http://www.citypaper.net/articles/101801/news.godfrey.shtml.

48. Abbey Papers, box 5.

49. Abbey, letter of Dec. 14, 1981, to Morton Kamins, Abbey Papers, box 3, folder 13.

50. Tim Sandlin, *New York Times Book Review*, Dec. 11, 1994, 11.

51. In *Confessions of a Barbarian*, editor David Petersen writes: "One considerable problem has been the difficulty of identifying all the many names Ed mentions as he goes along," many of which "can be identified only in context—for example, 'college friends'" (xii). The problem is that such guesswork sometimes leads him astray, as when he misidentifies "Popejoy and

Smith [more college friends]" (119), actually the University of New Mexico president and dean who fired Abbey and shut down *The Thunderbird* in 1951, and similarly "Stabley" (Rhodes Stabley, English Department chairperson and Abbey's professor at Indiana State Teachers College in 1947) as one of his "childhood friends" (188). Petersen incorrectly cites, for example, Abbey's high school graduation year as 1944 (3); claims that his first wife, Jean, had left Edinburgh by early November 1951 (3–4); misidentifies the "Judy" who called Abbey in the Albuquerque hospital in April 1960 as Judy Pepper (166), who in fact was a New Jersey teenager at the time and did not meet Abbey until over four years later; and misprints the date of "the night of the police riot at the Democratic convention in Chicago," in Abbey's entry remembering his daughter Susie's birth at the same time, as "1969" (260) instead of 1968 as Abbey had correctly written.

52. Hepworth, "The Poetry Center Interview" (1985), in Hepworth and McNamee, eds., *Resist Much, Obey Little* (1996), 49.

53. In "Love Letter," for example, Abbey had described flowers that "all are blazing up in yellow"—which became simply "all blazing yellow" in *Earth Apples* (1994), 39. In "The Gift," Abbey's lines "We waited, waited, while / our hearts withered in the heat" were printed as "We waited, while our hearts / withered in the heat" (40), with conjunctions added and punctuation deleted elsewhere in that poem. The word "much" was deleted from Abbey's line in "The Dry Season" describing how the wind was "today blowing much harder," and the published poem omitted his last two lines: "What can a man do? / What is a man supposed to do?" In "American Picnic" (96), individual words were added, deleted, and re-ordered, with some of the line divisions changed. I am thankful to Louis Hieb, formerly of the University of New Mexico and University of Arizona libraries, for pointing out these discrepancies.

54. Frank Allen, *Library Journal*, Aug. 1994, 90.

55. Bishop omits, for example, Abbey's migratory boyhood residences, his school career in Indiana County from 1934 until the end of 1947, his job with the Geological Survey during 1952–53, his two terms at Stanford studying with Wallace Stegner (1957–58), his stint as a newspaper editor in Taos during 1959–60, his semester teaching at Western Carolina University (1968), his seasons working at Organ Pipe Cactus National Monument (1968–70) and a great many other federal wilderness sites such as Glacier National Park (1975), his relationship with Ingrid Eisenstadter (beginning in 1970), his year-round position at Aravaipa Canyon (1972–74), the details of his life in Moab (1974–78) and Tucson (1971–74, 1978–89), the particulars of his dealings with Earth First! (1980–89), and many other major parts of Abbey's career.

56. In his undocumented book, Bishop claimed that Abbey was born in Home (xi). A photograph that is actually of Bill, Nancy, Iva, Mildred, and Ed Abbey—at John Abbey's funeral in 1987–was captioned by Bishop as "Brother Johnny Abbey, sister Nancy, a friend, and mother Mildred, 1986." Bishop mistakenly asserted that Mildred Abbey died in 1987 (56).

57. Bishop, *Epitaph for a Desert Anarchist*, 114. As further examples, Bishop had Abbey head west to the University of New Mexico in 1947 (66, 79), marry Jean "Schmechal" (88), work at "newspaper reporting . . . in Taos" in the early 1950s (88), marry Rita Deanin in December 1952 (91), collect his master's degree in 1956 (xi), first meet William Eastlake inaccurately and vaguely "in the 1950s" (25), marry Judy Pepper in August 1965 (115), work at Canyonlands National Park in 1966 (95), write *Black Sun* after Judy's death (155), marry Renée Downing in 1973 (119), meet Clarke Cartwright in 1978 (68), and, finally, die of pancreatitis (5, 43).

58. In early 2001, the "Abbeyweb" listserv was busily posting at abbeyweb@utsidan .se, and the elaborate "Abbey's Web" site was at http://www.abbeyweb.net. See Christer Lindh, "Weaving Abbey's Web," which appeared in *Arid Lands Newsletter* 38, and then at http://www .abbeyweb.net/articles/weaving-aw/index.html.

59. Abbey, *A Voice Crying in the Wilderness* (1990), 6. Originally published as *Vox Clamantis in Deserto* (1989).

60. "Ed Abbey's Truck Auctioned at SUWA Fund Raiser," Abbey's Web, accessed in Sept. 2000 at http://www.abbeyweb.net/edtruck/index.html.

61. "Redford Honors Activist," *Honolulu Star-Bulletin*, Oct. 1, 1996, n.p. The Abbey historical marker subsequently appeared on the World Wide Web at http://www.abbeyweb.net/marker.html.

62. Terry Tempest Williams "Edward Abbey," *Outside*, Oct. 1997, 140.

63. See Jerry Ignasewski, "Abbey Gave Us Words to Live By," *Arizona Republic*, Mar. 4, 1999, *The Rep* magazine, 2; Julie Newberg, "Abbey's Road," *Arizona Republic*, Mar. 4, 1999, *The Rep* magazine, 54–55; Steve Yozwiak, "Legacy on the Land: Environmentalists Still Follow Author Abbey's Call to Action," *Arizona Republic*, Mar. 7, 1999, E1–E4; Tricia Wasbotten Parker, "The Famous Mr. Ed," *New Times* (Phoenix), Mar. 11–17, 1999, 42; and Rhonda Bodfield, "Controversial Environmentalist Abbey Stirs Emotions 10 Years After His Death," *Arizona Daily Star*, Mar. 13, 1999, 1B–2B.

64. Lesley Hazleton, "Arguing with a Ghost in Yosemite," *New York Times*, May 11, 1997, 37.

65. See, for example, Todd Wilkinson, "In a Battle over Cattle, Both Sides Await Grazing Ruling," *Christian Science Monitor*, May 1, 2000, 2.

66. Morton Kamins, "Son of the Desert," *Gallery* 12, no. 4 (Apr. 1984): 102.

67. Abbey, "Free Speech: The Cowboy and His Cow," in *One Life at a Time, Please* (1988), 9.

68. Quoted in Eric Temple, "An Interview with Ed Abbey," *Canyon Country Zephyr*, Apr./May 1999, 12.

69. Abbey, "A Writer's Credo," in *One Life at a Time, Please* (1988), 174.

70. Abbey, *A Voice Crying in the Wilderness* (1990), 53.

71. Abbey, "Return to Yosemite," in *The Journey Home* (1977), 145.

72. Abbey, "A Writer's Credo," 177. One of those friends was Jack Loeffler, whose memoir *Adventures with Ed: A Portrait of Abbey* (Albuquerque: University of New Mexico Press, 2002) appeared after the publication of my book. It contains some lively stories but also a number of errors. Loeffler claims that Abbey was born in Home (pp. 3, 11), and that he knew Abbey for "more than two decades" (3), when by all appearances, even though Loeffler never dates it, they met slightly less than twenty years before Abbey's death. He combines Abbey's Swiss great-grandfather and his grandfather who moved to Creekside into one person (11), calls *Appalachian Wilderness* just *Appalachia* (113), and credits Abbey's infamous *Thunderbird* cover quotation to Voltaire (36) rather than Diderot, and the Arizona novel that Abbey reviewed, *Fade Out*, to Virginia Woolf rather than Douglas Woolf (67). Loeffler misdates Abbey's one LSD trip (88), claims that Abbey spoke at the University of Utah (instead of Utah State) on the first Earth Day in 1970 (96), states that he fell in love with Renée when she was seventeen (109) rather than sixteen, and misses some of his many jobs and geographical moves.

73. Berry, "A Few Words in Favor of Edward Abbey," in Hepworth and McNamee, eds., *Resist Much, Obey Little* (1996), 5; Nancy Abbey, quoted in Temple, *Edward Abbey: A Voice in the Wilderness* (1993 video).

74. Abbey, *Desert Solitaire* (1988 [1968]), 194.

75. Quoted in Bonnie Kime Scott, *Joyce and Feminism* (Bloomington: Indiana University Press, 1984), 117.

76. Frank O'Connor, foreword to his *Stories* (New York: Vintage, 1956), vii. Thanks to Ruth Sherry for locating this quotation for me.

Bibliography

PUBLICATIONS BY EDWARD ABBEY

The following is a chronological list of Abbey's publications, alphabetized under each year, with the many reprintings (and his audiorecordings) of individual books and essays included with the first appearance of each publication. It cannot include every item that Abbey ever published; doubtlessly there are other letters to the editor, reprinted excerpts in textbooks, and such that I have not located. But it is as extensive as I could make it. Limited to Abbey's own publications, it does not include (except for Abbey's 1988 self-interview in the *Whole Earth Review*) interviews with Abbey, many of which are cited in my notes. The first version of every publication is not always the preferable one, and thus in my notes I cite, for example, the 1985 edition of *The Monkey Wrench Gang* (1975) and the 1990 edition of *The Fool's Progress* (1988)—both of which include chapters not included in the first editions—and the revised 1988 edition of *Desert Solitaire* (1968).

1941
"America and the Future." *Marion Center [Pennsylvania] Independent*, December, n.p.

1942
"Another Patriot." Untitled Marion Center High School student compendium. Spring: n.p.

1944
"Abbey Walks 8,000 Miles by Adroit Use of Thumb." *High Arrow* (Indiana, Pennsylvania, High School), November 8: 4.
"Ambitious Aching Arm Aids Abbey's Ambulation." *High Arrow*, November 22: 2.
"Vagabond Lover Has Drink with Governor." *High Arrow*, December 20: 2.

1945
"Abbey Finally Arrives Home." *High Arrow*, May 10: 3.
"Abbey Hitch-Hikes to Jail After Viewing Blue Pacific." *High Arrow*, April 11: 3.
"Abbey on Last Lap Towards Home." *High Arrow*, April 25: 2, 4.
"Cougar Toys with Gastronomic Picture of Footsore Ed Abbey." *High Arrow*, March 28: 2.

1947
"A New Variation on an Old Theme." *The Indiana GI Writes, 1946–47*, edited and foreword by Rhodes R. Stabley. Indiana, Pa.: Indiana State Teachers College English Department. September: 5–6.

1948
"A Fugue in Time." *The Indiana Student Writes*, edited and foreword by Rhodes R. Stabley. Indiana, Pa.: Indiana State Teachers College English Department. December: 9–11.
"Moonlight Neurosis." Poem. *The Thunderbird* (Univ. of New Mexico) 4, no. 1 (September): 16.

1949

"The Analysis of Visions." Poem. *The Thunderbird* 5, no. 2 (December): 13.

"Arabesque." Poem. *The Thunderbird* 5, no. 2 (December): 12.

"Fugue." Poem. *The Thunderbird* 5, no. 2 (December): 13.

1950

"Marching through Moscow," "Near the Beach on a Stormy Evening," and "The Astronaut's Report." Poems. *Selections* (Univ. of New Mexico) 1, no. 1 (January): 14, 15, 19.

"String Quartet." Poem. *The Thunderbird* 5, no. 3 (March): 28–29.

"Turntable Talk: Dialogue on Duty." Review essay on classical music albums. *The Thunderbird* 5, no. 4 (May): 20–23.

"Turntable Talk: The Primitive in Music." Review essay on classical music albums. *The Thunderbird* 5, no. 3 (March): 14–16.

1951

"Some Implications of Anarchy." Short story. *The Thunderbird* 6, no. 3 (March): 3–9.

"A Specific Target." Letter about *Thunderbird* closure. *New Mexico Daily Lobo*, April 10: 2.

1954

Jonathan Troy. New York: Dodd, Mead. Brief excerpt reprinted in *Slumgullion Stew* (1984).

1956

The Brave Cowboy: An Old Tale in a New Time. New York: Dodd, Mead. Reprinted, London: Eyre and Spottiswoode/Western Book Club, 1957. Reprinted, New York: Pocketbooks, 1957. Revised edition (with corrections and a preface by Abbey), New York: Ballantine, 1971. Reprinted (with introduction by Neal Lambert), Albuquerque: University of New Mexico Press, 1977. Chapter 4 reprinted in *Southwest Fiction*, edited by Max Apple. New York: Bantam, 1980, 1–8. Reprinted, New York: Avon, 1982 (mass market) and 1992 (trade). New York: William Morrow, 1992. Chapter 11 reprinted in *Slumgullion Stew* (1984), 6–14. Reprinted (with introduction by Kirk Douglas), Salt Lake City: Dream Garden Press and Santa Barbara: Santa Teresa Press, 1993. Chapter 14 reprinted in *The Serpents of Paradise* (1995), 72–84.

1957

"Underground in Amerigo." *Accent: A Quarterly of New Literature* 17, no. 1 (Winter): 21–29. Reprinted, *Inside/Outside Southwest Magazine* (Durango), March/April 1999: 24–27.

1959

"Anarchism and the Morality of Violence." Master's thesis, Univ. of New Mexico, August 5.

"Christmas Greetings." *El Crepusculo de la Libertad: Weekly Newspaper of Taos County* (published by Craig S. Vincent), December 24: 2.

"The Eyes of Power Watch Taos County." *El Crepusculo de la Libertad*, October 29: 2.

"In Defense of Cottonwoods." *El Crepusculo de la Libertad*, October 29: 2.

"Let's Call a Town Meeting." *El Crepusculo de la Libertad*, December 17: 2.

Review of *Fade Out*, by Douglas Woolf. *New Mexico Quarterly* 29, no. 3 (Autumn): 383–84.

Review of *Watt*, by Samuel Beckett. *New Mexico Quarterly* 29, no. 3 (Autumn): 381–83.

"The Smell of Fraud." *El Crepusculo de la Libertad*, November 12: 2.

"TV Without Hucksterism." *El Crepusculo de la Libertad*, November 26: 2.

"Way Down South in Gallup." *El Crepusculo de la Libertad*, November 19: 2.

"What Is 'News' —? And What's Fair?" *El Crepusculo de la Libertad*, December 3: 2.

1960

"Amador." *Between Worlds: An International Magazine of Creativity* (Inter American University, Puerto Rico; published in Colorado) 1, no. 1 (Summer): 138–52. Excerpt from the unpublished New Mexico novel "Black Sun."

"For Future Beauty." *El Crepusculo de la Libertad*, January 14: 2.

"God Bless America—Let's Save Some of It." *El Crepusculo de la Libertad*, January 21: 2.

1962

Fire on the Mountain. New York: Dial. Reprinted, London: Eyre and Spottiswoode, 1963. Reprinted, Garden City, N.J.: Doubleday, 1963. Reprinted, New York: Ballantine, 1971. Reprinted (with introduction by Gerald Haslam), Albuquerque: University of New Mexico Press, 1978. Reprinted, New York: Avon, 1982 (mass market) and 1992 (trade). Excerpt from chapter 2 reprinted in *Slumgullion Stew* (1984), 16–23. Reprinted (paperback), New York: William Morrow, 1992.

1966

"Snake Dance." *Sage* (Fall 1966/Winter 1967): 22–25. Reprinted as "The Serpents of Paradise" in *Desert Solitaire* (1968). Reprinted in *The Wilderness Reader*, edited by Frank Bergon. New York: New American Library, 1980, 334–46. Reprinted in *The Norton Book of Nature Writing*, edited by Robert Finch and John Elder. New York: Norton, 1990, 679–92. Reprinted in *Reading the Environment*, edited by Melissa Walker. New York: Norton, 1994, 52–57.

"The West's Land of Surprises, Some Terrible." *Harper's* 233, no. 1399 (December): 98–99, 104–7. Reprinted and condensed as "West's Land of Surprises." *Reader's Digest* 90 (February 1967): 61–65. Reprinted as part of "Water" chapter in *Desert Solitaire* (1968). *Digest* version reprinted in *Reader's Digest, 50th Anniversary Treasury: A Selection of the Best of 50 years from The Reader's Digest*. Pleasantville, New York: Reader's Digest Association, 1972, 59–64. Full "Water" chapter reprinted in *Late Harvest: Rural American Writing by Edward Abbey, Wendell Berry, Carolyn Chute, Annie Dillard, William Gass, Garrison Keillor, Bobbie Ann Mason, Wallace Stegner, and Others*, edited by David R. Pichaske. New York: Paragon House, 1991, 377–90.

1967

"A Day in the Life of a Park Ranger." *Sage* (Fall): 10–17. Reprinted as part of "Cliffrose and Bayonets" chapter and also the first page of *Desert Solitaire* (1968).

"Death Valley Notebook." *Sage* (Spring): 14–19. Reprinted as "Death Valley" in *The Journey Home* (1977), 71–84. Reprinted in *Slumgullion Stew* (1984), 118–30. Excerpt reprinted in *The Sierra Club Desert Reader*, edited by Gregory McNamee. San Francisco: Sierra Club Books, 1995, 29–33.

"A River to Explore." *Sage* (Summer): 13–19. Reprinted as "Down the River with Major Powell" in *The Journey Home* (1977), 189–202.

"Sunflowers." *Western Review* 4 (Summer): 17–24. Excerpt from the unpublished New Mexico novel "Black Sun."

1968

Desert Solitaire: A Season in the Wilderness. New York: McGraw Hill. Reprinted (paperback), New York: Simon and Schuster, 1970. Reprinted (mass market), New York: Ballantine, 1971. Reprinted, Salt Lake City: Peregrine Smith, 1981. Excerpts from five chapters ("Cowboys," "The Moon-Eyed Horse," "Havasu," "The Dead Man at Grandview Point," and "Bedrock and Paradox") reprinted in *Slumgullion Stew* (1984), 26–

80. "The Dead Man at Grandview Point" and "Cowboys" recorded on *Freedom and Wilderness* (1987, sides 1 and 2, respectively). Revised edition (as *Desert Solitaire*, without subtitle), Tucson: University of Arizona Press, 1988. Reprinted, New York: Touchstone/Simon and Schuster, 1990. Original introduction, "The First Morning," "The Serpents of Paradise," "Polemic: Industrial Tourism and the National Parks," and "Tukuhnikivats, the Island in the Desert" reprinted in *The Serpents of Paradise* (1995), 95–97, 98–103, 104–9, 110–27, and 128–40.

"Glen Canyon Dam." *Sage* (Summer/Fall): 26–32. Reprinted as "The Damnation of a Canyon" in *Slickrock* (1971), 64–69. Reprinted in *Beyond the Wall* (1984), 95–104. Reprinted in *The Serpents of Paradise* (1995), 311–17.

"In Brief: Muchos Papeles." Reviews of *The Allagash*, by Lew Dietz; *Horse of a Different Color: Reminiscences of a Kansas Drover*, by Ralph Moody; *Jesse Stuart's Kentucky*, by Mary Washington Clarke; *Everyman's Eden: A History of California*, by Ralph J. Roske; *Earl Morris and Southwestern Archaeology*, by Florence C. Lister and Robert H. Lister; *Roads to Empire: The Dramatic Conquest of the American West*, by Harry Sinclair Drago; *The Apache Frontier*, by Max. L. Moorhead; *The Story of Adirondac*, by Arthur H. Masten; *Dranberry Lake from Wilderness to Adirondack Park*, edited by Albert Fowler; and *Rushton and His Times in American Canoeing*, by Atwood Manley. *New York Times Book Review*, October 27: 36, 38.

"Interview with Joseph Wood Krutch." *Sage* 2, no. 4 (Spring): 12–21. Reprinted and revised as "Preface" in Krutch, *The Great Chain of Life* (1956). Reprinted, Boston: Houghton Mifflin, 1978, v–xix. Reprinted as "Mr Krutch" in *One Life at a Time, Please* (1988), 179–93.

Review of *The Red Machines*, by F. D. Reeve. *New York Times Book Review*, May 26: 46.

"Running the Wild River." *Sage* 2, no. 3 (Winter): 2–8.

1969

"City of the Prophecies—A Hoboken Perspective." *Natural History* 78 (April): 24, 74–79. Reprinted as "Manhattan Twilight, Hoboken Night" in *The Journey Home* (1977), 89–101. Reprinted in *Slumgullion Stew* (1984), 131–42. Reprinted in *The Serpents of Paradise* (1995), 85–94.

"Escalante Canyon." *Natural History* 78, no. 9 (November): 58–63. Reprinted as "Fun and Games on the Escalante" in *Slickrock* (1971), 52–63.

"How to Save Our National Parks." *Field and Stream* 73 (March): 74, 105–14. Revised from "Polemic: Industrial Tourism and the National Parks" in *Desert Solitaire* (1968).

"Malcolm Brown: The Artist as Architect." *Sage* 3, no. 2 (Winter): 2–7.

"Of Cowboys, Indians and the Modern West." *Sage* 3, no. 2 (Winter): 28–31. Interview with William Eastlake. Published under the pseudonym Peter M. Kenyon.

"The Old West." Letter to the editor replying to an attack on his review of Stegner. *Arizona Daily Star*, August 18: B12.

Review of *A Betting Man and Other Stories*, by Brian Glanville. *New York Times Book Review*, October 19: 52.

Review of *Custer Died for Your Sins: An Indian Manifesto*, by Vine Deloria, Jr. *New York Times Book Review*, November 9: 46.

Review of *The Grand Colorado: The Story of a River and Its Canyons*, by T. H. Watkins and others, foreword by Wallace Stegner, photographs by Philip Hyde. *New York Times Book Review*, December 14: 10, 16.

Review of *The Inland Island*, by Josephine W. Johnson. *New York Times Book Review*, March 2: 8.

Review of *The Man Who Rediscovered America: A Biography of John Wesley Powell*, by John Upton Terrell. *New York Times Book Review*, October 5: 17.

Review of *The Sound of Mountain Water*, by Wallace Stegner. *New York Times Book Review*, June 8: 10.
Review of *The Varmints*, by Michael Frome; *Lost Wild America: The Story of Our Extinct and Vanishing Wildlife*, by Robert M. McClung; *America's Endangered Wildlife*, by George Laycock; *Animals in Danger*, by Frances and Dorothy Wood; and *Animals at Bay*, by Adrien Stoutenburg. *New York Times Book Review*, May 4: n.p.

1970

"Appalachian Pictures." *Audubon* 72 (September): 4–13. Reprinted from *Appalachian Wilderness* (1970). Reprinted as "Coming Home" in *MD Magazine* (August 1989): 38–45.
Appalachian Wilderness: The Great Smoky Mountains, by Eliot Porter (photographer) "with Natural and Human History by Edward Abbey." Epilogue by Harry Caudill. New York: Dutton. Reprinted, New York: Dutton, 1973. Reprinted, New York: Ballantine, 1973. Reprinted, New York: Chanticleer and Milan, Italy: Promontory, 1975. Excerpts reprinted in *Slumgullion Stew* (1984) as "Appalachia," 82–94. Reprinted (whole book), New York: Arrowood Press, 1988. "Appalachian Pictures" and "Appalachia, Goodbye" reprinted in *The Serpents of Paradise* (1995), 141–49 and 150–52.
"Hallelujah, on the Bum." *American West* 7 (July): 11–14. Reprinted in *The Journey Home* (1977), 1–11. Reprinted in *The Serpents of Paradise* (1995), 22–30.
"How to Live on This Planet Called Earth." *New York Times Book Review*, April 19: 2–3.
"Let Us Now Praise Mountain Lions." *Life* 68, no. 9 (March 13): 52B–58. Reprinted in *The Journey Home* (1977), 131–37. Reprinted as *In Praise of Mountain Lions: Original Praises by Edward Abbey and John Nichols*. Albuquerque: Albuquerque Sierra Club, 1984.
Review of *The Best American Short Stories 1970*, edited by Martha Foley and David Burnett. *New York Times Book Review*, August 30: 33.
Review of conservation books: *Wilderness Defender*, by Donald C. Swain; *Lost Heritage*, by Henry Savage, Jr.; *The Conservation Fraud*, by Charles Zurhorst; *The Environmental Handbook*, edited by Garrett De Bell; *A Question of Priorities*, by Edward Higbee; *The Environmental Crisis: Man's Struggle to Live with Himself*, edited by Harold W. Helfrich; *Challenge for Survival: Land, Air, and Water for Man in Megalopolis*, edited by Pierre Dansereau; *America's Changing Environment*, by Robert W. Patterson and Nathaniel Wollman; *Terracide: America's Destruction of Her Living Environment*, by Ron Linton; *Our Precarious Habitat*, by Melvin A. Bernarde; and *Conservation: Now or Never*, by Nicholas Roosevelt. *New York Times Book Review*, April 19: 2–3.
Review of *Where Is My Wandering Boy Tonight?* by David Wagoner. *New York Times Book Review*, November 22: 58.
"Short Stories: Auchincloss, Deck, Madden, and Others." Review of *Creased Samba and Other Stories*, by John Deck; *The Shadow Knows*, by David Madden; and *Second Chance: Tales of Two Generations*, by Louis Auchincloss. *New York Times Book Review*, August 30: 32.

1971

Black Sun. New York: Simon and Schuster. Reprinted as *Sunset Canyon*, London: Talmay, Franklin, 1971. Reprinted (under original title), Santa Barbara, Calif.: Capra, 1981. Reprinted, New York: Avon, 1982. Chapter 23 reprinted in *Slumgullion Stew* (1984), 96–99. Reprinted (whole novel), San Bernardino, Calif.: Borgo, 1989. Chapters 6 and 7 reprinted in *The Serpents of Paradise* (1995), 166–74. Reprinted (whole novel), Santa Barbara, Calif.: Capra, 1999.
"Canyonlands and Compromises." Excerpt from *Slickrock*. *Sierra Club Bulletin* 56, no. 1: 12. Reprinted in *Voices for the Earth: A Treasury of the Sierra Club Bulletin*, edited by Ann

Gilliam and introduced by Harold Gilliam. San Francisco: Sierra Club Books, 1979, 391–93.

"Living on the Last Whole Earth." Review of *Living on the Earth*, by Alicia Bay Laurel, and *The Last Whole Earth Catalog: Access to Tools*, edited by Stewart Brand. *Natural History* 80 (November): 84–88.

"The Park That Caught Urban Blight." *Life* 71 (September 3). Reprinted as "Return to Yosemite: Tree Fuzz vs. Freaks" in *The Journey Home* (1977), 138–45.

"Science with a Human Face?" *Wasatch Front* 58, no. 1 (Winter): 3–7. Reprinted in *Abbey's Road* (1979), 123–29. Reprinted in *Slumgullion Stew* (1984), 224–30.

Slickrock: The Canyon Country of Southeastern Utah. "Words by Edward Abbey. Photographs and commentary by Philip Hyde." New York: Scribner's and Sierra Club. Reprinted as *Slickrock: Endangered Canyons of the Southwest* (paperback), New York: Scribner's and Sierra Club, n.d. Excerpts, such as "Days and Nights in Old Pariah" and "How It Was," reprinted in *Beyond the Wall* (1984). Reprinted (whole book), Layton, Utah: Peregrine Smith, 1987.

1972

"Man and the Great Reef." *Audubon* 74 (January): 76–84, 86–89. Reprinted as "The Reef" in *Abbey's Road* (1979), 3–15. Reprinted in *A Thousand Leagues of Blue: The Sierra Club Book of the Pacific, a Literary Voyage*, edited by John A. Murray. San Francisco: Sierra Club Books, 1994, 203–17.

"On the Need for a Wilderness to Get Lost In." *New York Times*, August 28: L29. Combined with "Wilderness and Freedom" (1976) as "Freedom and Wilderness, Wilderness and Freedom" in *The Journey Home* (1977), 227–38. Recorded on *Freedom and Wilderness* (1987), side 4.

1973

Cactus Country. New York: Time-Life. Reprinted, New York: Time-Life, 1977. "The Ancient Dust" and "Down to the Sea of Cortez," reprinted in *Beyond the Wall* (1984).

"Great Overdone." Letter to the editor about Vietnam veterans. *Arizona Daily Star*, June 13, n.p.

"Merry Christmas, Pigs!" *Tucson Daily Citizen*, December 22: 3–4. Reprinted in *Abbey's Road* (1979), 138–41. Recorded on *Freedom and Wilderness* (1987), side 4.

Review of *So Far From Heaven*, by Richard Bradford. *New York Times Book Review*, October 14: 10.

"The Southwest: A Thirst for the Desert." In *Wilderness USA*. Washington, D.C.: National Geographic Society, 89–92, 101–16.

1974

"In Defense of Sheep." Letter to the editor on sexism. *Mountain Gazette* 28 (December): 33.

Letter to the editor defending his *Life* article on Yosemite. *Mountain Gazette* 24 (August): 36.

Letter to the editor attacking motors in the wilderness. *Moab Times-Independent*, Sept. 19: n.p.

Review of *Shelter*, edited by Lloyd Kahn. *Natural History* 83, no. 6 (June/July): 72–75.

"Shadows from the Big Woods." *Sierra Club Wilderness Calendar*. Reprinted in *The Journey Home* (1977), 223–26, and as the "Introduction" to *Sierra Club Wilderness Calender* (1984).

"A State Plan from Upstairs: It May Have Come From God, Or a Sharp Blow on the Head." *Arizona* 10 (March): 16–27. Reprinted as "God's Plan for the State of Utah" in *Mountain Gazette* 55 (March 1977): 10–13. Reprinted as "God's Plan for the State of Utah: A Revelation" in *The Journey Home* (1977), 102–13.

"Where's Tonto?" *Mountain Gazette* 28 (December): 5–7. Reprinted as "Strangers in the Night" chapter in *The Monkey Wrench Gang* (1975).

1975

"Desert Driving." *Mountain Gazette* 30 (February): 26–27. Revised as "Disorder and Early Sorrow" in *The Journey Home* (1977), 23–29.

"Dust: A Movie." *Not Man Apart*, September: 1–2. Reprinted in *The Journey Home* (1977), 239–42.

"Hardcase Survival Pinto Bean Sludge." In *John Keats's Porridge: Favorite Recipes of American Poets*, edited by Victoria McCabe and introduced by William Cole. Iowa City: University of Iowa Press, 21–22. Version reprinted within "My Friend Debris" in *Down the River* (1982), 224–25.

"The Lure of the Mountains." Introduction to *The Mountains of America: From Alaska to the Great Smokies*. New York: H. N. Abrams, 6–11. Reprinted, New York: Bonanza, 1981. Reprinted as "Mountain Music" in *The Journey Home* (1977), 209–22.

The Monkey Wrench Gang. New York: Lippincott. Reprinted, New York: William Morrow, 1976. Reprinted, London: Cannongate, 1978. Revised edition (illustrations by R. Crumb), Salt Lake City: Dream Garden Press, 1985. Reprinted, Salt Lake City: Dream Garden Press, 1990. Reprinted, Salt Lake City: Roaming the West, 1991. "The Wooden Shoe Conspiracy" and "The Raid at Comb Wash" reprinted in *The Serpents of Paradise* (1995), 219–32 and 233–54. Reprinted (whole novel), New York: HarperTrade, 2000.

Review of *The Forest Killers*, by Jack Shepherd; *The Southern Appalachians: A Wilderness Quest*, by Charlton Ogburn; and *Losing Ground*, by John G. Mitchell. *New York Times Book Review*, July 20: 6.

Review of *Reading the Rocks: A Guide to the Geologic Secrets of Canyons, Mesas, and Buttes of the American Southwest*, by David A. Rahm. *Mountain Gazette* 31 (March): 26.

Review of *Run, River, Run*, by Ann Zwinger, and *A River for the Living: The Hudson and Its People*, by Jack Hope. *New York Times Book Review*, October 12: 24.

Review of *Zen and the Art of Motorcycle Maintenance: An Inquiry into Values*, by Robert M. Pirsig. *New York Times Book Review*, March 30: 5.

"The Saga of Albert T. Husk." *Colorado Rocky Mountain West* 10 (March/April): 13–16, 38–41. Reprinted from "Rocks" chapter in *Desert Solitaire* (1968).

"The Second Rape of the West." *Playboy* 22 (December): 138, 194, 230–34. Revised and reprinted in *Aspen* 4, no. 33 (Fall 1977): 33, 52–54, and *The Journey Home* (1977), 158–88.

"Seldom Seen at Home." *Mountain Gazette* 36 (August): 8–9. Reprinted in *Slumgullion Stew* (1984), 102–6. Reprinted in *The Monkey Wrench Gang* (1985 revised edition), 221–24.

"Snow Canyon." *Audubon* 77, no. 4 (July): 2, 4, 9. Reprinted in *The Journey Home* (1977), 58–61.

"A Tale of the Sierra Madre." *Mountain Gazette* 35 (July): 10–17. Reprinted as "Sierra Madre" in *Abbey's Road* (1979): 81–97. Reprinted in *Slumgullion Stew* (1984), 201–18. Reprinted in *El Palacio: Magazine of the Museum of Mexico* 97, no. 3 (Summer/Fall 1992): 30–35, 58–63.

"Welcome to Canyonlands." Introduction to *Canyonlands Country: A Guidebook of the Four Corners Geological Society*, edited by James E. Fassett. N.p.: Four Corners Geological Society, iii. Revised as "Come On In" in *Plateau: The Magazine of the Museum of Northern Arizona* 49, no. 1 (Summer 1976): 3–5. Reprinted in *The Journey Home* (1977), 85–88. Recorded on *Freedom and Wilderness* (1987), side 1. Reprinted in *Desert Skin*, by Thomas Miller. Salt Lake City: University of Utah Press, 1994, 1–5.

1976

"Abbey's Road, Take the Other (Or Death Valley Acid)." *Mountain Gazette* 44 (April): 10–11. Reprinted as "Death Valley Junk" in *Abbey's Road* (1979), 170–75. Reprinted in *The Serpents of Paradise* (1995), 255–59.

"The BLOB Comes to Arizona." *New York Times*, May 16: 14, 28. Reprinted in *The Journey Home* (1977), 146–57.

"The Happiness Implosion." Letter to the editor criticizing Tom Wolfe. *Harper's* 253, no. 1516 (September): 6.

"Joy, Shipmates, Joy!" *High Country News* 8, no. 19 (September 24): 1, 4–5. Reprinted as "We Must Not Plan for Growth But Plan for War," in *Olé! The Tucson Daily Citizen Magazine*, November 20: 3–4.

Letter to the editor criticizing Jim Harrison's article "The Sporting Life." *Playboy* 23, no. 4 (April): 14.

"Notes from a Lookout Logbook." *Audubon* 78, no. 3 (May): 82–86, 105. Reprinted as "Fire Lookout: Numa Ridge" in *The Journey Home* (1977), 30–57. Reprinted in *The Great Bear: Contemporary Writings on the Grizzly*, edited by John A. Murray. Anchorage and Seattle: Alaska Northwest Books, 1992, 93–97.

"Nothing to Do." *New York Times Magazine*, August 15: sec. 6, p. 4.

Review of *Death Valley*, by George Laycock, and *Summit Lake: Four Seasons in the Sierras*, by Carl Heintze. *New York Times Book Review*, August 1: 16.

Review of *Woodswoman*, by Anne LaBastille; *A World of My Own*, by Mike Tomkies; and *The Year-Long Day*, by A. E. Maxwell and Ivar Ruud. *Natural History* 85 (November): 106–11.

"Telluride Blues: A Hatchet Job." *High Country News* 8, no. 21 (October 22). Reprinted, *Mountain Gazette* 51 (November): 12–17. Revised in *The Journey Home* (1977), 119–30. Reprinted in *Slumgullion Stew* (1984), 143–53.

"Walking." *Sierra Club Trail Calendar*. Reprinted in *The Journey Home* (1977), 203–5.

"Wilderness and Freedom." *Not Man Apart* 7 (July): 1–2, 8. Combined with "On the Need for a Wilderness to Get Lost In" (1972) as "Freedom and Wilderness, Wilderness and Freedom" in *The Journey Home* (1977), 227–38. Reprinted in *Earthworks: Ten Years on the Environmental Front*, edited by Mary Lou Van Deventer. San Francisco: Friends of the Earth, 1980, 87–92. Reprinted as "In Aravaipa Canyon, Face to Face with the Biggest Cat in the World" in *Defenders of Wildlife* (Washington, D.C.), June 1981: 14–15. Excerpt reprinted as "The Journey Home" in *The Earth Speaks: An Acclimatization Journal*, edited by Steve Van Matre and Bill Weiler. Greenville, West Virginia: Institute for Earth Education, 1983, 41–44. "Freedom and Wilderness, Wilderness and Freedom" recorded on *Freedom and Wilderness* (1987), side 4.

1977

"The Appalachian Trail, and Beyond: A Foreword." In *Appalachian Odyssey: Walking the Trail from Georgia to Maine*, by Steve Sherman and Julia Older. Brattleboro, Vermont: Stephen Greene Press, 1977, vii–x.

"The Crooked Wood." *Audubon* 77 (November): 24–27. Reprinted from *The Journey Home*, 206–8.

"Desert Island Solitaire." *Outside*, November: 56–63. Reprinted as "Isla Encantada: Six Days on a Desert Island" in *Backpacker* 5 (December 1977): 39–41. Reprinted as "A Desert Isle" in *Abbey's Road* (1979), 69–80. Reprinted in *Slumgullion Stew* (1984), 188–200.

"The Great American Desert." In *The Journey Home*, 12–22. Reprinted in part as "Foreword" to *A Sierra Club Naturalist's Guide to the Deserts of the Southwest*, by Peggy Larson with Lane Larson. San Francisco: Sierra Club Books, 1977, 7–9. Reprinted and condensed as "Desert Love Affair" in *Reader's Digest* 111 (October 1977). Reprinted in full as "The Great American Desert" in *Mariah* 3, no. 1 (February/March 1978): 18–24, 78–79. Reprinted in part as "Why Go into the Desert?" *Sierra* 64 (July 1979):

45. "The Great American Desert" reprinted in *Slumgullion Stew* (1984), 108–17; in *This Incomperable Lande: A Book of American Nature Writing*, edited by Thomas J. Lyon. Boston: Houghton Mifflin, 1989, 346–55; and in *The Literary West*, edited by Thomas J. Lyon. New York: Oxford University Press, 1999, 226–33.

The Hidden Canyon: A River Journey. Photography by John Blaustein, journal by Abbey, introduction by Martin Litton. New York: Viking (hardback) and Penguin (paperback). Text reprinted as "A Colorado River Journey" in *Beyond the Wall* (1984), 105–24. Reprinted in *The Serpents of Paradise* (1995), 272–86. Revised edition (whole book) as *The Hidden Canyon*. San Francisco: Chronicle Books, 1999.

The Journey Home: Some Words in Defense of the American West. Illustrations by Jim Stiles. New York: Dutton. Reprinted, New York: Penguin/Plume, 1991.

"Last Oasis." *Harper's* 254 (March): 8, 10. Reprinted as "Down There in the Rocks" in *Abbey's Road* (1979), 117–20. Reprinted in *Slumgullion Stew* (1984), 219–23. Recorded on *Freedom and Wilderness* (1987), side 2.

"Memories of an Indian Childhood." Review of *The Names: A Memoir*, by N. Scott Momaday. *Harper's* 254, no. 1521 (February): 94–95.

Review of *Desert Notes: Reflections in the Eye of a Raven*, by Barry Holstun Lopez. *Mountain Gazette* 54 (February): 34.

Review of *Land of Clear Light*, by Michael Jenkinson. *Western American Literature* 12, no. 2 (August): 149–50.

"The Right to Arms." *Playboy* 24 (January): 41. Reprinted in *Abbey's Road* (1979), 130–32. Reprinted in *The Redneck Review of Literature*, no. 15 (Fall 1988): 1–2.

Untitled list of suggestions for Jimmy Carter. Friends of the Earth's *Not Man Apart* 7, no. 2 (January): n.p.

"Voluntary Simplicity: Follow-up and Comment." *The CoEvolution Quarterly* 15 (Fall): 55.

"White Water Ramblers." *Playboy* 24, no. 8 (August): 88–90, 114, 167, 172–75. Reprinted in *Grand Canyon: An Anthology*, edited by Bruce Babbitt. Flagstaff: Northland Press, 1978, 203–18. Revised as part of *The Hidden Canyon* (1977) and as "A Colorado River Journey" in *Beyond the Wall* (1984), 105–24.

"The World of Anna Creek." *Mountain Gazette* 60 (August): 6–11. Reprinted as "Anna Creek" in *Abbey's Road* (1979), 16–32. Reprinted in *Slumgullion Stew* (1984), 156–73.

1978

"Back of Beyond: Out Back, Down Under and Into the Bush, Part III." *Mountain Gazette* 75 (November): 8–14. Reprinted as "Back of Beyond" in *Abbey's Road* (1979), 46–68.

"Dear Jimmy." Letter to the editor addressed to Jimmy Carter. *Not Man Apart* 8, no. 6 (April): n.p.

"Down Under, Out Back, and Into the Bush, Part II." *Mountain Gazette* 69 (May): 6–11. Reprinted as "The Outback" in *Abbey's Road* (1979), 33–45. Reprinted in *Slumgullion Stew* (1984), 174–87.

"Ed Abbey Would Prefer to Walk." *Outside*, July/August: 73–77. Reprinted as "A Walk in the Park" in *Abbey's Road* (1979), 107–16.

"Edward Abbey as Smokey the Cop." *Outside*, February: 44–47. Reprinted as "My Life as a P.I.G., or the True Adventures of Smokey the Cop" in *Abbey's Road* (1979), 147–57. Reprinted in *Out of the Noösphere—Adventure, Sports, Travel, and the Environment: The Best of Outside Magazine*. New York: Simon and Schuster, 1992, 232–37. Reprinted in *The Serpents of Paradise* (1995), 153–62.

"Flights of Reincarnation." *Outside*, November/December. Reprinted as "Watching the Birds: The Windhover" in *Down the River* (1982), 49–55. Reprinted in *Slumgullion Stew* (1984), 308–14. Recorded on *Freedom and Wilderness* (1987), side 3.

"God Bless America . . . Let's Save Some of It." *High Country News* 1 (May 19): 1, 4–5.

"Introductory Commentaries." In *Back Roads of Arizona*, by Earl Thollander. Flagstaff: Northland Press, 13, 45, 103, 127. Whole book reprinted as *Arizona's Scenic Byways*, 1979, same publisher and page numbers.

"The Journey Home." Letter to the editor about book review. *Outside*, January: 7–8.

Review of *Zen and the Art of Motorcycle Maintenance*, by Robert M. Pirsig. "Reviewed by Edward Abbey (former General Secretary, Velocipede Club, Winkleman, Arizona)." *Mountain Gazette* 74 (October): 23. Reprinted (with new introduction) as "Reviewing *Zen and the Art of Motorcycle Maintenance*" in *Down the River* (1982), 199–202.

"The Sorrows of Travel." *Harper's* 256 (February): 32–35. Revised in *Abbey's Road* (1979), 181–90. Reprinted in *Slumgullion Stew* (1984), 249–59.

"Treasure of the Canyon Country." In *Utah Wilderness Photography: An Exhibition*, curated by Greer Markle. Salt Lake City: Utah Arts Council.

1979

"Abbey on McGuane." Letter to the editor. *Mariah/Outside*, December 1979/January 1980: 4.

Abbey's Road. New York: Dutton. Reprinted, New York: Penguin/Plume, 1991.

"Abbey's Road." Letter to the editor about review of *Abbey's Road* by Lucinda Franks. *New York Times Book Review*, October 7: 45.

"Arizona Tomorrow." Excerpt from *Good News* (1980). *New Times* (Phoenix), July 4–10, 11–17, 18–24, and August 1–7: n.p.

Desert Images: An American Landscape. Text by Abbey, photographs by David Muench. New York: Harcourt, Brace, Jovanovich. Excerpts reprinted as "Desert Images" in *Beyond the Wall* (1984), 77–94. Reprinted, New York: Chanticleer/Gallery/W. H. Smith, 1986.

"Down the Tatshenshini: Notes from a Cold River." *Mariah/Outside*, December 1979/January 1980: 19–24, 66–67. Reprinted as "Notes from a Cold River" in *Down the River* (1982), 67–82. Reprinted in *Adventure Book II: 1000 Journeys to the Rivers, Lands and Seas of 7 Continents*, edited by Christine Kallen. Angels Camps, Calif.: Sobek's International Explorers Society, 1983, 66–87. Reprinted in *Outside*, October 1987 (special ten-year anniversary issue): 41–46, 140–42.

"Fire Lookout." In *Abbey's Road*, 176–80. Reprinted in *Slumgullion Stew* (1984), 243–48. Recorded on *Freedom and Wilderness* (1987), side 1. Reprinted in *The Uncommon Touch: Fiction and Poetry from the Stanford Writing Workshop*, edited by John L'Heureux. Palo Alto: Stanford Alumni Association, 1989, 1–4. Reprinted in *Go Tell It on the Mountain*, edited by Jackie Johnson Maughan. Mechanicsburg, Pa.: Stackpole Books, 1996, 1–6.

"Grow and Die." *Penthouse* 11 (September): 170–71.

"Guadalupe's Trails in Summer." *National Geographic* 156 (July): 134–41. Reprinted as "On the High Edge of Texas" in *Beyond the Wall* (1984), 125–36.

"In Defense of the Redneck." *Penthouse* 10 (April). Reprinted in *Abbey's Road*, 158–69. Reprinted in *Slumgullion Stew* (1984), 231–42. Reprinted in *The Redneck Review of Literature*, 12th annual (Spring 1987): 36–43. Recorded on *Freedom and Wilderness* (1987), side 3.

"Introduction." In *Pioneer Conservationists of Western America*, by Peter Wild. Missoula, Mont.: Mountain Press, xvi–xxiii. Reprinted as "The Conscience of the Conqueror" in *Abbey's Road*, 133–37.

"One Man's Nuclear War." *Harper's* 258 (March): 8–9, 16–18. Reprinted as "Of Protest" in *Down the River* (1982), 98–110. Reprinted in *Slumgullion Stew* (1984), 315–26.

"Preface: The Old Ruin Speaks." In *Headwaters: Tales of the Wilderness*, by Ash, Russell, Doog, and Del Rio. Covelo, Calif.: Island Press, 1979, i–iii.

"Relics in Repose: Meditations on a Ghost Town." *GEO* 1 (May 1979): 26–46. Reprinted as "Fool's Treasure" in *Down the River* (1982), 160–71.

"Up the Creek with the Downriver Rowdies." *Rocky Mountain Magazine* 1 (May): 40–47. Reprinted as "River Rats" in *Down the River* (1982), 175–87.

"Yes, There Is a Home, Pa." Letter to the editor. *Indiana Gazette*, August 24: 2.

1980

"Casting Shadows in the Desert." *Running*, November/December: 28–37. Reprinted as "Footrace in the Desert" in *Down the River* (1982), 188–98.

"Floating: The River of the Mind." *Rocky Mountain Magazine* 2 (April): 31–34. Reprinted as "Floating" in *Down the River* (1982), 230–39. Reprinted in *Slumgullion Stew* (1984), 344–53. Revised as "Every River I Touch Turns to Heartbreak" in *Environmental Action* 16, no. 7 (May/June 1985): 10.

"Game Remarks." Letter to the editor. *Rocky Mountain Magazine* 2 (March): 6.

Good News. New York: Dutton. Excerpt reprinted in *Slumgullion Stew* (1984), 262–70. Reprinted (whole novel), New York: Penguin/Plume, 1991. First two chapters reprinted in *The Serpents of Paradise* (1995), 287–97.

"Good News." *TriQuarterly* 48 (Spring): 273–95. From chapter one of *Good News.*

"Good News." *Tucson Weekly News* 1, no. 10 (March 26–April 1). From prologue to *Good News.*

"In the Canyon." *Outside*, February/March: 26–35. Reprinted in *Down the River* (1982), 144–48.

"A Walk in the Woods." Introduction to the *Sierra Club Wilderness Calendar*. Reprinted as "Meeting the Bear" in *Down the River* (1982), 56–60. Reprinted in *The Serpents of Paradise* (1995), 260–63.

1981

"Before the Boom: A Last Look at the Towns and Trails in the Shadow of MX." *Rolling Stone* 339 (March 19): 22–23. Reprinted as "MX" in *Down the River* (1982), 83–97.

Chapter 4 of *The Brave Cowboy* (1956), reprinted in *Southwest Fiction*, edited by Max Apple. New York: Bantam, 1–8.

"The Death of Empires, The Triumph of Trees." *Backpacker* 9 (August/September): 17. Reprinted as "Planting a Tree" in *Down the River* (1982), 61–63. Recorded on *Freedom and Wilderness* (1987), side 4.

"Down the River with Henry Thoreau." Introduction to *Walden*, by Henry David Thoreau. Salt Lake City: Gibbs M. Smith, ix–xli. Reprinted as "Encounters with Henry on Utah's Green River" in *High Country News* 13, no. 19 (October 2). Reprinted as "The Green River Dialogues: The Higher Laws, Lower Stirrings, and Midnight Visitations of Henry David Thoreau" in *Outside*, February/March 1982: 67–76. Reprinted as part of "Down the River with Henry Thoreau" in *Down the River* (1982), 13–60. Reprinted in *Slumgullion Stew* (1984), 272–307. Reprinted in *Words from the Land: Encounters with Natural History Writing*, edited and introduction by Stephen Trimble. Salt Lake City: Gibbs M. Smith/Peregrine Smith, 1988, 50–76. Reprinted in 1989 edition of *Words from the Land* with an added dedication to Abbey.

"Foreword." In *A River Runner's Guide to the History of the Grand Canyon*, by Kim Crumbo. N.p.: Johnson Books, v–vi.

"Holes in the Fence." Letter to the editor against Mexican immigration. *New York Review of Books*, December 18: 68.

"The Land of John DePuy." *Rocky Mountain Magazine* 3 (September/October): 72.

Review of *The Second Long Walk: The Navajo-Hopi Land Dispute*, by Jerry Krammer. *New York Times Book Review*, March 8: 13, 33.

"Waiting for the Fifth Card." *Rolling Stone* 359/360 (December 24): 66.

1982

"Abbey Reviews Drabelle." Letter to the editor about review of *Down the River*. *The Nation*, May 22: 608.

"The Bitter Journey." Letter to the editor. *Rocky Mountain Magazine* 4 (January/February): 8.

Down the River. Illustrations by Abbey. New York: Dutton. Reprinted, New York: Penguin/Plume, 1991.

"Ed Abbey Takes a Shot." Letter to the editor criticizing the contemporary West and the editorial direction of this magazine. *American West*, November/December: 8.

"In the Land of 'Laughing Waters.'" *New York Times*, January 3: sec. 10, p. 17. Reprinted as "Aravaipa Canyon" in *Down the River* (1982), 154–59. Reprinted in *The Serpents of Paradise* (1995), 264–68.

"My Friend Debris." *Bisbee Times*, February: 10–17. Reprinted in *Down the River*, 222–28. Reprinted in *Slumgullion Stew* (1984), 327–43.

Letter to the editor about the election. *Arizona Republic*, October 29: n.p.

Letter to the editor about immigration. *Arizona Daily Star*, May 22: n.p.

Letter to the editor about Tucson's growth. *Arizona Daily Star*, December 21: n.p.

"On Going Home Again." Review of *Recollected Essays 1965–1980* and *The Gift of Good Land*, by Wendell Berry. *Pacific Northwest*, January/February: 50.

"The Treasure of the Canyon Country." In *The Edward Abbey 1982 Western Wilderness Calendar*. Salt Lake City: Utah Wilderness Association and Dream Garden Press.

1983

"Abbey Strikes Back." Letter to the editor responding to Alfredo Gutierrez's criticism of "The Closing Door Policy." *New Times* (Phoenix), August 3–9: 3.

"Afterword." In *Everett Ruess: A Vagabond for Beauty*, by W. L. Rusho. Salt Lake City: Gibbs M. Smith/Peregrine Smith, 1983, 218. Reprinted as "A Sonnet for Everett Ruess" in *Earth Apples* (1994), 101.

"The Closing Door Policy." *New Times* (Phoenix), June 29–July 5: 8–9. Revised as "Immigration and Liberal Taboos" in *One Life at a Time, Please* (1988), 41–44. Reprinted in *The Serpents of Paradise* (1995), 373–76.

Letter to the editor about the film *Koyaanisqatsi*. *Arizona Daily Star*, October 4: n.p. Reprinted in the *High Country News*, December 26: 14.

Letter to the editor about James Bond movie *Octopussy*. *Arizona Daily Star*, June 27: n.p.

"One final paragraph of advice: Do not burn yourselves out." Excerpted from a speech. In *The Earth Speaks: An Acclimatization Journal*, edited by Steve Van Matre and Bill Weiler. Greenville, West Virginia: Institute for Earth Education, 1983, 57.

"Property vs. People?" Letter to the editor about the distinction between sabotage and terrorism. *Reason*, June: n.p.

"William Eastlake: *Para Mi Amigo.*" *The Review of Contemporary Fiction* 3, no. 1: 18–20.

1984

"Arizona's Future: How Big Is Big Enough?" *Arizona Daily Star*, January 29: C1. Reprinted as "Arizona: How Big Is Big Enough?" in *One Life at a Time, Please* (1988), 20–24.

Beyond the Wall: Essays from the Outside. New York: Holt, Rinehart, and Winston. Includes excerpts from *Slickrock* (1971) and chapters from *Desert Images* (1979).

"Coda: Cape Solitude." Excerpt from *Abbey's Road* (1979), 191–98. Reprinted in *Writers of the Purple Sage: An Anthology of Recent Western Writing*, edited and introduced by Russell Martin and Marc Barasch. New York: Viking, 141–49.

"Desert Images." Reprinted from *Desert Images* (1979), chapters entitled "Sand Dunes," "Scarce

Waters," "Wild Flowers," and "Images on Rock," in *Beyond the Wall,* 77–94. Reprinted in *The Serpents of Paradise* (1995), 298–310.

"Down the River." In *River Reflections: An Anthology,* edited by Verne Huser. Charlotte, N.C.: East Woods Press, 222–31. Reprinted from "Running the San Juan" in *Down the River* (1982), 125–43.

"Earth First! Proposal: More Land for Fewer People." *Tucson Citizen,* February 7: 9A. Reprinted as "Earth First! Proposes 6 Million National Forest Wilderness in Arizona, by Ed Abbey and Pablo Desierto" in *Earth First! Journal* 4, no. 4 (May 1): 8.

"Foreword." In *The Unnatural Enemy,* by Vance Bourjaily. Tucson: University of Arizona Press, vii–xii. Reprinted as "Hunting in Earnest." *Harper's* 276, no. 1653 (February 1988): 42–44. Shortened version reprinted as "Blood Sport" in *One Life at a Time, Please* (1988), 33–40. Reprinted in *A Hunter's Heart: Honest Essays on Blood Sport,* edited by David Petersen. New York: Henry Holt, 1996, 11–16.

"Forward!" In *Earth First! Journal* 5, no. 2 (December 21): 25–26. Reprinted in *Ecodefense: A Field Guide to Monkeywrenching,* by Dave Foreman. Tucson: Earth First!/Ned Ludd, 1985, 3–5. Reprinted as "Eco-Defense" in *One Life at a Time, Please* (1988), 29–32. Reprinted in *The Serpents of Paradise* (1995), 370–72. Reprinted in *Literature and the Environment: A Reader on Nature and Culture,* edited by Lorraine Anderson, Scott Slovic, and John P. O'Grady. New York: Longman, 1999, 345–47.

"Grease for the Mill: Remembering the Late John Gardner." Review of Gardner's *On Becoming a Novelist. Bloomsbury Review,* February/March: 31.

"Houseboat in the Desert." *New York Times Magazine,* October 7: sec. 6, pp. 89, 94–96. Reprinted as "Lake Powell by Houseboat" in *One Life at a Time, Please* (1988), 85–93.

"How It Was." Excerpt from *Slickrock* (1971), 18–31. Reprinted in *Beyond the Wall,* 51–67. Reprinted in *Southwest Stories: Tales from the Desert,* edited by John Miller and Genevieve Morgan. San Francisco: Chronicle Books, 1993, 166–85. Reprinted in *The Serpents of Paradise* (1995), 31–43.

"Introduction." *Sierra Club Wilderness Calendar.*

"The Last Pork Chop." *Outside,* March: 51–58. Reprinted as "Gather at the River" in *Beyond the Wall,* 163–203. Reprinted in *The Serpents of Paradise* (1995), 318–47. Reprinted (under original title) in *The Best of Outside: The First 20 Years.* New York: Random/Villard, 1997, 13–33.

Letter to the editor on James Watt. *Earth First! Journal* (February 2): 3.

Letter to the editor on Robinson Jeffers and Garret Hardin. *Earth First! Journal* (Nov. 1): 2.

Letters to the editor (a reply and a prank). *High Country News* 23 January: 13.

"My 40 Years as a Grand Canyoneer." *National Geographic Traveler* 1, no. 1 (Spring): 19. Reprinted as "Forty Years as a Canyoneer" in *One Life at a Time, Please* (1988), 123–26.

"My Recipe for a Long and Healthy Life?" *Environmental Action,* November/December: 18.

"Right to Own Guns." Letter to the editor. *Arizona Daily Star,* July 14: n.p.

"The Rio Grande: All Vigor Spent." *Great Rivers of the World,* edited by Margaret Sedeen. Washington, D.C.: National Geographic Society, 429–34. Reprinted as "Round River Rendezvous: The Rio Grande, October 1984" in *One Life at a Time, Please* (1988), 150–67.

"Sexual Evolution . . . Edward Abbey on the Future of Sex." Review of *Femininity,* by Susan Brownmiller, and *Outrageous Acts and Everyday Rebellions,* by Gloria Steinem. *Bloomsbury Review,* September: 7, 10. Reprinted as "The Future of Sex: A Reaction to a Pair of Books—Brownmiller's *Femininity* and Steinem's *Outrageous Acts*" in *One Life at a Time, Please* (1988), 199–205.

Slumgullion Stew: An Edward Abbey Reader. Edited and illustrated by Abbey. New York: Dutton.

Reprinted as *The Best of Edward Abbey*. San Francisco: Sierra Club, 1988. "From *The Rites of Spring* (novel-in-progress)," 355–83, revised as chapter 4, "April 1942: The Rites of Spring," in *The Fool's Progress* (1988), 84–101.

"This Antique and Empty Land." *GEO* 6 (April): 50–59, 114. Expanded as "A Walk in the Desert Hills" in *Beyond the Wall*, 1–49.

1985

"Another Taboo." Letter to the editor criticizing notions of prejudice. *New York Times Book Review*, March 3: 24.

"Big Bend: Desert Rough.and Tumble." *National Geographic Traveler* 2, no. 3 (Autumn): 94–107. Reprinted as "Big Bend" in *One Life at a Time, Please* (1988), 127–41.

Foreword to *Wild Horses and Sacred Cows*, by Richard Symanski. Flagstaff, Ariz.: Northland Press, ix–xi. Reprinted as "Wild Horses" in *One Life at a Time, Please* (1988), 45–48.

"Forward." In *The Rain and the Fire and the Will of God*, by Donald Wetzel. 2nd edition. Sag Harbor, N.Y.: Second Chance Press, n.p.

Letter to the editor about donating his royalties to Earth First! *Earth First! Journal* (May 1): 3.

Letter to the editor about technology. *Bloomsbury Review*, April: n.p.

Letter to the editor replying to attacks on "The Ungulate Jungle." *Northern Lights*, September/October: 22.

"Little Bighorn: Small Episode in a Large Tragedy." Review of *Son of the Morning Star: Custer and the Little Bighorn*, by Evan S. Connell. *Sunday Sun-Times* (Chicago), January 13: 24.

Review of *A Cloak of Light: Writing My Life*, by Wright Morris. *New York Times Book Review*, February 17: 9–10.

"The Ungulate Jungle." *Northern Lights* July/August: 7–14. Revised as "Even Bad Guys Wear White Hats: Cowboys, Ranchers, and the Ruin of the West" in *Harper's* 271 (January 1986): 51–55, and as "Taking Stock of the Cowboy Myth" in *Arizona Daily Star*, February 9, 1986: 1C, and February 10, 1986: 15A. Revised as "Free Speech: The Cowboy and His Cow" in *One Life at a Time, Please* (1988), 9–19. Original version ("Ungulate Jungle") reprinted as "Something about Mac, Cows, Poker, Ranchers, Cowboys, Sex, and Power . . . and Almost Nothing about American Lit" in *Northern Lights: A Selection of New Writing from the American West*, edited by Deborah Clow and Donald Snow. New York: Random House/Vintage, 1994, 137–58. Reprinted as "Free Speech: The Cowboy and His Cow" in *The Serpents of Paradise* (1995), 358–65.

1986

"Art: Ceremonies in the Sand. Painting the Myths and Legends of the Navajo." *Architectural Digest* 43 (March): 176–81.

Confessions of a Barbarian. Preface (never reprinted) and first chapter of what became *The Fool's Progress* (1988). Published with *Redknife Valley*, by Jack Curtis. Santa Barbara: Capra.

"Edward Abbey Replies." Letter to the editor responding to letters about "Even Bad Guys Wear White Hats: Cowboys, Ranchers, and the Ruin of the West." *Harper's* 272 (May): 71–72.

"Edward Abbey's Bay Area Journal." *San Francisco Examiner*, December 16: A4; December 17: A10; December 18: A12; and December 19: A10. Reprinted as "A San Francisco Journal" in *One Life at a Time, Please* (1988), 51–84.

"Foreword." In *Blessed by Light: Visions of the Colorado Plateau*, edited by Stephen Trimble. Layton, Utah: Gibbs M. Smith/Peregrine Smith, 1986, xv–xvii.

"Frederic Remington's West." *Architectural Digest Travels* (Fall): 28. Reprinted as "The Remington Studio" in *One Life at a Time, Please* (1988), 194–98.

"From *Confessions of a Barbarian*." First chapter of what became *The Fool's Progress* (1988). *ZYZZYVA, the Last Word: West Coast Writers and Artists* 2, no. 1 (Spring): 105–20.

"Glen Canyon Remembered." Review of *Ghosts of Glen Canyon*, by C. Gregory Crampton. *Desert Southwest Magazine* 1, no. 1 (Winter 1986–87): 27.

Letter to the editor about development in Gold Basin. *Moab Times-Independent*, July 3: n.p.

Letter to the editor about Martin Litton and Dian Fossey. *Outside*, September: n.p.

"A Reply to Schmookler on Anarchy." *Earth First! Journal* 6 (August 1): 22. Reprinted, *City Lights Review* 1 (1987): 93–95. Revised as "Theory of Anarchy" in *One Life at a Time, Please* (1988), 25–28. Reprinted, *The Serpents of Paradise* (1995), 366–69.

1987

Freedom and Wilderness: Edward Abbey Reads from His Work. Denver: Audio Press. Audio recording later distributed by Gibbs M. Smith and also NorthWord Audio Press.

"Leaving Tucson." *City Magazine* (Tucson) 2, no. 6 (June): 27–33. Extracted from chapter 3 of *The Fool's Progress* (1988).

Letter to the editor about chauvinism and racism. *Earth First! Journal* 8, no. 2 (December 22): 3.

Letter to the editor about motor vehicles at Arches. *Moab Times-Independent*, September 17: n.p.

"Reading Updike." *The Nation* 244, no. 12 (March 28): 409–10.

"River Solitaire: A Daybook." *Mother Earth News/American Country* 1, no. 3 (July): 20–25. Reprinted in *One Life at a Time, Please* (1988), 94–106. Reprinted in *The Serpents of Paradise* (1995), 348–57.

"When Spring Paints the Desert." Condensed from "Wild Flowers" chapter of *Desert Images* (1979), 112–16. *Reader's Digest* 130 (April 1987): 164, 167.

1988

"Abbey Interrogates Abbey: An Exercise in Existential Angst." *Whole Earth Review* 61 (Winter): 17.

"Abbey on Books—And Gurus." *Earth First! Journal* 9, no. 5 (May 1): 29.

"Attack of the Alien Monsters: Byrd Baylor's Books as Survival Manuals." *City Magazine* (April): 80–81.

"The Folly Wise Men Commit." Review of *More Die of Heartbreak*, by Saul Bellow. *Bloomsbury Review*, January/February: 9–10.

The Fool's Progress: An Honest Novel. New York: Henry Holt (hardback). Reprinted, London: The Bodley Head, 1989. Revised edition, New York: Avon, 1990 (paperback). Chapter 2 and parts of chapters 10 and 20 reprinted in *The Serpents of Paradise* (1995), 3–21, 59–71, 175–218. Reprinted (whole paperback), New York: Henry Holt, 1998.

"Fun Couple." Letter to editor about Charles Keating. *City Magazine* (October): 5.

"Funny and Too Real." Review of *Too Funny to Be President*, by Morris K. Udall. *Tucson Weekly*, August 8: n.p.

"A Harvest of Riches: Writers Select Their Favorite Books of 1988." *Bloomsbury Review*, November/December: 14.

Introduction to *The Land of Little Rain*, by Mary Austin. New York: Penguin, 1988. vii–xiii.

"Issue of Morality." Letter to the editor defending Dave Foreman and Earth First! *Arizona Daily Star*, September 20: 8A.

Letter to the editor about Alston Chase. *Outside*, January: 10.

Letter to the editor about Robinson Jeffers. *The Nation*, March 19: n.p. Reprinted, *Robinson Jeffers Newsletter* 74 (November): 4.

Letter to the editor responding to Bill McKibben's review of *One Life at a Time, Please*. *New York Review of Books*, November 10: n.p.

"Life and Death in the American Desert." *American Country* 2, no. 2 (Summer): 36–39.

One Life at a Time, Please. New York: Henry Holt. Includes many of Abbey's essays previously published in periodicals.

Review of *Fear at Work: Job Blackmail, Labor, and the Environment*, by Richard Kazis and Richard L. Grossman. *Earth First! Journal* (May 1): 25.

Review of *S.*, by John Updike. *Bloomsbury Review* 8, no. 4 (July/August): 9, 20.

"Stewardship Versus Wilderness." Review of *Home Economics*, by Wendell Berry. *Earth First! Journal* 8, no. 3 (February 2): 32.

"To the Wild Wanton Women of Moab, Utah." An open letter from Edward Abbey. *The Stinking Desert Gazette* (Moab) 3, no. 2 (September): n.p.

"The True Grit of A. B. Guthrie." *Chicago Sun-Times Book World*, October 30: n.p. Reprinted in *Images from the Great West*, with photographs by Marc Gaede, with essay by Guthrie. La Canada, Calif.: Chaco Press, 1990, 1–2.

"Who Benefits?" Letter to the editor attacking a proposed hyper-collider. *Arizona Daily Star*, March 17: 14A.

"Wolfe and Tolstoy." Letter to the editor. *New York Times Book Review*, October 9: 50.

1989

"Drunk in the Afternoon." *Chicago Tribune Magazine*, June 25: n.p. Reprinted in *Northwest: The Sunday Oregonian Magazine*, July 30: 24–25. Reprinted in *The Sound of Writing*, edited by Alan Cheuse and Caroline Marshall. New York: Doubleday/Anchor, 1991, 1–6. Reprinted in *The Serpents of Paradise* (1995), 44–49.

"Edward Abbey from *Vox Clamantis in Deserto*." *City Lights Review* 3: 87–92. Excerpts reprinted from *Vox Clamantis in Deserto*.

"Hard Times in Santa Fe." *Canyon Country Zephyr* 1, no. 1 (April): 8–9. Reprinted, *Inside/Outside Southwest Magazine* (Durango), March/April 1999: 28.

"Hayduke Lives!" Excerpt from chapter 1 of *Hayduke Lives!* (1990). *Mother Earth News*, November/December: 56–59.

"Introduction: Forward!" In *The Backcountry Handbook: An Illustrated Guide to the Techniques and Joys of the Wilderness Experience*, by the editors of *Mother Earth News*. New York: Simon and Schuster, 7.

"The River of No Return." *National Geographic Traveler*, July/August: 88–97. Reprinted from "River of No Return" in *One Life at a Time, Please* (1988), 107–22.

"The Secret of the Green Mask." *Condé Nast Traveler*, March: 154–56, 188.

Vox Clamantis in Deserto. Illustrations by Andrew Rush. Santa Fe, N.M.: Rydal. Reprinted as *A Voice Crying in the Wilderness (Vox Clamantis in Deserto): Notes from a Secret Journal*. New York: St. Martin's, 1990.

1990

"The Cleaning Lady." Excerpt from *Hayduke Lives! Buzzworm: The Environmental Journal* 2 (January/February): 106–9.

Hayduke Lives! Boston: Little, Brown. Reprinted (paperback), New York: New American Library/ Dutton, 1991. Reprinted (paperback), Boston: Little, Brown, 1991.

"Introduction to Bill Hoy." In *Spanish Terms of the Sonoran Desert Borderlands: A Basic Glossary*, by Bill Hoy. 3rd edition. Calexico, Calif.: Institute for Border Studies, 1990, iii–iv.

1991

"Benedictio." Excerpt reprinted from *Desert Solitaire* (1988). *Earth Prayers from Around the World: 365 Prayers, Poems, and Invocations for Honoring the Earth*, edited by Elizabeth Roberts and Elias Amidon. San Francisco: Harper Collins, 208.

"Ed Abbey to Earth First! Mabon [September] 1983." In *Earth First! Reader: Ten Years of Radical Environmentalism*, edited by John Davis. Salt Lake City: Peregrine Smith, 247–49.

"George Hayduke's Code of the Eco-Warrior: A Preface to Howie Wolke's Book, by George Hayduke as told to Edward Abbey." In *Wilderness on the Rocks*, by Howie Wolke. Tucson: Ned Ludd Books, 1991.

"Why Wilderness?" Excerpt from "Down the River" chapter of *Desert Solitaire* (1968). Reprinted in *The Best of the West: An Anthology of Classic Writing from the American West*, edited by Tony Hillerman. New York: Harper Collins, 466–69.

1994

Confessions of a Barbarian: Selections from the Journals of Edward Abbey, 1951–1989, edited and introduced by David Petersen, illustrations by Abbey. Boston: Little, Brown. Part of Journal IV reprinted in *The Serpents of Paradise* (1995), 50–55. Reprinted (whole book in paperback), Boston: Little, Brown, 1996.

Earth Apples (Pommes des Terre): The Poetry of Edward Abbey, edited by David Petersen, illustrations by Michael McCurdy. New York: St. Martin's. Reprinted, New York: St. Martin's Griffin, 1995.

"How to Pick a Woman." September 14, 1966, journal entry. *Esquire* 122 (August): 102–3. Reprinted from *Confessions of a Barbarian*, 203–5.

"Sheep Count." June 23 and 24, 1988, journal entries. *American Nature Writing 1994*, edited by John A. Murray. San Francisco: Sierra Club Books, 23–27. Reprinted in *Confessions of a Barbarian*, 344–47.

1995

"The Moon-Eyed Horse." Reprinted from *Desert Solitaire* (1968). *Great and Peculiar Beauty: A Utah Reader*, edited by Thomas Lyon and Terry Tempest Williams. Salt Lake City: Peregrine Smith, 746–58.

The Serpents of Paradise: A Reader, edited by John Macrae. New York: Holt. Reprinted (paperback), New York: Holt, 1996.

"A Writer's Credo." In *The Serpents of Paradise*, 377–89. Reprinted from *One Life at a Time, Please* (1988).

1999

"Abbey Speaks: From a Letter to the Editor of *High Country News*" (about Telluride and the imminent demise of industrial civilization). Reprinted in *Inside/Outside Southwest Magazine* (Durango), March/April: 29–31.

"The First Morning and Labor Day." Reprinted from *Desert Solitaire* (1968), the opening "First Morning" chapter and the beginning of the "Episodes and Visions" chapter. *Reading Culture: Contexts for Critical Reading and Writing*, edited by Diana George and John Trimbur. 3rd edition. New York: Longman, 253–56.

THE EDWARD ABBEY PAPERS AT THE UNIVERSITY OF ARIZONA, TUCSON

This extensive collection, running from 1947 to 1990, fills thirty boxes and (with the kind permission of Special Collections and Clarke Cartwright Abbey) is cited in my notes as "Abbey Papers," by box and folder number. Here follows a brief summary of the manuscripts and recordings in the collection, listed by box numbers:

1–2	Incoming correspondence, 1966–88
3	Incoming and outgoing (1969–89) correspondence
4–5	Journals, 1951–89
6	Logbooks and notes from trips and speeches
7	*The Brave Cowboy*, unpublished novels, and speeches
8	Speeches
9	*Abbey's Road, Beyond the Wall*, and unpublished New Mexico novel "Black Sun"
10	*Cactus Country* and unpublished novel "City of Dreadful Night"
11	*Desert Images, Desert Solitaire*, and *Down the River*
12	*Good News*
13–16	*The Fool's Progress*
17	Unpublished novel "The Good Life" and *Hayduke Lives!*
18	*Hayduke Lives!*
19	*The Journey Home* and *The Monkey Wrench Gang*
20	*The Monkey Wrench Gang*
21	*One Life at a Time, Please*
22	*Slickrock, Vox Clamantis in Deserto*, and screenplays
23	*The Monkey Wrench Gang* scripts, other scripts, and periodical articles
24	Periodical articles
25	Book reviews, play, poems, and articles and reviews about Abbey
26	Reviews of Abbey's books
27	Audiotapes of interviews, trips, and the Arches memorial
28	Copies of *El Crepusculo de la Libertad*, audiotapes, and videotapes
29	Royalty statements, calendars, and miscellaneous materials
30	Original masters of audiotapes and videotapes

INTERVIEWS BY THE AUTHOR

The following interviews were tape-recorded unless otherwise specified.

Abbey, Clarke Cartwright. Tucson, Ariz., February 6, 1996, and February 11, 1999.

Abbey, Howard. Chambersville, Pa., October 18, 1995, and August 27, 1998.

Abbey, Iva. Chambersville, Pa., October 18, 1995, and August 27, 1998.

Abbey, Nancy. Santa Cruz, Calif., December 2, 1995.

Abbey, William T. Chambersville, Pa., October 18, 1995; Marion Center, Pa., October 27, 1995, and August 27, 1998.

Abrams, Leonard. Indiana, Pa., September 22, 1995.

Alexander, Hubert Griggs. Albuquerque, N.M., October 15, 1997.

Alexander, Mildred B. Albuquerque, N.M., October 15, 1997.

Anonymous. Five important interviewees asked not to be identified for attribution.

Baker, Gail. Albuquerque, N.M., March 6, 1998.

Barassi, Lou. Tucson, Ariz., October 15, 1998.

Bence, Eugene. Indiana, Pa., September 22, 1995.

Benge, Bill. Moab, Utah, April 10, 1998.

Berry, Wendell. Port Royal, Ky., August 11, 1996.

Betts, William. Indiana, Pa., December 1, 1995.

Booth, Evelyn. Indiana, Pa., September 13, 1995.

Bounds, Katherine. Jersey City, N.J., March 27, 1998.

Bowden, Charles. Tucson, Ariz., January 19, 1999.

Brodell (McElheney), Karilyn. Jackson, Wyo., April 2, 1998.

Brown, Malcolm. Taos, N.M., February 13, 1998.

Brown, Rachel. Arroyo Seco, N.M., February 6, 1998.

Brown, Seth. Arroyo Seco, N.M., January 28, 1998.

Buchanan, Roberta. Indiana, Pa., September 22, 1995.

Bulow, Ernie. Gallup, N.M., February 20, 1998.

Carrico, James. Terlingua, Tex., September 27, 1998.

Carrico, Virginia. Terlingua, Tex., September 27, 1998.

Cohen, Ruth. Toronto, Ontario, December 7 and 8, 1998 (e-mail correspondence).

Congdon, Don. New York, May 15, 1998.

Coss, Harold. Tucson, Ariz., October 6, 1998.

Creeley, Robert. Buffalo, N.Y., March 17 and April 11, 1998 (e-mail correspondence).

Crews, Judson. Albuquerque, N.M., September 24, 1998.

De Puy, John. Questa, N.M., January 23, 1998.

Dusard, Jay. Douglas, Ariz., November 11, 1999.

Ensley, Robert. Indiana, Pa., May 23, 1996.

Felger, Richard. Tucson, Ariz., October 29–November 6, 1998 (e-mail correspondence).

Foreman, Dave. Albuquerque, N.M., November 17, 1998.

Furgiuele, Samuel. Indiana, Pa., November 17, 1995.

George, Betty. Indiana, Pa., October 27, 1995.

Gray, Cindy. Portola, Calif., January 20, 1998 (written correspondence).

Greenspan, Bob. Jackson, Wyo., March 13, 1998.

Grette, Roger. Amherst, Mass., April 10, 1998.

Hawkins, B. L. Boulder, Colo., May 3 and 5, 1998 (e-mail correspondence).

Hepworth, James R. Lewiston, Idaho, December 1, 1998.

Hieb, Louis A. Albuquerque, N.M., March 23, 1998 (e-mail correspondence).

Hoagland, Edward. Bennington, Vt., April 17, 1998.

Houck, Laura Lee. Moab, Utah, December 4, 1998.

Houston, Robert. Tucson, Ariz., January 28, 1999.

Howard, Anne. Reno, Nev., November 15, 1999 (e-mail correspondence).

Hoy, Bill. Bowie, Ariz., October 8, 1998.

Hull, Raymona. Indiana, Pa., January 29, 1996.

Keener, John. Indiana, Pa., September 22, 1995.

Kessler, Rod. Cambridge, Mass., April 9, 1998 (e-mail correspondence).

Kinter, William P. Hellertown, Pa., November 1, 1996 (written correspondence).

Kirkpatrick, Dick. Tempe, Ariz., December 16, 1995.

Klett, Mark. Tempe, Ariz., September 29, 1998 (e-mail correspondence).

Lee, Katie. Jerome, Ariz., June 2, 1998.

Lynch, Tom. Las Cruces, N.M., February 9 and 12, and December 15, 1999 (e-mail correspon-
     dence).

Lyon, Thomas J. Carlsbad, Calif., March 6, 1998.

Macrae, Jack. New York, February 27, 1998.

Marius, Richard. Belmont, Mass., December 8 and 10, 1998 (e-mail correspondence).

McClure, Donald. Indiana, Pa., November 30, 1995.

McGee, Ivan. Indiana, Pa., September 13, 1995.

McMurtry, Larry. Archer City, Tex., April 18, 2000 (written correspondence).

McNamee, Gregory. Tucson, Ariz., October 20, 1998.

Mears, Edward. Marion Center, Pa., October 4, 1995.

Miller, Katherine T. Edinboro, Pa., March 13, 1998.

Mitchell, John G. Chevy Chase, Md., October 27, 1998.

Mondt, Rod. Tucson, Ariz., February 2, 1999.

Moorhead, Judy. Indiana, Pa., September 22, 1995.

Nesbitt, Isabel. Naples, N.Y., December 2, 1995.

Newcomb, Ralph. Allegany, Ore., January 30, 1998.

Newmark, Linda. Tucson, Ariz., December 6, 1998.

Newmark, Sandy. Tucson, Ariz., December 6, 1998.

Norman, Gurney. Lexington, Ky., December 18, 1995.

Peacock, Douglas. Livingston, Mont., November 3, 1998.

Pierson, Lloyd. Moab, Utah, April 17, 1998.

Preston, Gilbert. Butte, Mont., April 14, 1998 (e-mail correspondence).

Rawlings, Donn. Prescott, Ariz., June 1, 1998.

Reedy, Penelope. Pocatello, Idaho, March 27 and 29, 1998 (e-mail correspondence).

Sanders, Ken. Salt Lake City, Utah, March 20, 1998.

Saum, Judith. Reno, Nev., January 29, 2000.

Schmechel, Jean. April 15, 1998.

Sharp, David. Wickenburg, Ariz., January 29, 2000.

Shelton, Richard. Tucson, Ariz., February 18, 1999.

Silko, Leslie Marmon. Tucson, Ariz., February 11, 1999.

Sleight, Ken. Moab, Utah, January 17, 1996, and December 10, 1998.

Snyder, Gary. Nevada City, Calif., September 18, 1998.

Stadtmiller, Bernard. Creekside, Pa., September 1, 2000.

Stiles, Jim. Moab, Utah, March 11, 1998.

Tallmadge, John. Cincinnati, Ohio, February 18, 1998 (e-mail correspondence).

Tecklin, Jerry. Nevada City, Calif., October 1, 1998.

Thomas, Raymond. Indiana, Pa., November 28, 1995.

Thompson, Tom. Oracle, Ariz., November 19, 1998.

Twining, Edward S. Denver, Colo., September 10, 1998.

Vincent, Jenny. San Cristobal, N.M., September 17, 1998.

Watta, John. Indiana, Pa., May 18, 1995.

Wild, Peter. Tucson, Ariz., November 2 and 8, 1998 (written correspondence).

Woodin, Ann. Oracle, Ariz., November 10, 1998.

Zierenberg, Nancy. Tucson, Ariz., February 2, 1999.

UNPUBLISHED INTERVIEWS BY OTHERS

Abbey, Paul Revere. By Jim Dougherty. Home, Pa., June 23, 1990. Special Collections, Indiana University of Pennsylvania.

Bowden, Charles. By Eric Temple. Tucson, Ariz., April 1992. Transcript courtesy of Eric Temple.

De Puy, John. By Eric Temple. April 1992. Transcript courtesy of Eric Temple.

Smith, D. Newton. By Randall Holcombe. Cullowhee, N.C., September 13, 1994. Typescript courtesy of Cindy Gray.

ESSENTIAL SECONDARY SOURCES

In my notes I cite a great many secondary sources beyond the short list of writings about Abbey's life and contexts offered here; the list below should be seen as a starting point for the interested reader. A definitive bibliography of scholarly and popular writings about Abbey, along the lines of my bibliography of his own publications, is a task for another day and a different scholarly forum.

"Abbey, Edward." *Contemporary Authors 45*. Detroit: Gale Press, 1974.

"Abbey, Edward." *Contemporary Authors: New Revision Series 41*. Detroit: Gale Press, 1994.

"Abbey, Edward." *Contemporary Literature Criticism 36*. Detroit: Gale Press, 1986.

"Abbey, Edward." *Contemporary Literature Criticism 59*. Detroit: Gale Press, 1989.

Abbey special issue. Edited by Thomas J. Lyon. *Western American Literature* 28, no. 1 (May 1993): 1–49.

Bishop, James, Jr. *Epitaph for a Desert Anarchist: The Life and Legacy of Edward Abbey*. New York: Atheneum, 1994.

Bowden, Charles. *The Sonoran Desert*, photographs by Jack W. Dykinga, text by Bowden. New York: Harry N. Abrams, 1992.

Cahalan, James M. "Edward Abbey, Appalachian Easterner." *Western American Literature* 31, no. 3 (Fall 1996): 233–53.

———. "'My People': Edward Abbey's Appalachian Roots in Indiana County, Pennsylvania." *Pittsburgh History* 79, nos. 3–4 (Fall/Winter 1996–97): 92–108, 160–78. Republished in 1997 at http://www.abbeyweb.net/articles/mypeople/index.html

"A Celebration of Edward Abbey." *Tucson Weekly*, April 5–11, 1989: 1–12.

"Eulogy to Edward Abbey." A collection of speakers' remarks at the May 20, 1989, Moab wake. *Journal of Energy, Natural Resources, and Environmental Law* 11, no. 1 (1990): 3–28.

Foreman, Dave. *Confessions of an Eco-Warrior*. New York: Harmony, 1991.

Hepworth, James R., and Gregory McNamee, eds. *Resist Much, Obey Little: Some Notes on Edward Abbey*. Tucson: Harbinger House, 1985; reprinted, 1989. Revised as *Resist Much, Obey Little: Remembering Ed Abbey*. San Francisco: Sierra Club, 1996.

Lee, Katie. "His Heart to the Hawks." *The Tab* (Flagstaff, Verde Valley, and Sedona) 1, no. 14 (April 27, 1989): 9, 14.

Loeffler, Jack. "Strolling Along the Edge of Mortality." *El Palacio: Magazine of the Museum of New Mexico* 99, nos. 1–2 (Winter 1994): 22–31.

Manes, Christopher. *Green Rage: Radical Environmentalism and the Unmaking of Civilization*. Boston: Little, Brown, 1990.

Martin, Russell. *A Story That Stands Like a Dam: Glen Canyon and the Struggle for the Soul of the West*. New York: Henry Holt, 1989.

McCann, Garth. *Edward Abbey*. Boise, Idaho: Boise State University Press, 1977.

Miller, Tom. "Fighting the Good Fight: Tucson's Literary Troika—Bill Eastlake, Ed Abbey, and Alan Harrington—Remembered." *Tucson Monthly*, January 1998, 56–61.

Pierson, Lloyd M. "Edward Abbey (1927–1989)." *Canyon Legacy: Journal of the Dan O'Laurie Museum of Moab, Utah* 25 (Winter 1995): 5–9.

Quigley, Peter, ed. *Coyote in the Maze: Tracking Edward Abbey in a World of Words*. Salt Lake City: University of Utah Press, 1998.

Ronald, Ann. "Edward Abbey." *Fifty Western Writers: A Bio-Bibliographical Sourcebook*, edited by Fred Erisman and Richard W. Etulain. Westport, Conn.: Greenwood Press, 1982, 3–12.

———. "Edward Abbey." *A Literary History of the American West*, edited by James H. Maguire, et al. Fort Worth: Texas Christian University Press, 1987, 604–11.

———. "Edward Abbey." *Updating the Literary West*. Fort Worth: Texas Christian University Press, 1997, 541–46.

———. *The New West of Edward Abbey*. Albuquerque: University of New Mexico Press, 1982. Reprinted, Reno: University of Nevada Press, 1988. Reprinted, with new postscript by Ronald and a new afterword by Scott Slovic. Reno: University of Nevada Press, 2000.

Rothman, Hal. *The Greening of a Nation? Environmentalism in the United States since 1945*. New York: Harcourt Brace, 1998.

Scarce, Rik. "Earth First!: Cracking the Mold." *Eco-Warriors: Understanding the Radical Environmental Movement*. Chicago: Noble Press, 1990, 57–95.

Sleight, Ken. "Abbey and Me." *Canyon Country Zephyr* (Moab) 11, no. 1 (April/May 1999): 8–9.

Temple, Eric. *Edward Abbey: A Voice in the Wilderness.* Video documentary. Eric Temple Productions, 1993.

Zakin, Susan. *Coyotes and Town Dogs: Earth First! and the Environmental Movement.* New York: Penguin, 1993.

Acknowledgments

The extent to which I have depended on help from other people in this project is reflected in my dedication at the beginning of this book. My debts are many enough that I fear I (absent-minded professor that I am) will surely forget someone. When I do, I can only hope that anyone whom I fail to name here will know that the oversight was not intentional. Also, because of the constraints on space, I will not be able to list again here all of the more than 100 interviewees named in my bibliography, or the various other particular people identified in my notes. I hope those individuals take my naming of them in those places as clear indication of my profound thanks to them. Everyone on my interview list was very generous with their time, knowledge, energy, and also their kind permission. Several of them not only allowed me to interview them but also followed up by sending me copies of letters from Abbey, photographs, or other valuable items. Obviously I cannot thank by name the handful of interviewees who wanted to remain anonymous. But they know who they are, and I am deeply grateful.

Here I want to thank, first of all, the several Abbeys who helped me so much: Ed's widow Clarke, his brothers Howard and Bill, his sister Nancy, Howard's wife Iva, and Abbey's maternal aunt Betty George. They all gave me, a stranger at first, multiple interviews, permission to study and quote various manuscripts and other Abbey materials, assistance in obtaining crucial records, and many other kinds of help. Without this, I could not have conducted my research, let alone complete it. Howard and Bill Abbey both saved me from errors that I would otherwise have made in this book, and they gave very generously of their time; they both rode around Indiana County pointing out their childhood homes, as did Betty George in the town of Indiana, identifying the very first houses where Ed Abbey lived. Howard and Iva lent me key items not to be found even in the Abbey Papers in Tucson, and Bill gave me the greatest and most generous of Christmas presents: an original copy of the first and only edition of *Jonathan Troy*. Clarke took me to Ed's grave, a big trip for which I shall remain forever thankful beyond words. I also enjoyed meeting Clarke's daughter Becky and son Ben, and Howard and Iva's sons Joe and Mike and daughter Cathy.

My book is not an "authorized biography," nor would I want it to be. These close relatives of Ed Abbey may not like or agree with everything (or even many things) that I have written here. The fact that they have nonetheless helped me so generously is therefore all the more impressive, and I will never forget it.

I am also deeply grateful, in much the same way, to the former Jean Schmechel, Ed's first wife. Even before we had met in person, she was willing to talk long-distance and correspond with me on more than one occasion, even though it meant dredging up often difficult memories from half a century ago. She then followed up our interviews by putting her library skills to work and sending me some very useful information (as cited in my notes) that helped me track Ed's whereabouts in New Mexico in the murky 1950s.

Another reflection of the special generosity of Clarke Cartwright Abbey was that she allowed me—again, initially a comparative stranger—to use the very extensive Abbey Papers at the University of Arizona in 1996, 1998, and 1999, and she granted me permission to cite unpublished materials in that essential collection. During all of my work with those papers, I received kind, intelligent, patient help from Roger Myers, director of the UA Special Collections, and all of the members of his staff. I am also grateful to various other staff of the UA main library and to my own home library at Indiana University of Pennsylvania, especially Carol Asamoah and her interlibrary-loan department. As recorded in my notes and interviewee list, I also incurred a special debt to Louis Hieb, formerly of the University of Arizona and the University of New Mexico libraries.

To pursue the writings of Edward Abbey, one needs more than conventional libraries. My deepest extracurricular debt in this regard is to Dean Shenk, a park ranger at Yosemite National Park and an insatiable collector of publications by Abbey. He sent me quite a few items that I had not found even in the UA Abbey collection, and he also read my manuscript. Jacek Macias similarly identified another publication that I had not been able to locate. Sally Armstrong sent me a very useful list of Abbey's publications, and the bibliography compiled by Carrie L. Marsh in 1990 (maintained as part of the UA Abbey Papers) was also very useful. I am indebted to my good friend Gary Ferguson (the noted Montana-based nature writer in Abbey's tradition) for a lot of good advice, generous help, and good times.

I am especially thankful to others who read my manuscript at one stage or another (sometimes at multiple stages): senior deans of Western letters Ann Ronald and Thomas Lyon; younger rising scholarly stars Tom Lynch and Steve Holmes; and my daughter Clare, avid environmentalist and budding artist. Lea Masiello—IUP professor of English, director of liberal studies English, and my spouse—also read the manuscript. She knows what I owe. My brother Bill gave me my first copy of *Desert Solitaire* in 1984.

I am very much indebted to each of the photographers listed in the photographic credits. Special recognition is due to filmmaker and videomeister Eric Temple, who spent a great deal of time rescuing quite a few old photographs that otherwise would have remained unavailable. Eric also kindly permitted me to cite his own interviews with Abbey and his associates, some of which were part of his excellent documentary *Edward Abbey: A Voice in the Wilderness*. Jim Wakefield, former IUP photographer, also went well beyond the call of duty in helping me. I am also grateful to IUP media resources whiz Doug Shumar and current IUP photographer Keith Boyer. Dirk Kirkpatrick, Lloyd Pierson, and Rod Mondt generously lent me their original slides, and Dick was also my energetic host during his March 1999 Ed Abbey week in Phoenix and Tempe. Howie Wolke identified his fellow Earth First! cofounder Bart Koehler in Peter Dustrud's photograph.

I have enjoyed the obvious advantages of living and working in Abbey's home Indiana County, Pennsylvania. As noted in my introduction, this project began while I was living next door to my friend John Watta, IUP professor emeritus of English and a 1947 classmate and longtime friend of Abbey. John was, fittingly, the very first person I interviewed, and I remain in his debt. I am also still very grateful to Ivan McGee—former executive director of the Indiana County Historical and Genealogical Society, and 1941–42 classmate of Abbey—who not only talked with me and steered me to other interviewees but who also helped me raise the money for the Abbey state historical marker that I sponsored in 1996 through the Historical and Museum Commission of Pennsylvania. Additionally, I am indebted to IUP professor emeritus of history Merle Rife, who made a crucial phone call on my behalf.

Until 1997, I thought that I was writing only a couple of articles about Abbey, one for Tom Lyon's *Western American Literature* and the other for Paul Roberts's *Pittsburgh History*. Working with two such excellent editors was a significant part of what hooked me into continuing to work on this subject, as was collaborating with Christer Lindh, webmaster of "Abbey's Web" across the sea in Sweden. Dan Philippon steered me to the microfilmed *Earth First! Journal*.

At the University of Arizona Press, I have enjoyed similar good luck. Christine Szuter has seen me all the way through, first as my acquisitions editor, then as editor-in-chief and interim director, and now as permanent director of the press; she has remained a persistent advocate and clear critic. I was startled and thrilled when a previous acquisitions editor—but at the opposite end of the country for a different publisher (Syracuse University Press) and in a different field (Irish literature)—rematerialized in Tucson in early 2000 as my new editor-in-chief, helping me again during her brief term there: Cynthia Maude. At the UA Press I have also appreciated the sage editorial advice of the assistant managing editor, Alan Schroder, and the design and production manager, Anne Keyl, as well as the friendly assistance of the former assistant to the director, Carolyn Clancy. Julia Zafferano (freelance copyeditor and former managing editor of Stanford University Press) edited my manuscript thoroughly, carefully, and insightfully.

In the UA English Department, I especially appreciate the generous help of Robert Houston, director of the creative writing program; Larry Evers, department head; and Peter Wild, Abbey's old office mate. Also in Tucson, I enjoyed on-the-spot help beyond the call of duty from Charles Bowden, Sandy Newmark, Tom Miller, Rod Mondt, Nancy Zierenberg, Jack Dykinga, Terry Moore, and Greg McNamee; in Oracle, from Tom Thompson; in Prescott, from Peter Quigley; in Jackson, Wyoming, from Karilyn McElheney. Within the New York City publishing world, I appreciated advice and help from Abbey's old agent Don Congdon, his veteran editor Jack Macrae, Penguin Putnam executive editor Michael Millman, and Lyons Press editors Nick and Tony Lyons. Thanks to Rachel Carson biographer Linda Lear for very helpful advice.

In Moab, Jim Stiles, editor of the remarkable *Canyon Country Zephyr*, not only interviewed with me but also sent me copies of postcards from Abbey and helped introduce me to other interviewees. José Knighton at Moab's Back of Beyond Books was another shrewd consultant. Across the country in Salem, Massachusetts, Rod Kessler was similarly a big help, following up our e-mail interview about being Abbey's student in 1981 by putting me in touch with several of his classmates and sending me copies of his photographs and notes. Cindy Gray introduced me to those who knew Abbey in Cullowhee, North Carolina, during his short-lived teaching stint there in 1968. Thanks for Karla Armbruster for sending me Abbey's review of Josephine Johnson.

John De Puy inspired me by doing my single longest interview as well as by advising me to "write an honest book" about Ed Abbey and always keeping generously and cheerfully in touch with me. Carl De Puy sent me the wonderful photo of John, his father, and even corresponded with his Swiss cousins on my behalf, after his mother, Judith Saum, very helpfully put me in touch with him after her own interview with me. Rachel, Malcolm, and Seth Brown helped me very kindly in several different ways. All of my interviews were memorable; I got to talk with people like Ralph Newcomb, Doug Peacock, Dave Foreman, Wendell Berry, Leslie Marmon Silko, Gary Snyder, and many other unforgettable people.

I am grateful to several IUP graduate assistants who contributed crucial work on this project, especially Richard Higgason and Thomas Caulfield, both of whom went far beyond the call of duty in providing key assistance and also becoming thoroughly interested in my project. Rich did some significant research for me, and Tom helped me immensely in compiling my bibliography. Rich, Mohammed El Nahal, Rebecca Steinberger, and Kristen Williams all transcribed quotations from my interviews—no easy task. Jaehwan Han and Yeonman Kim spent many hours helping me with my index.

I also thank Dawn Marano for her help with a page reference; Indiana University of Pennsylvania for a sabbatical that allowed me to live in Tucson, and for grants supporting my research; Pennsylvania's State System of Higher Education for two grants; the Arizona Humanities Council for a grant that allowed me to give presentations on Abbey and do research in Tucson and Prescott; the Pennsylvania Humanities Council for sponsoring my many presentations all across Abbey's native state; Pennsylvania's Historical and Museum Commission for approving the Abbey state historical marker; and various helpful staff members of the Universities of Arizona, New Mexico, and Utah; the Hudson County, New Jersey, Welfare Department; the Nevada and New Mexico state welfare departments; the U.S. federal civil and military records offices, as well as the FBI; the U.S. post office in Home, Pennsylvania; and the Rayne Township office near Home.

Again, the dedication of this book is for *everyone* who helped me.

INDIANA, PENNSYLVANIA

January 11, 2001

Illustration Credits

Young cowboy Ed in the 1930s (Photograph courtesy of Howard and Iva Abbey)

Postmodern cowboy Ed in the 1980s (Photograph by and courtesy of Terrence Moore)

Baby with a wheelbarrow, 1928 (Photograph courtesy of Eric Temple and Clarke Cartwright Abbey)

Adolescent Ed (Photograph courtesy of Eric Temple and Clarke Cartwright Abbey)

The bemused teenager (Photograph courtesy of Eric Temple and Clarke Cartwright Abbey)

As an army motorcycle cop, 1946 (Photograph courtesy of Eric Temple and Clarke Cartwright Abbey)

With Jean Schmechel, ca. 1950 (Photograph courtesy of Eric Temple and Clarke Cartwright Abbey)

Abbey and his dog Homer, ca. 1953 (Photograph courtesy of Eric Temple and Clarke Cartwright Abbey)

Rock-climbing in the Fiery Furnace, 1957 (Photograph by and courtesy of Lloyd Pierson, chief ranger that summer)

Family holiday meal, 1956 (Photograph courtesy of Howard and Iva Abbey)

The staff of *El Crepusculo de la Libertad*, 1959 (Photograph courtesy of Jenny Vincent)

Judy and baby Susannah, 1968 (Photograph courtesy of Eric Temple and Clarke Cartwright Abbey)

In the Utah canyon country, late 1960s (Photograph courtesy of Eric Temple)

John De Puy and his paintings, 1973 (Photograph courtesy of Carl De Puy)

With his ranger friends, 1969 (Photograph by and courtesy of Bill Hoy, Organ Pipe naturalist at the time)

In El Gran Desierto in Sonora, 1982 (Photograph by and courtesy of Terrence Moore)

Professor Abbey, 1981 (Photograph by and courtesy of Rod Kessler, who was one of Abbey's graduate students that semester)

Delivering a speech, 1982 (Photograph by and courtesy of Peter Dustrud)

With his parents, Paul and Mildred, 1983 (Photograph by and courtesy of James G. Wakefield)

Showing off *The Journey Home*, 1983 (Photograph by and courtesy of James G. Wakefield)

With William Eastlake, 1984 (Photograph by and courtesy of Richard Byrd)

With Clarke and baby Rebecca, 1984 (Photograph by and courtesy of Jay Dusard)

In his cabin study, 1984 (Photograph by and courtesy of Jay Dusard)

Near Tule Well in the Cabeza Prieta, 1987 (Photograph courtesy of Eric Temple and Clarke Cartwright Abbey)

With R. Crumb at Arches, 1985 (Photograph by and courtesy of Ernie Bulow)

Saying goodbye, Grand Gulch, Utah, 1988 (Photograph by and courtesy of Mark Klett)

His final public appearance, 1989 (Photograph © Charles Hedgcock)

Sunrise wake, 1989 (Photograph by and courtesy of Marc Gaede)

Doug Peacock speaking at the wake, 1989 (Photograph by and courtesy of Rod Mondt)

Abbey's gravestone, 1999 (Photograph by James M. Cahalan, March 15, 1999; heartfelt thanks to Clarke Cartwright Abbey)

Index

Abbey: LIFE AND THEMES (cont.)

20, 41, 152, 155; river trips, 64, 69, 73–74, 106–7, 109, 124, 203, 216–17; tire-burning and rolling, 40, 63; trees, 18; warm weather, 35, 50, 155, 165

JOBS AS RANGER: Aravaipa (1972–74), 125–26, 144–45, 146, 148–49, 151, 154, 167, 312n. 55; Arches (1956, 1957), 52, 64, 65–66, 68, 73, 83, 112, 166, 232, 235, 270; Atascosa (1968), 114–15, 312n. 55; Aztec Peak (1977, 1978, 1979), 164, 174–75, 178, 182, 195; Canyonlands (1965), 94, 95; Casa Grande (1958–59), 72, 83; Everglades (1965–66), 95, 98–99; Gila (1958), 72; Lassen (1966), 99–100; Lee's Ferry (1967), 106, 107–9, 111; North Rim (1961, 1969–71), 83–84, 116, 118, 124, 127, 139, 141; Numa Ridge (Glacier) (1975), 164, 165, 173, 312n. 55; Organ Pipe (1968–70), 109, 112, 116–17, 122, 312n. 55; Petrified Forest (1961), 81, 82, 83

JOBS, OTHER: bartender, Taos (1960), 81; caseworker, Albuquerque (1960), 85; caseworker, Hudson County, N.J., (1962–65), 88–89, 94; caseworker, Las Vegas (1965), 94, 232; clerk, Interior Water Resources division (1952–53), 52, 53, 54, 55, 312n. 55; consultant, *Lonely Are the Brave* (1961), 84; delivering *Grit* and *Gazette*, 21; Dumont TV factory (1953), 56–57; editor, *El Crepusculo de la Libertad* (1959–60), 74–78, 80, 210, 275, 312n. 55; engineering aid, Apache National Forest (1955–56), 64, 69; GE factory, Erie (1948–49), 39–40; laborer, Carson National Forest (1953), 52, 55, 69; oil crew, New Mexico (1950, 1951), 43; picking apples, 22; school bus driver, Death Valley (1966–67), 100; shoestore, 21; teaching, New School (1962), 86; teaching, Univ. of Arizona (1981–88), xiii, 86, 132, 173, 178, 195–201, 203, 208, 215, 219, 222, 229, 233, 234, 242, 243, 255, 260; teaching, Univ. of New Mexico (1956), 64, 86, 136, 195; teaching, Univ. of Utah (1970), 131–32, 137, 195; teaching, Western Carolina Univ. (1968), 115, 116, 195; technical writer, Western Electric, New York (1962), 86–87, 216; writer in residence, *San Francisco Examiner* (1986), 244

MAJOR LIFE EVENTS: army (1945–47), 27,

Abbey: LIFE AND THEMES (cont.)

33–35, 37, 225; burial, 262, 263–64, 276; buys Cadillac (1988), 235, 236; buys Esperero house (1971), 141; buys Moab house (1974), 154; buys Pack Creek land (1986), 237, 291n. 103; buys Tucson house (1978), 175; buys Vermillion Cliffs land (1980), 185; children, 64, 65, 140, 141–42, 148, 155, 157, 169, 174, 175, 178–79, 184, 185, 189, 190, 203, 204, 206, 208, 223–24, 232, 236, 237–38, 244, 256, 261; death, 261; divorces, 47, 94, 95, 98, 273; drug experiences, 100–101, 107, 118; Fulbright Fellowship (1951–52), xiii, 45, 47, 49, 51; funeral instructions, 205, 207–8, 231, 263, 264, 265; Guggenheim Fellowship (1974–75), xiii, 163–64, 246; hitchhiking and railroading in 1944, 26, 28–32, 73, 142, 159; hitchhiking in 1943, 22, 29; illnesses (1982–89), 205, 206–7, 217, 231–32, 234, 257–58, 259–61, 265, 266; knee surgery (1960), 80, 83; wake at Saguaro (March 1989), 262, 264–65; wake beside Arches (May 1989), 242, 262, 266–68; wake in Aspen (May 1989), 268

MARRIAGES: to Clarke Cartwright Abbey (1982–89), 177, 184–85, 204, 205, 206, 208, 217, 218, 224, 233, 234–35, 236–37, 256, 257, 260–61, 273; to Rita Deanin (1952–65), 49, 54–55, 57–58, 62–63, 64–65, 68–69, 72–73, 78, 79, 81, 85, 86, 87–88, 89, 91, 92, 93, 94, 98, 111, 118, 182, 184, 273; to Renée Downing (1973–79), 149, 151, 155–56, 165, 172–73, 174, 175, 176, 177, 181, 182, 184; to Judy Pepper (1965–70), 95, 96, 98, 100, 101, 110–11, 112, 113, 115, 118–19, 124, 126–27, 130, 182, 184, 273; to Jean Schmechel (1950–52), 27, 44, 46–47, 182, 184, 273

PLACES: Alaska, 86, 172, 176, 182, 186, 203, 216–17, 221; Albuquerque, 40, 42, 44, 57, 63, 64, 72, 85; Appalachia, xii, 3, 4, 14–16, 24, 25–26, 43, 90, 119, 121–22, 224, 246, 248–51, 275, 296n. 26; Australia, 164, 165–66, 187, 217–18, 255; Cabeza Prieta, 117–18, 224, 276; Death Valley, 100–101, 102–3; Esperero Canyon (1971–74), 125–26, 142–43, 144, 154, 157, 223; Glen Canyon, 52, 64, 73, 106; Grand Canyon, 30, 40, 274, 281n. 16; Half Moon Bay (Calif.), 72; Havasu Canyon, 40, 43, 64; Hoboken and New York, 68, 86, 89–90, 168; Home and Indiana, Pa., 3–4,

Alaska: Abbey and, 86, 172, 176, 182, 186, 203, 216–17

Albuquerque, 29, 30, 37, 38, 43, 47, 63, 72, 78, 80, 81, 82, 84, 226, 239; Abbey's apartments in, 40, 42, 44, 63, 64, 72, 85; growth of, 38

Alexander, Hubert (UNM professor), 55, 62, 63, 64, 86

All My Rivers Are Gone (Katie Lee), 139

Almanac of the Dead, The (Silko), 195

American Academy of Arts and Letters, 254

American West, 170, 209, 229, 279n. 46

Amerind Foundation, 255

Anatomy of Melancholy (Burton), 165

Antonioni, Michelangelo, 100

Aravaipa Canyon: Abbey and, 126, 135, 140, 144–45, 146, 148–49, 155, 167, 312n. 55

Arches National Park (formerly Monument), 52, 64, 65, 66, 68, 69, 89, 112, 166, 168, 169, 201, 230, 232, 235, 242, 247, 262, 266–68, 270

Arizona Cattle Growers' Association, 229

Arizona Daily Star (Tucson), 121, 144, 209, 210–11, 212, 220, 225, 228, 239, 263

Arizona Republic newspaper, 209, 212, 213

Arnold, Tom (friend), 151, 152, 155

Association for the Study of Literature and Environment (ASLE), 186

Atlantic, The, 211

Audubon, xiv, 118, 125, 141, 165, 170, 264

Audubon Society, 125, 137, 193

Austin, Mary, 178, 242, 257, 263

Australia: and Abbey, 141, 164, 165–66, 187, 199, 217–18, 244, 255

Back of Beyond Bookstore (Moab), 268

Bahm, Archie (UNM professor), 62, 63

Baird, Robert (student), 197, 198

Bakunin, Mikhail: influence on Abbey, 49, 74

Ballantine (publisher), 112, 125

Ballard, Carroll, 243

Barassi, Lou (Aravaipa attorney), 145, 148

"Bard of Oracle, The" (McNamee), 230

Baylor, Byrd, 225

Beckett, Samuel, 75, 132

Beliveux, Robert (Rita Abbey's husband), 207

Bellow, Saul, 222

Bence, Eugene (high school classmate), 21, 22

Benge, Bill (friend and attorney), 151, 155, 159

Berry, Wendell (friend and author), xiv, 18, 24, 60, 71, 89, 113, 119, 197, 229, 241–42, 260, 267, 274, 308n. 43

Beyond the Hundredth Meridian (Stegner), 263

Big Bend National Park, 40, 44, 48, 57, 151, 274

Big Rock Candy Mountain, The (Stegner), 17

Bishop, James P., 263, 270, 312nn. 55–57

Black, Cal: caricatured in *Monkey Wrench* and *Hayduke Lives!* 159

Black Mesa Defense Fund, 138, 150

Blaustein, John, 171

Bloomsbury Review, 222, 223

Bonfire of the Vanities, The (Tom Wolfe), 257

Bookchin, Murray, 240, 241, 242

Booth, Norah, 175

Bounds, Katherine, 89, 93, 126

Bourjaily, Vance, 146

Bowden, Charles (friend and author), 25, 208, 213, 221–22, 232, 235–36, 239, 255, 259, 265, 269, 272

Brautigan, Richard, 215

Brower, David, 53, 55–56, 108, 169, 242

Brown, Malcolm (friend and artist), 55, 57–58, 61, 62, 63, 105, 106–7, 126, 127, 141, 185, 218; model for two of Abbey's characters, 61, 219, 247, 308n. 53

Brown, Rachel (friend and artist), 57, 58, 61, 62, 63

Brown, Seth (son of Malcolm and Rachel), 63

Brownmiller, Susan, 135, 222

Bryce Canyon National Park, 134

Buchanan, Marcellus, 115

Bulow, Ernie (student and friend), 132, 142, 213, 221, 232; model for Don Williams character in *Fool's Progress*, 225, 247

Bureau of Land Management (BLM), 192, 266

Burroughs, John, 242

Cabeza Prieta (Black Head) game range and wilderness area, 117–18, 123, 145, 159, 160, 202, 224, 255, 263–64, 276

Canyon Country Zephyr (Moab), 256, 268, 269

Canyonlands National Park, 68, 69, 94, 95, 106, 151

Carrico, Jim (friend), 112, 117, 205

Carrico, Virginia (Ginny, Jim's wife), 205

About the Author

James M. Cahalan is the author of six previous books: *Great Hatred, Little Room: The Irish Historical Novel* (1983), *The Irish Novel: A Critical History* (1988), *Liam O'Flaherty: A Study of the Short Fiction* (1991), *Practicing Theory in Introductory College Literature Courses* (coedited with David Downing, 1991), *Modern Irish Literature and Culture: A Chronology* (1993), and *Double Visions: Women and Men in Modern and Contemporary Irish Fiction* (1999). He is Professor of English at Indiana University of Pennsylvania (IUP), where he received the Distinguished Faculty Award for Research in 1990. Dr. Cahalan has been a graduate Fulbright Fellow, a Commonwealth Speaker through the Pennsylvania Humanities Council, and the recipient of many grants.

Professor Cahalan teaches in the same building where Ed Abbey took his first college English courses in 1947, and his interest initially focused on the beginning of Abbey's life and his home region. In 1996, he published articles about Abbey in *Pittsburgh History* and *Western American Literature* and dedicated a Pennsylvania state historical marker that he sponsored for Abbey in Home. He pursued his research for this book through several trips west, beginning in 1994 and continuing through his 1999 sabbatical in Tucson. He has given many talks on Abbey throughout Pennsylvania as well as in Tucson, Prescott, Flagstaff, Albuquerque, Taos, and Big Bend National Park. From his house in the middle of the woods a mile from where Ed Abbey's father, Paul, first lived when he was seven years old, and within a few hundred yards of the old mine site where Paul worked as a young man, Jim enjoys taking bike rides all around Indiana County.